The Rough

Bali & Lombok

written and researched by

Lesley Reader and Lucy Ridout

ROUGH
GUIDES

NEW YORK · LONDON · DELHI

www.roughguides.com

Contents

Volcanoes and ricefields colour section following p.376

The crafts of Bali and Lombok colour section following p.184

◄◄ Gunung Agung ◄ Traditional Jukung, Sanur

Gili Islands & Senggigi (Lombok) △

△ Lembar (Lombok)

BALI

Lombok

Bali

Java

B A L I   S E A

Lombok Strait

Lombok

Lipah Beach

Amed

Jemeluk

Aas

Amlapura

Culik

Gunung Tulamben

Kubu

Tirtagangga

Candi Dasa

Tenganan

Padang Bai

Buyik Harbour

Sampalan

Gunung Agung ▲▲ Besakih

Semarapura

Ped

Toyapakeh

Nusa Penida

Songan

Sembirenteng

Gunung Batur ▲

Toya Bungkah

Penelokan

Gunung Kawi

Tampaksiring

Bangli

Mas Gianyar

Nusa Lembongan

Badung Strait

O C E A N

Tejakula

Ponjok Batu

Bondalem

Kintamani

Toya Bungkah

Pelaga

Pujung Kelod

Tegalalang

Petulu

Pejeng

Bedulu

Batuan

Sukawati

Batubulan

Jungutbatu

Air Sanih

Bukti

Ubud

Savan

Teges

DENPASAR

Sanur

Tanjung Benoa

Kubutambahan

Singaraja

Gunung Brukaru ▲

Bedugul

Batukaru

Jatiluwih

Sangeh Monkey Forest

Pura Taman Ayun

Mengwi

Ubung

Kuta Benoa Harbour

Nusa Dua

Lovina Beach

Dencarik

Munduk

Pupuan

Pura Luhur Batukaru

Sanda

Wongayagede

Penebel

Tabanan

Seminyak

Legian

Jimbaran

Buala

Seririt

Buddhist Monastery Ω

Bajera

Krambitan

Ngurah Rai Airport ✈

Dreamland

Pura Luhur Uluwatu

Pura Agung Pulaki

Antosari

Lalang Linggah

Yeh Gangga Beach

Pura Tanah Lot

Pekutatan

Pura Rambut Siwi

Medewi

Pemuteran

Negara

Perancak

B a l i   S t r a i t

N

Pulau Menjangan (Deer Island)

Labuan Lalang

BALI BARAT NATIONAL PARK

Cekik

Ketapang

Gilimanuk

Java

I N D I A N   O C E A N

feet	metres
9000	2743
7000	2134
5000	1524
3000	914
2000	610
1000	305
500	152
250	76
0	0

20 km

0

0

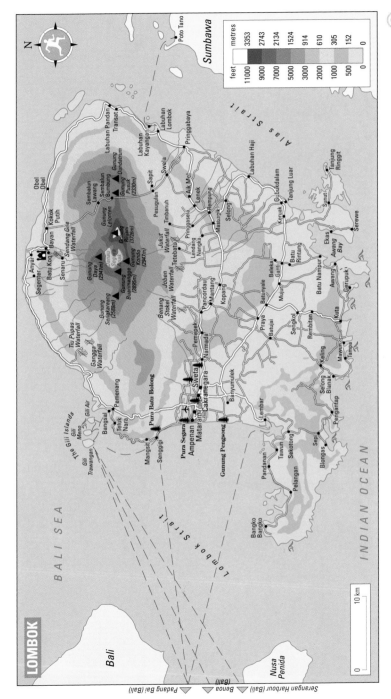

LOMBOK

feet	metres
11000	3353
9000	2743
7000	2134
5000	1524
3000	914
2000	610
1000	305
500	152
0	0

N

Sumbawa

Poto Tano

Alas Strait

Labuhan Pandan
Transat
Labuhan Lombok
Pringgabaya
Labuhan Kayangan
Labuhan Haji
Swela
Sapit
Aik Mel
Pesugulan
Lenek
Timbanuh
Pringgasela
Masbagik
Selong
Tanjung Luar
Gulukdalam
Kenak
Kerak
Synut
Tanjung Ringgit
Serewe
Ekas
Awang Bay
Gerupuk
Batu Nampur
Awang
Kuta
Mawin
Tampa
Selong Blanak
Pengantap
Biangas
Sepi
Pelangan
Bangko Bangko

Obel Obel
Kokok Putih
Sembalun Lawang
Sembalun Bumbung
Gunung Qundatum
Bayan
Sendang Gile Waterfall
Gunung Lejoren
Gunung Pusuk (2330m)
Sambalun
Gunung Rinjani (3726m)
Batu Koq
Senaru
Anyar
Segenter
Gunung Daya (2941m)
Gunung Condo (2947m)
Jukut Waterfall
Lendang Nangka
Jantuk
Rempung
Tiu Pupas Waterfall
Gunung Buanmangge (2895m)
Gunung Sengkaraang (258m)
Benang Stokel Waterfall
Joben Waterfall
Terebatul
Gangga Waterfall
Pancordau
Mantang
Kopang
Batuvale
Muju'
Batu Rintang
Beleku Ganti
Praya
Senggol
Rembitan
Pemenang
Bangsal
Pura Batu Bolong
Pampang
Narmada
Batujai
Keling
Gunung Pengsong
Lembar
Banyumulek
Sekotong
Tawun
Pandanan
Sepi

The Gili Islands
Gili Air
Gili Meno
Gili Trawangan

Mangsit
Senggigi
Teluk Nara
Ampenan
Mataram
Cakranegara
Sweta
Pura Segara

BALI SEA

Bali

Nusa Penida

LOMBOK STRAIT

INDIAN OCEAN

0 — 10 km

Serangan Harbour (Bali) ◁ ◁ Benoa ◁ Padang Bai (Bali)
(Bali)

Introduction to

Bali & Lombok

The islands of Bali and Lombok are part of the Indonesian archipelago, a 5200-kilometre-long string of over thirteen thousand islands, stretching between Malaysia in the west and Australia in the east. Sandy beaches punctuate the dramatically rugged coastlines, and world-class surf pounds both shorelines.

Both islands are small – Bali extends less than 150km at its widest point, Lombok a mere 80km – volcanic, and graced with swathes of extremely fertile land, much of it sculpted into terraced rice-paddies. Culturally, however, Bali and Lombok could hardly be more different. Bali remains the only **Hindu** society in Southeast Asia, and religious observance permeates every aspect of modern Balinese life; the Sasak people of Lombok, on the other hand, are **Muslim**, like the vast majority of other Indonesians.

With a tourist industry that dates back over eighty years, the tiny island of **Bali** (population 3.1 million) has become very much a mainstream destination, offering all the comforts and facilities expected by better-off tourists, and suffering the predictable problems of congestion, commercialization and breakneck Westernization. However, its original charm is still much in evidence, its distinctive temples and elaborate festivals set off by the lush landscape of the interior. Although tourist arrivals plummeted after the bombs of 2002 and 2005, causing an island-wide recession that continues to bite, visitors are returning in their previously high numbers (2.5 million in 2007). Meanwhile, **Lombok** (population 2.4 million) plays host to far fewer foreign visitors and boasts only a handful of burgeoning tourist resorts, retaining its reputation as a more adventurous destination than its neighbour, with plenty of unspoilt beaches, wide-open spaces and extensive areas that have yet to be fully explored by visitors.

> **Bali remains the only Hindu society in Southeast Asia, and religious observance permeates every aspect of modern life.**

Until the nineteenth century, both Bali and Lombok were divided into small **kingdoms**, each domain ruled by a succession of rajas whose territories fluctuated so much that, at times, parts of eastern Bali and western Lombok were joined under a single ruler. More recently, both islands endured years of colonial

▶ Bird of paradise, Bali Bird Park

Fact file

• Bali and Lombok are part of the **Republic of Indonesia**, an ethnically diverse democracy of 234 million people. Everyone over the age of 17 is eligible to vote in the national **elections**, held at least every five years. The electorate votes first for the 550 members of the House of Representatives (DPR), and subsequently for the **president** and vice-president.

• As one of 33 self-contained provinces (*propinsi*) of Indonesia, **Bali** is overseen by a governor who is elected by Bali's Regional House of Representatives (DPRD) for a five-year term. The province is divided into one municipality, Denpasar, and eight districts, or *kabupaten*. The *kabupaten* reflect the borders of the old regencies and are named after them: Badung, Gianyar, Klungkung, Karangasem, Bangli, Buleleng, Tabanan and Jembrana.

• **Lombok** and its eastern neighbour, Sumbawa, together form the province of Nusa Tenggara Barat (West Nusa Tenggara), which is governed from Mataram and is made up of six districts and one municipality.

• Both islands are **volcanic**; the highest peak in Bali's spine of volcanoes is **Gunung Agung** (3142m). Lombok's highest point is the summit of **Gunung Rinjani** (3726m), one of the tallest mountains in Indonesia. Separating the two islands is the **Lombok Strait** – just 35km wide, but 1300m deep in places.

Swimming with mola mola

The waters around Nusa Lembongan and Nusa Penida from July to October each year are the best chance most people will ever having of spotting a *mola mola* (a.k.a. oceanic sunfish), one of the most elusive and startling of underwater creatures. The heaviest bony fish in the world, it has an average weight of 1000kg. Some specimens weigh more than double that and grow up to three metres long, making it roughly the size of a small car. *Mola* is Latin for millstone, which it resembles in being huge, grey, rough and rounded in shape – it has no tail. Fortunately it is docile and no danger to divers, as it eats jellyfish and other gelatinous marine life. Much remains unknown about this gentle giant but it is thought to spend most of its life well below 200m.

For some reason the annual shift of ocean currents brings it up to shallow waters for a few months each year, which is when enthusiasts and the merely curious head to the seas around these two small islands in the hopes of spotting one.

▼ Dancer, Ubud

rule under the Dutch East Indies government, which only ended with hard-won **independence** for Indonesia in 1949. Since then, the Jakarta-based government of Indonesia has tried hard to foster a sense of national identity among its extraordinarily diverse islands, both by implementing a unifying five-point political philosophy, the Pancasila, and through the mandatory introduction of Bahasa Indonesia, now the lingua franca for the whole archipelago. Politically, Bali is administered as a province in its own right, while Lombok is the most westerly island of Nusa Tenggara, a chain of islands stretching east as far as Timor, which is divided into two provinces, West Nusa Tenggara and East Nusa Tenggara.

Where to go

B ali's best-known resort is **Kuta**, an eight-kilometre sweep of golden sand whose international reputation as a hangout for weekending Australian surfers is enhanced by neighbouring **Seminyak**'s fashionable restaurants and chic designer shops. Travellers seeking more relaxed alternatives generally head across the southern peninsula to **Sanur** or offshore to **Nusa Lembongan**; to peaceful **Candi Dasa** or **Amed** further east; or to the black volcanic

▲ Temple gateway, Nusa Penida

9

Rice farming

Emerald-green rice terraces, or *sawah*, are one of the most memorable sights on Bali and Lombok, and you'll see them almost everywhere – ranged in steps up hillsides, tumbling down steep-sided river valleys, and encircling villages. The fertile volcanic soil, plentiful sunshine and regular downpours create ideal growing conditions that sustain at least two crops a year, and an ancient system of *subak* irrigation co-operatives (see p.462) ensures that neighbours help each other where possible. Spiritual help is also enlisted from the rice goddess, Dewi Sri, who is courted with numerous rituals and worshipped at tiny shrines in every expanse of *sawah*.

Rice farming is unrelenting, back-breaking work, and on Bali and Lombok nearly all of it is still done by hand, from the painstaking planting of the seedlings to the harvesting and threshing of the paddy. The flooded fields are ploughed by buffaloes, or tractors in some areas, and the birds are kept away by wind-chimes, rows of flapping plastic bags, strange bamboo contraptions and the occasional small boy out looking for eels, frogs and dragonflies. The rice is ready to harvest in about five months. Ducks are then herded in to graze and fertilize the land and to gobble up any pests in preparation for the new cycle.

sands of **Lovina** on the north coast. Quieter, upmarket seaside options can be found at **Jimbaran** in the south and **Pemuteran** in the northwest. On Lombok, the **Senggigi** coastline offers the widest range of accommodation, while the nearby and rapidly developing **Gili Islands** have long been a favourite with backpackers. All these resorts make comfortable bases for **divers** and **snorkellers**, within easy reach of the islands' fine reefs; Bali also boasts an unusually accessible wreck dive. **Surfers** on Bali head for the famed southcoast swells (particularly around Uluwatu) and the offshore island breaks of Nusa Lembongan, though less experienced wave-riders find Kuta and Medewi more manageable. There's also plenty of surfing potential off Lombok's south coast.

Despite the obvious attractions of the beach resorts, most visitors also venture inland to experience more traditional island life. On Bali, the once-tiny village of **Ubud** has become a hugely popular cultural centre, still charming but undeniably commercialized, where traditional dances are staged every night and the streets are full of craft shops and purveyors of alternative therapies. **Tetebatu** on Lombok occupies a similarly cool position in the foothills, although, like the island as a whole, it lacks the artistic heritage of Bali. In general, the villages on both islands are far more appealing than the towns, but Bali's capital, **Denpasar**, its former capital, **Singaraja**, and Lombok's **Ampenan–Mataram–Cakranegara–Sweta** conurbation are all worth a day-trip for their museums, markets and temples.

Bali's other big draw is its proliferation of elegant Hindu **temples**, particularly the island temple of Tanah Lot and the extensive Besakih complex on the slopes of Gunung Agung. Temple **festivals** are also well worth attending: held throughout the island and at frequent intervals during the year, most are open to tourists.

Both islands hold a number of hiking possibilities, many of them up **volcanoes**. The best is undoubtedly the climb to the summit of Lombok's **Gunung Rinjani** – one of the highest peaks in Indonesia. The ascent of Bali's **Gunung Agung** is shorter and less arduous although still pretty challenging. The climb up **Gunung Batur** is much less taxing and therefore more popular. Bali's sole **national park**, Bali Barat, has relatively

> **Despite the attractions of the beach resorts, most visitors also venture inland to experience more traditional island life.**

few interesting trails, but is a rewarding place for **bird-watching**, as is the area around Danau Bratan in the centre of the island. Even if you don't want to go hiking, it's worth considering a trip to an inland village for

11

the change of scenery (often with some lovely rice terrace views) and refreshing temperatures; the villages of **Sidemen, Tirtagangga** and **Munduk** are all good bases.

When to go

▲ Danau Batur

Located in the **tropics**, just eight degrees south of the equator, Bali and Lombok enjoy fairly constant year-round temperatures, averaging 27°C in coastal areas and the hills around Ubud and 22°C in the central volcanoes around Kintamani. Both islands are hit by an annual **monsoon**, which brings rain, wind and a sometimes unbearable 97 percent humidity from October through to March.

The **best time to visit** is outside the monsoon season, from May to September, though monsoons are, like many other events in Indonesia, notoriously unpunctual, and you should be prepared to get rained on in Ubud at any time of year. However, the prospect of a daily rainstorm shouldn't put you off: you're far more likely to get an hour-long downpour than day-long drizzle; mountain-climbing, though, is both unrewarding and dangerous at this time of year. You should also be aware of the peak **tourist seasons**: resorts on both

12

▲ Pasir Putih near Candi Dasa

islands get packed out between mid-June and mid-September and again over the Christmas–New Year period, when prices rocket and rooms can be fully booked for weeks in advance.

Average monthly temperatures and rainfall

	Jan	Feb	Mar	Apr	May	Jun	Jul	Aug	Sep	Oct	Nov	Dec
Kintamani												
°C	22	22	22	22	22	21	21	21	22	22	22	22
mm	444	405	248	174	72	43	30	21	35	50	166	257
Kuta												
°C	28	28	28	28	27	27	26	26	27	27	28	28
mm	394	311	208	115	79	67	57	31	43	95	176	268
Mataram												
°C	27	27	26	26	26	25	25	25	26	27	27	27
mm	253	254	209	155	84	67	38	21	36	168	250	209
Singaraja												
°C	27	27	27	27	28	28	27	27	28	29	28	28
mm	318	318	201	123	57	36	31	7	21	54	115	180
Ubud												
°C	27	27	27	27	27	26	26	26	26	27	27	27
mm	412	489	274	224	101	172	128	132	142	350	374	398

32

things not to miss

It's not possible to see everything that Bali and Lombok have to offer in a single trip – and we don't suggest you try. What follows is a selective and subjective taste of the islands' highlights: memorable places to stay, outstanding beaches and spectacular hikes. They're arranged in five colour-coded categories, so you can browse through the very best things to see, do, buy and experience. All highlights have a page reference to take you straight into the Guide, where you can find out more.

01 Climbing Rinjani Page **394** • The most challenging and rewarding climb on the islands takes in forest, rocky peaks and a dramatic crater-lake with its own mountain rising from the waters.

02 Bali Museum, Denpasar Page **89** • Traditional architecture and a good ethnological introduction to the island.

04 Temple festivals Page **434** • Every one of Bali's 20,000 Hindu temples holds at least one annual festival to entertain the gods with processions and offerings, which involve much preparation.

03 Sanur Page **140** • Sumptuous hotel gardens and a distinct village atmosphere make this one of south Bali's nicest resorts.

05 **Gamelan music** Page **438** • The frenetic syncopations of the Balinese xylophone provide the island's national soundtrack.

06 **Pura Meduwe Karang** Page **297** • A wonderfully exuberant example of Bali's highly ornate northern temple architecture.

07 South Lombok beaches

Page **408** •
Some of the most glorious coastline on the islands features sweeping bays and pristine coves between dramatic headlands.

08 Sunrise from Gunung Batur

Page **282** • Pre-dawn climbers of Gunung Batur are rewarded by a fabulous sunrise silhouetting the mountains of Abang, Agung and Rinjani to the east.

09 Ubud

Page **174** • The arty heart of Bali has it all: beautifully sited accommodation, great restaurants, masses of craft shops and ricefields in every direction.

10 **Kerta Gosa paintings,**
Semarapura Page 232 •
Intricate and superbly crafted examples of
classical Balinese paintings.

11 **Gili Islands** Page 376 • Pure
white sand, crystal-clear turquoise
waters and a laid-back atmosphere make
these Islands a must-visit destination.

12 **Seminyak shopping** Page
120 • Imaginative but inexpensive
design infuses everything from luscious
silk drapes to sassy outfits and unusual
tableware.

13 **Kecak dance** Page 445 • Unforgettable spectacle featuring a cappella chorus of
at least fifty men.

14 **Rice-paddies of Iseh and Sidemen** Page **261** • Among the most beautiful of the many soaring terraces carved from the hillsides that adorn the islands.

15 **Tirtagangga Water Palace** Page **257** • Extensive pools, fountains and statues in attractive gardens, surrounded by ricefields and impressive mountains.

16 **Learning to cook, paint, carve or dance** Page **208** • Ubud is the best place to take short courses in Balinese crafts, cookery and performing arts.

19

17 **Nusa Lembongan**
Page **155** • Laid-back island life, surf-breaks, diving and snorkelling sites and great beaches are all just a short boat ride from the mainland.

19 **Nusa Penida's south coast** Page **162** • Stunning limestone cliffs rise sheer from the crashing ocean.

18 **Tanah Lot** Page **320** • Bali's most photographed temple sits serenely atop its own tiny island.

20 **Surfing** Page **49** • Awesome, challenging breaks at Uluwatu, Padang Padang and Lombok's Desert Point; beginners' waves at Kuta and Medewi.

21 **Gunung Agung** Page **241** • A perfectly conical summit, impressively visible from much of Bali.

22 **Amed** Page **262** • Total relaxation in the glorious bays in the far east of the island with great accommodation, fine restaurants and fabulous diving and snorkelling.

23 **Fine Dining** Page **46** • Splash out on creative gourmet cuisine at ultra-chic restaurants in Seminyak, Ubud, Lovina and Candi Dasa.

24 South Bali nightlife Page **118** • Seminyak is the place for sundowners on the beach and sophisticated DJ-bars, while Kuta is famous for its boisterous Aussie pubs.

25 Neka Art Museum, Ubud Page **192** • A breathtaking selection of the finest paintings in Bali, from seventeenth-century narratives to 1960s expressionism and contemporary abstracts.

26 Barong-Rangda dance Page **443** • This theatrical enactment of the battle between good and evil makes for a gripping show.

27 Pemuteran Page **344** • Appealingly low-key beach haven on Bali's northwest coast, close to the spectacular Menjangan reefs.

28 Tenganan Page **250** • An ancient Balinese village that is a centre for crafts, including weaving, basketmaking and calligraphy.

29 Spas Page **53** • Pamper yourself with some of the local beauty treatments, including the famous *mandi lulur* turmeric scrub.

30 The foothills of Gunung Batukaru Page **326** • Awesome mountain views, a garden temple and charming accommodation at Wongayagede and Sarinbuana.

31 **Diving and snorkelling** Page **50** • Teeming shallow reefs, submerged canyons and visiting oceanic sunfish are just a few of the underwater attractions.

32 **Seafood barbecues**, **Jimbaran** Page **127** • Fresh fish grilled to order at candlelit tables on the beach.

Basics

Basics

Getting there

There's no shortage of international and domestic flights to Bali's only airport, Ngurah Rai Airport – officially referred to as being in Denpasar (DPS), though it's actually 3km south of Kuta and 11km south of Denpasar (see p.100 for full details). The only international airline currently serving Lombok's Selaparang Airport, 2km north of Mataram, is the Singapore Airlines subsidiary Silk Air, but Lombok is on several domestic routes. International connections are set to increase enormously however when the new Lombok International Airport opens, possibly in 2010, in the south of the island.

The most expensive times to fly to Bali and Lombok are during **high season**, which on most airlines runs from the beginning of July through to the middle or end of August and also includes most of December and the first half of January. During these peak periods flights should be reserved several weeks in advance.

If Bali or Lombok is only one stop on a longer journey, you might consider buying a **Round-the-World (RTW)** ticket. Some travel agents can sell you an "off-the-shelf" ticket that will have you touching down in up to six cities (Denpasar is on many itineraries); others will tailor-make one for you. The only way to include Lombok on such a ticket is to go via Bali.

Flights from the UK and Ireland

There are no nonstop flights **from the UK or Ireland** to Bali. Singapore Airlines and Qantas/British Airways (code share) usually offer the fastest, most comfortable London–Denpasar flights; both require a (short) transfer in Singapore, but can get you to Bali in as little as 17hr. They are often competitively priced against the other major airlines that serve Bali, most of which require longer transit times and can take up to 22hr. At the time of writing there were no flights with Indonesia's national carrier Garuda from the UK or Ireland because all Indonesian airlines were banned from using any EU airport due to concern over poor safety standards; this ban is reviewed regularly. All fares quoted below include tax.

From London and Manchester **low-season fares** rarely cost less than £600, up to £900 in **high season**. Flying from Ireland, you'll need to add on the return fare to London. Many travellers stop in Denpasar en route between London and **Australia**: Qantas/BA fares for this cost about £900/1300 and may use the Qantas-owned budget airline Jetstar for the Denpasar–Australia leg. A typical one-year open **RTW ticket** from London taking in Bangkok, Denpasar, Sydney and Los Angeles can cost as little as £1000.

To Lombok

The most convenient way of getting **to Lombok** is to fly nonstop London–Singapore with Singapore Airlines and then change on to their subsidiary carrier, Silk Air, for the nonstop flight to Mataram (3 weekly; 3hr); the entire trip can be done in 17hr. The complete return journey from London costs around £680 in low season, £820 at peak times. You can buy the return Singapore–Mataram flight direct from the Silk Air website for about £165 inclusive, but it's hard to find a London–Singapore flight for under £500. Alternatively, take the cheapest available flight to Bali, from where a one-way flight to Mataram costs about £20, a bus £6, a tourist boat £11 or a ferry less than £2. For full details on getting from Bali to Lombok, see p.356.

Flights from the US and Canada

There's a big choice of flights to Bali **from North America**, although none goes direct. Continental is the only North American carrier currently serving Bali. Flights leaving from the **west coast** cross the Pacific to Asian hubs such as Taipei, Seoul, Tokyo, Hong Kong, Singapore or Kuala Lumpur, with connections on to Bali. The best journey times are around 24hr (crossing the Pacific in one hop), although considerably more than this is not unusual; slower journeys touch down midway, perhaps in Honolulu and/or Guam, while some schedules involve overnighting en route. From the **east coast**, airlines take a northern trajectory "over the top"; for example, New York–Tokyo is typically 14hr flying time, New York–Bangkok is 17hr. Best journey times are also around 24hr. Typically you'll be looking at a **fare** of

$1300 in low season and $1700-plus in high from either starting point.

RTW or **Circle Asia** multi-stop **tickets** put together by consolidators can cost little more than the return prices quoted above. Another possibility, which could also work out cheaper, is Cathay Pacific's "**All Asia Pass**", which costs from $1399 including flights from North America to Hong Kong with stops in all or some of 23 cities over 21 days. High season adds $450 to the cost, and you can buy extra time and cities.

To **Lombok** the route is from Denpasar on a local airline, or to Singapore and then connecting with the three-hour flight to Mataram on Silk Air.

Fly less – stay longer! Travel and climate change

Climate change is the single biggest issue facing our planet. It is caused by a build-up in the atmosphere of carbon dioxide and other greenhouse gases, which are emitted by many sources – including planes. Already, flights account for around 3–4 percent of human-induced global warming: that figure may sound small, but it is rising year on year and threatens to counteract the progress made by reducing greenhouse emissions in other areas.

Rough Guides regard travel, overall, as a global benefit, and feel strongly that the advantages to developing economies are important, as are the opportunities for greater contact and awareness among peoples. But we all have a responsibility to limit our personal "carbon footprint". That means giving thought to how often we fly and what we can do to redress the harm that our trips create.

Flying and climate change

Pretty much every form of motorized travel generates CO_2, but planes are particularly bad offenders, releasing large volumes of greenhouse gases at altitudes where their impact is far more harmful. Flying also allows us to travel much further than we would contemplate doing by road or rail, so the emissions attributable to each passenger become truly shocking. For example, one person taking a return flight between Europe and California produces the equivalent impact of 2.5 tonnes of CO_2 – similar to the yearly output of the average UK car.

Less harmful planes may evolve but it will be decades before they replace the current fleet – which could be too late for avoiding climate chaos. In the meantime, there are limited options for concerned travellers: to reduce the amount we travel by air (take fewer trips, stay longer!), to avoid night flights (when plane contrails trap heat from Earth but can't reflect sunlight back to space), and to make the trips we do take "climate neutral" via a carbon offset scheme.

Carbon offset schemes

Offset schemes run by **climatecare.org**, **carbonneutral.com** and others allow you to "neutralize" the greenhouse gases that you are responsible for releasing. Their websites have simple calculators that let you work out the impact of any flight. Once that's done, you can pay to fund projects that will reduce future carbon emissions by an equivalent amount (such as the distribution of low-energy light bulbs and cooking stoves in developing countries). Please take the time to visit our website and make your trip climate neutral.

Ⓦ**www.roughguides.com/climatechange**

Flights from Australia and New Zealand

From Australia, Jetstar, the Qantas low-cost carrier, flies nonstop from Sydney (5hr 30min) and Melbourne (6hr) to Denpasar for return fares that start at A$500/650 plus tax. Qantas and Garuda fly Perth–Denpasar (4hr) from A$550 plus tax, and Air North covers Darwin–Denpasar (2hr 30min) for a minimum of A$400 plus tax. The budget Asian airline Air Asia is also planning new routes to Bali from Darwin and Perth, due to be operational from late 2008.

There are no nonstop flights from **New Zealand** to Bali, but the fastest option is to go via Sydney or Melbourne on Qantas or Air New Zealand, making connections to Denpasar with Garuda. This can be done in 12hr from Auckland or 11hr from Christchurch, with through-fares starting from NZ$1300 inclusive in low season, NZ$1700 high. Alternatively, shop around for the cheapest Sydney flight then change on to budget airline Jetstar, described above.

There are no direct **flights to Lombok** from either country, so you'll either need to change in Bali on to a half-hour domestic Denpasar–Mataram flight (cheapest if booked through a Bali travel agent; see p.101 for details of domestic airlines) or take one of the cheaper ferry routes, as described on p.356.

Flights from South Africa

There are no nonstop flights **from South Africa** to Bali or Lombok but there are reasonably fast connections on to Denpasar with Malaysia Airlines via Kuala Lumpur, Singapore Airlines via Singapore and Cathay Pacific via Hong Kong; minimum travel time is 17hr. Choose Singapore Airlines for flights to Lombok, via Singapore. Fares on all routes start from R8000–10,000.

Airlines, agents and operators

For specialist diving and surfing tours it can work out cheaper to contact Bali- and Lombok-based operators direct; see p.146 and p.372 for dive operators and p.114 for surfing packages.

Online booking

ⓦ www.expedia.com
ⓦ www.lastminute.com (in UK)
ⓦ www.opodo.co.uk (in UK)
ⓦ www.orbitz.com (in US)
ⓦ www.travelocity.com
ⓦ www.travelonline.co.za (in South Africa)
ⓦ www.zuji.com.au (in Australia)

Airlines

Air North Australia ☎ 1800/627 474, ⓦ www .airnorth.com.au.
British Airways US and Canada ☎ 1-800/ AIRWAYS, UK ☎ 0870/850 9850, Republic of Ireland ☎ 1890/626 747, Australia ☎ 1300/767 177, New Zealand ☎ 09/966 9777, South Africa ☎ 114/418 600; ⓦ www.ba.com.
Cathay Pacific US ☎ 1-800/233-2742, Canada ☎ 1-800/2686-868, UK ☎ 020/8834 8888, Australia ☎ 13 17 47, New Zealand ☎ 09/379 0861, South Africa ☎ 11/700 8900; ⓦ www .cathaypacific.com.
China Airlines US ☎ 1-917/368-2003, UK ☎ 020/7436 9001, Australia ☎ 02/9231 5588, New Zealand ☎ 09/308 3364; ⓦ www.china-airlines.com.
Continental Airlines US and Canada ☎ 1-800/523-3273, UK ☎ 0845/607 6760, Republic of Ireland ☎ 1890/925 252, Australia ☎ 02/9244 2242, New Zealand ☎ 09/308 3350, International ☎ 1800/231 0856; ⓦ www.continental.com.
EVA Air US and Canada ☎ 1-800/695-1188, UK ☎ 020/7380 8300, Australia ☎ 02/8338 0419, New Zealand ☎ 09/358 8300; ⓦ www.evaair.com.
Garuda Indonesia US ☎ 1-212/279-0756, Canada ☎ 416/924 3175, UK ☎ 020/7467 8661, Australia ☎ 02/9334 9900, New Zealand ☎ 09/366 1862; ⓦ www.garuda-indonesia.com.
JAL (Japan Air Lines) US and Canada ☎ 1-800/525-3663, UK ☎ 0845/774 7700, Republic of Ireland ☎ 01/408 3757, Australia ☎ 02/9272 1111, New Zealand ☎ 09/379 9906, South Africa ☎ 11/214 2560; ⓦ www.jal.com or www.japanair.com.
Jetstar US and Canada ☎ 1-866/397 8170, Australia ☎ 13 15 38; ⓦ jetstar.com.
Korean Air US and Canada ☎ 1-800/438-5000, UK ☎ 0800/413 000, Republic of Ireland ☎ 01/799 7990, Australia ☎ 02/9262 6000, New Zealand ☎ 09/914 2000; ⓦ www.koreanair.com.
KLM (Royal Dutch Airlines) See Northwest/ KLM. US and Canada ☎ 1-800/225-2525, UK ☎ 0870/507 4074, Republic of Ireland ☎ 1850/747 400, Australia ☎ 1300/392 192, New Zealand

ⓣ 09/921 6040, South Africa ⓣ 11/961 6727; ⓦ www.klm.com.

Malaysia Airlines US ⓣ 1-800/5529-264, UK ⓣ 0870/607 9090, Republic of Ireland ⓣ 01/6761 561, Australia ⓣ 13 26 27, New Zealand ⓣ 0800/777 747, South Africa ⓣ 11-8809 614; ⓦ www.malaysia-airlines.com.

Northwest/KLM US ⓣ 1-800/225-2525, UK ⓣ 0870/507 4074, Australia ⓣ 1-300/767-310; ⓦ www.nwa.com.

Qantas Airways US and Canada ⓣ 1-800/227-4500, UK ⓣ 0845/774 7767, Republic of Ireland ⓣ 01/407 3278, Australia ⓣ 13 13 13, New Zealand ⓣ 0800/808 767 or 09/357 8900, South Africa ⓣ 11/441 8550; ⓦ www.qantas.com.

Qatar Airways US ⓣ 1-877/777-2827, Canada ⓣ 1-888/366-5666, UK ⓣ 0870/770 4215, Australia ⓣ 386/054 855, South Africa ⓣ 11/523 2928; ⓦ www.qatarairways.com.

Royal Brunei UK ⓣ 020/7584 6660, Australia ⓣ 1300/721 271, New Zealand ⓣ 09/977 2209; ⓦ www.bruneiair.com.

Silk Air Contact via Singapore Airlines ⓦ www .silkair.com.

Singapore Airlines US ⓣ 1-800/742-3333, Canada ⓣ 1-800/663-3046, UK ⓣ 0844/800 2380, Republic of Ireland ⓣ 01/671 0722, Australia ⓣ 13 10 11, New Zealand ⓣ 0800/808 909, South Africa ⓣ 11/880 8560 or 11/880 8566; ⓦ www.singaporeair.com.

Thai Airways US ⓣ 1-212/949-8424, UK ⓣ 0870/606 0911, Australia ⓣ 1300/651 960, New Zealand ⓣ 09/377 3886, South Africa ⓣ 11/455 1018; ⓦ www.thaiair.com.

Agents and operators

Adventure Center USA ⓣ 1-800/228-8747, ⓦ www.adventure-center.com. Adventure specialists offering overland trips including trekking (Rinjani is available) and cycling.

Airtreks USA ⓣ 1-877/AIRTREKS, ⓦ www .airtreks.com. Low fares and the website links to travel blogs.

Allways Dive Expeditions Australia ⓣ 1800/338239, ⓦ www.allwaysdive.com.au. Dive and accommodation packages to Bali plus liveaboard trips east to Komodo.

Asian Pacific Adventures USA ⓣ 1-800/825-1680, ⓦ www.asianpacificadventures.com. Small-group tours including "Bali: Through an Artist's Eye", fourteen days based in Ubud concentrating on arts, festivals and culture.

Backroads USA ⓣ 1-800/462-2848, ⓦ www .backroads.com. Cycling, hiking and multi-sport tours including the nine-day "Bali Biking", which includes cycling, hiking and whitewater rafting.

Destinations Unlimited New Zealand ⓣ 09/414 1680, ⓦ www.travel-nz.com. Discounted airfares.

ebookers UK ⓣ 0800/082 3000, ⓦ www .ebookers.com; Republic of Ireland ⓣ 01/488 3507, ⓦ www.ebookers.ie. Low fares.

Flight Centre US ⓣ 1-866/967-5351, Canada ⓣ 1-877/967-5302, UK ⓣ 0870/499 0040, Australia ⓣ 13 31 33, New Zealand ⓣ 0800/243 544, South Africa ⓣ 0860 400 727; ⓦ www .flightcentre.com. Guarantee to offer the lowest air fares; also sell package holidays and adventure tours.

Harvey World Travel Australia ⓣ 1300/855492, ⓦ www.harveyworld.com.au. Sells flights and package tours with all the big operators.

Imaginative Traveller UK ⓣ 0845/077 8802, ⓦ www.imaginative-traveller.com, Australia ⓣ 1300/135 088, ⓦ www.imaginative-traveller .com.au. Small-group adventure tours to Bali and Lombok, including treks to the crater rim on Rinjani.

Intrepid Travel US ⓣ 1-800/970-7299, Canada ⓣ 1-866/915-1511, UK and Ireland ⓣ 0203/147 7777, Australia ⓣ 1300/364 512, New Zealand ⓣ 0800/600 610; ⓦ www.intrepidtravel.com. Well-regarded, small-group adventure tour operator

Tying the knot

Plenty of specialist companies can make all the practical arrangements for anyone wishing to **get married in Bali** and will also advise on the paperwork and formalities. Prices vary enormously and it's important to check exactly what is included. It's also a good idea to check out postings on travel forums. Bali Weddings International (ⓦ www.baliweddingsinternational.com), Bali Paradise Weddings (ⓦ www.baliparadiseweddings.com), Romantic Bali Weddings (ⓦ www .romanticbaliweddings.com) and Bali Exotic Wedding (ⓦ www.bali-exoticwedding .com) all get good reports. Some top-class hotels, including the *Bali Intercontinental Resort* at Jimbaran Bay, will also plan the entire event for you. Many **boutique hotels** are happy to host wedding parties; unusual, characterful options include *Desa Seni* (see p.112) and *Mick's Place* (see p.130), or *Puri Taman Sari* (p.319), which can also arrange traditional wedding processions and entertainment.

that favours local transport and travellers'-style accommodation; tours to Ubud and Lombok.

North South Travel UK ☎01245/608 291, ⓦwww.northsouthtravel.co.uk. Travel agency whose profits support projects in the developing world.

STA Travel US ☎1-800/781-4040, UK ☎0871/2300 040, Australia ☎134 STA, New Zealand ☎0800/474 400, South Africa ☎0861/781 781; ⓦwww.statravel.com. Worldwide specialists in independent travel; good discounts for students and under-26s.

Surf Travel Company Australia ☎02/9222 8870, ⓦwww.surftravel.com.au. Flights and accommodation packages – resort-based or on yachts – to the best surf spots in Bali and Lombok.

Symbiosis Expedition Planning UK ☎0845/123 2844, ⓦwww.symbiosis-travel.com. Unusual

tailor-made holidays plus small-group specialist trips to Bali and Java focusing on arts and crafts.

Thompsons Tours South Africa ☎011/770-7677, ⓦwww.thompsons.co.za. Flights and package holidays.

Trailfinders UK ☎0845/058 5858, Republic of Ireland ☎01/677 7888, Australia ☎1300/780 212; ⓦwww.trailfinders.com. One of the best-informed agents for independent travellers.

Travel Cuts US ☎1-800/592-CUTS, Canada ☎1-866/246-9762; ⓦwww.travelcuts.com. Budget travel specialist.

Travel Online New Zealand ⓦwww.travelonline .co.nz. Flights, accommodation and package deals.

USIT Northern Ireland ☎028/9032 7111, Republic of Ireland ☎01/602 1906, ⓦwww.usit.ie. Discounted and student fares.

Health

Most travellers to Bali and Lombok end up with nothing more serious than a bout of traveller's diarrhoea ("Bali belly").

However, illness and accidents (including motorbike accidents and surfers' mishaps) can't be ruled out. In the event of serious illness or accident, you'll need private health-care and possibly medical evacuation to Singapore or back home, so it is vital to have adequate **health insurance** (see p.67).

Discuss your trip with your **doctor** or a specialist travel clinic (see p.35) as early as possible to allow time to complete courses of **inoculations**. If you've come directly from a country with yellow fever, you'll need to be immunized and you should carry the immunization certificate. Apart from this no inoculations are legally required for entry into Indonesia. However, inoculations against the following serious illnesses should be discussed with your medical advisor: diphtheria, hepatitis A, hepatitis B, Japanese encephalitis, polio, rabies, tetanus, typhoid, tuberculosis (see the sources of information on p.35 or *The Rough Guide to Travel Health*).

If you have any medical conditions, are pregnant or are travelling with children, it is

especially important to get appropriate advice. If you need regular medication, carry it in your hand baggage and take a certificate/letter from your doctor detailing your condition and the drugs – it can be handy for overzealous customs officials. It's also wise to get a dental check-up before you leave home.

Treatment in Bali and Lombok

You'll find **pharmacies** (*apotik*), village **health clinics** (*klinik*) and **doctors** across the islands and **public hospitals** in each district capital and in Denpasar, supplemented by **specialist tourist clinics** in the main tourist areas. In local facilities the prevalence of English-speaking staff and their ability to tackle accidents and common tourist ailments varies from area to area. Most Balinese use local facilities together with traditional healers (*balian*) as they believe that physical symptoms are a sign of spiritual illness (see p.463 for more on this).

If you need an **English-speaking doctor**, seek advice at your hotel (some of the luxury ones have in-house doctors). For more serious problems, you'll want to access private **clinics** in the main resorts. A couple of places on the outskirts of Kuta have good reputations for dealing with expat emergencies: Bali International Medical Centre (BIMC) and International SOS (see p.123) offer consultations (from Rp540,000) at the clinic, doctor call-out ($150) and ambulance and doctor call-out ($300). The only **recompression chamber** on the island is located in Denpasar (see p.50) and there is another on Lombok (see p.364). For details of local medical facilities including **dentists** (*doctor gigi*), see the "Listings" section of each city account.

Major diseases

Located as they are in the tropics, Bali and Lombok are home to a range of diseases endemic to Southeast Asia, most of which are not a threat in travellers' home countries. For this reason inoculations are needed to protect travellers.

Most Western travellers will have had inoculations against **polio, tetanus, diphtheria and tuberculosis during childhood**. Travellers should check that they are still covered against them and have booster injections if necessary.

Typhoid is one of the most serious diseases that can be passed through contaminated food or water and it can be lethal. It produces an extremely high fever accompanied by abdominal pains, headaches, diarrhoea and red spots on the body. Dehydration is the danger here as with all intestinal problems, so take rehydration salts and get medical help urgently. Alongside inoculation, personal hygiene is vital in prevention as is some discretion about choosing where to eat – if the bits you can see are filthy, imagine the state of the kitchen which you can't. Such places are best avoided.

Avoid contact with all animals, no matter how cute. **Rabies** is spread via the saliva of infected animals, most commonly cats, dogs or monkeys, and is endemic throughout Asia. If you get bitten, wash the wound immediately with antiseptic and get medical help. Treatment involves a course of injections, but

A traveller's first-aid kit

You might want to carry:
• Antiseptic cream
• Insect repellent
• Plasters/bandaids
• Water sterilization tablets or water purifier
• Lint and sealed bandages
• Rehydration sachets
• Emergency diarrhoea treatment
• Paracetamol/aspirin/Tylenol

you won't need all of them if you have had a course of pre-departure jabs.

Japanese encephalitis is a serious viral illness causing inflammation of the brain. It is endemic across Asia and is transmitted from infected birds and animals via mosquitoes. Those planning extended periods of travel in rural areas are at risk.

There are several strains of **hepatitis** (caused by viral infections) and vaccines can offer some protection against some. Symptoms in all of them are a yellow colouring of the skin and eyes, extreme exhaustion, fever and diarrhoea. It's one of the most common illnesses that afflicts travellers to Asia and can last for months and also lead to chronic illness. Hepatitis A is transmitted via contaminated food and water or saliva. Hepatitis B is more serious and is transmitted via sexual contact or by contaminated blood, needles or syringes, which means that medical treatment itself can pose a risk if sterilization procedures are not up to scratch.

Malaria

Both Bali and Lombok are within **malarial zones** and information regarding the prevalence, prevention and treatment of malaria is being constantly updated so you must seek medical advice at least a couple of weeks before you travel. Current advice seems to be that there is little risk of malaria in the major resorts on Bali but it is advisable to check the situation before you travel. Be sure to let them know if you're visiting other parts of Indonesia or Asia, even in transit. The latest information shows an increase in the most serious form of malaria across Asia and there are reports of resistance to certain drug treatments by some strains. Pregnant women and children need specialist advice.

Malaria, which can be fatal, is passed into humans in mosquito bites (one is all it takes). The appropriate prophylactic drug depends on your destination but all are taken to a strict timetable beginning before you enter the malarious area and continuing after leaving. If you don't follow instructions precisely, you're in danger of developing the illness. The symptoms are fever, headache and shivering, similar to a severe dose of flu and often coming in cycles, but a lot of people have additional symptoms. Don't delay in seeking help: malaria progresses quickly. If you develop flu-like symptoms any time up to a year after returning home, you should inform a doctor of your travels and ask for a blood test.

However, none of the anti-malarial drugs are one hundred percent effective and it is vital to try to stop the mosquitoes biting you: sleep under a **mosquito net** – preferably one impregnated with an insecticide especially suited to the task – burn mosquito coils, and use **repellent** on exposed skin. The most powerful repellents should be brought from home; DEET is effective but can be an irritant and natural alternatives are available containing citronella, eucalyptus oil or neem oil.

Dengue fever

Another reason to avoid mosquito bites is **dengue fever**, caused by a virus carried by a different species of mosquito, which bites during the day. There is no vaccine or tablet available to prevent the illness – which causes fever, headache and joint and muscle pains among the least serious symptoms, and internal bleeding and circulatory system failure among the most serious – and no specific drug to cure it. Outbreaks occur across Indonesia throughout the year, they are not linked to a particular season – the most recent serious one in Bali was in 2007. It is vital to get an early medical diagnosis and obtain treatment to relieve symptoms.

AIDS/HIV

Bali, Java and West Papua are the three most affected places in Indonesia for **HIV**

infection although bear in mind other travellers may also be infected. Many people with HIV are also infected with hepatitis. **Condoms** can be bought on both islands, but it's as well to bring your own.

General precautions

Precautions while you are travelling can reduce your chances of getting ill. Be scrupulous about **personal hygiene** and treat even small cuts or scrapes with antiseptic. Wear flip-flops or thongs in the bathroom rather than walk around barefoot.

Avoid **food** that has sat around in the heat and always opt for freshly cooked meals; food prepared in fancy tourist places is just as likely to be suspect as that from simple streetside stalls. **Ice** is supposedly prepared under carefully regulated conditions in Indonesia, but it's impossible to be sure how it has been transported or stored once leaving the factory. If you're being really careful, avoid ice in your drinks – a lot easier said than done in the heat.

Water hygiene

Do not drink untreated tap **water** on Bali or Lombok, it is likely to contain a huge population of disease-causing microorganisms. **Bottled water** is available everywhere and there are several methods of treating either tap water or natural ground water to make it safe for drinking (and this also avoids creating mountains of waste with your empty plastic water bottles); the most traditional method is boiling, although this isn't practical when you're travelling. However, **water purifying tablets**, **water filters** and **water purifiers** are all available in travel clinics (see p.35) and specialist outdoor-equipment retailers.

Heat and skin problems

Travellers are at risk of **sunburn** and **dehydration**. Limit exposure to the sun in the hours around midday, use high-factor sunscreen and wear sunglasses and hat. Make sure that you drink enough as you'll be sweating mightily in the heat. If you're urinating very little or your urine turns dark (this can also indicate hepatitis), increase your fluid intake. When you sweat you lose salt, so add some extra to your food or take oral rehydration salts (see below).

A more serious result of the heat is **heatstroke**, indicated by high temperature, dry skin and a fast, erratic pulse. As an emergency measure, try to cool the patient off by covering them in sheets or sarongs soaked in cold water and turn the fan on them; they may need to go to hospital, though.

Heat rashes, **prickly heat** and fungal infections are also common; wear loose cotton clothing, dry yourself carefully after bathing and use medicated talcum powder or anti-fungal powder if you fall victim.

Intestinal trouble

The priority with an **upset stomach** is to prevent dehydration. Start drinking **rehydration solution** as soon as the attack starts, even if you're vomiting as well, and worry about a diagnosis later. Rehydration salts are widely available in pharmacies (Oralit and Pharolit for example) but it makes sense to carry some with you. The home-made form of these is eight teaspoons of sugar and half a teaspoon of salt dissolved in a litre of clean water.

Stomach upsets can either be a reaction to a change of diet, or can signal something more serious. You should seek medical advice if the attack is particularly severe, lasts more than a couple of days or is accompanied by constant, severe abdominal pain or fever, blood or mucus in your diarrhoea or smelly farts and burps.

Drugs such as Lomotil and Imodium, which stop diarrhoea, should only be used if you get taken ill on a journey or must travel while ill; they are not a cure, and simply paralyse your gut, temporarily plugging you up, at a time when your insides need to get rid of the toxins causing the problem.

Cuts, bites and stings

Divers should familiarize themselves with potential **underwater hazards** and the appropriate first-aid although you're probably more at risk from the cold and scrapes from coral than from tangling with sharks, barracuda, sea snakes, stingrays, scorpionfish, jellyfish, stinging hydroids and sea

urchins. All cuts should be cleansed thoroughly, disinfected immediately, covered and kept dry until healed.

On the land, there are poisonous **snakes** on both Bali and Lombok although they are shy and are only likely to attack if you step on them – they are most often encountered in ricefields, so if you are exploring these look where you are stepping. In jungle areas wear long thick socks to protect your legs when trekking and walk noisily. If you're bitten, try to remember what the snake looked like, move as little as you can and send someone for medical help. Under no circumstances do anything heroic with a Swiss army knife. There are also a few poisonous **spiders** in Bali and Lombok, and if you're bitten by one you should also immobilize the limb and get medical help. If you get **leeches** attached to you while trekking in the jungle in the rainy season, use a dab of salt, suntan oil, or a cigarette to persuade them to let go, rather than just pulling them off.

Medical resources for travellers

Online

ⓦ **health.yahoo.com** Information on specific diseases and conditions, drugs and herbal remedies, as well as advice from health experts.
ⓦ **www.cdc.gov** The US government's official site for health.
ⓦ **www.fitfortravel.scot.nhs.uk** Scottish NHS website carrying information about travel-related diseases and how to avoid them.
ⓦ **www.tripprep.com** Travel Health Online provides an online-only comprehensive database of necessary vaccinations for most countries, as well as destination and medical-service-provider information.

UK and Ireland

Hospital for Tropical Diseases Travel Clinic; Travellers Healthline Advisory Service ☎ 020/7950 7799 (50p per minute), ☎ 020/7388 9600, ⓦ www .thehtd.org). Clinic and health information by telephone.
MASTA (Medical Advisory Service for Travellers Abroad) ⓦ www.masta.org. Online health briefings and a clinic network.
Tropical Medical Bureau ⓦ www.tmb.ie. Travel advice and clinics across Ireland.

US and Canada

Canadian Society for International Health
ⓦ www.csih.org. Extensive list of Canadian travel-health centres.
Centers for Disease Control ☎ 1-800/CDC-INFO and 1-877/FYI-TRIP, ⓦ www.cdc.gov. Publishes a vast amount of information for travellers.
International Society for Travel Medicine
☎ 1-770/736-7060, ⓦ www.istm.org. Has a full list of travel climics across the world.

Australia, New Zealand and South Africa

Travellers' Medical and Vaccination Centres
☎ 1300/658 844, ⓦ www.tmvc.com.au. As well as online advice lists travel clinics throughout Australia, New Zealand, South Africa and Singapore.

Getting around

Bali and Lombok are both small enough to traverse in a few hours by road (there's no rail transport on either island), although the lack of road or route numbers can make things confusing if you are driving yourself. The major roads are good, carrying at least two-way traffic, and are fairly well maintained, although they see a lot of large trucks. On less-frequented routes, the roads are narrow and more likely to be potholed, while off the beaten track they may be no more than rough tracks.

The state of the road is a reasonable indication of the frequency of **public transport**, which is generally cheap, but offers little space or comfort. In addition to the public transport system, **tourist shuttle buses** operate between major destinations on Bali and Lombok, and although these are more expensive, they are convenient. If you prefer to drive yourself, bicycles, motorbikes, cars and Jeeps are available to rent throughout the islands, or you can rent cars or motorbikes with a driver.

Getting **between Bali and Lombok** is easy by plane or boat. For details, see p.356.

Bemos and buses

On both Bali and Lombok, public transport predominantly consists of buses and bemos. **Bemos** are minibuses of varying sizes: tiny ones scurry around local routes, while larger versions travel further afield. **Buses** operate long-distance routes such as Denpasar to Singaraja, Denpasar to Amlapura, and Ampanan-Mataram-Cakranegra-Sweta to Labuhan Lombok. Because of the rise in motorbike ownership (see box opposite), bemos are declining on the islands year on year making public transport ever more time-consuming.

You can pick up a bus or bemo from the bus or bemo **terminal** in bigger towns or flag one down on the road. Fares are paid to the driver or conductor, if there is one. You can't buy tickets in advance – except for inter-island trips, such as from Bali to Java or Lombok.

No local person negotiates a **fare**. When they want to get off they yell "Stoppa", hop out and pay the fixed fare. This system has variable accessibility to tourists. Some bemo drivers insist on agreeing the price beforehand; tourists are usually charged several times the local fare. At a few of the main terminals on the islands there are fare charts of prices to major destinations, but it can be hard to find them. There's no substitute for asking a few local people what the fare should be. It's useful to carry small

Two feet good, two wheels better

Spend even five seconds in Bali or Lombok and you'll be bowled over, often literally, by the swarms of **scooters**, **mopeds** and **motorbikes** zipping, often at warp speeds, over every inch of the islands. Some are in pursuit of only speed and adrenaline. Others are modern beasts of burden laden with cages of chickens, mountains of plastic goods, fodder for the animals or any imaginable merchandise. Yet more are families on outings; dad drives with one tiny tot perched in front, mum rides pillion clutching infant two, while child number three needs to defy gravity in some more creative position. Some estimates reckon there is one motorbike on Bali for every two Balinese – it's easy to believe.

But there's a downside; kids who look about ten and are probably not much older (illegal but hey, who's looking?) use motorbikes to zip to and from school, often with classmates balancing on the back, **helmets** aren't as common as they should be and in the first eight months of 2007 alone almost 400 people died in **road traffic accidents** on Bali, with hundreds more being seriously injured.

Aggressive marketing is fuelling the myth that everybody can afford a motorbike; Rp50,000 or Rp100,000 as a down payment and an Indonesian ID card enables you to ride out of the showroom with a brand-new gleaming bike – and a debt that demands **repayment** at Rp1.5million monthly stretching far into the future. Given that the legal minimum monthly wage on the island varies from Rp685,000–805,000 a month it is clear that such a repayment is a fearful struggle for a lot of people. Miss a couple of repayments and the bike gets hauled back and you've lost the lot.

It's a vicious circle; as more bikes appear, there are fewer bemo passengers, bemo drivers give up the struggle to make a living, there are fewer bemos and travelling by **public transport** gets harder and harder for ordinary folk – who then need to buy motorbikes to get anywhere at all.

notes so you can pay the exact fare. If you sit with your luggage on your knees, you should not be charged extra for it but bulky rucksacks will entail a supplement of around Rp5000.

Tourist shuttle buses

The most established **tourist shuttle bus operator** is Perama (Wwww.peramatour .com) serving all major tourist destinations. Fares generally work out at least double that of public transport, but the big advantage is that their service is usually direct, while bemo routes often require connections; also there's room for luggage, wheelchairs, baby buggies and surfboards. For example, fares from Kuta are Rp30,000 to Ubud and Rp85,000 to Lovina, from Ubud Rp40,000 to Candi Dasa or Padang Bai and from Mataram to Kuta (Lombok) Rp90,000. You should try to book the day before, but you can sometimes get a seat the same day. Hotel pick-ups and drop-offs are available (Rp5000). The section "Travel details", at the end of every Guide chapter,

lists routes. Perama also run a tourist-boat service between Bali and Lombok. (see p.356 for details).

There are several **rival companies** operating on both Bali and Lombok who advertise throughout tourist areas and offer a similar service, but are not as high profile. These are worth checking out if, for example, the Perama office is inconveniently far from the town centre (as in Lovina and Ubud): a rival company may drop you more centrally. They can also make for a calmer arrival: every hotel tout on Bali and Lombok knows when and where the Perama bus arrives and waits to entice passengers to their lodging. This has advantages when beds are limited but a crowd of touts gathering to accost new arrivals can be an unpleasant entrance anywhere. Smaller companies attract less notice.

Ferries

Huge inter-island **ferries** connect Bali and Lombok with the islands on either side, from

Distance Charts (in kilometres)

Bali

	Amed	Candi Dasa	Denpasar	Gilimanuk
Ubud	68	54	23	157
Sanur	64	65	7	141
Nusa Dua	81	96	24	158
Ngurah Rai Airport	76	85	13	147
Lovina	89	139	89	79
Kuta	73	82	10	144
Gilimanuk	197	206	134	–
Denpasar	57	72	–	
Candi Dasa	32	–		
Amed	–			

Lombok

	Kuta	Labuhan Lombok	Lembar	Mataram
Tetebatu	62	53	85	59
Senggigi	66	105	39	13
Senaru	142	72	115	89
Sembalun Bumbung	105	44	128	102
Sapit	85	24	108	82
Pemenang	80	119	53	27
Mataram	53	92	26	–
Lembar	64	113	–	
Labuhan Lombok	95	–		
Kuta	–			

Gilimanuk to Java (see p.337), from Padang Bai to Lembar on Lombok (see p.253) and from Labuhan Lombok (see p.401) to Sumbawa. They run frequently and regularly day and night.

Access to Nusa Lembongan and Nusa Penida plus the many islands around the Lombok coast, most famously the Gili Islands, is by small local ferries. These either run on a timetable (Nusa Lembongan) or depart when full (Gili Islands); buy tickets beforehand at beachside ticket offices.

Tourist boats

The **Perama boat service** between Sanur and **Nusa Lembongan** is no faster or more luxurious than local boats but ties in with the Perama bus schedules between Sanur and other Bali destinations. Perama also operate a **tourist boat service** between Padang Bai on Bali and the **Gili Islands** and Sengiggi on Lombok. It is convenient, faster than the public ferry, and ties in with the Perama schedules between Padang Bai and other Bali destinations (see p.356).

Taxis

Metered **taxis** – with a "Taxi" sign on the roof – cruise for business in Kuta, Sanur, Nusa Dua, Jimbaran and Denpasar on Bali, and Ampenan-Mataram-Cakranegara-Sweta, Lembar and Senggigi on Lombok and are not expensive. On Bali there is Rp5000 flagfall, on Lombok Rp3750, and then Rp4000 per kilometre day or night. It's usual to round the fare up to the nearest Rp5000 when paying.

On Bali, there are several companies, the most common being the light-blue Bali Taksi (T0361/701111, W www.bluebirdgroup.com). Always check that the meter is turned on when you get in. As an example of fares, to get from Jalan Arjuna in Legian up to Jalan Laksmana in Petitenget will cost you around Rp20,000.

On Lombok, the light-blue Lombok Taksi (T0370/627000, W www.bluebirdgroup.com) have similar charges: to get from Mataram to central Senggigi costs around Rp40,000.

As an alternative, you can simply flag down an empty bemo and charter it like a taxi,

Kuta	Lovina	Ngurah Rai Airport	Nusa Dua	Sanur	Ubud
33	40	36	47	30	–
15	96	14	25	–	
14	113	11	–		
3	102	–			
99	–				
–					

Pemenang	Sapit	Sembalun Bumbung	Senaru	Senggigi	Tetebatu
86	43	63	99	72	–
25	95	118	87	–	
62	56	36	–		
129	20	–			
109	–				
–					

although you'll have to bargain hard before you get in.

Dokar/cidomo

The traditional form of transport on the islands is horse and cart. Called **dokar** on Bali and **cidomo** on Lombok, they usually ply the back routes, often transporting heavy loads. They're also used for city transport in Ampenan-Mataram-Cakranegara-Sweta and as tourist vehicles in Kuta and Senggigi. Negotiate a price before you get in.

Rental vehicles

There's a big selection of vehicles available for rental on the islands; think about your itinerary before you decide what you need. In the mountains, you need power for the slopes and on rougher terrain clearance is vital.

Renters must produce an **international drivers' licence** or **tourist driving licence**. On major holidays (like Galungan and Nyepi) vehicles are snapped up quickly by Balinese so make arrangements in advance. Rental vehicles need to have both Balinese and Lombok registration to travel on both islands, so you must tell the rental agency if you intend to take the vehicle between the islands, and check with them exactly what paperwork is required.

The multinational **rental agency** Avis (Ⓦ www.avis.com) has a Bali office although with their prices at $350–450 per week it's far more economical to rent a car locally after you arrive; see Listings for the major resorts for outlets or enquire at your hotel. Typically you'll be looking at Rp90,000–100,000 for a Suzuki Jimny for one day, Rp150,000 for a Kijang or Isuzu Panther and Rp175,000 for a Feroza. Discounts are available for longer rentals.

Some outfits offer partial **insurance** as part of the fee; typically, the maximum you'll end up paying in the event of any accident will be $150–500. The conditions of insurance policies vary considerably and you should make certain you know what you're signing. Bear in mind that under this system, if there is minor damage – for example if you

smash a light – you'll end up paying the whole cost of it.

Before you take a vehicle, **check** it thoroughly and record any damage that has already been done, or you may end up being blamed for it. Most vehicle rental agencies keep your passport as security, so you don't have a lot of bargaining power in the case of any dispute. Wherever you get the vehicle from, take a telephone contact number to get in touch in case of breakdown.

Tourist driving licences

If you don't have an international driving licence it's possible to obtain a **tourist driving licence**, which allows you to drive. They are available for cars or motorbikes (Rp200,000) from Pelayan Sim Tourist (Mon–Fri 8am–3pm, Sat 8am–1pm; ☎0361/243939) inside the Kantor Bersama Samsat on Jalan Cok Agung Tresna in the Renon district of Denpasar. Take a passport and home driving licence.

On the road

Traffic in Indonesia drives **on the left**. There's a maximum speed limit of 70kph. Fuel costs Rp4750 a litre, but may well rise.

Foreign drivers need to carry an **international driving licence** or **tourist driving licence** and the **registration documents** of the vehicle or you're liable to a fine. Seatbelts must be used. The police carry out regular spot checks and you'll be fined for any infringements.

In recent years, there have been reports of police stopping foreign drivers for supposed infringements and "fining" them on the spot – accepting only foreign currency – in what is essentially an extortion racket. Official clean-up campaigns have followed; if it happens the best advice is to keep calm and have some easily accessible notes well away from your main stash of cash if you have to hand some over.

It's worth driving extremely defensively. **Accidents** are always unpleasant, disagreements over the insurance situation and any repairs can be lengthy, and many local people have a straightforward attitude to accidents involving tourists – the visitor must be to blame. Don't drive at **night** unless you absolutely have to, largely because pedestrians, cyclists, food carts and horse carts all use the roadway without any lights. There are also plenty of roadside ditches.

Hiring a driver

Hundreds of drivers in tourist areas offer **chartered transport** – this means you rent their vehicle with them as the driver. Most have cars or Jeeps, but you can usually find somebody with a motorbike. You're expected to pay for the driver's meals and accommodation if the trip takes more than a day, and you must be very clear about who is paying for fuel, where you want to go and stop, and how many people will be travelling. With somebody driving who knows the roads, you've got plenty of time to look around and fewer potential problems to worry about, but it's very difficult to guarantee the quality of the driving. You'll pay Rp350,000–400,000 for the vehicle, driver and fuel, but you'll need to bargain. Try to get a personal recommendation of reliable drivers; we have listed our recommendations in Kuta (see p.103), Ubud (see p.180), Candi Dasa (see p.249) Lovina (see p.310) and Senggigi (see p.375) or check the Bali and Lombok Travel

Forum (www.travelforum.org/bali) or Lombok Lovers Forum (groups.msn.com/LombokLovers).

Motorbike and bicycle rental

Motorbikes available for rent vary from scooters through small 100cc jobs to more robust trail-bikes. Prices start at Rp50,000 per day without insurance with discounts for longer rentals. You'll need to show an international motorcycle licence or tourist driving licence. Conditions on Bali and Lombok are not suitable for inexperienced drivers, with heavy traffic on major routes, steep hills and difficult driving off the beaten track. There are increasing numbers of accidents involving tourists, so don't take risks. All motorcyclists, both drivers and passengers, must wear a helmet; these will be provided by the rental outlet, but most aren't up to much.

In most tourist areas, it's possible to rent a **bicycle** for around Rp25,000 a day; check its condition before you set off and carry plenty of water. Helmets and puncture repair kits are not provided so, if you intend to cycle a lot, it would be wise to take your own; bigger outfits

supply bike locks. There is occasional bag-snatching from bicycles in less populated areas, so attach your bag securely to yourself or the bike. Ubud is a popular area for cycling day-trips and guided rides (see p.180) and they are available in Lombok (see p.373). If you're planning to tour the island by bike, bear in mind that, should you get tired or stranded, bemos will be extremely reluctant to pick you and your bike up.

Planes

Bali's domestic terminal is adjacent to the international one at Ngurah Rai Airport, 3km south of Kuta; **Lombok's** domestic arrivals share the Selaparang Airport runway in Mataram with the handful of international flights. Domestic airlines have ticket sales counters in the domestic terminal at Ngurah Rai Airport, at Selaparang Airport and/or offices in nearby cities (see p.101 & p.363 for details). Fares depend on the airline and the conditions of the ticket but typical fares between Bali and Lombok are Rp365–450,000 and between Bali and Jakarta around Rp535,000.

Accommodation

Whatever your budget, the overall standard of accommodation in Bali and Lombok is high. Even the most inexpensive lodgings are enticing, nearly always set in a tropical garden and with outdoor seating. Interiors can be a bit sparse – and dimly lit – but the verandahs encourage you to do as local people do and spend your waking hours outdoors.

The majority of cheap places to stay are classed as **losmen**, a term that literally means homestay, but is most commonly used to describe any small-scale and inexpensive accommodation, be it in the grounds of the family home or not. Nearly everything else falls into the **hotels** category, most of which offer air-conditioning and a swimming pool. Rooms in both losmen and

hotels are often in "**cottages**" (sometimes known as "**bungalows**"), which can be anything from terraced concrete cubes to detached rice-barn-style chalets. **Villas** are private holiday homes, usually pretty luxurious, catering for couples, small groups and families.

Room rates in all classes of accommodation can vary considerably according to demand. **Internet** rates for hotel rooms are nearly always cheaper than walk-in prices; where available, hotels' own websites can offer good deals, but it's always worth checking online agencies as well (see box below, for some leads). During **low season** (Feb–June and Sept–Nov) many moderate and expensive hotels also offer good discounts on walk-in rates. In **peak season** (Jan, July, Aug & Dec) however rates can rise dramatically and rooms are at a premium so it's advisable to **reserve** ahead. **Check-out time** in losmen and hotels is usually noon.

Losmen

Many **losmen** (generally ❶–❸) are still family-run operations. Though a few still charge a bargain **price** of Rp50,000 for their simplest double rooms, the vast majority ask at least Rp70,000 and in high season rates can be hiked at whim so you should be prepared to pay a minimum of Rp100,000 – and as much as Rp200,000 on stratospherically popular Gili Trawangan. Very few losmen offer **single rooms** (*kamar untuk satu orang*), so lone travellers will normally get put in a double room at 75–100 percent of the full price.

Many losmen now offer a range of options, charging more for hot water, air-conditioning and the best views; an increasing number are building swimming pools too. But generally furnishings are simple and there's often a thin blanket rather than a top-sheet. Most rooms come with fans and netted windows (sticky tape comes in handy for repairing holes). Lighting is often dim, so some travellers pack their own high-wattage bulb, or you could buy a cheap portable desklight in a local supermarket.

Online booking agents
Asia Hotels ⓦwww.asiahotels.com
Bali Hotels ⓦwww.balihotels.com
Bali Life ⓦwww.balilife.com
Bali Online Hotels ⓦwww.indo
.com/hotels
Lombok Hotels ⓦwww
.lombokhotels.com
Travelethos ⓦwww.travelethos.com

The best losmen provide a complimentary flask of tea, and most include **breakfast** (*makan pagi*) in the price of the room. If you're lucky, this might run to fruit salad and banana pancakes, or may simply comprise toast and coffee.

Hotels

The least attractive type of lodgings on Bali and Lombok are the **cheap urban hotels** (❶–❹) such as those in Denpasar and Singaraja, which cater for short-stay Indonesian businesspeople and can feel soulless and lonely. Nonetheless, they are usually clean enough and tend to be located near transport terminals.

Accommodation in **moderately priced hotels** (❺–❼) is often in "cottages" or "bungalows" and facilities generally include air-conditioning and a swimming pool. Of all the **expensive hotels** (❽–❾) on Bali and Lombok, only one is high-rise – the nine-storey *Inna Grand Bali Beach* in Sanur – and this caused such consternation when built that a law now prevents any other hotel from being taller than a coconut palm. As a result, even the massive international hotels such as Sanur's *Bali Hyatt* and Lombok's *Sheraton Senggigi Beach Resort* are low-rise structures, many of them designed to evoke traditional Balinese palaces (*puri*) and temples (*pura*). This *puri-pura* style, dubbed **Bali baroque** or Baliesque because of its excessive use of ornamentation, works better in some buildings than others, but adds a distinct character to the upmarket resorts. Their grounds are usually equally grand, with ponds, endless lawns and profuse tropical shrubbery.

If you're looking for smaller-scale places with more character, opt for those that classify themselves as **boutique hotels**. Some comprise as few as half a dozen rooms, and they're generally stylish and luxurious; many are well priced, too. Outstanding examples include *Desa Seni* in Canggu, *Alam Jiwa* and *Tegal Sari* in Ubud, *Aquaria, The Watergarden* and *Kubu Bali* in Candi Dasa, *Damai Lovina Villas* in Lovina, *Cabé Bali* in Tirtagangga, *Sarinbuana Eco Lodge* in Sarinbuana, *Prana Dewi* in Wongayagede and *Sanda Butik Villas* in Sanda. They are rarer on Lombok but *Desa*

Dunia Beda on Gili Trawangan and *Villa Nautilus* on Gili Meno fit the bill.

An increasing number of Bali's and Lombok's **super-luxury hotels** (US$250–800) are designed in chic modern-Asian style and often comprise private garden-compounds, sometimes with personal plunge-pools as well. We've detailed some of these places, most notably the *Four Seasons Resort* in Jimbaran, *The Legian* in Seminyak, the *Tugu* in Canggu, the *Amandari* in Ubud, Candi Dasa's *Amankila*, *Spa Village Tembok* in northern Bali and the *Oberoi* in Lombok.

Villas

If you want posh accommodation for a family or small group, or extremely private accommodation for a couple, it's worth considering a **villa**. Sometimes the home of an expat, rented out for most of the year, or sometimes purpose-built for holiday rentals, villas are usually designed in appealing Balinese style and equipped with a private pool and kitchen. They can be rented by the day or the week, and prices (from $50 per night for two people but more commonly $50–100 per person per night) often include the services of a housekeeper and cook. Be aware though that some hotels advertise their poshest bungalows as "villas" even though they lack the self-sufficiency of genuine holiday homes. Note too that a growing number of villas operate illegally, without government licences, which means they could get closed down at any time; you may be able to check a villa's licence online, and licences must be displayed prominently on the premises. Online villa-rental **agencies** include ⓦwww.balion.com, ⓦwww.bali-tropical-villas.com and ⓦwww.balivillas.com.

Camping

There are so many cheap losmen near almost every decent beach on Bali and Lombok that it's hardly worth lugging a tent and sleeping bag all the way around the islands. It's not easy to get permission to **camp** in Bali Barat National Park and it's considered inappropriate to camp on the slopes of Bali's most sacred mountains, although camping on Lombok's Gunung Rinjani is normal practice and tents, sleeping bags and cooking equipment can be rented for the climb.

Long-term accommodation

Expat **house rental** is huge in Bali, particularly around Seminyak, Sanur and Ubud, and many local **real-estate agents** specialize in that market; try Bali Real Estate Agents (ⓣ0361/284069, ⓦwww.balirealestateagents.com), House of Bali (ⓣ0361/738996, ⓦwww.houseofbali.com)

Accommodation price codes

All the accommodation listed in this book has been given one of the following price codes, corresponding to the **least expensive double room** in high season if booked via the hotel website, where available, and excluding tax. Rates in low season may be up to fifty percent lower and booking via online agencies at any time may give you significant discounts. Nearly all losmen and hotels quote their rates exclusive of government **tax** (ten or eleven percent); many of the more expensive hotels add an extra ten percent **service charge** (in hotel-speak, these supplements are usually referred to as "plus-plus").

In general, losmen in the ❶–❹ categories post their prices in **rupiah**. The most upmarket hotels quote their rates in **US dollars**, or sometimes in **euros**, and usually accept cash, traveller's cheques or credit cards, but will also convert to rupiah. **Credit-card** transactions are always in rupiah, so check the in-house exchange rate.

❶ Under Rp85,000; under US$9
❷ Rp86,000–135,000; US$10–14
❸ Rp136,000–195,000; US$15–21
❹ Rp196,000–305,000; US$22–32
❺ Rp306,000–505,000; US$33–55

❻ Rp506,000–755,000; US$56–80
❼ US$81–130
❽ US$131–200
❾ above US$200

Bathrooms

The vast majority of losmen and all hotel rooms have en-suite **bathrooms** (*kamar mandi*), though the very cheapest places may offer cold water only. **Toilets** (*wc*, pronounced *way say*) are usually Western-style, though flushing is sometimes done manually, with water scooped from an adjacent pail. The same pail and scoop is used by Indonesians to wash themselves after going to the toilet (using the left hand, never the right, which is for eating), but most tourist bathrooms also have toilet paper.

Many Balinese and Sasak people still **bathe** in rivers, but indoor bathing is traditionally done by means of the scoop and slosh method, or **mandi**, using water that's stored in a huge basin. This basin is not a bath, so never get in it; all washing is done outside it and the basin should not be contaminated by soap or shampoo. Many losmen and all hotels in the bigger resort areas provide showers as well as *mandi*. Outside the bigger resorts, the very cheapest rooms may not have hot water (*air panas*).

In the more stylish places, bathrooms can be delightful, particularly if they are designed with open roofs and bedecked with plants. These "**garden bathrooms**" often have showers and *mandi* fed by water piped through sculpted flues and floors covered in a carpet of smooth, rounded pebbles.

or In Touch (☎0361/731049, ⓦwww .intouchbali.com). The free fortnightly *Bali Advertiser* (ⓦwww.baliadvertiser.biz) always carries a page or two of property ads, and is available at hotels, restaurants and supermarkets. If you're thinking about **buying** or building a house in Bali, check out the

advice on Owning Property in Bali (ⓦwww .baliproperties.com). Be very wary of any **time-share deal**: many tourists fail to read the small print and have found themselves making unwise investments and unable to claim back their money. See p.70 for related cons.

Food and drink

If you come to Bali or Lombok expecting the range and exuberance of the cooking elsewhere in Southeast Asia, you'll be disappointed. Somehow the ingenuity and panache don't seem to have reached this far, or maybe they've been elbowed out of the way by Japanese, Mexican and even Russian food. However, there's an impressive array of food available. Ironically, the most elusive cuisines on the islands are the native Balinese and Sasak.

At the inexpensive end of the scale, you can get a bowl of *bakso ayam* (chicken noodle soup) for Rp5000 from one of the **carts** (*kaki lima*) on the streets, at bus stations during the day and at night markets after dark. Slightly upmarket are **warung** or *rumah makan* (eating houses), ranging from a few

tables and chairs in a kitchen to fully fledged restaurants. There's usually a menu, but in the simplest places it's just rice or noodle dishes on offer. Most places that call themselves **restaurants** cater for a broader range of tastes, offering Western, Indonesian and Chinese food, while others specialize in a particular cuisine such as Mexican, Japanese or Italian. The multinational fast-food chains have also arrived in the tourist and city areas.

Vegetarians get a good deal, with tofu (*tahu*) and *tempeh*, a fermented soybean cake, alongside plenty of fresh vegetables.

Restaurant **etiquette** is pretty much the same as in the West, with waiter service the norm. If you're eating with friends, don't count on everyone's meal arriving together; there may be just one gas burner in the kitchen.

Prices vary dramatically depending on the location rather than the quality of the meals. In the humblest local rumah makan, a simple rice dish such as nasi campur is about Rp7000–8000, while basic tourist restaurant prices start at Rp12,000 for their version of the same dish up to Rp60,000 or more in the plushest location. If you choose non-Indonesian food such as pizza, pasta and steak, prices start at around Rp25,000 in tourist restaurants and the sky is the limit (Rp270,000 for example) for imported steaks with all the trimmings in swanky locations. Bear in mind that restaurants with more expensive food also have pricier drinks and, in addition, most places add anything up to 21 percent to the bill for tax and service.

See p.482 for a menu reader of dishes and common terms.

Styles of cooking

Throughout Bali and Lombok the most widely available food is **Indonesian** rice- and noodle-based meals, followed closely by **Chinese** (essentially Cantonese) food, as well as a vast array of **Western** food in the resorts. Native Balinese food on Bali, and Sasak food on Lombok, is something you'll need to search out. Should you wish to learn more about local food, cookery schools for visitors are available; see p.309.

Indonesian food

Based on rice (*nasi*) or noodles (*mie* or *bakmi*), with vegetables, fish or meat, **Indonesian food** is flavoured with chillies, soy sauce (*kecup*), garlic, ginger, cinnamon, turmeric and lemongrass. You'll also find chilli sauce (*sambal*) everywhere.

One dish available in even the simplest warung is **nasi campur**, boiled rice with small amounts of vegetables, meat and fish, often served with a fried egg and *krupuk* (huge prawn crackers). The accompanying dishes vary from day to day, depending on what's available. Other staples are **nasi goreng** and **mie goreng**, fried rice or noodles with vegetables, meat or fish, often with fried egg and *krupuk*. The other mainstays of the Indonesian menu are **gado-gado**, steamed vegetables served with a spicy peanut sauce, and **sate**, small kebabs of beef, pork, chicken, goat or fish, barbecued over a fire and served on a bamboo stick with spicy peanut sauce.

Fish is widely available; grilled, kebabed, baked in banana leaves or in curries. However, although tasty, by Western standards a lot of it is overcooked.

Inexpensive, authentic and traditionally fiery **Padang** fare is sold in rumah makan Padang, in every sizeable town. Padang food is cold and displayed on platters. There are no menus; when you enter you either select your composite meal by pointing to the dishes on display, or just sit down, the staff bring you a selection, and you pay by the number of plates you have eaten from at the end. Dishes include *kangkung* (water spinach), *tempeh*, fried eggplant, curried eggs, fried fish, meat curry, squid or fish curry, potato cakes, beef brain curry and fried cow's lung.

Balinese food

The everyday **Balinese** diet is a couple of rice-based meals, essentially nasi campur, eaten whenever people feel hungry, supplemented with snacks such as *krupuk*. The full magnificence of Balinese cooking is reserved for ceremonies. One of the best dishes is **babi guling**, spit-roasted pig, served with *lawar*, a spicy blood mash. Another speciality is **betutu bebek**, smoked duck, cooked very slowly – this has to be ordered in advance from restaurants.

The Balinese rarely eat desserts but, *bubuh injin*, **black rice pudding**, named after the colour of the rice husk, is available in tourist spots. The rice is served with a sweet coconut-milk sauce, fruit and grated coconut.

Rice cakes (*jaja*) play a major part in ceremonial offerings but are also a daily food.

Sasak food

According to some sources, the name "Lombok" translates as "chilli pepper" – highly appropriate considering the savage heat of traditional **Sasak food**. It's not easy to track down, however, and you'll find Indonesian and Chinese food far more widely available on Lombok. Traditional Sasak food uses rice as the staple, together with a wide variety of vegetables, a little meat (although no pork), and some fish, served in various sauces, often with a dish of **chilli sauce** on the side in case it isn't hot enough already. Anything with *pelecing* in the name is served with **chilli sauce**. Taliwang dishes, originally from Sumbawa, are also available on Lombok, consisting of grilled or fried food with, you've guessed it, a chilli sauce. All parts of the animals are eaten, and you'll find plenty of offal on the menu.

Fine dining

Just as it's possible to get by spending a dollar or less for a meal in Bali or Lombok, you can also enjoy some superb **fine dining** experiences on the islands. Plenty of innovative chefs, some Western, some Asian, have imported and adapted modern international gourmet cooking. They offer menus that are creative and imaginative and, best of all, taste great. Restaurants serving this food are invariably stylish, with excellent service, charging US$30–50 per head. This can seem a lot in the context of Indonesian prices, but when compared with restaurants of a similar standard in London or New York, it's decidedly good value. Top choices include the restaurants at *Damai Lovina Villas* in the north of the island (see p.308), *Kafé Warisan* and *Ku dé Ta* in Seminyak (see p.118), *Ma Joly* in Tuban (see p.117), *Mozaic* and *Lamak* in Ubud (see p.202) and *Seasalt* at the *Alila* in Candi Dasa (see p.247).

Fresh fruit

The range of **fresh fruit** available on Bali and Lombok is startling. You'll see **banana**, **coconut** and **papaya** growing all year round, and **pineapple** and **watermelon** are always in the markets. Of the citrus fruits, the giant **pomelo** is the most unusual to visitors – larger than a grapefruit and sweeter. **Guava**, **avocado** (served as a sweet fruit juice with condensed milk), **passion fruit**, **mango**, **soursop** and its close relative, the **custard apple**, are all common. Less familiar are the seasonal **mangosteen** with a purple skin and sweet white flesh; the hairy **rambutan**, closely related to the lychee; the **salak** or **snake-fruit**, named after its brown scaly skin; and the **starfruit**, which is crunchy but rather flavourless. **Jackfruit**, which usually weighs 10–20kg, has firm yellow segments around a large stone inside its green bobbly skin. This is not to be confused with the **durian**, also large but with a spiky skin and a pungent, sometimes almost rotten, odour. Some airlines and hotels ban it because of the smell, but devoted fans travel large distances and pay high prices for good-quality durian fruit.

Drinks

Bottled water is widely available throughout the islands (Rp2000–3000 for 1.5 litres in supermarkets), as are international brands of

Betel

One habit that you'll notice in Bali and Lombok, and throughout Southeast Asia, predominantly among older people, is the chewing of **betel**. Small parcels, made up of three ingredients – areca nut wrapped in betel leaf that has been smeared with lime – are lodged inside the cheek. When mixed with saliva, these are a stimulant as well as producing an abundance of bright red saliva, which is regularly spat out on the ground and eventually stains the lips and teeth red. Other ingredients can be added according to taste, including tobacco, cloves, cinnamon, cardamom, turmeric and nutmeg. You may also come across decorated boxes used to store the ingredients on display in museums.

soft drinks; you'll pay higher prices in restaurants. There are also delicious **fruit juices** although many restaurants automatically add sugar to their juices so you'll need to specify if you don't want that. Inexpensive tourist restaurants charge from Rp5000 for juice drinks, excluding tax and service.

Indonesians are great **coffee** (*kopi*) and **tea** (*teh*) drinkers. Locally grown coffee (*kopi Bali* or *kopi Lombok*) is drunk black, sweet and strong. The coffee isn't filtered, so the grounds settle in the bottom of the glass. If you want milk added or you don't want sugar, you'll have to ask (see p.482). Increasing numbers of cappuccino machines have arrived in the swisher tourist restaurants along with imported coffee, and Nescafé instant coffee is also available.

Alcohol

Locally produced **beer** includes Bintang, a light, reasonably palatable lager. Expect to pay from Rp8000–9000 for a 620ml bottle from a supermarket and Rp15,000 in a simple restaurant. Draught beer is available in some places. There are four varieties of locally brewed organic Storm beer from the palest (like a British bitter ale) to the darkest (a stout).

Many tourist restaurants and bars offer an extensive list of **cocktails** and imported spirits (Rp45,000 upwards).

Locally produced **wine** is available on Bali, made from grapes grown in the north of the island by Hatten Wines or from imported grape juice by Wine of the Gods (Rp175,000 upwards per bottle) – the Hatten rosé and the sparkling wines get the best reports. Imported spirits are available in major tourist areas, where wines from Australia and New Zealand, California, Europe and South America are also available, mostly Rp45,000 upwards for a glass and Rp350,000 upwards for a bottle. Local brews include *brem*, a type of rice wine, *tuak*, palm beer brewed from palm-tree sap, and powerful *arak*, a palm or rice spirit that is often incorporated into highly potent local cocktails.

Look out for **happy hours** in tourist areas – the most generous last all evening.

Festivals and events

Balinese festivals

Bali has a complex timetable of religious ceremonies and festivals both local and island-wide. One of the biggest is **Galungan**, an annual event in the *wuku* calendar, which means it takes place every 210 days. This ten-day festival celebrates the victory of good over evil and all the ancestral souls are thought to visit earth. Elaborate preparations take place: *penjor* – bamboo poles hung with offerings – arch over the road, offerings are prepared and animals slaughtered for the feasts. Galungan day itself is spent with the family, praying and making offerings. The following day, Manis Galungan, is the day for visiting friends. The final and most important day is **Kuningan**, when families once again get together, pray and make offerings as the souls of the ancestors return to heaven.

The main festival of the *saka* year is New Year, **Nyepi**, generally in March or April, the major purification ritual of the year. The days before Nyepi are busy: religious objects from temples are purified in sacred springs or the sea. The night before Nyepi the evil spirits are frightened away with drums, gongs, cymbals, firecrackers and huge **papier-mâché monsters** (*ogah-ogah*). On the day itself, everyone sits quietly at home to persuade any remaining evil spirits that Bali is completely deserted. Visitors are expected to stay quietly in their hotels.

Every temple has an annual **odalan**, an anniversary and purification ceremony. The majority of these are small, local affairs, but the celebrations at the large directional temples draw large crowds (see p.434). There are also local temple festivals related to the moon, some associated with full moon and some with the night of complete darkness.

Another annual event, **Saraswati**, in honour of the goddess of knowledge (see p.429), takes place on the last day of the *wuku* year. Books are particularly venerated and the faithful are not supposed to read, while students attend special ceremonies to pray for academic success. Other annual festivals are **Tumpek Kandang**, when all animals are blessed, and **Tumpek Landep**, a day of devotion to all things made of metal, including tools, motorbikes, cars and buses.

Nonreligious anniversaries that are celebrated in Bali include April 21, **Kartini Day**, commemorating the birthday in 1879 of Raden Ajeng Kartini, an early Indonesian nationalist and the first female emancipationist. Parades, lectures and social events are attended by women, while the men and children take over their duties for the day. September 20, the anniversary of the **Badung puputan** in Denpasar in 1906 (see p.421), is commemorated each year by a fair in Alun-alun Puputan. November 20 is **Heroes Day** in Bali, in remembrance of the defeat of the nationalist forces led by Ngurah Rai at Marga in 1946 (see p.423).

The huge month-long **Arts Festival** (ⓦwww.baliartsfestival.com) celebrates all Balinese arts and is held annually at Denpasar's Taman Budaya Arts Centre, usually from mid-June. Watersports competitions and parades are the highlights of the **Kuta Karnival** (ⓦwww.kutakarnival.com) which runs for a week, usually in September. Up in Ubud, there's the **Bali Spirit Festival** of world music, dance and yoga every March (ⓦwww.balispiritfestival.com) and the **Ubud Writers and Readers literary festival** (ⓦwww.ubudwritersfestival.com), with talks and workshops from an international cast of writers, every October.

Lombok festivals

In **Lombok**, festivals are a mixture of Hindu, Muslim and local folk festivals. **Ciwaratri** (in Jan) is celebrated by Hindus in West Lombok, where followers meditate without sleeping or eating for 24 hours to redeem their sins. **Nyale** (see p.403) takes place annually in February or March and is celebrated along the south coast when thousands of people flock to witness the first appearance of the sea worms. **The Anniversary of West Lombok**, a formal government event, takes place on April 17. **Harvest festival** is celebrated by Balinese Hindus in March/April at Gunung Pengsong, when they give thanks for the harvest by the ritual slaughter of a buffalo. **Lebaran Topat** occurs seven days after Ramadan, when Sasak people visit

Traditional calendars

There are two **traditional calendars** in Bali in addition to the Western calendar. The Hindu **saka** calendar operates with years comprising 354–356 days, is divided into twelve months, and runs eighty years behind the Gregorian year: 2010 is 1930 in the *saka* calendar.

Also in use is the magnificently complex **wuku**, *pawukon* or *uku* calendar, based on a 210-day lunar cycle; these cycles are unnumbered. The cycle is divided into weeks that are ten days long, nine days long, eight days long and so on down to weeks that are one day long. All of these weeks run concurrently and have specific names – for example, the three-day week is called *Triwara*, the five-day week *Pancawara* – and each day of each week has a specific name. This means that every day has a total of ten names, one from each of the weeks. To add to the complexity, each of the thirty seven-day weeks has its own name. You can buy calendars to keep track of all of this. They are vital for the Balinese as they're used to determine festival dates and other auspicious days but sources of tourist information (see p.75) publish dates of temple festivals.

Galungan Mar 18, 2009; Oct 14, 2009; May 12, 2010; Dec 8, 2010; July 6, 2011.
Kuningan Mar 28, 2009; Oct 24, 2009; May 22, 2010; Dec 18, 2010; July 16, 2011.

family graves and the grave of Loang Baloq at Batu Layar, 10km north of Mataram.

At the end of the year comes **Perang Topat**, celebrated at Pura Lingsar. Offerings are made here from October through to December, at the beginning of the rainy season, by Hindus and adherents of Wetu Telu to bring rain or give thanks for it. Also at this time, offerings are made at the crater lake of Segara Anak to ask for blessings, known as **Pekelem**, and the **Pujawali** celebration is held at Pura Kalasa temple at Narmada, at Pura Lingsar and at Pura Meru in Cakranegara. December 17 marks the anniversary of the political **founding of West Nusa Tenggara**. Finally, **Chinese New Year** (Imlek) sees many Chinese-run businesses closing for two days in January or February.

Outdoor activities

The sea and the mountains are the two great focuses of outdoor activities in Bali and Lombok. Bali in particular is renowned for its world-class surf breaks, and both islands offer excellent diving as well as several spectacular volcano hikes.

Surfing

Bali's volcanic reef-fringed coastline has made this island one of the great **surfing** Meccas of the world, with a reputation for producing an unusually high number of perfect and consistent tubes, and waves that regularly top five metres. With this kind of challenge, Bali's breaks are a great draw for advanced surfers, but there are also plenty of gentler beach breaks, which are ideal for beginners.

From April to October, the southeast trade winds blow offshore, fanning the waves off Bali's southwest coast and off Nusa Lembongan, and making this both the best time of year for surf, and the pleasantest, as it's also the dry season. The most famous and challenging of the southwestern breaks are around **Uluwatu** on the Bukit peninsula – at **Balangan** (see p.129), **Dreamland** (p.129), **Bingin** (p.129), **Padang Padang** (p.130) and **Suluban** (p.130). These are tough, world-class breaks and get very crowded, particularly from June to August; small, surfer-oriented resorts have grown up around each one. **Nusa Lembongan**'s six breaks can be less busy (see p.153). Novice and less confident surfers generally start with the breaks around **Kuta** (see p.113), **Canggu** (p.112) and **Medewi** (p.332). From November to March, the winds blow from the northwest, bringing rain to Bali's main beach breaks, though the lesser breaks off eastern Bali, around **Sanur** (see p.145) and **Nusa Dua** (p.138), are still surf-able at this time of year.

As for **Lombok**, readers of Australia's *Tracks* magazine voted **Desert Point** (see p.368) as their top surf spot in the world. Other breaks in Lombok pale in comparison, but the entire south coast is worth a look from Ekas Bay, east of Kuta, to Selong Blanak to the west.

Information, lessons and tours

For the best lowdown on the surfing scene in Bali, head for Kuta, where you'll find the biggest choice of surfer-oriented shops, tour agents and **surf schools** offering **lessons** for US$45 per half-day (see p.113).

There is also a **women-only** luxury surf camp, *Surf Goddess Retreats* (Wwww.surfgoddessretreats.com), in Seminyak, which offers an all-inclusive week of surfing lessons, yoga, and spa treatments from US$1995. Several companies in Bali organize **surfing tours** to the awesome breaks off Sumbawa, Java, Lombok and West Timor; see p.114 for details of the Kuta agents, and p.155 for other operators.

For detailed reviews of surf breaks, see the **book** *Indo Surf and Lingo*, available from Wwww.indosurf.com.au and from surfshops and bookshops in Bali. Good surf **websites** include Bali Waves (Wwww.baliwaves.com), Wanna Surf (Wwww.wannasurf.com) and Bali Surf Report (Wwww.balisurfreport.com).

Equipment

There are dozens of surfshops in Kuta (Bali) selling **equipment** from all the top international brands. Brand-new surfboards in Bali cost about US$700 – twice as much as in Australia – but you can also rent boards for about Rp50,000 per day on most of the surf beaches. Bring reef shoes for the coral, a helmet for the reef breaks, and an emergency ding-repair kit, though you'll be able to get repairs done on the beaches too.

Most **airlines** will take boards in the hold for free so long as your total luggage weight doesn't exceed 20kg, but call to check if they require special insurance. Board bags with straps are a good idea, as some breaks are only accessible by motorbike. Some **tourist shuttle buses** on Bali and Lombok refuse to carry boards, though Perama buses will take them for an extra Rp10,000 per board. Bemo drivers are similarly unaccommodating, so you're probably best off **renting a car** or a motorbike to get to the breaks. In Kuta, it's fairly easy to rent **motorbikes** with special surfboard clips already attached.

Health and safety

Bali's shoreline is notorious for its extreme currents and **rip tides**: lifeguards will show you where they are, but if you do get caught in one, stay calm and paddle sideways across the rip to get out of it; never try to paddle straight in or out of it. The beaches at both Kuta and Sanur have **surfers' lifeguard posts**, but at the other breaks you'll have to rely on help from other surfers.

Be sure to wash your **coral cuts** every night with a good disinfectant, and to remove sea-urchin spines without breaking them: urinating on the wound is supposed to help alleviate swelling. **Sunburn** and **heatstroke** are very real problems: sunblock is essential, and most surfers wear a rash-vest as well. It's also advisable to bone up on your first-aid knowledge, especially mouth-to-mouth resuscitation techniques, which can be life-saving if someone's been knocked out on a remote break. For general health considerations and details on health care in Bali and Lombok, see p.32.

Diving and snorkelling

Bali and Lombok are encircled by reefs that offer excellent and varied year-round **diving and snorkelling**. Staying as close as you can to one of the main diving areas (see box, p.52, for a roundup) means that not only will your dive trips be a little cheaper, but you won't have to suffer long journeys to the reefs, and you may be able to reach the dive sites before the day-trippers turn up. In reality though, most divers make excursions from the south as all dive operators offer transport from the main tourist centres. One health factor to consider is that you should not go anywhere that's more than **300m above sea level** for eighteen hours following a dive. This means you shouldn't fly, but it also renders certain inland destinations out of bounds, including Kintamani, Wongayagede and Sanda on Bali, and Senaru on Lombok.

Whether you're diving or snorkelling, you should be aware of your effect on the fragile **reef** structures. Any human contact with the microscopic colonies that make up a reef will do some damage, but you can significantly minimize your impact by not stepping on, or supporting yourself on, any part of the reef, and by asking your boatman not to anchor in the middle of one. Don't buy coral souvenirs, as tourist demand only encourages local entrepreneurs to dynamite reefs. See p.342 for more about reefs and reef fish.

Bali's **recompression chamber** is at Sanglah Public Hospital, Jl Kesehatan

Selatan 1, Sanglah, in Denpasar (Mon–Sat 9am–5pm ☎0361/227911–4 ext 123 or 232; outside these hours contact Dr Antonius Natasamudra ☎0361/420842), but any reputable dive centre should organize treatment for you in the very unlikely event that you need it. There is also a recompression chamber on Lombok (see p.364). If your travel insurance does not cover use of recompression chambers, ask your dive operators if their **insurance** covers you. It's essential for all divers to have travel insurance anyway, in case you need medical evacuation by plane.

See "Books" on p.474 for a recommended diving **book** on Bali and Lombok.

Diving trips and courses

There are dozens of **dive operators** on Bali and Lombok, so it's worth checking out several before committing yourself. If

possible, get recommendations from other divers as well. Always check the dive centre's PADI or equivalent accreditation and verify it at ☻www.padi.com. Some dive operators in Bali and Lombok do fake their PADI credentials, which is why it's good to get a second opinion; others are not PADI dive centres, though their staff may be individually certified. Technical diving using gases other than compressed air is gaining in popularity in Bali and Lombok; the relevant associations are Technical Diving International (☻www.tdisdi.com) and IANTD (☻www.iantd.com). Avoid **booking** ahead over the Internet without knowing anything else about the dive centre, and be wary of any operation offering extremely cheap courses: maintaining diving equipment is an expensive business in Indonesia, so any place offering unusually good rates will probably be compromising your safety. Ask to meet your instructor or dive leader, look

Top dives

Bali

Amed p.267. Some of the best and most varied coral in Bali, with plenty of fish. Wall dives down to about 43m; visibility up to 20m. Gili Selang has a pristine reef, pelagics and challenging currents.

Candi Dasa p.246. An underwater canyon (32m), steep wall dives and the occasional *mola mola* (oceanic sunfish). Currents can be strong.

Nusa Penida and Nusa Lembongan p.156. One of the best dive spots in Bali, but strong currents and drifts mean that some sites are only for experienced divers. Good chance of spotting *mola mola* (oceanic sunfish) here from August to October.

Padang Bai p.254. Plenty of coral, plus eels, wrasses, turtles, flatheads, lion fish, and the occasional shark.

PJ (Puri Jati) p.348. Great for muck-diving (diving on sandy bottoms in search of elusive, hidden marine life) and macrophotography; rich in juvenile fish and rare marine species.

Pulau Menjangan (Deer Island) p.341. Spectacular wall dives, 40–60m drop-offs, plenty of gorgonians and a deep wreck. Visibility up to 50m.

Secret Bay p.336. Another popular muck-diving destination, good for nudibranchs (unusual, exceptionally colourful molluscs).

Tulamben p.270. Hugely popular wreck dive (3–29m deep), with visibility from 12–15m, and night dives too. Many other excellent dives nearby and good muck-diving at Seraya.

Lombok

Gili Islands p.378. Dives for every level, with plenty of reef fish, some whitetip reef sharks and turtles, but some damage to coral.

South coast p.409. Rarely dived and only for very experienced, confident divers who can cope with current and surge. Occasional schools of hammerhead sharks.

at their qualifications, find out how many people there'll be in your group (four divers to one dive master is a good ratio) and whether they're a similar level to you, and look over the equipment, checking the quality of the air in the tanks yourself and also ensuring there's an oxygen cylinder on board.

Many of the dive operators in Bali have a main **office** in Sanur, Lovina or Candi Dasa and one or two branch offices, for example, in Tulamben or Pemuteran. For a list of some of the main dive operators in south Bali, see p.146; for those in Candi Dasa, see p.246; for Padang Bai, see p.254; for Amed, see p.267; for Tulamben, see p.270; and for Lovina, see p.306. Most dive centres on Lombok are based in Senggigi (see p.372) and/or on the Gili Islands (see p.378, p.380, p.385 & p.386). Most charge similar **rates** for dives and courses, though you'll save on transport costs if you're staying locally. One-day **dive trips** usually cost US$65–100 (or their euro equivalent) including equipment, and two- to five-day safaris cost US$135–180 per day all-inclusive.

All dive centres offer a range of internationally certified **diving courses**, generally with the first couple of days split between a classroom and a hotel pool, and the next couple of days out on the reef. Sample prices include four-day PADI Open Water courses for US$300–400 (dive shops must now include the dive manual and exam papers in this price) and two-day PADI Advanced Open Water courses for around US$300. Most dive centres also run PADI's introductory Discover Scuba course for novices, and Scuba Review for those needing a refresher.

Snorkelling

Snorkellers are generally welcome on dive excursions, and are usually charged fifty to sixty percent of the diver's fee, which should include the rental of mask, fins and snorkel. Snorkellers in Padang Bai, Lovina, on the Gili Islands and on Nusa Lembongan can charter their own boat fairly cheaply, as can anyone wanting to explore the spectacular Menjangan reefs (see p.341).

Hiking

Most **hikers** eschew the trails of Bali's lone national park, Bali Barat – which are only really of interest to bird-watchers (see p.52) – and head instead for the islands' grandest mountains. A trek up the volcano of Lombok's **Gunung Rinjani** (see p.394) usually involves a night spent on the crater rim or down inside the mountain by the crater lake. But the trip to the summit of what is Indonesia's second highest peak is usually a three- or four-day expedition, with some really hard work to get to the top. Guides are necessary on the routes to the summit and you can rent camping equipment and hire porters at the starting points. Bali's holiest peak, **Gunung Agung** (see p.241), also involves a very strenuous climb – and guides for this walk are essential – but the ascent and descent can be managed in one day. **Gunung Batur** (see p.282), also on Bali, is a much easier proposition and by far the most popular of the volcano walks; don't be put off by this, though, as the sunrise from the top is glorious. **Gunung Batukaru** is less commonly hiked but guides are available at the several start-points (see p.328).

Several tour companies in Bali run **guided hikes** to some of the island's best spots (see p.115 for contact details), including Gunung Batur, Gunung Batukaru and the Bedugul rainforests (see p.287). It's also possible to join hikes from Toya Bungkah (see p.283) and Ubud (see p.181). It's easy to organize a Rinjani trek from the starting points but if time is very tight a number of Lombok-centred companies will arrange the entire trip for you (see p.395).

Walks through rural Bali and its **ricefields** are usually much less tiring than volcano climbs and always offer lovely views. Ubud is a popular departure-point (see p.191), but there are dozens of other possibilities, including around Wongayagede (see p.327), Tirtagangga (see p.259) and Munduk (see p.291).

Bird-watching

Bali Barat National Park covers about 190 square kilometres of mountain and coast in far western Bali (see p.336) and is one of the islands' most rewarding places for bird-watching. Its most famous avian resident is the critically endangered Bali starling (see p.339), which has also recently been introduced on to the island of Nusa Penida. Visitors are prohibited from exploring Bali Barat alone, but guides are available for hire at the park headquarters.

Other worthwhile bird-watching areas include the forested hills around **Danau Buyan** and **Danau Tamblingan** (p.290); Bali's second highest mountain, **Gunung Batukaru** (p.329); and the settling ponds at **Nusa Dua** (p.138). *Udayana Eco Lodge* near **Jimbaran** on the Bukit (see p.128) is a small hotel that caters especially for bird-watchers, and regular half-day bird-watching excursions are also organized from **Ubud** (p.181). The **Bali Bird Park** (Taman Burung) in Batubulan houses dozens of unusual birds from all over the world. For reviews of the most useful guides to the birds of Bali and Lombok, see p.474.

Rafting, kayaking and horse-riding

Whitewater rafting on Bali's rivers ranges from Class 2 to Class 4, so there are routes for first-timers as well as the more experienced; you can book trips in all the major coastal resorts (see p.115) as well as in Ubud. It's also possible to go **kayaking** on the gentler rivers, as well as on Danau Tamblingan and off Gili Trawangan.

There's **horse-riding** in Kerobokan near Seminyak, on Pantai Saba, Kuta (Lombok) and Gili Trawangan.

Golf

There are five **golf courses** on Bali: 18-hole courses at the Bali Handara Kosaido Country Club in Bedugul (see p.288), the Bali Golf and Country Club in Nusa Dua (see p.138), New Kuta Golf on the Bukit peninsula (see p.129), and at *Le Meridien Nirwana* in Tanah Lot (see p.322); and a nine-hole course at the *Inna Grand Bali Beach* in Sanur (see p.146). For golf packages, including transfers, green fees and club rental, contact Bali Discount Golf (☎0361/285935, ⓦwww .golf-bali.com). Lombok has two 18-hole courses: near Sira Beach on the northwest coast (see p.390), and in the centre of the island (see p.397).

Spas, traditional beauty treatments and yoga

Herbal medicines or *jamu* (see p.208) and massages using oils and pastes made from locally grown plants have long played an important role in traditional Indonesian health care. In the last few years, this resource has been adapted for the tourist market, with dozens of spas and salons now offering traditional beauty treatments to visitors.

The biggest concentrations of hotel **spas** and **traditional beauty salons** are in Seminyak/Petitenget (see p.122), Ubud (p.207) and Nusa Dua (see p.139). In addition, there are plenty of recommended spas in Candi Dasa (p.248), Lovina (p.309) and Senggigi (p.373). We've singled out some of the best throughout the Guide but there are hundreds more; browse Bali Spa Guide (ⓦwww.balispaguide.com) for a comprehensive database. Most offer a range of similar massages and body rubs, plus a few in-house specialities, but many make their own distinctive oils and body pastes. The settings are often half the pleasure, usually enjoying tropical garden

Yoga and holistic therapies

Ubud-based Bali Spirit (ⓦwww.balispirit.com; see p.207) is an excellent resource for all things **holistic** in Bali, and the website carries a detailed programme of all upcoming yoga retreats. Regular **yoga sessions and courses** for all levels are held in Canggu (see p.123), Ubud (see p.207), Lovina (see p.309), Wongayagede (see p.328), Ume Anyar (see p.348), Sidemen (see p.261), Tejakula (see p.299) and Bondalem (see p.299).

surrounds, luxury fabrics and indulgent bathrooms.

Treatments

The most famous traditional treatment is the Javanese exfoliation rub, **mandi lulur**, in which you're painted and then gently massaged with a turmeric-based paste. Such is its apparent power to beautify, that Javanese brides are said to have a *lulur* treatment every day for the forty days before their wedding ceremonies. Another popular body wrap is the **Balinese boreh**, a warming blend of cloves, pepper and cardamom that improves circulation and invigorates muscles. There are dozens of other **body mask treatments**, using ingredients such as seaweed, aloe vera, coconut, salt and even coffee. Most scrub treatments are preceded by a gentle Balinese-style massage and followed by a moisturizing "milk bath" – actually a soothing mask treatment in which you're slathered in yoghurt or condensed milk; the whole package generally takes around ninety minutes. Prices vary enormously for these scrub packages, from Rp150,000 to US$150, depending on the poshness of the venue.

Most beauty centres can do several different types of **massage**, including Balinese (gentle), Thai (more vigorous), Hawaiian lomi-lomi (therapeutic), Japanese shiatsu (pressure points) and Swedish (very vigorous). Some also offer **aromatherapy** and traditional herbal massages to treat ailments such as coughs, headaches and insomnia. Prices start at Rp30,000 for a half-hour rub on the beach to $50 or more for an hour's massage at a top hotel. Some massage centres in Seminyak (see p.123) and Ubud (see p.207) also run massage **courses**. Every spa and beauty salon does manicures, pedicures, facials, and cream-bath deep-moisturizing hair treatments.

Spas and beauty salons in Bali and Lombok are very professional and treatment rooms are always private but some people prefer to take swimwear with them anyway. Many places are happy for couples to have massages and body wraps in the same room. Most masseuses and beauty therapists are women, but some salons use male masseurs for their male customers.

Culture and etiquette

The people of Bali and Lombok are extremely generous about opening up their homes, temples and festivals to the ever-growing crowd of interested tourists but, though they're long-suffering and rarely show obvious displeasure, they do take great offence at certain aspects of Western behaviour. The most sensitive issues on the islands are Westerners' clothing – or lack of it – and the code of practice that's required when visiting holy places.

Religious etiquette

Anyone entering a **Balinese temple** (*pura*) is required to show **respect** to the gods by treating their shrines with due deference (not climbing on them or placing themselves in a higher position than them) and by **dressing modestly**: skimpy clothing, bare shoulders and shorts are all unacceptable, and in many temples you'll be required to wear a sarong (usually provided at the gate of the most visited temples). In addition, you should wear a **ceremonial sash** around your waist whenever you visit a temple: these can be bought cheaply at most shops selling sarongs, and can be of any style (the Balinese sometimes make do with a rolled-up sarong wrapped around their waist or even a towel); they too are provided for visitors to popular temples.

When attending special **temple ceremonies**, cremations and other village festivals, you should try to dress up as formally as possible: sarongs and sashes are obligatory, and shirts with buttons are preferable to T-shirts. Don't walk in front of anyone who's praying, or take their photo, and try not to sit higher than the priest or the table of offerings. Never use a flash.

At temples, you'll be expected to give a **donation** towards upkeep (Rp5000–10,000 is an acceptable amount) and to sign the donation book. There's no need to be prompted into larger sums when you read how much the previous visitor donated – extra noughts are quite easy to add. Because the shedding of blood is considered to make someone **ritually unclean** (*sebel*) in Balinese Hinduism, women are not allowed to enter a temple, or to attend any religious ceremonies, during menstruation, and the same applies to anyone bearing a fresh wound. Under the same precepts, new mothers and their babies are also considered to be *sebel* for the first 42 days after the birth (new fathers are unclean for three days), and anyone who has been recently bereaved is *sebel* until three days after burial or cremation. These restrictions apply to non-Balinese as well, and are sometimes detailed on English-language notices outside the temple.

Mosques

On the whole, the **mosques** of Lombok and Bali don't hold much cultural or architectural interest for tourists, but should you have occasion to visit one, it's as well to be aware of certain Islamic practices. Everyone is required to take off their shoes before entering, and to wear long sleeves and long trousers; women should cover their shoulders and may also be asked to cover their heads (bring a scarf or shawl, as there probably won't be any provided). Men and women always pray in separate parts of the mosque, though there are unlikely to be signs telling you where to go. Women are forbidden to engage in certain religious activities during menstruation, and this includes entering a mosque. Finally, you should be aware that during the month of **Ramadan** (see p.72 for more), devout Muslims neither eat, drink nor smoke during daylight hours. If visiting Lombok during this time, you should be sensitive to this, although you'll certainly be able to find places to eat. Adherence varies across the island at this time: it is most apparent in the south and the east, but something you might not even notice in Senggigi.

...ess in the
...nesians are
...ess and nude
... attire in their
...ommand a great
...eep your shortest
...shoulders for the
...ially true in central
...where Sasaks do not
subsc...   ...tively relaxed attitudes
of their west-...   ...compatriots in Senggigi
and the Gili Islands.

The Balinese and Sasak people themselves regularly expose their own bodies in public when **bathing** in rivers and public bathing pools, but they are always treated as invisible by other bathers and passers-by. As a tourist you should do the same: to photograph a bathing Balinese would be very rude indeed.

If you bathe alongside them, do as they do – nearly all Balinese women wash with their sarongs wrapped around them – and take note of the segregated areas: in public pools, the men's and women's sections are usually clearly defined, but in rivers the borders are less tangible.

According to Hindu beliefs, a person's body is a microcosm of the universe: the **head** is the most sacred part of the body and the feet the most unclean. This means that you should on no account touch a Balinese person's head – not even to pat a small child's head or to ruffle someone's hair in affection; nor should you lean over someone's head or place your body in a higher position than their head without apologizing. You should never sit with your **feet** pointed at a sacred image (best to sit with them tucked underneath you) or use them to indicate someone or something.

Balinese caste and names

Balinese society is structured around a hereditary **caste system**, which, while far more relaxed than its Indian counterpart, does nonetheless carry certain restrictions and rules of etiquette, as ordained in the Balinese Hindu scriptures. Of these, the one that travellers are most likely to encounter is the practice of **naming** a person according to their caste.

At the top of the tree is the **Brahman** caste, whose men are honoured with the title **Ida Bagus** and whose women are generally named **Ida Ayu**, sometimes shortened to **Dayu**. Traditionally revered as the most scholarly members of society, only Brahmans are allowed to become high priests (*pedanda*).

Satriya (sometimes spelt Ksatriya) form the second strata of Balinese society, and these families are descendants of warriors and rulers. The Balinese rajas were all Satriya and their offspring continue to bear telltale names: **Cokorda**, **Anak Agung**, **Ratu** and **Prebagus** for men, and **Anak Agung Isti** or **Dewa Ayu** for women. The merchants or **Wesia** occupy the third most important rank, the men distinguished by the title **I Gusti** or **Pregusti**, the women by the name **I Gusti Ayu**.

At the bottom of the heap comes the **Sudra** caste, the caste of the common people, which accounts for over ninety percent of the population. Sudra children are named according to their position in the family order, with no distinction made between male and female offspring. Thus, a first-born Sudra is always known as **Wayan** (or, increasingly commonly, **Putu** or **Gede**), the second-born is **Made** (or **Kadek**), the third **Nyoman** (or **Komang**) and the fourth **Ketut**. Should a fifth child be born, the naming system begins all over again with Wayan/Putu, and so it goes on. In order to distinguish between the sexes, Sudra caste names are often prefaced by **"I"** for males and **"Ni"** for females, eg I Wayan. Some Wayans and Mades prefer to be known by their second names, and many have distinctive nicknames, but you will come across many more Wayans than any other name in Bali.

Unlike their counterparts in the far more rigid Indian caste system, the Sudra are not looked down upon or denied access to specific professions (except that of *pedanda*), and a high-caste background guarantees neither a high income nor a direct line to political power.

Balinese people will never walk under a **clothes line** (for fear of their head coming into contact with underclothes), so you should try not to hang your washing in public areas, and definitely don't sling wet clothes over a temple wall or other holy building. The **left hand** is used for washing after defecating, so the Balinese will never eat with it or use it to pass or receive things or to shake hands.

Social conventions

As elsewhere in Asia, Indonesians dislike **confrontational behaviour**, and will rarely show anger or irritation of any kind. Tourists who lose their cool and get visibly rattled tend to be looked down on rather than feared.

A major source of irritation for foreigners is the rather vague notion of **time-keeping** that pervades almost every aspect of Indonesian life, but lack of punctuality is such a national institution that there is even a word for it – *jam karet*, or rubber time. Public **displays of affection** are also subdued – you're more likely to see affectionate hand-holding and hugging between friends of the same sex than between heterosexual lovers.

Since the downfall of Suharto in 1998, and the subsequent democratic elections, Indonesian people seem to have become much more confident about discussing **political issues** and voicing critical opinions of the state. This is mirrored by a more open

press. Religious beliefs, however, are a much more sensitive issue, and it would be bad form to instigate a debate that questions a Balinese person's faith.

You will probably find Balinese and Sasak people only too eager to find out about your **personal life** and habits. It's considered quite normal to ask "Are you married?" and to then express sorrow if you say that you aren't, and the same applies to questions about children: marriage and parenthood are essential stages in the life of most Balinese and Sasaks.

Tipping

It's becoming increasingly common to **tip** on Bali or Lombok, generally about ten percent to waiters (if no service charge is added to the bill), drivers and tour guides; a few thousand rupiah to bellboys and chambermaids in mid-range and upmarket hotels; and a round-up to the nearest Rp5000 for metered-taxi drivers.

Photography

While Bali and Lombok are both incredibly photogenic, not all local people want to be the subject of visitors' holiday snaps; always ask by word or gesture whether it is okay to take a photograph, and respect the answer. Be especially sensitive during religious events such as cremations and take care never to get in the way of worshippers.

Shopping

Shopping can easily become an all-consuming pastime in Bali and Lombok: the range and quality of artefacts is phenomenal, and although the export trade has dulled the initial impact a little, the bargain prices are irresistible. Bali also has a well-deserved reputation for its elegant modern designs in everything from fashion to tableware, much of it dreamt up by expat designers and best sourced in Seminyak and Ubud. On Lombok, Senggigi has the widest choice of shops, but the real pleasure is visiting the craft villages in the centre of the island where pottery, basketware, woodcarving and textiles are local specialities.

Remember that touts, guides and drivers often get as much as fifty percent **commission** on any item sold to one of their customers – not only at the customer's expense, but also the vendor's. Many shops will organize **shipping**, but be prepared for a huge bill; the minimum container size is one cubic metre, which will set you back at least US$175, even to Australia. For parcels weighing under 10kg, use the postal system, as detailed on p.71. If you're planning on doing some serious shopping, buy a copy of the comprehensive **shopping guidebook**, *Shopsmart Bali and Lombok*, reviewed on p.474.

Arts and crafts

Locally produced arts and crafts include traditional and modern **paintings**, **pottery**, **textiles**, **basketware**, **stone sculptures** and **woodcarvings**. Though the big resorts stock a wide range of all these artefacts, there's much fun and better bargains to be had, at least on the high-quality versions, at the craft-producing **villages** themselves. For a round-up of where to buy what, see the box opposite; for an introduction to the crafts and their producers, see the colour section *The crafts of Bali and Lombok*; and for background information on the history, styles and techniques, see p.453.

A couple of practical points to note when choosing **woodcarvings**. Be warned that not all "sandalwood" (*cendana*), which is an extremely expensive material, is what it seems as the aroma can be **faked** with real sandalwood sawdust or oil. In either case, the smell doesn't last that long, so either buy from an established outlet or assume

that it's faked and reduce your price accordingly. **Ebony** is also commonly faked; compare its weight with any other wood: ebony is very dense and will sink in water. Most tropical woods **crack** when exported to a less humid climate: some carvers obviate this by drying the wood in kilns, while others use polyethylene glycol (PEG) to fill the cracks before they widen. Always check for cracks before buying.

Some **stonecarvings** are also not what they seem, though shops rarely make a secret of this. Specifically, the cheapest lava-stone *paras* sculptures are usually mass-produced from moulded lava-stone paste rather than hand-carved. They're sometimes referred to as **"concrete"** statues but can still be very attractive.

Soft furnishings, clothing and jewellery

Designers make delicious use of the sumptuous local fabrics for luxurious and unusual **soft furnishings**, including cushions, bedspreads, sheets, curtains, drapes and tablecloths. Seminyak, Legian, Sanur and Ubud have the best outlets.

Bali also produces some great **clothes**. Kuta–Legian–Seminyak have the classiest and most original boutiques, along with countless stalls selling beachwear. Brand-name surfwear and urban sportswear is also good value here, as are custom-made leather shoes, boots and jackets.

Bali's small but thriving **silver** and **gold** industry is based in the village of Celuk, where silversmiths create filigree pieces and larger items to order, and sell to the public

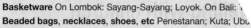

Basketware On Lombok: Sayang-Sayang; Loyok. On Bali:

Beaded bags, **necklaces**, **shoes, etc** Penestanan; Kuta; Ubu

Books Kuta; Ubud.

Ceramics Pejaten.

Fashion Kuta–Legian–Seminyak.

Furniture Modern furniture on Jl Bypass Sanur and in Kerobokan. R furniture from Batubulan, Mas, Seminyak and Senggigi.

Interior decor and soft furnishings Seminyak; Legian; Sanur; Ubud; Te Pujung road.

Jewellery and silver Celuk is Bali's main silver-producing village; shops in Kuta, Seminyak, Ubud, Lovina and Candi Dasa. Gold shops on Jl Hasanudin, Denpasar. Gold and silver jewellery in Kamasan, Lombok; pearls in Sekarbela and Karang Genteng, Lombok.

Leather shoes and jackets Kuta; Sanur.

Markets and pasar seni On Bali in Sukawati, Ubud and Denpasar. On Lombok in Senggigi; Ampenan, Cakranegara and Sweta; Gunung Sari; Lombok Handicraft Centre and Sayang Sayang Art Market north of Cakranegara.

Masks Mas; Singapadu; Labuapi.

Paintings Ubud area; Batuan; Kamasan.

Pottery On Lombok in Mataram; Senggigi; Banyumulek; Penunjak; Pejangik.

Puppets Sukawati.

Stone sculptures Batubulan.

Textiles Traditional *ikat* in Tenganan, Gianyar and Singaraja and in Sukarara on Lombok; traditional Sumba and Flores textiles in Kuta, Ubud and Candi Dasa. Batik and dress fabrics in Denpasar, especially Jl Sulawesi. Mass-produced and hand-printed batik sarongs in *pasar seni* and tourist shops in Kuta, Sukawati, Ubud, Lovina, Candi Dasa and Senggigi.

Woodcarvings Unpainted figurines from Mas, Ubud, Kemenuh and Nyuhkuning. Painted wooden artefacts from villages along the Tegalalang–Pujung road. On Lombok at Senanti.

from their workshops. For more unusual jewellery, you're better off scouring the jewellery shops in Kuta, Ubud, Lovina and Candi Dasa, where designs tend to be more innovative and prices similar, if not lower. Lombok's gold and silver workshops are centred on Kamasan. For **pearls**, head to Sekarbela, where the products of the pearl farms that dot the Lombok coastline are brought for sale.

Furniture

Several shops in Bali and Lombok advertise, quite ingenuously, "Antiques made to order". The **antiques** in question generally either come from Java or are **reproductions** of mostly Javanese items, chiefly **furniture**, screens, carved panels, window shutters and doors. Weather-worn or fashionably distressed, most of the furniture is heavy, made from teak to a Dutch-inspired design, but carved with typical Indonesian grace and whimsy. Check items for rot and termite damage (genuine teak is resistant to termites), as well as for shoddy restoration work.

There is an increasing demand for interesting **modern furniture** on Bali and aside from a few outlets in Seminyak the best places to browse are out of the main centres, along Jalan Bypass Sanur between Kuta and Sanur, and north of Seminyak in Kerobokan.

Travelling with children

The Balinese make a great fuss of their own and other people's children, and permit them to go pretty much anywhere.

One peculiar cultural convention you might encounter, though, is that the Balinese abhor young children crawling on the ground – a practice that's considered far too animal-like for young humans – and so kids are **carried** everywhere, either on the hip or in slings made from sarongs, until they're six months old. Don't be surprised if your child gets scooped off the ground for the same reason.

Activities for kids

There's plenty on Bali and Lombok to appeal to children. Aside from the beach and other water-based activities in the southern resorts, the enormous *Hard Rock* swimming pool and the nearby Waterbom Park are fun for all ages (see p.114). Many **dive centres** will teach the PADI children's scuba courses on request: their Bubblemaker programme is open to 8-year-olds and the Junior Open Water course is designed for anyone over 10. Active children may also enjoy **mountain- biking**, **whitewater rafting** and **horse-riding** (see box, p.115), and **wildlife attractions** such as the Elephant Safari Park at Taro, the Bird and Reptile parks in Batubulan, the Bali Treetop Adventure Park at the Botanical Gardens in Bedugul and the Bali Safari and Marine Park in Gianyar. **Ubud** is especially child-friendly, with a huge amount on offer that they will love (see box, p.180), including chances to try their hand at batik, gamelan and dancing, and a multi-lingual kids' library. The colour and dynamism of the **dance and music shows** could almost be tailor-made for children – from the beauty and grace of Legong to the drama of the Barong. Older, more fashion-conscious children will relish the varieties of brand-name **clothing** on offer and the endless offers to "plait your hair", while parents will appreciate the bargains to be had in the children's sections of department stores in Kuta and Denpasar and the specialist children's clothing stores.

Practicalities

Many upmarket **hotels** provide extra beds for one or two under-12s sharing a room with their parents and the best ones have a kids' club as well, and may also offer babysitting services. The Tuban area of south Kuta is particularly strong on family-oriented hotels, many of which have grounds that run right down to the sea: the *Bali Dynasty Resort* runs a well-regarded programme of kids' activities (see p.107). In Sanur, the mid-range *Swastika* is one of several family-friendly options, complete with children's swimming pool (see p.144). Up near Ubud, in the village of Mas, *Taman Harum Cottages* gets rave reviews from families, not least because of all its activities (see p.185); *Klub Kokos*, also near Ubud, has a kids' playroom and special family unit (see p.185). An increasing number of **losmen**, particularly in Kuta and Ubud, have a family bungalow available for rent, usually with at least two bedrooms and sometimes a kitchenette as well. Others offer adjoining rooms. **Villas** are the obvious top-whack alternative. On the whole, children who occupy their own seat on **buses** and **bemos** are expected to pay full fare. Most **domestic flight** operators charge two-thirds of the adult fare for children under 14, and ten percent for infants.

Although you can buy **disposable nappies** (diapers) in the supermarkets of Kuta, Sanur, Denpasar and Ubud, the Balinese don't use them, so prices are inflated. Bring a **changing mat**, as there are precious few public toilets in Bali and Lombok, let alone ones with special baby facilities (though posh hotels are always a useful option). For touring, child-carrier **backpacks** are ideal. Opinions are divided on whether or not it's worth bringing a **buggy** or three-wheeled **stroller** – pavements are bumpy at best, and there's an almost total absence of ramps; sand is especially difficult for buggies, though less so for three-wheelers. Buggies and strollers do, however, come in handy for feeding and even bedding small children, as highchairs and cots are only provided in the most upmarket hotels. Taxis and car-rental companies never provide baby seats, but you can rent **baby car seats**, backpacks and cots through Bali Family Holidays (ⓦwww.balifamilyholidays.com). A child-sized **mosquito net** might be useful. **Powdered milk** is available in every major tourist centre, but sterilizing bottles is a far more laborious process in Indonesian hotels and restaurants than it is back home.

Food on Bali and Lombok is generally quite palatable to children – not much spice and hardly any unfamiliar textures – but, as always, avoid unwashed fruit and salads, and dishes that have been left uncovered. Some restaurants offer special kids' menus.

The other main hazards are thundering traffic, huge waves and strong currents, and the **sun** – not least because the islands' main beaches offer almost no shade at all. Sun hats, sunblock and waterproof suntan lotions are essential, and can be bought in the major resorts. You should also make sure, if possible, that your child is aware of the dangers of rabies (see p.33); keep children away from animals, especially dogs and monkeys, and ask your doctor about rabies jabs.

Information and advice

The Bali for Families **website** (ⓦwww .baliforfamilies.com) is run by parents who have lots of first-hand experience of travelling in Bali; as well as child-friendly recommendations, there's also a travellers' forum. The more commercial Bali Family Holidays website (ⓦwww.balifamilyholidays .com) is another good resource, as is the "Kids To Go" bulletin board at ⓦthorntree .lonelyplanet.com.

Charities and volunteer projects

Despite the glossy tourist veneer, Bali and Lombok are part of a poor country with limited resources to provide good-quality education and health care to its citizens, whose opportunities, quality of life and very survival are compromised as a result. The bombs of 2002 and 2005 brought extra hardship to many. Below are some suggestions for charities who welcome help from visitors; most of their websites include information on volunteer work.

AdoptA ⓦadopta.info. A dressmaking cooperative run by and for women who were widowed by the 2002 Kuta bomb; they have a small shop in Candikuning (see p.287).

Anak Pertiwi (Child of the Earth Foundation) ⓦanakpertiwi.org. Based in Penginyahan in northern Bali (see p.285), this foundation provides for children whose parents cannot take care of them. Visitors are welcome, ask at *Restoran Coffeebreak* on the Kubutambahan–Kintamani road.

Bali Hati Foundation ⓦwww.balihati.org. Promotes access to education for all, provides student scholarships and sponsorship, offers community education and healthcare and runs an acclaimed elementary school in Mas. Their spa centre, Spa Hati, in Ubud (see p.207), helps fund the work.

Bali Key Foundation ⓦwww.pondokpiscesbali .com. Established by *Pondok Pisces* bungalows in Lalang Linggah to meet schooling expenses for local kids from low-income families.

Crisis Care Foundation ☏0812/377 4649, ⓦbalicrisiscare.org. Provides free health care for local people both in the clinic in Lovina and as outreach and is run on charitable donations, which are always needed. The driving force is an Englishwoman, Gloria, and visitors are welcome to see the work. There's more information and a Wish List on the website. If you can't make it to Lovina, donations can be dropped off with Kerry (the owner) in *Piggy's Bar* on Poppies 2 in Kuta.

East Bali Poverty Project ⊕0361/410071, ⓦwww.eastbalipovertyproject.org. Helps isolated mountain villages on the arid slopes of Gunung Agung and Gunung Abang in a number of ways, including education, nutrition, health and sustainable agriculture.

Help the Children of Gili Meno If you visit Meno look out for calendars or other products produced for sale to support children from Gili Meno who attend the secondary school in Gili Trawangan. With uniform, food and boat transfers it costs €250 per child per year and without this support most of the island children never progress beyond primary school.

IDEP Foundation ⓦwww.idepfoundation.org. An Ubud-based NGO that promotes sustainable-living programmes across Indonesia, including permaculture, micro-credit, fair trade and disaster response projects. Their handicrafts shop and info centre, Bali Cares (see p.206), helps fund Balinese charities.

Kupu-Kupu Foundation ⓦwww.yamp .com/kupukupu. Encourages sponsors and volunteers to help improve the lives of the 12,500 disabled children and adults in Bali. Sells inexpensive, high-quality handicrafts and jewellery made by disabled craftspeople at its shop in Ubud (see p.206).

Mitra Bali Fair-Trade Arts and Crafts NGO ⓦwww.mitrabali.com. Welcomes visitors to its HQ in Lodtunduh near Ubud (see p.171) to learn more about its work supporting Balinese craftspeople through fair trade. Also has a fair-trade shop on the Tegalalang road (see p.215) and another in the Bali Discovery Shopping Mall in Tuban, south Kuta.

Pondok Pekak Library and Learning Centre ©pondok@indo.net.id. A free library service in Ubud that offers all local children access to books and educational activities. Visitors can support the project by using the excellent adult-oriented library of English-language books (see p.210), by taking cultural classes here (see p.209) and by donating books and funds.

Yayasan Senyum ⓦwww.senyumbali.org. Dedicated to helping fund operations for Balinese people with cranio-facial disabilities such as cleft palate. Visitors can assist by donating secondhand goods to their Ubud charity shop, The Smile Shop; see p.206.

Travel essentials

Addresses

Because the government has outlawed the use of English-language names, demanding that Indonesian names be used instead, a number of street names in resort areas such as Kuta (Bali) are known by two names: where relevant, we have included both. Because of haphazard planning, frequent rebuilding, and superstitions about unlucky numbers, street numbers are not always chronological – and may not be present at all. It's also quite common to use "X" where an adjacent property has been added, with the original building being, say, Jl Raya 200 and the new one becoming Jl Raya 200X.

Cookery and cultural classes

Short courses in Balinese cookery are available in Ubud (see p.209), Seminyak (see p.123), Tanjung Benoa (see p.140), Sanur (see p.151), Lovina (see p.309) and Munduk (see p.291), and at the *Alila* hotel in Candi Dasa (see p.247). Ubud is the most popular place to take workshops in art, dance, music, carving and other Balinese arts and crafts (see p.208 for details). You can learn batik painting in Kuta (see p.123).

Costs

Foreign tourists visiting Bali and Lombok, wherever they come from, invariably find that hotel rooms at all levels of comfort, goods and services are relatively inexpensive when compared with their home countries. However, the range of accommodation, restaurants and other opportunities means that it is just as easy to have a fabulously extravagant experience as a budget one.

Many tourist businesses quote for their goods and services in **US dollars while others use euros (€)**; in the Guide, prices are given in these where this is the case. This includes hotels, dive operators, tour agents and car-rental outlets, particularly in the larger resorts. Even where prices are displayed in US dollars or euros, though, you have the option of paying with cash, traveller's cheques, credit card or rupiah.

If you're happy to eat in local places, stay off the beer, use the public transport system and stay in the simplest accommodation, you could scrape by on a **daily budget** of £6/US$12 per person if you share a room. For around £20/$40 a day per person if you share a room, you'll get quite a few extra comforts, like the use of a swimming pool, hot water and air-conditioning, three good meals and a few beers and you'll be able to afford tourist shuttle bus tickets to get around. Staying in luxury hotels and eating at the flashiest restaurants and chartering transport, you're likely to spend £75/$150 per day. The sky's the limit at this end of the market, with $1000-a-night accommodation, helicopter charters, dive or surf safaris, and fabulous gourmet meals all on offer.

Government-run museums and the most **famous temples** charge Rp3000–10,000 per person; **private art museums** and **tourist attractions** mostly charge Rp20,000–50,000. Youth and student **discounts** are rare but can be had where available. All visitors to any temple, however humble, are expected to give a small donation (about Rp10,000).

Bargaining

Bargaining is one of the most obvious ways of keeping your costs down. Except in supermarkets, department stores, restaurants and bars, the first price given is rarely the real one, and most stallholders expect to engage in some financial banter before finalizing the sale; on average, buyers will start their counterbid at about 30 to 40 percent of the vendor's opening price and the bartering continues from there. Pretty much everything, from newspapers and cigarettes to woodcarvings and car rental is negotiable, and even accommodation rates can often be knocked down, from the humblest losmen through to the top-end places where potential guests ask about "low-season discounts".

Bargaining is an art, and requires humour and tact – it's easy to forget that you're quibbling over a few cents or pennies, and that such an amount means a lot more to an Indonesian than to you.

Crime and personal safety

While incidents of crime of all kinds are relatively rare on Bali and Lombok, the importance of tourism to the economy, and the damage that adverse publicity could do, means that the true situation may be kept conveniently obscured. Certainly, the majority of visitors have trouble-free trips, but there have been instances of theft and assault on tourists.

It makes sense to take a few **precautions**. Carry vital documents and money in a concealed moneybelt: bum-bags are too easy to cut off in a crowd. Make sure your luggage is lockable (there are gadgets to lock backpacks) and beware that things can quickly be taken from the back pockets of a rucksack while you're wearing it without you knowing. Beware of pickpockets on crowded buses or bemos and in markets; they usually operate in pairs: one will distract you while another gets what they can either from your pockets or your backpack.

Check the **security** of a room before accepting it, make sure doors and windows can be locked, and don't forget access via the bathroom. Female travellers should make sure there are no peepholes through into neighbouring rooms. Some guesthouses and hotels have safe-deposit boxes, which neatly solves the problem of what to do with your valuables while you go swimming. A surprising number of tourists do leave their valuables unattended on the beach and are amazed to find them gone when they return.

Keep a separate **photocopy** of your passport and airline ticket so you can prove who you are and where you are going if you need to get replacements, and a separate list of traveller's cheque numbers along with the emergency phone number.

It's never sensible to carry **large amounts of cash**, and on Bali it's not necessary. However, on Lombok you may need to carry more than you would like because of the scarcity of moneychangers outside the resort areas. It's wise to keep a few dollars hidden somewhere away from your main stash of cash so that if you get your money stolen you can still get to the police, contact a consulate and pay for phone calls while you sort everything out. There are a number of potential rip-offs when you're changing money; see box on p.70.

Something else to watch out for on Bali is being approached on the street by somebody wanting to ask a few questions about your holiday. These seemingly innocuous questionnaires provide information for **time-share companies**, who have a reputation for hassling visitors once they've divulged their details. Another ruse is for the "researchers" to offer you a prize as a reward for participating – usually a free dinner or tour – which invariably involves a trip to the time-share company's office. Advice on this is to never sign anything unless you've thought about it extremely carefully, examined all the small print – and then thought about it some more.

It's also worth being alert to the possibility of **spiked drinks** and to be aware that **gambling** is illegal in Indonesia and problems can arise from foreigners getting involved in this.

It is foolish to have anything to do with **drugs** in Indonesia. The penalties are very tough, and you won't get any sympathy from consular officials.

If you're arrested, or end up on the wrong side of the law for whatever reason, you should ring the **consular officer** at your embassy immediately (see p.66 for a list).

If you're driving, the chance of entanglement with the police increases; see p.40 for more.

Women travellers

Bali and Lombok do not present great difficulties for **women travellers**, either travelling alone or with friends of either sex; basic

issues of personal security and safety are essentially the same as they would be at home. Women should take similar responsibility for their own safety, especially in bars and large parties.

However, an image of Western women as promiscuous and on holiday in search of sex is well established on both islands, although attitudes on Bali are a little more open-minded than on Lombok.

Observe how local women **dress** both on the streets and on the beach. While topless sunbathing is popular among tourists – and it's unlikely that local people will say anything directly – it's worth being aware how far outside the local dress code such behaviour is. Whatever you do on the beach, you should cover up when you head inshore, and visits to temples or festivals carry their own obligations regarding dress (see p.55).

There's a large population of **young men** on both Bali and Lombok known variously as Kuta Cowboys, mosquitoes (they flit from person to person) or gigolos, whose aim is to secure a Western girlfriend for the night, week, month or however long it lasts. Older women are increasingly targeted for attention. The boys vary considerably in subtlety and while the transaction is not overtly financial, the woman will be expected to pay for everything. You'll see these couples all over the islands, and if a Western woman and a local man are seen together, this is the first assumption made about their relationship. Local reaction is variable, from hostility in the more traditional villages through acceptance to amusement. Sex outside marriage is taboo in the Muslim religion, and young girls on Lombok are expected to conform to a strict code of morality. On Bali things are changing and while sex outside marriage is not actually approved of, it is accepted that it happens – although marriage is still expected once the girl becomes pregnant.

Women involved in relationships abroad, either with local men or other travellers, should be aware of **sexual health issues**; see p.34.

Reporting a crime or emergency

If you have anything **lost** or **stolen** you must get a **police report** for insurance purposes, so head for the nearest police

> In an emergency, call the police (☏110), ambulance (☏118) or fire service (☏113).

station (these are marked on the maps in the Guide). In areas without local police, such as the Gili Islands off the coast of Lombok, ask for the local village headman, *kepala desa* or *kepala kampung* in smaller villages, whose job it is to sort out the problem and take you to the nearest police. The police will usually find somebody who can speak some English, but it's a good idea to take along someone who can speak both Indonesian and English, if you can. Allow plenty of time for any bureaucratic involvement with the police. If you're unfortunate enough to be the victim of violent crime, contact your consulate at once (see consulate addresses on p.66).

Departure taxes

International: Rp150,000 from Bali, Rp100,000 from Lombok. Domestic: Rp30,000 from Bali and Lombok.

Electricity

Usually 220–240 volts AC, but outlying areas may still use 110 volts. Most outlets take plugs with two rounded pins. See ⓦwww .kropla.com for more.

Entry requirements

At the time of writing, only citizens of eleven (mostly Southeast Asian) countries are eligible for **visa-free visits** to Indonesia. Citizens of 66 other countries, including Britain, Ireland, most European states, Australia, New Zealand, Canada, the USA, South Africa and India, are able to buy thirty-day **visas on arrival** (VOA). Citizens of all other countries must buy their visas in advance.

For citizens of eligible countries, visas for **stays of up to thirty days** can be bought **on arrival** if entering and exiting Indonesia via one of the country's 37 **designated gateway ports**. In Bali, the visa-issuing gateways are Ngurah Rai Airport, Benoa Harbour and Padang Bai port; in Lombok, it's just Selaparang Airport. The fee of US$25 is payable in almost any currency; your passport must be valid for at least six months and you must be able to show proof of onward travel (a return or onward ticket). If you're staying seven days or fewer, the fee is US$10. The seven-day and thirty-day visas on arrival are non-extendable.

If you're not on the list of 66 countries, if you're entering via a non-designated gateway, or if you want to **stay for up to sixty days**, you must buy a **visa in advance** from an Indonesian embassy or consulate. Forms and detailed lists of requirements can be downloaded from most Indonesian embassy websites (see below). Fees for single-entry sixty-day visas are £35/US$45/AUS$60; for multiple entry £125/US$100/AUS$165. In addition, you will need two passport photos and proof of onward travel (a return or onward ticket), and your passport must be valid for at least six months, or one year if applying for a multiple-entry visa. Many but not all visa-issuing embassies also require a recent bank statement showing a minimum balance of £1000 and a recent letter from your employer, educational establishment, bank manager, accountant or solicitor certifying your obligation to return home/leave Indonesia by the designated date.

Penalties for **overstaying your visa** are severe. On departure, you'll be fined $20 for each day you've overstayed up to a limit of sixty days. If you've exceeded the sixty-day barrier you're liable for a five-year prison sentence or a fine of Rp25,000,000.

It's unlikely you'll be able to extend a visa of any type once in Indonesia, but it may be worth contacting the local government **immigration office** (*kantor imigrasi*) anyway; see p.95 for the Bali office and p.364 for Lombok office.

Indonesian embassies and consulates abroad

Australia 8 Darwin Ave, Yarralumla, Canberra, ACT 2600 ☏02/6250 8600, ⓦwww.kbri-canberra .org.au; 20 Harry Chan Ave, Darwin, NT 0801 ☏08/8943 0201, ⓦwww.kri-darwin.org; 72 Queens Rd, Melbourne, VIC 3004 ☏03/9525 2755, ⓦwww.kjri-melbourne.org; 134 Adelaide Terrace, East Perth, WA 6004 ☏08/9221 5858, ⓦwww .kri-perth.org.au; 236 Maroubra Rd, Maroubra, Sydney, NSW 2035 ☏02/9344 9933, ⓦwww .kjri-sydney.org.

Canada 55 Parkdale Ave, Ottawa, ON K1Y 1E5 ☏613/724-1100, ⓦwww.indonesia-ottawa.org; 129 Jarvis St, Toronto, ON M5C 2H6 ☏416/360-4020, ⓦwww.indonesiatoronto.org; 1630 Alberni St, Vancouver, BC V6G 1A6 ☏604/682-8855, ⓦwww.indonesiavancouver.org.

Malaysia 233 Jl Tun Razak, 50400 Kuala Lumpur ☏03/2116 4031, ⓦwww.kbrikl.org.my; 723 Jl Anyer Molek, 80000 Johor Bahru ☏07/221 2000; 467 Jl Burma, 10350 Penang ☏04/226 7412, ⓦwww.kjripenang.org.my; Lorong Kemajuan, Karamunsing, Kota Kinabalu, Sabah 88817 ☏088/218600.

New Zealand 70 Glen Rd, Kelburn, Wellington ☏04/475 8697, ⓦwww.indonesianembassy.org .nz; 2nd floor, Beca Carter Hollings & Femer Ltd, 132 Vincent St, Auckland ☏09/308 0842, ⓔimackley@beca.co.nz.

Singapore 7 Chatsworth Rd, Singapore 249761 ☏6737 7422, ⓦwww.kbrisingapura.com.

South Africa 949 Schoeman St, Arcadia, Pretoria ☏012/342-3350–2, ⓦwww .indonesia-pretoria.org.za; 212 Buitengracht St, Cape Town ☏021/423-2321, ⓦwww .indonesia-capetown.org.za.

Thailand 600 Phetchaburi Rd, Bangkok 10400 ☏02/252 3135–40, ⓦwww.kbri-bangkok.com.

UK and Ireland 38 Grosvenor Square, London W1K 2HW (personal callers: 38 Adams Row, W1) ☏020/7499 7661, ⓦwww.indonesianembassy .org.uk.

USA 2020 Massachusetts Ave NW, Washington DC 20036 ☏202/775-5200, ⓦwww .embassyofindonesia.org; 211 W Wacker Drive Chicago, IL 60606 ☏312/920-1880, ⓦwww .indonesiachicago.org; 10900 Richmond Ave, Houston, TX 77057 ☏713/785-1691, ⓦwww .indonesiahouston.org; 3457 Wilshire Blvd, Los Angeles, CA 90010 ☏213/383-5126, ⓦkjri-la.net; 5 E 68th St, New York, NY 10065 ☏212/879-0600–15, ⓦwww.indonesianewyork.org; 1111 Columbus Ave, San Francisco, CA 94133 ☏415/474-9571, ⓦwww.kjrisfo.org.

Worldwide listings at ⓦwww.deplu.go.id.

Foreign embassies and consulates

Most countries maintain an **embassy** in the Indonesian capital, Jakarta, and some also have **consulates** in Bali. Your first point of contact should always be the Bali consulate.

Australia Consulate in Bali: Jl Letda Tantular 32, Renon, Denpasar ☏0361/241118, ⓦwww.bali .indonesia.embassy.gov.au. Embassy: Jl H.R. Rasuna Said Kav C15–16, Kuningan, Jakarta ☏021/2550 5555, ⓦwww.austembjak.or.id.

Canada Contact the Australian consulate in Denpasar first. Embassy: World Trade Centre, 6th floor, Jl Jen Sudirman, Kav 29, Jakarta ☏021/2550 7800, ⓦwww.dfait-maeci.gc.ca/jakarta.

Ireland Contact the UK consul in Sanur first.

Malaysia Jl H.R. Rasuna Said, Kav X/6 1–3, Kuningan, Jakarta ☏021/522 4940.

New Zealand Contact the Australian consulate in Denpasar first. Embassy: Gedung BRII, 23rd floor, Jl Jen Sudirman, Kav 44, Jakarta ☏021/570 9460, ⓔnzembjak@cbn.net.id.

Singapore Embassy: Jl H.R. Rasuna Said, Blok X/4 Kav 2, Kuningan, Jakarta ☏021/5296 1433.

South Africa Embassy: Wisma GKBI, 7th Floor, Suite 705, Jl Jen Sudirman, Kav 28, Jakarta ☏021/574 0660, ⓦwww.saembassy-jakarta .or.id.

UK Consulate in Bali: Jl Tirta Nadi 20A, Sanur ☏0361/270601, ⓔbcbali@dps.centrin.net.id. Embassy: Jl M.H. Thamrin 75, Jakarta ☏021/2356 5200, ⓦwww.britain.or.id.

USA Consulate in Bali: Jl Hayam Wuruk 188, Renon, Denpasar ☏0361/233605, ⓔamcobali @indosat.net.id. Embassy: Jl Merdeka Selatan 5, Jakarta ☏021/3435 9000, ⓦwww .usembassyjakarta.org.

Customs regulations

Indonesia's **customs regulations** allow foreign nationals to import one litre of alcohol, 200 cigarettes or 50 cigars or 100g of tobacco, and a reasonable amount of perfume. Cars, laptops, TV sets and video cameras are supposed to be declared on entry and re-exported on departure. Import restrictions cover the usual banned items, including narcotics, weapons and pornographic material, and foreigners are also forbidden to bring in any printed matter written in Chinese characters, Chinese medicines, and amounts of Rp5,000,000 or more in Indonesian currency. Indonesia is a signatory to the Convention on International Trade in Endangered Species (CITES), and so forbids import or export of products that are banned under this treaty, which include anything made from turtle flesh or turtle shells (including tortoiseshell jewellery and ornaments), as well as anything made from ivory. Indonesian law also prohibits the export of antiquities and cultural relics, unless sanctioned by the customs department.

Gay and lesbian travellers

As members of a society that places so much emphasis on marriage and parenthood, the Balinese are generally intolerant of homosexuality within their own culture, to the point where gay Balinese men will often introduce themselves to prospective lovers as hailing from Java, so as not to cause embarrassment to their own people. It's not uncommon for men to lead a gay lifestyle for ten or fifteen years before succumbing to extreme social pressure around the age of thirty, getting married and becoming fathers. Lesbians are even less visible, but subject to similar expectations.

On the positive side, it's much more common in Bali and Lombok to show a modest amount of physical affection to friends of the same sex than to friends or lovers of the opposite sex, which means that Indonesian and foreign **gay couples** generally encounter less hassle about being seen together in public than they might in the West. Indonesian law is relatively liberal: the legal **age of consent** for both gay and heterosexual sex is 16.

Despite the indigenous aversion to gay culture, Bali's tourist industry has helped establish the island as one of the two main gay centres of Indonesia (the other being Jakarta). Young gay men from islands as far afield as Borneo gravitate to Bali in search of a foreign partner, and most end up in the Kuta area, where sophisticated Seminyak has become the focus of the island's small but enduring **scene**. Here, Jalan Dhyana Pura has a burgeoning number of boutique gay bars and larger more out-there clubs (with drag shows, theme nights and the like). A mixed gay crowd of Indonesians and foreigners congregates in certain other Kuta venues, where they're welcomed without a problem; see p.119 for details of all these places. There are also established **cruising** areas in north Petitenget at the far northern end of Kuta beach, and on Alun-alun Puputan in Denpasar. Everything is a lot quieter on Lombok, and you won't find anything resembling a gay scene in any of the resorts.

A lot of gay visitors and expatriates do have **affairs** with Indonesian men, and these liaisons tend to fall somewhere between holiday romances and paid sex. Few Indonesians would classify themselves as rent boys – they wouldn't sleep with someone they didn't like and most don't have sex for money – but they usually expect to be financially cared for by the richer man (food, drinks and entertainment expenses, for example), and some do make their living this way.

The Utopia website (ⓦwww.utopia-asia .com) is an excellent **resource** for gay travellers in Bali and the rest of Indonesia. The Bali-based tour agencies Bali Friendly (ⓦwww.balifriendlyhotels.com) and Gay Bali Tours (ⓦwww.bali-rainbows.com) recommend gay-owned and gay-friendly hotels, spas and package tours, while the Bali Gay and Lesbian Business Association has an online directory of gay-and lesbian-owned businesses (ⓦwww.balipinkpages .com). The umbrella organization for gays and lesbians in Bali and Lombok is Gaya Dewata (☎0361/234079).

Insurance

It is vital to arrange **travel insurance** before travelling to Bali or Lombok, covering for medical expenses due to illness or injury, the loss of baggage and travel documents plus cancellation or curtailment of your journey. Most exclude so-called dangerous sports unless an extra premium is paid: in Bali and Lombok, this can mean scuba diving, kayaking and whitewater rafting.

Before buying a **policy**, check that you're not already covered. Your home-insurance policy may cover your possessions against loss or theft even when overseas, or you can extend cover through your household-contents insurer. Many credit cards include some form of travel cover, and very limited medical cover is sometimes included if you pay for your trip with a credit card. Some private medical schemes include cover when abroad. In Canada, provincial health plans usually provide some cover for medical mishaps overseas, while holders of official student/teacher/youth cards in Canada and the US are entitled to meagre accident coverage and hospital in-patient benefits. Students may find that their student health coverage extends during the vacations and

Rough Guides travel insurance

Rough Guides has teamed up with Columbus Direct to offer **travel insurance** that can be tailored to suit your needs. Products include a low-cost **backpacker** option for long stays; a **short break** option for city getaways; a typical **holiday package** option; and others. There are also annual **multi-trip** policies for those who travel regularly. Different sports and activities (trekking, skiing etc) can usually be covered if required.

See our website (ⓦwww.roughguides.com/website/shop) for eligibility and purchasing options. Alternatively, UK residents should call ⓣ0870/033 9988; Australians should call ⓣ1300/669 999 and New Zealanders should call ⓣ0800/55 9911. All other nationalities should call ⓣ44 870/890 2843.

for one term beyond the date of last enrolment.

After exhausting the possibilities above, you should contact a **specialist travel insurance company**, or consider the travel insurance deal we offer (see box below). Many policies can be chopped and changed to exclude coverage you don't need. With regard to medical coverage, ascertain whether benefits will be paid as treatment proceeds or only after your return home, and be sure to carry the 24-hour medical emergency number and the policy number with you at all times. Always make a note of the policy details and leave them with someone at home in case you lose the original. When securing baggage cover, make sure that the per-article limit – typically under £500/US$900 – will cover your most valuable possession.

It can be more economical for couples and families travelling together to arrange joint insurance. Older travellers or anyone with health problems is advised to start researching insurance well in advance of their trip.

If you need to make a claim, you should keep receipts for medicines and treatment, and, if possible, contact the insurance company before making any major payment (for example, on additional convalescence expenses). In the event you have anything stolen, you must obtain an official report from the police.

Internet

There are scores of **Internet** centres in the main resorts on Bali and Lombok, most of which charge about Rp300 per minute, though big hotels usually charge very inflated

rates. Access is patchy in smaller towns and non-touristed neighbourhoods; where available, the main customers are often small boys playing online computer games. In the east of Bali the connection is via dial-up not broadband and as such is excruciatingly slow. Details are given throughout the Guide. **Wi-Fi** hotspots are also becoming more common in certain clued-up restaurants and hotels: those that provide this service for free are highlighted in the Guide.

If you plan to email from your **laptop** in Bali and Lombok, be advised that very few losmen have phone sockets in the room. The usual phone plug in Indonesia is the US standard RJ11; see ⓦwww.kropla.com for detailed advice on how to set up your modem before you go, and how to hardwire phone plugs where necessary. It's straightforward to become a temporary subscriber to public **local ISP** TelkomNet Instan (ⓦwww.telkom-indonesia.com; ⓣ147), which requires no registration or set-up fee: you simply dial ⓣ0809/89999 from your laptop, key the username "telkomnet@instan" and the password "telkom", and you're online. This service costs Rp165/minute with dial-up, but some hotels add surcharges or even bar ⓣ0809 numbers.

Language lessons

Indonesian language lessons are available in Denpasar (see p.95), Kuta (see p.123), Ubud (see p.209) and Munduk (see p.291).

Laundry

Most hotels and losmen have a laundry service, and tourist centres have plenty of services outside the hotels as well.

Left luggage

Most losmen and hotels will store luggage. Bali's Ngurah Rai Airport has a left-luggage facility (see p.100) and the shuttle-bus operator Perama will store luggage for its customers.

Living and working in Bali and Lombok

A few tourists manage to set themselves up as English- or Japanese-language teachers in Kuta and Ubud. Otherwise, the most common money-making ploy is the exporting of Indonesian goods (fabric, clothes, jewellery and other artefacts). The fortnightly free newspaper the *Bali Advertiser* (ⓦwww .baliadvertiser.biz) carries a "situations vacant" column.

For advice on renting accommodation long-term see p.43.

Mail

Every town and tourist centre on Bali and Lombok has a **General Post Office** (GPO; *kantor pos*) where you can buy stamps (*perangko*) and aerogrammes (*surat udara*), and can post letters (*surat*) and parcels (*paket*) and, in some cases, collect poste restante. Most *kantor pos* keep official government office **hours** (Mon–Thurs 8am–2pm, Fri 8–11am, Sat 8am–1pm; closed on festival days and public holidays); exceptions are detailed in the Guide. In larger towns and resorts, you can also buy stamps and send letters and parcels from **postal agents**, who charge official rates but often open longer hours than the *kantor pos*. Post boxes aren't widespread, so it's best to post letters at GPOs or postal agents. Postage is expensive, with the current rates for **airmail postcards/letters** under 200g as follows: Australia and New Zealand Rp7000/9000, Europe Rp10,000/16,000, USA and Canada Rp11,000/19,000. Airmail post takes about a week.

Details of **poste restante** services are given throughout the Guide. Letters are held for up to one month and should be filed by family name, but check under first-name initials as well.

If the *kantor pos* doesn't offer a **parcel-packing service**, there will be a stall next door for getting your stuff parcelled up; don't bother packing it yourself as the contents need to be inspected first. Postal rates for parcels are also high: a parcel weighing less than 500g costs R230,000 to be airmailed to Europe or Rp150,000 to Australia; a 6–10kg parcel sent by sea costs Rp234,000 to Australia and Rp242,000 to the UK and could take up to three months. *Kantor pos* won't handle any parcels over 10kg or more than a metre long, but most shops can arrange **shipping**; reputable drivers will also often help organize shipping and can be a good source of advice. Alternatively, try Nusa Trans Cargo (☏0361/461974, ⓦwww .nusatrans.com), who charge from $175 for shipping a crate of up to two cubic metres internationally.

Maps

For **Bali**, the best **maps** are Periplus Travel Maps (1:250,000; on sale worldwide) and *Bali Pathfinder* (1:200,000; only available in Bali, chiefly in Ubud bookshops), though neither is perfect. Periplus also produces the impressive *Bali Street Atlas*, which is exhaustively indexed and good for drivers. Studio Satumata publishes an attractive souvenir topographic relief map (1:74,000; sold at Ganesha Bookstore in Ubud), which shows the mountainous terrain with exceptional clarity.

Maps of **Lombok** are less easy to come by and are best bought abroad or in Bali rather than on Lombok itself. Go for the Periplus Travel Maps sheet covering Lombok and Sumbawa (1:200,000).

The media

Most Balinese **newspaper** readers buy the daily *Bali Post* (ⓦwww.balipost.co.id), while non-Indonesian speakers read the English-language daily *The Jakarta Post* (ⓦwww .thejakartapost.com; Rp5000, or more from hawkers and some shops) and the weekly *The Bali Times* (ⓦwww.thebalitimes.com; every Fri; Rp10,000). There's more incisive domestic and international coverage in the weekly **news magazine** *Tempo* (ⓦwww .tempointeractive.com*)*, published in both Indonesian and English versions, but not widely distributed on Bali or Lombok; and hard-hitting articles on social and political change in the online quarterly *Inside Indonesia* (Ⓦinsideindonesia.org). Major **international newspapers** are available in Bali's main tourist centres and digital-print services mean that some outlets can even sell them on the same day.

Locally produced **lifestyle magazines** are predictably glossy and glamorous and mostly concentrate on villas, spas, restaurants and clubs in the big Bali resorts; *The Yak & The Bud* (Ⓦwww.theyakmag.com; quarterly; Rp48,000) is all about Semin-*yak* and U-*bud* and carries some decent features on local design trends and personalities. For listings and tourist-oriented magazines, see p.75.

The government-operated **TV station** Televisi Republik Indonesia (TVRI) is dominated by soaps, but carries headline news and weather reports in English every afternoon. Bali's local station is TVRI Bali. Most hotels also have satellite TV, which

includes CNN, HBO, and sometimes BBC World and ABC.

Paradise FM (100.9 FM; daily 8am to 7pm) is a Bali-based English-language **radio** station aimed at tourists, broadcasting regular news bulletins and features from ABC's Australia Radio, as well as music and chat. Radio Republik Indonesia (RRI) broadcasts music, chat and news programmes 24 hours a day on 93.5 FM, with occasional English-language bulletins.

Money

The Indonesian **currency** is the **rupiah** (abbreviated to "Rp"). Notes commonly in circulation are Rp1000 (blue), Rp5000 (green and brown), Rp10,000 (pink), Rp20,000 (green), Rp50,000 (blue) and Rp100,000 (pink). They are all clearly inscribed with English numbers and letters. Be warned that most people won't accept ripped or badly worn banknotes, so you shouldn't either. You'll commonly come

Money-changing scams

Some unscrupulous exchange counters try to rip customers off, and there are several well-known **money-changing scams** practised in the bigger resorts, in particular in Kuta and Sanur on Bali.

Some common rip-offs
• Confusing you with the number of **zeros**. With nearly Rp20,000 to every pound it's easy for staff to give you Rp100,000 instead of Rp1,000,000.
• Giving you your money in Rp10,000 **denominations**, so that you lose track.
• Tampering with the **calculator**, so that it shows a low sum even if you use it yourself.
• **Folding notes** over to make it look as if you're getting twice as much as you are.
• Turning the lights out or otherwise **distracting** you while the pile of money is on the counter.
• **Stealing** some notes as they "check" it for the last time.
• Once you've rumbled them and complained, telling you that the discrepancy in the figures is due to "**commission**".

Some advice
• **Avoid** anywhere that offers a ridiculously good rate. Stick to banks or to exchange desks recommended by other travellers.
• Work out the total amount you're expecting beforehand, and write it down.
• Always ask whether there is commission.
• Before signing your cheque, ask for notes in **reasonable denominations** (Rp10,000 is unreasonable, Rp50,000 is acceptable), and ask to see them first.
• **Count your money** carefully, and never hand it back to the exchange staff, as this is when they whip away some notes without you noticing. You should be the last person to count the money.
• So long as you haven't already **signed** a traveller's cheque, you can walk away at any point. If you have signed the cheque, stay calm, don't get distracted, and count everything slowly and methodically.

across Rp100 (silver-coloured plastic), Rp500 (larger, round, bronze) and Rp1000 (large, round, bronze with silver rim) coins. Don't be surprised if cashiers in supermarkets give you sweets instead of small-denomination coins as change.

At the time of writing the **exchange rate** was US$1 to Rp9500, and £1 to Rp18,600. For the current rate check out the useful "Travellers Currency Cheat Sheets" at ⓦwww.oanda.com.

Cash and traveller's cheques

Before you leave home, exchange facilities should be able to get some **cash** rupiah for you but order at least a week ahead of your departure, as there is always a shortage of rupiah stocks outside Indonesia. However, rates are poor and you don't really need it; there are exchange counters at Bali's Ngurah Rai Airport and Lombok's Selaparang Airport which all open for arriving passengers and ATMs at Ngurah Rai (but see below). Some cash in **US dollars** can be useful to take with you, but take crisp new notes and avoid $100 bills, which can be hard to exchange and pre-1996 ones are not accepted at all.

Most people carry at least some of their money as **traveller's cheques**, which are widely accepted at banks and exchange counters across Bali and in the tourist centres of Lombok (Senggigi, the Gili Islands and the four-cities area of Mataram-Ampenan-Cakranegara-Sweta). Outside these areas on Lombok, facilities are rarer (see Guide chapters for details), so be sure to carry enough cash. The best cheques are those issued by the most familiar names, particularly American Express in US dollars or pounds sterling, though numerous other currencies are accepted in the largest resorts. Keep the **receipt** (or proof of purchase) when you buy your traveller's cheques, as you may need to show it. Be aware that if you lose your passport your traveller's cheques will be useless as you can't encash them, so a back-up access to funds (a credit or debit card) in case of emergency is useful.

In tourist centres, **exchange counters** are the most convenient places to cash your cheques. They open daily from around 10am–10pm and rates compare favourably

Lost or stolen credit cards/ traveller's cheques

American Express Cards and traveller's cheques
☎001-803-44-0176
MasterCard ☎001-803-1-887-0623
Visa Cards ☎001-803-1-933-6294
Traveller's cheques
☎001-803-011-2575

with those offered by the banks. However, be wary of money-changing scams (see box below), particularly in Kuta.

Normal **banking hours** are Monday–Thursday 8am–2pm, Friday 8am–noon and, in some branches, Saturday 8–11.30am, but these do vary. However, in many banks the foreign-exchange counter only opens for a limited period. Banks in smaller towns don't have foreign-exchange facilities.

Plastic

Major **credit cards**, most commonly Visa and MasterCard, are accepted by most mid- to top-end hotels and tourist businesses. However, outlets often add to your bill the entire fee that is charged to them (currently four percent), bumping costs up.

In Bali's and Lombok's biggest tourist centres you'll find **ATMs** that accept international cards, both Visa and MasterCard as well as **debit cards** on the Cirrus network. If you can't find one, track down the local Hardy's supermarket – there's always at least one ATM attached. See the relevant sections of resort and city accounts for ATM locations; for an up-to-the-minute list, check ⓦwww .mastercard.com and ⓦwww.visa.com. Note that currently some areas, notably Amed, Candi Dasa, Pemuteran and the Gili Islands, have no ATM. Remember that all cash advances on credit cards are treated as loans, with interest accruing daily from the date of withdrawal and, possibly, a transaction fee on top. Debit-card withdrawals are not liable to interest payments but check the flat transaction fee your bank will charge. Be aware that your home bank may well block your card when you initially try to use it abroad, even if you've warned them of your trip, and it may take a couple of phone calls to sort this out – take the relevant telephone number with you.

Be careful when using your card – unlike machines at home, some of the Bali and Lombok machines only return your card *after* they've dispensed your cash, making it easier to forget your card. Visa Travel-Money (ⓦwww.visa.com) and American Express's Travelers Cheque Card (see ⓦwww.americanexpress.com) are **pre-paid cards** that work like a debit card in ATMs, hotels and other businesses and allow you to top it up as and when you wish.

Wiring money

Wiring money through a specialist agent is a fast but expensive way to **receive money abroad** and is a last resort. Money should be available for collection in local currency, from the company's local agent within twenty minutes of being sent via Western Union (ⓦwww.westernunion.com) or Moneygram (ⓦwww.moneygram.com); both charge on a sliding scale, so sending larger amounts of cash is better value. Money can be sent via the agents, telephone or, in some cases, the websites (see above). **Western Union** has a larger network of agents in Bali and Lombok; many post offices are agents. Check the websites for locations and opening hours.

It's also possible to have money wired **directly** from a bank in your home country to a bank in Indonesia, but this can be tortuous. If you think you'll use it, check with your bank before travelling to see which branch of which bank they have reciprocal arrangements with, and precisely what details they'll need in order to complete the transaction.

Opening hours and public holidays

Opening hours are not straightforward in Bali and Lombok, with government offices, post offices, businesses and shops setting their own timetables.

Generally speaking, **businesses** such as **airline offices** open at least Monday–Friday 8am–4pm, Saturday 8am–1pm, with many open longer, but have variable arrangements at lunchtime. Normal **banking hours** are Monday–Thursday 8am–2pm, Friday 8am–noon and, in some branches, Saturday

8–11.30am, but these do vary and foreign-exchange-counter opening hours are often shorter. Main **post offices** operate roughly Monday–Thursday 8am–3pm, Friday 8am–1pm, Saturday 8am–noon, with considerable variations from office to office. Postal agents in tourist areas tend to keep later hours. In tourist areas, **shops** open from around 10am until 8pm or later, but local shops in towns and villages open and shut much earlier with the exception of supermarkets in shopping centres, which generally open at least 10am–10pm. Local **markets** vary; some start soon after dawn with business completed by 10am, others open all day and only close up towards the end of the afternoon.

Government offices are widely reported as open Monday–Friday 8am–4pm; in fact there is much variability in different areas and departments, most close early on Friday and you'll generally be most successful if you turn up between 9am and 11.30am. Official government hours shorten during Ramadan; the best advice is to ring offices at that time to check before you make a long journey.

National public holidays

In addition to **national public holidays** celebrated throughout Indonesia (see box below) there are frequent local **religious festivals** occurring throughout the Muslim, Hindu and Chinese communities. Each of Bali's 20,000 temples also has an anniversary celebration once every *wuku* year, or 210 days (see p.48), local communities host elaborate **marriage** and **cremation** celebrations, and both islands have their own particular secular holidays.

All major **Muslim festivals** are national holidays; see box opposite. These, based on a lunar calendar, move backwards against the Western calendar, falling earlier each year. The ninth Muslim month is **Ramadan**, a month of fasting during

---

Ramadan begins Sept 1, 2008, Aug 21, 2009, Aug 11, 2010, Aug 1, 2011. **Idul Fitri** Sept 30, 2008, Sep 20, 2009, Sept 9, 2010, Aug 30, 2011. Note that Islamic festivals depend on local sightings of the moon; actual dates may vary by a day or two.

National public holidays

January 1 New Year's Day (Tahun Baru).

January Muharram, Muslim New Year.

January/Febuary Chinese New Year.

March/April Balinese New Year (Nyepi).

March/April Good Friday and Easter Sunday.

March/April Maulid Nabi Muhammad, birth of the Prophet.

May Ascension of Jesus Christ (Isa Almasih).

May/June Waisak Day, anniversary of the birth, death and enlightenment of Buddha.

July/August Al Miraj, Ascension Day.

August 17 Independence Day (Hari Proklamasi Kemerdekaan).

October/November Idul Fitri, celebration of the end of Ramadan.

December Idul Adha, the Muslim day of sacrifice.

December 25 Christmas Day.

---

daylight hours. It is much more apparent on Muslim Lombok than on Hindu Bali. Followers of the Wetu Telu branch of Islam on Lombok (see p.437) observe their own three-day festival of **Puasa** rather than the full month. Many Muslim restaurants, although not tourist establishments, shut down during the day so it can be hard to get a meal in central and eastern parts of Lombok where you should not eat, drink or smoke in public at this time. However, in all other areas of Lombok you'll find Ramadan much less apparent. **Idul Fitri**, also called Hari Raya or Lebaran, the first day of the tenth month of the Muslim calendar, marks the end of Ramadan and is a national holiday. In fact, many businesses across Indonesia shut for a week and many hotels on Bali and Lombok get booked out with visitors from across the archipelago.

Phones

With mobile phones becoming increasingly common and Internet phoning also gaining in popularity, the variable efficiency of Indonesia's **telephone network** is a little less of a hindrance than it once was.

The cheapest way to make **international calls** (*panggilan internasional*) is generally via **Skype** or equivalent Internet technology at one of the more clued-up Internet centres, generally in the main tourist resorts; some Internet centres charge standard Internet rates for this service (around Rp300/min) but those with limited band-width capacity may charge up to Rp10,000/min.

Privately run "telephone shops" or **wartel** have traditionally been the main public phone centres and are found all over Bali and Lombok, even in the smallest towns; most have several booths and open long hours, typically 7am – 10pm. Because of special pre-paid VoIP (Voice over Internet Protocol) deals, many wartel in the biggest resorts are now able to offer a uniform cheap **rate** of Rp7000/min for any international call, regardless of the destination. Other wartel, particularly those in outlying areas, charge according to rates set by **Telkom**, the government telecommunications service (see box on p.74 for details), plus a little extra. To make international calls you preface your country code with either ⊕017 (Telkom) or ⊕001 (Indosat); rates for both services are identical, fixed by the government, and use identical time-bands for identical discounts.

It's increasingly difficult to find **card phones** (*telepon umum kartu*) and **coin-operated phones** (*telepon umum*), but call charges for these are standard Telkom rates. Phone cards (*kartu telepon*) are sold at the bigger supermarkets in denominations of Rp5000–100,000; if using a **coin phone**, in most cases you put the coins in only after the person you're calling has picked up and started to speak.

Some wartel will send and receive **faxes** (*fax*) for you but faxing is ever more unreliable;

hotels often seem unable to receive faxes, so using email is preferable.

Domestic calls are charged at various rates. A **local call** (*panggilan lokal*) is a call to any destination that shares the same area code; current Telkom rates for this are Rp83–163/min depending on distance and time of day. Calls to all other domestic destinations with a different area code are classed as **long-distance calls** (*panggilan inter-lokal*) and cost from Rp600–2300/min. Bali is divided into several **code zones**, and Lombok has two codes.

Calls to **mobile phones** – whose numbers begin ☎08 – are more expensive. Some businesses have to rely on **satellite phones** (code ☎086812), which are costlier still.

Mobile phones

Most **UK**, **Australian** and **New Zealand** mobiles use GSM technology, which works fine in parts of Indonesia, but contact your phone provider before leaving home to get international "roaming" switched on. Unless a **US** or **Canadian** phone is a special triband handset it probably won't work in Indonesia; check with your provider.

Buying a **local sim card** can be a useful alternative, especially as international calls from Indonesian mobiles can work out cheaper than via landlines. Mobiles are huge in Bali and Lombok and there are phone shops all over, even in some villages. Staff may have to unblock your phone first and will also advise on the best sim card for your needs, bearing in mind local and international coverage. They should also fill you in on promotions and access codes for discounted calls; travellers' forums are also a good source of advice (see below). Expect to pay around Rp50,000 for a sim card, which should include some credit. Top-up cards are sold at mobile phone stalls all over both islands.

Useful numbers and codes

International operator ☎101
International directory enquiries ☎102
Domestic operator ☎100
Local directory enquiries ☎108
Long-distance directory enquiries ☎106

Phoning home

Dial ☎017 or 001 + IDD country code + area code (minus its initial zero if applicable) + local number.

Telkom rates shown are for the **standard period** and do not include the inevitable **surcharge** applied by every wartel (usually rounded up to the nearest Rp1000). In addition, there's a 20-percent surcharge if calling during the weekday **peak** period, and a 25-percent discount during weekday **off-peak** periods, at weekends and on national holidays.

Australia Code ☎61. IDD rate: Rp8300/min (peak 9am–noon, off-peak 10pm–6am).
Ireland Code ☎353. IDD rate: Rp7150/min (peak 2–5pm, off-peak 3–11am).
New Zealand Code ☎64. IDD rate: Rp8300/min (peak 9am–noon, off-peak 11pm–7am).
South Africa Code ☎27. IDD rate: Rp5650/min (peak 2–5pm, off-peak 3–11am).
UK Code ☎44. IDD rate: Rp9400/min (peak 2–5pm, off-peak 3–11am).
US and Canada Code ☎1. IDD rate: Rp10,700/min (peak 9am–noon, off-peak 11pm–7am).

Calling Bali and Lombok from abroad

Dial your international access code (☎00 from the UK, Ireland and New Zealand, ☎011 from the US and Canada, ☎0011 from Australia) + 62 for Indonesia + area code minus its initial zero + local number.

Time

Bali and Lombok are on **Central Indonesian Time** (GMT+8, North American EST+13, Australian EST+2). There's no daylight saving.

Tourist information

Indonesia has no **overseas tourist offices** but in Australia is represented by Integra Tourism Marketing, Level 5, 68 Alfred St, Milsons Point, NSW 2061 ☏02 9959 4277, Ⓦwww.visit-indonesia.com.au.

District capitals across Bali and Lombok all maintain their own **government tourist office** (Mon–Thurs 8am–3pm, Fri 8am–noon; those in the main tourist centres keep longer hours) but they're generally concerned more with strategy and marketing than with travellers' queries. You may get more help from locally run information centres, where available, and perhaps from private entrepreneurs advertising "tourist information", though they will certainly want to sell you a tour or rent you some transport.

Government Travel Advice

Most Western governments maintain websites with travel information detailing some of the potential hazards and what to do in emergencies.

Australian Department of Foreign Affairs and Trade Ⓦwww.dfat.gov.au
Canadian Department of Foreign Affairs and International Trade Ⓦwww.dfait-maeci.gc.ca
Irish Department of Foreign Affairs Ⓦwww.irlgov.ie/iveagh
New Zealand Ministry of Foreign Affairs Ⓦwww.mft.govt.nz
Republic of South Africa Department of Foreign Affairs Ⓦwww.dfa.gov.za
UK Foreign and Commonwealth Office Ⓦwww.fco.gov.uk
US Department of State Ⓦtravel.state.gov

Tourist publications

Plenty of **free tourist magazines** supply information on Bali's and Lombok's sights, activities and events; they're generally available in hotels and restaurants in the main tourist centres.
Agung Small-format periodical detailing the east of Bali from Padang Bai to Amed.

Bali Plus Ⓦwww.baliplus.com. Compact monthly that covers tourist attractions, and lists and reviews restaurants, clubs, shops and spas.
Bali Travel News Ⓦwww.bali-travelnews.com. Fortnightly newspaper that details upcoming temple festivals and carries a long directory of useful contacts, but is of most interest for its punchy features on Balinese culture and its distinctive Bali-Hindu editorial voice.
the beat Ⓦwww.beatmag.com. Bali's premier nightlife listings magazine covers gigs, parties and clubs plus a few bars and restaurants. Fortnightly.
Lombok Times Ⓦwww.lomboktimes.com. Lombok's only tourist-oriented newspaper is published monthly and covers general info on all aspects of visiting Lombok.
What's Up? Bali Ⓦwww.whatsupbali.com. Weekly foldout featuring day-by-day listings of club and live-music events; dance performances; major festivals and church services; plus restaurant and shopping recommendations.

Websites and forums

Bali Blog Ⓦwww.baliblog.com. An expat blogs his Bali experiences – hiking up Batur, eating seafood, going surfing – and offers tons of Bali-related advice.
Bali Paradise Online Ⓦwww.bali-paradise.com. Features and links on everything from traditional architecture to car rental and the weather forecast. Also has a travellers' forum.
Bali Travel Forum Ⓦwww.balitravelforum.com. Active forum.
Lombok Hotels Ⓦwww.lombok.com. General tourist info, plus hotel booking.
Lombok Lovers Forum Ⓦgroups.msn.com/LombokLovers. Most active Lombok forum.
Lombok Sumbawa Ⓦwww.lomboksumbawa.com. General tourist info from the Lombok Sumbawa Tourism Promotion Board.
Mic's Bali Forums Ⓦmicbali.proboards21.com. Multi-stranded forum covering Lombok and Bali.

Travellers with disabilities

Indonesia makes few provisions for its disabled citizens, which clearly affects **travellers with disabilities**, although the situation is definitely improving year on year. At the physical level, kerbs are usually high (without slopes) and pavements/sidewalks uneven with all sorts of obstacles; access to most public places involves steps (very few have ramps); public transport is inaccessible to wheelchair users (although Perama tourist buses will take them); and the few pedestrian crossings on major roads have no audible signal. On the positive side, many hotels comprise bungalows in extensive grounds and/or have spacious bathrooms, while the more aware are increasingly making an effort to provide the necessary facilities. These hotels are highlighted in the Guide and the Bali Paradise site below carries a round-up of big hotels that have accessible facilities.

For all of these reasons, it may be worth considering an **organized tour** or holiday – the contacts listed below will help you start researching trips to Bali and Lombok. Arrange **travel insurance** carefully taking into account any medical difficulties you may have, and use your travel agent to make your journey simpler: airlines cope better if they are expecting you and pre-arranged transport at the other end makes arrival smoother. A medical certificate of your fitness to travel, provided by your doctor, is also extremely useful; some airlines or insurance companies may insist on it. Carry spares of any clothing or equipment that might be hard to find.

Make sure that you take sufficient supplies of any **medications**, and – if they're essential – carry the complete supply with you whenever you travel (including on buses and planes), in case of loss or theft. It's also a good idea to carry a doctor's letter about your drugs prescriptions with you at all times, particularly when passing through customs at Ngurah Rai or Selaparang airports, as this will ensure you don't get hauled up for narcotics transgressions.

Contacts for travellers with disabilities

ⓦ **www.bali-paradise.com** Follow the Special Needs Traveler link for detailed local information, suggestions and tips.
ⓦ **www.bootsnall.com/guides** An excellent guide to travelling with disabilities.
ⓦ **thorntree.lonelyplanet.com** The "Travellers with Disabilities" forum is useful.

Guide

Guide

1

South Bali

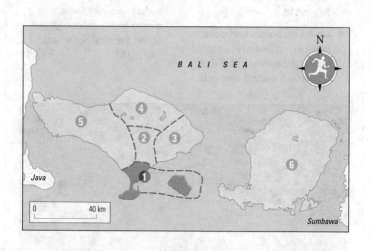

CHAPTER 1   # Highlights

* **Bali Museum, Denpasar** A tantalizing introduction to the island's cultural and religious heritage. See p.89

* **Seminyak** Some of the finest dining and most sophisticated shopping on Bali. See p.117

* **Kuta nightlife** Scores of easy-going bars, trendy clubs and packed dancefloors make Kuta a great place to party. See p.118

* **Jimbaran beach barbecues** Fresh fish grilled over coconut husks and served at candlelit tables on the sand. See p.127

* **Surf beaches** Awesome breaks and good beach vibes at Uluwatu, Dreamland, Bingin and Padang Padang. See p.129

* **Sanur** A green and relatively peaceful resort that makes an appealing alternative to Kuta. See p.140

* **Nusa Lembongan** Islanders, surfers and sun-seekers mingle on the great beaches and in the rural hinterland. See p.155

▲ Kuta beach

South Bali

he triangle of mainly flat land that makes up **the south** is some of the most fertile in Bali, and also the most densely populated, with more than 650 people resident on every square kilometre. Bali's administrative capital, Denpasar, is here and so too are the island's major tourist resorts, which have sprung up along the white-sand beaches: at Kuta and Jimbaran in the west, and Sanur, Nusa Dua and Tanjung Benoa in the east. The combination of large offshore reefs and a peculiarly shaped coastline have also made this area a genuine surfers' paradise, pounded by some of the most famous and challenging breaks in the world. Most of south Bali comes under the administrative district of **Badung** which, unsurprisingly given its many advantages and monopoly of the most lucrative tourist resorts, is the wealthiest in Bali – despite occupying under eight percent of the island's total land mass.

Most tourists treat **Denpasar** as little more than a transit point for cross-island journeys, but it holds the island's best museum and makes an interesting contrast to the more westernized beach enclaves. Instead, the vast majority of visitors head straight for brash, commercial **Kuta–Legian–Seminyak** which sprawls down the southwest coast just 3km north of Bali's airport and is as famous for its shopping and nightlife – the most happening on the island by far – as its surf.

Across on the southeast coast, beach life is quieter and greener at **Sanur**, more luxurious and manicured at five-star **Nusa Dua**, and more focused on water-sports at **Tanjung Benoa**. Offshore lie three islands: little-visited **Nusa Penida**, whose south coast consists of towering limestone cliffs; tiny **Nusa Ceningan**; and resolutely relaxed **Nusa Lembongan**, with its white-sand beaches and easy access from Sanur. South of Kuta and west of Nusa Dua, the **Bukit peninsula** offers peaceful, upmarket beachfront hotels at **Jimbaran** and fabulous **surf** and lively beach bases beneath the cliffs at and around **Uluwatu**, also the site of an important clifftop temple.

Denpasar

Despite roaring motorbikes and round-the-clock traffic congestion, Bali's capital, **DENPASAR**, remains a pleasant city at heart, centred on a grassy

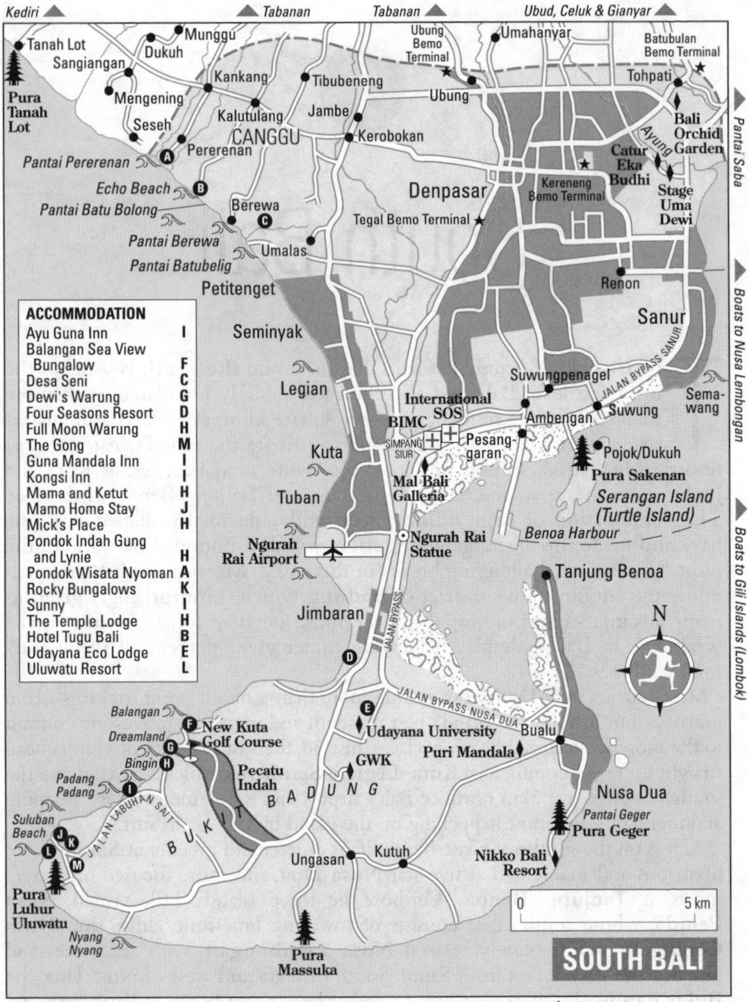

① (map label)

SOUTH BALI

Top map labels

▲ Kediri ▲ Tabanan Tabanan ▲ ▲ Ubud, Celuk & Gianyar

Munggu
Tanah Lot
Sangiangan
Dukuh
Pura Tanah Lot
Mengening
Seseh
Kankang
Tibubeneng
Kalutulang
Jambe
CANGGU
Pererenan
Pantai Pererenan Ⓐ
Echo Beach Ⓑ
Berewa
Pantai Batu Bolong
Ⓒ
Pantai Berewa
Pantai Batubelig
Petitenget

Seminyak

Legian

Kuta
BIMC
International SOS
SIMPANG SIUR
Pesang-garan
Mal Bali Galleria
Tuban

Ngurah Rai Airport
Ngurah Rai Statue

Jimbaran Ⓓ

Ubung Bemo Terminal
Umahanyar
Ubung
Kerobokan
Denpasar
Kereneng Bemo Terminal
Tegal Bemo Terminal ★
Renon

Batubulan Bemo Terminal ★
Tohpati
Bali Orchid Garden
Ayung
Catur Eka Budhi
Stage Uma Dewi

▶ Pantai Saba

Sanur

Suwungpenagel
Ambengan
Suwung
Semawang
Pojok/Dukuh
Pura Sakenan
Serangan Island (Turtle Island)
Benoa Harbour

▶ Boats to Nusa Lembongan

▶ Boats to Gili Islands (Lombok)

Tanjung Benoa

JALAN BYPASS NUSA DUA
Bualu
Nusa Dua
Udayana University Ⓔ
GWK
Puri Mandala
Pantai Geger
Pura Geger
Nikko Bali Resort

Balangan
Ⓕ **New Kuta Golf Course**
Dreamland
Ⓖ
Bingin Ⓗ
Pecatu Indah
Padang Padang
Ⓘ
B A D U N G
Suluban Beach
Ⓙ Ⓚ
Ⓛ Ⓜ
B U K I T
Pura Luhur Uluwatu
Nyang Nyang
Ungasan
Kutuh

Pura Massuka

0 — 5 km

N

ACCOMMODATION

Ayu Guna Inn	I
Balangan Sea View Bungalow	F
Desa Seni	C
Dewi's Warung	G
Four Seasons Resort	D
Full Moon Warung	H
The Gong	M
Guna Mandala Inn	I
Kongsi Inn	J
Mama and Ketut	J
Mamo Home Stay	H
Mick's Place	H
Pondok Indah Gung and Lynie	A
Pondok Wisata Nyoman	K
Rocky Bungalows	I
Sunny	H
The Temple Lodge	B
Hotel Tugu Bali	E
Udayana Eco Lodge	L
Uluwatu Resort	L

Bottom map labels

▲ Padang Bai

Batubulan
DENPASAR
Seminyak
Legian
Sanur
Kuta
Ngurah Rai Airport
Benoa Harbour
Jimbaran
Tanjung Benoa
Bualu
Nusa Dua

Nusa Lembongan
Ped
Jungutbatu
Buyuk Harbour
Toyapakeh
Sampalan
Nusa Penida
Badung Strait

▶ Gili Islands (Lombok)

INDIAN OCEAN

N

0 — 10 km

square, with just a few major shopping streets crisscrossing the core. Department stores and malls do feature but the older neighbourhoods, especially those in the north of the city, are still dominated by family compounds grouped into traditional *banjar* (village association) districts, where time-honoured community events, such as gamelan and dance rehearsals, take place as frequently as in the island's rural villages. What makes Denpasar different is the marked influence of the sizeable immigrant communities, notably Javanese Muslims, Sasaks from Lombok, and Chinese-Indonesians, who together constitute around thirty percent of the city's population of 400,000.

Most tourists whiz into Denpasar as part of a day-trip from one of the southern resorts, lingering just long enough to tour the wide-ranging **Bali Museum** and browse the traditional **markets**. Hardly any visitors stay overnight and the choice of lodgings is correspondingly poor. But the lack of tourist facilities is an attraction in itself, offering a rare chance to experience unadulterated urban Bali, not to mention cheaper food and shopping; the city also makes a feasible base for trips by public transport to local attractions such as Tanah Lot, Mengwi, Sangeh and Batubulan.

Some history

Until the early twentieth century, control of the city – then known as **Badung**, like the regency it governed – was divided among several rajas, most notably those at the courts of Pemecutan (southwest Denpasar) and Kesiman (east Denpasar). Supremacy was wrested from them however by the insatiably expansionist Dutch, whose invasion of Badung in 1906 resulted in the ritual suicide of hundreds of Badung citizens, and the subsequent end to raja autocracy on Bali. The original **royal districts** survive to this day, but though some of the ancestral places remain, the royal families have lost their political power. After Bali won independence from the Dutch in 1949, the island's administrative **capital** was moved to Badung from the north-coast town of Singaraja and the city was renamed Denpasar. Almost fifty years later Denpasar's status was upgraded again when, in 1992, it became a self-governing municipality, no longer under the auspices of Badung district.

Moving on from Denpasar

Denpasar's four main bemo terminals serve destinations across the island; see the plan on p.87 for an overview. **Tegal** bemo terminal covers routes south of Denpasar, including Tegal–Kuta–Legian (Rp5000), Tegal–Kuta–Tuban/Airport (Rp5000), Tegal–Jimbaran–Bualu–Nusa Dua's Bali Collection (Rp10,000) and Tegal–Renon–Sanur (Rp5000), though frequencies on all these routes vary due to an ongoing drop in demand. **Kereneng** terminal covers Sanur (Rp5000), and these services are also quite erratic. **Batubulan** terminal (described on p.170) runs regular services to the Ubud area; to east Bali; parts of north Bali; and Nusa Dua, via Sanur (dropping passengers on the outskirts at the *Sanur Paradise Plaza* hotel) and the eastern outskirts of Kuta (see p.106). **Ubung** terminal (see p.318) runs frequent transport to north and west Bali, as well as to Padang Bai (for Lombok) and Java.

There are smaller bemo terminals on **Jalan Gunung Agung**, for transport to Canggu and Kerobokan; near the **Sanglah** hospital, for Benoa Harbour and Suwung; at **Wangaya** for Sangeh and Pelaga; and at **Suci** for Pulau Serangan.

For **airport** departure details, see p.100.

Arrival, information and city transport

If you're arriving in Bali by air, you'll land at **Ngurah Rai Airport**, which is not in Denpasar as sometimes implied, but just beyond the southern outskirts of Kuta. For full information on airport arrival, departure and onward transport, see the box on p.100.

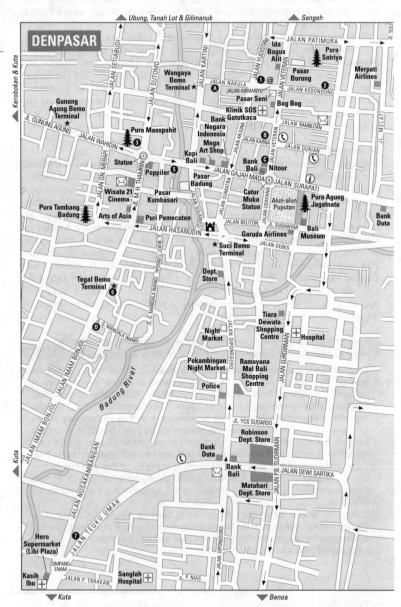

Arriving in Denpasar by bemo or public bus from other parts of the island, you'll almost certainly be dropped at one of the four main **bemo terminals**, which lie on the edges of town: **Tegal**, on Jalan Imam Bonjol, in the southwest corner; **Kereneng**, off Jalan Hayam Wuruk, in east central Denpasar; **Ubung**, in its own suburb way off to the northwest on the main road to Tabanan (see p.318); and, even further out, **Batubulan** on the northeast fringes (see p.170).

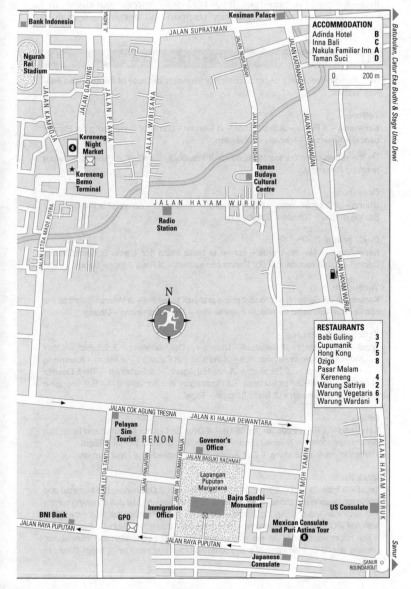

ACCOMMODATION

Adinda Hotel	B
Inna Bali	C
Nakula Familiar Inn	A
Taman Suci	D

0   200 m

RESTAURANTS

Babi Guling	3
Cupumanik	7
Hong Kong	5
Ozigo	8
Pasar Malam Kereneng	4
Warung Satriya	2
Warung Vegetaris	6
Warung Wardani	1

Sanur

The plan opposite shows which terminal covers which routes. Getting from one bemo terminal to another is fairly easy, but connections can be quite time-consuming, as you have to wait for your bemo to fill up at each transit point.

Information

Denpasar's **tourist office** is conveniently located near the Bali Museum on the northern perimeter of Alun-alun Puputan, at Jalan Surapati 7 (Mon–Thurs 7.30am–3.30pm, Fri 8am–1pm; ℡0361/234569). Specific questions can be answered here, particularly about city transport and upcoming festivals, but don't expect much more.

Cross-city bemo routes

As outlined below, some routes alter slightly in reverse because of the extensive one-way system.

Yellow

Kereneng – Jl Plawa – Jl Supratman – Jl Gianyar – corner of Jl Waribang (for Barong dance) – Kesiman – Tohpati – **Batubulan**.

On the return route bemos travel down Jl Kamboja instead of Jl Plawa just before reaching Kereneng.

Grey-blue

Ubung – Jl Cokroaminoto – Jl Gatot Subroto – Jl Gianyar – corner of Jl Waribang (for Barong dance) – Tohpati – **Batubulan**.

Dark green

Kereneng – Jl Hayam Wuruk – corner of Nusa Indah (for Taman Budaya Cultural Centre) – Sanur roundabout (for Renon consulates) – Jl Raya Sanur – **Sanur**.

Turquoise

Kereneng – Jl Surapati (for tourist office and Bali Museum) – Jl Veteran (alight at the corner of Jl Abimanyu for *Nakula Familiar Inn*) – Jl Cokroaminoto – **Ubung**.

Yellow or turquoise

Tegal – Jl Gn Merapi – Jl Setiabudi – Ubung – Jl Cokroaminoto – Jl Subroto – Jl Yani – Jl Nakula (for *Nakula Familiar Inn*) – Jl Veteran – Jl Patimura – Jl Melati – **Kereneng** – Jl Hayam Wuruk – Jl Surapati – Jl Kapten Agung – Jl Sudirman – Tiara Dewata Shopping Centre – Jl Yos Sudarso – Jl Diponegoro (for Ramayana Mal Bali shopping centre) – Jl Hasanudin – Jl Bukit Tunggal – **Tegal**.

Beige

Kereneng – Jl Raya Puputan (for GPO) – Jl Dewi Sartika (for Matahari and Robinson department stores) – Jl Teuku Umar – junction with Jl Imam Bonjol – **Tegal**.
The return route runs along Jl Cok Agung Tresna instead of Jl Raya Puputan.

Dark blue

Tegal – Jl Imam Bonjol – Jl Teuku Umar – junction with Jl Diponegoro (for Matahari and Robinson department stores) – Jl Yos Sudarso (for Ramayana Mal Bali shopping centre) – Jl Sudirman – Jl Cok Agung Tresna – junction with Jl Panjaitan (alight for the 500m walk to GPO) – Jl Hajar Dewantara – Jl Moh Yamin – Sanur roundabout – **Sanur**.
The return route goes all the way along Jl Raya Puputan after the roundabout, passing the GPO, then straight along Jl Teuku Umar and north up Jl Imam Bonjol to Tegal.

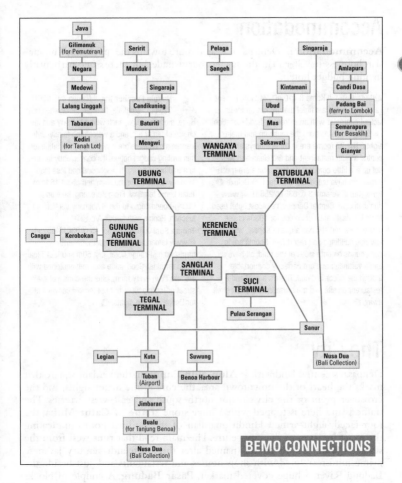

BEMO CONNECTIONS

City transport

As in many other areas of Bali, public transport in Denpasar is in decline because of the huge rise in motorbike ownership. Although **public bemos** continue to shuttle between the city's bemo terminals, they now run at increasingly infrequent intervals, only departing when enough passengers show up, which could mean waiting for anything between five minutes and an hour. Nonetheless, we've detailed the most convenient routes in the text and there's a summary of the most useful routes opposite. Nearly all Denpasar bemos have at least their first and last stop printed on the vehicle, and most are colour coded. Wave to hail one and state your exact destination before getting in. **Prices** are supposed to be fixed, but tourists are often obliged to pay more – generally Rp3000 for a cross-city ride. For impartial advice on bemo routes and prices, ask at the controller's office rather than in the bemos themselves. If you can't face the bemo system, metered **taxis** also circulate around the city (Rp5000 flagfall, then Rp4000 per km).

Accommodation

Accommodation in Denpasar is geared more towards the quick-stop Indonesian business traveller than the fussier tourist trade, but there's one particularly inviting budget hotel.

Adinda Hotel Jl Karna 8 ☎0361/240435. Decent-value mid-range a/c hotel that makes up for its lack of character with an extremely handy location just a few minutes from the museum and main sights. The 27 rooms are in three storeys around a central atrium restaurant and are clean and well set up if a little compact. Deluxe rooms are much larger and have balconies. Standard ❸ Deluxe ❹

Inna Bali Jl Veteran 3 ☎0361/225681, ⓦwww.innabali.com. Central Denpasar's oldest hotel used to be the destination of choice for 1930s cruise passengers and still has a quaint appeal, with its low-rise buildings and resort feel. Rooms are in compounds on both sides of the road, all have a/c and a verandah and are perfectly comfortable, though the decor is dated. There's a pool and a restaurant on site and the museum is a short stroll away. ❺

Nakula Familiar Inn Jl Nakula 4 ☎0361/226446, Ⓔnakulafamiliar_inn@yahoo.com. Huge, modern rooms, each with a balcony and the choice of fan or a/c, and a welcoming family-style losmen atmosphere are a winning combination for this inviting budget option. It's conveniently located in a traditional northern neighbourhood less than 10min walk from the museum and about 15 from Tegal bemo terminal. From Kereneng, take an Ubung-bound bemo to the Jl Abimanyu/Jl Veteran junction. Rooms with fan ❶ A/c ❷

Taman Suci Jl Imam Bonjol 45 ☎0361/485254, ⓦwww.tamansuci.com. Modern, decently furnished mid-range hotel, just 50m south of Tegal bemo terminal. Good value and well equipped with a/c and TV in every room, plus the choice of main-street or rooftop view, but not terribly convenient for Denpasar's big sights. ❹

The City

Denpasar's central landmark is **Alun-alun Puputan**, the verdant square that marks the heart of the downtown area, the core of the major sights, and the crossover point of the city's major north–south and east–west arteries. The traffic island here is topped with a huge stone **statue** of **Catur Muka**, the four-faced, eight-armed Hindu guardian of the cardinal points, indicating the exact location of the city centre. The main road that runs west from the statue is **Jalan Gajah Mada** (named after the fourteenth-century Javanese prime minister), lined with shop-houses and restaurants and, just beside the Badung River, a huge covered market, **Pasar Badung**. A couple of blocks further west stands the historic **Pura Maospahit** temple, but the more visited attractions dominate the eastern fringes of Alun-alun Puputan itself – the rewarding **Bali Museum** and the state temple, **Pura Agung Jagatnata**.

Denpasar's eastern districts are less enticing, but the art gallery at the **Taman Budaya Cultural Centre** is worth a look, while the suburb of **Renon** is home to consulates and government offices. Modern Denpasar is epitomised on **Jalan Teuku Umar**, a long, neon-lit strip crammed with restaurants, malls and scores of mobile-phone outlets.

Alun-alun Puputan

Grassy **Alun-alun Puputan** or Taman Puputan (Puputan Square) commemorates the fateful events of September 20, 1906, when the Raja of Badung marched out of his palace gates, followed by hundreds of his subjects, and faced the invading Dutch head on. Dressed entirely in holy white, with each man, woman and child clasping a golden kris (dagger), the people of Badung had psyched themselves up for a **puputan**, or ritual fight to the death, rather than submit to the Dutch colonialists' demands. Historical accounts vary, but it's thought that the mass suicide took place on this square and was incited by Badung's chief priest who, on a signal from the raja, stabbed his king with the royal kris. Hundreds of citizens followed suit, and those that didn't were shot down by Dutch bullets; the final death toll was reported to be somewhere between six hundred and two thousand. The palace itself, just across Jalan Surapati on the north edge of the modern square, was razed and has since been rebuilt as the imposing official residence of Bali's governor. The huge bronze statue depicting figures bearing sharpened bamboo staves and kris on the northern edge of the park is a memorial to the citizens who died in the *puputan*; it's an image that you'll see repeated in towns and villages across the island.

The square hosts a commemorative **fair**, with food stalls and *wayang kulit* shows, every year on September 20.

The Bali Museum

Overlooking the eastern edge of Alun-alun Puputan on pedestrianized Jalan Mayor Wisnu, the **Bali Museum** (Museum Negeri Propinsi Bali; Sat–Thurs 8am–3pm, Fri 8am–12.30pm; closed public hols; Rp2000, children Rp1000; on the turquoise Kereneng–Ubung bemo route) is Denpasar's top attraction and makes a worthwhile introduction to the island's culture, past and present. The museum compound itself is also charming, divided into traditional courtyards complete with *candi bentar* (split gates), *kulkul* (bell) tower, shrines and flower gardens. Work on the museum began in 1910 under the direction of the Dutch Resident, whose idea it was to construct the museum in *puri-pura* style, mixing elements from traditional palace (*puri*) architecture with temple (*pura*) features; the collection is housed in four separate buildings, each designed in a specific regional and historical style. The most rewarding is Gedung Karangasem.

Gedung Timur

The two-storey **Gedung Timur**, located at the back of the entrance courtyard, is the least informative of the collections. Its downstairs hall makes a desultory attempt at introducing key events in the island's **history**, with cases of stone axes and bronze jewellery set alongside a massive **stone sarcophagus** that was hewn from soft volcanic rock around the second century BC. The black-and-white **photographs of the 1906 puputan** are unfortunately rather murky but show the landing of the Dutch troops at Sanur and gruesome scenes of massacred bodies in what is now Alun-alun Puputan. The upstairs gallery is given over to an unexceptional display of traditional **paintings and woodcarvings**.

Gedung Buleleng

Through the traditional gateway that leads left off the entrance courtyard, the compact **Gedung Buleleng** is designed in Buleleng (or Singaraja) style and holds fine examples of Balinese **textiles**. The plainest, most common style displayed here is **endek**, sometimes referred to as *ikat*, in which the weft threads are dyed to the finished pattern before being woven – hence the distinctive fuzzy-edged look (see p.458 for more on this and other traditional textiles). **Gringsing**, or double-*ikat*, is a far rarer material that involves a complex dyeing and weaving technique practised only by the villagers of Tenganan.

Gedung Karangasem

Built to resemble the long, low structure of an eighteenth-century Karangasem-style palace, the **Gedung Karangasem** introduces the **spiritual and ceremonial life** of the Balinese – the cornerstone of the average islander's day-to-day existence – and is the most fascinating section of the museum. The displays focus on the five main religious ceremonies of Balinese Hinduism, the *panca yadnya*: rituals performed for the gods; for ancestors; for humans; for saints and priests; and for the neutralising of evil spirits.

In the *dewa yadnya* display about rituals for the gods, on the far left-hand wall, the bronze image of **Sanghyang Widi Wasa** (the supreme god or being, who is also known as Acintya) is immediately recognizable because of his peculiar stance – the right leg drawn up so that his flame-shaped right foot rests against his left knee. In the same section, look out for the two statuettes constructed from a thousand ancient **Chinese coins** strung together, meant to invoke the god of wealth. Although these coins, or *kepeng*, are no longer legal tender, they are hoarded by Balinese to use as offerings.

Along the back wall, in the *manusa yadnya* display about rituals for humans, the birth-rites exhibit contains a bell-shaped **bamboo cage** still used by some villagers to mark the first cycle of a baby's life. Babies are never allowed to crawl on the ground, as the Balinese eschew any animal-like behaviour, and are continually carried around until their 210th day. On completion of its first cycle, the baby is placed in the cage and ceremonially lowered to the ground, after which it is expected to totter on two legs.

The Balinese **calendars** on the right-hand wall are immensely complex compositions derived from mathematical, astrological and religious calculations. The painted one is in traditional Kamasan style (see p.453), while the carved wooden calendar is much rarer. Though these examples are quite old, the calendar system they depict is still widely used to determine all sorts of events from temple festivals to the starting day for the construction of a new house. For an explanation of the workings of the Balinese calendar, see p.48.

Gedung Tabanan

The theme of the **Gedung Tabanan**, a replica of a Tabanan regency palace, is **music and dance**, and its exhibits include masks, costumes and puppets. Most impressive are the Barong costumes, representing legendary creatures that feature in nearly every Balinese dance performance. The shaggy-haired **Barong Ket**, symbolizing the forces of good, is probably the most popular character, and looks like a cross between a lion, a pantomime horse and a Chinese dragon. The witch-like figure of **Rangda** who stands next to him is the embodiment of all that is evil, with her pointed fangs, unkempt hair, snarling mouth and huge lolling tongue (the box on p.226 tells Rangda's story). Less commonly seen on tourist stages are the two towering **Barong Landung**, huge humanoid male and female puppets that are worn by holy men when chasing away evil spirits. See p.443 for more on these ritual performances.

Pura Agung Jagatnata

Just over the north wall of the Bali Museum stands the modern state temple of **Pura Agung Jagatnata**, set in a fragrant garden of pomegranate, hibiscus and frangipani trees. Founded in 1953, it is dedicated to the supreme god, Sanghyang Widi Wasa, who is here worshipped in his role as "Lord of the World", or Jagatnata.

Carvings of lotus flowers and frogs adorn the tiny stone bridge that spans the moat around the temple's central gallery (access at festival times only) and scenes from the Hindu epics the *Ramayana* and *Mahabharata* decorate the gallery's outer wall. On the east wall you'll see the famous *Ramayana* episode in which Rama shoots the golden deer, thereby precipitating Sita's kidnap and the subsequent bookful of battles between Rama and Rawana (see box, p.444).

The temple's focal point is the looming five-tiered **padmasana** tower in the inner courtyard, supporting the customary empty throne and itself balanced on a huge cosmic turtle. Built entirely from blocks of white coral, the tower is carved with demons' heads and the bottom level displays the face and hands of Bhoma, the son of the earth, whose job is to repel evil spirits from the temple. The lotus throne at its summit is left empty for Sanghyang Widi Wasa to fill when descending to earth at festival times – the god is represented in a gold relief embossed on the back. In the southeast corner of the outer compound stands the **kulkul** tower, its split wooden bell still used to summon locals to festivals, meetings and temple-cleaning duties.

As a state temple, Pura Agung Jagatnata is effectively open to all devotees (village temples are not). Twice a month, on the occasion of the full moon and new (or dark) moon, **festivals** are held here and *wayang kulit* shows are sometimes performed, from around 9pm to 11pm; ask at the nearby tourist office for details.

Pasar Badung and Pasar Kumbasari

The Chinese shop-houses and glossy department stores of modern Denpasar are nowhere near as interesting as the city's old-fashioned Balinese **markets**. The biggest and best is the chaotic **Pasar Badung** located downtown in a traditional three-storey covered stone-and-brick *pasar* beside the Badung River, set slightly back off Jalan Gajah Mada. Approaching the market building, you may find yourself landed with a **guide**: local women hang out around the Jalan Sulawesi entrance – some even wait for their prey way up on Gajah Mada – offering to accompany you around the stalls. You'll be steered towards certain outlets, and anything you buy will include a commission for your guide. Trading at Pasar Badung takes place 24 hours a day, with buyers and sellers pouring in from all over the island. You'll find fresh fruit, veg and spices on the lower floors but the most browsable section is the art market upstairs, with hundreds of stalls selling well-priced sarongs, handicrafts, Balinese and western clothes, ceremonial parasols and more.

Until it burnt down in May 2007, the one place that used to rival Pasar Badung on price and variety was the four-storey traditional art market **Pasar Kumbasari**, which overflowed with clothes, souvenirs, textiles, woodcarvings, paintings and sarongs. If it gets rebuilt you'll find it just west across the narrow Badung River from Pasar Badung, a few metres south of Jalan Gajah Mada.

Pura Maospahit

Pura Maospahit on Jalan Sutomo, northwest of Pasar Badung, has a long and significant history. It's thought that the temple's oldest section may have been brought from East Java, either following the 1343 conquest of the island by the Majapahit empire, or in the sixteenth century by the Hindu aristocracy forced to flee the Islamic invasion there. The style is typically Majapahit – constructed entirely from brick, and remarkable for its total absence of superfluous ornamentation – but much of what you see today is reconstructed, as the temple was badly damaged in the 1917 earthquake.

Pura Maospahit is rarely visited by tourists, which adds to its charm. Its rooftops are visible from Jalan Sutomo, but **access** is via the *gang* that runs along the compound's southern wall. Once inside, look up at the tree to your immediate right to see an unusual *kulkul* tower, built into its own little treehouse. Through the towering, chunky and unadorned *kori agung* gateway, the **inner courtyard** is packed with about a dozen thatched brick shrines. The central, and most important, structure here is the squat red-brick *candi raras* Maospahit, guarded by two ancient terracotta figurines, and was probably constructed in honour of the Majapahit ancestors of the Balinese people.

Painter and woodcarver Ida Bagus Alit

In the traditional northern neighbourhood not far from *Nakula Familiar Inn* – and across Jalan Veteran from the Pasar Burung bird and pet market – stands the home of the idiosyncratic and multitalented **painter and woodcarver**

▲ Pasar Badung

Ida Bagus Alit (☎0361/226824, ✉alit_satria@telkom.net). There is no gallery sign but during daylight hours visitors are welcome to browse his paintings and carvings at his house, Geria Satria, located at no. 69, Gang V. Alit's style is unusual and his work includes charming, surreal, *wayang*-style folk art, abstract watercolours, acrylics on paper, and sinuous, statuesque woodcarvings. He speaks good English, is widely travelled and has exhibited all over the world.

Taman Budaya Cultural Centre

In the eastern part of town, on Jalan Nusa Indah, fifteen minutes' walk from the Kereneng bemo terminal, or direct on a Sanur-bound bemo, the **Taman Budaya Cultural Centre** (daily 8am–3pm; Rp250) was designed by one of Indonesia's most renowned architects, Ida Bagus Tugur, and aims to cover the history of Balinese painting and celebrate the island's contemporary artistic life. It doesn't always succeed at this, but if you don't have time to visit the far superior Neka Art Museum in Ubud, it will at least give you a taste. If you're in Denpasar during the annual **Arts Festival** (usually staged between mid-June and mid-July; see ⊛www.baliartsfestival.com for details), it's worth dropping by the centre for the huge programme of special exhibitions and dance shows.

The main **exhibition hall**, towards the back of the compound, opens with an overview of Balinese **painting**, with a few examples in the classical *wayang* style, followed by works from several different schools, taking in the Ubud, Batuan and Young Artists styles (see p.454 for an explanation of these). Unfortunately, the presentation and labelling is less than helpful. A selection of religious and secular **woodcarvings** fills the next room, together with an assortment of *Ramayana* and *topeng* **masks**. More ambitious carvings are housed downstairs along with a collection of **contemporary paintings**, spanning batik style through to works influenced by Cubism and Post-Impressionism.

Renon and Bajra Sandhi

Denpasar's administrative district, **Renon**, is on the southeastern edge of the city, near the resort of Sanur and served by Sanur-bound bemos. In among its wide tree-lined boulevards and imposing government offices stands the huge grey lava-stone **Bajra Sandhi** ("Balinese People's Struggle") monument (Mon–Fri 8.30am–5pm, Sat & Sun 9.30am–5pm; Rp2000; entrance just off Jl Raya Puputan), at the heart of the **Lapangan Puputan Margarana** park. Designed by Taman Budaya's architect Ida Bagus Tugur to resemble a priest's bell, the monument's structure also symbolises the date of Indonesia's Declaration of Independence – August 17, 1945 – with its eight entrances, seventeen corners and height that measures 45m. The upper floor contains a series of 33 mildly interesting dioramas illustrating edited episodes from Balinese history (much is made of the several wars against the Dutch, but the civil war of 1965 is omitted). Climb the spiral stairs to get a view across Denpasar rooftops.

Eating and drinking

There are few tourist-oriented **restaurants** in Denpasar, so this is a good chance to sample Bali's cheap, authentic neighbourhood eateries. Smaller restaurants generally shut by 9pm.

Babi Guling Next to the Pura Maospahit compound on Jl Sutomo. The roast suckling pig (*babi guling*) at this simple warung is considered the best in the city, and it's cheap too, at Rp10,000 a plate. There's no sign, but look for the warung with low tables next to Pura Maospahit, opposite Bale Banjar Gerenceng. Daily from mid-morning to about 10pm.

Cupumanik Jl Teuku Umar 112B. Great Thai food at this small, modern, style-conscious little restaurant just north of Simpang Enam round-about on southern Denpasar's big commercial drag. Check out the delicious green and Penang curries (around Rp26,000), or the mouthwatering deep-fried aubergine with chilli and the sweet basil seafood salad.

Hong Kong Jl Gajah Mada 99. Moderately priced a/c Chinese restaurant offering a huge variety of set meals and à la carte choices, including seafood and some Western dishes. Popular with middle-class Indonesian families and has karaoke at night.

Pasar Malam Kereneng Just off Jl Hayam Wuruk, adjacent to Kereneng bemo terminal. Over fifty vendors convene at this night market from dusk to dawn every night, dishing out super-cheap soups, noodle and rice dishes, *babi guling*, fresh fruit juices and cold beers for consumption at the trestle tables set around the marketplace.

Warung Satriya Jl Kedondong 11. Neighbourhood restaurant serving very cheap nasi campur (veg and non-veg from Rp10,000), seafood sate, *nasi soto ayam* (chicken rice soup) and lots of other chicken dishes. Convenient for the *Nakula Familiar Inn* and stays open till 10pm.

Warung Vegetaris Tegal bemo terminal, Jl Imam Bonjol. Tiny, cheap vegetarian food-stall inside the Tegal bemo-terminal compound.

Warung Wardani Jl Yudistira 2. The locals' favourite for good, filling plates of nasi campur, *nasi soto ayam*, *soto babat* (meat soup) and gado-gado, most of them costing just Rp10,000. Shuts by 4pm.

Entertainment

The city's main **cinema** complex is the five-screen Wisata at Jalan Thamrin 29 (T0361/423023; tickets Mon–Fri Rp10,000, Sat & Sun Rp15,000). Films are usually shown in the original language with Indonesian subtitles; programmes are listed in the free tourist publication *What's Up Bali* and in the weekly English-language paper *The Bali Times*.

Tourist-oriented performances of traditional **Balinese dance** are staged daily at several venues in greater Denpasar. Tickets arranged through tour agents generally cost US$10–15 per person including return transport, or buy them at the door for Rp50,000. For background information on all the dances, see p.440. The **Barong** is performed at the Catur Eka Budhi on Jalan Waribang, in Denpasar's eastern Kesiman district (daily 9.30–10.30am); Batubulan-bound bemos from Ubung and Kereneng pass the corner of Jalan Waribang, from where the stage is a short signposted walk. The spectacular "Monkey Dance", or **Kecak**, is performed nightly at the Stage Uma Dewi, which is also on Jalan Waribang in Kesiman, about 300m south of the Barong dance stage (daily 6.30–7.30pm). Bemo access is as above, but you'll probably have to get a taxi back.

Denpasar's main **live-music venues** for Balinese bands include the bar-restaurant *Ozigo* at Jalan Moh Yamin 59, which favours pop, and the Ngurah Rai Stadium on Jalan Melati, which hosts several big Bali music events a year.

Shopping

For **crafts and souvenirs**, the most rewarding places to browse, and bargain, are Pasar Kumbasari and Pasar Badung, described on p.91. The best place for lengths of **fabric**, including rolls of batik, is Jalan Sulawesi; its entire course, from Jalan Hasanudin in the south to Jalan Gajah Mada in the north, is devoted to cloth of all descriptions, including batik, *songket* brocades and saree silks. Fabric shops also spill out east along Jalan Gajah Mada as far as Jalan Sumatra. The city's **gold quarter** has lots of outlets for jewellery and is centred on the stretch of Jalan Hasanudin that runs west from Jalan Diponegoro to the river.

The Ramayana Mal Bali shopping centre, Jalan Diponegoro 103 (Kereneng–Tegal and Tegal–Sanur bemos), the Matahari department store at Jalan Dewi Sartika 4 (Tegal–Sanur bemo), and the Tiara Dewata shopping centre at Jalan Sutoyo 55 (Kereneng–Tegal bemo) all carry high-street **fashions** and a few handicrafts. Matahari stocks some English-language novels and **books** about Bali in its basement Gramedia bookstore and also has a **children's department** upstairs, with everything from baby clothes to bottles and mosquito nets.

Department stores **open** daily from 9.30am–9pm, but many small shops in Denpasar close on Sundays.

Arts of Asia Gallery Blok C5 27–37, Jl Thamrin (behind Bank Maya Prada) ☎0361/423350, ⓔantique@indo.net.id. The antique Southeast Asian artefacts displayed here in the family home of veteran collector Verra Darwiko have been painstakingly gathered from all over Indonesia. They include some astonishing Majapahit era (13th–15th century) gold jewellery from East Java, an extraordinary 2000-year-old Bronze Age kettle drum from Lumajang in East Java, and centuries'-old glass beads and tiny shell "coins" found in the same area but probably originating from China. Some but not all items are for sale; interested browsers are welcome. Mon–Sat 9am–5pm.

Bhineka Jaya Kopi Bali Jl Gajah Mada 80 ⓦwww.kopibali.com. At this downtown outlet for Indonesia's Butterfly Globe Brand coffee you can sit down and sample a cup of premium, creamy Bali Gold and then choose which grade of beans to take away – from Bali, Sumatra or Kalimantan. Mon–Sat 9am–4pm.

Bog-Bog: Bali Cartoon Arcade Jl Veteran 39A. The studio and merchandise centre for Bali's bilingual monthly cartoon magazine *Bog-Bog* ("Bullshit" in Balinese) sells back-copies of the mag plus T-shirts and cards featuring the irreverent artwork. Daily 9am–9pm.

Mega Art Shop Jl Gajah Mada 36. Fairly good quality, local arts and crafts including Kamasan-style cloth paintings, Javanese batik sarongs, silver jewellery and woodcarvings. Prices are fixed but reasonable. Mon–Sat 9am–5pm.

Poppiler Jl Gajah Mada 117. Specializes in traditional batik prints, selling ready-made shirts and sarongs as well as some designs by the metre. Mon–Sat 9am–5pm.

Listings

Airline offices Garuda has a city check-in on the southeast corner of Alun-alun Puputan at Jl Sugianyar 5 (Mon–Thurs 7.30am–4.30pm, Fri 7.30am–5pm, Sat & Sun 9am–1pm; 24-hour national call centre ☎0804/180 7807 or ☎021/2351 9999 if calling from a mobile), where you can get your boarding pass 4–24 hours in advance. For other international and domestic airline offices, see p.100.

Banks and exchange Most central Denpasar banks have exchange counters and there are ATMs on all main shopping streets.

Embassies and consulates See p.66.

Hospitals, clinics and dentists Sanglah Public Hospital (Rumah Sakit Umum Propinsi Sanglah, or RSUP Sanglah) at Jl Kesehatan Selatan 1, Sanglah (five lines ☎0361/227911–227915; Kereneng–Tegal bemo and Tegal–Sanur bemo) is the main provincial public hospital, with an emergency ward and some English-speaking staff. It also has Bali's only divers' recompression chamber (ext 123). The more central Klinik SOS Gatotkaca at Jl Gatotkaca 21 (☎0361/223555) is a tiny 24hr private hospital that is fine for minor ailments, but not equipped for emergencies; most expats use BIMC or International SOS, both near Kuta, instead (see p.123), and also go to Kuta dentists.

Immigration Office Corner of Jl Panjaitan and Jl Raya Puputan, Renon (Mon–Thurs 8am–4pm, Fri 8–11am, Sat 8am–2pm; ☎0361/227828).

Internet access On Jl Abimanyu (near Jl Nakula) and inside the main shopping centres including on the top floor of the Ramayana Mal Bali on Jl Diponegoro.

Language lessons Courses in Indonesian language at Indonesia Australia Language

Foundation (IALF), Jl Raya Sesetan 190 ⓣ0361/225243, ⓦwww.ialf.edu.

Pharmacies Several along Jl Gajah Mada and inside all the major shopping centres.

Phone offices There are Telkom offices at Jl Teuku Umar 6 and on Jl Durian, and wartels all over the city.

Police There are police stations on Jl Patimura and Jl Diponegoro; the main police station is in the far west of the city on Jl Gunung Sanghiang (ⓣ0361/424346).

Post offices Denpasar's poste restante (Mon–Fri 8am–7pm, Sat 8am–6pm) is at the GPO, located on Jl Raya Puputan in Renon. The Sanur–Tegal and Kereneng–Tegal bemos pass the front door;

otherwise, take the Tegal–Sanur bemo, get out at the Jl Cok Agung Tresna/Jl Panjaitan junction and walk 500m south. There's a more central post office on Jl Rambutan, north of Alun-alun Puputan.

Travel agents Domestic airline tickets can be bought from Nitour next to the *Inna Bali* hotel, Jl Veteran 5 ⓣ0361/234742, ⓔnitourbali @denpasar.wasantara.net.id, and international and domestic airline tickets from Puri Astina Tour, Jl Moh Yamin 1A, Renon ⓣ0361/223552, ⓔastina@denpasar.wasantara.net.id. Get Pelni boat tickets from Jl Diponegoro 165 ⓣ0361/234680, and train tickets (for Java) from Jl Diponegoro 150 Blok B4 ⓣ0361/227131.

Kuta–Legian–Seminyak

The biggest, loudest, brashest resort in Bali, the **KUTA–LEGIAN–SEMINYAK** conurbation continues to expand from its epicentre on the southwest coast, 10km southwest of Denpasar. Packed with hundreds of losmen, hotels, restaurants, bars, clubs, souvenir shops, fashion boutiques and tour agencies, the eight-kilometre strip plays host to several hundred thousand visitors a year, many of them regular visitors from Australia and all of them here to party, shop or surf. It's a hectic place: noisy, full of hassling touts, and constant building work. The narrow main drag, **Jalan Legian**, is often so packed that traffic just crawls along it, every inch jammed with taxis and tourist buses, minibuses, bemos and motorbikes. Yet the hustle is mostly good-humoured and there are as yet no strip bars or high-rises (nothing over the height of a tall coconut tree, in fact).

For many travellers, it's not only the crowds and the assault on the senses that are off-putting, it's that the place seems so un-Balinese: *McDonald's*, Rip Curl and *Hard Rock* are all here; *Time* and *The Sydney Morning Herald* are sold on every street corner; Hollywood blockbusters show regularly at the dozens of tourist cafés; and almost every bartender, waiter and losmen employee slides effortlessly into slang-ridden English or Japanese banter. But the resort is, in truth, distinctly Balinese: villagers still live and work here, making religious offerings, attending *banjar* meetings and holding temple festivals. Every morning and afternoon, the women of Kuta–Legian–Seminyak don their temple sashes and place **offerings** in doorways and under tables; you're more than likely to find a tiny palm-leaf basket filled with flowers and rice on the steps of your verandah first thing in the morning. All three former villages have their own **temples**, but none is outstanding and nearly all lock their gates to tourists except at festival times, when visitors are welcome to attend as long as they are suitably attired (see p.55).

Some history

For centuries, Kuta was considered by the Balinese to be little more than an infertile stretch of coast haunted by malevolent spirits and a dumping ground for lepers and criminals. Compounding this unpleasant image was Kuta's history as a **slave port** in the seventeenth and eighteenth centuries, when hundreds of thousands of people were sold by the Balinese rajas to their counterparts in Java

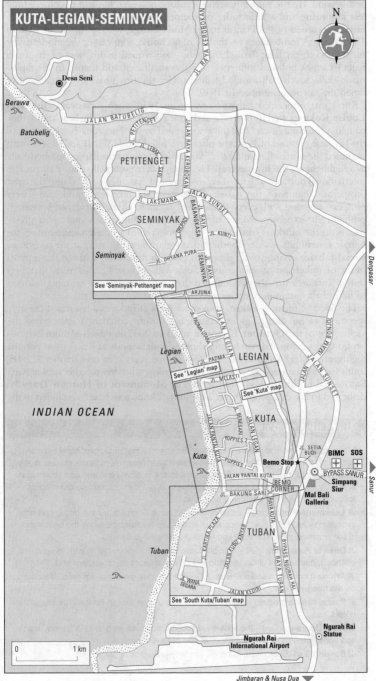

KUTA-LEGIAN-SEMINYAK

N

SOUTH BALI

Canggu

Berawa

Batubelig

Desa Seni

JALAN BATUBELIG

JL. PETITENGET

PETITENGET

JL. LEBAK SARI

JALAN RAYA KEROBOKAN

JALAN SUNSET

JL. RAYA BASANGKASA

SEMINYAK

JL. LAKSMANA

DRUPADI

JL. RAYA SEMINYAK

JL. KUNTI

Seminyak

JL. DHYANA PURA

See 'Seminyak-Petitenget' map

JL. ARJUNA

JALAN LEGIAN

JL. PADMA UTARA

Legian

JL. PADMA

LEGIAN

See 'Legian' map

JL. MELASTI

Denpasar

JALAN SUNSET

BYPASS SUNUR

JALAN KUTA

INDIAN OCEAN

JALAN PANTAI KUTA

JL. BENESARI

KUTA

See 'Kuta' map

POPPIES 2

POPPIES 1

Kuta

JALAN PANTAI KUTA

Bemo Stop ★

JL. SETIA BUDI

BIMC   SOS

✚   ✚

Simpang Siur

BEMO CORNER

JL. BAKUNG SARI

RAYA KUTA

Mal Bali Galleria

Sanur

Tuban

JL. KARTIKA PLAZA

JALAN KUBU ANYAR

TUBAN

JL. RAYA NGURAH RAI

JL. BYPASS NGURAH RAI

JL. WANA SEGARA

JALAN KEDIRI

JL. RAYA TUBAN

See 'South Kuta/Tuban' map

Ngurah Rai Statue

0   1 km

Ngurah Rai International Airport

Jimbaran & Nusa Dua ▼

and beyond. By the mid-nineteenth century, however, life had become a little less inhumane and a little more prosperous – thanks in part to the energetic business acumen of the Danish trader **Mads Lange**, who set up home here in 1839. (Lange's tomb stands on the site of his house, 50m east of the modern-day night market, on Jalan Tuan Langa, the road named in his honour, in south Kuta.) Lange's political influence was also significant and thanks to his diplomatic skills, south Bali avoided falling under the first phase of Dutch control when the north succumbed in 1849.

Kuta's image received a drastic revision in 1936 when Americans **Bob and Louise Koke** spotted its potential and built a small hotel on the beachfront; they named it the *Kuta Beach Hotel* (now succeeded by the *Inna Kuta Beach*) and, until the Japanese invasion of 1942, the place flourished. World War II and its aftermath stemmed the tourist flow until the 1960s, when young travellers established Kuta as a highlight on the **hippie trail**. Homestays were eventually joined by smarter international outfits, and Kuta–Legian–Seminyak has since evolved into the most prosperous region of the island. Wages here are relatively good, and career prospects improve with every English and Japanese phrase learnt, but housing is prohibitively expensive. Many of the transport touts and waiters rent grotty rooms on the outskirts of the resort and only return to their village homes for temple ceremonies – a development that is starting to eat away at the traditional **social fabric**, leaving young people to establish themselves without the support of their families and *banjar* members. Some villages now have so many members in the Kuta area that they've founded their own expat *banjar*, enabling villagers to fulfil their community duties away from home.

The flood of fortune-seekers from other parts of Indonesia has raised the ugly spectre of racism and religious tension, but no one could have anticipated the viciousness of the **October 12 bomb** attack in 2002, in which Muslim extremists from Java detonated two bombs almost simultaneously at Kuta's most popular nightspots, *Paddy's Pub* and the *Sari Club*. Three years later, on October 1, 2005, south Bali was targeted again by a terrorist group, who detonated bombs at Kuta Square and in Jimbaran, killing twenty. The **Monument of Human Tragedy**, dedicated to the 202 people from 22 countries known to have been killed in the

Alternative road names

Many roads in the resort were initially named after the first or biggest hotel or restaurant along them; though the roads have all now been given more formal names, many local residents, taxi drivers and maps stick to the original versions, and streetsigns are rarely consistent. **Alternative road names** are given in brackets on our maps; the following are the most confusing examples:

Jl Laksmana (Petitenget) – often referred to as Jl Oberoi, after the hotel, and now increasingly as "Eat Street" because of all the new restaurants; along the beachfront, Jl Laksmana is more correctly known as Jl Pantai Kayu Aya.

Jl Dhyana Pura (Seminyak) – officially known as Jl Abimanyu (along with its southern offshoot), and also as Jl Gado-Gado after the restaurant at its western end.

Jl Arjuna (Legian) – also known as Jl Double Six after the famous nightclub located on the nearby beach.

Jl Pantai Arjuna (Legian) – informally known as Jl Blue Ocean Beach after one of its hotels.

Jl Werk Udara (Legian) – the east–west section is also referred to as Jl Bagus Taruna and sometimes as Jl Rum Jungle after one of its restaurants.

Jl Bakung Sari (South Kuta/Tuban) – formerly known as Jl Singo Sari.

2002 attack, now occupies the "Ground Zero" site of the original *Paddy's*, across from the Poppies 2 junction on Jalan Legian, and a peace park is slated for the *Sari Club* plot across the way. *Paddy's* has been rebuilt just down the road. For more background on the bombings, see Contexts, p.424.

Orientation and arrival

Kuta, Legian and Seminyak all started out as separate villages but it's now impossible for the casual visitor to recognize the demarcation lines. We've used the most common perception of the neighbourhood borders: **Kuta** stretches north from the Matahari department store in Kuta Square to Jalan Melasti; **Legian** runs from Jalan Melasti as far north as Jalan Arjuna; and **Seminyak** extends from Jalan Arjuna to the *Bali Oberoi* hotel, where **Petitenget** begins. Petitenget feeds into Kerobokan and then north up to the string of isolated little **Canggu** area beaches, not strictly within the Kuta boundaries but close enough to share facilities. Kuta's increasingly built-up southern fringes, extending south from Matahari to the airport, are defined as **south Kuta/Tuban**.

The resort's main road, which begins as **Jalan Legian** and becomes Jalan Raya Seminyak, runs north–south through all three main districts, a total distance of 5km. The bulk of the resort facilities is packed into the 600m-wide strip between Jalan Legian in the east and the coast to the west, an area crisscrossed by tiny *gang* (alleyways) and larger one-way roads.

The other main landmark is **Bemo Corner**, a minuscule roundabout at the southern end of Kuta that stands at the Jalan Legian–Jalan Pantai Kuta intersection. The name's a bit misleading as the Denpasar bemos don't actually depart from this very spot, but it's a useful point of reference.

Arrival

For information on **airport arrivals**, see the box on p.100.

Public bemos have limited routes through the Kuta area. Coming **from Denpasar's** Tegal terminal, the most convenient option is the dark blue **Tegal–Kuta–Legian bemo** that goes via Bemo Corner and runs clockwise via Jalan Pantai Kuta, Jalan Melasti and north up Jalan Legian as far as Jalan Padma, then does a U-turn to travel back south down Jalan Legian to Bemo Corner again. For destinations a long way north of Jalan Padma, you're probably better off getting a taxi.

The dark blue **Tegal–Kuta–Tuban (airport)–Bualu** route is fine if you're staying in the southern part of Kuta as drivers generally drop passengers on the eastern edge of Jalan Bakung Sari – a five-minute walk from Bemo Corner – before they turn south along Jalan Raya Kuta. Coming by bemo **from Jimbaran**, you'll probably be dropped off at the same place.

If arriving in Kuta by **shuttle bus**, you could be dropped almost anywhere, depending on your operator. Perama drivers drop passengers at their office on Jalan Legian, about 100m north of Bemo Corner, but may stop at spots en route if asked.

Information and local transport

The official, though not very clued-up, **Badung tourist office** is at Jalan Raya Kuta 2 (Mon–Thurs 8am–3pm, Fri 8am–noon, Sat 8am–4pm; ☎0361/756175),

All Bali's international and domestic flights come into the busy **Ngurah Rai Airport**, in the district of Tuban, 3km south of Kuta. For all arrival and departure **enquiries**, call ℡0361/751011 ext 1454.

Arrival

Queues can be lengthy at **immigration**, where citizens of most countries have to buy a **visa on arrival**: the fee of US$25 (for a thirty-day visa) or US$10 (for a seven-day visa) is payable in any currency (see Basics, p.67, for more info). Once inside the baggage-claims hall, you'll find several **ATMs** and **currency exchange** booths, while just outside the Arrivals building there are a number of **hotel reservations desks** (room rates starting at $15), along with **car rental** outlets for Europcar (℡0361/744 1142, ℮bali@indorent.co.id) and Indotrans Astri (℡0361/757650, ℮indotransastri @hotmail.com). The 24-hour **left-luggage** office (Rp20,000–25,000 per day per item) is located outside, midway between International Arrivals and Departures. The **domestic terminal** is in the adjacent building, where you'll find offices of nearly all the domestic airlines serving Bali.

For **onward transport**, most mid-priced and upmarket hotels can arrange pick-up at the airport. Otherwise, the easiest but most expensive mode of transport anywhere on the island is **pre-paid taxi**, for which you'll find counters beyond the customs exit doors in the International Arrivals area, and just outside the Arrivals doors at Domestic; pay at the counter before getting into the taxi. **Fares** are fixed: currently Rp40,000 to Tuban/south Kuta; Rp45,000 to central Kuta (Poppies 1 and 2); Rp50,000 to Legian (as far as Jalan Arjuna); Rp55,000 to Seminyak; Rp60,000 to outer Seminyak/Petitenget. Further afield, you'll pay Rp50,000 to Jimbaran; Rp65,000 to Denpasar; Rp85,000 to Sanur or Nusa Dua; Rp175,000 to Ubud; or Rp300,000 to Candi Dasa.

Bear these rates in mind before you start bargaining with the transport **touts** who gather round both the International and Domestic Arrivals areas. Write down the agreed price and be very firm about which hotel you're heading for, or you could easily end up at the driver's friend's losmen, miles from anywhere. **Metered taxis** ply the road immediately in front of the airport gates (turn right outside International and walk about 500m – they're not licensed to pick up inside the compound); their rates for rides into Kuta–Legian–Seminyak are around thirty percent lower than the pre-paid taxi equivalents – the light blue Bali Taksi cars are the most reliable.

Cheaper still are the dark blue **public bemos** whose route (daylight hours only) takes in Jl Raya Tuban, about 700m beyond the airport gates. Keep in mind that their schedules are random and may run no more than hourly, and that it's difficult to stash large backpacks in crowded bemos. The northbound bemos (heading left up Jalan Raya Tuban) go via Kuta's Bemo Corner, Jl Pantai Kuta, Jl Melasti and Jl Legian (see p.99 for details), before continuing to Denpasar's Tegal terminal. You should pay around Rp5000 to Kuta, Legian or Denpasar, or twice that if you've got sizeable luggage.

If you want to go straight from the airport to **Ubud**, **Candi Dasa** or **Lovina**, the cheapest way (only feasible during daylight hours) is to take a bemo, first to Tegal

with a counter beside the lifeguard post on the beach off Jalan Pantai Kuta (Mon–Fri 10am–3pm; ℡0361/755660). You'll get a lot more tourist information and details about forthcoming events from the bevy of **tourist newspapers and magazines** available at hotels and some shops and restaurants; see Basics, p.74, for details.

The **Kuta Karnival** (🌐www.kutakarnival.com) was inaugurated in 2003 in response to the 2002 bombing and has since become an annual fixture.

terminal in Denpasar and then on from there; see the plan on p.87 for route outlines. A bemo journey to Ubud will involve two changes and cost around Rp17,000. More convenient, but a little more expensive, is to take a bemo or pre-paid taxi from the airport to Kuta's Bemo Corner, then walk 100m north up Jalan Legian to Perama's shuttle-bus office, where you can book yourself on to the next tourist shuttle-bus, most of which run three or four times a day (see p.106).

Departure

For a small fee, any tour agent in Bali will **reconfirm** your air ticket for you if necessary. Most hotels in Kuta, Sanur, Nusa Dua and Jimbaran will provide **transport to the airport** for about Rp50,000–70,000. **Metered taxis** should be a little cheaper and **shuttle buses** are cheaper still: about Rp15,000 from Sanur, Rp30,000 from Ubud, Rp40,000 from Candi Dasa or Rp100,000 from Lovina. During daylight hours, you could also take the rather unreliable Tegal (Denpasar)–Kuta–Tuban **bemo** from Denpasar, Kuta or Jimbaran, which will drop you just beyond the airport gates for about Rp5000.

Airport **departure tax** is Rp150,000 for international departures and Rp30,000 for domestic flights. Ngurah Rai Airport operates the same strict **security regulations** for liquids and gels in carry-on luggage as many other airports around the world, so you'll be restricted to 100ml containers within a single, one-litre, clear plastic bag.

Airline offices in Bali

Most **airline offices** are open Mon–Fri 8.30am–5pm and some also open Sat 8.30am–1pm; some close for an hour's lunch at noon or 12.30pm. Except where stated, all the following offices are at Ngurah Rai Airport. Websites are given here for domestic airlines only; websites for international carriers are given in Basics, p.29.

Adam Air Jl Raya Sesetan 12B, Denpasar ☏0361/227999, ⓦwww.adamair.co.id; **Air Asia** ☏0804/133 3333; **Batavia** ☏0361/751011 ext 5336, ⓦwww.batavia-air.co .id; **Cathay Pacific** ☏0361/753942; **China Airlines** ☏0361/757298; **Continental Airlines** ☏0361/768358; **Eva Air** ☏0361/759773; **Garuda** ☏0804/180 7807 or ☏021/2351 9999 if calling from a mobile (both 24-hour), ⓦwww.garuda-indonesia .com, city check-ins in Sanur (see p.151), south Kuta/Tuban (see p.123), Nusa Dua (see p.140) and Denpasar (see p.95); **JAL** Jl Bypass Ngurah Rai 100X, Tuban ☏0361/757077; **Jetstar** contact Jakarta ☏021/385 2288; **Korean Air** ☏0361/768377; **Lion Air/Wings** ☏0804/177 8899, ⓦwww.lionair.co.id; **Malaysia Air** ☏0361/764 995; **Mandala** ☏0804/123 4567 or ☏021/5699 7000 from a mobile, ⓦwww.mandalaair .com; **Merpati** Jl Melati 51, Denpasar ☏361/235358, ⓦwww.merpati.co.id; **Northwest** *Inna Grand Bali Beach* hotel, Sanur ☏0361/287841; **Qantas** *Inna Grand Bali Beach* hotel, Sanur ☏0361/288331; **Qatar Airways** *Discovery Kartika Plaza* hotel, Tuban ☏0361 752222; **Royal Brunei** Soka Bali Arcade 8, Jl Bypass Ngurah Rai, Tuban ☏0361/759736; **Singapore Airlines/Silk Air** ☏0361/768388; **Sriwijaya Air** Jl Teuku Umar 97B, Denpasar ☏0361/228461, ⓦwww.sriwijayaair-online.com; **Thai Airways** *Inna Grand Bali Beach* hotel, Sanur ☏0361/288141; **Trans Nusa/Trigana/Pelita Air** ☏0361/754421, ⓦwww.transnusa.co.id.

Highlights of the week-long carnival, held in early September, include parades, surfing and skateboarding competitions, gigs by Balinese and national bands, and an outdoor food festival.

Bemos

As more and more Balinese buy their own motorbikes, public **bemos** are in decline and it can now be as much as an hour between services. All Kuta bemos are dark blue and they all originate at Denpasar's Tegal terminal. For details of the routes, see "Arrival" on p.99; local trips cost Rp3000.

Taxis and touts

Dozens of **metered taxis** circulate throughout the resort, all with a "Taxi" sign on the roof. The most reliable are the light blue Bali Taksi (⑦0361/701111) and the dark blue Ngurah Rai Airport Taxis (⑦0361/724724); north Seminyak and Petitenget are covered by the Liberty Group (⑦0361/7455229). All charge

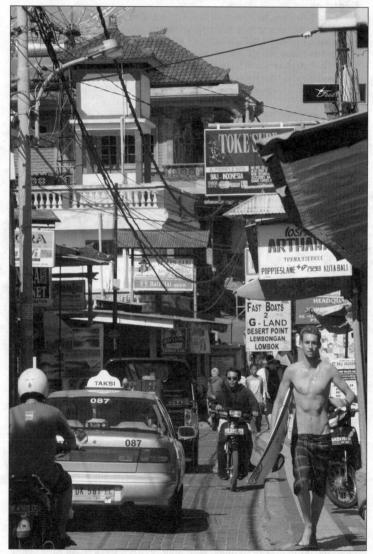

▲ Poppies 2

Rp5000 flagfall and then Rp4000 per kilometre day or night; always double-check that the meter is turned on. A ride from, say, Jalan Arjuna in Legian up to Jalan Laksmana in Petitenget will cost you around Rp20,000. You can often save yourself both time and money by walking a short distance to pick up a taxi on its way out of Kuta's long-winded one-way system; some drivers refuse to go along the narrow lanes of Poppies 1 and Poppies 2 anyway, forcing you to walk out to the main street.

Another option is the informal taxi service offered by the "Transport! Transport!" **touts** who hang around on every corner. For brief journeys the bargaining is often more hassle than it's worth but they can be worthwhile for longer trips.

Cars, bikes and motorbikes

Every major road in the resort is packed with tour agents offering **car rental**: see Basics, p.39, for price guidelines and advice. Where it is legal to **park** beside the road, attendants generally charge Rp2000 to wave you in and out and keep an eye on your vehicle. For a similar fee, you can use the public car parks opposite Poppies 2 on Jalan Legian and under the Matahari department store in Kuta Square.

Most car-rental outlets can also provide a **driver** for the day, which is a good way of organizing a private tour of sights or shops. A recommended freelance English-speaking guide and driver is Wayan Artana (℡0812/396 1296, ⓔiartana@hotmail.com).

You can also rent **motorbikes** from many car-rental outlets, as well as from Chitchat on Legian's Jalan Werk Udara (℡0361/752192); see p.41 for information on costs and insurance. Chitchat also rents **bicycles** as do some other motorbike-rental places and losmen.

Accommodation

Of south Bali's main beach resorts, Kuta–Legian–Seminyak has by far the greatest amount of **accommodation**, and also the biggest range of cheap and moderately priced rooms.

The inexpensive losmen are mainly concentrated in **Kuta**, though **Legian** has some too, along with a decent share of good-value mid-range places. **Tuban**, **Seminyak** and **Petitenget** are dominated by expensive, and often very stylish accommodation, a lot of it right on the beach. The scene is much quieter in the **Canggu** area, whose beaches, at Batubelig, Berewa, Batu Bolong and Pererenan, are served by just a handful of hotels.

Kuta

The vibe in **Kuta** is young and fun, bordering on the trashy. Hugely popular with backpackers and surfers, this is the most frantic part of the resort, and also the cheapest. The narrow lanes known as Poppies 1 and 2 are the main accommodation hubs; most of the smaller lanes off are a bit calmer. The beach gets crowded, but it's a long stretch of clean, fine sand and undeniably inviting.

Inexpensive

Adus Beach Inn Off Gang Lebak Bene ℡0361/755419. Rooms at this old-style losmen are dotted round the large family compound down a quiet residential lane that's handy for all the restaurants and surf shops of nearby Jl Benesari. They're simple but all have fans and cold-water bathrooms and are among the cheapest in Kuta. ❶

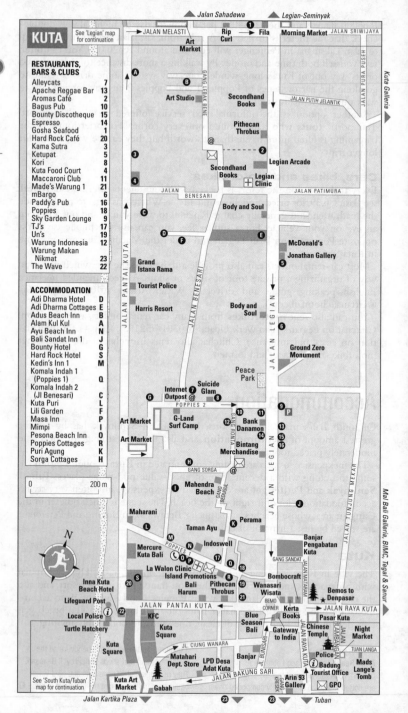

KUTA

See 'Legian' map for continuation

RESTAURANTS, BARS & CLUBS

Alleycats	7
Apache Reggae Bar	13
Aromas Café	2
Bagus Pub	10
Bounty Discotheque	15
Espresso	14
Gosha Seafood	1
Hard Rock Café	20
Kama Sutra	3
Ketupat	5
Kori	8
Kuta Food Court	4
Maccaroni Club	11
Made's Warung 1	21
mBargo	6
Paddy's Pub	16
Poppies	18
Sky Garden Lounge	9
TJ's	17
Un's	19
Warung Indonesia	12
Warung Makan Nikmat	23
The Wave	22

ACCOMMODATION

Adi Dharma Hotel	D
Adi Dharma Cottages	E
Adus Beach Inn	B
Alam Kul Kul	A
Ayu Beach Inn	N
Bali Sandat Inn 1	J
Bounty Hotel	G
Hard Rock Hotel	S
Kedin's Inn 1	M
Komala Indah 1 (Poppies 1)	Q
Komala Indah 2 (Jl Benesari)	C
Kuta Puri	L
Lili Garden	F
Masa Inn	P
Mimpi	I
Pesona Beach Inn	O
Poppies Cottages	R
Puri Agung	K
Sorga Cottages	H

0 — 200 m

N

See 'South Kuta/Tuban' map for continuation

104

SOUTH BALI

Ayu Beach Inn Poppies 1 ⓣ0361/752091, ⓦwww.ayubeachinn.baliklik.com. Well-located and efficiently run budget option with 38 plain rooms set back from the road in one- and two-storey blocks. Also has a good-sized pool. Rooms with fan ❷ With a/c ❸

Bali Sandat Inn 1 Jl Legian 120 ⓣ0361/753491. Clean and well-maintained terraced rooms set round a garden right in the heart of the action, just a few metres from the main nightspots and shopping. The a/c rooms are especially good, decorated with mango-coloured walls and nice wooden furniture. Rooms with fan ❶ With a/c ❸

Kedin's Inn 1 Poppies 1 ⓣ0361/756771. Backpackers' favourite, offering 30 large, attractively refurbished losmen rooms, built in two storeys around a garden compound and swimming pool at the heart of Poppies 1. Rooms with fan ❷ With a/c ❸

Komala Indah 1 (Poppies 1) Poppies 1, #20 ⓣ0361/751422. Handily located, compact square of seven terraced bungalows set around a courtyard garden. Rooms have fans and are clean and cheap. ❶

Komala Indah 2 (Jl Benesari) Jl Benesari ⓣ0361/754258. Friendly spot offering 50 rooms, the simplest of which are among the cheapest in town (you pay more for a thicker mattress). Occupies a pleasant garden on a quiet part of Jl Benesari, just a couple of minutes' walk from the beach. Rooms with fan ❶ With a/c ❸

🏃 **Lili Garden** Jl Benesari ⓣ0361/750557, ⓔduarsa@dps.centrin.net.id. A simple but inviting haven in a good location between Jl Legian and the beach, this small, friendly, family-run losmen offers a dozen clean, fan-cooled red-brick bungalows set around Ibu Lili's refreshingly green garden. Also has a good-value five-bed family house with kitchen. ❶ Family house ❹

Masa Inn Poppies 1, #27 ⓣ0361/758507, ⓦwww.masainn.com. Very central, very well-priced hotel that's efficiently run, has two good pools and a sociable garden area, and serves decent breakfasts. Rooms in the two- and three-storey blocks are unexciting but comfortable and all come with a/c, cable TV and safety box. ❹

🏃 **Mimpi** Gang Sorga, off Poppies 1 ⓣ0361/751848, ⓔkumimpi@yahoo.com .sg. Just seven characterful, thatched, fan-cooled Balinese cottages dotted round an attractive, shady garden with a reasonable-sized pool. There's also a large villa-style house that sleeps 4 and has a separate living area and roof terrace. Reservations advisable. Cottages ❸–❹ House ❺

Pesona Beach Inn Poppies 1, #31 ⓣ0361/765778. Nice little hideaway of just ten decent-sized but otherwise typical losmen-style fan and a/c rooms in a two-storey block set in a garden that's at the heart of Poppies 1 but away from the main fray. ❷

Puri Agung Gang Bedugul, off Poppies 1 ⓣ0361/750054. Welcoming little losmen comprising twelve sprucely kept and very cheap rooms packed into two storeys around a dark, minuscule courtyard. ❶

Sorga Cottages Gang Sorga, off Poppies 1 ⓣ0361/751897, ⓦwww.angelfire.com/nb /sorgacott. Forty-eight good-value rooms in a three-storey block set round a smallish pool and restaurant. Lacks style but is comfortably furnished and well run. Rooms with fan ❸ With a/c ❹

Moderate and expensive

Adi Dharma Hotel and Cottages Access from both Jl Legian 155 and Jl Benesari: hotel ⓣ0361/754280, cottages ⓣ751527, both ⓦwww.adhidharmahotel.com. A surprisingly appealing package-tourist-oriented operation with 37 pleasant, contemporary-styled a/c "cottage" rooms in blocks of four just off Jl Legian, and 86 similarly furnished hotel rooms in a separate building off Jl Benesari. They all have good bathrooms and there are two pools, a spa and a games room. ❺

Alam Kul Kul Jl Pantai Kuta ⓣ0361/752520, ⓦwww.alamkulkul.com. Sophisticated, award-winning boutique-style hotel with 80 rooms and 23 villas packed village-style into a long, narrow compound across the road from the beach. Decor is modish but welcoming, and though there's no real garden, each room has a terrace, plus there are two pools and a spa. ❼

Bounty Hotel Poppies 2 ⓣ0361/753030, ⓦwww.bountyhotel.com. Long-established favourite of young partying Australians on week-long packages, this place is good value even if you don't fit the profile. The 165 well-maintained terraced bungalows all have a/c and cable TV and are set around two different pools so you can choose whether to stay in the "lively" area of the complex, near the 24-hour pool – or not. ❺

Hard Rock Hotel Jl Pantai Kuta ⓣ0361/761869, ⓦwww.hardrockhotelbali.com. Aimed at the well-heeled, mainstream rock fan, with sleek, contemporary rooms and rock hall-of-fame iconography and memorabilia all over the place. Occupies a prime location across from the beach, and boasts a fantastic series of swimming pools, a spa and a kids' club. ❼

🏃 **Kuta Puri** Poppies 1 ⓣ0361/751903, ⓦwww.kutapuri.com. Occupying an ideal location less than a minute from the beach and

Moving on from Kuta

Bemos

To get from Kuta to most other destinations in Bali by **bemo** will almost always entail going via Denpasar, where you'll probably have to make at least one cross-city connection.

Dark blue bemos to **Denpasar**'s Tegal terminal (Rp5000; 25min) run throughout the day though the service can be sporadic and you may have to wait up to an hour; the easiest place to catch them is at the Jl Pantai Kuta/Jl Raya Kuta intersection, about 15m east of Bemo Corner, where they wait to collect passengers, although you can also get on anywhere on their loop around Kuta (see p.99 for details). From Tegal, other bemos run to **Sanur** and to Denpasar's other bemo terminals for onward connections; full details are on p.83 and on the map on p.87. Note that, to get to Batubulan terminal (departure point for **Ubud**), the white Damri bus service from Nusa Dua is quicker than taking a bemo to Tegal and another to Batubulan; you can pick it up at the Kuta fuel station on the intersection of Jl Imam Bonjol and Jl Setia Budi, about ten minutes' walk northeast of Bemo Corner. Dark blue bemos from Tegal to Bualu and **Nusa Dua's** Bali Collection also pass this intersection, and will pick you up on Jl Setia Budi if you signal. Some Tegal–Bualu bemos serve **Jimbaran** on the way, and there's also a dark blue Tegal–Jimbaran bemo.

Shuttle buses and taxis

If you're going anywhere beyond Denpasar, the quickest public-transport option from Kuta is to take a tourist **shuttle bus**, which run to all the obvious tourist destinations on Bali as well as to some major spots on Lombok and the Gili Islands. Every agency in Kuta–Legian–Seminyak offers "shuttle bus services": some are little more than one man and his minivan, others are big buses run by professional operators. Prices are always competitive; most travellers choose according to convenience of timetable and pick-up points. Drop-offs are usually at the operator's office at the destination rather than specific hotels.

Bali's biggest and best-known shuttle-bus operator is **Perama**, whose unobtrusive head office is located 100m north of Bemo Corner at Jl Legian 39 (daily 7am–10pm; ⊕0361/751875, ⓦwww.peramatour.com). This is the departure point for all Perama buses, although you can pay an extra Rp5000 to be picked up from your hotel (and another Rp5000 for a precise hotel drop-off) and can buy tickets on the phone; shuttle-bus tickets sold by other agencies are almost certainly not for the Perama service, whatever you're told. Typical fares include Rp30,000 to Ubud, Rp85,000 to Lovina and Rp240,000 to the Gili Islands (including boat transfer). See "Travel details", p.163, for a full list of destinations and frequencies.

If there are several of you, **taxis** can be good value for transport to other areas of south Bali: a ride to Denpasar will cost around Rp45,000, and to Nusa Dua or Sanur about Rp70,000.

Transport to other islands

Many Kuta travel agents (see p.124 for a list) sell **boat tickets** to Lombok, Nusa Lembongan and other Indonesian islands; Perama (described above) also offer integrated shuttle-bus and boat transport, and Island Promotions (see p.124) specializes in the Gili Islands. Details of the local Pelni office (for long-distance ferries to other parts of Indonesia) are on p.124.

All Kuta travel agents sell **domestic air tickets**. Sample one-way fares are Rp350,000 to Mataram on Lombok, Rp250,000–375,000 to Yogyakarta, and Rp79,999 (on budget airline Air Asia) – 535,000 to Jakarta. Full airport information is on p.100.

just a bit further from Kuta Square shops, this set of bungalows enjoys an unusually spacious setting, with a charming garden, large pool, and on-site massage service. The terraced a/c "cottage" rooms and more luxurious freestanding bungalows (60 rooms in all) are in Balinese style and attractively furnished, and some have pretty garden bathrooms. Deservedly popular, so booking is advisable. ⑤–⑥

Poppies Cottages Poppies 1
☏0361/751059, ⓦwww.poppiesbali.com. Just 20 elegant, traditional-style a/c cottages secluded within a tranquil tropical garden of arbours, miniature bridges and a bougainvillea-shaded swimming pool. Rooms are charmingly furnished in local fabrics and all have shady terraces and garden bathrooms plus all the mod cons. Extremely popular so reserve ahead. ⑦

South Kuta/Tuban

A few hundred metres south of Jalan Pantai Kuta, beyond Kuta Square's Matahari department store, Kuta beach officially becomes **Tuban** beach and things quieten down a bit. This area is often the first choice of Australian families, not least because many hotels here enjoy direct access to the beach (though the shore's not as appealing as further up) and can be booked at bargain rates through tour operators. There are plenty of restaurants and small shops along the main drag, Jalan Kartika Plaza, as well as the colossal Discovery Shopping Mall. No bemos run this way but it's only ten minutes' walk from *Bali Dynasty* to Kuta Square, either along the road or via the beachfront promenade.

Bali Dynasty Resort Jl Kartika Plaza
☏0361/752403, ⓦwww.balidynasty.com. Large, lively, mid-market hotel that's a hit with Australian family groups because kids' suites feature bunk beds and a PlayStation, and there's a busy programme of activities. Also offers an adults-only pool and spa, wheelchair-accessible

accommodation, and the Irish-style *Gracie Kelly's* pub (serving Guinness pie and fish and chips). The hotel has no direct beach access but it's just 50m down a *gang* to the sea. ⑥
Bunut Gardens Gang Puspa Ayu ☏0361/752971, ⓔbunutgarden@yahoo.com. Just thirteen rooms set round a small yard down a quiet, residential

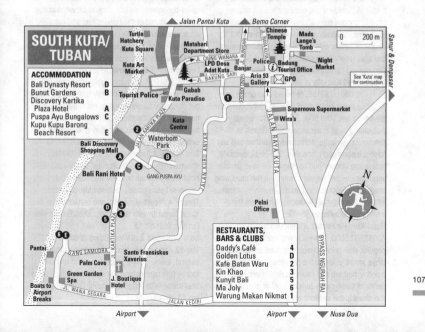

lane, about 800m from the beach and the shops. Rooms are decent and all have fans and nice bamboo furniture. ❶

Discovery Kartika Plaza Hotel Jl Kartika Plaza ☎0361/751067, ⓦwww.discoverykartikaplaza .com. Large, quite sophisticated beachfront outfit with rooms arranged in a U-shape around the lush tropical garden. There's a huge freeform pool right on the shore. ❼

Kupu Kupu Barong Beach Resort (formerly The Sandi Phala) Jl Wana Segara ☎0361/753780, ⓦwww.kupubarong.com. Classy beachside boutique hotel with just eleven rooms and suites, all

elegantly furnished in Bali-minimalist style, with added warmth from deep red rugs; many also have private plunge pools. There's a beautifully sited, seafront hotel swimming pool and the stunning *Ma Joly* restaurant is also here. ❾

Puspa Ayu Bungalows Gang Puspa Ayu ☎0361/756721. The most popular accommodation on this refreshingly peaceful residential street occupies a quiet and pleasant spot with sixteen typical Bali-style rooms and bungalows (fan and a/ c) set round a garden 200m off the main road. Rooms with fan ❸ With a/c ❹

Legian

Slightly calmer than Kuta, and with less-crowded sands, **Legian** is more popular with Australian families and package tourists than backpackers. It has plenty of shops and restaurants, and a wider choice of mid-range hotels than Kuta. If you've got your eye on a beachfront hotel in Legian, note that the shorefront road between Jalan Melasti and Jalan Arjuna is open only to toll-paying drivers and is therefore very quiet: most vehicles have to go the long way round.

Ayodya Beach Inn Gang Three Brothers ☎0361/752169, ⓔayodyabeachinn@yahoo.com. Cheap and friendly losmen with fifteen terraced fan rooms, most of them fairly basic, in a small garden compound just 75m from Jl Legian. ❶

Blue Ocean Jl Pantai Arjuna ☎0361/730289. A five-star location at one-star prices, this place occupies a prime, spacious spot on the beachfront road. The 24 rooms all have fans and most are huge, if simply furnished; many have kitchen facilities and some can sleep four. Maintenance is not exactly tip-top but it's a laid-back place with a loyal clan of returning guests and a no-reservations policy. The Rip Curl School of Surf (see p.113) has its headquarters here. ❸

🏃 **Hotel Kumala** Jl Werk Udara ☎0361/732186, ⓦwww.hotelkumala.com. With two pools and a good location just 250m from the beach and 50m from Jl Arjuna, this small, welcoming hotel is excellent value. Rooms in all categories are large, attractively furnished and all have a/c and good bathrooms. Top-end ("deluxe") rooms and bottom-end "cottages" all have private verandahs while "superior" rooms in the main wing share an outdoor seating area. Sometimes known as the *Grand Kumala* to distinguish it from the nearby *Kumala Pantai*. ❸–❹

Hotel Kumala Pantai Jl Werk Udara ☎0361/755500, ⓦwww.kumalapantai.com. Hugely popular, well-priced beachfront hotel comprising 90 large, smart, comfortable a/c rooms, each with a balcony, bathtub and cable TV. Rooms are in a series of three-storey buildings set in grounds that run down to the seafront road. Has a good-sized

pool and two restaurants. Decent discounts outside peak season but reservations are essential. ❻

Hotel Padma Jl Padma 1 ☎0361/752111, ⓦwww.hotelpadma.com. Typical upper-bracket resort hotel set in extensive tropical gardens that run down to the beachfront road. The hotel is assiduous about maintenance so rooms tend to be consistently high standard but not necessarily up-to-the-minute-stylish. Choose between accommodation in one of the hotel wings and more attractive deluxe "chalets"; some are wheelchair-accessible. Has two pools, a spa and a complimentary kids' club and nursery. ❼

Legian Beach Bungalow Jl Padma ☎0361/751087, ⓔgading_lbb@yahoo.com. A small, inviting place with friendly staff and 20 simple but pleasantly furnished rooms set in a spacious garden close to the shops and not far from the beach. Very well priced considering its location and swimming pool. Rooms with fan ❷ With a/c ❸

Suri Wathi Jl Sahadewa 12 ☎0361/753162, ⓔsuriwati@yahoo.com. Popular, family-run little hotel with 46 small but well-maintained bungalow rooms set either side of a long strip of garden. There's a decent-sized pool and restaurant on site too. A favourite with returning guests. Rooms with fan ❸ With a/c ❹

Su's Cottages 2 Jl Werk Udara ☎0361/752127. The 22 comfortably furnished rooms at this central, losmen-style place are set in a two-storey row overlooking the small pool. A/c rooms also come with fridge and cable TV. Rooms with fan ❸ With a/c ❹

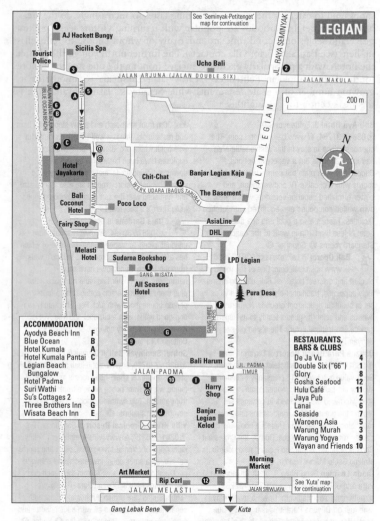

LEGIAN

See 'Seminyak-Petitenget' map for continuation

AJ Hackett Bungy

Sicilia Spa

Tourist Police

Ucho Bali

JALAN ARJUNA (JALAN DOUBLE SIX)

JALAN NAKULA

JL. RAYA SEMINYAK

JL WERK UDARA

JL. PANTAI ARJUNA (BLUE OCEAN BEACH)

JALAN LEGIAN

0   200 m

N

Hotel Jayakarta

Chit-Chat

Banjar Legian Kaja

JL. WERK UDARA (BAGUS TARUNA)

The Basement

Bali Coconut Hotel

Poco Loco

Fairy Shop

AsiaLine

DHL

Melasti Hotel

Sudarna Bookshop

GANG WISATA

LPD Legian

All Seasons Hotel

Pura Desa

JALAN PADMA UTARA

GANG THREE BROTHERS

Bali Harum

JL. PADMA TIMUR

JALAN PADMA

Harry Shop

Banjar Legian Kelod

JALAN LEGIAN

JALAN SAHADEWA

Art Market

Rip Curl

Fila

Morning Market

JALAN MELASTI

JALAN SRIWIJAYA

See 'Kuta' map for continuation

Gang Lebak Bene ▼   ▼ Kuta

ACCOMMODATION

Ayodya Beach Inn	F
Blue Ocean	B
Hotel Kumala	A
Hotel Kumala Pantai	C
Legian Beach Bungalow	I
Hotel Padma	H
Suri Wathi	J
Su's Cottages 2	D
Three Brothers Inn	G
Wisata Beach Inn	E

RESTAURANTS, BARS & CLUBS

De Ja Vu	4
Double Six ("66")	1
Glory	8
Gosha Seafood	12
Hulu Café	11
Jaya Pub	2
Lanai	6
Seaside	7
Waroeng Asia	5
Warung Murah	3
Warung Yogya	9
Wayan and Friends	10

Three Brothers Inn Gang Three Brothers ☎0361/751566, @www .threebrothersbungalows.com. One of the most characterful places in the area, this lush, rambling, typically Balinese garden complex holds dozens of large, attractive bungalows and a pool. There are numerous room types (though all are a good size and have garden-view verandahs): among the nicest are the upstairs fan-cooled ones with four-poster beds. Rooms with fan ④–⑤ With a/c ⑤–⑥ **Wisata Beach Inn** Gang Wisata, off Jl Padma Utara ☎0361/755987. Quiet little place at the back of a beauty parlour, with just four bungalows in a small garden, each offering plain, split-level accommodation with one bedroom and balcony upstairs and another one downstairs. ① For four people ②

Seminyak and Petitenget

Upmarket **Seminyak** and its sophisticated, almost swanky, neighbour **Petitenget** are the favourite haunt of Euro-expats, so just as the bars, clubs, restaurants and shops tend to cater for these more discerning tastes so, increasingly, do the areas' hotels. Both neighbourhoods are popular with returning visitors seeking extra peace and seclusion second time around, many of whom choose to rent villas up here (see Basics, p.43, for villa contacts). The further north you go the classier the hotels, with a particularly exclusive enclave fronting the fine stretch of shore south of the temple in Petitenget. Nearby Jalan Laksmana is famous for its growing number of upscale restaurants while Seminyak's Jalan Dhyana Pura is the area's centre for gay nightlife.

Bali Ayu Hotel Jl Petitenget 99X ☎0361/731264, ⓦwww.baliayuhotel.com. The cheapest place to stay in this fashionable area has just 32 rooms but a variety of options. Choose between plain but comfortable standard rooms with a/c, cable TV and verandah, and better-furnished superior versions, within their own walled compound and equipped with kitchen facilities. There's also a pool and spa and the hotel is less than 10min walk to the beach. Standard rooms ❹ Superior ❺

Bali Oberoi Jl Laksmana ☎0361/730361, ⓦwww.oberoibali.com. One of the most elegant and discreet hotels on Bali, offering charmingly appointed, traditional-style rooms and villas set in beautiful beachfront grounds. Numerous awards and celebrity guests testify to its superb service and tranquil luxury. There's an on-site Banyan Tree Spa. ❾

Dhyana Pura Beach Resort Jl Dhyana Pura ☎0361/730442, ⓦwww.hoteldhyanapura.com. Good-value hotel with 118 pleasantly furnished if slightly old-fashioned a/c rooms, some in two-storey terraced blocks, others in cottages set around the grassy lawns (renovations and new room blocks are planned). There's a pool, and the garden runs down to the sea. Run by the Protestant Christian Church of Bali and located next door to its striking Santo Mikael church. ❺

Inada Losmen Gang Bima 9, off Jl Dhyana Pura and Jl Raya Seminyak ☎0361/732269, ⓔputuinada@hotmail.com. Down a quiet leafy lane just off Dhyana Pura, this is a great-value spot offering a dozen large, clean, typical losmen rooms set round a garden yard. ❶

The Legian Jl Pantai Kayu Aya ☎0361/730622, ⓦwww.ghmhotels.com. *The* choice of weekending Asian sophisticates, who love the muted minimalist style and enormous deluxe apartment-style rooms (the bathrooms have to be the biggest in Bali). Huge private verandahs make the most of the unparalleled ocean views, and there's a shorefront pool and a spa. Published rates from US$400. ❾

Puri Cendana Jl Dhyana Pura ☎0361/730869, ⓦwww.puricendana.com.

Just 30m from the beach and a few steps from bars and restaurants, this is a well-priced, characterful little hotel whose a/c, Balinese-style two-storey duplexes have huge bathrooms as well as downstairs living areas, making them very good value. The single-storey rooms are also a good size and furnished with the same pretty, boho-antique look. There's a pool too. ❺

Raja Gardens Jl Dhyana Pura ☎0361/730494, ⓔjdw@eksadata.com. Six unusual, nicely furnished bungalows (one of which has a/c) in a spacious garden one minute's walk from the beach. Bungalows have garden bathrooms, four-poster beds and mosquito nets, plus there's a two-person cottage and a four-person house (both with a/c). Peaceful, family run and good value, with a big pool and free Wi-Fi. Reservations strongly advised. Bungalows ❹ Cottage ❺ House ❻

Sofitel Seminyak Bali Jl Dhyana Pura ☎0361/730730, ⓦwww.sofitelbali.com. Cheerfully stylish, upmarket chain-hotel rooms and villas (some with private pools) set in a tropical beach-front garden. Two swimming pools, a spa and several tennis courts. ❽

Villa Kresna Tropical Resort Jl Sarinande 19 ☎0361/730317, ⓦwww.villa-kresna.com. A tiny compound of colonial-style suites, villas and rooms set around a small bougainvillea-shaded saltwater pool, just one minute's walk from the beach and five minutes from Jl Dhyana Pura. The six a/c "Lotus Suites" are stylish but homely, most with separate living areas and all with a kitchenette and a balcony or terrace. Rooms with fan ❻ Suites ❼ Villas ❾

Vila Lumbung Jl Raya Petitenget 100X ☎0361/730204, ⓦwww.hotellumbung.com. Modern *lumbung*-style villas set in a mature tropical garden less than ten minutes' walk from the beach make this a more affordable alternative to the big hitters on the seafront. Most are spacious two-bedroom, two-storey affairs with antique-style furniture, and can also be rented separately. Additional rooms are housed in a block and there's also a pool. Rooms ❻ One-bed *lumbung* ❼ Three bedrooms with kitchen ❾

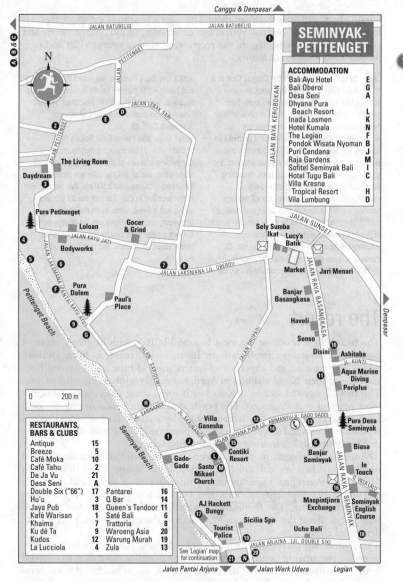

SEMINYAK-PETITENGET

ACCOMMODATION

Bali Ayu Hotel	E
Bali Oberoi	G
Desa Seni	A
Dhyana Pura Beach Resort	L
Inada Losmen	K
Hotel Kumala	N
The Legian	F
Pondok Wisata Nyoman	B
Puri Cendana	J
Raja Gardens	M
Sofitel Seminyak Bali	I
Hotel Tugu Bali	C
Villa Kresna Tropical Resort	H
Vila Lumbung	D

RESTAURANTS, BARS & CLUBS

Antique	15
Breeze	5
Café Moka	10
Café Tahu	2
De Ja Vu	21
Desa Seni	A
Double Six ("66")	17
Hu'u	3
Jaya Pub	18
Kafé Warisan	1
Khaima	7
Ku dé Ta	9
Kudos	12
La Lucciola	4
Pantarei	16
Q Bar	14
Queen's Tandoor	11
Saté Bali	6
Trattoria	8
Waroeng Asia	20
Warung Murah	19
Zula	13

Canggu beaches: Batubelig, Berewa, Batu Bolong and Pererenan

North of Petitenget, the coastline unfurls via a rapid succession of wild, isolated little surfing beaches at **Batubelig**, **Berewa**, **Batu Bolong** and **Pererenan** (see map, p.82) – all of which can be dangerous for swimming. This area is loosely referred to as **Canggu** rather than Kuta, but is so easily reached from Petitenget, 3km to the south of Batubelig, that surfers, tourists and expats are constantly buzzing back and forth between them. There are a couple of exceptional places to stay around here, but few restaurants or services. Inland, village streets and ricefields still dominate, despite the recent explosion of tourist villas and ugly pseudo-modernist expat homes.

🏃 **Desa Seni** 100m from the Canggu Club at Jl Kayu Putih 13, Pantai Berewa, Canggu ☎0361/844 6392, ⓦwww.desaseni.com. This gorgeous little hotel consists of ten original wooden homes sourced from all over Indonesia and reassembled here as a village, within a garden that supplies the hotel restaurant. Each house is unique and exquisitely furnished with antique artefacts and guests are provided with a room book describing their provenance. There are plenty of extras, including free daily yoga classes, complimentary bicycles, a pretty saltwater pool, and great food (see p.117). The hotel is a 5-minute cycle from the beach at Batubelig (see map, p.97) and 20min from Petitenget restaurants. ❼–❽ Family houses ❾ **Pondok Wisata Nyoman** Pantai Pererenan ☎0812/394 5967, Ⓔpondoknyoman@yahoo.com.

Just a few steps from the sea – and the Pererenan surf break – this friendly, family-run losmen caters mainly to wave riders with its four large, nicely furnished fan-cooled rooms and shoreview *Surfwatch Café*. ❷
Hotel Tugu Bali Pantai Batu Bolong ☎0361/731701, ⓦwww.tuguhotels.com. Comprising a series of traditional polished-teak houses that are all built to different designs and furnished with beautiful antiques, this hotel is one of the loveliest in Bali. Each of the 21 elegant suites has a living room, bedroom and garden bathroom, and some have private plunge-pools. There's a hotel pool, restaurant, gorgeous spa, tennis court and library, and free transport to Kuta. ❾

The resort

The **beach** here is one of the most beautiful in Bali, with its gentle curve of golden sand stretching for 8km from Tuban to Petitenget, its huge breakers, which lure amateur and experienced surfers alike, and the much-lauded Kuta sunsets – at their blood-red best in April, but streaky-pink at any time of year. The most congested swathe is Kuta beach itself, along Jalan Pantai Kuta; the most peaceful is at Petitenget. The beach around Jalan Pantai Arjuna in north Legian makes a pleasant alternative, fronted by a barely used road and graced with sunloungers and several restaurants where you can laze away the sweltering midday hours while admiring the local surfing talent.

North of Petitenget, in the **Canggu** area, the sand darkens around the rougher little beaches at Batubelig, Berewa, Batu Bolong, Echo Beach (Batu Mejan) and Pererenan. These are mainly the province of surfers and there's no real resort development up here, just villas, a few places to stay, and the occasional warung. *The Beach House* warung at Echo Beach, five minutes' walk south along the shore from Pererenan, is the most famous place to eat, drink and chill.

The waves that make Kuta such a great beach for surfers can make it treacherous for **swimming**, with a strong undertow as well as the rollers to contend with. The current is especially dangerous at the Canggu beaches. Always swim between the red-and-yellow striped flags, and take notice of the warning signs that dot the beach. If you need extra discouragement, check the last decade's tally of rescue attempts, drownings and disappearances listed on a board at the Surf Rescue centre on Kuta Beach: in 2006, 26 people drowned and another 248 were rescued. **Lifeguards** are stationed in special towers all along Bali's southwest coast from Uluwatu on the Bukit to Seseh near Pererenan (15 in all), with six in the Kuta–Legian–Seminyak stretch and one each at Batubelig and Berewa; the central lifeguard post is on the beach at the corner of Jalan Pantai Kuta.

Despite the crowds, Olive Ridley **turtles** return to Kuta's shores every year between June and October to lay their eggs late at night. To protect these much sought-after eggs from poachers and help the hatchlings survive, a hatchery has been established by the NGO ProFauna and the Satgas community police beside the latter's office on the beach near the corner of Jalan Pantai Kuta. The babies are then released safely into the sea, usually in public ceremonies. For more on turtles in Bali, see p.134.

Surfing

Surfing is huge in Kuta and Poppies 2, Poppies 1 and Jalan Benesari in particular are crammed with board rental and repair shops, surfwear outlets and surfer-oriented bars. It was off this stretch of shore in 1936 that surfing was supposedly introduced to Bali by American hotel-owner Bob Koke. The first pro-am competition was organized here in 1980, and local and international surf championships have since become regular events. The best **time of year** for surfing off Kuta is during the dry season (April–Oct), when the southeast trade winds blow offshore; they're at their strongest in July and August. From November to March, the wind arrives from the northwest, bringing rain and blowing onshore, sending most surfers east to Sanur and Nusa Dua.

As Kuta is a sandy beach with no coral or rocks to wipe out on, it's the best place in Bali to learn to surf. The **breaks** offer consistent, almost uniform waves, with lots of tubes. Kuta Beach (beyond the Jalan Pantai Kuta lifeguard station) is particularly appealing for beginners because it's fun but not too daunting, and there are slightly more advanced breaks further south in Tuban, accessed by boats from the lot at the west end of Jalan Wana Segara (Rp50,000 or less including waiting time). North of Seminyak, in the Canggu area, there are reef breaks at Batu Bolong, Echo Beach, and Pererenan. For general surfing info, see p.49; for surfari tours see p.114.

Surfing **lessons** ("If you're not standing on your board by the end of your first lesson, the next one's free") are offered by the Rip Curl School of Surf, based at the *Blue Ocean* hotel on Jalan Pantai Arjuna in Legian (℡0361/735858, Ⓦwww.ripcurlschoolofsurf.com), Odyssey's Surf School at the *Mercure Kuta*

▲ Waiting for the surfers, Seminyak

113

Bali on Jalan Pantai Kuta (℡0361/742 0763, Ⓦwww.odysseysurfschool.com), Pro Surf School at the *Grand Istana Rama* on Jalan Pantai Kuta (℡0361/7441466, Ⓦwww.prosurfschool.com), and Ombak Bagus in Canggu (℡0818/0550 4551, Ⓦwww.ombakbagus.com). Prices average $45 for a half-day introduction, or $205 for three full days.

Diving and other activities

Most south-Bali **dive** centres are based not in Kuta but in Sanur (see p.146 for a list) and as there's no diving directly off Kuta's shores they all include free transport to dive sites. A notable local outfit, based in Seminyak, is AquaMarine Diving, at Jalan Raya Seminyak 2A (℡0361/730107, Ⓦwww.aquamarinediving.com).

Watersports also happen elsewhere, in Tanjung Benoa (described on p.137). It's easy and usually cheaper to make your own way there and organize equipment rental yourself, but any Kuta tour agent can make the arrangements if you prefer.

Water parks and pools

Kuta's **Waterbom Park** on Jalan Kartika Plaza, Tuban (daily 9am–6pm; adults US$21, 2 to 12-year-olds $11, family tickets $58; children under 12 must be accompanied by an adult), is a hugely popular aquatic adventure park, with water slides, a 150-metre-long macaroni tube, a lazy river with inner tubes, water trampolines, a climbing wall and a kids' area for 2 to 10-year-olds. Another good aquatic option is the **Hard Rock swimming pool** (daylight hours; adults Rp100,000, kids Rp50,000), inside the *Hard Rock Hotel* complex on Jalan Pantai Kuta. It's a huge, fantastic construction, hundreds of metres long, with water chutes, a sandy beach area and volleyball net. You can even rent a little waterside cabana for the day, complete with day bed and room service. A lot more self-consciously hip is the dazzlingly white Petitenget dining, drinking and lounging experience that is **Day Dream**, a nightclub that opens at 7.30am (and shuts at 2am) and tempts punters in during the day with its large pool, outdoor cinema screen and quality food and drink; it's just north of *Hu'u* at Jalan Petitenget 2000XX. On a much smaller scale, non-guests can use the charming little bougainvillea-shaded swimming pool at *Poppies Cottages* on Poppies 1 for Rp18,000.

Adrenaline kicks

Should you be so inclined, you can **bungee jump** off a 45-metre-high swimming-pool tower in the grounds of the *Double Six* nightclub on Jalan

---

Surfaris

Numerous agents in Kuta sell **"surfari"** surfing tours for all abilities to the mega-waves off East Java (including the awesome G-Land surfbreak; mainly March–Oct but ask about out-of-season options), West Java, Lombok, Sumbawa and West Timor. Prices start from US$300 for a six-night package at G-Land, or $390 for five days at Sumbawa's Lakey Peak. G-Land operators include Wanasari Wisata, Jl Pantai Kuta 8B (℡0361/755588, Ⓦwww.grajagan.com), and G-Land Surf Camp, Okie House, Poppies 2 (℡0361/750320, Ⓦwww.g-landsurfcamp.com). Surf Travel Online on Jl Benesari (℡0361/750550, Ⓦwww.surftravelonline.com) runs trips to breaks all over, or you can charter a liveaboard surf boat to pretty much any break in the region through Bali Boat Trips on Poppies 2 (℡0812/365 8239, Ⓦwww.surfdesertstorm.com).

Active days out

All the following **activities** can also be booked through travel agents, but the bigger adventure-tour operators – Bali Adventure Tours (☎0361/721480, ⓦwww .baliadventuretours.com) and Sobek (☎0361/844 6194, ⓦwww.99bali.com /adventure/sobek) – offer discounts for direct online booking. All operators do free picks-up from hotels in Kuta, Sanur, Nusa Dua and Ubud, and some will pick up from Candi Dasa.

Elephant trekking At the Elephant Safari Park in Taro (see p.216), with Bali Adventure Tours.

Hikes Guided walks through ricefields, rainforest and villages. Bali Adventure Tours and Sobek.

Horse-riding At the Umalas Equestrian Resort in Kerobokan (☎0361/731402, ⓦwww.balionhorse.com). Lessons (from $25) and rides along the beach and through village areas ($60 for 2 hrs).

Mountain-biking and quad-biking Bike downhill from north- and west-Bali volcanoes through villages and rural areas ($62/40) with Bali Adventure Tours, Sobek and SeeBali Adventures (☎0361/794 9693, ⓦwww.seebaliadventures.com); quad-bike through plantations and muddy paddyfields (see p.327) with SeeBali Adventures.

Paragliding In tandem with an instructor, off the Bukit cliffs; through Bali Adventure Tours (Sept–May; 20mins; $71).

Whitewater rafting and river kayaking Year-round rafting on the Class 2 and 3 rapids of the Ayung River near Ubud with Bali Adventure Tours and Sobek (around US$70/45). Kayaking on the Ayung River with Bali Adventure Tours.

Arjuna, care of A.J. Hackett Bungy (daily noon–8pm and Fri & Sat night 2–6am; $59); the **2am jumps** on weekends are predictably popular with tripped-out clubbers. Or head skywards instead, via the **Bali Slingshot**, which catapults you 52m into the air in just over one second ("Wear ya brown jocks" as the publicity advises) and captures your terror on video; it operates in front of the Kuta Centre at Jalan Kartika Plaza 8X in Tuban (daily 11am until late; Rp200,000).

Eating

There are hundreds of **places to eat** in Kuta–Legian–Seminyak, from tiny neighbourhood warung to design-obsessed dining experiences. Unless otherwise stated, all places listed below are open daily from breakfast-time through to at least 10pm. In general, the most sophisticated, interesting – and expensive – restaurants are located in Seminyak and Petitenget, while Kuta and Legian are dominated by low-grade but decent enough tourist restaurants and international fast-food joints.

Kuta's main **night market** (*pasar senggol*) on Jalan Blambangan at the southern edge of Kuta is another enjoyable culinary event, with hawkers cooking everything from noodle soup to barbecued corn, and the adjacent warung offering very cheap, barbecued fresh fish.

Kuta

Alleycats Behind Internet Outpost off Poppies 2. The home-from-home for hungry Brits, this courtyard café prides itself on dishing out authentic full English breakfasts (Rp32,000), Sunday roasts, monster mixed grills (Rp95,000) and kormas and Punjabi curries (pick your fire rating up to level 15).

Aromas Café Jl Legian. Delicious vegetarian food served in a garden dining room set away from the street. The menu includes Mexican, Italian, Indian and Indonesian dishes (Rp25,000–45,000), mostly made with organic ingredients. Also does cheese-cakes, chocolate mousse, good Italian coffee and lots of vegetable juices.

Ketupat Behind the Jonathan Gallery jewellery shop at Jl Legian 109. Not only is this Kuta's most romantic dining experience but the food is interesting too. The focus is on dishes from around Indonesia (Rp40,000–70,000), which include recommended deep-fried calamari with pickles and rainbow sauce (*chumi chin chin*), prawns in spicy Sulawesi sauce, and lime-stewed chicken from Kalimantan. The eponymous *ketupat* – doughy cakes of rice steamed in banana-leaf parcels – are eaten all over the archipelago but can be a bit heavy. Choose to dine in a private wooden cabana, poolside, or on one of the balconies.

Kori Poppies 2. Refined dining in a sophisticated setting, where the menu features dishes that you grill yourself on sizzling hot stones: pork medallions (Rp62,000), lobster mornay, and a seafood spa of scallops, calamari and fresh fish (Rp120,000). Also does good home-made ice cream, sticky-toffee pudding, plus various cocktails including chocolate Martinis. Not great for vegetarians, but otherwise worth the price tag, especially if you order before 7pm, when you're entitled to a ten percent discount.

Kuta Food Court Jl Pantai Kuta. Outdoor version of a shopping-mall food court with 20 food stalls serving cheap regional specialities from across Indonesia. Graze as many stalls as you like and then grab a table in the central yard area. Daily from about 5pm.

Maccaroni Club Jl Legian 52. Mixing Seminyak chic with Kuta populism, this place exudes a relaxing loungey vibe with its mellow DJ sounds, comfy armchair seating, free Internet access and Wi-Fi and extensive list of twenty Absolut cocktails and a hundred Australian wines (from Rp190,000 a bottle). The predominantly Italian food (Rp30,000–80,000) is variable – great gnocchi with four cheeses, less inspiring woodfired pizzas, tempting tropical fruit pannacotta.

Made's Warung 1 Jl Pantai Kuta. Long-standing if rather overpriced haven set serving Indonesian and Balinese fare (Rp20,000–100,000) that ranges from nasi campur to chicken rice-porridge and black-rice ice cream. Also does seafood, including good snapper in garlic sauce, as well as cappuc-cino and cakes.

Poppies Poppies 1 ☎0361/751059. This seduc-tively tranquil haven set away from the hustle beneath bougainvillea-draped pergolas is another venerable Kuta institution, established in 1973 and so famous the road is named after it. Though the food is less notable, and pretty pricey (Rp47,00–145,000), the menu does feature Indonesian specials such as *tongseng kambing* (lamb and vegetables cooked in coconut milk and spices), beef curry and *rijsttafel* (Rp160,000 for two). Worth reserving a table a few hours in advance.

TJ's Poppies 1. Popular, long-running Californian/Mexican restaurant with tables set around a water garden. The menu covers the full gamut of tortillas, fajitas, buffalo wings and enchiladas (around Rp45,000), and includes mango cheesecake, Kahlua-spiked coffees and especially good margaritas and strawberry daiquiris.

Un's Poppies 1. Small, upmarket Italian place with a pleasant courtyard dining area that specializes in pretty good home-made pasta (Rp40,000–70,000) including a "four-in-one combo" of two raviolis (one of them stuffed with Balinese herbs), gnocchi and tortellini, plus risotto and seafood.

Warung Indonesia Gang Ronta. Welcoming surfer-friendly warung where you can fill up on your own assortment of veg and non-veg nasi campur dishes for just Rp7500 or splash out on *bihun kuah* (rice-noodle soup) or *soto ayam*.

South Kuta/Tuban

Daddy's Café Jl Kartika Plaza. Greek restaurant with a good selection of mezze, including aubergine imam, cheese saganaki, and delicious potatoes stuffed with spinach, feta and aromatic herbs. Good-value mixed-seafood platters (Rp90,000 for two), plus a variety of hearty, set breakfasts from Rp25,000.

Golden Lotus Inside the *Bali Dynasty Resort* on Jl Kartika Plaza. Upmarket Chinese restaurant that's a hit with local Chinese and Indonesian families, especially for the all-you-can-eat Sunday buffets of 60 different types of dim sum (10.30am–2.30pm; Rp60,000, kids Rp30,000). On other days, dim sum is served from 11.30am–2.30pm and dinner from 6–10pm.

Kafe Batan Waru Jl Kartika Plaza. South-Kuta branch of the Ubud stalwart, this streetside café directly opposite Waterbom Park serves wholesome specialities from across Indonesia (mostly Rp40,000–70,000), including spicy, Manado-style chicken (*ayam ayam rica*), jackfruit, papaya and coconut *lawar* salad, and *tenggiri* fish steaks in turmeric sauce. Also does international salads and sandwiches.

Kin Khao Jl Kartika Plaza 170. Reliable, mid-priced Thai restaurant serving good deep-fried chicken wings with chilli sauce, aromatic *tom yam kung* soup, and a range of red, green and yellow curries (from Rp35,000).

Kunyit Bali Jl Kartika Plaza. Breezy pavilion restaurant specializing in fairly classy Balinese food (mains from Rp38,000), including house duck in spicy sauce (*bebek tutu Kunyit*) and traditional Balinese sausage deep-fried with garlic and ginger.

Ma Joly *Kupu Kupu Barong Beach Resort*, Jl Wana Segara ⊕ 0361/753708. Tuban's most sophisticated dining experience occupies a glorious spot right on the sand, with the sea view artfully framed. Its angle is expensive, top-notch French-fusion cuisine – grilled *mahi mahi* with chilli and mango salsa, snail stew with mushrooms and garlic, strawberry millefeuille – with an emphasis on seafood. Predictably popular at sunset but also great for lunch. Main courses Rp83,000–140,000.

Warung Makan Nikmat just off Jl Kubu Anyar (next to the main entrance of *Hotel Baking Sari*, 50m west from the southern end of Gang Kresek or 300m west of Supernova). The ultra-popular lunchtime choice of everyone from office workers to Kuta girls and surfers, where you assemble your own nasi campur from around 50 different East Java-style dishes – water spinach with chilli, curried eggs, chicken curry, beef rendang, *urap*, tempeh and much more – for a bargain Rp6500. Fresh fruit juices cost just Rp4500 and there are fresh fruit salads too. Shuts when the food runs out, usually around 2.30pm.

Legian

Glory Jl Legian 445, 200m north of Jl Padma. Long-running tourists' favourite that's known for its huge Rp29,500 "outback breakfasts", creamy chicken pancakes, barbecued spare ribs (from Rp55,000) and reliably good fresh seafood. Also popular for its Balinese buffets on Sunday lunchtimes (noon–3pm; Rp25,000).

Gosha Seafood Jl Melasti 7. For years this has been the most popular seafood restaurant in Legian. The speciality is lobster (Rp38,000/kg) cooked any number of ways. Also does steaks, frogs' legs and rice dishes.

Lanai Jl Pantai Arjuna. One of a string of good, busy eateries set beside the traffic-free beachside road, boasting a wide-ranging menu and generous portions: nachos with assorted Mexican dips; barbecued tuna, prawns and calamari (Rp58,000); sushi and sashimi; pizza and calzones; and white chocolate mousse.

Seaside Jl Pantai Arjuna. Choose your preferred ocean-view spot – streetside cushioned benches or terrace-top for breezy wave panoramas – at which to enjoy this decent menu (Rp35,000–65,000) that ranges from tortillas and other Mexican favourites to home-made soups. Also does California-style burgers and salads, fish – *mahi mahi* fillet a

speciality – and a veggie selection that includes a tasty mezze plate.

Waroeng Asia Jl Arjuna 23. Shady café that's an expat fave for its palate-tingling, well-priced Thai food (most mains around Rp25,000), including deliciously chilli-hot green chicken curry and creamy, peanut-laced massaman (beef or veg). Get there before 7pm to guarantee a table.

Warung Murah Jl Arjuna. A popular haunt for economy-minded expats: select your own nasi campur medley from various curries, tempeh chips, corn and potato fritters and chilli-spiked water spinach. From Rp12,000 for a plate of two meat servings, two veggies plus rice.

Warung Yogya Jl Padma Utara 79. Another busy, unpretentious and cheap Indonesian eatery, where nasi campur (veg or non-veg) costs Rp12,000 and juices Rp5000. Also does *nasi pecel* and fried chicken.

Wayan and Friends Jl Padma. Favourite Aussie hangout that's known for its design-it-yourself sandwiches (from Rp26,000): crusty white baguettes filled with your chosen mix of fillings such as cold cuts, tuna, cheese and salads.

Seminyak and Petitenget

Antique Abimanyu Arcade 7, Jl Dhyana Pura. Dinner only; closed Mon. Creative Asian cuisine with strong Thai, Japanese and Indonesian influences: try the *nasi jingo Antique*, a tasty chicken-and-*urap* combo steamed and served in a banana leaf, or the "prawn delight" (prawn samosas, skinny spring rolls and fritters), and finish up with the irresistible chocolate passionfruit tart. Cosy, unpretentious and good value (mains from Rp32,000–45,000).

Café Moka Jl Raya Seminyak. Wholemeal loaves, baguettes and imported Parma ham make this a perfect place for a lunchtime sandwich (from Rp26,000), or indeed for one of its famously good coffees (soya milk also available) and a millefeuille or tarte tatin.

Café Tahu Jl Raya Petitenget. *Tahu* means tofu and this is the place for your soy-bean fix with over 20 different tofu-based dishes on offer, from deep-fried combos to salads, stir-fries to soups. Don't expect haute cuisine, but it's cheap at Rp9000 a dish, and there are some seafood options as well.

Desa Seni Jl Kayu Putih 13, Pantai Berewa, Canggu; see map, p.97. All the vegetables used in the kitchen at this charismatic little boutique village hotel (see p.112) are organic, grown either in the hotel garden or up in the hills. The dishes (Rp45,000–65,000) are delicious: scrumptious house salad made with pomelo and gorgonzola;

mouthwatering Portobello porcini and shitake mushroom rigatoni; grilled tuna topped with Spanish-olive salsa.

Kafé Warisan Jl Raya Kerobokan 38, about 1km north of the Jl Laksmana turn-off ☎0361/731175. Mon–Sat lunch & dinner, Sun dinner only; reservations strongly advised. Outstanding, beautifully cooked gourmet French food – grilled rosemary rack of lamb, duck confit, raspberry soufflé – is the hallmark of this long-running expats' favourite overlooking the ricefields. Also has an extensive wine list from all over the world. A genuine fine-dining experience. Mains Rp95,000–150,000.

Khaima Jl Laksmana. Atmospheric Moroccan place with authentic decor, belly dancers on Fri & Sat nights, and deliciously tender meat dishes (Rp45,000–85,000). Especially good are the perfectly spiced tajines made with imported Australian lamb, and the top-notch beef *mechoui* (kebabs).

Ku dé Ta Jl Laksmana ☎0361/736969. Opinions are divided on this, one of the most talked-about restaurants in south Bali. The look – a dramatic, mostly open-roofed beachfront piazza embraced by a cloister that frames a stunning sea-view – is as breathtaking as the prices (Rp190,000 for saffron risotto, Rp270,000 for prosciutto-wrapped veal cutlet) and the modern-European food is variable. Many people prefer to soak up the setting over a long, lazy breakfast, but others come for the club vibe that dominates from 11pm–2am.

La Lucciola Jl Petitenget, accessed only by a footpath from the Pura Petitenget car park, or from the beach ☎0361/730838; reservations advisable, especially for a sea-view table. Built right on the edge of the shore, this open-sided pavilion is a popular spot for sunset cocktails and romantic dinners under the glow of flaming torches. The Mediterranean-inspired menu (Rp40,000–150,000)

doesn't always live up to the setting, but includes prawn and snapper pie, grilled Black Angus steak, and an array of tropical fruit sorbets.

Pantarei Jl Raya Seminyak 17. Mid-priced place that focuses on Greek classics including perfect mixed-meat kebabs (Rp65,000), good salads (Rp18,000), grilled swordfish, some mezze dishes and the famous (and famously expensive, at Rp150,000) spaghetti lobster.

Queen's Tandoor Jl Raya Seminyak 73. Notably good Indian food served in stylish surrounds, either on the streetside terrace or in the upstairs dining room. Opt for the especially delicious chicken curry with cashew nuts, the creamy dhal makhani, or the mutton kadai – or come at lunchtime to sample a bit of everything in the veg and non-veg thalis. Most mains cost Rp40,000–55,000.

Saté Bali Jl Pantai Kayu Aya ☎0361/736734. Tiny, inviting place specializing in classy, authentic Balinese cuisine, especially sates, meat and seafood *rijsttafels* (Rp160,000 for two), *ayam betutu* (spicy chicken that's slow-cooked overnight), and minced duck in spiced coconut milk. Also runs cooking classes (see p.123).

Trattoria Jl Laksmana ☎0361/737082; opens evenings only and doesn't accept credit cards. Outstanding, home-style Italian cuisine where the extensive, constantly rotating menu may include rucola salad with artichoke hearts, octopus-stuffed ravioli, spinach pappardelle with mushrooms and cream, and any number of thin-crust pizzas. Most mains cost Rp35,000–45,000 and the house Côtes du Rhône is reasonable at Rp70,000 a half-litre. Very popular, so worth booking.

Zula Jl Dhyana Pura 5. Tasty vegetarian fare, predominantly organic, including nasi campur-style "planet platters" (Rp40,000), daily grain specials, booster juices, soya-milk smoothies, interesting salads and lots more.

Nightlife and entertainment

Kuta–Legian–Seminyak has the liveliest and most diverse **nightlife** on the island, with dozens of clubs and bars, many featuring live bands. Most places stay open until at least 1am, with several clubs continuing to churn out the sounds until 6am; there are always plenty of metered taxis running down the main drag.

Women are unlikely to get serious hassle, although you will get seriously chatted up by the resident gaggle of **gigolos** who haunt the dancefloors and bars. Most of the long-running Kuta clubs now try to discourage this by making locals pay a cover charge (redeemable against beer), but it's still very much part of the Kuta scene. Female prostitution is also on the increase.

Drugs are also part of the Kuta scene and are widely available, but be aware that police setups are quite common and even the possession of small quantities for personal consumption can land you with a ten-year jail sentence.

Cultural entertainment doesn't get much of a look-in around Kuta, but tour agents can organize trips to local dance shows and there's a cinema on the edge of the resort.

Bars, clubs and live music

Kuta's nightlife is mostly loud, laddish and good-humoured. It's the home of the jam jar (lethal, pint-sized cocktails of multiple spirits and mixers) and countless happy hours, and the province of drunken Australians and partying backpackers; just start at *Paddy's Pub* and follow the crowds. Up in **Legian, Seminyak and Petitenget** the scene is more self-consciously sophisticated, with an ever-changing choice of trendy little dance- and lounge-bars, a number of very chic spots, plus several **gay bars** on Jalan Dhyana Pura. All the clubs stage frequent live-music and special events, listed in the free fortnightly **magazine** *the beat*, which is available at restaurants and nightlife venues.

Kuta and Tuban

Apache Reggae Bar Jl Legian 146. Kuta's primary reggae spot is dark and loud, with a sunken dance-floor and dread-heads grooving to the Rasta beats played by the four house bands and resident DJs. Nightly 11pm–2am.

Bagus Pub Poppies 2. Large and loud tourist restaurant and video bar.

Bounty Discotheque Behind *Paddy's* on Jl Legian, just south of Poppies 2 intersection. Infamous hub of bare-chested Australian excess, housed in and around a novelty replica of Captain Bligh's eighteenth-century galleon. DJs play hip-hop and mainstream dance music, bands (mostly rock and punk) do their stuff at one of the live-music stages, and foam parties happen a lot. Jam jars are of course the signature drink. 6pm till late.

Espresso Jl Legian 83. Capacity crowds at this small and always rockin' live-music bar where punters with decent voices or guitar-playing skills are often invited to join in. Nightly 8pm–3am.

Hard Rock Café Jl Pantai. This place has a good reputation for its live music (including from Balinese bands) and stage shows, which attract huge crowds of Asian visitors. Check flyers for big-name appearances. Most shows start at 11pm; closes 2am (weekends 3am).

Kama Sutra Jl Pantai Kuta. Large, plush club and live-music venue that attracts capacity crowds of domestic and other Asian tourists with big-name bands from Jakarta and beyond.

mBargo Jl Legian, just north of Poppies 2 intersection. Great music from hip-hop and R&B DJs ensures packed dancefloors every night at this trendy lounge bar and dance club that's brought a dash of sophistication to the Kuta scene. Opens at 8pm but kicks off from 1–4am.

Paddy's Pub Jl Legian 66, just south of Poppies 2 intersection. Part of the *Bounty* complex and just as popular, this huge, open-sided place gets crammed with Australian drinkers who need little encouragement to enter the frequent drinking competitions and foam parties. Regular live music and reasonably priced beer (happy hour 7.30–11pm), plus a fair few working girls. Daily 4pm–4am.

Sky Garden Lounge Upstairs at the *ESC Urban Food Station* restaurant, Jl Legian 61, across from the Poppies 2 intersection. DJs, regular margarita nights, comfy chairs on a small, shrub-lined terrace and a fourth-floor view across to the Ground Zero monument makes this intimate, open-sided bar a more classy place for a cocktail than nearby *Paddy's*.

The Wave Jl Pantai Kuta. Three-in-one venue occupying a prime beachside spot, with the surf 'n' turf *SailFin* restaurant and coffee terrace upstairs and an a/c club (nightly 8pm–2am) at street level. The club hosts regular live music from local indie bands, and has DJs, theme nights, and "sexy dancers". Most events cost Rp20,000 including one beer.

Legian, Seminyak and Petitenget

Breeze At the *Samaya* hotel, Jl Laksmana, Petitenget. Unfurl yourself along the breeze-cooled, al fresco sofas that line the shorefront boardwalk, enjoy the unparalleled sea-view, swaying paper lanterns and illuminated palm trees, and hopefully you won't mind paying the top-dollar prices at this swanky hotel spot (Rp70,000 for a cocktail, Rp80,000 for a glass of wine).

De Ja Vu Jl Pantai Arjuna 7X, Legian. Happening, sleek and slender beach-view lounge-bar whose in-house DJs spin progressive house, electro and chill-out sounds to big crowds. Nightly 9pm–4am.

Double Six ("66") Jl Pantai Arjuna, Legian. Large, lively, Legian institution that's currently massive with the loved-up gay crowd who congregate here after 2am for the hardcore dance music. The airy, open-sided dancefloor can pack in 1500 ravers and is often fronted by visiting big-name DJs (check flyers for info). Nightly 11pm–6am; Rp30,000 including one free drink.

Hulu Café 23A Jl Sahadewa, Legian. Cosy café-bar that's famous for its drag cabarets, performed twice nightly at 10pm & 11.15pm, free to anyone who cares to stop by for a drink. Daily from 1pm.

Hu'u Jl Laksmana, Petitenget. There's style and atmosphere aplenty at this hip drink 'n' dine experience that is constantly giving itself new looks. Sofas and beanbag mattresses under the trees invite you to lounge or you can do the romance thing at the candlelit tables set around

the gem-like swimming pool. A mellow lounge-band entertains until the DJ takes over around midnight and the pace ratchets up, aided by the bar's famous lychee Martinis and unusual shots. Daily noon–2am.

Jaya Pub Jl Raya Seminyak 2, Seminyak. Fairly sedate live-music venue and watering hole that's popular with older tourists and expats. Daily 5pm–2am.

Kudos Jl Dhyana Pura, Seminyak. Big with the gay crowd, this DJ lounge and dance bar hosts regular drag, cabaret and go-go shows, though everyone's welcome. Nightly 9pm–4am; Rp30,000 incl one drink on Sat.

Q Bar Jl Dhyana Pura, Seminyak. Seminyak's main gay venue stages different events every night, including drag shows, cabarets and retro nights. Most of the action is downstairs around the dimin-utive dancefloor, while upstairs is the chill-out zone and restaurant. Daily 4pm–2am.

Entertainment

The traditional Balinese **dances** the Kecak and the Barong are performed every day in Denpasar (see p.94) and Batubulan (see p.170), both well worth seeing and within easy reach of Kuta. Tour agencies charge US$10–15 per person, including return transport but if you make your own way there, tickets on the door cost just Rp50,000.

Kuta's Cineplex **cinema** is inside the Mal Bali Galleria shopping complex at the Simpang Siur roundabout on Jalan Bypass Ngurah Rai, near the road to Sanur (☎0361/767021; Mon Rp15,000, Tues–Fri Rp20,000, Sat & Sun Rp25,000). Most mainstream films are shown in their original language with subtitles; the weekly freebie *What's Up? Bali* publishes the programme, as does the English-language weekly *The Bali Times*.

Shopping

Kuta–Legian–Seminyak has the best and most diverse **shopping** in Bali, especially for clothes, kids' wear, surfing gear, homewares and souvenirs. And there's nowhere better to start than on Jalan Legian, whose six kilometres of shops begin at the southern end with an emphasis on cheap, mass-market stuff and gain in style and price as you reach Seminyak.

For basic necessities, cosmetics, groceries and kids' items, head for either the **Matahari department store** in Kuta Square (daily 10am–10pm), or the colossal seafront **Discovery Shopping Mall** (10am–11pm) in south Kuta/ Tuban; Discovery is also not a bad one-stop shopping venue, packed with scores of international and local brand-name clothing stores plus several beachside cafés for sustenance. You can also get **mobile phones** and local SIM cards at Matahari and Discovery, as well as at any of the countless little mobile-phone shops throughout the resort. Most stores stay open until at least 9pm.

Serious shoppers should plan their campaign with the exhaustive **retail therapy guidebook** *Shopsmart Bali & Lombok* (reviewed on p.474), on sale at Periplus.

Books, DVDs and mu...

There are second hand **bookstores** along ...
Jalan Padma Utara, but prices are not as ...
The resort is full of shops selling recently ...

Bombocraft Jl Pantai Kuta 8C, Kuta. Handmade musical instruments, mainly African-inspired *jimbeh* drums carved from teak and mahogany, and bamboo didgeridoos.

Periplus This outstanding chain of English-language bookshops has branches at Discovery

Sho...
Bypa...
Made...
on Jl Ku...

Bali Harum Jl Pantai Kuta 28A, Kuta, and ...
419, Legian. Small, local chain speciali...
prettily packaged aromatherap...
oils and incense. ...
Bintang Capture Shop #...
2, Kuta. Capture ...
some take-h...
T-shirts ...
ap...

SOUTH BALI

shopping

Clothes and jewellery

Bali's **clothing** industry is based here, and the shops ... ...at designs.
The most stylish and exclusive boutiques are on north... ...Legian and Jalan Raya Seminyak.

Animale Kuta Square. One of Bali's most popular womenswear chains, with a good line in stylish, unstructured trousers, dresses and tops.

Biasa Jl Raya Seminyak 36. Specializes in elegant chiffon, cotton and silk clothing for women.

Body and Soul Kuta Square and Jl Legian 162, Kuta, plus a factory outlet at Jl Raya Seminyak 16C. Young street and beach fashions.

Fairy Shop Jl Padma Utara. Paradise for pint-sized princesses: cheap, shiny fairy dresses in every shade of pink plus the requisite accessories. From Rp80,000.

Harry Shop Jl Padma. Selling billions of beads strung – by hand – in a thousand different ways, this is one of several shops in this part of Legian specializing in cheap beaded necklaces, bracelets and belts. Try also the bead shops south down Jl Legian from Jl Padma.

Jonathan Gallery Jl Legian 109, Kuta. Stunning, idiosyncratic (and expensive) silver and semi-precious jewellery, plus some antique trinkets from other parts of Indonesia.

Kuta Kidz Jl Pantai Kuta (Bemo Corner) and Jl Bakung Sari. Bright fabrics and cute designs for boys and girls under 12.

Paul Ropp Jl Raya Seminyak 39, and Jl Laksmana 68, Seminyak. Expensive, elegant, boho-chic fashions hand-tailored from stunning silk and cotton fabrics that are all custom-made in India.

Pithecan Throbus Jl Pantai Kuta, and Jl Legian 368, Kuta. Attractive traditional batik-print sarongs, shirts and skirts, and unusual, classy handicrafts.

Suicide Glam Jl Poppies 2 and Jl Legian. Well-made, fair-trade, punk-metal-chic clothes, designed to evoke "maximum rock 'n'roll couture", so lots of skinny black outfits with attitude.

Surfwear shops Dozens of outlets including Jungle Surf, Mambo, Quiksilver, Rip Curl and Surfer Girl – along Jalan Legian and every other shopping street in the resort. All stock brand-name surf- and skate-wear, plus some surfing equipment.

Uluwatu Jl Pantai Kuta and several branches on Jl Legian. The original Balinese chain specializing in white, handmade Balinese lace and cotton clothes.

Handicrafts, souvenirs and homewares

The shops and stalls that line Poppies 1 and the Kuta end of Jalan Legian are the place to start looking for **artefacts**, **antiques** and other **souvenirs** from all over Indonesia. As with fashions, the most interesting and better-made **handicrafts** and **homewares** are found in the shops of Legian and Seminyak.

Arin 93 Gallery Gang Kresek 5, off Jl Bakung Sari, south Kuta. Batik, oil and mixed-media paintings in traditional, surrealist and modern styles by master artist Heru, plus cheaper pictures by his students (from Rp50,000). Heru also gives batik-painting lessons (see "Courses and classes", p.123) and sells dyes and waxes.

Ashitaba Jl Raya Legian 353, Legian, and Jl Raya Seminyak 6, Seminyak. Intricate *ata*-grass basket-ware from Tenganan, fashioned into everything from mats to bowls.

Asialine Jl Legian 457, Legian. Hand-painted batik-print masks, picture frames and boxes from Java, plus other tasteful artefacts from across Indonesia.

121

...l Legian
...zing in
...iletries, soaps,

..., between Poppies 1 and
...at Bintang hangover feeling with
...ome Bintang Beer merchandise:
..., stubby holders, drinks mats, cuddly toys
...d more.

Disini Jl Raya Seminyak 6, Seminyak. Known for its fine cotton and linen sheets, pillowcases and bed covers, which come in a range of charming, natural dyes.

Haveli Jl Raya Seminyak 15, Seminyak. Upscale homewares, including hand-woven cotton drapes, tablecloths and cushions.

Senso Jl Dhyana Pura 4C, Seminyak, and Jl Raya Basangkasa 13, Seminyak. Eye-catching droplet-shaped polymer lights with easy-to-change fabric covers in dramatic designs. Very light to transport.

Toko Kuta Suci Pasar Kuta, Jl Blambangan 127, south Kuta. Supplier of workaday offertory paraphernalia to local residents, including cheerily painted square offering-baskets (*sok*) and wooden pedestals for fruit offerings (*dulang*).

Sarongs and traditional textiles

The cheapest places to buy everyday rayon and cotton **sarongs** are the street stalls and art markets of Kuta.

Lucy's Batik Jl Raya Basangkasa 88, Seminyak. Breathtakingly beautiful collection of Javanese batik sarongs and scarves, from the cheapest stamped cotton wraps (from Rp65,000) to hand-drawn batik cotton sarongs in intricate designs and exquisite silk sarongs (some woven with pineapple leaf fibre) that cost up to Rp2,000,000 and may take four months to make.

Sely Sumba Ikat Jl Raya Basangkasa, Seminyak. Distinctive, mass-produced "primitive style" *ikat*

wall hangings, scarves, bags and jackets from Sumba and Flores.

Ucho Bali Jl Arjuna 28X, Legian. One of many shops on this road devoted to bright, modern rayon sarongs in a variety of looks (tie-dyed, beachy, lurid); around Rp17,000.

Wira's 50m south of Supernova Supermarket, Jl Raya Kuta. Enormous emporium stuffed full of fabrics sold by the metre, with everything from plain linen to thick cotton weaves and brightly printed rayons.

Spas and beauty treatments

Many of Kuta's high-end hotels have their own spas but there are also plenty of smaller **day-spas** offering good-value massages, facials and manicures, as well as the ever-popular Javanese *mandi lulur* body scrub (for a description of this see p.54). Or head down to the sea for a beach-side kneading from one of Kuta's conical-hatted massage women (Rp30,000 for 30min).

Bodyworks Jl Kayu Jati 2, Petitenget ☎0361/733317. Housed in earthy, Moroccan-style rooms set around a courtyard, this long-running and well-regarded treatment centre offers an extensive menu of massages (from Rp155,000) including Balinese, Javanese (*mandi lulur*), Thai, shiatsu, hot stone and aromatherapy. Hair treatments, manicures, facials and waxing are also available.

Jari Menari Jl Raya Basangkasa 47, Seminyak ☎0361/736740, ⓦwww.jarimenari.com; reservations advisable. One of Kuta's most raved about massage centres, not least because its masseurs are all male as, apparently, "they can maintain pressure more consistently from the beginning to

the end of the treatment". Offers various programmes and massage styles (from Rp200,000 for 75mins) and runs massage courses (see opposite).

Putri Bali *Wisata Beach Inn*, Gang Wisata, off Jl Padma Utara, Legian ☎0361/755987. Inexpensive treatments in charming massage rooms at this small, local, beauty salon, including hour-long *mandi lulur*, Balinese *boreh* (blood-circulation), and coconut (after-sun) scrubs for Rp75,000 each.

Sicilia Spa Jl Arjuna, Legian ☎0361/736292, ⓦwww.siciliaspa.com. Offers a range of popular massages and treatments (*mandi lulur* from Rp115,000) in its cute, airy little rooms.

Courses and classes

Balinese Cookery Saté Bali restaurant, Jl Pantai Kayu Aya 22A, Petitenget (℡0361/736734, ℮satebali@yahoo.com). Led by the former chef of Jimbaran's *Hotel InterContinental*; Rp250,000 incl lunch.

Batik-painting Arin 93 Gallery, Gang Kresek 5, off Jl Bakung Sari, south Kuta (℡0361/765087, ℮arin93batik@hotmail.com). Taught by painter and batik artist Heru at his home; 3-day workshops cost Rp500,000 incl materials.

Indonesian language Seminyak English Course, Gang Villa Lalu, off Jl Raya Seminyak, Seminyak

(℡0361/733342). Rp2,000,000–4,200,000 for 40 hours, depending on class size.

Massage Jari Menari, Jl Raya Basangkasa, Seminyak (℡0361/736740, ⓦwww.jarimenari .com). Day courses at this famously good massage centre, every Tues (9am–3.30pm; $170) and longer versions also available.

Yoga and meditation Desa Seni hotel, Canggu (see p.112 for details). Two or three times daily at Rp70,000/class; see ⓦwww.desaseni.com for the schedule.

Listings

Airline offices Garuda has a sales office and city check-in (4 to 24 hours before departure) inside the *Kuta Paradiso* hotel in Tuban (Mon–Fri 7.30am–4.30pm, Sat & Sun 9am–1pm; national call centre ℡0807/180 7807). For other international and domestic airline offices, see p.101.

Banks and exchange There are ATMs every few hundred metres throughout the resort and a Moneygram agent at Bank Danamon just south of the Poppies 2 intersection on Jl Legian. Be very careful about being ripped-off at exchange counters in Kuta: many places short-change tourists by using several well-known scams (see p.70 for details). One chain of recommended money-changers is PT Central Kuta, which has several branches on Jl Legian plus one on Jl Melasti. There's another reputable money-changer just a few metres north up Jl Legian from Bemo Corner, on the east side of the road, and in Seminyak go to Maspintjinra at Jl Raya Seminyak 16A. If you do get caught in a money-changing scam, contact the community police (see below).

Dentist Bali Dental Clinic 911, Mal Bali Galleria, Simpang Siur roundabout, Jl Bypass Ngurah Rai ℡0361/7449911.

Embassies and consulates See p.66.

Hospitals and clinics The nearest hospitals are in Denpasar; see p.95. In the Kuta area, most expats go to one of two very reputable small, private 24-hour hospitals on the outskirts of Kuta, both of which have English-speaking staff, A&E facilities, ambulance and medivac services: Bali International Medical Centre (BIMC) at Jl Bypass Ngurah Rai 100X, near the Simpang Siur roundabout on the road to Sanur ℡0361/761263, ⓦwww.bimcbali .com; and International SOS (Klinik SOS Medika), just a few hundred metres further east at Jl Bypass

Ngurah Rai 505X ℡0361/710505, ⓦwww .sos-bali.com. Consultations cost from Rp540,000. Smaller, cheaper places in the heart of the resort include Legian Clinic on Jl Benesari, Kuta, ℡0361/758503, which offers 24hr consultation and dental services, and La Walon Clinic on Poppies 1 ℡0361/757326. Nearly all the large, upmarket hotels have an in-house doctor.

Internet access You're rarely more than 500m away from an Internet centre here. Prices are competitive, with most places charging Rp200–300/min.

Left luggage All hotels and losmen will store your luggage if you reserve a room for your return; some charge a nominal fee. There's also left luggage at the airport (see p.100), at Internet Outpost on Poppies 2 (℡0361/763392; daily 9am–1am; large locker Rp30,000/day or Rp150,000/week) and, for Perama customers, at the Perama office, Jl Legian 39, Kuta (daily 7am–10pm; ℡0361/751875; Rp10,000 a week or part thereof).

Pharmacies Inside the shopping malls and department stores; on every major shopping street (see map for other locations); next to Legian Clinic 1 on Jl Benesari, Kuta; and at La Walon Clinic on Poppies 1.

Phones There are dozens of private wartels in the resort, most of them open from 8am–midnight and most offering calls at Rp7000/min whatever the destination. Most Internet cafés also have Skype (from Rp200/min).

Police The helpful and energetic local community police, Satgas Pantai Desa Adat Kuta, are English-speaking and in 24hr attendance at their office on the beach in front of *Inna Kuta Beach Hotel* (℡0361/762871). The government police station is at Jl Raya Kuta 141, south Kuta (℡0361/751598).

Post offices Kuta's GPO is on indistinct, unsignposted Gang Selamat, between Jl Raya Kuta and Jl Blambangan in Tuban (Mon–Sat 8am–5pm); services include parcel packing and poste restante. There are many small postal agents elsewhere in the resort, including on the ground floor of the Matahari department store in Kuta Square; see maps for other locations.

Travel agents Domestic and international airline tickets are available from the following agents, some of which also sell express boat tickets: Perama, Jl Legian 39, Kuta ☏ 0361/751875, ⊛ www.peramatour.com; KCB Tours, Jl Raya Kuta 127 (the main road to Denpasar, on the eastern outskirts) ☏ 0361/751517, ⊛ www.kcbtours.com; Satriavi Tour, *Bali Rani Hotel*, Jl Kartika Plaza ☏ 0361/751369 ext 179, ⊛ www.aerowisata .com. Gili Islands transport and accommodation booking at Island Promotions, The Gili Paradise Shop, Poppies 1 #12 ☏ 0361/753241, ⊛ www .gili-paradise.com. Pelni boat tickets from the Pelni office, about 500m south of Supernova Supermarket at Jl Raya Tuban 299 ☏ 0361/763963.

The Bukit peninsula and Nusa Dua

Some 4km south of Kuta, Bali's **Bukit peninsula** narrows into a sliver of land at Jimbaran before bulging out again into a harsh, scrubby limestone plateau that dangles off the far southern end of the island. Officially called **Bukit Badung** (*bukit* means "hill" in Bahasa Indonesia), the plateau has more in common with the infertile scrub of Nusa Penida across the water than with the generously lush paddies elsewhere in Bali. Farming is almost impossible here, but it's the dramatic, craggy coastline that fuels the local economy: surfers flock to the Bukit's famously challenging breaks, particularly those at Uluwatu and Padang Padang, while everyone else simply enjoys the glorious clifftop views from the burgeoning number of expat villas and coastal hotels.

This account follows an anti clockwise route around the peninsula, beginning at the fishing town of **Jimbaran**, which lies just a couple of kilometres south of the airport on the isthmus and has a fine beach and several luxury hotels. Continuing southwest, the road passes a number of pretty **surf beaches** before reaching **Uluwatu**, site of world-class breaks as well as one of Bali's major clifftop temples, perched on the island's far southwestern tip. Across on the southeast coast sits **Nusa Dua**, a purpose-built resort offering deluxe facilities but distinctly lacking in character, and its adjacent alter-ego **Tanjung Benoa**, a centre for watersports and cheaper accommodation.

Public **transport** in the Bukit is sporadic at best, so the best option is to rent your own wheels. Motorbikes are often more practical than Jeeps for negotiating the potholed tracks down to the surfing beaches.

Jimbaran

With its safe, crescent-shaped bay of soft, golden sand fronted by a string of well-spaced, mostly upmarket, hotels, **JIMBARAN** makes a quieter, slightly more authentic alternative to purpose-built Nusa Dua, and is just a few kilometres'

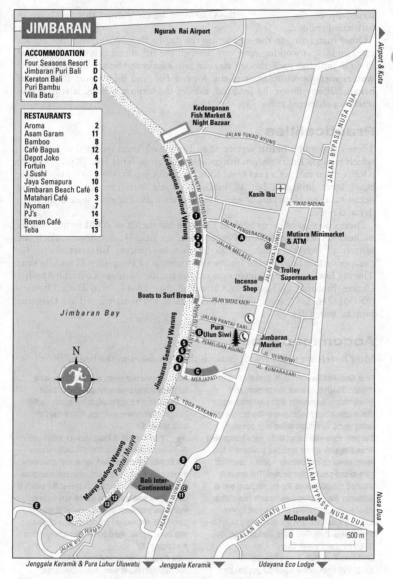

JIMBARAN

Ngurah Rai Airport

ACCOMMODATION

Four Seasons Resort	E
Jimbaran Puri Bali	D
Keraton Bali	C
Puri Bambu	A
Villa Batu	B

RESTAURANTS

Aroma	2
Asam Garam	11
Bamboo	8
Café Bagus	12
Depot Joko	4
Fortuin	1
J Sushi	9
Jaya Semapura	10
Jimbaran Beach Café	6
Matahari Café	3
Nyoman	7
PJ's	14
Roman Café	5
Teba	13

Kedonganan
Fish Market &
Night Bazaar

JALAN TUKAD AYUNG

Kasih Ibu

JL. TUKAD BADUNG

JALAN PENGERACIKAN

Mutiara Minimarket
& ATM

JALAN MELASTI

Trolley
Supermarket

Incense
Shop

Jimbaran Bay

Boats to Surf Break

JALAN BATAS KAUH

JALAN PANTAI SARI

Pura
Ulun Siwi

Jimbaran
Market

JL. PEMELISAN AGUNG

JL. ULUNSIWI

JL. KUMARASARI

JL. MERJAPATI

JL. YOGA PERKANTI

Bali Inter-
Continental

McDonalds

JALAN BYPASS NUSA DUA

JALAN ULUWATU II

0   500 m

Airport & Kuta

Nusa Dua

Jenggala Keramik & Pura Luhur Uluwatu   *Jenggala Keramik*   *Udayana Eco Lodge*

drive from the temptations of Kuta. Its location right next to the airport also makes it a handy stop at the beginning or end of a Bali holiday.

Jimbaran's raison d'être is **fish**, and every morning at dawn, the town's fishermen return with hundreds of kilos of sardines, tuna, mackerel, snapper and baby sharks for sale at the covered fish market in Kedonganan, the *banjar* at the far northern end of Jimbaran beach. The market stays open all day and you can join the locals and get your freshly purchased fillet grilled at one of the stalls just outside its entrance for about Rp6000. In the evening, the day's catch is served up on the seafront at the dozens of beach warung that specialize in barbecued seafood.

Other than lazing in the sun during the day (with a bit of plane-spotting for extra kicks) and working your way through the fish menu at night, there's little to do in Jimbaran itself, though you can rent kayaks and boogie boards from the **watersports** booth in front of the *Keraton Bali*, and the Airport Rights **surf break**, halfway down the Jimbaran side of the airport runway, is within easy reach via chartered *prahu*.

Practicalities

There's a sporadic **bemo** service from Denpasar's Tegal terminal to Jimbaran, which runs via Kuta's eastern fringes and then on to Nusa Dua (Rp,10,000; see p.83), or you can get a **taxi** from Kuta for about Rp30,000. No tourist shuttle buses serve Jimbaran, but all Jimbaran hotels run transport to Kuta and occasionally to Nusa Dua as well. Metered taxis also circulate around Jimbaran day and night.

There's no post office or bank in Jimbaran but there's an **ATM** in the Mutiara minimarket across from Jalan Pengeracikan on Jalan Raya Uluwatu. There are wartels all over the place and all hotels have (pricey) **Internet** access: for cheaper surfing head for the Internet centres spaced along Jalan Raya Uluwatu. The big hotels all have **doctors** on call, or try the 24-hour Kasih Ibu Medical Centre Jimbaran at Kompleks Citra Bali No. 13–14, Jalan Raya Uluwatu (℡0361/746 3382); more serious medical cases will be transferred to a Denpasar hospital (see p.95).

Accommodation

Most **hotels** are upscale with grounds that run down to the beach.

Four Seasons Resort South Jimbaran ℡0361/701010, ⓦwww.fourseasons.com /jimbaranbay. A favourite with honeymooners, this is consistently voted one of the top ten hotels in the world. Accommodation is in private Balinese-style villa compounds, each comprising three elegantly styled thatched pavilions – for living, sleeping and bathing – plus a courtyard garden and private plunge pool. The resort is situated cliffside above the far southern end of Jimbaran Bay and facilities include two clifftop infinity-edge swimming pools, a spa, tennis courts, a kids' club and complimentary babysitting service. Published rates start at US$630 ($700 for a sea view). ⑨

Jimbaran Puri Bali Jl Yoga Perkanti ℡0361/701605, ⓦwww.jimbaranpuribali.com. Rather stylish small hotel whose 42 charmingly designed cottage compounds each have an elegantly furnished bedroom (and separate living area in the more deluxe versions), garden bathroom and patio seating within their own walled garden. The large hotel pool is right on the beachfront. ⑧

Keraton Bali Jl Merajapati ℡0361/701961, ⓦwww.keratonjimbaranresort.com. This mid-sized, mid-range hotel has smart and tastefully furnished rooms housed in a series of Bali cottage–style buildings dotted around the peaceful tropical garden that stretches down to the beach. Facilities include a swimming pool, spa, tennis court and table tennis. ⑦

Puri Bambu Jl Pengeracikan, Kedonganan, north Jimbaran ℡0361/701468, ⓦwww .puribambu.com. This comfortable and deservedly popular place keeps its prices reasonable because there's no shorefront access. However, the beach is about 3min walk away and the 48 very large a/c rooms are positioned around a series of charming plant- and statue-filled courtyards, one of which also holds a good-sized pool. Upper-storey rooms are brighter. ⑤

Villa Batu Jl Pemelisan Agung 21A ℡0361/703186, ⓦwww.balivillabatu.com. Jimbaran's cheapest option comprises a dozen unusual losmen-style rooms (some rather dark) with adobe-look walls, funky bathrooms and the option of connecting rooms and a living area, all set in a compound across the road from the beach. Also here are two appealing villas, sleeping two to four, both with kitchen/living area and sharing a small pool. Rooms with fan ③ With a/c ④ Villas ⑤

Eating

Jimbaran is famous across Bali for its fresh fish served at the countless almost identical **seafood warung** strung along the beachfront. All the posh hotels have seafront **restaurants**, but to find the cheapest, most authentic local food you merely need to take a stroll along Jalan Raya Uluwatu.

The seafood warung

The **fresh fish barbecues** at Jimbaran's beachfront **seafood warung** are so good that diners travel here from Kuta, Nusa Dua and Sanur (often in bus-loads), and restaurants across the island try to re-create the taste in their "Jimbaran-style fish barbecues". There are over fifty of these warung, grouped in three clusters along the shore: the **Kedonganan** group is in the north, nearest to *Puri Bambu*; the **Jimbaran** collective is in the middle; and the **Muaya** restaurants are between the *Intercontinental* and *Four Seasons* hotels in the south. Both the Jimbaran and Kedonganan groups are run by village collectives.

The setup is similar in every one, with tables on the sand and **the day's catch** grilled in front of you over smoky fires of coconut husks. Lobster, prawns, red snapper, squid, mussels and crab are almost always on the menu. Though food is served during the day, the warung are at their liveliest from sunset; eat at the busier places to ensure that the fish really is fresh. Prices are competitive (Rp60,000–90,000 per kg of snapper with trimmings) and include a generous spread of rice and vegetables. In the past some warung had a reputation for rigging their scales and, though complaints seem to be less common now, you can always do your own scales check with a full bottle of water. The most commonly recommended warung in each group are labelled on the map on p.125.

Restaurants

Asam Garam Across from the *Intercontinental* at Jl Uluwatu 18X. There's classy international cuisine at this secluded spot within the grassy gardens of boho-chic *Villa Balquisse*. The menu ranges from tuna sashimi to lamb medallions, calamari risotto with ginger to five-spices crème brûleé (Rp50,000–125,000) and there's a kids' menu too.

Depot Joko Jl Raya Uluwatu, just south of the Jl Pengeracikan intersection. Locally popular restaurant serving prawns, chicken, fish and veg cooked half-a-dozen different ways, including Chinese style, sweet and sour, deep fried and in *angioso* sauce; nothing costs more than Rp13,000.

J Sushi Jl Raya Uluwatu 62. Japanese restaurant specializing in a dozen different sushi sets for around Rp78,000.

Jaya Semapura Jl Raya Uluwatu 33. Another no-frills local favourite that does Chinese and Indonesian dishes (mostly chicken and seafood) for a well-priced Rp10,000–15,000.

PJ's Southern beachfront, also accessible via Jl Bukit Permai, south Jimbaran ☏ 0361/701010. This *Four Seasons* restaurant has a Bali-wide reputation for exquisite, and pricey, Mediterranean food (Rp185,000–485,000), as well as for wood-fired pizzas with innovative toppings. It occupies a fine position in a couple of gazebos beside the sand and three times a week runs extravagant dining events on the beach: brunch on Sun, buffet with entertainment on Tues, and the spectacular candlelight gourmet Beds on the Beach dinner every Fri (Rp200,000–950,000 per person).

Shopping

Shopping is pretty low-key in Jimbaran, with just a few sarong and souvenir stalls operating along the beach, and normal Balinese town shops along Jalan Raya Uluwatu. The town-centre **market** across from Pura Ulun Siwi is worth checking out for its square offertory baskets (*sok*), and there's a shop that sells nothing but **incense** on the west side of the road between the market and Jalan Melasti. The place that draws in the coach parties though is the ceramic specialist **Jenggala Keramik Bali** (daily 9am–6pm), which is well known for its sophisticated range of unusual designs (at correspondingly high prices); their premises on Jalan Uluwatu ll houses their flagship store and factory, as well as a café and workshop space for kids' pot-painting classes.

Around the Bukit

Just south of Jimbaran, the road climbs up on to the limestone plateau, with views back across southern Bali. Once up on the "hill", past a massive limestone quarry, the typical **Bukit landscape** of cracked earth and leafless silver-grey trees begins, an eerily beautiful scene where the long brown pods of the ubiquitous kapok trees hang like bats from the bare, dry-season branches and the occasional bougainvillea bring dramatic flashes of pink or purple. The thin, dusty soil supports just a few crops up here, mainly cassava tubers, used to make tapioca flour, and grass-like sorghum, whose seeds are also pounded into flour. It's a tough existence so, not surprisingly, many locals have eagerly cashed in on the area's new status as prime real estate. Property development has taken off, and the Bukit is now home to an ever-growing number of expats' dream homes, villas for rent and tiny boutique hotels – most appealingly at **Bingin**, formerly just a surfers' hangout, now a lively little beach enclave.

A good place to get a handle on the Bukit's unusual ecology, and a perfect spot for bird- and butterfly-watching, is the environmentally conscious **Udayana Eco Lodge** (☏0361/747 4204, ⊛www.ecolodgesindonesia.com; ●), which is managed by the environmental organization the Indonesian International Rural and Agricultural Development Foundation and occupies a peaceful hilltop position within the grounds of Udayana University. The *Lodge* environs harbour a couple of short trails with good **bird-watching** potential (there are 50 local species, with kingfisher and bulbul the most common) and guests are provided with bird lists, reference books and binoculars. The ten rooms are comfy though not particularly stylish, and all have a/c and fans that run partly on solar power. There's a pool and restaurant, and bird-spotting trips are offered; the lodge is also home to a cricket club. It's 1km from the so-called *McDonald's* junction on Jalan Bypass Nusa Dua, a couple of kilometres southeast of Jimbaran (see map, p.82).

Garuda Wisnu Kencana (GWK)

Not far from *Udayana Eco Lodge*, but usually accessed via the main Jimbaran–Uluwatu road, the monumental **Garuda Wisnu Kencana** cultural park, or **GWK** (pronounced "Gay Way Kah"; daily 8am–10pm; Rp15,000, cars Rp5000, motorbikes Rp1000), is a massive and controversial project that's still being carved out of the hillside but welcomes tourists nonetheless. The focal point is a towering statue of the Hindu god Vishnu astride his sacred vehicle, the half-man, half-bird Garuda, which will measure 146m when eventually completed. Though it is intended to serve as a Welcome-to-Bali landmark for passengers arriving at Ngurah Rai Airport, 9km to the north, critics have deplored the commercial rather than religious motivation of the venture and accused GWK's supporters of trying to turn Bali into a Hindu theme-park (see p.467 for more on the "touristification" of Balinese culture). The build is way behind schedule but visitors can climb the partially constructed statue and enjoy the commanding views of south Bali's coastlines from the restaurant. Big concerts and other performances are also sometimes staged here.

Surfing beaches

The Bukit's greatest assets are the **surfing beaches** along its southwest coast – breathtakingly craggy shorelines that get relentlessly pounded by the most thrilling and tantalizingly difficult breaks in Bali. Where once only hard-core surfers would endure the pot-holed tracks to get to them, lightweight sybarites and party-hungry backpackers are now following suit as the roads get improved and new hotels are hollowed out of the clifftops. To date, the atmosphere in these secluded little enclaves – at **Balangan**, **Dreamland**, **Bingin**, **Padang Padang** and **Suluban** – is still pleasingly sand- and wave-oriented, with little room for the shops and glossy commercialism that dominate nearly every other beach resort in Bali (though some big resort hotels are in the pipeline). The swimming is variable however, and can be dangerous because of rips and reefs. The breaks are at their best from April to October when the southeast winds blow offshore.

Balangan and Dreamland

The quietest and most northerly of the surfing beaches is white-sand **BALANGAN**, a long, wild stretch of shoreline fringed by a shallow reef that makes swimming tricky but powers a speedy left-hand break at high tide. The atmospheric lava-stone *pura dalem* (temple of the dead) marks the northern limit of the beach and a handful of warung serving food and drink occupy the southern end, near the main break. You can stay up on the clifftop plateau here at *Balangan Sea View Bungalow* (T081/2376 1951, E robbyandrosita@hotmail .com; ●, *lumbung* ●), either in a room with a shared ocean-view terrace above the restaurant and pool, or in a *lumbung*-style bungalow that sleeps five. Road access to Balangan is via Dreamland, described below.

West around Balangan's rocky southern point is the famous **DREAMLAND** beach, a stunning chunk of coast with great surf, gloriously white if rather congested sands, and breathtakingly aquamarine waters. Reached via a long flight of steep steps, it's a popular spot both with day-trippers and surfers who come for the fast left and right peak and the chance of grabbing some unusually long rides. Unfortunately much of the access land around Dreamland beach is now part of the controversial **Pecatu Indah condo project**, which has resulted in the forcible relocation of the cliffside warung from the northern end of the beach into an unsightly concrete structure built into the channel that runs down to the shore. Those warung offering **accommodation** on the southern part of the beach were, at the time of writing, still fighting to keep theirs open: if they win, you'll still be able to stay at *Dewi's Warung* (T0815/555 1722; ●), which has simple rooms with shared bathrooms.

Access to both Dreamland and Balangan is via the ostentatious entrance to the Pecatu Indah condo project and its eighteen-hole **New Kuta Golf Course** (T0361/8481327, W www.hole17.com; $140), guarded by enormous statues of Garuda and Hanoman beside the main Uluwatu road. Follow the wide boulevards through the condo project for about 4km until signed down a short dirt track to the Dreamland parking area (Rp5000); for Balangan follow the signed road running north from near the Dreamland car park.

Bingin

Fast developing into the liveliest of the Bukit surf beaches, **BINGIN** enjoys the same great coastal scenery as its neighbours and equally rewarding **breaks** – short left-hand tubes close to shore and the long and peeling left-handers of "Impossibles" further out – but wins out with a superior choice of accommodation. The beach is soft and sandy, if a bit narrow, but as with all these wave-lashed, reefy little gems, be careful where you swim as currents can be treacherous and there are large expanses of shallow reef just offshore. Access to the beach is via two different sets of very steep steps.

To reach Bingin, take the **coastal road**, Jalan Labuhan Sait, which is signed west off the main Uluwatu road and then follow signs to Bingin, via a two-kilometre side road to the parking area (Rp3000 fee). There is also a four-wheel-drive-only track from Dreamland. *Jiwa Juice* restaurant on Labuhan Sait about 200m south of the Bingin turn-off has **Internet** access and fresh bread, while nearby *Warung Yeyes* does pizza.

Accommodation

The cheapest **places to stay** are the warung that almost literally tumble down the cliff-face, many of them built hard against the rock; the more comfortable options are on the clifftop.

Full Moon Warung Halfway down the northerly steps. Reasonably comfy accommodation in four upstairs en-suite rooms that all open onto a wide sea-view terrace. ②

Mama and Ketut At the top of the northerly steps. Ultra-basic, thin-walled rooms with shared bathrooms. ①

🏃 **Mick's Place** On the clifftop above the northerly steps ☎0812/391 3337, ⓦwww .micksplacebali.com. Occupying a stunning position right on the cliff edge, this lovely spot comprises just six exceptionally elegant, contemporary-styled circular huts, their open design making the most of the location. It's candlelight-only at night and there is a tiny infinity pool in the garden. You can get married here, too, if you want. ⑦

Pondok Indah Gung and Lynie A few metres back from the northerly cliff edge ☎0361/847 0933. Welcoming place offering a dozen rather tasteful, ochre-painted fan-cooled rooms set round a garden, some of them in pretty coconut-wood-and-thatch bungalows. ④

🏃 **The Temple Lodge** On the clifftop near the southerly steps ☎0813/3776 9477, ⓦwww .thetemplelodge.com. Enjoying an unrivalled cliff-edge view of the surf breaks, this creatively designed jewel has been constructed around existing rocks and trees from an inspired mix of limestone coral, reclaimed wood and Indonesian antiques. Its three sinuously shaped bungalows (sleeping 2–4) are beautifully appointed in individual style plus there's a pool, yoga classes and Ayurvedic-influenced cuisine. ⑦

Padang Padang

Back on Jalan Labuhan Sait, **PADANG PADANG**'s accommodation begins almost immediately, lining the roadside between the Bingin turn-off and the bridge that marks the steps down to the famous Padang Padang **break**. This is considered one of the classiest and most exciting surf spots in Indonesia, not least because of a twist in the final section. There are distinctive *lumbung*-style **bungalows** at the popular *Ayu Guna Inn* (☎0815/575 6294, ⓔayugunabali @yahoo.com; ②), 400m west along Jalan Labuhan Sait from the Bingin turn-off and about the same from the Padang Padang bridge, where you get a mattress on the floor, fan, balcony and private outside bathroom. Near the bridge, *Kongsi Inn* (①) has four simple losmen rooms, while almost next door the new, purpose-built *Guna Mandala Inn* (☎0361/847 0673; ②) is a spruce, modern place with twenty good, clean fan rooms in two-storey blocks plus a restaurant. The other side of the bridge, *Sunny* (☎0361/769887; ①) has seven unexpectedly huge brick-and-woven-bamboo huts beside the road. Within the main Padang Padang accommodation cluster you'll also find several restaurants, motorbike rental, exchange and Internet facilities.

Suluban

SULUBAN is another mesmerizing spot, its turquoise water, crashing white surf and olive-green seaweed framed by the distant golden curves of Kuta and Legian. But it's the famous **Uluwatu surf breaks** (named after the nearby temple) that are the headliners here: five separate left-handers, all of them consistent and surfable at anything from two to fifteen feet. Access to the breaks is either down the steep steps beside the ultra-posh *Blue Point* villas (parking Rp3000/car or Rp2000/motorbike) or from nearby *Uluwatu Resort*.

There's plenty of **accommodation** on the clifftop above the breaks and along the adjacent road: *Uluwatu Resort* (℡0361/769855, ⓦwww.uluwaturesort.com; ❼) occupies a prime spot along the cliff's edge and offers thirteen attractive rooms, stylishly furnished with four-poster beds and linen drapes, each enjoying an uninterrupted surf view from enormous windows and balcony. There's a pool too, and the panoramic café makes an ideal viewpoint for admiring the action below. More affordable accommodation is available at *Mamo Home Stay* (℡0361/769882; ❹) just beside the *Blue Point* parking barrier, 300m from the path down to the beach; its six large, solid, sparklingly maintained fan rooms are set around the garden of the family home. A little further back from the coast, the fourteen comfortable fan and a/c rooms at *Rocky Bungalows* (℡0817/346209; ❺) are about 500m further north, down a side road off the Uluwatu road, but still enjoy long-range sea views from their verandahs, and there's a pool here too. Heading south about 700m from *Uluwatu Resort*, on the road to Pura Luhur Uluwatu, the chilled and friendly surfers' favourite, *The Gong* (℡0361/769976, ⓔthegongacc@yahoo.com; ❷), run by ex-surfer Nyoman and family, has six fan-cooled terraced losmen rooms, rents motorbikes and sells warung-style food and travellers' breakfasts.

Pura Luhur Uluwatu

One of Bali's holiest and most important temples, **Pura Luhur Uluwatu** (dawn to dusk; Rp3000 including sarong and sash rental) commands a superb position on the edge of a sheer rocky promontory jutting out over the Indian Ocean, 70m above the foaming surf, at the far southwestern tip of Bali – 18km south of Kuta and 16km west of Nusa Dua. Views over the serrated coastline to left and right are stunning, and it's a favourite spot at sunset, especially with tour buses. The temple structure itself, though, lacks magnificence, being relatively small and for the most part unadorned.

Accounts of Uluwatu's early **history** are vague, but the Javanese Hindu priest Empu Kuturan almost certainly constructed a *meru* (multi-tiered thatched shrine) here in the tenth century. Six hundred years later, Nirartha, another influential Hindu priest from Java, added his own cliffside shrine here. Pura Luhur Uluwatu is now sanctified as one of Bali's sacred **directional temples**, or *kayangan jagat* – state temples having influence over all the people of Bali, not just the local villagers or ancestors. It is the guardian of the southwest, is dedicated to the spirits of the sea and its festivals are open to all; during the holy week-long period of Galungan, Balinese from all over the island come here to pay their respects.

The temple complex

Climbing the frangipani-lined stairway to the temple's **outer courtyard**, you'll get your first brush with Uluwatu's resident troupe of macaques, who are proficient at stealing earrings, sunglasses and cameras. The outer courtyard is dominated by the elegant **candi bentar** that connects this area with the middle courtyard, built of greyish-white coral blocks to an unusual winged design. Images of the elephant god Ganesh flank the entrance.

If you peer through the gate into the middle courtyard (only worshipers are allowed in), you'll see the **kori agung**, the archway that divides the middle from the inner courtyard, which is studded with mythological images and crowned by a three-pronged tower. The **inner sanctum** extends to the cliff edge and over its low walls you can see the three thatched *meru* and the stone *padmasana*. A tiny courtyard off the temple's outer courtyard contains a locked shrine housing an ancient statue, thought by some to be Nirartha, who possibly achieved his own spiritual liberation, or *moksa*, on this very spot.

You'll get some of the best **views** of Pura Luhur Uluwatu's dramatic position if you follow the pathway that heads off to the right, standing with your back to the temple stairway. This track winds its way along the cliff-edge for a few hundred metres, affording fine, silhouetted vistas of the three-tiered *meru* perched daintily atop the massive, sheer wall of limestone.

Practicalities

There is no public **transport** to Uluwatu, so if you don't have your own wheels the easiest option is to join a "Sunset Uluwatu" **tour** with a south Bali-tour operator for around Rp200,000. These are timed to take in the nightly performances of the **Kecak and Fire Dance** (Sanghyang Jaran) at Uluwatu (6–7pm; Rp50,000).

Nusa Dua and Tanjung Benoa

Bali's most artfully designed high-end beach resort luxuriates along a coastal stretch of reclaimed mangrove swamp some 14km southeast of Kuta. This is **NUSA DUA**, a pristine, gated enclave that was purpose-built to indulge the whims and smooth away the grievances of upmarket tourists, while simultaneously protecting local communities from the impact of mass tourism (see p.466 for the full story). The dozen or so five-star hotels here all boast expansive grounds running down to a white-sand beach, but other than the Bali Collection tourist-shopping complex and the Pasifika art museum there's nothing else in Nusa Dua: no losmen or mid-range hotels and no markets, *banjar* or noodle stalls.

There are more signs of real life along the narrow sand-bar that extends north from Nusa Dua. **TANJUNG BENOA**, as this finger-like projection is known, is dominated along its east-coast strip by more mid-market hotels, tourist-oriented restaurants, shops and watersports facilities. But west of its Jalan Pratama thoroughfare, village life rumbles on among the palm groves, an area well worth exploring by bicycle if only to remind you that you are still in Bali. Tanjung Benoa's chief drawback is the beach: the northern stretch is scruffy and unappealing, and though the smarter, more southerly, hotels have trucked in their own sand and cordoned off safe swimming enclaves, these areas still suffer from the revving of the jet skis hired from nearby watersports centres. In addition, Tanjung Benoa has the dubious distinction of being the centre of Bali's turtle trade (see box, p.134).

Sandwiched between Nusa Dua and Tanjung Benoa, the village of **BUALU** is where you'll find the densest concentration of *banjar*, temples, warung,

Don't confuse Tanjung Benoa with **Benoa Harbour** (Pelabuhan Benoa; described on p.152), which lies about a kilometre north across the water from Tanjung Benoa's northern tip, but is only accessible to the public by a circuitous land route. Fast boats to Lombok, Pelni boats to other parts of the Indonesian archipelago, sea planes, and many excursion boats depart from Benoa Harbour, not Tanjung Benoa.

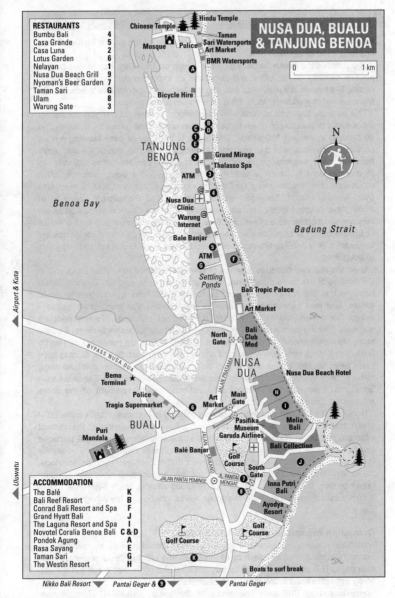

RESTAURANTS

Bumbu Bali	4
Casa Grande	5
Casa Luna	2
Lotus Garden	6
Nelayan	1
Nusa Dua Beach Grill	9
Nyoman's Beer Garden	7
Taman Sari	G
Ulam	8
Warung Sate	3

NUSA DUA, BUALU & TANJUNG BENOA

0 _____ 1 km

Hindu Temple
Chinese Temple
Taman Sari Watersports
Mosque
Police
Art Market
BMR Watersports
A
Bicycle Hire
C B
E D
TANJUNG BENOA
1
2
Grand Mirage
3 Thalasso Spa
ATM
@
4
Nusa Dua Clinic
Warung Internet **@**
Bale Banjar
Benoa Bay
Badung Strait
5
F
ATM
G
Settling Ponds
Bali Tropic Palace
Art Market
North Gate
Bali Club Med
NUSA DUA
BYPASS NUSA DUA
Nusa Dua Beach Hotel
Bemo Terminal
Police
Tragia Supermarket
Art Market
Main Gate
H
I
Melia Bali
BUALU
6
Pasifika Museum
Garuda Airlines
Bali Collection
Puri Mandala
Balé Banjar
Golf Course
J
South Gate
Inna Putri Bali
JALAN PANTAI PEMINGE
JALAN PANTAI MENGIAT
8
7
Ayodya Resort
Golf Course
Golf Course
K
Boats to surf break
Nikko Bali Resort
Pantai Geger & **9**
Pantai Geger

Airport & Kuta
Uluwatu

ACCOMMODATION

The Balé	K
Bali Reef Resort	B
Conrad Bali Resort and Spa	F
Grand Hyatt Bali	J
The Laguna Resort and Spa	I
Novotel Coralia Benoa Bali	C & D
Pondok Agung	A
Rasa Sayang	E
Taman Sari	G
The Westin Resort	H

family homes and commerce common to any small Balinese town, particularly along Jalan Srikandi. The cluster of tourist restaurants on the Bualu side of Nusa Dua's South Gate, and to a lesser extent the stalls around the Main Gate, are a useful enticement to explore beyond the too-perfect confines of Nusa Dua itself.

Tanjung Benoa and the turtle trade

Bali's role in the **turtle trade** is a complex one and the fishing port of Tanjung Benoa has long been at the heart of it.

The meat of the **green turtle**, which can weigh up to 180kg, has always been a popular delicacy on the island and also plays an important part in certain religious rituals. The flippers are made into sate and the flesh ground down into the ceremonial *lawar* served at weddings, tooth-filing ceremonies and cremations.

This puts the Balinese at odds with international conservation organizations, for Indonesia's population of green turtles is in severe decline (down by an estimated 90 percent in the last 130 years). This is partly because of **over-hunting** – it's a profitable business, with a single turtle fetching up to a million rupiah – and partly because many **nesting** grounds have disappeared. Female turtles will only lay their eggs on the beach where they themselves were born, which is often thousands of kilometres away. On Bali these include beaches at Kuta, Sanur, Nusa Dua, Tanjung Benoa, Serangan Island, Jimbaran and Pemuteran, nearly all of which have become either unusable because of tourist developments (turtles are very sensitive creatures and will not come ashore if there's too much light or noise) or unsafe because of hunters and egg poachers. And even where conditions are favourable, only one in a thousand eggs produces a turtle that survives thirty years to adulthood.

Over the last two decades a series of **laws** have aimed to reduce Bali's role in the decline of the turtle population, with varying success. In 1990 Tanjung Benoa became the island's only legal centre for landing, holding and trading green turtles, and nine years later the trade in green turtles was banned altogether – except for a fixed quota to be used for religious purposes. To few people's surprise, Tanjung Benoa fishermen continued catching turtles regardless, if a little more clandestinely, with holding pens and slaughterhouses here (and on nearby Serangan Island) now heavily guarded and hidden from outside eyes. Quotas have since been flouted, bribes offered and enforcers attacked. At one point, so many turtle importers from all over Indonesia were also using Tanjung Benoa as their base that it became the centre for an estimated eighty percent of the entire Indonesian turtle trade.

However, it's thought that things are now starting to improve. Where some 2000 green turtles were once landed at Tanjung Benoa every month, the current estimate is around 600, though that's still some way above the **ritual-purpose quota** of 5000 a year. An interesting breakthrough was made in 2005 when the Hindu Dharma Council of Indonesia decreed that substitutes such as drawings, cakes or other animals could be used for any endangered species, including green turtles, traditionally required for religious rituals. Such high-level global thinking could yet prove to be the most useful weapon in the struggle to save Bali's turtles.

Campaign organizations and hatcheries

Travellers can support the unnecessary slaughter of turtles by avoiding all products made from turtle flesh or tortoiseshell (the latter is illegal under an international CITES agreement), and by boycotting restaurants that serve turtle meat. Many **organizations** in Indonesia are dedicated to conserving local turtle populations, including ProFauna Indonesia in Denpasar (℡0361/424731, ⓦwww .profauna.or.id), and the Jakarta branch of the World Wide Fund for Nature (℡021/576 1070, ⓦwww.wwf.or.id). Several concerned groups have established small **turtle hatcheries** on Bali and Lombok, including near the Satgas police post on Kuta beach (see p.113), at Reef Seen Aquatics in Pemuteran (see p.347), and on the Gili islands.

Arrival

For information on **airport arrivals** and transfers to Nusa Dua, see p.100.

Public **transport** can work okay if you're just coming for a day out at the beach or shopping centre, but to get to one of the hotels in either Nusa Dua or Tanjung Benoa it's more efficient, and often more economical, to get a metered **taxi** (about Rp70,000 from Kuta). White Damri **buses** run from Denpasar's Batubulan bemo terminal (see p.170) to Nusa Dua's Bali Collection shopping centre, via the western edge of Sanur and the eastern outskirts of Kuta (hourly until 3pm; 1hr; Rp6500 flat fare); the sporadic **bemo** service from Denpasar's Tegal terminal (see p.83) also runs via Kuta's eastern pick-up point, then Jimbaran and Bualu before also terminating at the Bali Collection (45min; Rp10,000 flat fare).

Transport and tours

As the resorts, restaurants and shops are strung over a distance of some 6km from the northern tip of Tanjung Benoa to southern Nusa Dua, getting around can be a hot and time-consuming business. The shortest route between hotels is nearly always via the paved beachfront **walkway**, which begins in front of the *Ayodya Resort* at the far southern end of Nusa Dua and runs north to Tanjung Benoa's *Grand Mirage*; it takes about thirty minutes to walk from the *Ayodya Resort* to the *Bali Club Med*, or around an hour to the *Grand Mirage*.

Alternatively, the free Bali Collection **shuttle bus** does a loop between all the big hotels in both resorts and the shopping centre (approximately hourly, 10am–9pm), and pale brown Kowinu Bali **metered taxis** (☎0361/773030; Rp5000 flagfall, then Rp4000 per km) circulate around both resorts. Many hotels run free transport to Kuta.

Or you could capitalize on the flat terrain by **renting a bicycle** (around Rp20,000 per hour from hotels or Rp70,000 per day from independent outlets along Jalan Pratama). **Car rental**, with or without driver, can also be arranged through Nusa Dua hotels (from $35 per day) or from Tanjung Benoa rental outlets on Jalan Pratama. All the big hotels in Nusa Dua offer organized tours to major sights in Bali and beyond.

Accommodation

In **Nusa Dua**, four- and five-star **accommodation** is the norm. Rates booked via hotel websites or through agents start at around US$125, excluding tax and a possible high-season supplement, which makes them very good value.

Tanjung Benoa caters for a wider span of budgets, with some lower- and mid-range hotels at the north end of the peninsula and a burgeoning number of four- and five-star operations on the beachfront further south.

Nusa Dua

The Balé ☎0361/775111, ⓦwww.thebale.com. Super-sleek minimalist boutique hotel built from dazzlingly white Java stone in stepped terraces up the hillside. Each of the 29 pavilions has its own good-sized pool (at least 8m long) and tiny lawn within its private, screened compound. There's a notable absence of greenery and the look is stark chic – plus it's isolated, with the nearest (seaweed-farming) beach, at Pantai Geger, a couple of minutes' drive away – but it's hugely popular, especially with honeymooners. No kids under 16. Published rates from $520. ⑨

Grand Hyatt Bali ☎0361/771234, ⓦwww.bali.grand.hyatt.com. Massive 650-room resort whose terraced rooms and cottages (some of which are suitable for wheelchair users) are grouped into "villages" surrounded by sumptuous grounds filled with ponds, fountains and tropical blooms. Has an amazing series of free-form swimming pools complete with water chutes, bridges and sunken bars, plus a spa, tennis and squash courts, and a kids' club. Free shuttle bus to the *Bali Hyatt* in Sanur. ⑧

The Laguna Resort and Spa ⓣ0361/771327, ⓦwww.luxurycollection.com/bali. A luxury hotel whose 270 rooms are set around a series of seven lagoon-like swimming pools, complete with little sandy beaches, islands and waterfalls. The most expensive rooms have direct lagoon-access and all have 42-inch plasma TVs, DVD players and broadband access. There are six restaurants on site, a spa with charming hydro-therapy pool centre, and beachfront cabanas with Wi-Fi access. ⑧

The Westin Resort ⓣ0361/771906, ⓦwww.westin.com/bali. A typical *Westin* hotel, with a central block of 355 contemporary-styled rooms done up in neutral tones and centred round the trademark, ultra-luxurious "heavenly" bed, plus a spa, gym and kids' club as well as some enticing beachfront lounging pavilions. Some rooms have been modified for wheelchair users. Also has fresh-water, salt-water and kids' pools, plus broadband and Wi-Fi access in every room. ⑦

Tanjung Benoa

Bali Reef Resort Jl Pratama ⓣ0361/776291, ⓦwww.balireef-resort.com. Small, intimate, peaceful beachfront hotel with just 28 smart a/c bungalows (all with Wi-Fi and DVD player) lining a long, narrow tropical garden that runs down to the sea. There's a pool and spa, Internet access in the lobby, and a seaside restaurant and bar. ⑦

Conrad Bali Resort and Spa Jl Pratama 168 ⓣ0361/778788, ⓦwww.ConradHotels.com/Bali. Dramatic architecture, strong, uncluttered lines, pale cream stone and dark wood give this deluxe chain hotel a modish air, and the stylish rooms are surprisingly pretty. A 33-metre-long lagoon pool snakes its way right round the resort and all rooms have some sort of sea view, though the beach itself is not great here (the hotel has created its own sandy shorefront embankment). Service always

gets great reviews, there's a spa and kids' club, and some rooms are wheelchair-accessible. ⑧

🏃 **Novotel Coralia Benoa Bali** Jl Pratama ⓣ0361/772239, ⓦwww.novotelbali.com. Chic, charming and contemporary, this comfortable low-rise hotel spreads over both sides of the road. The cheaper rooms (non-beach side) all have a balcony or small garden and are furnished with cream drapes and coconut-wood furniture and flooring. Beach-side options include good-value tropical terrace bungalows with larger gardens and modern styling. The beautifully planted grounds run down to a decent stretch of beach and facilities include three pools, a children's club and tennis courts. Has a good baby-sitting service and is child-friendly. ⑥–⑦

🏃 **Pondok Agung** Jl Pratama 99 ⓣ0361/771143, ⓔroland@eksadata.com. Exceptionally welcoming and classy homestay, offering just eleven stylish and comfortably furnished rooms, all with good, contemporary-look bathrooms and some with terraces, in cottages overlooking the prettily designed gardens. Great value. Rooms with fan ② With a/c ③–④

Rasa Sayang Jl Pratama 88X ⓣ0361/771643, ⓔrsbind@yahoo.com. Small, friendly, budget hotel in central Tanjung Benoa offering twenty perfectly decent if rather unremarkable rooms with verandahs in a terraced block; upstairs rooms are lighter. Rooms with fan ① With a/c ②–③

🏃 **Taman Sari** Jl Pratama 61B ⓣ0361/773953, ⓦwww.tamansarisuite-bali.com. The mellowest place in Tanjung Benoa, comprising just ten nicely designed Balinese-Japanese-style a/c bungalows, each with a four-poster bed and garden bathroom, plus six deluxe villas. Aside from a spacious garden, there's a large lagoon-pool, a charmingly traditional spa (see p.140) and a good restaurant. As there's no beach access, the hotel runs free transport to its beach club on Pantai Geger (see opposite). ⑧ Villas ⑨

The resorts

Nusa Dua beach is long, white and sandy, and reasonably wide even at high tide, though at low tide the reef is exposed and you're better off beachcombing than swimming. Halfway down the shoreline, the land blossoms out into two little clumps, or "islands" (Nusa Dua means "Two Islands"), on which stand two of the area's original temples. The shorefront here is shaded with trees, and at weekends it's a popular picnicking spot, with the inevitable food carts in attendance and kids swimming in the sheltered water between the two islets.

Few people swim or sunbathe on the northern part of **Tanjung Benoa beach** as it's strewn with debris and dominated by watersports facilities and the constant whine of jet-skis. Shore-life is more appealing further south, from the *Bali Reef Resort* downwards, though still not as inviting as at Nusa Dua.

Inland Tanjung Benoa has a few points of interest, best absorbed by bicycle. At the northern tip, there's an impressive coral-carved Hindu temple, a gaudy red-painted Chinese temple and the restrained contours of a mosque within a few hundred metres of each other. Follow any of the lanes running west from the middle stretch of Jalan Pratama to find typical Balinese warung, fruit and veg stalls and family compounds set amongst the remaining stands of palm trees and bamboo.

For a different beach experience, head south of the Bali Golf and Country Club, towards the *Nikko Bali Resort & Spa*, and follow signs for **Pantai Geger** (about a one-kilometre drive from the golf course or fifteen minutes' walk along the beach from *Ayodya Resort*). Much of the broad, white-sand beach here is given over to seaweed farming (for more on which, see p.162), especially at the southern end, below the clifftop temple, Pura Geger (which is also accessible via a more southerly road). There are sunloungers for rent and the recommended *Nusa Dua Beach Grill* (see p.139). An informal taxi service operates from the beach, or it's Rp2000 to park your own car.

Sports and other activities

Tanjung Benoa is south Bali's **watersports** playground, with the protected waters off the peninsula's northern tip perfect for thrillseekers wanting to try parasailing, water-skiing, jet-skiing, kayaking, wakeboarding and the rest. At least a dozen similar watersports centres operate from shorefront premises along here, including Taman Sari (☎0361/772583) and BMR (☎0361/771757, ⊛www.bmrbali.com). Prices are the same at all of them: $15–25 per 10–15-minute session. Their **snorkelling** trips are less interesting, and overpriced at $25 per person; all boats make for the one location known as White Tower, a few minutes offshore, where the fish gather to gorge on the bread they're fed

▲ Parasailing off Tanjung Benoa

throughout the day. Be wary of **dive** courses and expeditions offered by Tanjung Benoa watersports centres as most of these places are not PADI certified, though some of their instructors may be. Sanur is better equipped for divers; see the box on p.146 for full information.

Nusa Dua's **surf breaks** catch the most swell of all the breaks in Bali, though currents can get pretty vicious. The main Nusa Dua break is a right-hander about 1km offshore (accessible by boat from a signposted point south of the *Ayodya Resort* and the golf course), while further north, a brief paddle beyond the *Bali Club Med*, "Sri Lanka" is a short, speedy right-hander.

The world-class, eighteen-hole, championship **Bali Golf and Country Club** (☎0361/771791, ⓦwww.baligolfandcountryclub.com) dominates the southern end of Nusa Dua and is open to all: green fees are $142 including cart and caddy, and you can rent clubs for $45.

For **bird-watchers**, the settling ponds around the mangrove swamp and sewage works to the north and west of Nusa Dua's North Gate are a rewarding place to spend an early morning; you're likely to see several species of kingfisher here, as well as lots of water birds including white-vented Javan mynahs, Sunda teals and white-browed crakes.

Nusa Dua is not known for its cultural highlights, but the new art gallery, **Pasifika: Museum Pacific Asia** (daily 10am–6pm; Rp50,000), just north across the access road from the Bali Collection, houses a wide-ranging and reasonably interesting, if poorly labelled, display of art and artefacts from Asia and the Pacific. Nearly all the Bali-related work here is by mediocre foreign artists, though famous expats also feature, including Arie Smit, Han Snel, Rudolph Bonnet, Le Mayeur, Covarrubias, Theo Meier and Donald Friend. More engaging are pieces by the Balinese artists, particularly the vivacious ink paintings from the 1940s by Batuan artist Ida Bagus Nyoman Rai, and works by modern masters Nyoman Gunarsa and Made Wianta. There's also an impressive collection of tribal masks and statues from Vanuatu, plus several dozen striking bark paintings from the Pacific Islands.

Eating and drinking

You'll find the cheapest and most authentic Balinese **food** at the warung along the back lanes of Tanjung Benoa and on Jalan Srikandi in Bualu village. At the pricier tourist restaurants on the **Bualu** side of Nusa Dua's South Gate the atmosphere is livelier and less stilted than in Nusa Dua, though prices are still pretty high. The same goes for **Tanjung Benoa**, which has a few notables among its many unremarkable identikit options. In **Nusa Dua**, the Bali Collection shopping complex houses a dozen restaurants, including ones specializing in Japanese, tapas, surf'n'turf and Balinese food. Recommended hotel restaurants include *Spice* at the *Conrad*, which serves contemporary cuisine from the Middle, Near and Far East (dinner only).

For those restaurants in Tanjung Benoa and Bualu that offer **free transport**, we have included the phone number.

Bumbu Bali Jl Pratama, Tanjung Benoa ☎0361/771256. Founded and managed by renowned expat chef and food writer Heinz von Holzen, this is the most famous restaurant in the area. It serves classy, if variable, fairly expensive Balinese cuisine, including duck roasted in banana leaves (Rp380,000 for two), seven-course *rijsttafels* (vegetarian and meat options, from Rp130,000),

seafood platters and sate set meals. Diners have an open-plan view of the chefs at work, and Balinese cooking lessons are offered here (see p.140).
Casa Grande Jl Pratama, Tanjung Benoa ☎0361/777942. In among the Indonesian standards and seafood dishes you'll find decent Greek food here (Rp39,000–80,000), including souvlaki and dolmades.

Casa Luna Jl Pratama, Tanjung Benoa ℡0361/773845. Popular spot with attractive decor that's known for its wood-fired pizzas, cooked in a traditional-style brick oven. Also offers plenty of interesting seafood dishes (Rp45,000–90,000), including Balinese seafood stew flavoured with lemongrass, and crab in a spicy nut sauce. Live music or dance performances nightly.

Lotus Garden Near the Main Gate on Jl Bypass, Bualu ℡0361/773378. The Bualu branch of this prolific Bali-wide chain serves moderately priced Italian dishes (Rp37,000–100,000), including its trademark wood-fired pizza, plus pasta and seafood.

Nelayan Jl Pratama 101, Tanjung Benoa ℡0361/776868. Deservedly popular mid-priced place offering good Balinese curries – vegetable, prawn, chicken and beef – and a range of fresh fish and seafood dishes (Rp30,000–95,000). Delicious rum-and-raisin ice cream, too.

Nusa Dua Beach Grill Pantai Geger ℡0361/743 4779; daily 8am–10pm. Breezy café on the low-key beach at Pantai Geger (see p.137) that's a favourite with expats. Watch the waves – and the seaweed harvesters – while scoffing the special fisherman's basket (Rp35,000) or any number of fish dishes and salads, and refuelling with a spirulina-laced power smoothie. Easiest road access is via the rough track to Pura Geger temple just south of *The Balé* villas.

Nyoman's Beer Garden Near the South Gate on Jl Pantai Mengiat, Bualu ℡0361/775746. Very popular, long-established, German-run place that spices up the usual tourist menu with German specialities such as sausage salad, steaks and rostis, plus tofu stroganoff and aubergine spaghetti for veggies (Rp45,000–90,000). Live music nightly, plus a decent cocktail menu.

Taman Sari Beside *Taman Sari* bungalows, Jl Pratama 61B, Tanjung Benoa ℡0361/773953. Known for its Thai cuisine (Rp53,000–71,000) – try the fried chicken with cashew nuts, or the spicy squid salad – and its quality fish meals, including slow-grilled marinated snapper, and lobster and asparagus salad.

Ulam Near the South Gate at Jl Pantai Mengiat 14, Bualu ℡0361/771590. Locally famous Balinese seafood restaurant whose menu includes grilled lobster with garlic butter, steamed crab, and seafood baskets (Rp45,000–85,000).

Warung Sate Jl Pratama, Tanjung Benoa ℡0361/772299. Another successful and enjoyable branch of Heinz von Holzen's specialist Balinese restaurants. Here the focus is on set meals based around sate sticks and giant spit-like skewers to share (seafood, meat and veggie versions; Rp27,000–125,000), all grilled over charcoal braziers and served with generous spreads of Balinese veg dishes including *lawar* (long-bean coconut salad), *urap*, *sambal*, rice cakes and peanut sauce. Wash it down with home-brewed *arak*, Hatten wine or local, organic Storm beer.

Shopping

Nusa Dua's shopping facilities are grouped in one centrally located complex, the **Bali Collection** (daily 11am–10pm), served by a free shuttle-bus service from all the big hotels in Nusa Dua and Tanjung Benoa. Though it has yet to be fully occupied, the complex offers a reasonable range of upscale, fixed-price retail temptations, including Sogo Department Store, Coco super-market, an Art Market handicrafts emporium, plus local and international brand-name stores such as D&G, Body and Soul, Roxy and Uluwatu Lace. Cheaper souvenirs and clothes are sold at the stalls on Jalan Pantai Mengiat just outside the Main Gate in Bualu and the small shops on Tanjung Benoa's Jalan Pratama.

Spa treatments

Many of the top hotels have **spas** offering a full menu of traditional Balinese, Thai, Swedish and aromatherapy massages, as well as the popular Javanese *mandi lulur* (see p.54); reservations are advisable.

Mandara Spa *Nikko Bali Resort*, south of Nusa Dua ℡0361/773337, ⓦwww.mandaraspa.com. Part of the respected chain of East–West spas, this location has beachside spa villas and a cave

Jacuzzi and offers the signature Mandara massage using two therapists and five styles.

Nusa Dua Spa *Nusa Dua Beach Hotel*, Nusa Dua ℡0361/771210, ⓦwww.nusaduahotel.com/spa.

One of the best-known and longest-established spas in Bali, this award-winning venue enjoys a beautiful water-garden setting. Treatments include a jet-lag massage.

Taman Sari Spa *Taman Sari* hotel, Tanjung Benoa ☎0361/773953, ⓦ www.tamansarisuite-bali.com. Charmingly traditional spa in the gardens of this low-key boutique hotel. Massages are cheaper than many, from $35.

Thalasso Bali Spa *Grand Mirage* hotel, Tanjung Benoa ☎0361/773883, ⓦ www.thalassobali.com. Specializes in therapies using heated sea water and seaweed.

Listings

Airline offices Garuda has a sales office and city check-in in the Bali Collection complex, just inside Entrance 1 (west entrance; Mon–Fri 7.30am–4.30pm, Sat & Sun 9am–1pm; 24-hour national call centre ☎0804/180 7807 or 021/2351 9999 if calling from a mobile). For other international and domestic airline offices, see p.101.

Banks and exchange There are several ATMS and moneychangers on Jl Pratama in Tanjung Benoa, and big hotels in both resorts do exchange. See p.70 for advice on moneychangers' scams.

Cooking lessons Balinese cooking lessons offered at *Bumbu Bali* restaurant in Tanjung Benoa (Mon, Wed & Fri; from $65 with chef and food writer Heinz von Holzen, or Rp250,000 with another teacher; ☎0361/771256, ⓦ www.balifoods.com).

Email and Internet At all major hotels (for about ten times usual street price) and some smaller ones; also far cheaper at a couple of places south of Nusa Dua Clinic on Jl Pratama in Tanjung Benoa, including at Warung Internet café.

Hospitals and clinics Nusa Dua Clinic, Jl Pratama 81A, Tanjung Benoa (daily 24hr; ☎0361/778098), staffed by English-speaking medics. All Nusa Dua hotels provide 24hr medical service. See also p.123 for expat-oriented clinics near Kuta and p.95 for Denpasar hospitals.

Sanur and around

With a fairly decent, five-kilometre-long sandy beach, plenty of attractive accommodation in all price brackets and a distinct village atmosphere, **SANUR** makes an appealing, more peaceful alternative to Kuta, and is not as manufactured as Nusa Dua. Because it lacks the clubs and all-night party venues of Kuta, it can seem a bit tame to younger travellers (hence its nickname, "Snore"), but there are plenty of restaurants to keep most visitors entertained, and nearly everyone appreciates the calmer ambience. It's also a good place to bring the kids, is south Bali's main centre for diving, and works well as a base for exploring the island: Kuta is just 15km to the southwest, Ubud a mere forty minutes' drive north and Nusa Lembongan a ninety-minute boat ride away.

The written history of Sanur dates back to 913 AD, as inscribed on the ancient stone pillar **Prasasti Blanjong**, which is enshrined in a glass case at the back of Pura Blanjong on Jalan Danau Poso in southern Sanur. You can't actually see the inscriptions, as the two-metre-high pillar is wrapped in cloth, but they tell of a Javanese king who arrived in Sanur to set up a Mahayana Buddhist government.

Fast-forward several centuries, and Sanur was chosen as the site of Bali's first major beach hotel in the 1960s, during the initial attempt at planned tourism during the Sukarno era. This was the **Grand Bali Beach**, an ugly high-rise that remains a blot on the Sanur seafront (currently part of the *Inna* hotel group). Though fashionable at the time, its architecture did not, thankfully, go down well locally and the Bali-wide edict against building anything higher than a coconut tree has held good ever since.

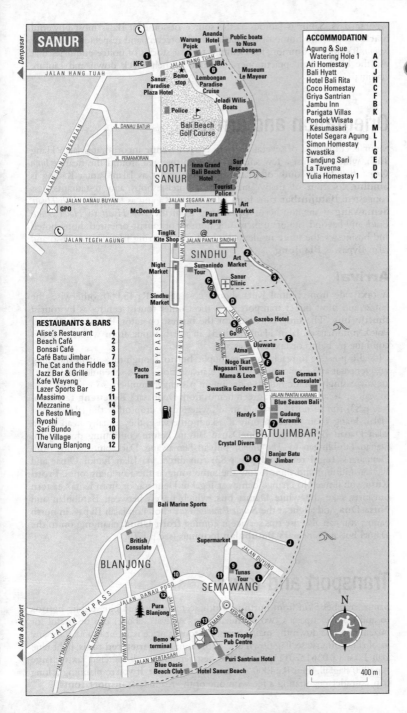

SANUR

Denpasar ◄

Kuta & Airport ◄

JALAN HANG TUAH

JALAN HANG TUAH

KFC

Warung Pojok

A

Ananda Hotel

Public boats to Nusa Lembongan

Sanur Paradise Plaza Hotel

Bemo stop

JBA

Lembongan Paradise Cruise

Museum Le Mayeur

Police

Jeladi Wilis Boats

JL. DANAU BATUR

JL. PEMAMORAN

Bali Beach Golf Course

NORTH SANUR

Inna Grand Bali Beach Hotel

Surf Rescue

JALAN DANAU BUYAN

JALAN SEGARA AYU

GPO

McDonalds

Pergola

Pura Segara

Art Market

Tourist Police

JALAN TEGEH AGUNG

Tinglik Kite Shop

JALAN PANTAI SINDHU

SINDHU

Night Market

Sumanindo Tour

Art Market

2

Sanur Clinic

C

4

D

3

Sindhu Market

Gazebo Hotel

5

Go

@

Uluwatu

E

GANG BUMI AYU

Atma

6

F

Gili Cat

JALAN PUNGUTAN

JALAN BYPASS

Nogo Ikat

Nagasari Tours

Mama & Leon

German Consulate

Swastika Garden 2

JALAN PANTAI KARANG

Blue Season Bali

G

Hardy's

Gudang Keramik

7

BATUJIMBAR

RESTAURANTS & BARS

Alise's Restaurant	4
Beach Café	2
Bonsai Café	3
Café Batu Jimbar	7
The Cat and the Fiddle	13
Jazz Bar & Grille	1
Kafe Wayang	1
Lazer Sports Bar	5
Massimo	11
Mezzanine	14
Le Resto Ming	9
Ryoshi	8
Sari Bundo	10
The Village	6
Warung Blanjong	12

Pacto Tours

Crystal Divers

Banjar Batu Jimbar

H

B

I

Bali Marine Sports

British Consulate

BLANJONG

Supermarket

JALAN DUKUH

J

SEMAWANG

Tunas Tour

9

11

K

M

Pura Blanjong

JALAN DANAU POSO

12

Bemo terminal

13

14

The Trophy Pub Centre

JALAN MERTASARI

Puri Santrian Hotel

Blue Oasis Beach Club

Hotel Sanur Beach

JALAN BYPASS

JALAN TANJUNG

JL. PANGEMBAK

JALAN SEKAR WARU

JALAN SUDAMALA

JL. KESUMASARI

ACCOMMODATION

Agung & Sue Watering Hole 1	A
Ari Homestay	C
Bali Hyatt	J
Hotel Bali Rita	H
Coco Homestay	C
Griya Santrian	F
Jambu Inn	B
Parigata Villas	K
Pondok Wisata Kesumasari	M
Hotel Segara Agung	L
Simon Homestay	I
Swastika	G
Tandjung Sari	E
La Taverna	D
Yulia Homestay 1	C

N

0   400 m

These days, Sanur is famous as the source of some of Bali's most powerful **black magic** and home of the most feared sorcerers and respected healers or *balian*. It's not uncommon, for example, to hear stories of police enquiries that use the black-magic practitioners of Sanur to help track down and capture criminals.

Orientation and arrival

Sanur is comprised of several districts. **North Sanur** incorporates Jalan Hang Tuah, which has just a few small hotels, and the area around the nearby *Inna Grand Bali Beach*; south of Jalan Segara Ayu as far as Jalan Pantai Karang is **Sindhu**, location of many guesthouses, hotels, shops and restaurants; less congested, **Batujimbar** runs from Jalan Pantai Karang as far as the *Bali Hyatt*. **Semawang** is the southern coastal strip from the *Bali Hyatt* to *Hotel Sanur Beach* and beyond, site of an increasing number of tourist-oriented shops, hotels and businesses; the more residential inland area covering Jalan Danau Poso and Jalan Bypass is **Blanjong**.

Arrival

A **taxi** ride from central Kuta should cost about Rp45,000; otherwise, the fastest and most direct transport from most other tourist centres is by tourist **shuttle bus**. The drop-off point for the biggest operator, Perama, is Warung Pojok minimarket, Jalan Hang Tuah 31 in north Sanur, from where you can continue by bemo or taxi if necessary.

It's also possible to reach Sanur by public **bemo**, though this entails travelling via Denpasar and changing at least once; in addition, bemo schedules in this area are increasingly erratic due to a decline in passenger numbers, so you may have to wait up to an hour. Dark green bemos from Denpasar's **Kereneng terminal** (see p.83) run to north Sanur (15min), where they drop off at the Jalan Bypass /Jalan Hang Tuah junction only if asked; otherwise, they usually head down Jalan Danau Beratan and Jalan Danau Buyan, before continuing down Jalan Danau Tamblingan to *The Trophy* pub in Semawang. Dark blue bemos from Denpasar's **Tegal terminal** (see p.83) run direct via Jalan Teuku Umar and Renon (30min) and then follow the same route as the Kereneng ones. **From Kuta**, you'll need to change bemos at Tegal in Denpasar or, from Kuta's eastern outskirts, take the white Damri **bus**, which travels between Batubulan and **Nusa Dua**, and alight at the *Sanur Paradise Plaza* hotel on Jalan Bypass in north Sanur; you can also use this service if coming **from Ubud**, changing on to the Damri bus at Denpasar's **Batubulan** terminus (see p.170).

Transport and tours

Sanur stretches 5km from north to south, so the green and blue public **bemos** to and from Denpasar's two terminals (see "Arrival", above) can be useful for buzzing up and down the main streets; the tourist price is about Rp3000 for any local ride. Otherwise, flag down one of the numerous **metered taxis**: light blue Bali Taksi (℡0361/701111) have the best reputation; all metered taxis charge Rp5000 flagfall, then Rp4000 per km, day and night. If you're planning a long trip, consider negotiating a fee with one of the roadside **transport touts**.

Most hotels and losmen will arrange transport to the **airport** for around Rp70,000, or you can hail a metered taxi for slightly less.

The most painless way of moving on to most tourist destinations is by **tourist shuttle bus**, tickets for which are sold by tour agents. The largest, most reliable operator is Perama and their main agent and pick-up point is Warung Pojok minimarket, Jl Hang Tuah 31 in north Sanur (℡0361/285592, ⍟www.peramatour .com); other Perama ticket outlets, where you may also be able to get picked up, include the more central Nagasari Tours, at Jl Danau Tamblingan 102 in Sindhu (℡0361/288096), and Tunas Tour, further south at Jl Danau Tamblingan 105, Semawang (℡0361/288581). Sample fares include Rp15,000 to Kuta/the airport, Rp40,000 to Padang Bai and Rp85,000 to Lovina. See "Travel details", p.164, for destinations and frequencies.

Moving on by **bemo** to anywhere on Bali entails going via the Denpasar terminals at Kereneng or Tegal. For **Kuta** and **Jimbaran**, it's easiest to go via Tegal (see p.83). For most other destinations, the Kereneng service is more efficient (see p.83), though you then have to make a cross-city bemo connection to the Ubung terminal for **the west and the north** (see p.318), or the Batubulan terminal for **Ubud and the east** (see p.170); the alternative for Ubud connections is to pick up the white Damri **bus** service, which runs direct to the Batubulan terminal (hourly until about 3pm), collecting passengers from near the *Sanur Paradise Plaza* hotel on Jl Bypass in north Sanur.

Sanur is the main departure point for **boats to Nusa Lembongan**, which leave from a jetty at the eastern end of Jl Hang Tuah in north Sanur. There are currently two public boats a day, one Perama shuttle boat, a couple of speedboat services and various charter options as well; see p.154 for full details. Gili Cat, a **catamaran service to Gili Trawangan and Lombok**, runs free transfers from Sanur to the departure point in Padang Bai (see p.377 for details); its Sanur office is at Jl Danau Tamblingan 51, Sindhu (℡0361/271680, ⍟www.gilicat.com).

The transport touts also **rent cars** and **motorbikes**, as do many hotels and tour agencies. JBA is one of the few Sanur agencies to sell car insurance, and will also supply a **car with driver**; it's located inside the compound of the *Diwangkara Hotel*, Jalan Hang Tuah 54 in north Sanur (℡0361/286501, Ⓔjbadwkbl@denpasar.wasantara.net.id). See Basics, p.39, for vehicle rental advice and price guidelines, and for first-hand recommendations of Sanur drivers check the archives of the online travellers' forums listed on p.74.

Sanur is an ideal place for **bicycles**, which are available for rent (Rp20,000–35,000) at spots all along Jalan Danau Tamblingan, near *The Trophy* pub in Semawang, and also along the beachfront promenade.

Most tourist businesses in Sanur offer **sightseeing tours** around Bali and to neighbouring islands. See "Listings", p.151, for some recommended travel agents.

Accommodation

There's a surprising amount of low-key, low-budget homestay **accommodation** in Sanur, none of it more than ten minutes' walk from the beach, and many of the mid-range and expensive hotels are also small, personable places, set in lovely gardens, the best of which run down to the shore.

Inexpensive and moderate

Agung & Sue Watering Hole 1 Jl Hang Tuah 37, north Sanur ⊕0361/288289, ⓦwww.wateringholesanurbali.com. Long-established, family-run place offering the cheapest rooms in this part of Sanur, only 250m from the beach. Set in two-storey blocks around a small courtyard, all rooms are of a high standard, clean and comfortable, and the larger ones have a/c and a streetside balcony. Also has a good restaurant. Very handy for boats to Nusa Lembongan, and there's luggage storage, too (Rp10,000 per day). Rooms with fan ❷ With a/c ❸

Ari (formerly Luisa) Homestay Jl Danau Tamblingan 40, Sindhu ⊕0361/289673. One of three very similar losmen clustered together in family compounds behind streetside businesses. Elementary but cheerful and very cheap accommodation in ten rooms, some with hot water. Large breakfasts included. Rooms with fan ❶ With a/c ❷

Hotel Bali Rita Jl Danau Tamblingan 152, Batujimbar ⊕0361/282630, ⓔbalirita@hotmail.com. A dozen exceptionally good-value Bali-style brick-and-concrete bungalows in a garden that's set well off the main road. All bungalows have a/c and quite chic furnishings plus partially open-air bathrooms. The top-end ones have kitchenettes and living rooms. ❸ With kitchen ❹

Coco Homestay Jl Danau Tamblingan 42, Sindhu ⊕0361/287391. Archetypal homestay offering just eight budget rooms (four upstairs and four down) behind the family art shop. Some of the cheapest accommodation in Sanur. ❶

Jambu Inn Jl Hang Tuah 54, north Sanur ⊕0361/286501, ⓔjbadwkbl@denpasar.wasantara.net.id. Tiny, quiet place next to, and owned by, JBA tour agent on the edge of the *Diwangkara Hotel* compound. The eight bungalows are set round a cute little shady garden complete with pool and gazebo. Rooms are a good size and the pricier a/c ones have a living area as well as a spacious verandah. Rooms with fan ❷ With a/c ❸ With living area ❹

Pondok Wisata Kesumasari Jl Kesumasari 6, Semawang ⊕0361/287824. Located just ten metres from the beach, this is the cheapest shoreside accommodation in Sanur. The dozen rooms are decent, standard losmen style, some of them with traditional painted and carved wooden doors. Rooms with fan ❸ With a/c ❹

Hotel Segara Agung Jl Duyung 43, Semawang ⊕0361/288446, ⓦwww.segaraagung.com. Occupying a very quiet spot down a beautifully floral residential *gang* just a couple of minutes' walk from the beach, this is an attractive place of sixteen bungalows set around soothing green lawns and a pool. The cheapest have fans and unusually big windows, the most expensive have a/c, and there are family options too. Rooms with fan ❹ With a/c ❺

Simon Homestay Down a tiny *gang* at Jl Danau Tamblingan 164D, Batujimbar ⊕0361/289158. Small losmen with six decent rooms in the family compound, set back off the main road. Rooms with fan ❶ With a/c ❷

Swastika Jl Danau Tamblingan 128, Batujimbar ⊕0361/288693, ⓦwww.swastika-bungalows.com. Deservedly popular mid-range place, whose 78 comfortable rooms (many with beautifully painted carved wooden doors and window shutters) are set round a delightful garden with three pools. Most of the fan-cooled rooms have pretty garden bathrooms and shrubbery-enclosed verandahs, and many of the a/c ones have private garden-view gazebos. Named after the ancient Buddhist symbol, not the Nazi emblem. Rooms with fan ❹ With a/c ❺

Yulia Homestay 1 Jl Danau Tamblingan 38, Sindhu ⊕0361/288089. This is the largest, longest-running and best of the several similar homestays in this area. It's a friendly, family-run place that's filled with birdsong, as the owner breeds and trains prize-winning songbirds. There's a range of different accommodation in twenty appealing, comfortably equipped, terraced, fan-cooled bungalows, some of which have hot water; the deluxe option has striking modern furniture and a couch. ❶ With hot water ❷ Deluxe ❷

Expensive

Bali Hyatt Jl Danau Tamblingan, Semawang ⊕0361/281234, ⓦwww.bali.resort.hyatt.com. The 36 acres of exceptionally gorgeous, award-winning tropical gardens are the highlight of this long-established, 390-room upmarket chain hotel. Accommodation is in a trio of ocean-facing or garden-view blocks and facilities include several swimming pools, a well-regarded spa, watersports equipment, a kids' club, tennis courts and grounds that extend to the beach. Some rooms are designed for wheelchair users. ❽

Griya Santrian Jl Danau Tamblingan 47, Sindhu ⊕0361/288181, ⓦwww.santrian.com. Popular mid-sized place with 98 roomy, detached and semi-detached a/c bungalows scattered around a garden compound that runs down to the beach. The newly built "deluxe" rooms are far lighter and more contemporary than the old-style standard and superior options, and well worth the extra money. Also has an art gallery which hosts interesting

exhibitions, and three pools (one shoreside). ❻
Deluxe ❼

La Taverna Jl Danau Tamblingan 29, Sindhu
☎0361/288497, ⓦwww.latavernahotel.com.
Small, seafront hotel offering characterful and cosy
bungalows, including some stylish split-level and
family ones. Interiors are pleasingly furnished with
carved panels and antique doors and all have a/c;
most have verandahs overlooking the garden, and
the grounds, with pool, run down to the beach. ❻
Family ❼

Parigata Villas Jl Duyung 99, Semawang
☎0361/270133, ⓦwww.parigatahotelsbali.com.
Search the Web for online agents' discounts and
this complex of 18 villas becomes a remarkable
bargain, not least because each villa has its own

plunge pool. Accommodation is in individual walled
compounds, each with a bedroom area designed in
cool creams, an indoor-outdoor bathroom, plus a
patio area with private pool. There's also a hotel
pool and restaurant. ❾

Tandjung Sari Jl Danau Tamblingan 41,
Sindhu ☎0361/288441, ⓦwww
.tandjungsari.com. Sanur's original boutique hotel
comprises 28 elegant, beautifully appointed traditional-style cottage compounds, each with its
own living area, courtyard garden, shaded gazebo
and garden shower. Many rooms feature original
antique Chinese floor-tiles and all have refined
Javanese batik furnishings. There's a swimming
pool, and the garden runs down to the shore. ❽

The resort

The entire length of Sanur's five-kilometre **shoreline** is fronted by a partially
shaded, paved esplanade, so it's easy to wander (or cycle) down the coast in
search of the perfect spot. There are busy patches of beach around the *Inna
Grand Bali Beach* in the north and, further south, in Sindhu, between the Sindhu
Art Market and the *Gazebo Hotel*. Semawang's shorefront is much quieter: the
area around Jalan Kesumasari is mainly the province of fishermen and their
brightly painted wooden *jukung*, while the bit in front of the *Hotel Sanur Beach*
is pleasant and fairly peaceful. The views are great from almost any point along
this coast: on a clear day, Gunung Agung's imposing conical profile dominates
panoramas to the northeast, while out to sea you should get a clear look at the
cliffs of Nusa Lembongan.

A huge expanse of Sanur's shore gets exposed at low tide and the reef lies only
about 1km offshore at high tide; the **currents** beyond it are dangerously strong.
This makes it almost impossible to swim here at low tide (though it's okay for
paddling kids), but at other times swimming is fine and watersports are
popular.

Watersports and golf

Sanur is a popular base for **divers** (see the box on p.146 for details of local dive
operators and courses), but its own **dive sites**, along the east-facing edge of the
shorefront reef, are only really of interest for refresher diving ($60 inclusive).
The coral is not that spectacular, and visibility is only around 6–10m, with dives
ranging from 2–12m, but the area does teem with reef fish.

Several outlets along the beachfront offer **snorkelling** trips ($20 per person per
hour including gear) and three-hour fishing excursions ($60 per person). They
also rent out **watersports** equipment, including kayaks ($6 per hour), windsurfers
($20 per half-day) and jet skis ($20 for 15min), and can arrange parasailing,
wakeboarding and water-skiing. In north Sanur, contact Jeladi Wilis Boat Co-
operative (☎0361/284206), in front of the *Inna Grand Bali Beach*; in Semawang,
try the Blue Oasis Beach Club (☎0361/288011) in front of *Hotel Sanur Beach*.
Blue Oasis also runs **courses** in windsurfing ($25/hr) and sailing ($80).

From September to March, when the northwest winds blow offshore, there
are several decent **surf breaks** off Sanur, including directly in front of the *Inna*

Grand Bali Beach, in front of *Tandjung Sari* hotel, and about 1.5km offshore from the *Bali Hyatt*. You can rent surfboards and boogie boards ($6–10) along the beachfront.

Sanur has its own nine-hole **golf course** in the grounds of the *Inna Grand Bali Beach*; clubs and shoes can be rented at the club house (℡0361/287733; Rp564,000 for 18 holes).

Museum Le Mayeur

One of Sanur's earliest expat residents was the Belgian artist Adrien Jean Le Mayeur de Merpres (1880–1958), whose home has remained standing for more than seventy years and is now open to the public as **Museum Le Mayeur**

Diving in south Bali

Many of the outfits that sell **dive** excursions from shops in Kuta and Nusa Dua have their headquarters in Sanur. South Bali's dive sites are good for learners and those needing a refresher, but experienced divers usually prefer the dives off the east and north coasts of Bali, either arranging them from the south, or basing themselves nearer those places. For **general advice** on diving in Bali and Lombok, see p.50.

There is one **divers' recompression chamber** on Bali, located at Sanglah Public Hospital, Jl Kesehatan Selatan 1 in Denpasar (℡0361/227911–4 ext 123).

Dive courses and excursions

All the centres listed below run internationally **certificated diving courses**, including four-day PADI Open Water **courses** (about $380) and two-day PADI Advanced Open Water courses ($315); most also offer introductory dives for non-certificated divers ($100, depending on dive site). Prices are competitive, but be sure to check whether equipment rental and insurance are included; PADI requires that course materials are always included in the price. Be wary of extremely cheap courses: maintaining diving equipment is an expensive business in Bali so any place offering unusually good rates will probably be cutting corners and compromising your safety.

All dive centres offer **one-day dive excursions** to superior reefs beyond south Bali, including to Tulamben and Amed; to Pulau Menjangan (Deer Island); and to the islands of Nusa Lembongan and Nusa Penida (see relevant sections of the Guide for descriptions). Prices average $100, which includes two tanks but not necessarily all equipment. Three-day **diving safaris** to a selection of top sites cost $425–560 per person all-inclusive.

Dive centres

All tour agents in south Bali sell diving trips organized by Bali's major **dive centres**, but it's always a good idea to discuss your requirements with the dive centres directly. Some of the most established PADI-certified dive centres in south Bali include:

AquaMarine Diving Jl Raya Seminyak 2A, Kuta ℡0361/730107, ⓦwww .aquamarinediving.com. UK-run PADI five-star Gold Palm Resort.

Bali Scuba Jl Danau Poso 40, Blanjong, Sanur ℡0361/288610, ⓦwww.baliscuba .com. PADI five-star IDC centre that's known for its technical diving courses.

Blue Season Bali Jl Tamblingan 69XX, Batujimbar, Sanur, and Jl Bunisari 50, Kuta ℡0361/282574, ⓦwww.baliocean.com. PADI five-star IDC centre. UK/Japanese-run.

Crystal Divers Jl Danau Tamblingan 168, Batujimbar, Sanur ℡0361/287314, ⓦwww .crystal-divers.com. PADI five-star IDC centre. Also run liveaboards to all the main Bali sites. UK/Danish-run.

(Mon–Thurs & Sun 8am–3.15pm, Fri 8am–12.45pm; Rp2000, kids Rp1000); access is via the beachfront just south of Jalan Hang Tuah in north Sanur. Le Mayeur arrived in Bali at the age of 52 and after travelling down from the north pitched up in the village of Klandis near Denpasar. The teenage Ni Pollok was at this time the chief Legong dancer of Klandis and considered by many to be the best dancer in the whole of Bali. An outstandingly beautiful young woman, she began to pose regularly for the middle-aged Le Mayeur. Romance blossomed, and by 1935 the two were married and had moved to this house on Sanur beach. Ni Pollok outlived her husband but, following her death in 1985, the marital home became the Museum Le Mayeur.

Le Mayeur's house dates back to the mid-1930s and is idyllically located right on the shore, with a compound gate that still opens on to the sand. Much more interesting than the tattered paintings it contains, the single-storey house is a typical low-roofed wooden building, sumptuously carved with red and gold painted doors, lintels and pediments, and partitioned into rooms by walls that stop short of the ceiling. Le Mayeur did most of his painting in the courtyard garden – a compact tropical wilderness filled with stonecarvings, shrines and tiny *bale* – which features in many of his paintings and photographs. Inside the house, dozens of the artist's **paintings** and charcoal and crayon sketches are displayed, though they are mostly in poor condition, and the relentless gallery of Balinese beauties with dreamy expressions and ridiculous pouts soon gets wearying.

Bali Orchid Garden

The Balinese have a passion for tropical gardens and many buy their plants from the nurseries that line the roads between Sanur and Denpasar. The **Bali Orchid Garden** (daily 8am–6pm; Rp50,000; Ⓦwww.baliorchidgardens.com) has turned itself into a paying attraction and encourages tourists who probably aren't thinking of taking a shrub home to come and browse the beautiful blooms anyway. The grounds are pleasingly landscaped and alongside the huge variety of orchids are other lovelies including heliconias, bromeliads and tree ferns. You can also order gift boxes of cut flowers for taking overseas. The garden is 3km north of Sanur on Jalan Bypass, just beyond the junction with the coast road to Pantai Saba and Kusamba (see p.227).

Eating

Sanur has dozens of inexpensive, almost indistinguishable tourist-oriented **restaurants** but lacks the fine-dining choices found in Kuta and Ubud. The most enjoyable places to while away an evening are the beachfront cafés, nearly all of which set candlelit tables on the sand and offer fresh seafood grilled on the beach. You'll find the most authentic Indonesian food at restaurants beyond the main drag, particularly along predominantly residential Jalan Danau Poso in Blanjong. The **night market** that sets up inside the Sindhu Market at the Jalan Danau Tamblingan/Jalan Danau Toba intersection is another good place for cheap local eats. Many restaurants offer **free pick-ups** for diners within the Sanur area: for these places we've listed the telephone number.

Alise's Restaurant Part of the *Tamukami Hotel*, Jl Tamblingan 64X, Sindhu ☎0361/282510. The genial Belgian proprietor is likely to be on hand to explain the extensive and inventive menu at this thoughtfully run place, which offers both Indonesian and European cuisine and includes several daily specials and set menus. The snapper stuffed with spinach (Rp56,000) is good,

▲ Beachfront restaurant, Sanur

and there's Balinese champagne plus some well-priced Australian and Balinese wines. Live crooners nightly.

🏃 **Beach Café** Beachfront walkway south off Jl Pantai Sindhu, Sindhu. The most sophisticated of the beachfront cafés has sea-view couches indoors as well as tables right on the sand. An especially good spot for breakfast – eggs Benedict, frittatas, lattes and full English (Rp35,000) – but also offers good dinner options including "taster platters" that feature a selection of meat or seafood dishes (Rp65,000), plus a kids' menu.

Bonsai Café Beachfront walkway just north of *La Taverna* hotel, access off Jl Danau Tamblingan, Sindhu. Breezy shorefront restaurant and late-opening bar that serves typical tourist fare, including Mexican enchiladas and fajitas, seafood, and specials like roast duck (Rp72,000) and prawns in honey sauce. Also does good-value cocktails. The owner's impressive nursery of artfully pruned bonsai is out back, beside the access path to the main road.

🏃 **Café Batu Jimbar** Jl Danau Tamblingan 75A, Batujimbar. This long-established Sanur institution has been remodelled with a modish dining area, easy chairs and a streetfront terrace. Their menu (Rp35,000–150,000) is similarly contemporary – with a touch of Ubud

organics – and includes roast vegetable salads, home-made spinach-stuffed ravioli, and minted lamb medallions, as well as mulberry pie, home-baked cakes, good breads, herbal teas and Bali-brewed Storm Beer. Live music Tues, Thurs & Sat from 8pm.

Le Resto Ming Jl Danau Tamblingan 105, Semawang ⓣ 0361/281948; evenings only. Atmospheric spot known for its French cuisine and especially its seafood, including lobster thermidor, sweet and sour prawns and Parma-ham-wrapped salmon fillets (main courses Rp60,000–165,000). The cosy restaurant and its cute courtyard garden are filled with Balinese artefacts and paintings.

Massimo Jl Danau Tamblingan 228, Semawang. The home-made *gelato* ice cream (Rp16,500) at this genuinely south-Italian restaurant is outstanding, and there are more than 50 types of pizza on offer, including some sweet ones. Also serves pasta specialities from Lecce like fettuccine and lamb in spicy tomato sauce. Most mains cost about Rp37,000.

Mezzanine Part of *Puri Santrian* hotel, at Jl Danau Tamblingan 63, Semawang. The impressively chic barn-like dining hall, complete with comfy chairs for aperitifs and coffee, adds a touch of class to an unexceptional but decent enough menu of fairly pricey Thai fusion dishes (from Rp75,000), including duck red curry, Thai seafood platter with lemongrass, and rack of lamb with blue cheese and miso.

Ryoshi Jl Danau Tamblingan 150, Batujimbar. As well as a decent selection of sushi, this branch of the Bali-wide chain of Japanese restaurants has a great menu of appetizers that includes spinach and sesame salad, deep-fried tofu, barbecued chicken, and baked aubergine (Rp40,000–80,000).

Sari Bundo Jl Danau Poso, Blanjong. Typical, very cheap Masakan Padang place (see p.45 for details) serving spicy Sumatran dishes 24 hours a day.

The Village Part of *Griya Santrian* hotel, at Jl Danau Tamblingan 47, Sindhu. Classy Italian food – especially fish carpaccio and scallopini – in stylish contemporary surroundings, either on the streetside terrace or in air-conditioned cool. Pizza, pasta and seafood from Rp65,000.

Warung Blanjong Jl Danau Poso 78, Blanjong ☎0361/285613. Specializes in good-value Balinese dishes, all of them cheap (Rp11,000–30,000), including exceptionally good veggie delights such as *tipat* (fried vegetables with sticky rice cakes and peanut sauce), veggie nasi campur, and non-veg specialities like *pepes pe pasih* (grilled fish in banana leaves). Also serves wholemeal sandwiches and burgers. Runs cooking classes (see p.151) and there's free delivery to Sanur hotels.

Nightlife and entertainment

Reggae **bands** and cover groups entertain drinkers and diners most nights at one or other of the beachside restaurants between *La Taverna* and Jalan Pantai Sindhu, but for clubbing action you'll need to head for Kuta. If you're carousing in Sanur after 10pm you might find it difficult to find a taxi, so ask bar staff to phone Bali Taksi (☎0361/701111).

Bars and live music

The Cat and the Fiddle Opposite *Hotel Sanur Beach*, Jl Danau Tamblingan, Semawang. There's live Irish music at least three nights a week at this Ireland-focused bar-restaurant. Plus draught Guinness of course, as well as Guinness pie and Irish bangers and mash.

Jazz Bar & Grille Komplek Pertokoan Sanur Raya 15, next to *KFC* at the Jl Bypass/Jl Hang Tuah crossroads, north Sanur. In the downstairs bar, some of Bali's best jazz, blues and pop bands play live sets nightly from about 9.30pm (on Sun it's more of a jam session); the atmosphere is mellow and it attracts a mix of locals, expats and the occasional tourist. The upstairs restaurant serves quality food (Rp40,000–70,000) including barbecued fish, red Thai curry with salmon, and a bizarre but tasty banana pizza. There's a pool table, too. Daily 10am–2am.

Kafe Wayang Komplek Pertokoan Sanur Raya 12–15, same building as *Jazz Bar & Grille*, north Sanur. Bar and restaurant that stages regular live music from interesting Balinese artists.

Lazer Sports Bar Opposite *Gazebo Hotel* at Jl Danau Tamblingan 68, Sindhu. Rowdy place dominated by big-screen-TV sports coverage and with pool tables and live music from local MOR bands to fill in the gaps.

Entertainment

Agung & Sue Watering Hole I hotel and restaurant at Jalan Hang Tuah 37 puts on a **Balinese dancing** Legong show with buffet dinner every Thursday (Rp75,000; 8pm); other restaurants sometimes stage classical dancing for their diners: check boards for details. To see two of Bali's most spectacular dances – the exuberant **Barong** lion dance, and the spectacular "Monkey Dance", or **Kecak** – you'll need to head out to the daily tourist shows in the Kesiman district on Denpasar's eastern fringes, just 3km by taxi from Sanur's Jalan Hang Tuah (see p.94 for details). Sanur tour agencies offer trips for about $25 including return transport, but tickets cost Rp50,000 tickets at the door so it's cheaper to make your own way there.

Shopping

Compared to Kuta there are far fewer **shops** to browse in Sanur, though the cheaper souvenir shops sell much the same range. Designer boutiques and trendy homewares outlets feature in moderation but most lack the panache of the better Seminyak versions. Periplus **bookstore** has a branch in Hardy's Grosir supermarket.

Animale Next to *Swastika* bungalows on Jl Danau Tamblingan, Batujimbar. One of Bali's most popular womenswear chains, with a good line in well-made, loose-fitting trousers, dresses and tops in plain cottons and bold prints.

Art markets Sanur's *pasar seni* (art market) stalls selling cheap cotton clothes, beachwear, sarongs, woodcarvings and other souvenirs are mainly clustered along the beachfront south from Jl Pantai Sindhu to the *Hyatt* hotel.

Ashitaba Jl Danau Tamblingan 39, south of the Gazebo Piazza, Sindhu. Part of a small chain of good-quality Balinese basketware shops selling placemats, containers, handbags and more, all made from *ata* grass in Tenganan.

Bali Harum Jl Danau Tamblingan 97, Semawang. Balinese chain selling aromatherapy products and attractively presented toiletries, soaps, oils and incense.

Bé Opposite *Tandjung Sari* hotel, Jl Danau Tamblingan 80, Sindhu. Quality handicrafts, including palm-leaf books of handmade paper, coconut-shell spoons, bowls and tablemats, and batik wallets.

Gudang Keramik Jl Danau Tamblingan, Batujimbar. Ceramics shop that's an outlet for seconds produced by the high-quality Jenggala Keramik ceramics emporium in Jimbaran (see p.128). Slight imperfections get you a thirty percent discount.

The Hanging Tree Jl Danau Tamblingan 210, Semawang. Phenomenal choice of leather and woven-rattan handbags and baskets.

Hardy's Grosir Jl Danau Tamblingan 193, Batujimbar. The entire first floor of Sanur's main supermarket is devoted to local handicrafts, with a large, if uninvitingly displayed, range of reasonably priced, fixed-rate souvenirs, from baskets to woodcarvings. Among other things, the ground-floor supermarket sells groceries, pharmacy items, sandals and motorbike helmets. Daily 6am–10.30pm.

Mama & Leon Opposite *Griya Santrian*, at Jl Danau Tamblingan 99A, Sindhu. Elegantly under-stated mid-priced women's fashions in plain-coloured natural fabrics.

Nogo Ikat Jl Danau Tamblingan 100, Sindhu. Pricey but high-quality fabric shop that specializes in *ikat* cloth (also known as *endek*; see p.458) that's sold by the metre. Ready-made soft furnishings and clothes are also sold here; they will also make almost anything to order.

Tingklik Kite Shop Jl Tendakan, Sindhu. Sanur is famous for its fantastic, creative, and often enormous kites, and for its annual inter-village kite festival, which is held on the beach every July. This is one of several places where you can buy charismatic ready-made papier-mâché kites, and you can get them custom-made here, too.

Uluwatu Jl Danau Tamblingan, Sindhu. Balinese chain specializing in handmade Balinese lace and quality womenswear made in white and cream cotton and linen.

Spa treatments

Many of the more expensive hotels have luxurious **spas** offering a range of treatments (from about $75), including aromatherapy and traditional Balinese massages, and the Javanese *mandi lulur* exfoliation scrub (see p.54), as well as facials and hair treatments. Sanur's most famous hotel spa is the traditional village-style spa complex at the *Bali Hyatt* (℡0361/281234). Smaller, cheaper day-spas include Atma at Jalan Danau Tamblingan 96 in Sindhu (℡0361/283850), which charges Rp190,000 for a two-hour *mandi lulur*. Or there's always the massage-and-manicure ladies who hang out on the beach and charge Rp30,000 for a half-hour massage.

Listings

Airline offices Garuda has a sales office and city check-in inside the *Hotel Sanur Beach*, Semawang (Mon–Fri 7.30am–4.30pm, Sat & Sun 9am–1pm; 24-hour national call centre ☎0804/180 7807 or 021/2351 9999 if calling from a mobile), where you can get your boarding pass 4–24 hours in advance. For other international and domestic airline offices, see p.101.

Banks and currency exchange There are ATMs and exchange counters all over Sanur; see p.70 for advice on how to avoid exchange scams.

Cookery classes Learn to make Balinese dishes at the *Warung Blanjong* restaurant, Jl Danau Poso 78, Blanjong (Mon–Sat 8am–1pm; $25; ☎0361/285613).

Email and Internet At Internet centres every few hundred metres on all main roads.

Embassies and consulates See p.66.

Hospitals and clinics All the major hotels provide 24hr medical service; if yours doesn't, try the doctor at the *Inna Grand Bali Beach* ☎0361/288511, or the *Bali Hyatt* ☎0361/288271. Expats tend to use the two international clinics on the edge of Kuta (see p.123); the nearest hospitals are all in Denpasar (see p.95).

Pharmacies Several on Jl Danau Tamblingan, including Guardian Pharmacy next to Hardy's Grosir in Batujimbar.

Phones There are plenty of private wartels in central Sanur, and Direct Dial public phones in the basement shopping arcade of the *Inna Grand Bali Beach*.

Police The police station is on Jl Bypass in north Sanur, just south of the *Paradise Plaza* hotel ☎0361/288597.

Post office Sanur's main post office is on Jl Danau Buyan, Sindhu. There are postal agents opposite *Respati Bali* hotel at Jl Danau Tamblingan 66, Sindhu (poste restante c/o Agen Pos, Jl Danau Tamblingan 66, Sanur 80228), and inside the Trophy Pub Centre in Semawang.

Travel agents International and domestic flights, plus organized tours from: JBA, inside the compound of the *Diwangkara Hotel*, Jl Hang Tuah 54, north Sanur ☎0361/286501, ✉jbadwkbl@denpasar.wasantara.net.id; Nagasari Tours, Jl Danau Tamblingan 102, Sindhu ☎0361/288096, ⊛www.balinagasari.com; Sumanindo Tour, Jl Danau Tamblingan 22, Sindhu ☎0361/288570, ✉sumantravel@dps.centrin.net.id; and Tunas Tour, Jl Danau Tamblingan 107, Semawang ☎0361/288581, ⊛www.balitunastour.com. Tickets for speedboats to Mushroom Bay on Nusa Lembongan from Lembongan Paradise Cruise, Jl Hang Tuah 78, north Sanur (☎0361/281974 ⊛www.mushroom-lembongan.com; see p.154 for details).

Serangan (Turtle) Island

A few hundred metres off southern Sanur's coastline, almost blocking the entrance to Benoa Harbour, lies the sand-bar settlement of Pulau Serangan, more commonly referred to as **Serangan Island** or **Turtle Island**. The site of a very important temple, Pura Sakenan, Serangan is no longer an island, having been connected to the mainland in the mid-1990s by a kilometre-long causeway. This was phase one of a controversial **development project** associated with Tommy Suharto, the unpopular son of the former president, which also tripled the size of the island by encircling it with "reclaimed" land made up of dredged sand and limestone. The planned hotel and casino developments have not been realized, but the project has caused a great deal of resentment locally, not least because of the widespread destruction of mangrove forest, the pollution, and the resulting decline in the fish population, as well as the significant change in tidal patterns, which eroded Sanur's beaches so quickly that the missing sand then had to be restored, at vast expense.

As for Serangan's former tourist attractions, the surrounding **reefs** have all been pulverized, while the **turtles** who used to return en masse to give birth here are long gone, though the trade in live green turtles continues (see p.134 for more on this). There is, however, an embryonic Turtle Conservation and Education Centre here now, sponsored by WWF Indonesia, which aims to employ and educate islanders in turtle conservation projects.

Pura Sakenan

On the northwest coast of this small, beleaguered island stands **Pura Sakenan**, which is believed to have been founded in the sixteenth century by the Javanese priest Nirartha (the same man associated with the coastal temples at Tanah Lot, Uluwatu and Rambut Siwi). It figures very importantly in the spiritual life of the people of south Bali, for whom it's a public temple – as opposed to an ancestral or village temple. The **annual festival** held here during Kuningan celebrations lasts for several days and attracts throngs of worshippers in full ceremonial gear. At low tide when boats are unable to make the crossing, devotees have traditionally waded across the exposed mud flats from Tanjung Benoa, sarongs hoisted up around their knees and piles of offerings balanced on their heads. It is a scene that recurs in numerous traditional Balinese paintings but is fast being consigned to the history books now that cars, bemos and bikes can drive on to the island.

Benoa Harbour (Pelabuhan Benoa)

BENOA HARBOUR (Pelabuhan Benoa) is located off the end of a long causeway 5km southwest of southern Sanur, and is the arrival and departure point for many sailing trips and tourist **boat services**, including fast boats to the Gili Islands (see p.377), luxury trips to Nusa Lembongan (see p.154), as well as for all Pelni ships from elsewhere in Indonesia, plus cruise liners.

Despite the shared name, there's just over a kilometre of sea between the harbour and the northern tip of the Tanjung Benoa peninsula, and the journey between the two has to be done the long way round, by land. The easiest way to reach Benoa Harbour is by **metered taxi**; it's a short ride of about Rp35,000 from Kuta. Occasional public **bemos** also run here from near Denpasar's Sanglah hospital, and there is also a sporadic return service.

Tickets for long-distance **Pelni** boats to other islands must be bought in advance (booking opens three days before departure), either through travel agents or at the Pelni offices in Benoa Harbour (Mon–Fri 8am–4pm, Sat 8am–12.30pm; ℡0361/723689) or Kuta (see p.124). **Tickets** for tourist boats to Nusa Lembongan, fast boats to Lombok and sailing trips can be booked through any tour agent and include transfers to the harbour.

Nusa Lembongan, Nusa Ceningan and Nusa Penida

Southeast of the mainland just across Badung Strait, the islands of Nusa Lembongan, Nusa Ceningan and Nusa Penida rise alluringly out of the ocean and are ideal escapes from the hustle and bustle of the south. Nearest to the

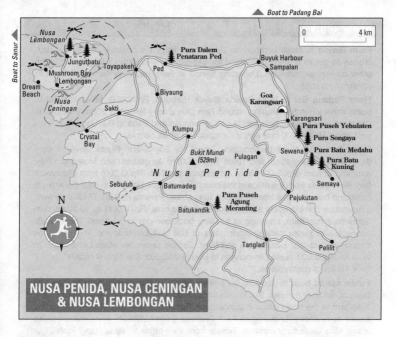

NUSA PENIDA, NUSA CENINGAN & NUSA LEMBONGAN

mainline, just forty minutes away by speedboat, is **Nusa Lembongan**, encircled by a mixture of white-sand **beaches** and mangrove. Seaweed farming is the major occupation here, supplemented by the tourist income from surfers, day-trippers and those seeking attractive beaches, a bit of gentle exploring and an addictively somnolent atmosphere. All price ranges are catered for: Jungutbatu is best for those on a budget while Mushroom Bay to the southwest is home to luxury hotels, and the area in-between; the Hill, Chelegimbai and the nearby bays, features moderately-priced options. Although pretty sleepy for most of the year, during **peak season** (mid–July to mid–September) it is vital to reserve accommodation.

Only a few hundred metres separates Nusa Lembongan from tiny **Nusa Ceningan**, just 4km long by 1km wide. For a glimpse of a totally rural island life right away from all tourist facilities take a stroll, cycle or motorbike across the bridge from Nusa Lembongan (see p.159). To stay longer, Village Ecotourism Network, JED (☏0361/735320, ⓦwww.jed.or.id), organizes overnight visits to the island, staying in the village and offering the opportunity to experience local life first-hand.

Further east from Nusa Lembongan is **Nusa Penida**, roughly 20km long, dominated by a harsh, dry, limestone plateau reminiscent of the Bukit, the far southern tip of the mainland south. The island is crisscrossed by miles of small lanes ripe for exploring and its south coast has some of the most spectacular scenery in Bali. There are few tourist facilities here and the island the gets almost no visitors.

The best **surfing** is from June to September, although full moons during other months are worth a try. The most popular breaks are offshore from Jungutbatu with others off Mushroom Bay and in the channel between Nusa Lembongan and Nusa Ceningan. To range further afield sign up for a **surf**

Boats and trips to and from the islands

From Benoa to Nusa Lembongan (Mushroom Bay). It's possible to use the day-cruises to get to or leave the island for $15–20 one way without taking part in the other day-cruise activities. Departing Benoa at 9am, returning 4pm. Call them to confirm availability.

From Padang Bai to Nusa Penida (Buyuk Harbour). Rp18,000; takes 1hr. Public boats leave when full, starting around 7am plus a daily ferry at 1.30pm (Rp20,000). **Charters** are possible between Nusa Lembongan and Padang Bai/Candi Dasa: it'll cost about Rp700,000 one way for a maximum of six people.

From Sanur to Nusa Lembongan. Takes 1hr 30min–2hr. Boats leave at 8am (Rp33,000) to Jungutbatu and 10am (Rp60,000) to Jungutbatu and Mushroom Bay, returning at 8am (Rp33,000) from Jungutbatu and 7am (Rp33,000) from Mushroom Bay. Buy tickets from the office at the beach end of Jalan Hang Tuah near the *Ananda Hotel* and from the beachfront office in Jungutbatu. Perama (℡0361/751875, ⓦwww.peramatour.com) operate a daily **tourist shuttle** boat (Rp70,000) at 10.30am from Sanur to Jungutbatu, returning at 8.30am; book one day in advance. These boats connect with buses serving other parts of Bali and Lombok and you can book through-tickets that include bus and boat. Sample prices are Nusa Lembongan to Kuta for Rp85,000, Nusa Lembongan to Ubud Rp90,000. See "Travel details", p.163, for a full list of destinations.

Public speed boat to Jungutbatu. Leaves Sanur at 4pm, Jungutbatu at 3pm and takes about forty minutes. Buy tickets from vendors on Sanur beach near Jalan Hang Tuah and at the ticket office in Jungutbatu; Rp150,000 one way, Rp250,000 return. **Scoot speedboat** (Lembongan Fast Cruises; ℡0361/285522, ⓦwww.scootcruise.com), also takes forty minutes. Tickets from their office at Jalan Hang Tuah 27 or office in Jungutbatu (℡0361/780 2255). *Scoot* leaves Sanur Beach at 9:30am and 4 pm (plus 1.30pm during peak season), departing Nusa Lembongan 8.30am and 3pm (plus 11.30am in peak season), $18 one way and $35 return. It's also possible to **charter** a private boat for a Lembongan day-trip from the Jeladi Wilis Boat Cooperative booth on the beachfront in front of the *Grand Bali Beach* (℡0361/284206); they charge $35 per person (minimum six people).

Luxury trips

A day-trip to the luxury resorts on the islands or to watersports pontoons moored offshore can be a pleasant, if pricey, way to visit Nusa Lembongan or Nusa Penida. All are widely advertised in the south. The trips are popular so don't sign up if you are looking for peace and tranquillity. The best resorts have pools and there are plenty of activities to choose from, including free snorkelling and watersports. Lunch and transfers between your hotel and the boat are included. Prices vary considerably so shop around and be aware that not all of the trips use resorts right on the beach. See p.157 for more on the accommodation add-ons on offer.

Bali Hai ℡0361/720331, ⓦwww.balihaicruises.com. The biggest operator uses the *Lembongan Island Beach Club* at Mushroom Bay.

Bounty ℡0361/726666, ⓦwww.balibountycruises.com. Water activities off the coast and/or onshore at *Mutiara Villas*.

Island Explorer ℡0361/728088, ⓦwww.bali-cruise.com. Uses *Coconuts Beach Resort* where it's a short walk to the beach.

Lembongan Paradise Cruise ℡0361/281974, ⓦwww.mushroom-lembongan.com. Visitors use *Mushroom Beach Bungalows* on the headland.

Quicksilver ℡0361/742 5161, ⓦwww.quicksilver-bali.com. The watersports pontoon is offshore at Toyapakeh where there are also beachside facilities.

Sail Sensations ℡0361/725864, ⓦwww.bali-sailsensations.com. Visitors use the facilities at the *Anchorage* resort on the coast at Mushroom Bay.

safari which combines Nusa Lembongan along with Lombok and Sumbawa; try Dreamweaver (☎0361/842 7110, ⓦwww.dreamweaver-surf.com).

Nusa Lembongan

Just 4km long and less than 3km wide, **NUSA LEMBONGAN** is sheltered by coral reefs that provide excellent snorkelling and create the perfect conditions for seaweed farming (see box, p.162). You can **walk** around the island in three to four hours, and **bicycles** (from Rp40,000 per day) and **motorbikes** (Rp25,000–30,000 per hour, Rp100–150,000 per day) are widely available for rent in Jungutbatu. A bridge, sturdy enough for motorbikes, spans the narrow strait that separates Nusa Lembongan and Nusa Ceningan.

Most budget accommodation is in **Jungutbatu** on the west coast, with the mid-and top-end places on **the Hill** to the south of Jungutbatu beach and further south at **Coconut Beach** and **Chelegimbai**, **Mushroom Bay** (Tanjung Sanghyang), informally named after the mushroom coral in the offshore reef, and **Dream Beach**. The island is developing fast – a bare patch of land today is a plush set of bungalows tomorrow.

Jungutbatu

Spread out along the west coast for well over 1km, the attractive, low-key village of **JUNGUTBATU** is home to the bulk of the island's tourist facilities. Drop-off points for the boats depend on the tide – you'll wade ashore wherever you land.

There are no ATMs but you can **change money** at the moneychangers along the beach or at Bank Pembangunan Daerah Bali (Mon–Fri 10am–1pm); rates are dires so it's best to bring plenty of cash. There's a **wartel** marked on the map and several cafés and hotels have **Internet access** (about Rp1000 per minute or Rp45,000 per hour) but there's no post office. The Perama office (daily 7am–6pm) is north of *Pondok Baruna*. There's a health centre, *klinik*, in the village (marked on the map), with a doctor who is used to dealing with traveller problems; contact the *klinik* through your accommodation. The **ticket offices** for public boats and for *Scoot* speedboat are towards the southern end of the beach.

Accommodation

Most of the **accommodation** is right on the beach north of Jungutbatu, with a couple of places to the south. Buildings are mostly concrete and tile, although some bamboo-and-thatch places do remain. All have en-suite bathrooms and fans but breakfast is not included. Some hot water and a/c is available. These reviews include places on the Hill that are easily accessible from Jungutbatu. Don't come to the island without a reservation in the peak season (mid-July to mid-September)

Agung ☎0366/24483. Basic but adequate rooms in a concrete building with some two-storey thatched places. ①–②

Bunga Bungalo ☎0361/742 9185, ⓦwww .bunga-bungalo.com. At the southern end of the beach this popular place has attractive rooms in two-storey buildings in a cosy compound. ③

Bungalo No. 7 ☎0366/24497, ⓦwww .bungalo-no7.com. Good-value rooms at the far southern end of the beach, all with balconies or verandahs. There's a sunbathing area overlooking the beach. ③

Ketut ☎0361/747 4638, ⓦwww .ketutlosmenbungalows.com. Well-built,

Diving and snorkelling

The area around the islands is popular for **diving**, although the sea can be cold with treacherous currents, so it is important to dive with operators familiar with the area (see p.51 for general notes on choosing an operator). Toyapakeh, SD Point and Mangrove are the most reliable and frequently dived sites, and can get busy. Toyapakeh offers huge coral boulders and pillars, which protect an inland area of gorgonians and soft coral bushes, and it's possible to see pelagics such as manta rays, hammerhead sharks and *mola mola* from June to October. At SD Point there are large coral heads, a diverse collection of sponges, and the possibility of green and hawksbill turtles, manta rays, sea snakes, octopus and white-tipped reef sharks. Mangrove is an easy dive and used frequently for beginners. It has a forty-five-degree sloping reef with excellent coral coverage off the northeast corner of Nusa Lembongan. Manta Point off the south coast of Nusa Penida is renowned for *mola mola*.

The most established operator on the islands is the highly professional **World Diving Lembongan** (℡0812/390 0686, ⓦwww.world-diving.com), a PADI five-star international resort, based at *Pondok Baruna* in Jungutbatu. They offer dives for certified divers ($70 for a one-day two-dive package), introductory dives, scuba reviews and PADI courses up to Divemaster level (PADI Open Water $370, Advanced Open Water $280). As well as the usual sites, they also dive a few sites rarely visited by other companies.

It is also possible to charter boats from Nusa Lembongan to go **snorkelling** (arrange this through your accommodation or with the boat captains on the beach). Some of the best spots are Mushroom Bay, Mangrove Corner, Malibu Point, Crystal Bay, off Nusa Penida, which is renowned for clear waters, and the Penida Wall off Toyapakeh. Prices depend on distance; with negotiation it's around Rp150,000 for two hours for two people including equipment around Nusa Lembongan, Rp250,000 to the Penida Wall and Rp350,000 to Crystal Bay. World Diving also take snorkellers, if the site is suitable, for Rp100,000 per person, including equipment, for about four hours.

attractive rooms, a cut above the rest in attention to detail, set in pleasant grounds. A/c and hot water available. ❸–❹

Linda Bungalows ℡0812/360 0867, ⓔbcwcchoppers@yahoo.com. Rooms are in well-built two-storey buildings with good-quality furnishings. The Aussie owners pride themselves on cleanliness. ❷

Mainski Inn ℡0366/24481. The new swimming pool at the front indicates that this hotel, which was being renovated at the time of writing, is moving upmarket. Rooms are decent and the more expensive ones have a/c. ❷–❸

Minami's Villa Nusa ℡0812/460 7407. Imposing two-storey houses facing seawards contain gleaming rooms with a/c and hot water. The most upmarket place on the beach. ❹

Nusa Indah ℡0366/24480. Set back slightly from the beach behind the *Surfer's Beach Café*, bungalows are new and good quality. ❷

Playgrounds ℡0366/24524, ⓦwww.playgroundslembongan.com. Six rooms in a big house perched on the cliff overlooking Jungutbatu beach. There are fans or a/c, cold-water bathrooms and cable TV and a small pool, but the real highlight is the balconies, which offer one of the most spectacular views on Lembongan. ❺–❻

Pondok Baruna ℡0812/390 0686, ⓦwww.world-diving.com. A few hundred metres south of the main accommodation area, this place has basic rooms set in a garden, overlooking the beach. World Diving Lembongan is based here. ❶–❷

Puri Nusa ℡0366/24482. A variety of rooms all with good verandahs or balconies towards the north end of the beach. A/c and hot water are available at the top end. ❶–❹

The Villas ℡0813/3857 4436, ⓦwww.lembongantravel.com. Just a few minutes' walk from the southern end of Jungutbatu Beach, the villas (one-and two-bedroom) are excellent value and enjoy fine views across the whole of Jungutbatu. Next door to *Playgrounds*. ❺–❼

Eating

Most of the accommodation options have their own restaurants, usually right on the beach with sea views and a cooling breeze. All offer a good range of international and Indo-Chinese favourites, local seafood and the usual travellers' fare. Expect mains to be Rp20–35,000. If you are exploring the **northern tip** of the island during the day, there are a few tiny warung that are ideal for a drink. Most of the places below are along the beach in Jungutbatu but if you fancy going **further afield**, *Café Bali* (☎0812/466 8422) at Mushroom Beach and *Café Pandan* (☎0812/398 3772) at Dream Beach offer free transport (see p.159 for reviews).

Agung The usual menu, but worth a visit for the great daytime views from their upper storey.

Ketut's Warung Behind the beach, accessed north of *Agung*, there's a sign for this warung which is well worth searching out for excellent local food and a variety of Thai dishes.

Linda Excellent Thai food. The small menu is supplemented by regular specials.

Nyoman's Warung About 10min walk north of *Puri Nusa* on the road, *Nyoman* serves splendid Balinese dishes, mostly fish, at great prices (Rp35,000 for a meal).

Pondok Baruna Everything is good but, if you like it hot, their *ikan pepes* and Baruna curry are especially recommended. Lassis to die for.

Scooby Doo Bar Satellite TV supplements the food and drink here.

Surfer's Beach Café Shows surfing videos and does a good-value seafood barbecue (Rp70,000).

Ware-Ware For something a bit pricier (Rp35–40,000 for mains) this place on the Hill serves a mixture of local and Western dishes and is good at seafood.

Around the coast

Around the coast southwest of Jungutbatu, the glorious white-sand bays of **Coconut Beach**, **Chelegimbai** (also known as Selegimpak) and **Mushroom Bay**, together with the footpaths linking them, offer a wide range of mid-price and top-end accommodation. This area is the destination for day-trippers from the mainland, which can disturb the peace in the middle of the day but can't detract from the idyllic white sand and turquoise waters. Slightly further afield, **Dream Beach**, around on the south coast of the island, is about as remote as it gets in this part of Bali.

You can **charter a boat** to Mushroom Bay from Jungutbatu or head over on the back of a **motorbike** (about Rp50,000 per person). **On foot**, the most attractive route is to walk around the coast. Climb the steps that lead up from the extreme southern end of the beach at Jungutbatu to a path that leads along the hillside past *Playgrounds* and *Coconuts Beach Resort* to Coconut Beach, then up the far side of the bay to Chelegimbai beach. Another path leads up from the far southern end of Chelegimbai past *Tamarind Beach Bungalows* and passes above a couple of tiny bays before descending to the Mushroom Bay accommodation. To reach Dream Beach, follow the signs off the road between Lembongan village and Mushroom Bay.

Accommodation

The **accommodation** here is more upmarket than in Jungutbatu, although some are over-priced. It's worth doing some research; many of the luxury places are best booked as an add-on to a day-cruise (see p.154). This will ensure the best rates as well as a luxurious trip to and from the mainland. If you don't book accommodation this way, most of the hotels offer free transport to and from the boat drop-off points in Jungutbatu.

Coconuts Beach Resort ☏0361/728088, ⓦwww.bali-cruise.com. Accommodation is in circular, thatched bungalows (with fans or a/c) ranged up the hillside. There are two pools, and the beach is a short walk away. ⑥–⑦

Dream Beach Bungalows ☏0812/398 3772. In peaceful isolation in the far south above a fantastic white-sand beach, the large, well-kept rooms have fans and cold-water bathrooms. Take care if swimming as the waves can be big and there's an undertow. ③–④

Hai Tide Huts ☏0361/720331, ⓦwww.balihaicruises.com. At this large resort, guest rooms are housed in attractive, two-storey brick-and-thatch huts with great lounging platforms; beachfront rooms have fine views but cost extra. Bathrooms are not attached to each hut. The huge pool has a small island in the middle. Book as part of a package with a Bali Hai cruise. ⑨ including cruise

Morin ☏ 0812/385 8396, ⓦwww.morinlembongan.com. Just three bungalows on the hillside with fans and cold-water bathrooms. Great views, pretty gardens and just a short walk to the beach. ⑤

Mushroom Beach Bungalows ☏0366/24515, ⓦwww.mushroom-lembongan.com. On the headland at the eastern end of Mushroom Bay. You're paying for the brilliant location and the lovely little swimming pool although the rooms are fine; the more expensive have a/c and hot water. Can be booked as an add-on to Lembongan Paradise Cruise. ④–⑥

Mutiara Villas ☏0361/745 3857, ⓦwww.mutiara-villa.com. Located on the hillside a short walk from Coconut and Chelegimbai beaches, all rooms have a/c, hot water and TV. Standard rooms are small and have beds on a platform reached via a ladder, but the facilities are great. There are two pools, tennis court, sauna, and access to a coastal cave and beach (spiral staircase this time) and with gorgeous views and excellent lounging areas. ⑤–⑧

Nusa Lembongan Resort ☏0361/725864, ⓦwww.nusa-lembongan.com. The most luxurious resort on the island with a lovely infinity pool. Accommodation is in twelve superb villas at the far western end of Mushroom Bay. Can be arranged as an add-on to a Sail Sensations cruise, but day-visitors won't disturb hotel guests, as they use another location. ⑧

Sunset Villas ☏ 0813/3859 5776, ⓦwww.thesunsetvillas.com. Clean bungalows with fans and attached cold-water bathrooms perched on the cliff

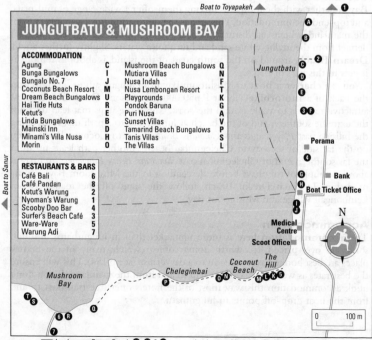

Boat to Toyapakeh

JUNGUTBATU & MUSHROOM BAY

ACCOMMODATION

Agung	C	Mushroom Beach Bungalows	Q
Bunga Bungalows	I	Mutiara Villas	N
Bungalo No. 7	J	Nusa Indah	F
Coconuts Beach Resort	M	Nusa Lembongan Resort	T
Dream Beach Bungalows	U	Playgrounds	K
Hai Tide Huts	R	Pondok Baruna	G
Ketut's	E	Puri Nusa	A
Linda Bungalows	B	Sunset Villas	V
Mainski Inn	D	Tamarind Beach Bungalows	P
Minami's Villa Nusa	H	Tanis Villas	S
Morin	O	The Villas	L

RESTAURANTS & BARS

Café Bali	6
Café Pandan	8
Ketut's Warung	2
Nyoman's Warung	1
Scooby Doo Bar	4
Surfer's Beach Café	3
Ware-Ware	5
Warung Adi	7

Boat to Sanur

Jungutbatu

Perama

Bank

Boat Ticket Office

N

Medical Centre

Scoot Office

Mushroom Bay

Chelegimbai

Coconut Beach

The Hill

0   100 m

Lembongan, Dream Beach, ⓤ, ⓥ & ⑧   Lembongan, Mushroom Bay & Dream Beach ▼

between Mushroom Beach and Dream Beach. There are great views and wonderful nearby beaches. **4**

Tamarind Beach Bungalows ☎ 0812/398 4234. Huge, high-ceilinged bungalows with fans and attached cold-water bathrooms, plus good views along Chelegimbai beach from their location at the far eastern end, near an excellent sunset-viewing spot. **4**

Tanis Villas ☎ 0361/743 2344, ⓦ www .tanisvillas.com. Excellent bungalows with fans or a/c in an attractive garden just behind Mushroom Beach. Lovely pool as well. **5–6**

Eating

As with Jungutbatu, most hotels here have **restaurants**, with ambience, decor and price in direct relation to the luxury and cost of the rooms. The cheapest place to eat in this part of the island is *Warung Adi*, a few hundred metres up the road towards Lembongan village from Mushroom Bay, offering a small Indonesian and travellers' menu with mains at Rp8000–10,000. A reasonably priced alternative is *Café Bali* (☎0812 466 8422) in a prime spot on the beach next to *Hai Tide Huts*, with good views and a large menu of Indonesian and international food (Rp20–40,000) and an especially appealing dessert menu. For views with your food, the restaurants at *Mushroom Beach Bungalows* and *Mutiara Villas* are unbeatable. Further around the coast *Café Pandan* at *Dream Beach Bungalows* (☎0812/398 3772) offers free transport, a huge list of cocktails and a wide-ranging menu in a similar price range.

Around Nusa Lembongan

For a trip **around Nusa Lembongan**, it's best to walk or cycle in a clockwise direction, avoiding a killer climb out of Jungutbatu to the south. The road is tarmac most of the way, although a bit rough in places. Allow three to four hours to walk around the island, two hours to cycle, or less than an hour by motorbike. Allow for more time if you want to pop over and explore Nusa Ceningan.

Heading north on the tarmac road that runs parallel to the coast about 200m behind the beach, the road splits a couple of kilometres north of Jungutbatu. The left-hand fork follows the coast and a few hundred metres later passes **Pura Sakenan**, recognizable by its highly decorated central shrine. This road continues a couple of kilometres to the northernmost tip of the island. The right fork leads to **Pura Empuaji**, notable for its highly carved doorway, which is the most venerated temple on the island (take a sarong and sash if you want to visit). The road continues south for four kilometres between the mangroves on the coast and scrub and cacti on the right. A few derelict salt-makers' huts are still scattered about but production has now been replaced by more lucrative **seaweed farming**. Gradually the mangrove clears and there are views of Nusa Ceningan just across the water with Nusa Penida rising up dramatically behind. At the point where the channel between Nusa Lembongan and Nusa Ceningan is narrowest, matching temples face each other across the water and a **bridge** links the islands: you can walk, cycle or ride a motorbike above the crystal-clear waters for a look at the totally rural island.

Continuing round the island, a steep hill climbs up from the coast into **LEMBONGAN**, the largest village on the island, 3km south of Jungutbatu. The island's only sight is here, the **Underground House** (open on request; donation), dug by a local man, Made Byasa, between 1961 and 1976, inspired by part of the *Mahabarata* (see p.442). It consists of several rooms, a well and ventilation shafts, and isn't for the claustrophobic. If you want to visit, show up at the house and somebody will open it up.

All roads heading uphill through the village eventually join to become the main road up past the school and over the hill to Jungutbatu. A left turn on the climb up through the village is well signed with the names of the accommodation at Mushroom Bay, and it is about a kilometre down to the coast if you want a side-trip. A left turn on the way down to Mushroom Bay, also signed, leads to Dream Beach and *Sunset Villas*.

Nusa Penida

To the Balinese, **NUSA PENIDA** is regarded as *angker*, a place of evil spirits and ill fortune, and the home of the legendary figure **I Macaling**, also known as Jero Gede Macaling, who is believed to bring disease and floods across to the mainland; he requires regular appeasement to avert these dangers. Many Balinese make regular pilgrimage to Pura Dalem Penataran Ped, the home of I Macaling, to ward off bad luck. The gigantic black I Macaling and his white-faced wife, Jero Luh, appear in the drama **Barong Landung** (for details, see p.444), which is performed throughout Bali to protect villages from illness and evil spirits.

Nusa Penida is too dry to cultivate rice, and while you'll see maize, cassava, beans and tobacco in the fields during the rainy season, there's nothing grown during the dry season. The island can only sustain a small population and many local people leave to work on the mainland or as part of the government's *transmigrasi* programme (see p.424).

Sampalan

SAMPALAN, on the northeast coast, is the largest town on the island, and has a shady street of shops, a bemo terminal and market spread out behind the coast. The Pura Dalem, close to the cemetery near the football field, has a six-metre-tall gateway adorned with five leering Bhoma and a pendulous-breasted Rangda.

There are several **warung** in the main street, serving rice and noodles, and a **place to stay**. *Nusa Garden Bungalows* (℡0813/3855 7595; ❶) has simple fan rooms with attached bathrooms.

Toyapakeh and around

Some 9km from Sampalan, the village of **TOYAPAKEH** is separated from Nusa Ceningan by a channel less than 1km wide but over 100m deep in places. There's an attractive white **beach,** peaceful atmosphere, small daily **market** and a tiny mosque serving the town's Muslim population. There are plans for **accommodation** just behind the beach; check out ⓦwww.penida .com for progress.

Pura Dalem Penataran Ped, dedicated to I Macaling and built from volcanic sandstone and local limestone, lies 5km east of Toyapakeh on the Sampalan road. The size of the courtyards and the grand entrances emphasize the prestige of the temple. The *odalan* festival here is well attended by pilgrims hoping to stave off sickness and ill fortune; every three years a larger *usaba* festival draws enormous crowds.

Around Nusa Penida

The best way to see Nusa Penida is by **motorbike** – ask at your guesthouse for rental details – although you'll need to be confident on steep terrain. The island is a maze of lanes and signposts are few, so start early and have plenty of fuel. A full circuit is only about 70km, but allowing time to visit the major attractions and to get lost a few times, it takes most of a day. The road between Toyapakeh and Sampalan is the busiest on the island and roughly follows the coast; traffic elsewhere is much lighter.

▲ Man weaving a basket for odalan festival at Pura Dalem Penataran Ped

Seaweed farming

Areas of Nusa Penida, Nusa Lembongan and Nusa Ceningan, the Geger beach in south Bali and some areas of Lombok are big producers of **seaweed**, source of two lucrative substances: **agar**, a vegetable gel used in cooking, and **carrageenan**, used in cosmetics and foodstuffs. Seaweed is fussy stuff; it can only be cultivated in areas protected from strong currents but needs a flow of water through it. The temperature must not get too high, the salinity needs to be constant and, at low tide, the seaweed must remain covered by water. To **"farm"** seaweed, a bamboo frame is made to support lengths of twine. Farmers tie small pieces of seaweed – both green *cotoni* and red *spinosum* varieties (*cotoni* produces better-quality carrageenan and fetches at least twice the price) – to the twine, harvesting the long offshoots after 45 days. The seaweed is then dried and compressed into bales; 8kg of wet seaweed reduces to 1kg when dry.

Seaweed is responsible for the increased prosperity in these areas over the last few decades although it's hard physical work, drying anything in the rainy season is distinctly tricky and, like all producers of raw materials that sell on a world market, they remain subject to price fluctuations and market forces way beyond their control.

About 10km south of Sampalan, the tiny entrance to the limestone cave of **Goa Karangsari** is a short climb above the road and is tight, but opens up into an impressive cavern. Choose the local guide with the best pressure-lantern. The cave houses small shrines and emerges after 300m onto a ledge with fine views over a peaceful grove surrounded by hills. The Galungan festival (see p.47) is celebrated with a procession and ceremony inside the cave.

On the way to **SEWANA** (or Suana), you'll pass **Pura Puseh Yehulaten** perched on a cliff edge offering great views back along the coast. Look out for the attractive **Pura Songaya** at the southern end of Sewana village backed by a sheer cliff. Just beyond, a side-road to the left leads 2km further down the coast to **SEMAYA** passing the large **Pura Batu Medahu** and **Pura Batu Kuning**, with some fabulous carvings, on the way. Semaya itself is a small fishing village around a long bay and pretty enough for a brief stop.

Returning to the main road, you climb dramatically up to the central plateau. Approaching the village of **PEJUKUTAN**, 6km from Sewana, the land is dotted with giant concrete dishes for catching rainwater, which is then stored in massive underground tanks. Some 2km further on, a right fork heads to **TANGLAD**, a cool, upland village, with an ancient throne to the sun god, Surya. Traditional weaving is the local speciality here, carried out in local houses. Nestled among hills 9km from Tanglad is the village of **BATUKANDIK**, whose **Pura Puseh Agung Meranting** houses a remarkable, supposedly prehistoric and much eroded, carving of a woman supporting the top of a stone altar. The amazing south coast of the island is accessible from here, consisting of dramatic limestone cliffs rising sheer out of the ocean and views that are utterly spellbinding. From Butukandik a side road leads south to the edge of the cliffs and a staircase to the fresh water spring at their base. This is typical of the whole southern coast of the island; there are several spots where equally hairy descents to the sea are possible – ask locally. **BATUMADEG**, 6km beyond Batukandik, is the island's second-largest village.

Turn left at Batumadeg to **SEBULUH**, where the road ends a couple of hundred metres beyond the village green. There are numerous paths through the village to the cliffs. There are two **temples** here, one on a promontory linked to the mainland by an exposed ridge, and the other at the bottom of a path that winds down the face of the cliff to a freshwater spring.

Returning to Batumadeg, the road turns inland and skirts close to the summit of **Bukit Mundi**, at 529m the highest point on the island, where the goddess Dewi Rohini, a female manifestation of Siwa, is said to dwell. The road reaches the edge of the plateau, dropping down through the small, red-roofed village of **KLUMPU**, shortly after which the left fork continues to **SAKTI**, from where you can head to the glorious white-sand beach at **Crystal Bay** or continue straight back to Toyapakeh.

Travel details

Bemos and public buses

It's almost impossible to give the frequency with which bemos and public buses run: see Basics, p.36, for details. Journey times given are the minimum you can expect. Only the direct bemo and bus routes are listed; for longer journeys you'll have to go via one of Denpasar's four main bemo terminals (full details on p.83).

Denpasar (Batubulan terminal) See p.218.
Denpasar (Kereneng terminal) to: Sanur (15–25min).
Denpasar (Tegal terminal) to: Jimbaran (40min); Kuta (25min); Ngurah Rai Airport (35min); Nusa Dua (Bali Collection; 35min); Sanur (25min).
Denpasar (Ubung terminal) See p.350.
Denpasar (Wangaya terminal) to: Sangeh Monkey Forest (45min).
Jimbaran to: Denpasar (Tegal terminal; 40min); Kuta (15min); Ngurah Rai Airport (10min).
Kuta to: Nusa Dua (Bali Collection; 20min); Denpasar (Tegal terminal; 25min); Jimbaran (15min); Ngurah Rai Airport (10min).
Ngurah Rai Airport to: Nusa Dua (Bali Collection; 20min); Denpasar (Tegal terminal; 35min); Kuta (10min); Jimbaran (10min).
Nusa Dua (Bali Collection) to: Denpasar (Batubulan terminal; 1hr); Denpasar (Tegal terminal; 35min); Kuta (20min); Ngurah Rai Airport (20min).
Sanur to: Denpasar (Kereneng terminal; 15–25min); Denpasar (Tegal terminal; 25min).

Perama shuttle buses

Kuta to: Bedugul (daily; 2hr 30min–3hr); Candi Dasa (3 daily; 3hr); Gili Islands (daily; 9hr 30min); Kintamani (daily; 2hr 30min); Lovina (daily; 4hr); Mataram (Lombok; 2 daily; 8hr 30min); Nusa Lembongan (daily; 2hr 30min); Padang Bai (3 daily; 2hr 30min); Sanur (4 daily; 30min); Senggigi (Lombok; 2 daily; 9hr); Ubud (4 daily; 1hr–1hr 30min).
Nusa Lembongan (including boat transfer to Sanur and on from Padang Bai where relevant) to: Bedugul (daily; 5hr); Candi Dasa (daily; 3hr–3hr 30min); Gili Islands (daily; 9hr); Kuta/Ngurah Rai Airport (daily; 2hr 30min–3hr); Lovina (daily; 7hr); Mataram (daily;10hr); Padang Bai (daily; 3hr); Senggigi (daily;10hr); Ubud (daily; 3hr).
Sanur to: Bedugul (daily; 2hr–2hr 30min); Candi Dasa (3 daily; 2hr–2hr 30min); Gili Islands (daily; 9hr); Kintamani (daily; 2hr 15min); Kuta/Ngurah Rai Airport (5 daily; 30min–1hr); Lovina (daily; 2hr 30min–3hr); Mataram (Lombok; 2 daily; 8hr); Nusa Lembongan (daily; 2hr); Padang Bai (3 daily; 1hr 30min–2hr); Senggigi (Lombok; 2 daily; 8hr 30min); Ubud (4 daily; 30min–1hr).

Boats

Pelni

Denpasar (Benoa Harbour) Except where indicated, services twice a fortnight to: Bima (Sumbawa; 3 times a fortnight; 21–31hr); Bitung (Sulawesi; 5 days); Ende (Flores; 2 days); Kupang (West Timor; fortnightly; 26hr); Labuanbajo (Flores; 30hr); Makassar (Sulawesi; 2–4 days); Maumere (Flores; fortnightly; 3 days); Surabaya (Java; fortnightly; 23hr); Waingapu (Sumba; 26hr).

Others

Benoa Harbour to: Gili Islands (1–2 daily; 2hr–2hr 30min).
Buyuk Harbour (Nusa Penida) to: Padang Bai (2 daily; 1hr).
Jungutbatu (Nusa Lembongan) to: Sanur (6 daily; 1–2hr); Toyapakeh (daily; 45min);
Mushroom Bay (Nusa Lembongan) to: Sanur (daily; 1–2hr);

Sanur to: Jungutbatu (Nusa Lembongan; 6–7 daily; 40min–2hr); Mushroom Bay (Nusa Lembongan; 3 daily; 30min–2hr).

Toyapakeh (Nusa Penida) to: Jungutbatu (Nusa Lembongan; daily; 45min).

Domestic flights

Denpasar (Ngurah Rai Airport) to: Bima (Sumbawa; 1–2 daily; 1hr 15min); Ende (Flores; weekly; 2hr); Jakarta (Java; 21 daily; 1hr 40min); Kupang (West Timor; 3 daily; 1hr 40min); Labuanbajo (Flores; 10 weekly; 2hr 20min); Makassar (Sulawesi; 2 daily; 1hr 10min); Mataram (Lombok; 7–8 daily; 30min); Maumere (Flores; daily; 2hr 20min); Padang (3 weekly; 3hr 30min); Surabaya (Java; 13 daily; 45min); Waingapu (Sumba; 5 weekly; 1hr 10min); Yogyakarta (Java; 6 daily; 1hr 10min).

2

Ubud and around

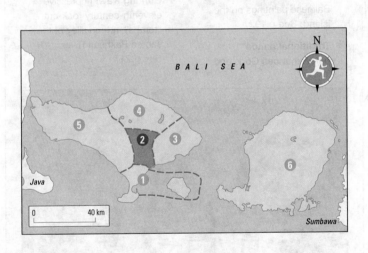

CHAPTER 2   # Highlights

* **Bali Bird Park** A vast and beautifully landscaped aviary, with elusive Bali starlings in residence. See p.170

* **A walk through the rice-paddies** Classic vistas of emerald terraces and coconut groves, framed by distant volcanoes. See p.191

* **Neka Art Museum, Ubud** The finest collection of Balinese paintings on the island. See p.192

* **Traditional dance performances** Gods and demons flirt and fight by torchlight. See p.203

* **Alternative therapies** Take up yoga, experiment with herbal tonics, have a massage. See p.207

* **Cultural classes** Return home with a new skill in batik painting, silversmithing or Balinese cookery. See p.208

* **Gunung Kawi** Impressive eleventh-century rock-cut "tombs" in the valley of the sacred Pakrisan River. See p.217

▲ Rock-cut "tombs" at Gunung Kawi

Ubud and around

The inland town of **Ubud** and its surrounding area form Bali's cultural heartland, home to a huge proliferation of temples, museums and art galleries, where Balinese dance shows are staged nightly, a wealth of craft studios provide absorbing shopping, and traditional ceremonies and rituals are observed on a daily basis. It's also surrounded by a stunning physical environment of lush, terraced paddies watered by hundreds of streams – and much higher rainfall than in the south – giving plenty of scope for leisurely hikes and bicycle rides. The route to Ubud **north of Denpasar** takes you through a string of craft-producing little towns dubbed the "tourist corridor", where you can watch artisans at work and browse their wares. You'll need to venture out to the villages around Ubud, however, for a sense of old-fashioned Bali – to the classic adobe-walled settlements of **Penestanan** and Peliatan, for example, or to Pejeng, which still boasts relics from its Bronze Age inhabitants.

Ubud and everywhere else described in this chapter lie within the boundaries of **Gianyar district**, formerly an ancient kingdom. (Gianyar itself, 10km east of Ubud, lies on the main route into east Bali and is described in Chapter 3, as are all the villages east of the T-junction at Sakah.) Roads within the Ubud region tend to run north–south down river valleys, making it difficult in places to travel east–west; this chapter reflects that restriction.

Ubud has always played second fiddle to the royal and political centre of Gianyar, and it has only been with the advent of mass tourism in the last few decades that it has assumed such a dominant role. Ubud's development was closely bound to the fortunes of the **Sukawati family**, who for centuries ruled over much of Gianyar regency from their court, 10km south of Ubud, where the modern-day market town of Sukawati now stands. The Sukawati royal household was established in the early eighteenth century by **Dewa Agung Anom**, who gathered musicians, dancers, puppeteers, artists and sculptors from all over the island to his court. This was the foundation of the strong **artistic** heritage of the area, and over the next two hundred years Dewa Agung Anom's descendants established satellite courts in Peliatan, Ubud and Singapadu, among others. The 1930s saw the arrival of a bevy of expat artists in Ubud, injecting a new vigour into the region's arts and crafts, which have thrived ever since.

North of Denpasar

The stretch of road running 13km **north of Denpasar** to Ubud passes through an almost unbroken string of **arts- and crafts-producing towns**, all of which – despite their modern-day commercialization – have genuine histories as centres of refined artistic activity. Most were renowned for a particular speciality and this still applies today: Mas, for example, is the place for **woodcarvings**, Celuk for **silverwork**, and Batubulan for **stone sculptures**.

Nearly all towns described below lie on the main bemo route between Denpasar's Batubulan terminal and Ubud. With private transport they are easily visited on a day-trip from Ubud or the southern resorts; access from Sanur is particularly easy, with Batubulan less than 10km north of its northern outskirts.

Batubulan

Barely distinguishable from the northeastern suburbs of Denpasar, **BATUBULAN** acts as the capital's public-transport interchange for all bemos heading east and northeast, but it's also an important little town in its own right, home of the most famous Barong **dance troupes**, and respected across the island for its **stonecarvers**. There's also a **bird park** and a **reptile park** here. The town is strung out over 3km along the main road, defined by the bemo station in the south and the huge **Barong statue** at the Singapadu/Celuk junction in the north. Beyond the Barong statue, along the minor road to Singapadu, the northern stretch of the town is known as **Tegaltamu**.

Roadsides throughout Batubulan are crowded with orderly ranks of **stone statues**, grouped in front of the dozens of workshops and galleries. Most of these **shops** deal in a range of images and stone types, for both indoor and outdoor use (see the colour section, *The crafts of Bali and Lombok*, for a guide), and many appear to sell a surfeit of the same things – serene Buddhas, pagoda lanterns, sinuous Saraswatis (the goddess of learning) and elephant-headed Ganesh – but there is variation in quality, price and interpretation. Some shops sell carvings imported from Java, where much of the stone now originates, and most also deal in cheaper, mass-produced artworks that are moulded (rather than carved) from lava-stone "concrete"; see Basics, p.58, for details.

One of Batubulan's most famous stonecarving outlets is **I Made Sura**, west across the main road from the side road to Pura Puseh (about 250m south of the Barong statue), where you can watch the sculptors working on good-quality, freestanding pieces and friezes: a 60cm Garuda carved from limestone or sandstone can cost Rp3,000,000 here. At the other end of the scale, tiny, family-run **Bali Frog**, just north of the Barong statue on the way to the Bird Park, on the west side of the road at Jalan Raya Singapadu 96 (in Banjar Seraya), produces much cheaper, more portable figurines in slinky white Javanese limestone, particularly cute primitives and the eponymous humorous frogs; prices here start at Rp25,000. Many shops can organize shipping; see Basics, p.71, for shipping info.

In among the stonecarving outlets, you'll also come across a number of woodcarving places specializing in elegant **antique-style furniture**, doors and window frames. Just south of the Batubulan bemo terminal and officially in Tohpati, signed off Jalan W.R. Supratman, U.C. Silver is a large, upscale **silver workshop** and gallery with a good reputation for original contemporary designs, much of it set with semi precious stones (earrings with stones cost from

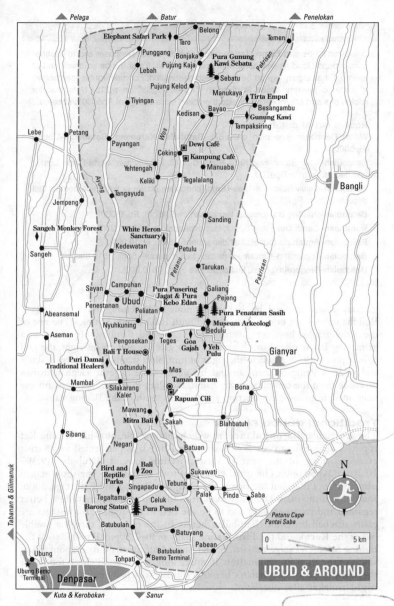

UBUD & AROUND

Rp350,000). Techniques used are the same as in the smaller workshops in nearby Celuk, but the choice here is huge.

Pura Puseh

As you'd expect in a town so renowned for stonecarving, the main temple, **Pura Puseh**, is exuberantly decorated. Its unusual design features a five-tiered

Batubulan public transport

Batubulan's **bus and bemo station** runs services across Denpasar and to destinations around Ubud as well as to east and north Bali. It's at the far southern end of town and has clearly signed bays for each destination. For main routes, see below; a guide to **journey times** is given in "Travel details" on p.218. Note that for **rucksacks** and other bulky baggage there's an extra charge of Rp5000 on bemos.

Routes out of Batubulan

Within **Denpasar** (see plan on p.87): **Batubulan–Kereneng**; **Batubulan–Ubung** (Rp5000).

Batubulan–west Sanur–east Kuta–**Nusa Dua** (Bali Collection; white Damri buses; last departure 3pm; Rp6500).

Batubulan–Celuk–Sukawati–Mas–**Ubud** (chocolate-brown or light blue bemos; last departure 6pm; Rp7000).

Batubulan–Padang Bai (bemos; last departure 5.45pm; Rp20,000).

Batubulan–Candi Dasa (big buses; last departure 6pm; Rp10,000).

Batubulan–Amlapura (buses; last departure 5.45pm; Rp10,000).

Batubulan–Tegalalang–**Kintamani** (buses; last departure 5pm; Rp10,000).

Batubulan–Singaraja (buses; last departure 5pm; Rp10,000).

gateway tower inspired by Indian religious architecture, and a number of Buddha images not normally associated with Bali's Hindu temples. The rest of the iconography, however, is characteristically and flamboyantly Balinese: a grimacing Bhoma head overlooks the main gateway and, to his right, the god Wisnu poses astride a bull; to the right of him, Siwa stands ankle-deep in skulls and wears a string of them around his neck, while majestic elephant torsos protrude from the central stairway balustrade. Pura Puseh is 250m east off the main road, from a signed junction about 250m south of the Barong statue.

Traditional dance shows

The spectacular **Barong dance**, in which the loveable, lion-like Barong Ket is pitted against the macabre widow-witch Rangda, is performed for tourists every morning of the year at various venues around Batubulan (9.30–10.30am; Rp50,000). The usual choice of tour operators is the show staged next to Pura Puseh but the one at the Denjulan Barong and Kris stage, 300m south down the main Denpasar road from the Pura Puseh junction, is better regarded and its dancers are said to be the best in the region. Both stages are easily reached by Ubud–Batubulan bemo. In the evenings, there's a double bill of the **Kecak** and the **Fire Dance** (daily 6.30–7.30pm; Rp50,000) at the Barong Sahadewa stage on Jalan SMKI, signed off the main road about 500m south of the Pura Puseh junction. If you're looking for good cheap food after the show, head to Batubulan's bemo terminal, which is transformed into a **night market** after sundown.

Bali Bird Park and Bali Reptile Park

Both the Bali Bird Park and the Bali Reptile Park (not to be confused with the vastly inferior reptile park in Mengwi) are fun places for children and fairly interesting for adults too. The parks are next door to each other, about 500m north of the Barong statue at the Singapadu/Celuk intersection, then west about 400m, or about 3.5km northwest of Batubulan bemo terminal. All bemos between Batubulan and Ubud or Gianyar can drop you at the intersection.

There's a good but expensive **restaurant** inside the bird park, or you can get cheap food at a tiny warung about 30m outside the car park.

Home to some 250 species of bird, mostly from Indonesia, the **Bali Bird Park** (**Taman Burung**; daily 9am–5.30pm; ⓦwww.bali-bird-park.com; $13.75, kids $7.10, family ticket $34.75) is beautifully landscaped around its enormous walk-in aviaries. Highlights include various birds of paradise, bright scarlet egrets, the weird-looking rhino hornbill, and iridescent blue Javanese kingfishers. And you shouldn't miss this rare chance to see the fluffy white Bali starling, Bali's only endemic bird and a severely endangered species (see the box on p.339 for more). There is also a pair of two-metre-long Komodo dragons.

All the tanks and cages at the **Bali Reptile Park** (**Rimba Reptil**; daily 9am–5pm; $9, kids $4.5) are instructively labelled too: look out for the green tree pit viper, which is very common in Bali, and very dangerous, as well as for the astonishing eight-metre-long reticulated python, thought to be the largest python in captivity in the world. There are Komodo dragons here too, and visitors are invited to pick up and cuddle one of the park's scaly green iguanas.

Singapadu and the back roads to Ubud

The main road from Denpasar divides at Batubulan's Barong statue roundabout, the principal artery and bemo routes veering right (east) to Celuk (see p.172), and the left-hand (north) prong narrowing into a scenic **back road**. This runs past the Bali Bird Park and on through traditional villages as far as Sayan, a few kilometres west of Ubud, before continuing to Payangan and eventually to Kintamani.

Just over 1km north of the T-junction, you'll pass through the charming village of **SINGAPADU**, a classic central-Bali settlement of house and temple compounds that hide behind low walls and effusive roadside shrubbery. Some of Bali's most expert mask-carvers come from this village, but as most of them work only on commissions from temples and dance troupes, there's no obvious commercial face to this local industry. Singapadu is also the site of the **Bali Zoo** (**Kebun Binatang Bali**; ⓦwww.bali-zoo .com; daily 9am–5pm; $18, kids $9, family $48.80), which is home to a walk-in aviary as well as a range of creatures – including crocodiles, cassowaries, lions, tigers and Komodo dragons – mostly housed in depressingly bare enclosures, though an ongoing collaboration with Western Australia's Peel Zoo aims to improve that.

Some 13km north of Singapadu the road runs through the village of **SAYAN**, located in the spectacular Ayung river valley, site of several top-flight hotels (see Ubud accommodation, p.186) and a couple of **white water-rafting** centres. Ubud is just 3km east from Sayan, via Penestanan and Campuhan.

For a more direct, quieter and even more scenic route to Ubud, turn east off the Sayan road a couple of kilometres north of Singapadu, in the heart of the kite-making and ceramic-egg-painting village of **NEGARI**. This route soon takes you over the wide Wos River, north via **MAWANG** and on through beautiful countryside interspersed with the art galleries and mask-making workshops of **LODTUNDUH**, before arriving in Pengosekan on the southern edge of Ubud. Lodtunduh, about 3km south of Ubud, is the site of some appealingly affordable little villas for rent, reviewed on p.184. En route, a minor easterly diversion before Mawang brings you to the headquarters of the Mitra Bali **fair-trade arts and crafts** NGO on Jalan Gunung Abang in Banjar Lodsema (off the Negari–Batuan road; see map, p.169; Mon–Fri 8am–5pm; ☏0361/295010, ⓦwww.mitrabali.com). Here you can learn more about Mitra Bali's groundbreaking work and browse the small display of crafts and silver jewellery made by their fair-trade producers. They do wholesale and retail and are happy to make to order (see p.62 for more info).

Celuk

Immediately east of Batubulan is **CELUK**, known as the "silver village" because it's a major centre for **jewellery** production. Celuk silversmiths have extended their homes to include workshops and salerooms and welcome both retail and wholesale customers, though designs are often less innovative than in Kuta's shops. The best-priced Celuk outlets are along Jalan Jagaraga (a back road to Singapadu), which runs north from the western end of the main road, Jalan Raya; among dozens of possibilities, you could try small, family-run Ketut Sunaka at no. 28, which has a workshop at the back. The larger, more upmarket, factory-style Ana's II, signed off the eastern end of Jalan Raya, also has a good reputation. (For one of the largest nearby silver outlets, see Batubulan, p.168). Batubulan–Ubud **bemos** pass through Celuk, but be warned that the shops and workshops are spread out over a three-kilometre stretch.

Sukawati and around

The lively market town of **SUKAWATI**, 4km east of Celuk, is an important commercial centre and a major stop on the tourist arts-and-crafts shopping circuit. It's especially convenient for anyone reliant on public transport as Ubud–Batubulan **bemos** stop right in front of the central market.

Sukawati's chief draw is its **art market** (*pasar seni*), which trades every day from dawn till dusk inside a traditional covered two-storey building on the main road, Jalan Raya Sukawati. Here you'll find a tantalizing array of artefacts, paintings, fabrics, clothing and basketware, piled high on stalls that are crammed together so tightly you can barely walk between them. Sarongs and lengths of *ikat* cloth are excellent buys, as are ceremonial temple parasols and huge decorative fans made from locally produced *perada* cloth. If you can't face the scrum, there are several good basket shops outside, on Jalan Raya, just to the north.

Sukawati is also famous for its *wayang kulit* **shadow-puppet makers and performers**, a traditional form of entertainment that's still very popular across the island (for more on which, see Contexts, p.447). The puppets (*wayang*) are made out of very thin animal hide, perforated to let the light shine through in intricate patterns, and designed to traditional profiles that are instantly recognizable to a Balinese audience. Several of Sukawati's puppeteers (*dalang*) make, and perform with, both *wayang kulit* puppets and the wooden *wayang golek* puppets, selling their creations from workshops inside their homes. **I Wayan Nartha** (☏0361/299080) has a shop on Jalan Padma (the road that runs east off Jalan Raya, one block south of the *pasar seni*); and **I Wayan Mardika** (☏0361/299646) sells from inside his home on Jalan Yudisthira, the road that runs parallel to the east of Jalan Raya, reached by walking east down Jalan Ciung Wanara (opposite the *pasar seni*) and then walking left for about 100m. Both workshops are in the *banjar* of Babakan and are signed off Jalan Raya Sukawati.

There are several cheap **warung** on Jalan Raya Sukawati, including the tiny *Warung Vegetarian Karuna Vittala*, about 1km north of the Pasar Seni on the east side of the road, which is run by a follower of the famous Indian guru Sai Baba.

Batuan

Northern Sukawati merges into southern **BATUAN**, another ribbon-like roadside development, which was the original home of the **Batuan style of**

painting and is now a commercial centre for all the main Balinese styles. The Batuan style first evolved in the 1930s when Ida Bagus Made Togog, Ida Bagus Made Wija and others started experimenting with black ink, peopling their visions with dozens of figures cowering beneath ominously dense forests; see Contexts, p.455, for more about the evolution of this style.

The public face of modern Batuan is now dominated by **galleries**: huge emporia line the main road, while smaller studios are tucked away within those houses in the traditional neighbourhoods, west of the main road, that hang "painter" signboards above their gateways. One of the larger, quality outlets is the **I Wayan Bendi Gallery**, on the west side of the main road, named after the contemporary artist whose Batuan-style pictures are exhibited all over the world as well as in Ubud's Neka Art Museum. A few examples of Wayan Bendi's work hang in the gallery (not for sale) along with a sizeable collection by other artists. Another worthwhile if undeniably commercial gallery is the sprawling **Dewa Putu Toris**, 250m west off the southern end of the main Batuan–Ubud road in the *banjar* of Tengah: turn west at the *raksasa* (demon-giant) statue and follow the signs. Just before the gallery you'll pass Batuan's main temple, **Pura Desa-Pura Puseh** (dawn to dusk; donation), graced with appropriately elaborate gold-painted woodwork.

At the northern limit of Batuan, a plump stone statue of a well-fed baby Brahma (officially known as Brahma Rare and unofficially as the **Fat Baby statue**) marks the Sakah turn-off to Blahbatuh and points east (see p.227), while the main road continues north.

Mas

Long established as a major **woodcarving** centre, **MAS** is a rewarding place both to browse and to buy, but be warned that it stretches 5km from end to end – and its reputation means that prices are high.

The woodcarvers of Mas gained great inspiration from the innovative **Pita Maha arts movement** during the 1930s, which encouraged the carving of secular subjects as well as traditional masks and religious images, and championed individual expression. Today, the range of carvings on display in the Mas shops is enormous; you'll find superbly imaginative portraits of legendary creatures and erotic human figures, alongside tacky cats, dogs and fish. Some of the woodcarving outlets in Mas are managed by the carvers and their families, but many are larger commercial enterprises.

The best place to start is the gallery and home of one of Bali's most famous woodcarving families, the **Nyana Tilem Gallery**, located approximately halfway along the Mas–Ubud road, about 2km north of the baby Brahma statue. Born in 1912, **Ida Bagus Nyana** (also spelt Njana) was one of the most prolific and innovative craftsmen of the 1930s and 1940s, closely associated with the Pita Maha arts movement, and credited with introducing the sleek, simple and slightly surreal style of elongated figures that's now so popular (for more, see p.456). His son, the late **Ida Bagus Tilem**, was renowned for highly expressive pieces using gnarled and twisted wood. The compound of this high-caste family (whose descendants still run the place) contains both a shop selling works by students of the two men and a gallery displaying some of their finest originals. The quality and craftsmanship here is breathtaking, notable for the exquisite attention to the grain and peerless sinuosity; in the upstairs showroom, the 1.2-metre-tall carving of a fisherman casting his net is a case in point. This extraordinary, painstaking piece of work was carved from a single piece of wood and took nine months to complete, not least because the mesh of the net was gouged out millimetre by millimetre.

Though many works at Nyana Tilem will be priced (and sized) beyond the reach of most visitors, they do set a benchmark. Once you've seen the best, you're ready to browse the street, but you'll probably want to avoid the other big galleries, which tend to charge way over the odds ($150 for an unremarkable 20-centimetre-high figurine).

Practicalities

All Ubud–Batubulan **bemos** zip through Mas. At its northern end, Mas merges into the village of Teges, which is about 2.5km from Peliatan on the outskirts of Ubud. *Taman Harum Cottages*, at the southern end of Mas, makes a charming place to stay and is reviewed on p.185. Non-guests are welcome to eat at its **restaurant**, or you could try *Rapuan Cili* (daily 8am–6pm), which overlooks a pretty ricefield panorama, serves wood-fired pizzas, and offers diners free use of the swimming pool; to find it, continue beyond *Taman Harum* for 500m, then follow the signs 300m east down a side road.

Museum Rudana, Teges

Sandwiched between Mas to the south and Peliatan to the north, the main attraction in the woodcarving village of **Teges** is not wood but contemporary Balinese painting, displayed with panache at the **Museum Rudana** (daily 9am–5pm; Rp20,000; Ⓦwww.museumrudana.com), which was founded by local politician Nyoman Rudana. Although the exhibitions change, and do not always focus exclusively on modern art, the museum's core collection includes an impressive number of works by the big hitters of the contemporary scene. They include **Nyoman Gunarsa** (see p.234), **Made Budhiana** and **Nyoman Erawan**, all of whom are associated with the influential Sanggar Dewata Indonesia style, best described as Balinese Hindu abstract expressionism, which has been the dominant form of modern Balinese painting since the 1970s (there's more on Balinese painters on p.453). Huge picture-windows offer inspiring views over adjacent rice-paddies and a contemplative garden, and there's a showroom with art for sale next door. Museum Rudana is 800m north of the Nyana Tilem gallery in Mas and about 1.5km south of the junction with Jalan Peliatan; it's a ten-minute ride on the Batubulan bemo from central Ubud or an hour's walk.

Ubud

Ever since the German artist Walter Spies arrived here in 1928, **UBUD** has been a magnet for any tourist with the slightest curiosity about Balinese arts and traditions. It is now a fully fledged resort, visited by nearly every holiday-maker on the island, even if only as part of a day-trip to the much-publicized Monkey Forest.

Although it's fashionable to characterize Ubud as the "real" Bali, especially in contrast with Kuta, it bears little resemblance to a typical Balinese town. Organic cafés, riverside bungalows and craft shops crowd its central market-place, chic expat homes occupy some of the most panoramic locations, and sidestreets are dotted with spas and alternative treatment centres. It even hosts an annual literary **festival**, the Ubud Writers and Readers Festival (🔌www .ubudwritersfestival.com), every October, and the Bali Spirit Festival of world music, dance and yoga every March (🔌www.balispiritfestival.com). There is major development along the central **Jalan Monkey Forest** (officially known as **Jalan Wanara Wana**), a kilometre-long street of hotels, restaurants, tour agencies and souvenir shops, and the core village has expanded to take in the neighbouring hamlets of **Campuhan**, **Penestanan**, **Sanggingan**, **Nyuhkuning**, **Padang Tegal**, **Pengosekan** and **Peliatan**. Yet traditional practices are still fundamental to daily life in Ubud – arguably more so than anywhere else on Bali – and the atmosphere remains undeniably seductive, an appealing blend of ethnic integrity and tourist-friendly comforts. The people of Ubud and adjacent villages really do still paint, carve, dance and make music, and religious rituals here are so rigorously observed that hardly a day goes by without there being some kind of festival celebrated in the area. Appropriately, Ubud is now a recognized centre of **spiritual tourism**, a place where visitors can experience indigenous healing practices as well as dabble in any number of imported therapies.

The surrounding countryside and traditional hamlets give ample opportunity for exploration on foot or by bike, and **shopping** tends to become a major pastime too, with Balinese carvers and painters selling their wares at every corner and plenty of outlets run by expat fashion designers and artists. The **restaurants** and **accommodation** also set Ubud apart: imaginative menus are the norm here (with vegetarians well catered for), and hotels and homestays tend to be small and charming. It's true that Ubud does take itself rather seriously, and the place can feel pretentious, especially if you're just whizzing through. But linger for several days, preferably in family-run accommodation, and you'll get an intriguing glimpse of the daily rhythms of traditional Bali. In fact, an increasing number of travellers are now choosing to base themselves in Ubud for the duration of their holiday: the volcanic peak of Gunung Batur and its crater lake are just 40km north; local tour operators offer sunrise treks up Gunung Agung; and it takes less than two hours on a tourist shuttle bus or bemo to reach the east-coast beach of Candi Dasa.

Some history

Ubud became a royal seat only towards the end of the nineteenth century, when Sukawati scion **Cokorda Gede Sukawati** was made a *punggawa* (ruling nobleman) and chose to establish his court north of his home town, at Ubud. Territories and allegiances were in constant flux during that period and in 1900 the Ubud court was obliged to join its influential neighbour, the Gianyar royal family, in asking for the protection of the Netherlands Indies government against other land-hungry rajas. As a Dutch protectorate with no more wars to worry about, the Sukawati family and the people of Ubud were then able to get on with the business of making carvings and paintings and refining their dancing and gamelan skills. Cokorda Gede's son, **Cokorda Gede Agung Sukawati** (1910–78), focused his energy on the cultivation of the arts, and began to actively encourage foreign artists to live in his district. The most significant of these early visitors was the artist and musician **Walter Spies**, who established himself in the hamlet of Campuhan on the western border of Ubud in 1928. Over the next nine years, Spies introduced influential new ideas to Ubud's already vibrant **artistic community** and helped secure foreign patronage. In his wake came a crowd of other Western intellectuals, including the Dutch artist Rudolph Bonnet, the American musician Colin McPhee, and

ACCOMMODATION

Alam Jiwa	Z
Alam Sari Keliki Hotel	A
Amandari	D
Ananda Cottages	F
Artja Inn	T
Bali T House	aa
Family Guest House	V
Four Seasons Resort Bali	N
Gusti's Garden 2	S
Gusti's Garden Bungalows	P
Hotel Tjampuhan	O
Klub Kokos	B
Kori Agung Bungalow	J
Londo 2	I
Londo Ricefield Bungalows	R
Melati Cottages	Q
Sari Bungalows	Y
Sayan Terrace	M
Sri Sunari	U
Sunrise Villas	E
Swasti Cottage	X
Taman Bebek	L
Taman Harum Cottages	bb
Taman Indrakila	G
Taman Rahasia	K
Tegal Sari	W
Uma Ubud	C
Waka di Ume	H

White Heron Sanctuary ▲

Rumah Lingkungan ▲

Bangkiang Sidem, Keliki & ▲

Payogan ▲

Payangan & Gunung Batur ▲

Lungsiakan ▲

Kedewatan ▲

Petanu

Wos Timur

Wos Barat

Blangsuh

Ayung

JALAN ANDONG

JALAN SUWETA

JALAN RAYA SANGGINGAN

JALAN RAYA CAMPUHAN

JL. LUNGSIAKAN

Spa Hati

Mitra Bali Fair Trade

Police

Ubud Botanic Garden

Threads of Life

Ubud Palace

Ubud Sari

Museum Puri Lukisan

Pura Dalem

Ibah Spa

Museum Blanco

Ubud Clinic

Pura Gunung Lebih

Dewa Bharata Bungalows

Warung Cinema

Meditation Shop

Neka Art Museum

Bali Botanica Day Spa

Bintang Supermarket

Simon's Studio

Sobek

Bali Adventure Tours

PELIATAN

KUTUH

SAMBAHAN

UBUD

CAMPUHAN

SANGGINGAN

PENESTANAN

SAYAN

LUNGSIAKAN

KEDEWATAN

See Central Ubud & Padang Tegal map for detail

JL. SANDAT (JL. TIRTA TAWAR)

JL. TIRTA TAWAR

JALAN RAYA UBUD

JALAN KAJENG

See Central Ubud & Padang Tegal map for detail

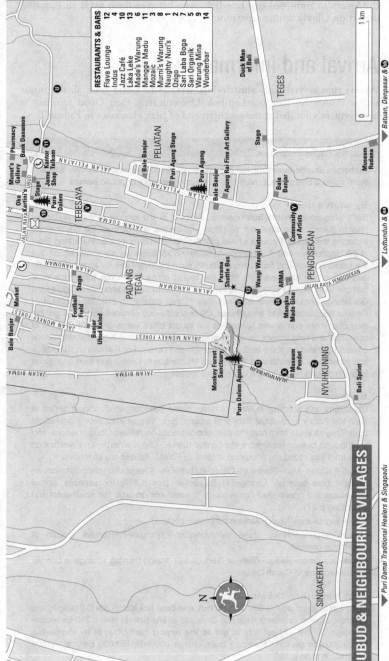

RESTAURANTS & BARS	
Flava Lounge	12
Indus	4
Jazz Café	10
Laka Leke	13
Made's Warung	6
Mangga Madu	11
Mozaic	3
Murni's Warung	8
Naughty Nuri's	1
Ozigo	2
Sari Laba Boga	7
Sari Organik	5
Warung Mina	9
Wunderbar	14

0   1 km

Duck Man of Bali

TEGES

Museum Rudana

PELIATAN

Bale Banjar

Puri Agung Stage

Pura Agung

Agung Rai Fine Art Gallery

Bale Banjar

Stage

JALAN PELIATAN

JALAN PELIATAN

Munut's Gallery

Pharmacy

Bank Danamon

Jamu Kantor Shop Telkom

Oka Kartini's UBUD

Stage

Pura Dalem

JALAN RAYA UBUD

TEBESAYA

JALAN SUKMA

Community of Artists

ARMA

PENGOSEKAN

JALAN RAYA PENGOSEKAN

Mangku Made Gina

Wangi Wangi Natural

Perama Shuttle Bus

PADANG TEGAL

JALAN HANOMAN

JALAN HANOMAN

Stage

Market

Bale Banjar

Football Field

Banjar Ubud Kelod

JALAN MONKEY FOREST

JALAN MONKEY FOREST

JALAN BISMA

Monkey Forest Sanctuary

Pura Dalem Agung

JALAN NYUH BULAN

Museum Pendet

NYUHKUNING

Bali Sprint

N

UBUD & NEIGHBOURING VILLAGES

SINGAKERTA

the American anthropologist Jane Belo, who between them made an enduring impact on Ubud's artistic reputation.

Arrival and information

Perama runs several daily **shuttle-bus** services to Ubud from all the major tourist centres on Bali and Lombok. Unfortunately, their Ubud terminus is inconveniently located at the southern end of Jalan Hanoman in Padang Tegal,

Moving on from Ubud

Numerous **shuttle buses** run out of Ubud every day to destinations all over Bali, and there's also a cheaper but more time-consuming network of public **bemos**.

By shuttle bus
Bali's ubiquitous **shuttle-bus** operator, Perama, is the longest running and most reliable transport provider out of Ubud and serves all major tourist destinations including the airport. **Perama's** head office is inconveniently located in Padang Tegal at the far southern end of Jl Hanoman (☏0361/973316, ⓦwww.peramatour.com), but the buses do pick-ups from central Ubud's main thoroughfares for an extra Rp5000 and tickets are also available from the tourist office and some travel agencies. Sample fares include Rp30,000 to Kuta, Rp85,000 to Lovina and Rp240,000 to the Gili Islands (including boat transfer). See "Travel details", p.218, for a full list of Perama destinations and frequencies. Other shuttle-bus services come and go, but may offer more convenient schedules: the tourist office keeps an up-to-date list of operators and sells tickets, as do travel agents. The alternative is the transfer service offered by transport touts and some losmen and hotels. For Pemuteran, Gilimanuk and other parts of **northwest Bali**, take a shuttle bus to Lovina and then change on to a westbound bemo for the last coastal stretch.

By bemo
Ubud runs only a limited number of direct **bemo** services, which should depart at least half-hourly from about 6am until around 2pm, then at least hourly until about 5pm. They all leave from near the central crossroads on Jl Raya Ubud; the east- and southbound bemos leave from the central market, and the north- and westbound ones from just round the corner on Jl Monkey Forest. **Routes** are as follows:

Ubud–Peliatan–Mas–Sukawati–Celuk–**Batubulan** (Denpasar; chocolate-brown or light blue bemos). Change in Batubulan (see p.170) for services across **Denpasar** and convoluted connections to **southern resorts**, the **southwest** and **Java** (see p.87).

Ubud–Tegalalang–Pujung–**Kintamani** (brown bemos).

Ubud–Campuhan–Neka Museum–Kedewatan–Payangan–**Kintamani** (brown or bright blue bemos).

Ubud–Goa Gajah–Bedulu–**Gianyar** (turquoise or orange bemos). Change in Gianyar for connections to **Candi Dasa**.

Boat and airline tickets
Many Ubud travel agents sell Perama **bus and boat tickets** for the Gili Islands and Lombok, as well as international and domestic **airline tickets** (see p.210 for recommendations). The easiest way to **get to the airport** from Ubud is by shuttle bus (Rp30,000 per person); transport touts charge about Rp150,000 per car. Airport information is on p.100.

about 750m from the southern end of Jalan Monkey Forest, and 2.5km from the central market. As there's no local bemo or taxi service from here, you can either choose to pay an extra Rp5000 for the Perama drop-off service (which entails a change of van at the terminus and only serves the main roads in central Ubud) or you can take your chances with touts offering free transport to whichever accommodation they are promoting. Other shuttle-bus operators are more likely to make drops either on Jalan Monkey Forest or near the market on Jalan Raya Ubud (some even offer a door-to-door service), but check this before booking.

All public **bemos** terminate in front of Ubud's central marketplace, at the junction of Jalan Raya Ubud and Jalan Monkey Forest (signed as Jalan Wanara Wana, but rarely referred to as such). If coming from Batubulan (Denpasar) you can alight in **Peliatan** en route; if heading for **Campuhan**, **Sanggingan** or **Penestanan**, you can shorten the walk by connecting on to a west-bound service at the market (see "Moving on", opposite). For **Nyuhkuning**, you'll either have to walk from the market (about 30min) or negotiate a ride with a transport tout.

Information

Ubud's **tourist office** (daily 8am–8pm; ☎0361/973285) is centrally located just west of the Jalan Raya Ubud/Jalan Monkey Forest intersection. It's run by a village organization and posts schedules of dance performances and upcoming festivals on its useful outdoor noticeboards. The staff sell tickets for dance shows and organize free transport to the less accessible venues, run their own inexpensive day-trips to local sights and sell shuttle-bus tickets for Perama and their competitors. They also dish out copies of the excellent free **Ubud Community booklet**, which carries a calendar of temple ceremonies and dance performances as well as interesting features.

If you're planning to do any serious walking or cycling around the Ubud area, buy the worthwhile *Bali Pathfinder* **map** from any local bookstore. Another good investment, though less widely available, is the slim, offbeat volume of **guided walks**, *Bali Bird Walks*, written by the local expat ornithologist Victor Mason.

Transport, tours and activities

The most enjoyable way of seeing Ubud and its immediate environs is **on foot**, making your way via the tracks through the rice-paddies and the narrow *gang* that weave through the more traditional *banjar*.

Bicycles make a pleasant alternative, and can be rented from the efficient Mutiara Cycles, next to the tourist office on Jalan Raya, as well as from many streetside outlets along Jalan Monkey Forest (from Rp20,000). There are countless possibilities for interesting **bike rides** in the area. If you're fit and have decent gears, the Campuhan ridge walk described on p.196 could be fun, or you might consider cycling up to Tegalalang, about 13km north of Ubud, via Jalan Suweta in central Ubud, a back road that's both calm and fairly traffic-free, if a little hilly. There have been some instances of bag snatching from bicycles by passing motorcyclists in the more remote areas so secure it to the basket if you have one.

There are no metered **taxis** in Ubud, so you have to bargain with the **transport touts** who hang around on nearly every corner; typically, you can expect to pay around Rp10,000–20,000 for local rides on a motorbike, a bit more in a car. Most outlying hotels provide free transport in and out of central Ubud.

It's also possible to use the public **bemos** for certain short hops (generally charged at Rp5000): to get to the Neka Art Museum, flag down any bemo heading west (such as the turquoise ones going to Payangan); for Pengosekan or Peliatan take any bemo heading for Batubulan; and for Petulu use the orange bemos to Pujung or the brown bemos to Tegalalang and Kintamani.

Most transport touts and tour agencies along Jalan Monkey Forest offer **car and motorbike rental**; see Basics, p.41, for price guidelines and advice. A reputable and efficient car-rental place that also offers optional third-party insurance is Ary's Business and Travel Service (℡0361/973130, ✉arys_tour @yahoo.com), next to Ary's Bookshop on Jalan Raya Ubud. Note that if you're driving up to the Kintamani volcanoes or to the north coast from here, it's worth getting a more powerful Kijang rather than opting for the cheaper Jimny.

Tours and other activities

Although the Ubud tourist office and all travel agencies offer programmes of standard **tours** (Rp125,000–200,000 per person, generally for minimum two people), it's usually more rewarding to hire your own **driver** and design your own itinerary. A day-trip to Kintamani, for example, could cost you just Rp300,000 all-in, for up to four people. Recommended freelance drivers include Putu Purnawan (℡0816/471 6857, ✉putu09@yahoo.com) and Nyoman Suastika (℡0813/3870 1962; ⑭www.nyoman-suastika.tripod.com), or you can arrange one through almost any car-rental outlet.

Most tour agencies advertise inclusive trips to local **festivals** and **cremations** (for more on which, see p.464), though for those within walking distance of Ubud you can simply check the details on the board outside the tourist office. Note that whether you go to a temple ceremony with a group or on your own, formal dress (sashes and sarongs) is required. Agencies also sell **diving packages** run by the dive operators of south Bali (see box, p.146).

Guided walks, treks and other activities

Ubud is especially good for unusual **guided walks**. These and all other tours can be booked direct or through agencies.

Ubud for kids

Many of the **courses and workshops** listed on p.209 welcome younger participants. In particular, Studio Perak welcomes all over-eights to make their own silver **jewellery**, and Pondok Pekak runs children's classes in **gamelan** and Balinese **dance**, which are suitable for most over-sixes. Pondok Pekak also has a library of **children's books**.

Traditional **dance-drama performances** (see p.203) can also be entertaining for kids, particularly the Kecak (Monkey Dance), and the *wayang kulit* shadow-puppet shows. Both are staged several nights a week in the Ubud area; the tourist office keeps a schedule.

There are a number of animal parks within 45 minutes' drive of Ubud that make fun days out for children of most ages. The **Elephant Park** in Taro (see p.216) gives everyone the chance to feed the elephants and watch them bathe, and you can also join a short elephant safari ride. At the **Bali Safari and Marine Park** in Gianyar (see p.227) a safari bus gives visitors close-ups of the resident lions, rhinos, white tigers and the rest. In Batubulan, the attractively landscaped **Bali Bird Park** (see p.170) houses plenty of pretty birds, while the **Bali Reptile Park** next door has all sorts of slimy creatures, including huge pythons, chameleons and little Komodo dragons.

Most **whitewater-rafting** operators (see opposite) also accept children (depending on the course), but river kayaking is unsuitable for children under 14.

Bicycle tours Downhill rides from Gunung Batur, via villages, temples and traditional homes. Bike Baik Tours ⓦwww.balispirit.com/tours, ☎0813/3867 3852; Rp350,000.

Bird walks Bird-spotting walks in the Campuhan area, organized by expat author Victor Mason. Bali Bird Walks ☎0812/391 3801, ⓦwww.balibirdwalk .com; Tues, Fri, Sat & Sun 9am; US$33, including lunch and the use of shared binoculars.

Cultural and ecological walks Guided walks with an emphasis on learning about rural traditions and meeting village craftspeople. Keep Walking Tours, c/o Bali Spirit, Jl Hanoman 44B ☎0361/970581, ⓦwww.balispirit.com/tours; from Rp95,000 (minimum two people).

Elephant treks At the Elephant Safari Park in Taro, 13km north of Ubud; see p.216.

Sunrise mountain treks Up Gunung Batur (from $45) and Gunung Agung ($100). Bali Sunrise 2001, Jl Raya Tegalalang 88 ☎0818/552669, ⓦwww .balisunrise2001.com, with another office in Toya Bungkah (see p.283); and Keep Walking Tours, c/o Bali Spirit, Jl Hanoman 44B ☎0361/970581, ⓦwww .balispirit.com/tours/bali_tour_keep_walking.html.

Traditional medicine walks Traditional herbalists Ni Wayan Lilir and I Made Westi show how to identify native medicinal plants on an educational walk through Ubud countryside. Herb Walk ☎0361/975051, ⓔsupadupa@dps.centrin.net.id; 3–4hr; $18.

Whitewater rafting and kayaking On the Ayung River just west of Ubud. The 2hr courses cover about 8km and cross Class 2 and 3 rapids; $70 or $45 for under-12s where appropriate. Bali Adventure Tours ☎0361/721480, ⓦwww .baliadventuretours.com; and Sobek ☎0361/844 6194, ⓦwww.99bali.com/adventure/sobek.

Accommodation

Ubud is known for its intimate **accommodation**, especially its family homestays in traditional compounds. There are plenty of more upscale options too and many offer rice-paddy or river views (usually best from upper-floor rooms). Light sleepers might want to bring earplugs as Ubud's frog population is ubiquitous, loud, and stays up late.

Few places on Jalan Monkey Forest have a road number but all listed accommodation is marked on a **map** – either the Central Ubud and Padang Tegal map (p.182) or the Ubud and neighbouring villages map (p.177).

Central Ubud and Padang Tegal

The kilometre-long **Jalan Monkey Forest** is the most central, but also the most congested and commercial part of town. It has few genuine homestays, with the emphasis instead on small mid-range or upmarket hotels comprising just a dozen bungalows and a pool. The tiny roads that run off Jalan Monkey Forest or parallel to it have a very different feel and, amazingly, still retain a peaceful village atmosphere. Much of the accommodation on these conveniently central lanes – Jalan Karna, Jalan Maruti, Jalan Gootama, Jalan Kajeng and Jalan Bisma, for example – is in small, archetypal homestays, where just a handful of rooms have been built in the family compound; they're usually very friendly places, though some people find the compounds claustrophobic.

The *banjar* of **Padang Tegal**, which is centred on Jalan Hanoman, merges with the eastern borders of central Ubud, so staying here means you're rarely more than a fifteen-minute walk from Jalan Monkey Forest, though you may be quite a hike from the marketplace. It's quieter than Jalan Monkey Forest but has plenty of shops and restaurants.

Inexpensive

Artja Inn Jl Kajeng 9 ☎0361/974425. Set away from the road behind a typical family compound in a pretty garden with a stream and wooded surrounds, this classic losmen offers six simple but pleasant bamboo-walled cottages with open-roofed, cold-water *mandi*. ❶

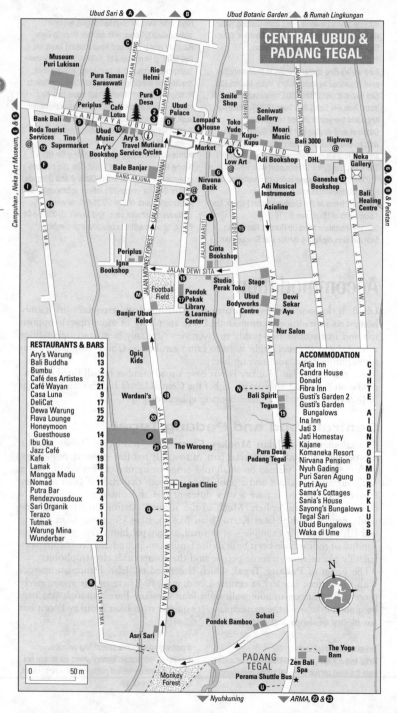

CENTRAL UBUD &
PADANG TEGAL

Ubud Sari & Ⓐ ▲ ▲ Ⓑ **Ubud Botanic Garden** ▲ **& Rumah Lingkungan**

Museum
Puri Lukisan

Pura Taman
Saraswati

Rio
Helmi

Jalan Kajeng

Jalan Suweta

Smile
Shop

Jalan Sandat (Jl. Tirta Tawar)

Periplus
Café
Lotus

Pura
Desa Ⓒ

Ⓓ

Ⓔ

Ubud
Palace

Lempad's
House

Seniwati
Gallery

Moari
Music

Bali 3000

Highway

Bank Bali
Ⓞ

JALAN RAYA UBUD

Toko
Yude

Kupu-
Kupu

Neka
Gallery

Roda Tourist
Services
@

Tino
Supermarket

Ubud
Music

Ary's
Bookshop

Ary's
Travel Mutiara
Service Cycles

ⓘ

JALAN RAYA UBUD

Market

Low Art
@

Adi Bookshop

DHL

Ganesha
Bookshop

Bali
Healing
Centre

Bale Banjar

GANG ARJUNA

Nirvana
Batik

Adi Musical
Instruments

Asialine

JALAN BISMA

JALAN MONKEY FOREST (JALAN WANARA WANA)

JALAN KARNA

JALAN WANARA WANA

Periplus
Igna
Bookshop

Cinta
Bookshop

JALAN DEWI SITA

JALAN MARUT

JALAN GOOTAMA

JALAN SUGRIWA

JALAN JEMBAWAN

Football
Field

Ⓜ

Pondok
Pekak
Library
& Learning
Center

Studio
Perak Toko

Stage

Ubud
Bodyworks
Centre

Dewi
Sekar
Ayu

Banjar Ubud
Kelod

Nur Salon

JALAN HANOMAN

Opiq
Kids

Wardani's

Ⓝ

Bali Spirit
Tegun

Ⓞ

The Waroeng

Pura Desa
Padang Tegal

Legian Clinic

JALAN MONKEY FOREST (JALAN WANARA WANA)

Ⓠ

Ⓡ

JALAN BISMA

Ⓢ

N

Ⓣ

Asri Sari

Pondok Bamboo

Sehati

PADANG
TEGAL

The Yoga
Bam

Zen Bali
Spa

Monkey
Forest

Perama Shuttle Bus

Nyuhkuning ▼ ▼ **ARMA,** 22 **&** 23

0 ——— 50 m

182

RESTAURANTS & BARS

Ary's Warung	10
Bali Buddha	13
Bumbu	2
Café des Artistes	12
Café Wayan	21
Casa Luna	9
DeliCat	17
Dewa Warung	15
Flava Lounge	22
Honeymoon	
Guesthouse	14
Ibu Oka	3
Jazz Café	8
Kafe	19
Lamak	18
Mangga Madu	6
Nomad	11
Putra Bar	20
Rendezvousdoux	4
Sari Organik	5
Terazo	1
Tutmak	16
Warung Mina	7
Wunderbar	23

ACCOMMODATION

Artja Inn	C
Candra House	J
Donald	H
Fibra Inn	T
Gusti's Garden 2	E
Gusti's Garden	
Bungalows	A
Ina Inn	I
Jati 3	Q
Jati Homestay	N
Kajane	P
Komaneka Resort	O
Nirvana Pension	G
Nyuh Gading	M
Puri Saren Agung	D
Putri Ayu	R
Sama's Cottages	F
Sania's House	K
Sayong's Bungalows	L
Tegal Sari	U
Ubud Bungalows	S
Waka di Ume	B

Candra House Jl Karna 8 ☎0361/976529. Nine typical losmen-style rooms inside the family compound on this quiet but central *gang*. All rooms have fans, cold-water bathrooms, verandas and good breakfasts. ❶

🏃 **Donald** Jl Gootama 9 ☎0361/977156. Tiny but well-run and very friendly homestay offering four exceptionally cheap, quite nicely furnished bungalows (two with hot water) in a secluded garden compound. ❶

Gusti's Garden 2 Jl Abangan, about 150m walk north along a path from the aqueduct on western Jl Raya Ubud (see map, p.177): follow signs from *Abangan Bungalows* ☎0361/971474, ⓔgusti-garden@yahoo.com. Occupying a quiet spot overlooking the paddies on the far western fringes of central Ubud, this cluster of seven nicely designed, contemporary rooms is deservedly popular so reservations are advisable. Also has a grotto-like swimming pool. Phone for pick-up within the Ubud area. ❸

🏃 **Gusti's Garden Bungalows** Jl Kajeng 27 ☎0361/973311, ⓔgustigarden@yahoo .com. Fifteen pleasant, above-average losmen rooms, all with hot water, set around a swimming pool in an attractive, stepped garden, and a peaceful location. ❸

🏃 **Ina Inn** Off Jl Bisma ☎0361/973317, ⓦwww.inainn.com. Located in a panoramic spot on a small *gang* surrounded by ricefields, these twelve attractively furnished cottages all have four-poster beds, bathtubs and hot water (but no a/c). The most expensive penthouse rooms have a spacious living area and huge windows affording wide views, and there's a great rooftop pool. Exceptionally good value. Cottages ❸ Penthouse rooms ❹

Jati 3 Off Jl Monkey Forest ☎0361/973249, ⓔjati3_ubud@yahoo.com. Located at the end of a quiet *gang* (if arriving by car, access is via the *Lotus Lane* car park next door), this place offers five good-quality losmen-style bungalows in a courtyard, plus a small spa. But the real attractions are the four split-level bungalows in an adjacent plot that slopes down to the river. Each of these has huge glass windows and can accommodate up to four people. Losmen bungalows ❷ Riverside bungalows ❸ For four ❹

Jati Homestay Jl Hanoman, Padang Tegal ☎0361/977701, ⓦwww.jatihs.com. Set well away from the road, the ten rooms here are all nicely outfitted with good bamboo furniture and decent, hot-water bathrooms, plus they all enjoy pretty outlooks over the adjacent rice-paddies (upstairs rooms have premier views and cost more). Run by a family of well-known painters so there's an art

gallery and small library on site and art lessons are available. ❷–❸

Nirvana Pension and Gallery Jl Gootama 10 ☎0361/975415, ⓦwww.nirvanaku.com. Six comfortably and artistically furnished rooms in the traditional house compound of painter and batik teacher Nyoman Suradnya (see p.209). ❹

Nyuh Gading Jl Monkey Forest ☎0361/973410. Seven standard bungalows set in a pretty garden behind a restaurant, plus one family house with kitchen. Family run and very central. Bungalows ❷ Family house ❹

🏃 **Sama's Cottages** Jl Bisma ☎0361/973481, ⓦwww.balilife.com /sama's. Neither the cheapest nor the most pristine of its kind, this place is nonetheless a lovely, ultra-typical Ubud hideaway. The eight fan-cooled, brick cottages are built on steep tiers that drop into the river gully and each has a sizeable terrace screened by profuse tropical shrubbery. Breakfasts are large, and there's a cute little pool. ❸

Sania's House Jl Karna 7 ☎0361/975535, ⓔsania_house@yahoo.com. Everything about this hugely popular backpackers' place is well done: bungalow rooms are ultra-clean and well furnished, breakfasts are enormous, and there's a small pool. The drawback is that with twenty-one bungalows (some in three-storey towers) crammed into the smallish compound it can feel lacking in privacy. Rooms with fan ❶–❸ With a/c ❹

Sayong's Bungalows Jl Maruti ☎0361/973305. Eight simply furnished bungalow rooms in a variety of sizes, set around a typical losmen garden at the end of a very quiet residential *gang*. Swimming pool across the lane. ❷–❸

Moderate and expensive

Fibra Inn Jl Monkey Forest ☎0361/975451, ⓦwww.fibrainn.com. A tiny hotel whose ten a/c rooms are furnished in traditional style (downstairs ones have garden bathrooms) and set in an elegant little tropical sculpture garden. There's also a pool and the exceptionally pretty Wibawa Spa. ❺

Kajane Jl Monkey Forest ☎0361/972877, ⓦwww .kajane.com. Very popular and outstandingly good-value, environmentally conscious resort with eleven multi-bedroom villa compounds set around a large tree-filled area on both sides of the river. Villas sleep two to eight and all have a private saltwater pool. Interiors are chic modern Balinese and have VCD players, Wi-Fi and garden bathrooms. Some are wheelchair accessible. ❽–❾

🏃 **Komaneka Resort at Monkey Forest** Jl Monkey Forest ☎0361/976090, ⓦwww.komaneka.com. Sophisticated boutique hotel comprising twenty large, light, a/c bungalows, stylishly appointed with sleek furnishings, plenty of thoughtful extra touches and verandas overlooking the paddy-fields. Also has some villas with private pools plus a beautiful hotel pool and a spa. ⑨

Puri Saren Agung Jl Raya Ubud ℡ 0361/975057. This series of eight pavilions occupies part of the palace belonging to Ubud's influential Sukawati family (see p.188), which means you've daily dance performances literally on your doorstep. Accommodation is styled on traditional palace lines so most rooms have plain interiors but flamboyantly carved doors, sculpted wall panels, and elegantly old-fashioned outdoor sitting-rooms (plus a/c). ⑥

🏃 **Putri Ayu** Far southern end of Jl Bisma, access on foot also from southern end of Jl Monkey Forest and via the *Pertiwi* compound ℡ 0361/972590, ⓦ www.putriayucottages.com. Occupying a stunning position surrounded on three sides by unadulterated (for the moment at least) ricefields and coconut groves, this place has just eight enormous rooms in two buildings, with those in the upper storeys well worth the extra money. Floor-to-ceiling windows, huge verandas (which connect, so they're good for families), big bamboo beds, a pool and great breakfasts. ⑤–⑥

🏃 **Tegal Sari** Jl Hanoman, Padang Tegal ℡ 0361/973318, ⓦ www.tegalsari-ubud .com. Exceptionally appealing set of 21 tastefully furnished rooms, all with both fan and a/c, in two-storey blocks strung out alongside the paddy-fields. With thoughtful service, massage facilities and a pool, this is a deservedly popular spot. Also runs a cooking school and does day-treks. Located just across the road from the Perama shuttle-bus office; free local transport is provided. ⑤–⑥

Ubud Bungalows Jl Monkey Forest ℡ 0361/971298, ⓦ www.ubudbungalow.com. Good-value, comfortable, detached fan and a/c bungalows set in a well-tended garden with an attractive pool at the bottom. ⑤

Waka di Ume About 1.8km north along Jl Suweta from Ubud market, in the hamlet of Sambahan ℡ 0361/973178, ⓦ www .wakaexperience.com. Delightful set of sixteen thatched bungalows designed in the *Waka* group's distinctive natural-chic style. Each bungalow has a picture-perfect rice-paddy view and the hotel has two beautifully sited pools (one for kids), a spa and a restaurant. Regular shuttle buses into central Ubud. ⑧

Tebesaya, Peliatan, Mas, Nyuhkuning and Lodtunduh

To the east of Padang Tegal, **Tebesaya** is an appealing, almost entirely residential area centred on Jalan Sukma, around fifteen minutes' walk from Ubud market; east again, **Peliatan** is dominated by the main road, but harbours a couple of nice, quiet places to stay. There's just one charming hotel in the woodcarving centre of **Mas**, some 6km south of Peliatan.

Stretching south from the Monkey Forest, **Nyuhkuning** is peaceful and village-like, and retains some of its ricefields, but is just ten minutes' walk from the bottom of Jalan Monkey Forest. The one drawback is having to walk or cycle through the eerie Monkey Forest if you're going into central Ubud in the evening. The village of **Lodtunduh** is 3km further out, with little tourist activity.

🏃 **Alam Jiwa** Nyuhkuning ℡ 0361/977463, ⓦ www.alamindahbali.com. Ten large, gorgeously located bungalows, secluded alongside a small river, each one enjoying dramatic views of ricefields and Gunung Agung from the bathtub and balcony. Upstairs rooms have fans, downstairs ones have a/c. Staff are charming; there's a pool and free transport into Ubud, and food is supplied by the *Café Wayan* restaurant chain. ⑥–⑦

Bali T House About 3km south of Ubud in northern Lodtunduh ⓦ www.balithouse.com. These unusual, idiosyncratic little wood-and-thatch houses were

designed to be uncluttered, cosy and environmentally harmonious. They're all owned by expats but are available for rent by the day and the week. Each has kitchen facilities, a living area, pretty views and use of a pool. ⑤–⑥

🏃 **Family Guest House** Jl Sukma 39, Tebesaya ℡ 0361/974054. Exceptionally friendly place offering ten very spacious and well-designed fan-cooled bungalows in the family compound, all of them with stylish furniture and most with large river-view verandas. The top-end ones are enormous, luxurious and especially good value. Famous for its excellent breakfasts. ③–④

The crafts of Bali and Lombok

Bali and Lombok are among the world's best destinations for traditional crafts, as famous for their flamboyant stone-carved temples as their sumptuous gold brocades. Woodcarvings, sandstone sculptures and handwoven fabric are some of the most tempting buys, particularly in the Ubud area and in the villages of East Bali, while Lombok produces beautiful pots. There is surprising diversity too, with age-old forms still popular but increasingly updated with a sleek, contemporary twist.

Stonecarving

Stonecarvings are Bali's most public art form, gracing the facades and interiors of homes, hotels and temples. Because many are chiselled from quick-to-erode volcanic tuff, they need to be renewed often, so the craft thrives. Religious and secular buildings tend to feature similar **iconography**, with deities and demons appearing alongside playful scenes of daily life. North Bali **temples** in Jagaraga, Sangsit and, most famously, Kubutambahan (see p.297) are sculpted with scenes of everything from love-making to beer-drinking parties. Bali's most famous stonecarving centre is **Batubulan**, where roadside stalls sell statues of mythical figures, Buddha heads and pagoda lanterns as well as modern, indoor abstracts carved from slinky white Javanese limestone.

Stone-carved statue at the Bali Museum, Denpasar ▲

Roadside sculpture workshops in Batubulan ▼

Woodcarving

The oldest Balinese **woodcarvings** are those that decorate the doors and pillars of **temples** and **palaces**, often in the shape of mythological beings that protect the building from evil influence. Denpasar's Bali Museum has some good examples (see p.89), and many losmen and hotels boast beautiful traditional-style wooden **doors**. Reproduction antique-style doors and furniture are sold in Batubulan, Mas, Seminyak and Senggigi. **Mas** is a centre for the best and most expensive woodcarving outlets, but more affordable carvings are produced in **Nyuhkuning** and **Ubud**. Villages along the Tegalalang-Pujung road churn out non-traditional artefacts like brightly painted mobiles. On Lombok, head to the wood carving centres of **Senanti** and **Labuapi**.

Wooden figurine of Gwan Yin, Goddess of Mercy ▼

Art markets and how to bargain

Some of the most enjoyable places to shop for lower-grade crafts are the traditional *pasar seni,* or **art markets**. Visitors will find everything from sarongs and ceremonial fabric to woodcarvings and T-shirts for sale. Every sizeable town has a *pasar seni*, but some of the best are in Denpasar, Ubud, Sukawati and Senggigi. These markets are also great places to hone your **bargaining** skills (for more advice, see p.63). It's standard practice all over Indonesia to haggle for your purchase and in general, assume that the vendor's opening price is well over the odds. Begin with a counter offer that's at least thirty percent less and negotiate from there – and always remain good-humoured.

Traditional textiles

Nearly a century after Western fashions started filtering into Indonesia, **cloth** still has a **ritual purpose** on Bali and Lombok where it is worn, given or hung at important rites-of-passage ceremonies such as tooth-filing and first hair-cutting. **Pacung** in north Bali is a renowned centre for sacred striped *bebali* cloth. Bali's indigenous textile industry has always focused on the **ikat** technique, in which the yarn is tie-dyed into the finished design before weaving begins, particularly the weft-*ikat* or *endek* of **Gianyar** and the highly complex double *ikat* or *gringsing* of **Tenganan**. It's possible to see weavers at work in both those places, as well as in **Singaraja**. To see brocaded weft-*ikat* or *songket* being woven, visit **Sukarara** on Lombok, which produces exuberantly coloured versions that are popular

▲ Craft stalls on the Tegalalang–Pujung road

▼ Gringsing double-ikat from Tenganan

Baskets woven from ata grass ▲

A Lombok potter works the clay by hand in Banyumulek ▼

for weddings. Javanese-style **batik** is currently more fashionable for sarongs and shirts; the shops on Denpasar's Jalan Sulawesi stock hundreds of batik designs (see p.94). For exquisite examples of locally woven cloth, go to the Bali Museum in Denpasar (see p.89) and the Threads of Life Textile Arts Center in Ubud (see p.190).

Basketware

The historic Balinese village of **Tenganan** is celebrated for its distinctive, very finely woven basketware made from *ata* grass, while **Pengosekan** is known for its palm-leaf baskets in eye-catchingly bold designs. On Lombok, the village of **Loyok** specializes in bamboo baskets.

Lombok pots

Traditional **pottery** has become big business in Lombok and most of the items sold in Bali have been shipped across the water. It's centred in the villages of **Banyumulek**, **Penujak** and **Masbagik Timur**, where the techniques for producing the distinctive water vessels, as well as the more modern bowls, vases and lamp bases, are passed down from mother to daughter. They work the local grey clay by hand using a round stone and a wooden paddle. After firing, the potters apply slip (liquid clay) and polish the surface to a deep shine. Modern designs incorporate etching, inlays and paintings.

For background on crafts traditions, see Contexts, pp.456–459; for advice on where and how to shop, see Basics, p.58.

Sari Bungalows Off the southern end of Jl Peliatan, Banjar Kalah, Peliatan ☎0361/975541. The fifteen simple bungalows here are some of the cheapest in Ubud and many of them are fronted by verandas affording views over the paddies beyond. Great value. ❶

Sri Sunari 700m east off Jl Peliatan on Jl Gunung Sari, Peliatan (follow signs for neighbouring *Maya Ubud* hotel) ☎0361/970542, ⓦwww.sunari-bali-inn.com. This is a good place to come if you want to be distant from the commercial heart of Ubud, whose market is about 2km away. Overlooking an expanse of paddy-fields just off a quiet village road, the family-friendly guesthouse comprises just four large, tastefully furnished fan-cooled rooms (with good views) and a saltwater pool. Cycle rental and Wi-Fi access available. ❺

Swasti Cottage Nyuhkuning ☎0361/974079, ⓦwww.baliswasti.com. Thoughtfully tended

French-run hideaway whose six spacious fan and a/c rooms, and one family house, are attractively furnished, enjoy partial ricefield views and also overlook the garden with its low tables, pool and organic vegetable patch. The well-designed menu fuses French, Thai and Indonesian cuisines, and yoga, art and meditation sessions are all offered. ❺ House ❻

Taman Harum Cottages In the compound of Tantra Gallery, Jl Raya, southern Mas ☎0361/975567, ⓦwww.tamanharumcottages .com. The standard rooms at this charming little hotel are pleasant if unexceptional, but the two-storey villas and suites are delightful and great value, affording fine ricefield views from upstairs; they're ideal for families with children. All rooms have a/c, there's a pool and a restaurant, free transport to Ubud, and an interesting on-site programme of cultural classes. Rooms ❺ Villas and suites ❻–❼

Campuhan, Sanggingan, Bangkiang Sidem and Keliki

West of central Ubud, **Campuhan** and **Sanggingan** hotels can only be reached via Jalan Raya, the busy main road, which is not a particularly pleasant walk, but public bemos run this way, and some hotels offer free transfers. Rural **Bangkiang Sidem**, on the other hand, is accessible via a delightful path from the edge of Campuhan. If you're staying in the remote but charming village of **Keliki**, you'll probably need transport.

Alam Sari Keliki Hotel Keliki ☎0361/981420, ⓦwww.alamsari.com. The twelve attractively furnished a/c bungalows here are pettily located on a slope overlooking the terraced ricefields and coconut groves of Keliki village, about 10km north of Ubud. There's also a spa, swimming pool and kids' programme, and art and culture classes are available. Ubud is about two hours' walk away, though the hotel has bikes for rent and runs a free shuttle. ❻

Ananda Cottages Jl Raya Sanggingan, Sanggingan/Campuhan ☎0361/975376, ⓦwww.anandaubud.com. Atmospheric collection of bungalows set in attractive gardens that include miniature rice-paddies, a pretty swimming pool, and paths lit by flaming torches at night. Most rooms have carved doors, antique furniture and garden bathrooms: the upper-level fan ones are the nicest and enjoy paddy views, though the contemporary a/c bungalows are also tempting. A half-hour walk or 5min bemo ride from central Ubud; bicycles, motorbikes and cars are available for rent. Rooms with fan ❺ With a/c ❻

Klub Kokos Bangkiang Sidem ☎0361/978270, ⓦwww.klubkokos.com. Located on the edge of

the remote ridge-top village of Bangkiang Sidem, partway along the Campuhan ridge walk (see p.196), this is a good spot from which to soak up village life. The seven bungalows are plainly but comfortably furnished; there are family units as well as a saltwater pool, restaurant, on-site art gallery, library, Internet access and kids' games room. A lovely 25min (1500m) walk from the Campuhan bridge, following signs from the *Warwick Ibah* hotel (or 45min from Ubud market); also accessible by car via Payogan. ❻ Family unit ❼

Sunrise Villas Jl Raya Sanggingan, Sanggingan/Campuhan ☎0361/979356, ⓦwww.indopac.com, ⒺΣsunrise_villa@indo.net.id. Four large, sumptuously well-appointed, three-tiered thatched houses, each with two bedrooms, tons of space, hardwood or marble floors, breezy verandas (with day beds) and a basement kitchen – plus glorious views of the Campuhan ridge right ahead. The villas share a pool. One bedroom ❻ Both bedrooms ❽

Taman Indrakila Jl Raya Sanggingan, Sanggingan/Campuhan ☎0361/975017. Offering a five-star view at two-star prices, this is a low-key operation with half a dozen cottage rooms ranged along the hillside, all affording spectacular panoramas over the Campuhan ridge. Rooms are traditional style with carved doors, netted beds, plain decor and fans. Also has a pool. ❹

Hotel Tjampuhan Jl Raya Campuhan, Campuhan ☏ 0361/975368, ⓦ www.tjampuhan.com. Built on the site of the 1920s' home of German artist Walter Spies (see p.192), the cottages here are stunningly positioned on terraces that drop down to the Wos Barat river. The large and elegantly designed fan and a/c rooms are secluded amid the stepped tropical gardens, which also contain tennis courts, two pools and a grotto-like spa complex. Not ideal

for guests with mobility problems. 15min walk from Ubud market. ❼–❽

Uma Ubud Jl Raya Sanggingan ☏ 0361/972448, ⓦ www.uma.como.bz. Japanese-designed minimalist resort of 29 all-white walled compounds set along the side of the Wos river valley next to the Neka Museum. Most rooms have private gardens and many enjoy distant views of the Campuhan ridge. Part of the *Como* group, there's an emphasis on well-being, with yoga mats in every room, a communal yoga pavilion, and complimentary daily classes and morning walks. ❾

Penestanan

Occupying a ridgetop and river valley between Campuhan and Sayan, **Penestanan** offers some very affordable hilltop bungalows with lordly views over Sanggingan to the east or across ricefields to the west, plus some appealing mid-range options down in the peaceful village. Access can be a bit tortuous: some village accommodation is quite a trek from Ubud, and all ridgetop places are inaccessible to cars, so you've either got to get transport to the nearest drop-off point (phone ahead for help with luggage) or slog up the steep steps from Jalan Raya Campuhan. Penestanan is also a popular area for villa rentals – see Basics, p.43, for leads.

Kori Agung Bungalow Northern ridgetop ☏ 0361/975166. A little bit more luxurious than nearby *Londo 2*, and correspondingly more expensive, with six well-furnished rooms, each with a large terrace and some with nice westerly paddy views. Accessible only on foot, via the Campuhan steps on Jl Raya Campuhan. ❸

Londo Ricefield Bungalows Southern ridgetop ☏ 0361/976548, ⓦ www.londobungalows.com. Ultra-friendly, family-run little place up on the ridge offering four large two-storey west-facing cottages. Interiors are unadorned but each has two double bedrooms, verandas and a kitchenette. Guests can use the pool at *Melati Cottages* next door. Car access to *Dewa Bharata Bungalows* on Jl Raya Penestanan, then 75m walk. ❷

Londo 2 Northern ridgetop ☏ 0361/976764. Located towards the end of the track that runs north from the top of the Campuhan steps on Jl Raya Campuhan, the three two-storey bungalows here offer spectacular west-facing views of the surrounding ricefields and palm groves. The bungalows are simply furnished but sleep four, have spacious balconies

and kitchen facilities and are amazingly good value. Run by one of the original Young Artists, I Nyoman Londo, whose studio is here too. Accessible only on foot, via the Campuhan steps on Jl Raya Campuhan. ❶

Melati Cottages Jl Raya Penestanan ☏ 0361/974650, ⓦ www.melaticottages.com. Small hotel offering 22 large, traditional-style fan and a/c rooms with huge picture windows, some of which enjoy partial paddy views. There's a pool and restaurant on site, and direct car access. Room with fan ❹ With a/c ❺

Taman Rahasia Penestanan Kaja ☏ 0361/979395, ⓦ www.balisecretgarden.com. A classy little boutique hideaway deep in the heart of the village, about 10min walk from Campuhan via the Campuhan steps or 1.5km by road via the Museum Blanco. The seven large a/c rooms are pleasingly furnished with four-poster beds, tasteful artworks and local fabrics and there's a small pool, a spa, and a charming lounging and dining area in the garden. Also has a cooking school (see p.209). Not recommended for children. Direct car access. ❼–❽

Sayan and Kedewatan

Overlooking the spectacular Ayung river valley about 3km west of central Ubud, **Sayan** and **Kedewatan** are famous for their luxurious five-star resorts, all of which capitalize on the dramatic panoramas, though the views are losing impact now because of all the new developments.

Amandari Kedewatan ℡0361/975333, ⓦwww
.amanresorts.com. Exclusive thirty-room hotel (part
of the *Aman* chain) that is repeatedly voted one of
the best in the world. Guests live in their own traditional thatched compounds, enclosing a garden
bathroom and minimalist-chic accommodation;
some also have private plunge-pools. Glorious
views out over the Ayung River, a stunning cliff-
edge pool, and a lotus-pond spa. Published rates
from $750. ❾

Four Seasons Resort Bali at Sayan Sayan/
Kedewatan ℡0361/977577, ⓦwww.fourseasons
.com/sayan. Considered to be one of the world's
top hotels, this innovatively designed, ultra-
modern five-star deluxe hotel is built on several
levels in the Ayung river valley. The style is
unadorned chic, and the suites and villas are
beautifully appointed, each with a huge living area
and private garden; villas also have plunge pools.

However, because of the tiered design it's not
ideal for kids or guests with mobility problems.
Published rates from $460. ❾

Sayan Terrace Sayan ℡0361/974384, ⓦwww
.sayanterraceresort.com. Just eleven enormous fan
and a/c rooms (some of them designed for
families), all with wooden floors and huge windows
that make the most of the fine Ayung River views.
Has a pool and a restaurant. A 10min drive from
central Ubud. ❻–❽

🏃 **Taman Bebek** Sayan ℡0361/975385,
ⓦwww.baliwww.com/tamanbebek. Top
choice here are the three delightful self-contained
valley-view villas, built in airy colonial style (no a/c)
with verandas, sliding screens, carved doors and
furniture, and views over the Ayung River terraces.
Each villa has a separate living area and kitchen
facilities, and there's a pool and restaurant. A
10min drive from central Ubud. ❼–❽

Central Ubud

Covering the area between Jalan Raya Ubud in the north and the Monkey Forest in the south, and between the Campuhan bridge in the west and the GPO in the east, **Central Ubud**'s chief draws are its restaurants and shops. However, it does hold a few notable sights, including the atmospheric lotus-garden temple, **Pura Taman Saraswati**, Ubud's oldest art museum, **Puri Lukisan**, and the modern **Seniwati Gallery of Art by Women**.

Museum Puri Lukisan

Although billed as central Ubud's major art museum, the **Museum Puri Lukisan** on Jalan Raya Ubud (daily 9am–5pm; Rp20,000; ⓦwww.mpl-ubud .com) suffers from poor labelling and inadequate information and should be visited only as an adjunct to the far superior Neka Art Museum, 2km west in Sanggingan.

Set in attractive gardens, complete with lotus-filled ponds and shady arbours, Puri Lukisan ("Palace of Paintings") was founded in 1956 by the Ubud *punggawa* Cokorda Gede Agung Sukawati (whose descendants are still involved with the museum) and the Dutch artist Rudolf Bonnet. Both men had amassed a significant collection of work by local artists through the **Pita Maha** arts association, which they had established in 1936 to stimulate experimentation and combat the decline in artistic standards caused by an influx of souvenir-hungry cruise-liner tourists. Pita Maha became very influential and those works which met the founders' exacting criteria were exhibited and sold.

Almost the whole of the **First Pavilion**, located at the top of the garden, is still given over to Pita Maha paintings and woodcarvings (identifiable by the words "donated by Rudolf Bonnet" on the label). Some of these are **wayang-style** canvases, but most are black-and-white **Batuan-style** and early **Ubud-style** pictures, depicting local scenes (see p.453 for more on all these styles). There's also a good selection of distinctive ink drawings by Pita Maha co-founder I Gusti Nyoman Lempad (see opposite). Several finely crafted Pita Maha–style **woodcarvings** from the 1930s, 1940s and 1950s are also displayed here, including the elegantly surreal earth-goddess *Dewi Pertiwi* by Ida Bagus Nyana, and Nyoman Cokot's weird and now much emulated *Garuda Eating Snake*.

The poorly lit **Second Pavilion**, to the left of the First Pavilion, showcases works in the naive expressionist **Young Artists** style that originated in nearby Penestanan in the 1960s. I Nyoman Mundik is an especially prolific painter in this style. Also in this pavilion you'll find a few paintings in the **Ubud style**, including one by Anak Agung Gede Sobrat, as well as works in the so-called **modern traditional** style, such as Ida Bagus Nadera's *Story of Rajapala*. The **Third Pavilion**, to the right of the First Pavilion, houses temporary exhibitions.

Pura Taman Saraswati

Commissioned in the 1950s by Cokorda Gede Agung Sukawati, **Pura Taman Saraswati** is the work of the prolific royal architect and stonecarver I Gusti Nyoman Lempad, who set the temple complex within a delightful lotus-pond garden. It's dedicated to Saraswati, the goddess of learning, science and literature. A **restaurant**, *Café Lotus*, now capitalizes on the garden view.

Access to the temple is via the restaurant. A forest of metre-high lotus plants leads you to the red-brick *kori agung* whose main entrance is blocked by an unusual **aling-aling** (the wall device built into nearly every temple to disorient evil spirits), which is in fact the back of a rotund statue of a *raksasa* demon guardian. Inside the **courtyard** on the right, you'll find a *bale* housing the huge costumes for the lion-like Barong Ket and the wild boar Barong Bangkal, both used for exorcism rituals. Nearby, the main lotus-throne **shrine** is covered with a riot of *paras* carvings, with the requisite cosmic turtle and *naga* forming the base, while the tower is a swirling mass of curlicues and floral motifs. The walk-in shrine occupying the northeast corner of the complex displays some more distinguished Lempad carvings, the central wall-panel describing a farewell scene.

Puri Saren Agung (Ubud Palace)

From the late nineteenth century until the 1940s, Ubud and its catchment area was ruled by the Sukawati clan from **Puri Saren Agung** (**Ubud Palace**), opposite the main market on Jalan Raya. Despite its modern incarnation as a hotel and dance stage, the palace compound has retained much of its original style and elegance. Casual visitors are welcome to walk around the compact central courtyards, and every night the outer courtyard is transformed into a spectacular backdrop for traditional dance performances.

Built to a classic design that is really just a grander version of the traditional family compound, the palace was divided into a series of **pavilions**, each serving a particular purpose. The centrepiece was the open-sided reception *bale*, its imposing wooden pillars, sculpted stone panels and huge guardian statues of elephants, lions and *raksasa* still much as they were in the Sukawatis' heyday. The veranda is still furnished with Dutch-style carved wooden armchairs, and piles of old photograph albums lie heaped on the floor, full of early pictures of the Ubud gentry. The small thatched *bale* nearby is decorated with stonecarvings and painted wooden reliefs ascribed to I Gusti Nyoman Lempad. Most of the **hotel rooms** have been adapted or purpose-built, but retain authentic features (see p.184).

Lempad's house

Many of Ubud's most important buildings are associated with the venerable sculptor, architect and artist **I Gusti Nyoman Lempad** (c.1862–1978), among them Puri Lukisan, Pura Taman Saraswati and Ubud Palace. Famously bright and idiosyncratic, Lempad came to Ubud with his family at the age of 13, where he soon found favour in the court of the Sukawatis, for whom he worked for most of his life. A versatile and innovative artist who designed temples, carved stone reliefs, built cremation towers and produced spare, humorous ink cartoons, Lempad was an influential figure in Ubud. He was also an important member of the Pita Maha arts association, which he co-founded with his friends Cokorda Gede Agung Sukawati and Rudolf Bonnet. A traditionalist in certain matters, Lempad would only work on propitious days and is said to have waited quite a while for a suitably auspicious day on which to die; by that time he was approximately 116 years old.

Lempad lived on Ubud's Jalan Raya for almost a century, in a **house** that still belongs to his family but is now also open to the public (daily 8am–6pm; free). Disappointingly, there's little evidence of the great man on show here, as the place functions chiefly as a showroom for artists working under the "Puri Lempad" by-line, some of whom are descendants of I Gusti Nyoman. A few of Lempad's original ink drawings are exhibited here, but the Neka Art Museum and Museum Puri Lukisan have many more. The *bale* at the back of the compound displays some **memorabilia**, including photos of Lempad, the Piagam Anugerah Seni certificate – government recognition of his lifetime's contribution to the island's cultural heritage – and a magazine article on the biographical film, *Lempad of Bali*, made by expats John Darling and Lorne Blair in 1980.

Seniwati Gallery of Art by Women

Balinese women feature prominently in the paintings that fill the Neka Art Museum and the Museum Puri Lukisan, but there is barely a handful of works by women artists in either collection. To redress this imbalance, British-born artist Mary Northmore-Aziz established the **Seniwati Gallery of Art by Women** at Jalan Sriwedari 2B (Tues–Sun 9am–5pm; free; ⓦwww.seniwatigallery.com), which now represents about seventy local and foreign women resident in Bali, many of whom have pictures in the gallery's permanent collection. Another element of the project is the regular art classes held at the gallery, and there's a small shop selling cards as well as their famous *Women Artists of Bali* calendar.

The Seniwati Gallery's small but charming permanent collection covers the range of mainstream Balinese art styles, and the works are supported by excellent information sheets and well-informed gallery attendants. Notable exhibits include a classical Kamasan-style depiction of the *Vindication of Sita* by **Ni Made Suciarmi**, whose childhood was spent helping with the 1930s' renovations on the Kerta Gosa painted ceilings in Semarapura. Batuan-born **Ni Wayan Warti** continues the traditional style of her village, producing dark and highly detailed scenes, while the already well-known young painter **I Gusti Agung Galuh** works chiefly in the popular Ubud style. Pengosekan resident **Gusti Ayu Suartini** also reflects her roots, concentrating on the pastel bird and flower compositions characteristic of the Pengosekan Community of Artists. **Tjok Istri Mas Astiti**, on the other hand, tackles less traditional subjects, such as fading Legong dancers and poverty. The works of the late Gusti Ayu Kadek Murniasih, better known as **Murni** (1966–2006), are even bolder: disregarding

▲ Walking through Ubud Kaja

sexual and social taboos, she was notorious for her witty, provocative and uninhibited style, which made her one of Bali's most famous modern artists.

Threads of Life Textile Arts Center

The small **Threads of Life Textile Arts Center and Gallery** (Mon–Sat 10am–6pm; Ⓦ www.threadsoflife.com) at Jalan Kajeng 24 is devoted to exquisite textiles that have been hand-woven to traditional ritual designs in Bali, Sumba, Flores, Lembata and Sulawesi. Though they were all produced using natural dyes and ancient methods, the textiles are modern works, commissioned by the Threads of Life fair-trade foundation in an attempt to keep Indonesia's historic textile art alive. It's a complex and highly skilled art, and severely endangered, not least because a single weaving can take two years to complete. There's plenty of information on the ritual use for the textiles, the specialized tools involved and the meaning of the most important motifs. The centre also sells beautiful, if pricey, **textiles** and runs regular **classes** on traditional textile appreciation (see p.209).

Campuhan, Sanggingan and Penestanan

Sited at the confluence of the rivers Wos Barat and Wos Timor, the hamlet of **CAMPUHAN** (pronounced *cham-poo-han*) officially extends west from Ubud only as far as the *Hotel Tjampuhan*, and is famous as the home of several of Bali's most charismatic expatriate painters, including the late **Antonio Blanco**, whose house and gallery have been turned into a museum; the late **Walter Spies**, whose delightful early twentieth-century villa has become the centre-piece of the *Hotel Tjampuhan*; and **Symon**, who still paints and presides at his enticing studio-gallery across the road from the hotel.

North up the Campuhan hill from this knot of artistic abodes, Campuhan turns into **Sanggingan** (though few people bother to distinguish it from its neighbour), and it's here that you'll find Bali's best art gallery, the **Neka Art Museum**.

Otherwise, Campuhan and Sanggingan comprise little more than a sprinkling of residences sandwiched between the road and the rivers, some notable restaurants and a growing number of prettily sited hotels, plus a few commercial galleries. Campuhan/Sanggingan also makes a good starting-point for **walks** around Ubud, including the picturesque route to the neighbouring and still quite traditional hamlet of Penestanan. If you don't fancy walking or cycling along the busy main road that tears through its heart, you can take any west-bound bemo from in front of the tourist information office on Jalan Raya Ubud.

In the 1960s, Campuhan's westerly neighbour **Penestanan** became famous for its so-called **Young Artists**, who forged a naive style of painting that's since been named after them. Some are still painting, but Penestanan's current niche is **beadmaking**, and the village now has several little shops selling intricately strung belts, bags, bracelets and other accessories.

A rice-paddy walk through Ubud Kaja

Running east of, and almost parallel to, the Campuhan ridge walk (see p.196) is a track defining an almost circular **rice-paddy walk** that begins and ends in the northern part of Ubud known as Ubud Kaja (*kaja* literally means "upstream, towards the mountains"). The walk – also detailed on the *Bali Pathfinder* map – takes two and a half hours round-trip and is flat and not at all strenuous, but there's no shade for the first hour. About 800m into the walk the *Sari Organik* café makes a lovely place for a break (see p.203) and you can refill water bottles here too. You can also shorten the walk by taking a shortcut about 500m beyond *Sari Organik*: this will reduce the total time to about one hour.

The walk begins from the western end of **Jalan Raya Ubud**, just before the overhead aqueduct, where a track leads up to the *Abangan Bungalows* on the north side of the road. Head up the slope and, at the top, follow the track which bends to the left before straightening out, passing *Gusti's 2* and heading north to *Sari Organik*. From here the route is straightforward, following the dirt track for about 3km as it slices through gently **terraced ricefields** fringed with coconut palms; you should see scores of beautifully coloured dragonflies, and plenty of birdlife, including, possibly, iridescent blue Javanese kingfishers.

After about 1hr 10min, the track ends at a sealed road. Turn right here to cross the river, then look for the **southbound track** that starts almost immediately after the bridge and runs east of the river. The southbound track becomes indistinct in places and for the next 10min you should try to follow the narrow paths along the top of the ricefield dykes and stick to a southerly direction by keeping the river in view on your right. Get back on the proper track as soon as you see it emerging from the woods alongside the river; don't forget to look back at the amazing **views of Gunung Agung** (cloud cover permitting): with the mountain in the background and the conical-hatted farmers working in the glittering ricefields, these views are perfect real-life versions of the Walter Spies-style paintings you see in the museums and galleries of Ubud. This track will take you back down to Ubud Kaja, finishing at the far northern end of Ubud's **Jalan Kajeng**, the little road paved with graffitied stones that runs all the way down to Jalan Raya Ubud. The stones are inscribed with the names, messages and doodlings of the Ubud residents and businesses who helped finance the paving of the lane.

To do the **shorter version** of the loop look for a huge frangipani tree on your left about 500m north of *Sari Organik*: across from here a path takes you down to a bridge on your right and puts you back on the southbound track described above, about 1km before it turns into paved Jalan Kajeng (see map, p.177).

The Neka Art Museum

Boasting the most comprehensive collection of traditional and modern Balinese paintings on the island, the well-curated **Neka Art Museum** (daily 9am–5pm; Rp20,000; ⓦ www.museumneka.com) is housed in a series of pavilions set high on a hill overlooking the Wos Barat river valley, alongside the main Campuhan/ Sanggingan road, about 2.5km from Ubud market.

It was founded in 1982 by the Ubud collector **Wayan Suteja Neka**, son of the Pita Maha woodcarver I Wayan Neka, to "document the history of paintings inspired by the Balinese environment", so Balinese as well as expatriate and visiting artists are all represented. Informative English-language labels are posted alongside every one of the museum's several hundred paintings, but the museum shop also sells a couple of recommended **books** about the collection: *Perceptions of Paradise: Images of Bali in the Arts* by Garrett Kam, and *The Development of Painting in Bali: Selections from the Neka Art Museum* by Suteja Neka and Garrett Kam. For more on the styles of art on display, see pp.453–456.

First Pavilion: Balinese Painting Hall

Divided into fairly distinct sections, the first pavilion surveys the three major schools of **Balinese painting** from the seventeenth century to the present day. The collection opens with an introduction to the earliest-known "school", the two-dimensional narratives inspired by *wayang kulit* shadow puppets (also displayed here) and dubbed **Kamasan style** after the east-Bali town where most were produced. The Kamasan style dates back to the seventeenth century, but the nineteenth-century pictures displayed here are typical. Episodes from popular *wayang* stories, in particular the *Ramayana* and *Mahabharata* epics, continue to inspire contemporary Kamasan artists such as the late **Ketut Kobot**. A former puppet-maker himself, Kobot introduced softer pastel shades and added more

Walter Spies in Campuhan

The son of a German diplomat, **Walter Spies** (1895–1942) left Europe for Java in 1923, and relocated to Bali four years later. He set up home in Campuhan and began devoting himself to the study and practice of Balinese art and music. He sponsored two local gamelan orchestras and was the first Westerner to attempt to record **Balinese music**. Together with the American composer Colin McPhee, he set about transposing gamelan music for Western instruments, and with another associate, Katharane Mershon, encouraged Bedulu dancer I Wayan Limbak to create the enduringly popular **Kecak**.

Spies was an avid collector of Balinese **art**, and became one of the founding members of the Pita Maha arts association in 1936, hosting their weekly meetings in his Campuhan house. He is said to have inspired, if not taught, a number of talented young Ubud artists, among them the painter Anak Agung Gede Sobrat, and the woodcarver I Tegelan. Characteristic of Spies's own Balinese works are dense landscapes of waterlogged paddies set within double or triple horizons, and peopled with elongated silhouettes of conical-hatted farmers, often accompanied by water buffaloes – a distinctive style that is still much imitated. There's currently only one Walter Spies painting on show in Bali; it's at the Agung Rai Museum of Art in Pengosekan.

In 1937, Spies retired from his increasingly hectic social life in Ubud to the tranquil hillside village of Iseh in the Karangasem district. He turned his Campuhan home into a **guesthouse**, the first of its kind in the Ubud area, and employed a couple of Germans to manage it. He died in 1942, and the guesthouse became *Hotel Tjampuhan*.

decorative motifs, as you can see from *Rajapala Steals Sulasih's Clothes*. Similarly, *The Pandawa Brothers Disguised as Common Beings*, painted in black and white by **Ida Bagus Rai**, fuses classical elements with a more modern sensuality.

The other galleries in the first pavilion trace the evolution of the *wayang* style and the influence of foreign art. In the 1930s, Ubud artists began to paint scenes from daily life and to experiment with perspective and the use of light and shadow. This is now known as **Ubud style**, and one of its finest examples is *The Bumblebee Dance* by **Anak Agung Gede Sobrat**, a prolific member of the Pita Maha group who was said to have been much influenced by the German artist Walter Spies; the painting shows a traditional flirtation dance (Oleg Tambulilingan), which is still regularly performed on local Ubud stages.

Of all the four major Balinese art styles, the dark and densely packed **Batuan style** canvases (named after the nearby village which spawned the style in the 1930s) lend themselves most to humour, political observation and social commentary. The most dramatic examples here include **I Wayan Bendi**'s depiction of the 1949–50 *Indonesian War of Independence* and his wry, two-metre-long portrait of the effect of tourism on the island, *Busy Bali*. **I Made Budi**'s very detailed 1987 work, *President Suharto and His Wife Visit Bali*, is a similarly satirical take.

Second Pavilion: Arie Smit Pavilion

The second pavilion is devoted to the hugely influential Dutch expatriate artist **Arie Smit**, a Campuhan resident who has been based in Bali since 1956, and to works by the Young Artists with whom he was associated. You enter via the upstairs gallery, which is filled with pictures by Smit – instantly recognizable from their bold, expressionist tone; many feature imaginative Ubud-inspired landscapes, generally depicted in vibrant oils and often either pierced by fractured light or splintered into blocks of broken colour rimmed in black, like stained glass. Among many breathtakingly beautiful works, *A Tropical Garden By the Sea* has a Cézanne-like quality.

The ground-floor hall exhibits works in the **Young Artists style**, a term coined by Smit to describe the naive, expressionistic pictures created by a group of teenagers living in Penestanan in the 1960s. **I Wayan Pugur**'s *In the Village* is typical. Also on show downstairs are works by other Balinese artists who are not so easily classifiable, including 1960s' ink paintings by renowned Sanur artist **Ida Bagus Nyoman Rai**, as well as an energetic abstract, *Water of Life*, by **I Made Sumadiyasa**.

Third Pavilion: Photography Archive Center

The third pavilion houses a fascinating archive of black-and-white **photographs** from Bali in the 1930s and 1940s, all of them taken by the remarkable American expatriate **Robert Koke**. He and his wife Louise founded the first hotel in Kuta in 1936 and spent the next six years entertaining guests there as well as getting involved with artists, dancers and musicians from all corners of Bali. His photographic record includes some stunning shots of village scenes, temple festivals and cremations, but its highlights are the pictures of the Legong and Kecak performances and the portraits of the charismatic Kebyar dancer Mario and of the Kecak choreographer I Wayan Limbak. The photos are labelled with extracts from Louise Koke's enjoyable book *Our Hotel in Bali* (reviewed on p.471).

Fourth Pavilion: Lempad Pavilion

The late **I Gusti Nyoman Lempad** (see p.189) is the subject of the small fourth pavilion, which holds the largest collection of his pictures in Bali. A highly regarded architect and stonecarver, Lempad took up painting fairly late in his long and varied artistic career, using deceptively simplistic, almost cartoon-like line drawings in black Chinese ink to describe scenes from religious mythology and secular folklore. Some of his best-known works are from a series on **Men and Pan Brayut** (see box below), a humorous reworking of the well-known folk story about a poor couple and their eighteen children. Lempad shows the family in various states of harmony and discord, either engaged in typical domestic activities, as in *Scene 3: Making Pork Saté*, or in wryly observed comical situations as in *Scene 5: Mother Brayut Eats the Offerings* (she is reduced to doing this, apparently, because looking after her huge brood leaves her too tired to cook).

Fifth Pavilion: Contemporary Indonesian Art Hall

The fifth pavilion focuses on works by Indonesian artists whose style is sometimes labelled "**Academic**" because the painters were academically trained, mostly at the Yogyakarta Academy of Fine Arts on Java. Many are associated with the Sanggar Dewata Indonesia art movement, whose abstract expressionist style has dominated modern Balinese art since the 1970s. Outstanding examples include a couple of large oils by Javanese-born **Anton H** (Anton Kustia Widjaja), who moved to Ubud in 1969: *Three Masked Dancers*, which ponders the role of traditional Topeng dancers, and *Divine Union*, which shows the symbolic fusion of the male and female aspects of the Hindu deity Siwa, which

The tale of Men and Pan Brayut

Blessed – or lumbered – with an unruly brood of eighteen children, **Men and Pan Brayut** ("Mother and Father Brayut") may be desperately poor, but their scrapes are typical of any Balinese family. So goes the popular Balinese folk tale, which has inspired countless artists including **I Gusti Nyoman Lempad**. They also star in the classical *wayang*-style murals of Semarapura's Bale Kambang hall (see p.233), and in the earthy stonecarved reliefs at Pura Dalem Jagaraga, near Singaraja (see p.297). The fullest account of their story is related in an epic poem called *Gaguritan Brayut*, housed in Singaraja's Gedong Kirtya library.

According to one version of the **story**, the reason that Men Brayut has so many children is her uncontrollable appetite. When hungry, she gets irritable and rows with her husband, Pan Brayut. After fighting, the couple always make up in the time-honoured fashion – hence the constantly expanding clan. Another version puts the size of the family down to Pan Brayut's insatiable desire for his wife, which he acts upon regardless of place or circumstance.

Men Brayut is both full-time mother and part-time weaver, so her husband does most of the domestic chores. Lempad shows him cleaning the yard and cooking ceremonial dishes, and in his spare time he studies religious practice. One of the highlights of their story is the **wedding ceremony** of their amorous son I Ketut Sabaya (an episode pictured in the Bale Kambang murals). Eventually, after all their hard parenting, Men and Pan Brayut renounce the material world and enter a retreat (still common practice, especially among elderly Balinese men), leaving their home and its contents to be divided among the children.

Although illustrations of the Brayut story always emphasize its **Hindu** elements with lots of scenes showing offerings and temple ceremonies, Men Brayut is also associated with **Buddhist** lore. In this mythology she is said to have evolved from an evil ogress named Hariti who spent her time devouring children until she converted to Buddhism and became not only a protector of children, but also a fertility goddess. Statues of Men Brayut in her Hariti manifestation can be found at Goa Gajah, near Ubud, and at the temple in Candi Dasa.

resulted in the creation of the world. Also displayed in this pavilion is **Abdul Aziz**'s cute and much-reproduced diptych entitled *Mutual Attraction*.

Sixth Pavilion: East–West Art Annex

Portraits of the Neka family by various famous contemporary artists open the sixth pavilion and on this floor you'll also find some striking works by Javanese expressionist **Affandi**, notably his rendition of fighting cocks, *Fight to the Finish*, and his depiction of a Barong and Rangda dance.

The upstairs galleries feature the paintings of **foreign artists in Bali**, including the Dutch painter **Rudolf Bonnet**'s sensual portrait of the *Mahabharata* hero, *Temptation of Arjuna*. Bonnet's style is said to have been very influential in creating what became known as the Ubud style. Although Bonnet's friend **Walter Spies** also influenced many artists with his distinctive use of light and dark in landscapes peopled by elongated silhouettes of farmers, Spies is only represented in the Neka collection by a photographic reproduction of his *The Death of Arya Penringsang*.

The bright Gauguin-esque oils of Swiss-born **Theo Meier** draw on the lurid light and tropical emotions of Bali, in contrast to the Dutchman **Willem Gerard Hofker**'s minutely observed crayon studies of temples, such as *Temple at Campuhan, Ubud*, and his romanticized soft-focus portraits of local women. Also on show are some erotically charged portraits by the Catalan-born **Antonio Blanco**, whose studio-gallery is nearby; the Australian **Donald Friend**'s charmingly fanciful Chagall-esque evocation of his Sanur home, *Batujimbar Village*; and the Dutchman **Han Snel**'s striking *Girls Carrying Offerings*.

Symon's Studio

With its eye-catching outdoor parade of vivacious paintings and weird suspended artefacts, the studio-gallery of American-born artist **Symon** (daily until about 9pm; free; ⓦwww.symonbali.com), across the road from the *Hotel Tjampuhan* complex, is hard to ignore. Inside, the multi-levelled gallery houses unconventional displays of Symon's paintings, sculptures and other creations, as well as a working atelier for the artist and his assistants. Symon has lived in Bali since 1978 and is best known for his bold portraits of sensual young Balinese men, done in vivid tropical colours and often to an exaggerated scale. He has a second gallery and workshop, the Art Zoo, in AlasSari on the northeast coast (see p.298). An insightful book about Symon's work, *Property of the Artist* by Philip Cornwel-Smith, is available at the Ubud studio, as well as at some local bookshops.

Museum Blanco

Just down the main road into Ubud from Symon's Studio and *Hotel Tjampuhan*, beside the Penestanan turn-off, the ostentatious gateway announcing in huge curly letters "Antonio Blanco", and then in a slightly smaller script "The Blanco Dynasty", sets the tone for the Blanco experience beyond. This is the entrance to the former home of the flamboyant Catalan artist – complete with gilded pillars and sweeping Spanish balustrades – now open to the public as the enjoyably camp **Museum Blanco** (daily 9am–5pm; Rp20,000; ⓦwww.blancobali.com).

Dubbed "the Bali Dali", Blanco (1911–99) specialized in **erotic paintings** and drawings, particularly portraits of Balinese women in varying states of abandon. As with countless other Western male artists before and since, Blanco fell for a local girl, Ni Ronji, soon after arriving in Ubud in 1952, singling her out as his top model and later marrying her. Aside from his erotica, Blanco's collection also includes multimedia pieces, many of them surreal and mischievous flights of poetic fancy, plus lots of idiosyncratic picture-frames created from unorthodox materials. The museum garden contains several small aviaries, including one housing a pair of rare **Bali starlings** (see p.339).

The Campuhan ridge walk

Campuhan means "the place where two rivers meet" and the confluence itself is marked by **Pura Gunung Lebah** (sometimes known simply as Pura Campuhan), which occupies the tip of the spur that divides the Wos Barat from the Wos Timor, just across the road from Museum Blanco. The track that extends north along the grassy spine behind Pura Gunung Lebah forms part of a very pleasant ninety-minute circular **walk** around the outskirts of Campuhan, returning you to the main road about 1.5km northwest of the Neka Art Museum. Alternatively, if you continue the complete length of the ridge, you'll eventually reach the tiny village of **Keliki** (7km), renowned for its intricate miniature paintings of Barong dances, beyond which the track, asphalted in some sections, proceeds to **Taro** (13km) before eventually joining the main Sayan road to **Kintamani** (32km). All routes are feasible on a **mountain bike**, but be prepared for some significant undulations and a few steps: see the *Bali Pathfinder* map for details.

If you're starting the walk **from central Ubud**, walk (or take a bemo) west from Ubud market almost as far as the Campuhan bridge, turning north off the main road about 100m before the bridge, into the entrance of the *Warwick Ibah* hotel, where an immediate left fork, signed for *Klub Kokos* hotel, takes you down some steps to the back of Pura Gunung Lebah. From here, the **track** (which is paved for the first 1500m) undulates for a stretch before levelling out along the flattened ridgetop between the two river valleys. The perspective from this elevated route is breathtaking: to the left, you'll see the steep, increasingly developed westerly banks of the Wos Barat valley. To the right, the eastern panorama across the Wos Timor valley remains almost unadulterated – little else but savannah, coconut grove and rocky river-gorge. There are few trees along this first stretch, and therefore no shade, just a seemingly endless long-haired carpet of **alang-alang grass** swaying in the breeze. The grass is a valuable resource, essential for thatching houses and shrines. Down below, the rocky river-beds harbour a rich supply of **volcanic sandstone**, or *paras*, swept down from the mountains, which is quarried out in blocks for carving.

About twenty minutes from Pura Gunung Lebah, the track passes through the first little ridgetop settlement, site of the *Klub Kokos* hotel (see p.185) and restaurant. Nearly all the grassland beyond has been sculpted into ricefields, irrigated by a complex system of water channels that draw on the Wos Barat below. About 1500m further on, the track enters the hamlet of **Bangkiang Sidem**, skirting a row of family compounds built mainly from adobe bricks and *alang-alang* thatch, a warung, a *bale banjar* and a temple. Just beyond the temple, the route **forks**: left for the round trip back to the Campuhan road, straight on for Keliki. On a clear day you get a superb view of **Gunung Agung** from this junction.

The left-hand branch of the track is sealed, but is only used for local access so is still a pleasant walk. It cuts through a swathe of ricefields – which attract several **bird** species, in particular the iridescent blue Javan kingfisher and the chubby, brown cisticola warbler – before dropping down quite steeply towards the Wos Barat. Fifteen minutes after crossing the river, you pass through the adjacent, still fairly traditional hamlets of **Payogan** and **Lungsiakan**, before reaching **Jalan Raya Sanggingan**, from where you can either flag down any bemo heading east for the ten-minute ride into Ubud, or continue walking for twenty minutes east down to the Neka Art Museum, or twenty minutes west to Kedewatan and the main Kintamani road.

Penestanan

Just west of the Campuhan bridge, but invisible from the main road, the hamlet of **PENESTANAN** is more old-fashioned than its neighbour and makes a good focus for a pleasant two-hour circular walk. It's accessible from a side road that turns off beside Museum Blanco, but the most dramatic approach is via the steep flight of steps a few hundred metres further north along Jalan Raya Campuhan, just south of Symon's Studio. The steps climb the hillside to a narrow west-bound track, which passes several arterial north–south paths leading to panoramic and inexpensive hilltop accommodation, then drops down through ricefields into the next valley, across a river and through a small wooded area, before coming to a crossroads with Penestanan's main street; for restaurants in this area, see p.202. Go straight across (west) if you're heading for Sayan (600m away), right for *Taman Rahasia* hotel (200m), or left for the walk through the village to Museum Blanco in Campuhan (1.5km).

Penestanan's main claim to fame is as the original home of the **Young Artists**. When the Dutch painter Arie Smit settled here in the 1960s he began encouraging village children to experiment with Western subjects and techniques. The resulting works were bold and naive, and were warmly received by collectors. One of the first young artists to come under Smit's influence, albeit briefly, was I Nyoman Londo. Now in his sixties, Londo is still painting in the same style and has a studio attached to his *Londo 2* bungalow accommodation on the hilltop (see p.186).

You can still find scores of painters in Penestanan and about a dozen browsable **galleries**, showcasing various styles. The people of Penestanan are also the most skilful **bead**-workers on the island, adorning an amazing array of items – from shoes and handbags to baskets, belts, caps, earrings and bracelets – with hundreds of painstakingly strung beads. Their work is on sale in shops in Penestanan and across Bali.

The Monkey Forest and Nyuhkuning

Ubud's best-known tourist attraction is its **Monkey Forest Sanctuary** (8am–6pm; Rp15,000, kids R7500), which occupies the land between the southern end of Jalan Monkey Forest and the northern edge of the woodcarvers' hamlet of **Nyuhkuning**.

The focus of numerous day-tours because of its resident troupe of over one hundred malevolent but photogenic long-tailed macaques, the forest itself is actually small and disappointing, traversed by a concrete pathway and with little exceptional flora to look at. The only way to visit is on foot: the entrance is fifteen minutes' walk south from Ubud's central market, and a stroll around the forest and its temple combines well with a walk around neighbouring Nyuhkuning.

Pura Dalem Agung Padang Tegal

Five minutes into the forest, you'll come to **Pura Dalem Agung Padang Tegal**, the temple of the dead for the *banjar* of Padang Tegal (you can borrow the requisite sarong and sash at the temple entrance, for which a small donation is requested). *Pura dalem* are traditionally places of extremely strong magical power and the preserve of *leyak* (evil spirits); in this temple you'll find half a dozen stonecarved images of the witch-widow **Rangda** (see p.226) flanking the main stairway – hard to miss with her hideous fanged face, unkempt hair, metre-long tongue and pendulous breasts. Two of the Rangda statues are depicted in the process of devouring children – a favourite occupation of hers.

The inner sanctuary is kept locked, but in the outer courtyard you can see the ornate *kulkul* **drum tower**, built in red brick and lavishly decorated with *paras* carvings of Bhoma heads and Garuda. When not being used to summon villagers to a cremation or a festival, the drums sit high up on the red-and-gold-painted platform, swathed in lengths of holy black-and-white-checked *kain poleng*.

You can stop for **refreshments** just south of the temple at the *Laka Leke* café, beside the road into Nyuhkuning; the café also stages free dance performances for diners (Mon & Thurs 8pm). There are several other small restaurants further along the road.

Nyuhkuning

Continuing south from the Pura Dalem Agung Padang Tegal, the road enters the **woodcarvers' village** of **NYUHKUNING**, a pleasingly quiet place for a wander and the site of several attractively sited small hotels. Though the road is dotted with shops selling the carvers' handiwork, the atmosphere is a lot more low-key and workshop-oriented than in the more famous woodcarving centre of Mas – and prices are much cheaper too. Many of the carvers will give woodcarving lessons to interested tourists. Works by the famous Nyuhkuning carver, the late I Wayan Pendet, are exhibited in the tiny **Museum Pendet** (daily 10am–5pm; free), alongside some sparse, cartoon-like line-drawings by his son, the prolific *Bali Post* cartoonist I Wayan Gunasta, better known as GunGun. Just beyond the museum, beside the football field, the road branches. Heading straight on, along the peaceful **main street**, you'll pass walled family compounds where many of the carvers have their workshops. At the southern end of the main street, a 600-metre walk, the left arm of the T-junction leads into the next village of Pengosekan (1km to the east; see below), while the right one completes the circular tour of Nyuhkuning, taking you west past the *Bali Spirit* hotel, overlooking the River Wos, and north again to the football field at the top of the village, from where you can head back to the Monkey Forest and central Ubud.

Pengosekan, Peliatan and Petulu

The villages of **Pengosekan**, **Peliatan** and **Petulu** lie to the east of central Ubud, and can be reached fairly easily on foot in an hour or less from the main market.

Pengosekan

At the southern end of Jalan Hanoman, the road enters **PENGOSEKAN**, known locally as the centre of the Pengosekan Community of Artists, a cooperative founded in 1969 by I Dewa Nyoman Batuan and his brother I Dewa Putuh Mokoh, to help villagers share resources, exhibition costs and sales. The cooperative was so successful that most of the original members have since established their own galleries, but the spirit of the collective lives on in the **Pengosekan Community of Artists showroom** (daily 9am–6pm), which stands just east of the river on the Pengosekan–Peliatan road. As with other local communities of artists, the Pengosekan painters developed a distinct style, specializing in large canvases of birds, flowers, insects and frogs, painted in gentle pastels and depicted in magnified detail. Their art also features increasingly on carved picture-frames, boxes and small pieces of furniture.

Agung Rai Museum of Art (ARMA)

Pengosekan's main attraction is the impressive **Agung Rai Museum of Art**, or **ARMA** (daily 9am–6pm; Rp25,000; Ⓦ www.armamuseum.com). Founded by influential Ubud art-dealer Anak Agung Rai, its collection nearly matches that of the Neka Art Museum; there's also an excellent public-access **library** and research centre here, and an open-air dance stage. Access is either via Jalan Hanoman or through the main gateway next to the *Kokokan Club* restaurant on the Pengosekan–Peliatan road.

From the main entrance, pass through the temporary exhibition hall and across the garden to the large **Bale Daja** pavilion. Its upstairs **Ruang Pita Maha** gallery gives a brief survey of the development of Balinese art, though the labels aren't that helpful. Historically speaking, you should begin with the **wayang style** (also known as Kamasan style) canvases that are hung high up on the walls overlooking the central well. These all depict episodes from the *Mahabharata* and are in typical seventeenth-century style, though they probably date from much later. Ida Bagus Belawa's *Cockfight* was probably painted in the 1930s or 1940s and is a good example of a modern subject done in traditional two-dimensional style.

Most **Batuan-style** art focuses on real life too and there are lots of pictures in this style – instantly recognizable by the volume of detail and activity. *Life in Bali* by the innovative and very popular I Wayan Bendi is a fine example: crammed with archetypal Balinese scenes, it's also laced with satire, notably in the figures of long-nosed tourists who are always poking their camera lenses into village events. If you look closely you'll find a surfer in the picture too. Anak A. Sobrat's *Baris Dance* is a typical **Ubud-style** painting, and look out also for the pen-and-ink cartoons of I Gusti Nyoman Lempad, an important Ubud character whose former house is open to the public (see p.189). The **downstairs** gallery in the Bale Daja houses temporary exhibitions.

Across the garden, the **Bale Dauh** is dedicated to works by expatriate artists. The middle gallery, **Ruang Walter Spies**, reads like a directory of Bali's most famous expats, with works by Adrien Jean Le Mayeur, Rudolf Bonnet, Antonio Blanco and Arie Smit. The highlight is *Calonarang* (1930) by **Spies** himself, a very dark portrait of a demonic apparition being watched by a group of petrified villagers; this is the only Spies painting currently on show in Bali. The other major work is the double portrait of the *Regent of Magelan and His Wife* (1837) by the Javanese artist **Raden Saleh**, considered to be the father of Indonesian painting. In the adjacent **Ruang Affandi** gallery, you'll find a classic Affandi picture of a cockfight, as well as portraits of ARMA founder Anak Agung Gede Rai and his wife Agung Rai Suartini, both by Srihadi Sudarsono.

Peliatan

To the Balinese, **PELIATAN** is best known as the home of one of the island's finest **dance troupes**, and particularly for its highly skilled pre-pubescent female Legong dancers. When a Balinese dance group was invited to perform at the Paris Colonial Exhibition in 1931, it was the Peliatan dancers that made the grade, and contributed to the first serious wave of European interest in Bali and Balinese culture. Peliatan dancers again represented Bali on a 1952 tour of Europe and the United States. There are currently over a dozen different dance and gamelan groups active in the village – including, very unusually, a women's gamelan – most of which perform in Peliatan and Ubud on several nights every week.

The best way to approach Peliatan from central Ubud is via Jalan Sukma, which runs south from Jalan Raya Ubud through the *banjar* of Tebesaya. The upper part of residential Jalan Sukma is peppered with losmen and a few warung, but the architecture is very traditional and the pace of life still gentle so it's a pleasure to wander through. Peliatan's eastern flank, however, is the heavily trafficked Denpasar–Ubud–Kintamani road, lined with arts and crafts shops.

Petulu

Every evening at around 6pm, hundreds of thousands of white herons fly in from miles around to roost in certain trees in the village of **PETULU**, immediately northeast of Ubud – quite a spectacle. To find this **white heron sanctuary**, follow Jalan Andong north from the T-junction at the eastern edge of Ubud for about 1.5km, then take the left-hand (signed) fork for a further 1.5km. You will be asked to give a donation just before reaching the roosting area. Lots of public bemos ply Jalan Andong, but you'll have to walk the section from the fork.

With binoculars, you might be able to distinguish between the four different species of wading birds that frequent the heronry. The **Javan pond heron** is easiest to spot during the breeding season, when its usual plumage of grey feathers streaked with white darkens to brown on the breast and black along the back. The three types of egret are harder to differentiate: the **plumed egret** is the largest and has pure white plumage, a long neck, black legs and either a black or a yellow beak; the shorter-necked **little egret** also has white feathers, black legs and a black beak. The smaller, yellow-billed **cattle egret** is at its most distinctive during the breeding season, when its normally white feathers become flecked with reddish brown.

No one knows for certain why the herons and the egrets have chosen to make their home in Petulu, though locally it's claimed that the birds are **reincarnations** of the tens of thousands of men and women who died in the civil war that raged through Bali in 1966. Many of the victims were buried near here, and the birds are said to have started coming here only after an elaborate ceremony was held in the village in memory of the dead.

Ubud Botanic Garden

Lush, tranquil **Ubud Botanic Garden** (daily 8am–6pm; Rp50,000; ⓦ www .botanicgardenbali.com) occupies five hectares of a steep-sided river valley in the *banjar* of Kutuh Kaja, 1.7km north of Jalan Raya Ubud, and combines well with a visit to the heron sanctuary at nearby Petulu. The garden features plants from all over Indonesia, grouped together in enclaves that include a gorgeous heliconia hill, a diverse orchid nursery, a bromeliad collection, a semi-formal Islamic garden and a maze, but there's frustratingly little information to educate the inexpert wanderer. It works better as a green retreat, with its thoughtfully designed open-air meditation court and strategically sited seating. The garden is signed off eastern Jalan Raya Ubud via Jalan Tirta Tawar and takes about half an hour to reach on foot, passing through a typically pleasant mix of villages and ricefields.

Eating

Ubud is packed full of **places to eat**, many with a higher proportion of vegetarian and organic dishes than anywhere else on the island. Most restaurants shut at about 10pm. Where phone numbers are given for restaurants outside central Ubud it's worth calling to ask about free transport (generally provided when business is good).

Central Ubud and Padang Tegal

Ary's Warung Jl Raya Ubud. Sleek and chic but also overpriced and rather pretentious, *Ary's* street-side lounge bar and upstairs dining terrace are very much places to see and be seen. The contemporary Asian menu includes veal cutlets with wasabi sauce (Rp170,000) and slow-roasted duck in Balinese spices (but not much of a vegetarian selection) plus frozen lemongrass parfait and over a hundred imported wines. Best for dinner, unless you splash out on the four-course lunchtime tasting menu (Rp170,000).

Bali Buddha Jl Jembawan 1. The café that started the Ubud trend for wholesome organic eateries, this chilled-out spot has couches and comfortable chairs, takeaways from its organic shop downstairs, plus a noticeboard for yoga and language classes and houses for rent. The menu includes organic juices, soy milk and traditional *jamu* health drinks, sandwiches made with rye, country and focaccia breads, brownies and cinnamon rolls, as well as raw-food meals, salads and pastas (Rp25,000–37,000).

Bumbu Jl Suweta 1. Wide choice of Indian and Balinese fare, with plenty of veggie options, served in a pleasant water-garden setting. The menu includes

banana and coconut curry, smoked duck platter (Rp45,000), vegetarian, meat and prawn thalis (from Rp35,000), rose-petal ice cream, and excellent iced coffees. Also runs cookery classes (see p.209).

Café des Artistes Jl Bisma 9X. Sophisticated place with changing exhibitions by local artists and a top-notch Belgian-accented menu that features half-a-dozen steak dishes (from Rp60,000) including au poivre and with mushroom sauce, home-made pastas, pear, blue cheese and sundried tomato salad (Rp45,000) plus a good-value monthly special (Rp150,000 for 4 courses). Also offers over forty imported wines – and some cigars.

Café Wayan Jl Monkey Forest. Long-established place that's known for its breads and cakes (eat in and takeaway), which include the signature temptation, "Death by Chocolate" (Rp23,000), apple strudel (Rp13,000) and much more. Also does Indonesian, Thai and European dishes (from Rp40,000), and produces occasional traditional Balinese feasts, served buffet style.

Casa Luna Jl Raya Ubud (same menu also delivered to *Honeymoon Guesthouse* restaurant on Jl Bisma). Another popular Ubud institution specializing in mid-priced breads (multigrain, rye, baguettes) and cakes (from Rp17,000), but also offering good salad, (from Rp25,000), plus plenty of

---

Be a good tourist...

... and **recycle** your plastic water bottle. Discarded plastic bottles pose a major problem in Bali, as they don't decompose and tend to pile up in nasty heaps at the back of hotels and restaurants; they're also relatively expensive and wasteful to manufacture. To help minimize this problem, you can reuse your plastic water bottle by **refilling** it with the filtered water supplied at certain clued-up outlets in Ubud for less than what it would cost to buy a replacement.

These include:

Jl Dewi Sita: *Tutmak* restaurant; and Pondok Pekak Library and Learning Centre.

Jl Karna: the *Candra House* shop at #8.

Jl Kajeng: *Rumah Roda* losmen at #24.

Jl Jembawan: *Bali Buddha* café.

Jl Bisma: *Roda Internet Café*.

Jl Hanoman: *Kafe* restaurant at #44B; and *Tegal Sari* hotel.

Rice-paddy walk: *Sari Organik* café.

veggie dishes, as well as Sunday-brunch specials (served until 2pm). Also runs cookery classes (see p.209) and has free Wi-Fi.

DeliCat Off Jl Dewi Sita. Run by an Icelander, this rustic-look deli restaurant has a loyal expat clientele and is the place to come if you've a hankering for a glass of wine and accompanying Camembert or Danish Blue on rye, salami or chorizo (sandwiches from Rp30,000), or meatballs and mash. It's a sociable spot as customers share the large outdoor tables overlooking the football field.

Dewa Warung Jl Gootama. This typical Balinese warung sells *cap cay*, nasi campur, nasi goreng and the like at typical Balinese prices (mostly a bargain Rp6000), so it attracts a mixed clientele of savvy foreigners and local lads who often end up having to share tables.

Ibu Oka Jl Suweta. Considered by many to make the best, and among the spiciest, *babi guling* (roast suckling pig) in Bali, this little warung attracts queues of diners from as far away as Denpasar. Early lunchers get the best cuts – and the choicest crackling – as the meat's cooked fresh every morning. Rp10,000/portion with rice and *sambal*. Open daily from 11am to about 2.30pm.

Lamak Jl Monkey Forest ☏0361/974688. Outstanding, exceptionally creative food is the hallmark of this large, fashionable restaurant, which is sectioned into several modishly designed dining areas (including an a/c room) and boasts a cocktail bar and wine cellar as well. There is much to recommend on the innovative modern-Asian menu, including curried yoghurt-coated smoked butterfish medallions (Rp75,000), avocado, asparagus and radicchio salad with mango dressing, and hot raspberry soufflé. Also has a blow-out six-course tasting menu for Rp245,000, a long and varied vegetarian menu and a kids' menu. Well worth the money.

Nomad Jl Raya Ubud 35. Having dished out travellers' food since 1979, this place has perfected the art of serving unusually tasty standards with style and at reasonable prices. The home-made pumpkin ravioli (Rp24,000) is good and the gado-gado stands out too. Black rice pudding is also on the menu.

Terazo Jl Suweta. Above-average Mediterranean cuisine including delicious gazpacho, very good porcini fettuccine and lots of daily specials (Rp60,000–80,000), served in a split-level dining area with boho-chic decor.

Tutmak Jl Dewi Sita. A favourite place for Ubud's expats to gossip over exceptionally good coffee and cakes, this is also a great spot for breakfasts – smoked-salmon bagels for Rp60,000, full English breakfast at Rp35,000.

Peliatan, Campuhan, Sanggingan, Penestanan and Sayan

Indus Jl Raya Sanggingan ☏0361/977684. Occupying a fine position overlooking the Campuhan ridge, this is a good place for breakfast (muffins on the menu from 7.30am), or at sunset, as you'll miss out on the view after dark. Run by the same team behind *Casa Luna* in central Ubud, the moderately priced menu here features lots of dishes using local *tenggiri* river fish – cooked in Thai, Vietnamese or Indian style – plus the trademark cakes, home-made breads, vegetable juices and healthy salads. Free shuttle from *Casa Luna* in central Ubud and live Latino music every Mon from 7.30pm.

Made's Warung Penestanan ridge, between the steps and the river. Homely spot that's handy for the ridgetop losmen and serves well-priced travellers' favourites, including cheap juices (Rp6000), good nasi campur (Rp12,500), pancakes, and (with 24hr notice) Balinese smoked duck (Rp115,000 for two).

Mangga Madu Jl Gunung Sari 1, Peliatan. Cheap, popular Indonesian warung known for its tuna dishes – sweet and sour, fried or curried – though it also does veggie curry, nasi campur and *nasi pecel* (Rp6000–15,000). Popular with locals and budget-minded expats.

Mozaic Jl Raya Sanggingan ☏0361/975768; closed Mon. The poshest and most expensive restaurant in Ubud (main courses from Rp100,000) serves a multi-award-winning menu inspired by contemporary French and Asian cuisine. It includes duck foie gras with mandarin sauce and kumquats, honey-soy caramelized suckling pork, and dark chocolate fondant with sour-cherry chutney. Also offers tantalizing six-course tasting menus (Rp450,000). Reservations essential.

Murni's Warung Jl Raya Campuhan. Follow the stairs all the way down to the lowest level of this multi-tiered restaurant and you'll appreciate the setting, for it's built into the wall of the steep-sided Wos river valley. The restaurant is an Ubud institution and serves curries, home-made soups and Indonesian specialities (Rp20,000–65,000) as well as a good line in sweet things, such as strawberry cheesecake, and banana and caramel cake. Also has free Wi-Fi.

Naughty Nuri's Jl Raya Sanggingan. Long-running warung and favourite expat hangout where the spare ribs and fresh tuna steaks, sashimi and sate are the highlights and barbecues are a regular event. All sorts of Indonesian standards too (from Rp25,000), plus great Martinis.

Sari Laba Boga Jl Raya Penestanan. Cheap and tasty travellers' fare and Indonesian favourites – including good *urap* and *nasi kuning* – plus a long menu of vegetarian options (from Rp15,000).

Sari Organik Off Jl Abangan, about 800m walk north along a path from the aqueduct on western Jl Raya Ubud: follow signs from *Abangan Bungalows* ☎ 0361/780 1839. Gorgeously sited in the ricefields (about 10 mins into the Ubud Kaja ricefield walk described on p.191) on a plot of land that's run as an organic garden and experimental station for indigenous strains of rice, this ultra-chilled-out café makes the most of the views – and the home-grown produce. Food (Rp17,000–35,000) is almost entirely home-made (even the tofu) and includes great veggie kebabs, delicious chicken, and lots of salads. Fireflies add extra sparkle in the evening. Daily 8am–8pm.

Warung Mina Jl Gunung Sari 2, Peliatan. Sit in your private gazebo and choose from the range of authentic east-Bali banana-leaf set meals, featuring either freshwater fish (*gurame*), prawns or chicken (Rp15,000–27,000).

Nightlife and entertainment

Ubud is hardly a hotbed of hedonistic **nightlife**. Many tourists spend the early evening at one of the many Balinese **dance performances** staged every night in the area before catching last orders at a restaurant at around 9pm. Alternative entertainment is limited to the **live music** staged at some of Ubud's **bars** and restaurants.

There's no proper cinema in Ubud but Warung Cinema in Penestanan Kelod shows different mainstream **films** nightly on its outdoor screen (Tues–Sun 7.30pm; Rp10,000); pick up a monthly schedule from restaurants around town or phone ☎0813/3773 9762. The Yoga Barn at the southern end of Jalan Hanoman in Padang Tegal hosts an interesting programme of Monday Night Movies (mostly documentaries) every other Monday from 7.30pm (Rp20,000 or Rp60,000 incl dinner from 6pm; ☎0361/970992, ⊛www.balispirit.com).

Bars and live-music venues

The **bar** scene can be very quiet in Ubud, so choose a **live-music night** to be sure of a decent crowd. Where phone numbers are given, free transport within the Ubud area is usually available.

Flava Lounge Jl Raya Pengosekan, Pengosekan. It's open mic on Wed nights at this pizza and Mexican-accented restaurant, when musicians of all styles and nationalities converge to play solo and in harmony.

Indus Jl Raya Sanggingan, Sanggingan ☎0361/977684. Mon night is Latino and salsa night at this locally famous restaurant on the western edge of town. 7.30–10.30pm.

Jazz Café Jl Sukma 2, Peliatan ☎0361/976594; free transport from *The Waroeng* restaurant on Jl Monkey Forest. Ubud's long-running jazz bar and restaurant stages quality live jazz Tues–Sat from 7.30pm.

Ozigo Jl Raya Sanggingan, Sanggingan ☎0812/367 9736. Expat bar with a small dancefloor, bar snacks, DJs, theme nights and live music nightly from 10pm.

Putra Bar Jl Monkey Forest. Ubud's most Kuta-style bar has a dancefloor, live international sports on the TV, and live music at weekends.

Rendezvousdoux Jl Raya Ubud 14. Live world-music sets from talented expat musicians at this second hand bookshop and café, usually followed by a jam session, every Thurs from 8pm.

Wunderbar Jl Raya Pengosekan, Pengosekan. There's a pool table at this German-run a/c bar-restaurant, and live music every Fri & Sat. Closed Mon.

Dance and drama

The Ubud region is an important centre of **Balinese dance** and **gamelan** and boasts dozens of performance groups. Between them they stage up to nine different dance shows every night in the area; the tourist office publishes the schedule (which is also available at Ⓦ www.ubud.com) and arranges **free transport** to outlying venues. **Ticket prices** are fixed and cost Rp50,000–80,000 from the tourist office, touts and at the door. Performances generally start between 7pm and 8pm, and it's free seating, so arrive early for the best spot.

A lot of the dance groups combine up to eight different dances into a medley show. The **Kecak** (Monkey Dance) and the **Barong** (Lion Dance) are the most accessible and visually interesting, while the **Legong** is more refined and

▲ Dance class at Ubud Palace

understated. Unusual shows worth seeking out include the village exorcism, **Calonarang**; Javanese shadow-puppet dramas, or **wayang kulit**; and the unique **all-female gamelan**. Although not detailed in its publicity, the Sadha Budaya group's Legong programme at Ubud Palace includes the brilliantly eloquent flirtation dance **Oleg Tambulilingan** (Bumblebee Dance) and the touching **Topeng Tua** (Old Man's Mask Dance). Similarly, the Tirta Sari show in Peliatan features the superb melodramatic solo, the **Kebyar Trompong**. For more on Balinese dance, see p.440.

If you have only one evening to catch a show, consider seeing whatever is playing at **Puri Saren Agung (Ubud Palace)**, opposite the market in the centre of Ubud. The setting is atmospheric, with the courtyard gateway and staircase furnishing a memorable backdrop. You can also watch dance classes here (Sun 9.30am–noon, Tues 3–5.30pm; free). The Kecak that's staged twice a month on the nights of the full and dark moon at the **ARMA** in Pengosekan (see p.199) is also worth a special effort as it's an unusually fiery and humorous version.

Shopping

Shopping for arts and crafts is a major pastime in Ubud: there are enjoyably browsable outlets in all its neighbourhoods, but if you're short on time the northern stretch of Jalan Hanoman has a concentration of interesting, quality handicraft shops. The **pasar seni** "art market" in central Ubud is another good one-stop venue and overflows with stalls selling cheap, mass-produced sarongs, trinkets and clothes; it also has several inexpensive tailors. You might also want to explore the specialist "craft villages" on the Denpasar–Ubud road (see pp.168–174), and the handicraft outlets around Tegalalang (see p.215) before making any significant purchases. Tino Supermarket, on Jalan Raya Ubud, and Bintang Supermarket, on Jalan Raya Campuhan, stock all major essentials, from suntan lotion to beer. Most Ubud shops **open** daily, often until 9pm; many can organize shipping if required.

Art

Agung Rai Fine Art Gallery Jl Peliatan. High-quality outlet for paintings of all styles, owned by the man behind the ARMA in Pengosekan.

Duck Man of Bali Jl Raya Goa Gajah, about 1.5km east along the road to Goa Gajah. Known for its phenomenal gallery of wooden ducks in all sizes and styles, carved by "the duck man", Ngurah Umum, and his assistants.

Graphic Art Jl Kajeng 22 and Jl Bisma 3B. Javanese artist F. Malik creates extraordinary pictures of classic Balinese landscapes with nothing but black and green rotring pens, painstakingly drawing in every rice plant in pictures that can be 2m wide. Originals cost at least Rp1,000,000, but framed limited-edition prints start at Rp200,000.

Low Art Jl Raya Ubud 8. Unmissable gallery and outlet for popular "street" art, film posters and kitsch from Bali and elsewhere. Especially

intriguing are the vinyl picture-mats used in the *kocokan* gambling game played at temple festivals, which feature different casts of popular characters, including cartoon creatures, TV personalities, politicians and mythological figures.

Munut's Gallery Far eastern end of Jl Raya Ubud. Recommended dealer in paintings of all styles, with a large selection on display.

Neka Gallery Eastern end of Jl Raya Ubud. Classy, highly reputable gallery owned by the founder of the Neka Art Museum. Specializes in good-quality works, many by well-known artists such as Nyoman Gunarsa, I Wayan Bendi and Arie Smit.

Pandi Jl Bisma 3C. Striking and deceptively simple pop-naive paintings by the idiosyncratic Pandi – nearly always featuring his trademark bird somewhere on the canvas.

Rio Helmi Jl Suweta 5. Small gallery and showroom of prints by the respected expat photographer.

Need to make room in your luggage for new purchases? Donate unwanted clothes, books, bric-a-brac and anything else "so long as it's not alive" to the Yayasan Senyum **charity shop**, The Smile Shop, on Jl Sriwedari (Tues–Sat 10am–4pm, Sun noon–4pm; Ⓦ www.senyumbali.org). Profits help fund operations for Balinese people with cranio-facial disabilities such as cleft palate. You can of course also buy cheap second-hand stuff at the shop too.

Books

Ary's Bookshop Jl Raya Ubud. Extensive stock of books and maps on Bali and Indonesia. Also sells foreign newspapers and magazines.

Cinta Bookshop Jl Dewi Sita. Alphabeticized secondhand books for sale plus some for rent.

Ganesha Bookshop Jl Raya Ubud, corner of Jl Jembawan Ⓦ www.ganeshabooksbali.com. The best bookshop in Bali, with a huge stock of new books on all things Balinese; also sells maps and some secondhand books, and has an online ordering service.

Periplus North end of Jl Monkey Forest, Jl Raya Ubud and inside Bintang Supermarket on Jl Raya Campuhan. Well-stocked Bali-wide chain.

Pondok Pekak Library and Learning Centre Jl Dewi Sita. Plenty of well-priced secondhand books available for sale, rent and part-exchange.

Rendezvousdoux Jl Raya Ubud 14. Secondhand bookshop and café with decent food and comfy chairs so you can try buy before you buy.

Clothes, jewellery and accessories

Kamar Sutra Jl Monkey Forest. Stunning batik designs on very expensive silk and crêpe scarves, wraps and shawls.

Opiq Kids Jl Monkey Forest. Cute kids' clothes and accessories (newborns up to age 10) made from distinctive, bright cotton prints.

Prama Shop Jl Hanoman 23. Central Ubud outlet for some of the Penestanan beadworkers, selling beaded belts, bags, bracelets, etc.

Studio Perak Toko Jl Raya Ubud and Jl Hanoman. Stylish silver jewellery from the people who run Ubud's silversmithing courses (see p.209).

Suarti Jl Monkey Forest. Jewellery shop specializing in original designs.

Crafts, textiles and homewares

Asialine Jl Hanoman 8. Classy handicrafts from across Indonesia, especially wooden frames and bowls painted with intricate batik-print motifs.

Bali Cares Inside *Kafe*, Jl Hanoman 44B. Tiny outlet for handicrafts, clothing and toiletries, proceeds from which are used to fund the work of Balinese charities. Run by the IDEP foundation (see Basics, p.62).

Kupu-Kupu Jl Raya Ubud. Small outlet for inexpensive works produced by disabled woodcarvers, kite-makers, painters, beadworkers and weavers, under the auspices of the Kupu-Kupu foundation (see Basics, p.62). Staffed by the artists.

Mangku Made Gina Near ARMA at the southern end of Jl Hanoman. Stunning selection of exquisite palm-leaf baskets made by a family of Pengosekan basket-weavers.

Oleh-Oleh: Outer Island Treasures Jl Monkey Forest. Artefacts from all over Indonesia including porcupine-quill necklaces from Irian Jaya, bronze horses from Java, carved Timorese panels and Balinese wooden figurines.

Tegun Jl Hanoman 44. Attractive Indonesian artefacts, including puppets, jewellery, and wooden bowls hand-painted with batik motifs.

Toko Yude Jl Raya Ubud. Stunning array of sarongs from Java including hand-painted cotton classics from Yogya (from Rp350,000) and silk beauties from Rp1,000,000.

Wardani's Jl Monkey Forest. Ubud's best fabric shop, with a range of cotton *ikat*, silks and cottons sold by the metre, and ready-made soft furnishings.

Musical instruments, CDs and DVDs

Adi Musical Instruments Jl Hanoman 7. Fun collection of small, cheap, quirky instruments that you can shake, twang, pluck, squeeze and bang. Mostly made from wood and bamboo and perfect for kids.

Ganesha Bookshop Jl Raya Ubud, corner of Jl Jembawan Ⓦ www.ganeshabooksbali.com. CDs and tapes of Indonesian and Balinese music; online ordering also available.

Moari Music Jl Raya Ubud. Specializes in traditional Balinese musical instruments, from bamboo flutes to full-sized gamelan.

Pondok Bamboo Off the far southern end of Jl Monkey Forest, Padang Tegal. Sells the full range of Balinese instruments made from bamboo, with everything from *genggong* to the component parts of the *gamelan joged bumbung*, the bamboo gamelan. The musician owner teaches music and is also a *dalang* shadow-puppet master; he performs here every Mon & Thurs at 8pm.

Ubud Music Jl Raya Ubud. One of Ubud's main outlet for cheap CDs and DVDs.

Spa treatments, yoga and alternative therapies

Arty, spiritual-minded Ubud is Bali's centre for **holistic practices** and **alternative therapies**, and also offers lots of opportunities to indulge in traditional **spa and beauty treatments** (for more on which see Basics, p.53). Except where stated, all listed centres open daily until at least 7pm. For more information on holistic activities and therapies in Ubud and the rest of Bali, visit the website of the Ubud-based **Bali Spirit** network (Ⓦwww.balispirit.com). Bali Spirit also runs Ubud's annual Bali Spirit Festival of world music, dance and yoga every March.

Bali Botanica Day Spa Jl Raya Sanggingan ☎0361/976739, Ⓦwww.balbotanica.com. Cute little day-spa overlooking a small flower garden and river where the signature treatments are Ayurvedic (2hr 30min; Rp450,000) and herbal massage. Also does half-day packages including hotel pick-up from Rp350,000.

Bali Spirit and The Yoga Barn Jl Hanoman 44B and southern Jl Hanoman ☎0361/970992, Ⓦwww.balispirit.com and Ⓦwww.theyogabarn .com. *The* hub for Ubud's community of yoga and therapy practitioners, Bali Spirit incorporates a holistic information centre and wholesome yogi-friendly restaurant – *Kafe* – plus the fairtrade Bali Cares shop (see opposite) at 44B and the Yoga Shop, for brand-name yoga mats and clothes, next door. It also manages The Yoga Barn studio (located further south along Jl Hanoman), which runs a big programme of yoga classes in various disciplines (see website for schedules) and can arrange many other therapies.

Balinese Traditional Healing Centre Jl Jembawan 5, but in 2008 due to move to Wayan's house at Rumah Lingkungan, Banjar Jungjungan, about 1.5km north of Ubud Botanic Garden ☎0852/3710 4401. Fourth-generation Balinese healer Ni Wayan Nuriasih uses a combination of local herbal medicine plus Chinese and Ayurvedic practices, massage and *jamu* to treat her clients. Tourists generally receive a traditional health spa treatment designed to improve circulation and rejuvenate the skin (3hr; Rp550,000) which includes a generalized diagnosis, a three-hour massage and poultice application, plus various *jamu* to take away. Her popularity has soared since the publication of Elizabeth Gilbert's bestselling spiritual memoir, *Eat, Pray, Love* (reviewed on p.471), in which Wayan plays a major role.

Meditation Shop Jl Raya Penestanan. The local Brahma Kumaris meditation group holds free meditation sessions every evening for anyone who's interested, and runs five-day meditation courses.

Nur Salon Jl Hanoman 28 ☎0361/975352, Ⓔnursalonubud@yahoo.com. Ubud's first massage and beauty salon has been in operation since the 1970s and enjoys a very good reputation; the *mandi lulur* treatments are especially famous (from Rp145,000). The salon occupies a traditional Balinese compound and treatment rooms are designed in keeping. Uses male masseurs for male customers.

Puri Damai Traditional Healers About 5km west of Ubud in Banjar Tunon, Singakerta ☎0361/744 5798; see map, p.169. Traditional healer Ida Ayu Rusmarini is well respected locally for her extensive garden of herbs and her knowledge of their medicinal properties. She offers a health consultation package that includes diagnosis via reflexology plus a one-hour massage and relevant *jamu* herbal medicine for Rp200,000–350,000. She speaks adequate English (and is employed by one of Ubud's top hotels) but for complicated problems go with an Indonesian speaker. Phone to book and get directions.

Spa Hati Jl Andong 14, Peliatan ☎0361/977578. Small, unpretentious spa offering a small programme of two- and four-hand massages and *lulur* treatments (from Rp135,000) and use of the Jacuzzi and ricefield-view swimming pool. Profits help fund the work of Bali Hati Foundation community projects (for more on which see Basics, p.61).

Ubud Bodyworks Centre Jl Hanoman 25 ☎0361/975720, Ⓦwww.ubudbodyworkscentre .com. Well-respected centre for massage and spiritual healing where you can book an appointment with master healer Ketut Arsana ($50) or with one of his staff (from Rp135,000). Also offers traditional baths and massages, beauty treatments, acupressure, energy balancing, herbal healing and reflexology, and yoga sessions, and sells essential oils.

Ubud has long been famous for its **herbal medicine**, known both for the medicinal plants that flourish around the Campuhan river gullies and gave the village its name – *ubad* means "medicine" in Balinese – and for the local healers who know how to use them.

The pills, pastes and potions distilled from medicinal herbs are collectively known as **jamu** and are widely used throughout Bali (and the rest of Indonesia), both in the treatment of serious ailments and for general wellbeing. Healers usually **make their own** *jamu* from herbs they may have picked or even grown themselves and will have a standard range of special, secret, mixtures to prescribe to their patients as pills or for use in infusions; often they'll custom-make *jamu* for particular conditions as well. Commonly used mainstream plants include turmeric, ginger, galangal and garlic, but there are countless others and recipes are always carefully designed for balance and holism. See p.207 for details of a couple of Ubud healers who also treat tourists and p.181 for info on guided herb-walks. Some *jamu*-makers don't offer healing sessions but simply hawk their home-brews around the market, dishing out measures of their half-a-dozen different muddy-coloured concoctions, usually laced with roots and leaves and stored in old glass bottles, to their regular customers and anyone else who feels in need of a boost. Several Ubud spas and cafés also serve ready-made *jamu* drinks to tourists, including *Bali Buddha*, reviewed on p.201.

Commercially produced *jamu* is also a huge industry and tends to focus more, but not exclusively, on the wellbeing side of things. Sex and beauty enhancers for men and women are predictably big sellers – in fact some people consider all *jamu*, both home-made and commercial, to be aphrodisiacs. Diet and breast-enlargement elixirs are similarly popular, but there are also plenty of products for cleansing the blood, easing joint pain and muscle ache, improving circulation and dealing with skin conditions. The reputable brands use entirely natural ingredients, often to recipes that are familiar to those who make their own and, like home-made *jamu*, should have no side effects at all (though it's always best to seek local advice first). Pharmacies sometimes sell these commercial powders and pills (around Rp25,000 a course) but there are also dedicated *jamu* shops, like the one towards the eastern end of Ubud's Jalan Raya. Commercial *jamu* is distinctively packaged, often carrying a helpful graphic, like a pulsating knee joint (arthritis) or a smiling, muscular male (better sex), and the most vital information is usually also given in English.

Ubud Sari Health Resort Jl Kajeng 35 ☏0361/974393, ⓦwww.ubudsari.com. The most serious, and expensive, of Ubud's health and beauty centres, with an on-site swimming pool and health restaurant. Treatments (from $15) include massage, aromatherapy, reflexology, reiki, sports massage and yoga. You can also stay at the resort's tranquil bungalows (ⓖ) or book an all-inclusive healing week for $200 per day.

Courses and workshops

With so many creative types in residence, Ubud is a great place to get learning: there are tourist-oriented **courses** here in everything from making offerings to creating jewellery, from traditional Balinese dance to textile appreciation. In addition to the more formal venues listed, it's always worth asking advice from the more traditional homestays, whose managers are often dancers, musicians or painters. For yoga courses, see p.207.

Arts, crafts, music, dance and traditional culture

ARMA Cultural Workshops Jl Raya Pengosekan ☎0361/976659, Ⓦwww.armamuseum.com. Museum-endorsed classes (mostly 2hr; $22–50) in Balinese painting, woodcarving, batik, gamelan, dance and theatre, traditional architecture, Hinduism, astrology and making offerings.

Asri Sari Jl Monkey Forest ☎0361/296633, Ⓔas_silver@telkom.net. Contact the Asri Sari silver shop for the chance to learn the main silver-making techniques at their small workshop in Batubulan (Rp100,000/day excluding materials).

Dewi Sekar Ayu Jl Hanoman 26 ☎0361/975350. If you have a serious interest in Balinese dance, Ayu will be happy to arrange a tailor-made course for you.

Kite Workshop Jl Suweta ☎0813/3876 4495. Make your own kite in the family compound of a local kite-maker. Designs and sizes to suit; Rp250,000–350,000.

Museum Puri Lukisan Cultural Workshops Jl Raya Ubud ☎0361/971159, Ⓦwww.mpl-ubud .com. Serious, reputable classes (mostly one-day; Rp350,000) run by and at Ubud's oldest art museum. Courses in batik, woodcarving, beadwork, classical painting, basketry, kite-making, mask-painting, shadow-puppet making, gamelan and Balinese dance.

Nirvana Batik Course Jl Gootama 10 ☎0361/975415, Ⓦnirvanaku.com. Renowned Ubud painter, village activist and batik artist I Nyoman Suradnya runs one- to five-day courses in batik painting ($35/day, including materials). His family also runs the *Nirvana Pension* guesthouse (see p.183).

Nyuhkuning woodcarving shops Nyuhkuning. There are plenty of willing teachers in this village of woodcarvers; just ask at any of the shops.

Pondok Pekak Library and Learning Centre Jl Dewi Sita ☎0361/976194, Ⓔpondok@indo.net.id. "Art of Bali" beginners' classes in dance, gamelan, painting, woodcarving, making offerings and bamboo weaving (Rp50,000–200,000).

Sari Api Jl Dewi Sita ☎0361/977917 Ⓔsariapi @indo.net.id. Courses in ceramic making from the Canadian ceramicist whose works are sold at the Sari Api shop. From Rp200,000/half-day.

Sehati Off the southern end of Jl Monkey Forest, Padang Tegal ☎0361/976341, Ⓦwww .sehati-guesthouse.com. Learn to play the gamelan and other Balinese instruments, or to master the rudimentary elements of Balinese dance from a graduate of Denpasar's prestigious school of performing arts. Rp50,000/hr.

Studio Perak Jl Hanoman ☎0812/365 1809, Ⓦwww.studioperak.com; closed Sun. Courses in silversmithing: in half a day you can produce your own ring (Rp175,000 inclusive).

Threads of Life Textile Art Center Jl Kajeng 24 ☎0361/972187, Ⓦwww.threadsoflife.com. Scheduled classes and workshops on Indonesian textile appreciation (from Rp50,000), indigo dyeing and batik making. Phone for details.

Cookery and language

Bumbu restaurant Jl Suweta 1 ☎0361/974217, Ⓔbumbu_bali@plasa.com. Half-day workshops in Balinese cooking, which begin with a trip to the local market and culminate in lunch. Rp150,000.

Casa Luna restaurant Jl Raya Ubud ☎0361/973282, Ⓦwww.casalunabali.com. Famous, long-running half-day Balinese cooking workshops run by *Fragrant Rice* author Janet de Neefe; see website for schedules. Rp250,000.

Pondok Pekak Library and Learning Centre Jl Dewi Sita ☎0361/976194, Ⓔpondok@indo.net.id. Intensive Indonesian language courses (24hr, usually over 4 weeks; Rp720,000) and lessons (Rp120,000/2hr); plus Balinese lessons(Rp150,000/2hr).

Secret Garden Cooking School *Taman Rahasia* hotel, Penestanan Kaja ☎0361/979395, Ⓦwww .balisecretgarden.com. One- and two-day intensive courses in Balinese cooking; see website for schedules. From $65.

Tegal Sari hotel Jl Hanoman, Padang Tegal ☎0361/973318, Ⓦwww.tegalsari-ubud.com. Half-day courses in Balinese and Indonesian cuisine. Rp350,000 including lunch.

Listings

Banks and exchange There are ATMs throughout Ubud and its environs. Many tour agents offer exchange services, but see p.70 for details of common scams. Western Union agents include the GPO, and Bank Mandiri on Jl Raya Ubud.
Embassies and consulates See p.66.

Hospitals, clinics and dentists For minor casual-ties, go to the Legian Clinic, Jl Monkey Forest ☎0361/970805, or to the Ubud Clinic, which also has a dental service, at Jl Raya Campuhan 36 ☎0361/974911. Both are open 24hr, are staffed by English-speakers, and will respond to emergency call-outs. For anything serious, the nearest hospitals are in Denpasar (p.95).

House rental Check the noticeboards at *Bali Buddha* café, Jl Jembawan; Bali Spirit, Jl Hanoman 44B; *Casa Luna* restaurant, Jl Raya Ubud; and Bali 3000 Internet café, Jl Raya Ubud.

Internet access Efficient Internet centres (daily 8am–9pm) include: Highway, Jl Raya Ubud (high-speed connection and laptop hookups; open 24hr); Bali 3000, Jl Raya Ubud; Roda Tourist Services, Jl Bisma 3; and Ary's Business and Travel Service, Jl Raya Ubud.

Libraries The Pondok Pekak Library and Learning Centre off Jl Dewi Sita (daily 9am–9pm) has lots of books about Bali, English-language novels, and a comfortable upstairs reading room. Their children's library welcomes donations of Indonesian- and English-language books; see p.62 for more details. The Agung Rai Museum of Art (ARMA) has the island's best library of books about Bali, including famous esoteric works and language books. *Rendezvousdoux* café, Jl Raya, also has a small reference library of Bali books.

Pharmacies On Jl Raya Ubud, Jl Monkey Forest and Jl Peliatan.

Phones The government Wartel Telkom is at the eastern end of Jl Raya Ubud (daily 8am–9pm) and also has credit-card phones outside. There are IDD direct-dial phones outside the GPO on Jl Jembawan and in front of the market; phone cards are sold at Bintang Supermarket, Jl Raya Campuhan. Most Internet centres offer international phone services and many also have Skype.

Police The main police station is on the eastern edge of town, on Jl Andong. There's a more central police booth at the Jl Raya Ubud /Jl Monkey Forest crossroads.

Post offices The Ubud GPO on Jl Jembawan (Mon–Sat 8am–5pm, Sun & hols 9am–4pm) keeps poste restante, and there's a parcel-packing service at the back. There are postal agents throughout Ubud where you can buy stamps and send mail and parcels.

Safety boxes For rent at Ary's Business and Travel Service, Jl Raya Ubud (℡ 0361/973130).

Travel agents Ary's Business and Travel Service, Jl Raya Ubud (℡ 0361/973130, ✉ arys_tour @yahoo.com); Perama, Jl Hanoman, Padang Tegal (℡ 0361/973316, ⊛ www.peramatour.com).

East of Ubud

Slicing through the region immediately **east of Ubud**, the sacred rivers Petanu and Pakrisan flow down from the Batur crater rim in parallel, framing a narrow strip of land imbued with great spiritual and historical importance. This fifteen-kilometre-long sliver has been settled since the Balinese Bronze Age, around 300 BC, and now boasts the biggest concentration of antiquities on Bali. From the stone sarcophagi and Bronze Age gong of **Pejeng** to the eleventh-century rock-hewn hermitage at **Goa Gajah** and fourteenth-century **Yeh Pulu reliefs**, these relics all lie within 7km of Ubud.

Access by bemo is very easy from Ubud – take any Gianyar-bound one – and similarly straightforward by bike or motorbike. This area also combines well with Tirta Empul and Gunung Kawi, 11km further north, and direct bemos connect the two.

Goa Gajah

Thought to have been a hermitage for eleventh-century Hindu priests, **Goa Gajah** (Elephant Cave; 8am–6pm; Rp6000, children Rp3000, including sarong rental) is a major tourist attraction, owing more to its proximity to the main Ubud–Gianyar road than to any remarkable atmosphere. Besides the cave itself, there's a traditional bathing pool here, as well as a number of ancient stone relics.

The pool and the cave

Descending the steep flight of steps from the back of the car park, you get a good view of the rectangular **bathing pool**, whose elegant sunken contours dominate the courtyard below. Such pools were usually built at holy sites, either at the source of a holy spring as at Tirta Empul or, like this one, near a sacred spot so that devotees could cleanse themselves before making offerings or prayers. Local men and women would have bathed here in the segregated male (right-hand) and female (left-hand) sections, under the jets of water from the Petanu tributary channelled through the protruding navels of the full-breasted statues lining its back wall. Although the water still flows, the pool is now maintained for ornamental purposes only.

The carvings that trumpet the entranceway to the hillside cave are impressive, if a little hard to distinguish. The **doorway** is a huge gaping mouth, framed by the upper jaw of a monstrous rock-carved head that's thought to represent either the earth god Bhoma, or the widow-witch Rangda, or a hybrid of the two. It would have served both as a repeller of evil spirits and as a suggestion that on entering you were being swallowed up into another, holier, world. Early visitors interpreted it as an elephant's head, which is how the cave got its modern name.

Passing into the monster's mouth, you enter the dank and dimly lit T-shaped **cave**, hewn by hand from the hillside to serve as meditation cells, or possibly living quarters, for the priests or ascetics. As with most of Bali's rock-cut monuments, the mythical giant Kebo Iwa is also associated with Goa Gajah, and legends describe how he gouged out the cells and the carvings here with his powerful fingernails, a feat that took him just one night. A statue of the Hindu elephant-headed god Ganesh sits in a niche to the left of the far end, while to the right are three lingga, phallic emblems of the god Siwa.

Outside the cave, in the small pavilion to the left of the gateway, sits a weather-worn statue of a woman surrounded by a horde of kids. This is the folk heroine **Men Brayut**, who has come to epitomize a mother's resolute struggle against poverty (see box, p.194). Men Brayut is known as the goddess Hariti in Buddhist literature, and this statue, along with a number of other relics found nearby, have led archeologists to believe that the site may have a **Buddhist** as well as a Hindu history. There are a few other Buddhist relics at the base of the concrete steps that drop down into the ravine just beyond the bathing pool, including the relief of a multi-tiered stupa carved into a chunk of rock.

Practicalities

To get to Goa Gajah, either walk, cycle or drive the 3km east from Ubud's Jalan Peliatan, or take one of the numerous (usually orange) Ubud–Gianyar **bemos**, which pass the entrance. The site car-park borders the main Ubud–Gianyar road. You can also walk here from the Yeh Pulu rock carvings (see below), along the irrigation channels that zigzag through the ricefields, but you'll need to hire one of the guides who hang around both at Yeh Pulu and Goa Gajah.

Yeh Pulu

In contrast with the overcrowded and overrated carvings at Goa Gajah, the rock-cut panels amidst the ricefields at **YEH PULU** (daylight hours; Rp6000, kids 3000 including sarong rental) are delightfully engaging, and the site is often empty.

Chipped away from a cliff face, the 25-metre-long series of Yeh Pulu **carvings** are said to date back to the fourteenth or fifteenth century. They are thought by some historians to depict a five-part story and, while the meaning of this story has been lost, it's still possible to make out some recurring characters and to speculate on the connections between them; local people, however, simply describe the carvings as showing daily activities from times past.

The series begins with an **introductory panel** separated from the others, showing a man with his arm raised, thought to be the Hindu god Krishna. In the **first scene**, a man carrying two jars of river water on a shoulder pole follows a woman of higher caste, who is bedecked with jewels. **Scene two** shows a different woman, seated, with her right arm stretched out towards a man carrying a hoe. To his left sits a figure whose distinctive turban-like hat indicates that he is either a priest or an ascetic (modern Balinese priests still wear very similar headdresses). A sarong-clad boy stands alone at the end of this panel, beside a kneeling statue of a Jaga Desa, the mythical village giant who protects the village from evil spirits. **Scene three** features a boar-hunting scene, above which two figures kneel either side of a water jar. **Scene four** shows two men carrying five boars away on a pole. In **scene five**, another hunter looks set to gallop off, and is either aided or hindered by a woman pulling on the animal's tail. Just as the story opened with a religious image, so the **concluding panel** is carved into a niche containing the elephant-headed god Ganesh.

The small **spring** after which the site is named (*yeh* means "holy spring", *pulu* "stone vessel") rises close by the statue of Ganesh and is sacred – hence the need for all visitors to wear temple dress; for the same reason, you may be asked for a donation when you get to this point. The Balinese believe that all water is a gift from the spirits so whenever the spring fails, special ceremonies are required to restore a harmonious flow.

Practicalities

The prettiest approach to Yeh Pulu is **on foot** along the dykes that skirt the sculpted rice terraces behind Goa Gajah, but you'll need to hire a guide to lead the way – they wait for customers at both sites and charge Rp100,000 for two or three people. Guides can also take you on the two-hour return ricefield **walk** from Yeh Pulu to the rice temple Dukuh Kedongan, with the chance of a dip in the Petanu River (prices as above); or there are longer, hotter variations (3–5hr), which continue either to the village of Segana or to the Durga Kutri temple, Pura Bukit Dharma Durga Kutri, in the village of Kutri (see p.225), and cost Rp250,000.

If you're using the Ubud–Gianyar **bemo**, get off at the Yeh Pulu signs just east of Goa Gajah or west of the Bedulu crossroads, then walk the kilometre south through the hamlet of Batulumbang to Yeh Pulu. If driving, follow the same signs through Batulumbang to where the road peters out, a few hundred metres above the stonecarvings. *Made's Warung* occupies a pretty position at the end of this road and serves a perfectly respectable menu of **snacks** and rice dishes. There's a four-room **losmen** almost next door, *Pondok Wisata Lantur* (T0361/942399; ①), which offers simple accommodation on the edge of the family compound.

Pejeng

Inhabited since the Bronze Age, and considered a holy site ever since, the village of **PEJENG** and its immediate environs harbour a wealth of religious antiquities, from carvings and rock-cut *candi* to bronze artefacts and massive stone statues. Some of these have been left in their original location, alongside riverbeds or buried in the paddy-fields, while others have been housed in local temples; several have also been carted off to museums, here and in Denpasar, Jakarta and Amsterdam. The remains have rather an esoteric appeal, and the area gets relatively few visitors and rarely features on the tour-bus circuit.

Practicalities

Pejeng's three main temples all lie within a few hundred metres of each other on the Bedulu–Tampaksiring road and are clearly signposted.

Coming from Ubud, take an orange, Gianyar-bound **bemo** to the Bedulu crossroads and then either wait for a bluey-grey Tampaksiring-bound one, or walk the kilometre to the temples. The alternative route from Ubud – by bike or motorbike – is the quiet, fairly scenic but quite severely undulating five-kilometre **back road** that heads east from the Jalan Raya Ubud/Jalan Peliatan junction at the eastern edge of Ubud, passes the posh *Maya Ubud* hotel, and then zigzags through paddies and small villages before finally emerging at the market on the main road, just 25m north of Pura Penataran Sasih (turn right for the temple).

Although the major temples are clearly signed, you might want to employ one of the local **guides** who wait at Pura Penataran Sasih. Entry to each temple is by **donation**; the obligatory sarong and sash can be borrowed at each one.

For **food** in Pejeng, try *Warung Pejeng*, between Pura Pusering Jagat and Pura Kebo Edan.

Pura Penataran Sasih

Balinese people believe **Pura Penataran Sasih** to be a particularly sacred temple, because this is the home of the so-called Moon of Pejeng – hence the English epithet **Moon Temple**.

The moon in question is a **large bronze gong**, shaped almost like an hourglass, suspended so high in its tower at the back of the temple compound that you can hardly see the decorations scratched onto its surface. It probably dates from the Balinese Bronze Age, from sometime during the third century BC, and – at almost two metres long – is thought to be the largest such kettle-drum ever cast. Etched into its green patina are a mass of geometric and abstract **designs** and, between its handles, a chain of striking heart-shaped **faces** with huge round eyes and distended earlobes. Legend tells how the gong fell towards earth one day from its home in heaven, where it had served as the wheel of a chariot that transported the moon through the skies. At that time, the wheel shone just as brightly as the moon itself, and when its fall was broken by a tree in Pejeng, a local thief became so incensed by the incriminating light it gave out that he tried to extinguish it by urinating over it. The wheel exploded with a thunderous echo, killed the thief, and dropped to the ground in its present form. Ever since, the Balinese have treated the Moon of Pejeng as sacred, making offerings to it whenever they need to move it, and always keeping a respectful distance.

Though now faded and rather dilapidated, the **temple** itself was once the most important in the area, and there's little doubt that, whatever the origins of the gong, it would have been used for much the same purposes as its modern counterpart, the *kulkul* – sounded with a stick to summon the people of Pejeng to ceremonies, to announce war, and also to invite rain to fall.

Pura Pusering Jagat

About 100m south down the main road from Pura Penataran Sasih, **Pura Pusering Jagat**, the "Temple of the Navel of the World", is famous for its elaborately carved metre-high stone jar, used for storing holy water. Carved in the fourteenth century from a single block of sandstone, the jar's reliefs are rather worn but are thought to depict a scene from the Hindu myth "**The Churning of the Sea of Milk**", in which the gods and the demons compete for the chance to extract, distil and drink the elixir of immortal life. Together they churn the Cosmic Soup (the Sea of Milk), using a holy mountain as their whisk and serpentine *naga* as ropes. Eventually, through a combination of trickery and good sense, the gods outdo the demons and are first with the elixir. Though some of the jar's detail is indistinct, you can make out several figures, including the undulating *naga* ropes and a number of dancing deities supporting them.

Housed in a nearby pavilion is another significant icon, the metre-high phallic *linggam* and its female receptacle, the *yoni* – an important shrine for newlywed and infertile couples.

Pura Kebo Edan

Pura Kebo Edan, some 200m south of Pura Pusering Jagat, is also considered lucky for childless couples. The attraction here is a massive lifelike phallus, attached to the huge stone body of a man, nicknamed the **Pejeng Giant**. In fact, this giant, nearly four metres tall, is said to possess six penises in all; aside from the one swinging out for all to see, one is supposed to have dropped to the ground during his very vigorous dancing, and four more are said to be hidden inside him, awaiting the correct point of the dance before emerging. His principal penis is pierced from front to back with a huge bolt-like pin, probably a realistic reference to an age-old Southeast Asian practice designed to increase women's sexual pleasure. With his hands on his hips, the giant – his face hidden behind a blank mask – dances on a prone female figure thought to represent the earth. The giant's identity is debatable; some think he's Bhima, one of the chief characters from the *Mahabharata*, while others see him as a manifestation of the Hindu deity Siwa, who harnessed enormous cosmic power whenever he danced.

Museum Arkeologi

As the main treasure-house of such a historically significant region, Pejeng's government-run **Museum Arkeologi**, 500m south of Pura Penataran Sasih (Mon–Fri 7.30am–2.30pm; Rp5000), makes disappointing viewing. Its four tiny pavilions house a small, eclectic assortment of artefacts found in the area, ranging from Paleolithic chopping tools to bronze bracelets and Chinese plates. Objects are poorly labelled, and the more valuable pieces have all been snapped up by the Bali Museum in Denpasar.

The most interesting exhibits are the dozen **sarcophagi** at the back of the compound. These massive coffins, up to three metres long and fashioned from two fitted sections of hollowed-out stone, probably date back to around 300 BC. It's thought that they were all designed to hold adult skeletons (those placed in the smallest vessels would have been flexed at knees, hips and shoulders), as only the more important members of a community would have merited such an elaborate burial. Bronze jewellery, coins and weapons were found in some of the sarcophagi, though most of the tombs are thought to have been robbed at a much earlier date.

North of Ubud: routes to Gunung Batur

All three major roads **north of Ubud** lead eventually to the towering peak of Gunung Batur and its huge crater. Whether you go via **Payangan** to the west, **Tegalalang** directly to the north, or **Tampaksiring** to the east, the villages and paddy-fields along each route make for a pleasant drive. Distances are comparable, about 40km to Batur whichever way you go, but the most significant tourist sights are located along the most easterly route, around the Tampaksiring area.

The most frequent and reliable **bemo** service running north from Ubud is the brown fleet that covers the **central route** via Tegalalang and Pujung; there are frequent turquoise and brown bemos along the first section of the **westerly route**, as far as Payangan, but only some of them continue as far as Kintamani. For the **easterly route** via Tampaksiring, you'll need to change bemos at the Bedulu crossroads.

Although there's little of specific interest on the westerly route, which takes you via Campuhan and Payangan, this is the quietest, least congested and prettiest of the three, and the best if you have **private transport**. The villages on the way are exceptionally picturesque, interspersed with lychee, durian and pineapple plantations, and in Payangan you pass the village's famously huge roadside banyan tree. The road eventually brings you to the impressive Pura Ulun Danu Batur (see p.279) on the Batur–Kintamani road, about 5km west of Penelokan.

Tegalalang, Sebatu and Taro

The **central route** up to Gunung Batur begins at the eastern edge of Ubud, from the point where Jalan Raya Ubud intersects with Jalan Peliatan; if heading up here on a bicycle, you might prefer the more peaceful route that starts on central Ubud's Jalan Suweta.

Tegalalang, Sebatu and around

The village of **TEGALALANG**, 7km north of Ubud, and its environs produce a wide range of **handicrafts** and **home accessories**, chiefly to order for wholesale and export, but also available to passing tourists. Consequently, the entire length of the twelve-kilometre-long Ubud–Tegalalang–Pujung road is lined with shops displaying their wares, which include **painted wooden mobiles**, animals and figurines; **wrought iron** lampstands, tables and artefacts; glass mosaic and wooden **frames** for pictures and mirrors; and much else besides. You can show your support for local craftspeople by stopping at the little shop run by the **Mitra Bali Fair Trade** organization (see p.62 for more on them), which is about 700m north of the Ubud junction, in **ANDONG**, the first *banjar* along the main road. Next up is **PETULU**, famous for its nightly heron-roosting spectacle, described on p.200.

One a clear morning the **views** get increasingly spectacular as you pass through Tegalalang, with Bali's greatest mountains looming majestically ahead – Gunung Batur to the north, and Gunung Agung to the east – and rice terraces providing the classic foreground. In **CEKING**, the village just north of Tegalalang, several **restaurants** make the most of these vistas, including the prettily situated *Kampung Café*, which is built on two levels overlooking the valley and serves classy *nouvelle cuisine* and Southeast Asian dishes; a few hundred metres further north, the more homely *Dewi Café* enjoys an even better view.

If you continue north along the main road for another 18km, you'll reach the Gunung Batur crater rim. Alternatively, a right turn at *Dewi Café* takes you along the scenic back-road to the village of **SEBATU**, site of the refreshingly uncrowded **Pura Gunung Kawi Sebatu** water-temple complex (daylight hours; Rp6000/3000, including sarong rental). Not to be confused with the quite different and more-visited Gunung Kawi in nearby Tampaksiring, the Sebatu temple is built on the site of holy springs, whose water is channelled into seven walled bathing-pools – four for public bathing and three, built at the spring itself, for special cleansing rituals. Many of the temple's wooden shrines and *bale* are carved with exquisite, brightly painted floral motifs.

Taro and the Elephant Safari Park

Turning left off the main Kintamani road a couple of kilometres beyond Pujung Kelod, a signposted little road leads you 6km west to the village of **TARO** and the Elephant Safari Park. This area is known for its distinctive grey-and-black-flecked tufa stone, used all over Bali to build temples, houses and hotels, and there are lots of **sculpture workshops** in the villages here. Taro itself is famous as the home of a small herd of sacred white **Brahmin cows**. Balinese people come here to pay their respects to the cows, who play an important role in certain temple ceremonies; as you pass into the Elephant Safari Park itself, you may be asked by the local priest to give a donation for their upkeep.

The **Elephant Safari Park** (daily 9am–5pm; $16, kids $8, family discounts available) occupies a landscaped area of fields and village forest and is home to more than two dozen elephants brought over from Sumatra, where they had been trained to work in the logging industry but were then abandoned when the industry declined. The park admission fee allows you to feed the animals, admire their painting skills – the trunk is apparently as adept with a paintbrush as the human hand, and some of their work has been exhibited internationally – and watch them having their twice-daily baths. There's also an elephant museum and luxurious on-site accommodation at the *Elephant Safari Park Lodge* (◎). The chief attraction, however, is the rather pricey half-hour elephant safari ride through sparse forest (an additional $45, kids $32). Most people visit the park as part of a **tour**, which includes transport, lunch and the safari ride ($75/50); book at any travel agent or, for a discount, direct with Bali Adventure Tours (℡0361/721480, ⓦwww.baliadventuretours.com).

Tampaksiring

The most **easterly route** from Ubud to the mountains takes you along the Bedulu–Penelokan road, passing through Pejeng before reaching **TAMPAK-SIRING**, 11km further on. A fairly nondescript town that's really only interesting as the access point for nearby **Tirta Empul** and **Gunung Kawi**, Tampaksiring is nonetheless well stocked with craft and souvenir shops: carved wooden chess sets and knick-knacks made from bone are a speciality. The bluey-grey Gianyar–Bedulu–Tampaksiring **bemos** terminate near the market in the centre of the long settlement, close by several warung. The bemo service between Tampaksiring and Penelokan, about 20km north, is patchy and unreliable at best, but you should at least be able to charter a bemo.

Gunung Kawi

Hewn from the rocky walls of the lush, enclosed valley of the sacred Pakrisan River, the eleventh-century royal "tombs" at **Gunung Kawi** (8am–5.30pm; Rp6000, kids Rp3000) occupy a lovely, impressive spot and are a lot quieter than most other archeological sites, not least because you have to descend 315 steps to reach them. Access is east off the main road, a few hundred metres north of Tampaksiring's bemo terminus, opposite the basic *Warung Vegetarian*, which serves cheap nasi campur made with soya meat.

The most likely **theory** about these "tombs", or *candi*, is that they were erected as memorials to the eleventh-century king Anak Wungsu and his queens. The four Queens' Tombs are thought to be for Anak Wungsu's minor consorts, while the five Royal Tombs across the river probably honour the king and his four favourite wives. As there are no signs of bones or ashes in the *candi*, they weren't actual tombs, yet over the false door of each were found inscriptions (most of them unreadable) thought to be names or titles.

At the bottom of the steps, before crossing the river, turn sharp left for the **Queens' Tombs**. Like the larger, more important structures on the other side of the river, these four *candi* are huge square-tiered reliefs, chiselled from the riverside cliff face to resemble temple facades. Originally the surface would have been decorated with plaster carvings, but now all that's left are the outlines of a single false door on each one. The design of the *candi* is very similar to that of structures in central and east Java, built in three clear sections to reflect a hell–earth–heaven cosmology, and with a stone-lidded hollow dug at the foot of each.

Crossing the Pakrisan River you enter the Gunung Kawi temple complex, which contains an unusual **cloister**, whose courtyard, rooms and cells are entirely cut from the ravine rock wall. It probably accommodated the tombs' caretakers. The five **Royal Tombs** at the back of the complex are in better condition than the Queens' Tombs, with distinct false doors and facades. The slightly higher *candi* at the far left end is believed to be Anak Wungsu's.

Returning across the river, follow the exit signs up the track beside the rice-paddies and then branch off left through the fields to reach the so-called **Tenth Tomb**, an often slippery five-minute walk away. Thought to have been erected in memory of an important member of the royal household who died after the king and his wives, possibly a prime-ministerial figure, this *candi* stands on its own, framed only by rock-cut cloisters.

Tirta Empul

Balinese from every corner of the island make pilgrimages to **Tirta Empul** (7am–5pm; Rp6000, kids Rp3000), signposted off the main Tampaksiring–Kintamani road, about 500m north of the turn-off to Gunung Kawi. They come to spiritually cleanse themselves and cure their physical ailments by bathing in the **holy springs**. Legend describes how the springs were first tapped by the god Indra during his battle with the evil Mayadanawa, an early ruler of the Pejeng kingdom. Mayadanawa had poisoned the nearby river and made hundreds of Indra's retainers sick, so Indra pierced the earth to release a spring of pure and sacred water – the elixir of immortality – that would revive his flagging troops. The new spring was named Tirta Empul, and has been considered the holiest in Bali ever since the tenth century, if not longer. A temple was built around the springs and special bathing-pools constructed for devotees, and the complex is now an extremely popular destination, both for Balinese and foreign tourists.

The shallow red-brick **bathing pools** are sunk into the ground of the temple's outer courtyard, fed by the slate-blue water from the springs in the inner sanctuary. Men, women and priests have segregated sections in which to immerse themselves, though most just splash their faces and smile for the camera. However, for pregnant women and anyone who's just recovered from a long illness, Tirta Empul is one of three places in which they must bathe for a special ritual called *melukat*. This ceremony requires immersion in the waters of each of Bali's three holiest springs: the "holy waters of the mountain" at Tirta Bungkah, the "holy springs of the plain" here at Tirta Empul, and the "holy springs of the sea" at Tirta Selukat.

Travel details

Bemos and public buses

It's almost impossible to give the frequency with which bemos and public buses run: see Basics, p.36, for details. Journey times given are the minimum you can expect. Only the direct bemo and bus routes are listed; for longer journeys, you'll have to go via Denpasar's Batubulan terminal or Gianyar (see p.224).

Batubulan (Denpasar) to: Amlapura (2hr 30min); Candi Dasa (2hr); Celuk (10min); Gianyar (1hr); Kintamani (1hr 30min); Mas (35min); Nusa Dua (1hr); Padang Bai (for Lombok; 1hr 40min); Peliatan (45min); Semarapura (1hr 20min); Singaraja (Penarukan terminal; 3hr); Sukawati (20min); Tegalalang (1hr 15min); Ubud (50min).

Ubud to: Campuhan/Sanggingan (5–10min); Celuk (40min); Denpasar (Batubulan terminal; 50min); Gianyar (20min); Goa Gajah (10min); Kedewatan (10min); Kintamani (1hr); Mas (15min); Peliatan (5min); Pujung (25min); Sukawati (30min).

Perama shuttle buses

Ubud to: Bedugul (daily; 1hr 30min); Candi Dasa (3 daily; 1hr 30min–2hr); Gili Islands (daily; 8hr); Kintamani (daily; 45min); Kuta/Ngurah Rai Airport (5 daily; 1hr–1hr 30min); Lembongan (daily; 2hr 30min); Lovina (daily; 1hr 30min–2hr); Mataram (Lombok; 2 daily; 7hr); Nusa Padang Bai (3 daily; 1hr–1hr 30min); Sanur (5 daily; 30min–1hr); Senggigi (Lombok; 2 daily; 7hr 30min).

③

East Bali

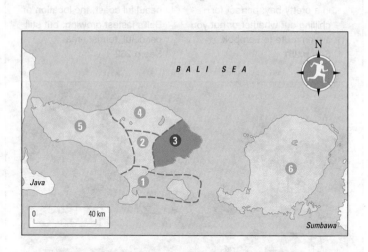

CHAPTER 3 # Highlights

* **Gunung Agung** Volcano towering majestically over the entire east of the island – everyone can enjoy the sight, the seriously fit can climb it. See p.241

* **Candi Dasa** This relaxed resort with great hotels is an ideal base for exploring the east. See p.242

* **Padang Bai** Laid-back village in a pretty bay; perfect for chilling out whether or not you are en route to Lombok. See p.251

* **Tirtagangga** Glorious mountain views, an attractive water-palace set amongst verdant rice terraces, and cool temperatures. See p.257

* **Iseh and Sidemen** Small villages famed for picturesque rice terraces, a perfect rural retreat. See p.261

* **Amed** Around 14km of beautiful coast, the location of Bali's fastest growing, but still peaceful, tourist area. See p.262

▲ Candi Dasa lagoon

East Bali

The **east of Bali** is dominated both physically and spiritually by the towering volcano **Gunung Agung**, and the **Besakih** temple high on its slopes. The landscape ranges from soaring peaks through sweeping rice terraces, to the dry, rocky expanses of the far east. Many visitors speed through the east on their way to the beaches known collectively as Amed. However, those lingering for a day or two en route are rewarded with an authentic Bali of fishing and farming villages, market towns, prestigious temples and glorious scenery – all far away from the crowds.

The biggest draw is the **coast**, which includes the black-sand bays south of Gianyar, **Amuk Bay** and the peaceful beaches at **Amed** in the far northeast. There's excellent diving and snorkelling; **Candi Dasa**, **Padang Bai**, **Tulamben** and **Amed** are the best areas. The beaches of Amed are developing fast as they entice increasing numbers of visitors away from the more established resorts with peace and quiet, excellent accommodation and restaurants, and great coastal scenery.

Inland, Gunung Agung and Besakih temple are the major attractions, although the hassles from the touts and guides and mist at the temple frequently disappoint visitors. However, there are other impressive **temples** – especially Pura Kehen in Bangli, Pura Lempuyang Luhur, accessible from Tirtagangga, and Pura Pasar Agung, above Selat. The villages of **Tirtagangga** and **Sidemen** both have plenty of accommodation for those in search of cooler temperatures and some gentle walking among the ricefields. **Tenganan**, close to Candi Dasa, is a traditional Bali Aga village, home to descendants of the early inhabitants of Bali and a must-see if you're interested in craftwork, especially **textiles**.

Formerly divided into a multitude of kingdoms, the area witnessed vicious battles and power struggles, followed later by the incursions of the invading **Dutch**. During the fourteenth century, the first Majapahit capital was in **Samprangan**, now a small village just east of **Gianyar**, and, in the following centuries, each of the towns of the area had its own royal dynasty. The now sleepy village of **Gelgel** once ruled a kingdom stretching from the island of Sumbawa in the east to Java in the west. Evidence of these ancient courts remains in the Taman Gili, the remnants of the royal palace in **Semarapura**, the Puri Agung in **Amlapura** and the **Puri Gianyar**, but these relics of past glory are now surrounded by busy towns with traffic pouring past the walls.

Practicalities

The east is easily **accessible**; Jalan Prof Dr Ida Bagus Mantra, from Tohpati, just north of Sanur, to Kusamba, west of Padang Bai, makes travel to the area speedy, and the traffic thins dramatically the further east you go. There's a

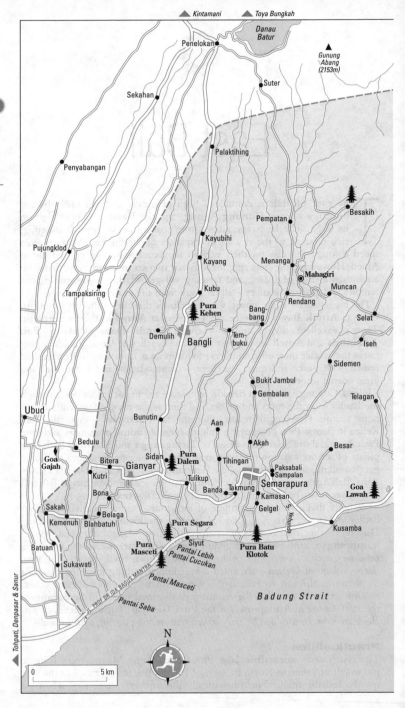

Kintamani   Toya Bungkah

Danau Batur

Penelokan

Gunung Abang (2153m)

Suter

Sekahan

Penyabangan

Palaktihing

Besakih

Pempatan

Kayubihi

Menanga

Mahagiri

Pujungklod

Kayang

Muncan

Kubu

Rendang

Selat

Tampaksiring

Pura Kehen

Bang-bang

Iseh

Demulih   Bangli

Tembuku

Sidemen

Bukit Jambul

Gembalan

Telagan

Bunutin

Aan

Ubud

Akah

Besar

Bedulu

Sidan   Pura Dalem

Tihingan

Goa Gajah

Bitera   Gianyar

Paksabali
Sampalan

Goa Lawah

Kutri

Tulikup

Semarapura

Bona

Banda   Takmung

Kamasan

Sakah

Belaga

Pura Segara

Gelgel

Kusamba

Kemenuh   Blahbatuh

Batuan

Pura Masceti

Siyut
Pantai Lebih
Pantai Cucukan

Pura Batu Klotok

Sukawati

Pantai Masceti

PROF DR IDA BAGUS MANTRA

Pantai Saba

Badung Strait

Tohpati; Denpasar & Sanur

N

0   5 km

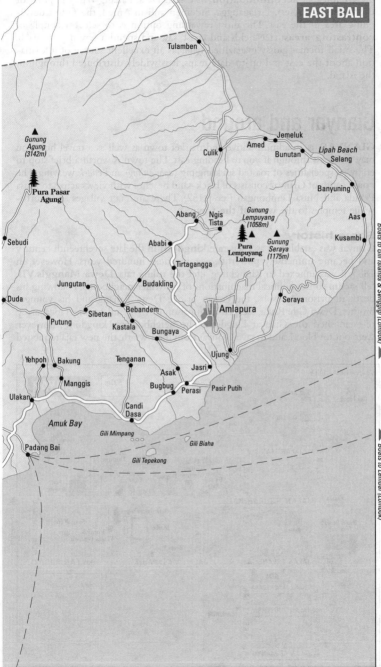

Kubu & Singaraja

Tulamben

Gunung
Agung
(3142m)

Pura Pasar
Agung

Jemeluk
Culik   Amed
                Bunutan   Lipah Beach
                            Selang

                            Banyuning

Sebudi

Abang   Ngis   Aas
        Tista
Ababi   Gunung
               Lempuyang   Kusambi
               (1058m)
Tirtagangga   Pura   Gunung
               Lempuyang Seraya
               Luhur   (1175m)

Jungutan   Budakling
Duda
        Sibetan Bebandem   Seraya
Putung
        Kastala   Bungaya   Amlapura

Yehpoh Bakung   Tenganan   Ujung
        Manggis   Asak   Jasri
Ulakan   Bugbug Perasi
                Candi   Pasir Putih
                Dasa

Amuk Bay
        Gili Mimpang   Gili Biaha
Padang Bai
                Gili Tepekong

Boats to Gili (Islands & Senggigi (Lombok)

Boats to Lembar (Lombok)

Boats to Nusa Penida

223

great choice of **accommodation** in Candi Dasa, Padang Bai (the port for the Lombok ferries), Tirtagangga, Sidemen and in Amed, the fastest developing area of the east. The most rewarding option is to select a couple of **contrasting areas**: rice fields and coast, say, and spend a few days in each. The small-format glossy magazine, *Agung*, is an excellent source of information about the east and up-to-date maps; it is widely distributed throughout the island.

Gianyar and around

GIANYAR is an administrative and market town as well as a travel hub; you may well pass through if you're heading east. The town is worth a brief stop to enjoy its specialities of roasted suckling pig (*babi guling*) and *endek* weaving. The **coast** south of Gianyar consists of black-sand beaches with views across to Nusa Penida and Nusa Lembongan (see p.152). There are craft villages and worthwhile temples to the **west of the town**.

Some history

Gianyar was established as a separate **kingdom** in the late seventeenth century and became immensely powerful over the next hundred years. However, in 1883, it was annexed to Klungkung after the ruling raja, **Dewa Manggis VII**, fell victim to the political machinations of his wilier neighbours. Following his death in prison, his sons, the crown prince Dewa Pahang and his younger brother, Dewa Gde Raka, escaped from prison in 1893 and, raising a local army, re-established the Gianyar kingdom. The neighbouring kingdoms, however, were out for blood, and to save Gianyar from their wrath, the new raja requested

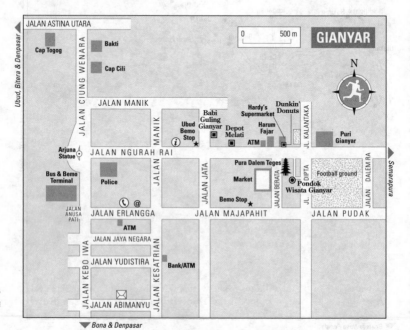

the protection of the Netherlands Indies government. In March 1900 Gianyar became a **Dutch Protectorate** and was spared the fighting that other southern Balinese kingdoms suffered at the hands of the Dutch. Instead, the kingdom flourished and became a centre for the arts. The aristocratic line and lifestyle continued; in the 1930s, the raja drove a Fiat with a solid-gold *garuda* radiator cap. These days the royal family still live in Puri Gianyar retaining ceremonial rather than political duties.

The Town

The town centres on the main road just west of the royal palace, **Puri Gianyar**, first built in 1771 but destroyed by the 1917 earthquake and largely rebuilt. Still the home of the descendants of the Gianyar royal family, it's not open to the public. Nearby, on Jalan Berata, the main **market** occurs every three days, although there are always some stalls here. The best time to visit is from 6am until noon.

Gianyar is well known for **endek weaving** (see p.458), produced in the workshops on the western outskirts of town; Cap Cili and Bakti on Jalan Ciung Wenara and Cap Togog on Jalan Astina Utara (see map; all daily 8am–5pm except bank holidays, workshops 9am–4pm). Prices start at Rp60,000 a metre for cotton *endek* and Rp135,000 for sarongs, rising dramatically as the silk content gets higher. There are also plenty of small gift items plus a lot of imported batik cloth from Java.

Practicalities

Heading east **from Denpasar** (Batubulan terminal), most public transport heads to Gianyar via Sakah, Kemenuh, Blahbatuh, Kutri and Bitera, although there are also bemos from Blahbatuh through Bona and Belega. Coming **from Ubud**, get a bemo to the large junction at Sakah and pick up Gianyar transport there.

The Gianyar government **tourist office**, Jalan Ngurah Rai 9 (Mon–Thurs 7.30am–3pm, Fri 6.30am–2pm; ☏0361/943401), gets few visitors but staff will do their best to help. The main **telephone office** is on Jalan Erlangga (8am–10pm); just east of it are a few small shops with **internet access**. The **post office** (a Western Union agent) is at Jalan Abimanyu 4 (Mon–Sat 8am–4.30pm). For exchange, BNI is on Jalan Kesatrian and there are international **ATMs** there, on Jalan Erlangga and near the Harum Fajar shopping centre.

With Ubud so close, there's no reason to stay overnight and the **accommodation** in town is basic. If you get stranded try *Pondok Wisata Gianyar*, Jalan Anom Sandat 10x (☏0361/942165; ❶), just off Jalan Ngurah Rai, with rooms in a small compound.

To sample Gianyar's famous *babi guling*, which is suckling pig stuffed with chillies, rice and spices, served with rice and *lawar* (chopped meat, vegetables and coconut mixed with pig's blood), try *Depot Melati*, Jalan Ngurah Rai 37, or just around the corner at *Babi Guling Gianyar* on Jalan Jata; expect to pay about Rp11,000. They serve from early morning until they sell out of pigs; get there by noon to be sure of a feast. For fast-food snacks there's a *Dunkin' Donuts* counter at the front of the Harum Fajar shopping centre.

West of Gianyar

It's worth exploring the **villages** to the west and southwest of Gianyar. **KUTRI**, 4km west of Gianyar, is home to the **Pura Bukit Dharma Durga Kutri**.

Rangda

The image of **Rangda**, Queen of the Witches, is everywhere in Bali: you'll see her in dance-dramas and on masks, temple carvings, paintings and batiks. She has a long mane of hair with flames protruding from her head, bulging eyes, a gaping mouth, huge teeth or tusks, and a long tongue often reaching to her knees. Her fingernails are long and curled, and she has enormous, pendulous breasts. She wears a striped shirt and pants, with a white cloth around her waist.

It's possible that Rangda is based on a real woman, Mahendratta, a Javanese princess who married the Balinese prince Udayana and bore him a son, Erlangga, in 1001 AD. According to legend, the king later banished Mahendratta for practising witchcraft. When Udayana died, Mahendratta, now a *rangda* (widow), used her powers to call a plague upon Erlangga's kingdom. Erlangga, learning the source of the pestilence, dispatched a troop of soldiers who failed to kill Rangda despite stabbing her in the heart. In desperation, the king sent for a holy man, Empu Bharadah, whose assistant stole Rangda's book of magic, with which he was able to restore Rangda's victims to life, and destroy the witch by turning her own magic on herself.

The Rangda story is widely enacted across the island, most commonly during the **Barong** and **Calonarang** dramas (see p.443). She always speaks in the ancient Kawi language and alternates between high whining, loud grunts and cackles. To the Balinese, Rangda represents evil, death and destruction. Even in performances of the story the figure of Rangda is believed to have remarkable powers, and prayers precede each show to protect the actors from the evil forces they are invoking.

Head up the staircase from the inner courtyard to the top of the hill, where you'll find the statue of the many-armed goddess **Durga** slaughtering a bull, brandishing a conch shell, flames, bow and arrow, javelin and shield shrouded in holy white cloths and shaded by parasols. Many people believe, however, that the carving depicts **Mahendratta**, the source of the legendary Rangda (see box above), and that this is her burial place. It's also possible to walk to Kutri (3–5hr) from the Yeh Pulu rock carvings east of Ubud, but you'll need to hire a guide (see p.212).

At the village of **BLAHBATUH**, 5km south of Kutri, the main road is lined with bamboo-furniture workshops. A few hundred metres along the Bona road, **Pura Gaduh** is guarded by stone elephants outside and mounted horsemen inside and was rebuilt following an earthquake in 1917. The highlight is a gigantic carved head with bulging eyes, supposedly the legendary **Kebo Iwa**, who is said to have created this and many other temples in the area.

The villages of **BONA** and neighbouring **BELAGA** are packed with shops selling bamboo furniture and baskets, wind chimes, rain sticks, lamps and boxes made from bamboo, rattan, lontar palm and *alang-alang* grass. Prices start at Rp5000 for tiny items.

Kemenuh and Sakah

At **KEMENUH**, 7km southwest of Gianyar, the speciality is **woodcarving** and an extensive range of subject, style and wood is on show in the workshops, where visitors can watch the craftsmen at work. Sembahyang is one of the larger workshops, about 100m north of the main road; turn left at the traffic lights in Kemenuh 1.5km from Blahbatuh. With workshops dotted along its length, enthusiasts may want to explore this twisting road all the way through to the northern end at Goa Gajah, a distance of about 5km. A tourist development committed to sustainable and socially responsible village tourism, *Sua Bali*

(Ⓣ0361/941050, Ⓦwww.suabali.com; ❻) is located on the northern side of Kemenuh, near the hamlet of Medahan. It was developed in consultation with the local community, which continues to be involved with the project. *Sua Bali* offers simple accommodation in attractive bungalows set on the banks of the Petang River. Cooking, language and craft courses can be arranged; contact them directly for details; reservations are essential.

Some 1.5km west of Kemenuh, at the junction of the road and bemo route north to Ubud, sits the small village of **SAKAH**, with its giant Buddha statue resembling a podgy baby.

The coast south of Gianyar

The coast **south of Gianyar** is an attractive but little-visited part of Bali, best accessed by private transport, with long beaches of pure black sand. It offers some fine views of Gunung Agung and the mountains of the east as you travel further from Sanur. Aside from a couple of spots that are opening up for experienced surfers, this is an area for beach walks rather for swimming, as the Badung Strait between the mainland and Nusa Lembongan is treacherous. There are plenty of temples to explore here; all are fabulous during festivals and ceremonies but pretty deserted otherwise.

The **road** eastwards, Jalan Prof Dr Ida Bagus Mantra, starts at **Tohpati**, 4km north of Sanur, where stonecarving workshops and nurseries including the **Bali Orchid Garden** (see p.147) feature big time. The garden is just north of the junction of Jalan Bypass with Jalan Prof Dr Ida Bagus Mantra.

Jalan Prof Dr Ida Bagus Mantra begins at a giant arch bearing its name. For 25km it snakes behind the coast, veering between a few hundred metres and several kilometres inland. Access to the coast is via the multitude of side-roads that head south. You could easily spend a day exploring each little lane that branches seawards; the most worthwhile are detailed below.

Pantai Saba to Pantai Cucukan

Seven kilometres from Tohpati, Pantai Saba is the base for Bali Horse Riding (Ⓣ0361 292523, Ⓦwwwhorseridingbali.com) where $56 gets you a couple of hours riding along the beach on a sturdy local mount plus lunch and a hotel pick-up from southern Bali, Ubud or Candi Dasa. Be aware that this is a dramatic, but largely shadeless area and it pays to avoid the midday heat.

Three kilometres to the east, Pantai Masceti is the location of the beachside **Pura Masceti,** to the left behind a huge parking area. One of Bali's directional temples, or *kayangan jagat* (see p.431), serving the south of the island, it is highly ornate and is especially busy on the day before Nyepi (see p.47), when religious objects are brought here for purification.

Experienced surfers are discovering the breaks off **Pantai Cucukan**, another kilometre to the east. Accommodation is plentiful in private villas and although it is an attractive sweep of sand, there are more beautiful spots in Bali with better facilities.

A few hundred metres past the Pantai Cucukan turning, **Bali Safari & Marine Park** (Ⓣ0361/950000, Ⓦwww.balisafarimarinepark.com; Mon–Fri 9am–5pm, weekends and holidays 8.30am–5pm; $25) houses animals from Indonesia, India and Africa. The highlight is the hour-long bus (they call it a tram) trip that passes extremely close to lions, tigers, rhinos, hippos, zebras, crocs and bears. At the time of writing the facilities were quite new and incomplete but the animals appeared relaxed and comfortable in large enclosures and this is a rare opportunity to see white tigers.

Pantai Lebih to Pantai Batu Klotok

Another kilometre further along the coast, **Pantai Lebih** is a picturesque and popular beach crowded with fishing boats and tiny warung serving the day's catch. Many of the warung are open throughout the day and close at 10pm or later, after their last customer has departed. This is an extremely popular spot with Balinese people in the evenings and is heaving during national holidays. *Sate languan, ikan bakar, ikan pepes, ikan goreng* and *nasi sela* are the specialities. A A meal of *sate languan, nasi sela*, fish soup and vegetables will set you back Rp9000 or so, while a fish meal depends on its size but expect to pay around Rp30,000. Across the main road the entrance of **Pura Segara** (Sea Temple) is imposing, but there's no real hint of the importance of this site. Magical forces are believed to be focused on the temple, and an annual ceremony placates the demon I Macaling, who is believed to bring disease and ill-fortune to the mainland frtom Nusa Penida (p.160).

One of the most picturesque areas of the south coast is at **SIYUT** where the bay stretches in a wide sweep for several kilometres, while inland the rice terraces form an attractive foreground to the bulk of the more distant Gunung Agung. You'll share the beach with fishermen and there are several drinks stalls here.

Moving eastwards the land becomes greener and more fertile. Another 3km on, **Pantai Batu Klotok**, or Watu Klotok, is the site of the highly revered Pura Batu Klotok, one of the four state temples of Klungkung regency, in a beachside position. The sacred statues from the "Mother Temple" Besakih, are brought here during the annual cleansing ritual of *malasti*. During the 1963 and 1979 Eka Dasa Rudra ceremonies at Besakih (see box, p.240), the procession to the sea was over a mile long, and tens of thousands gathered on the beach for the rituals, which included the sacrificial drowning of a buffalo. An imposing statue of Dewa Baruna, the god of the sea, stands beside the temple holding a container of holy water. It was built following the 2001 appearance of an unusual turtle bearing sacred markings, which died on the local beach and was cremated in the temple. The turtle was believed by local people to be a manifestation of Dewa Baruna, who was bestowing good fortune on the village.

From here it is nine kilometres on to Kusamba (see p.255) and then 20km to Candi Dasa (see p.242).

Northeast of Gianyar

Essential viewing for anyone interested in Balinese temples is the Pura Dalem at **SIDAN**, 1km north of the main Gianyar–Semarapura road. To reach it, turn off the main road about 2km east of Gianyar on the Bangli road. This temple of the dead, dating from the seventeenth century, drips with gruesome carvings and statues of the terrible Rangda squashing babies and the punishments that await evil-doers in the afterlife – which include having your head sawn off or being boiled up in a vat. There are occasional performances of the **barong** including the **kris** dance (see p.443 for more), generally during full-moon ceremonies; see p.203 for details.

At **BUNUTIN**, 3km north of Sidan and 7km south of Bangli, **Pura Penataran Agung** (also known as Pura Langgar), is located east of the main road. Its **red-brick shrine** with the two-tiered red roof and four doors is the main point of interest. A local story tells of a seventeenth-century Hindu prince whose brother became very sick; seeking advice from a traditional healer, a *dukun*, the prince was told about a Muslim ancestor, originally from Java, who had settled in the Bunutin area and the prince was instructed to build a temple to honour the ancestor. The prince designed one that partly incorporated Muslim principles, with four doorways corresponding to the directions of the four winds. The sick brother recovered, and the descendants of his family are said to still abstain from eating pork in honour of their ancestor.

Bangli and around

Situated between Gianyar and the volcanoes of Batur, **BANGLI** is a cool and spacious market town that it fits into any itinerary to or from Batur, but don't be fooled by its proximity to Besakih: there are no public bemos on the Bangli–Rendang road.

Some history

While it was never one of the major Balinese kingdoms, Bangli played a crucial role at pivotal points in Balinese history. Originally set up under the rule of the **Majapahit** dynasty based in Gelgel, Bangli gradually asserted its **independence**. By the nineteenth century, all the kingdoms were involved in a complex dance of attempted expansion during which **Gusti Ngurah Made Karangasem**, ruler of Buleleng in the north, annexed the entire Batur area from Bangli. Between 1841 and 1843, the princes of Bali signed "friendship agreements" with the Dutch government. The disparity between the Dutch and Balinese interpretation of these eventually led to a crisis in which it became clear that the Dutch would use force against Buleleng. Gaining his revenge for the loss of Batur, the Bangli raja, **Dewa Gde Tangkeban**, announced his support for the Dutch, refusing help to Buleleng, and reoccupied the Batur area. Following a **Dutch victory** in 1849, Dewa Gde Tangkeban reclaimed his former lands and also annexed Gianyar and Mengwi. Fighting between the kingdoms dominated the second half of the nineteenth century, until the common threat from the Dutch diverted attention. Following the defeat of Badung regency and the *puputan* in Denpasar in 1906, the Dutch forced Dewa Gde Tangkeban to sign away his powers. In January 1909, when Bangli became a **Dutch Protectorate**, the whole of Bali came under outside control.

The Town

Most visitors come to Bangli for the ancient **Pura Kehen**, one of the gems among Bali's temples (daily 6am–6.30pm; Rp3500 including car or motorbike entrance/parking), 1.5km north of the town. Rising in **terraces**, Pura Kehen is large and imposing and fierce Bhoma leer above fabulously carved doors. The **outer courtyard** contains a massive banyan tree with a *kulkul* tower built among the branches and a small compound, guarded by *naga* under a frangipani tree, houses a stone that reportedly glowed with fire when the site of the temple was decided. The **inner courtyard** contains an eleven-roofed *meru*, dedicated to Siwa, and other shrines dedicated to mountain gods.

Just across the road the lavishly restored **Pura Penyimpenan** (Temple for Keeping Things) contains three ancient bronze inscriptions (*prasasti*) dating from the ninth century. This suggests Kehen was a site of ancient worship long before the generally accepted founding of the temple around 1206.

A short distance southeast from Pura Kehen, the grand but often somnolent **Sasana Budaya Arts Centre**, one of the largest arts complexes in Bali, hosts

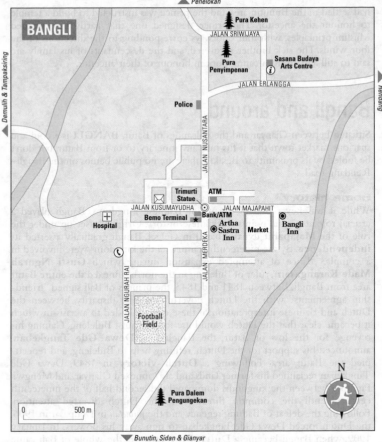

Demulih & Tampaksiring

Rendang

Penelokan

BANGLI

Pura Kehen

JALAN SRIWIJAYA

Pura
Penyimpenan

Sasana Budaya
Arts Centre ⓘ

JALAN ERLANGGA

Police

JALAN NUSANTARA

Trimurti
Statue

ATM

✉

JALAN KUSUMAYUDHA

Bemo Terminal ★

Bank/ATM

JALAN MAJAPAHIT

Hospital ✚

Artha
Sastra
Inn

Bangli
Inn

JALAN MERDEKA

Market

🕐

JALAN NGURAH RAI

Football
Field

N

Pura Dalem
Pengungekan

0   500 m

Bunutin, Sidan & Gianyar

occasional exhibitions and performances; enquire locally for details. It is only open when there's an event.

At the opposite end of town, it is a pleasant stroll through the town to the temple of the dead, **Pura Dalem Pengungekan**. The outside walls depict the fate of souls in hell and heaven as witnessed by Bhima, one of the Pandawa brothers, while trying to retrieve the souls of his parents from hell (see box, p.442). The carvings are a riot of knives, pleading victims, flames and decapitated bodies. You'll also see plenty of images of the evil witch Rangda and stories of Siwa, Ganesh, Uma and Rakshasha.

Practicalities

To reach Bangli, take the turn-off from the main road 2km east of Gianyar or pick up a bemo in Gianyar bus station. Buses plying the route between Denpasar (Batubulan terminal) and Singaraja (Penarukan terminal) pass through Bangli.

The Bangli government **tourist office** is in the grounds of the Sasana Budaya Arts Centre at Jl Sriwijaya 23 (☎0366/91537) but opening hours remain uncertain. There are **exchange** facilities at Bank Rakyat Indonesia at the junction of Jalan Kusumayudha and Jalan Merdeka in the town centre, where there is an international **ATM**; there's another one further north on Jalan Nusantara. The **warung telkom** (6am–midnight) is on Jalan Ngurah Rai and the **post office** is at Jl Kusumayudha 18. Bangli's **market** bursts into activity every three days.

There are a couple of places **to stay**. The best option is the *Bangli Inn*, Jl Rambutan 1 (☎0366/91518; ❷), which has clean rooms with attached cold-water bathrooms built around a small courtyard. The *Artha Sastra Inn*, Jl Merdeka 5 (☎0366/91179; ❶), is opposite the bus/bemo terminal close to the market (there is no sign). Guests can enjoy the kudos of staying in the ancient royal palace of Bangli, though there are just two basic rooms, which are nowhere near as grand as the family living quarters nearby. During the day, the bus/bemo terminal has several **food** stalls and after dark it transforms into a small **night market**.

Semarapura (Klungkung) and around

Just 16km from Gianyar, **Semarapura**, also known as Klungkung, is a lively market town, most famous for the remains of the royal palace, the **Taman Gili**. The highlight is the **painted ceiling of the Kerta Gosa**, one of the remaining pavilions within the palace grounds. The ceiling is the only surviving example of classical *wayang* painting in situ on the island (see p.453 for more on the *wayang* style). Although the pictures are decidedly grubby, located on the corner of a busy crossroads, they remain required viewing. The modern centre of classical-style Balinese painting is at **Kamasan**, a few kilometres south of town, while the **Nyoman Gunarsa Museum of Modern and Classical Art** to the west houses an extensive but little-visited collection of art. South of Semarapura, the sleepy village of **Gelgel** is a shadowy remnant of the thriving royal capital that ruled Bali for three hundred years. There is good-quality accommodation if you want to enjoy this pleasant town for more than a few hours.

Some history

Following the **Majapahit conquest** of Bali led by Gajah Mada in 1343, the conquerors set up a court in Samprangan, moving in 1400 to **Gelgel**, just south of modern Semarapura. From here, Bali was ruled by a dynasty appointed by Gajah Mada, and each ruler took the title *dewa agung* (Great God). When the Majapahit empire in Java collapsed in 1515, large numbers of Javanese royalty in exile swelled the community in Bali. In 1550, when **Batu Renggong** became *dewa agung*, his area of influence increased and the Gelgel court flourished, becoming a centre for art, literature and culture. However, decline set in, and under the rule of Batu Renggong's grandson, Di Made, control of the empire was gradually lost. Towards the end of the seventeenth century the palace and the court moved to **Semarapura**, the result of a belief that there was a curse upon the Gelgel palace. But it was downhill from then on: Gianyar was established as a separate kingdom in 1667, and the *dewa agung* never again reached such influential heights.

The Dutch attacked southern Bali in 1906, and by 1908 had subdued all the kingdoms except Klungkung and Bangli. When the Dutch set up their weapons outside the Semarapura palace on April 28, 1908, the *dewa agung* led two hundred members of his family and court in the traditional **puputan**. When he

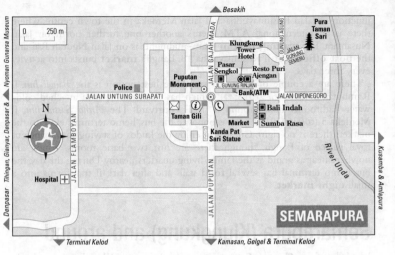

marched into the guns and was killed, six of his wives surrounded his body and stabbed themselves with their kris. The rest of the entourage were either shot or killed themselves. The monument opposite the Taman Gili in Semarapura commemorates the *puputan*. Surviving members of the royal family were then exiled to Lombok and didn't return until the 1920s.

The Town

Semarapura centres on a crossroads, marked by the **Kanda Pat Sari statue**, which guards the four cardinal directions. The Taman Gili is beside it, with the Puputan Monument opposite and the central market just to the east. The bus and bemo terminal is about a kilometre south.

The Taman Gili and Museum Daerah Semarapura

The **Taman Gili** (daily 7am–6.30pm; Rp5000), meaning "Island Gardens", has its entrance on Jalan Puputan. Built around 1710, and largely destroyed by the fighting in 1908, the only remains of the original Semarapura palace are the Kerta Gosa (Consultation Pavilion for Peace and Prosperity), the Bale Kambung (Floating Pavilion), a *kulkul* tower, and a massive red-brick **gateway**, which was the entrance to the palace's inner courtyard. Legend tells how the gateway was created by two craftsmen who, while sleeping in separate temples, each dreamt about half of a massive doorway. When they met and compared their dreams they realized that their visions fitted together perfectly, and they brought their dream to life. Legend also claims that at the time of the *puputan* in 1908, the doors sealed themselves shut and nobody has been able to open them since.

Perched on one corner of the main crossroads, the **Kerta Gosa** is a raised open *bale*. It's sometimes described as a criminal court, which adds poignancy to the pictures of gruesome punishments on the ceiling, but it's more likely that it was a debating pavilion for the king and his ministers. The **painted ceiling** is a superb example of the Kamasan or *wayang* style of classical painting. They underwent major restorations in the 1930s, in 1960 and 1982, so should be due for some TLC soon.

There are nine levels of paintings here. **Level one**, nearest the floor, shows scenes from an Indonesian version of the *Thousand and One Nights*, in which a girl, Tantri, weaves tales night after night. **Levels two and three** illustrate the Bhima Swarga story (part of the *Mahabharata* epic; see p.442), and the punishments meted out to souls in the afterlife, such as having your intestines extracted through your anus for farting in public. Bhima is the aristocratic-looking chap with moustache, tidy hair, a big club and a long nail on his right thumb. **Level four** shows the Sang Garuda, the story of the Garuda's search for *amerta*, the water of life, so that he can free his mother, Winita, and himself from eternal slavery to the thousand *naga*. **Level five** is the *palalindon*, predicting the effects of earthquakes on life and agriculture, while **levels six and seven** are a continuation of the Bhima Swarga story. **Level eight** is the Swarga Roh, which shows the rewards the godly will receive in heaven; unfortunately, it's so far above your head that it's hard to see whether good behaviour is worth it. **Level nine**, the *lokapala*, right at the top of the ceiling where the four sides meet, shows a lotus surrounded by four doves symbolizing good luck, enlightenment and salvation.

The **Bale Kambung**, almost beside the Kerta Gosa, was the venue for royal tooth-filing ceremonies (see p.463). Its ceiling is less famous than its neighbour's but equally detailed and well-drawn; six levels of paintings cover Balinese astrology, the tales of Pan Brayut (see box, p.194) and, closest to the top, the adventures of Satusoma, a legendary Buddhist saint.

The **Museum Daerah Semarapura** in the Taman Gili grounds is worth a quick look. It contains a motley collection including kris, textiles and Barong costumes, but labels are scant.

Pura Taman Sari

Less than one kilometre northeast from the town centre, **Pura Taman Sari** (Flower Garden) is a relaxing spot. The eleven-roofed *meru* stands in the middle of a moat resting upon a beady-eyed stone turtle. During the reign of the *dewa agung* in Bali, this was the site of an annual ceremony in which offerings were made to the kris and other weapons belonging to the royal family.

▲ The Bale Kambung (Floating Pavilion) at Taman Gili

Practicalities

The main **bus and bemo terminal**, Terminal Kelod, also known as Terminal Galiron after the market that bustles around it, is about 1km south of the town centre; pick up all public transport here. In addition, a few bemos pass along Jalan Gunung Rinjani just north of the main crossroads, en route to Rendang and Menanga for Besakih (see p.237).

The Klungkung government **tourist office** is in the same building as the Museum Daerah Semarapura, Jl Untung Surapati 2 (Mon–Thurs 7.30am–3pm, Fri 6.30am–2pm; ☎0366/21448). Across the road from the Kerta Gosa is the **warung telkom** (daily 24hr), while the **post office** is just west of the museum on Jalan Untung Surapati. Several banks along Jalan Diponegoro to the east of the main crossroads **change money**, and there's an international **ATM** in the main street.

There's **accommodation** at the comfortable *Klungkung Tower Hotel*, Jl Gunung Rinjani 18 (☎0366/25637, ✉towerhotel07@yahoo.co.id; ●), which has a/c rooms with hot-water bathrooms. Climb to the top of the tower for a panoramic view of the city. There are plenty of inexpensive **places to eat**: on Jalan Nakula, *Bali Indah* at no. 1 and *Sumba Rasa* at no. 5 have small English menu. Pasar Sengkol, at the western end of Jalan Gunung Rinjani, has a few food stalls during the day and becomes a vibrant night-market after dark. The *Resto Puri Ajengan* attached to the *Klungung Tower Hotel* is also worth a look. There's a **supermarket**, Cahaya Melati, on Jalan Puputan opposite the entrance to the Taman Gili.

Around Semarapura

There are several places worth a trip **around Semarapura**, especially if you're interested in arts and crafts, and all are easily accessible.

Nyoman Gunarsa Museum and Tihingan

Some 5km west of Semarapura, the **Nyoman Gunarsa Museum** (Mon–Sat 9am–4pm; Rp25,000) is just beyond the village of Takmung on the Gianyar road; look out for the massive Trimurti statue with mock policemen at the base. All Gianyar-bound public transport passes by it. The museum holds a vast collection of historical objects and traditional art, including painting, embroidery, sculpture, masks and ancient furniture. Scenes from the *Mahabharata*, the *Ramayana* and the *Karmapala* feature extensively. It's an attractive hoard to wander through, although they get hardly any visitors.

The museum also contains works by **Nyoman Gunarsa**, the museum's founder. Born in nearby Banda village, he is one of the foremost modern Balinese painters. Initially his work appears quite abstract, but resolves into the forms of dancers and musicians, the artist's constant theme. His studio within the grounds is occasionally open to visitors.

From the museum a side-road leads 3km to **TIHINGAN**; bemos ply this route through the villages of Banda and Penasan. Tihingan is renowned for its **gong-makers**, and there are a few showrooms on the main street (from 8am). If you come early, you may be able to see the craftsmen creating bronze gongs ranging in size from tiny tourist models no bigger than a handspan, to giants 1m in diameter and costing several million rupiah.

Kamasan

South of Klungkung, 500m beyond the Kelod bemo terminal, is the turning to the village of **KAMASAN**, the centre of **classical wayang painting**

Why Bali has remained Hindu

Gelgel is home to an Islamic community, who are believed to be the descendants of Islamic missionaries who came to Bali to convert the population and were too ashamed to go home when they failed. Legend tells that the *dewa agung*'s main objection to Islam was circumcision. The missionaries explained that the bamboo knife used was very sharp. The *dewa agung* demanded to see the knife, tried to cut his fingernail and failed. He then tried to cut the hairs on his arm and failed. Refusing to allow the knife near any other parts of his anatomy, he gave it back and declared that he and Bali would remain Hindu.

(see p.453). *Wayang* style depicts religious subjects, astrological charts and calendars, in muted reds, ochres, blues, greens and blacks.

After visiting a few studios, many of them family-owned, it's easy to pick out the better-quality work, identified by fine but solid outlines, the absence of large unfilled spaces on the canvas, and detailed colouring and shading. While the artists obviously want to make sales, the atmosphere is pleasant and relaxed – although you should shop around and bargain hard. **I Nyoman Mandra** has a fine reputation. **Ni Made Suciarmi** is one of very few **women artists** working in Kamasan in what is very much a male preserve; many women mix colours and fill in the outlines, but she does the drawing, too. She comes from a family of artists and was involved in the 1930s renovation of the Kerta Gosa ceiling in Semarapura when she was a very young girl. Her work is represented in the Seniwati Women's Art Gallery in Ubud (see p.189).

Gelgel and beyond

The ancient court centre of **GELGEL**, 4km south of Semarapura, is a somnolent village with nothing but its history to offer visitors; large numbers of its ancient stones have been removed to museums elsewhere. There are bemos from Terminal Kelod in Semarapura.

Pura Dasar on the main street is the most imposing temple, with massive courtyards, *bale*, and nine- and eleven-roofed *meru* in the inner courtyard. Each year this temple is the site of the **Pewintenan ceremony**, held on the fourth full moon of the Balinese calendar (check the sources of information on p.74 for dates), which attracts pilgrims from all over Bali. The ceremony purifies those ready to become *pemangku* (village priests) and at midnight culminates with the new *pemangku* walking over the skin and sometimes the head of a dead buffalo.

Besakih and Gunung Agung

The major draw in the east of Bali is undoubtedly the Besakih temple complex (daily 8am–5pm; Rp10,000, parking Rp2000), the most venerated site in Bali, situated on the slopes of **Gunung Agung**, the holiest and highest mountain on the island. The sheer volume of people can be overwhelming: it's worth **arriving early** in the morning or **late** in the afternoon to get the best of the atmosphere.

Besakih is totally schizophrenic. On the one hand it is the most sacred spot on Bali for Balinese Hindus, who believe that the gods occasionally descend to earth

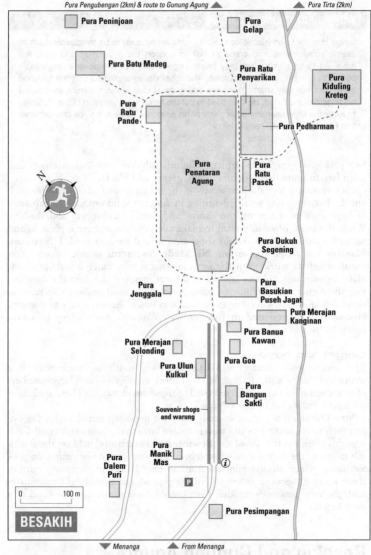

Pura Pengubengan (2km) & route to Gunung Agung ▲   ▲ Pura Tirta (2km)

Pura Peninjoan

Pura Gelap

Pura Batu Madeg

Pura Ratu Penyarikan

Pura Kiduling Kreteg

Pura Ratu Pande

Pura Pedharman

Pura Penataran Agung

Pura Ratu Pasek

N

Pura Dukuh Segening

Pura Jenggala

Pura Basukian Puseh Jagat

Pura Merajan Kanginan

Pura Merajan Selonding

Pura Banua Kawan

Pura Ulun Kulkul

Pura Goa

Pura Bangun Sakti

Souvenir shops and warung

Pura Manik Mas

Pura Dalem Puri

P

ⓘ

0   100 m

BESAKIH

Pura Pesimpangan

▼ Menanga   ▲ From Menanga

and reside in the temple, during which times the worshippers don their finery and bring them elaborate offerings. The complex's sheer scale is impressive, and on a clear day, with ceremonies in full swing, it is a wonderful place. On the other hand, Besakih is a jumble of buildings, unremarkable in many ways, around which has evolved the habit of separating foreign tourists from their money as quickly as possible. Even the stark grandeur of Besakih's location is often shrouded in mist, leaving Gunung Agung towering behind in all-enveloping cloud and the splendid panorama back south to the coast an imaginary delight. You can well end up wondering why you bothered.

Arrival and information

Without your own transport, the easiest way of getting to Besakih is to take an **organized tour**, but check how much time you'll have there; anything less than an hour isn't worth it.

If you are using **public transport**, bemos from Semarapura go as far as Menanga from where there are ojeks (Rp 5000–10,000) to the temple. In Semarapura pick up bemos on Jalan Gunung Rinjani (see map, p.232). Bemos also run from Amlapura via Selat and Muncan to Rendang, with some going on to Menanga. Most bemos run in the morning, but dry up in the afternoon. There are no public bemos north of Menanga to Penelokan, or between Rendang and Bangli.

The **tourist office** (daily 8am–7pm), on the right just beyond the car park, is staffed by guides from the local organization of guides who will pressure you to make a donation and engage their services (both are unnecessary but difficult to resist).

Besakih

The **Besakih complex** consists of more than twenty separate **temples**, spread over a site stretching for more than 3km. The central temple – the largest on the island – is **Pura Penataran Agung**, with the other temples ranged around it (see map opposite).

Unless you're praying or making offerings, you're **forbidden to enter** any of the temples and most remain locked unless there's a ceremony. However, a lot is visible through the gateways and over walls. The rule about wearing a sarong and sash appears to be inconsistently applied but you'll definitely need them if you're in skimpy clothing; **sarong and sash rental** is available, with negotiable prices. It's easier to bring your own.

Some history

It's likely that Besakih was a religious site long before the start of recorded history; Pura Batu Madeg (Temple of the Standing Stone), in the north of the

---

Guides at Besakih

Besakih has established an appalling reputation over the last decade as a place of nonstop hassle, leaving many visitors angry and insulted. The problem stemmed from the hundreds of local men who styled themselves as **guides**, **guardians** or **keepers** of the temple, insistently attached themselves to tourists and then demanded large sums in payment for their "services". The authorities periodically claim to have addressed this problem, and the official advice is only to engage a guide who has an official guide badge and is wearing a traditional **endek** shirt as uniform. They hang around the tourist office, so you're unlikely to miss them. But guides are hardly needed; stick to the paths running along the walls outside the temples shown on the map opposite, wear a sarong and sash, and you'll be in no danger of causing any religious offence. If you do engage a guide, establish the **fee** beforehand. Rp20,000 is reasonable, and you can always add extra if you feel you've received a good service. Be aware that if you're escorted by a guide into one of the temples to receive a blessing from a priest you'll be expected to make a "donation" to the priest, the amount negotiable through your guide.

If you're including Besakih in your own tour using a Balinese driver, you may find they're reluctant to bring visitors to Besakih because of the problems and they can suggest other temples to visit. If you do come, they will warn you of the problems although they'll be unable to intervene on your behalf.

complex, suggests megalithic connections through its ancient terraced structure based around a central stone. However, Besakih's founder is generally believed to be **Sri Markandeya**, a priest who came from eastern Java at the end of the eighth century with a party of settlers. Markandeya's son became the first high priest of the temple, attracting priests and successive rulers of the island, many of whom built shrines or temples. An important ceremony occurred in 1007, widely thought to be the cremation rites of Queen Mahendratta, origin of the Rangda legend (see box, p.226). **Empu Bharadah**, the holy man attributed with subduing Rangda, took part and there are shrines dedicated to him throughout the complex.

Already an important temple by the time of the **Majapahit** conquest of Bali in 1343, Besakih's pre-eminent position was confirmed as it became the state temple of the powerful Gelgel and Semarapura courts. An **earthquake** damaged the buildings in 1917 but it was repaired by the Dutch and underwent more restoration following damage in 1963 during the eruption of Gunung Agung (see box, p.240). As a result, the temples in the complex are a vibrant mix of old and new, and fresh building and restoration work is always ongoing.

The temples

To get the best out of Besakih, it's a good idea to see Pura Penataran Agung first, and then wander; most of the tourist crowds stick to the area around the central temple. The *meru* of Pura Batu Madeg, rising among the trees in the north of the complex, are enticing, while Pura Pengubengan, the most far-flung of the temples, is a good 2km through the forest. Pura Dalem Puri, the Temple of the Dead, is especially significant for the Balinese and, during the seventh lunar month, pilgrims come to pray for the souls of the dead.

Look out for representations of the manifestations of the supreme God, in particular differently coloured **flags and banners**: black for Wisnu (the preserver), red for Brahma (the creator) and a multicoloured array for Siwa (the destroyer).

Pura Penataran Agung

The Great Temple of State, or **Pura Penataran Agung**, is the central and most dramatic building in the complex. It is built on **six ascending terraces**, with more than fifty *bale*, shrines and stone thrones inside; about half are dedicated to specific gods, while the others have ceremonial functions, such as receiving offerings, providing seating for the priests or the gamelan orchestra, or as residences for the gods during temple festivals.

A giant stairway, lined by seven levels of **carved figures**, leads to the first courtyard; the figures to the left are from the *Mahabharata* and the ones to the

---

Besakih ceremonies

Every temple in Besakih has its timetable of **ceremonies**; see sources of information in Basics, on p.74, for exact dates. The most important annual ceremony is the Bhatar Turun Kabeh (The Gods Descend Together), which takes place in March or April and lasts a month, with the high point on the full moon of the tenth lunar month. At this time, the gods of all the shrines are believed to come and dwell in Besakih; worshippers converge here from all over the island. Besakih's most revered ceremony is Eka Dasa Rudra (see box, p.240), held every hundred years. More frequently, the Panca Wali Krama occurs every ten years and involves a forty-two-kilometre, three-day procession from the coast to the temple.

LEVEL I

1. Candi bentar An earlier entrance was toppled in the earthquake following the 1963 eruption.
2–3. Bale kulkul Contains the wooden kulkul (slit gongs).
4. Bale pegat Two-part *bale* to symbolize pilgrims passing from the material to the spiritual world.
5–6. Bale palegongan and **bale pagambuhan** Used for dance performances during festivals.
7–8. Bale ongkara Represent the sacred syllable *om*.

LEVEL II

9. Kori agung Gateway into next courtyard.
10. Bale gong For the gamelan orchestra.
11. Bale pawedan Where high priests prepare holy water.
12. Bale kembangsirang For conducting rituals.
13. Panggungan Place for offerings.
14. Bale agung For meetings.
15. Bale kawas Dedicated to Ida Bhatara Ider Buwana.
16. Padma capah Throne dedicated to Ida Ratu Sula Majemuh, lord of the weather.
17. Bale paruman alit Containing a stone *lingam*.
18. Nine-roofed meru Dedicated to Sanghyang Kubakal, god of instruments used in ceremonies.
19. Eleven-roofed meru Dedicated to Ratu Manik Maketel.
20. Bale pepelik For offerings.
21. Bale tegeh Dedicated to Empu Bharadah.
22. Padmatiga Triple lotus throne and centrepiece of the temple, where homage is paid to the supreme god Sanghyang Widhi Wasa in his three manifestations.
23. Bale pasamuhan agung Home of the gods at festival time.
24. Bale pepelik For offerings.

LEVEL III

25–30. Meru and shrines Dedicated to spirits
31–32. Shrines To the ancestors of a clan from the Besakih area.
33. Bale pepelik For offerings.
34–35. Shrines To the ancestors of another local clan.
36. Panggungan For offerings during ceremonies at the shrines.
37. Seven-roofed meru Dedicated to Saraswati, Hindu goddess of learning.
38. Panggungan For offerings during ceremonies at the shrines.
39. Bale pepelik For offerings.
40. Eleven-roofed meru Dedicated to Ida Ratu Maspahit.
41. Three-roofed kehen Temple store for sacred objects.

LEVEL IV

42. Bale Containing ancient statues.
43. Gedong Dedicated to Ida Ratu Ulang Alu, god of wandering salesmen.
44. Gedong Dedicated to Ida Ratu Ayu Subandar, god of merchants.
45. Bale pepelik For offerings.
46. Bebaturan Dedicated to Ida Ratu Sedahan Panginte.
47. Bale pepelik For offerings.
48. Eleven-roofed meru Dedicated to Ida Ratu Sunaring Jagat, god of the light of the world.
49–51. Bale tegeh Dedicated to the courtiers and nymphs of heaven (*widadara* and *widadari*).

LEVEL V

52–53. Bale pepelik For offerings.
54. Three-roofed meru Dedicated to Ida Ratu Ayu Mas Magelung, goddess of performing arts.
55. Eleven-roofed meru Dedicated to Sanghyang Widi Wasa.

LEVEL VI

56. Gedong Dedicated to Ida Ratu Bukit Kiwa, god of the left mountain.
57. Gedong Dedicated to Ida Ratu Bukit Tengen, god of the right mountain.

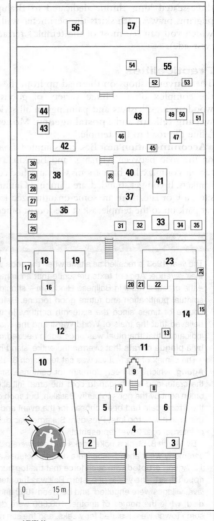

PURA PENATARAN AGUNG

0   15 m

right from the *Ramayana*. As worshippers process through the first courtyard they symbolically sever their connection with the everyday world, before proceeding through the *kori agung* into the second courtyard – the largest and most important courtyard in the temple, which contains the **padmatiga**, the three-seated lotus throne dedicated to Brahma, Siwa and Wisnu, where all pilgrims pray. A path skirts the perimeter wall of Pura Penataran Agung, from which you can see most of the temple's terraces (the best views are from the west side).

Practicalities

The **souvenir** shops on the road up from the car park and dotted throughout the complex offer a huge variety of goods including bedspreads, clothes, woodcarvings, baskets and paintings in all styles. In the car park you'll find a **warung telkom** and a **postal agency**. **Moneychangers** – offering poor rates – line the road to the temple.

Accommodation near Besakih is limited. *Lembah Arca* hotel (☎0366/23076; ②) on the road between Menanga and Besakih, a couple of kilometres before the temple complex, has basic rooms with attached cold-water bathrooms and provides blankets. If you get stranded, are climbing Gunung Agung, or want to explore the site early or late, there are some unauthorized lodgings behind the road from the car park up to the temple; ask at the tourist office. Further afield, about 9km from

---

1963

The year **1963** is recalled as a time when the gods were displeased with Bali and took their revenge. Ancient texts prescribe that an immense ceremony, **Eka Dasa Rudra** – the greatest ritual in Balinese Hinduism – should be held every hundred years for spiritual purification and future good fortune. Before 1963, it had only been held a couple of times since the sixteenth century. In the early 1960s, religious leaders believed that the trials of World War II and the ensuing fight for independence were indicators that the ritual was once again needed, and these beliefs were confirmed by a **plague of rats** that overran the entire island in 1962.

The climax of the festival was set for March 8, 1963, but on February 18, **Gunung Agung**, which had been dormant for centuries, started rumbling; fire glowed within the crater and ash began to coat the area. Initially, this was interpreted as a good omen sent by the gods to purify Besakih, but soon doubts crept in. Some argued that the wrong date had been chosen for the event and wanted to call it off. However, by this time it was too late: President Sukarno was due to attend, together with a group of international travel representatives.

By March 8, black smoke, rocks and ash were billowing from the mountain, but the ceremony went ahead, albeit in a decidedly tense atmosphere. Eventually, on March 17, Agung **erupted** with such force that the top hundred metres of the mountain was ripped apart. The whole of eastern Bali was threatened by poisonous gas and molten lava, villages were engulfed, and between 1000 and 2000 people are thought to have died, while the homes of another 100,000 were destroyed. Roads were wiped out, some towns were isolated for weeks, and the ash ruined crops, causing serious food shortages.

Despite the force of the eruption and the position of Besakih high on the mountain, a relatively small amount of damage occurred to the temples, and the **closing rites** of Eka Dasa Rudra took place on April 20. Subsequently, many Balinese felt that the mountain's eruption at the time of the ceremony was an omen of the civil strife that engulfed Bali in 1965 (see p.423).

In 1979, the year specified by the ancient texts, Eka Dasa Rudra was held again, this time passing off without incident.

Besakih, in Rendang, *Mahagiri* is the most luxurious accommodation in the area (see p.262) and by far the most comfortable place to stay.

There's reasonably priced **food** at *Lembah Arca* and at the *Warung Mawar* in Menanga, just on the left as you turn off to Besakih. There are a few warung on the walk up to Besakih from the car park.

Gunung Agung

According to legend, **Gunung Agung** was created by the god Pasupati when he split Mount Meru (the centre of the Hindu universe), forming both Gunung Agung and Gunung Batur. At 3142m Agung is the highest Balinese peak and an impressive sight from anywhere in east Bali. The spiritual centre of the island, the Balinese believe the spirits of their ancestors dwell here. Villages and house compounds are laid out in relation to the mountain, and many Balinese people habitually sleep with their heads towards it (see p.460).

Climbing the mountain

Two main routes lead up Gunung Agung, both long and hard. One starts from Besakih and the other from Pura Pasar Agung on the southern flank of the mountain (see p.261). Whichever route you take, you'll need to set out in the middle of the night to be at the top for the **sunrise** (6–7am). It's essential to take a **guide** and you'll also need strong footwear, a good flashlight – ideally a head lamp to leave both hands free for climbing – and water and snacks; for the descent, a stout stick is handy.

Climbing is not permitted at certain times of the year because of **religious ceremonies** at Besakih or Pura Pasar Agung. Fortunately, it is rare that these ceremonies coincide. **Weather**-wise, the dry season (April–mid-Oct) is the best time to climb; you may get a few dry days during the rainy season but don't contemplate it during January and February, the wettest months.

From Pura Pasar Agung, it's at least a three-hour climb with an ascent of almost 2000m, so you'll need to set out at 3am or earlier from the temple, depending on how fit you are. The track initially passes through forest, ascending onto bare, steep rock. It doesn't go to the actual summit, but ends at a point on the rim that is about 100m lower. From here, the summit masks views of part of the island and, between April and September, the sunrise on the horizon, but you'll be able to see Gunung Rinjani, the south of Bali and Gunung Batukau and look down into the five-hundred-metre crater.

From Besakih, the climb is longer (5–7hr) and much more challenging; you'll need to leave between 10pm and midnight. This path leads to the summit of Agung with views in all directions. The initial climb is through forest, but the path gets very steep, very quickly, even before it gets out onto the bare rock, and you'll soon need your hands to haul yourself upwards. The descent is particularly taxing from this side and feels very precarious when you're already exhausted; allow at least five hours to get down.

A less-used route, **from Dukuh Bujangga Sakti**, inland from Kubu on the north coast, is offered by one company, M&G Trekking (see below). Starting out at 300m altitude, the climb is greater but not as steep as the other routes. It is also less painful as you start climbing in the afternoon, camp on the mountain at 1750m and complete the three hours to the summit pre-dawn. The north of Bali is generally drier so it is less often shrouded in cloud. You can walk round the rim to the absolute summit if you climb from this side and can see the sunrise on the horizon all year round.

Practicalities

This is a serious trek: talk to potential **guides** and satisfy yourself that they have the necessary experience. There are guides from the local organization of trekking guides on standby at Pura Pasar Agung at any time of the day or night. With negotiation you'll be looking at Rp350,000 for a guide for one or two people but you'll need to provide all your own food and water. If you're at Besakih, guides can be arranged at the tourist office; they can also help with nearby lodgings. The going rate from this side is Rp700,000 per guide, for two people. Bear in mind that the level of English among local guides is variable and some don't have a lot of experience with tourists so you may feel more comfortable dealing with one of the agencies below.

Closest to **Pura Pasar Agung**, in Muncan, 4km east of Rendang, I Ketut Uriada (℡0812/364 6426) has climbed Agung over two hundred times, although these days, he rarely climbs himself but has trained several local guides. His house is on the left as you enter Muncan from the east; anybody in the village will direct you. Expect to pay $30 for a guide for one or two people from Pura Pasar Agung or $50 from Besakih. Larger groups may need more than one guide. I Ketut Uriada will help you arrange a bemo charter between Muncan and the start of the climb. There's basic **accommodation** at *Pondok Wisata Puri Agung* (℡&℻0366/23037; ❷–❸) in Selat, 4km east of Muncan on the Amlapura road, who can also provide a guide for the climb, quoting Rp350,000 for one or two people, Rp450,000 for three or four. This doesn't include accommodation or transport to and from Pura Pasar Agung. In Selat, Gung Bawa, Jl Sri Jaya Pangus 33 (℡0366/24379, ⓦwww.gb-trekking.blogspot.com), is an experienced guide and charges Rp350,000 per person from Pura pasar Agung and Rp500,000 per person from Besakih including overnight accommodation in Selat. He also offers a trek leaving Selat at midday and climbing to a camping spot at 2560m, leaving a climb of one to two hours the next morning to the summit ($120).

Inevitably, prices are higher if you arrange the trek **from further afield**. The *Pondok Lembah Dukuh* and *Geria Semalung* losmen in Ababi near Tirtagangga arrange climbs (see p.258). M&G Trekking (℡0363/41464 or 0813/315 3991, ⓔmgtrekking@hotmail.com) has an office in Balina, Candi Dasa (see p.246). They quote Rp890,000 per person for a minimum of two people for the longer, but potentially more rewarding, climb from Dukuh including transport from the Candi Dasa area, walking stick, hat, jacket and food. Bali Sunrise 2001 in **Ubud** (℡0818/552669, ⓦwww.balisunrise2001.com) will arrange pick-ups for the trek from pretty much anywhere on Bali, charging from $100 per person depending on the pick-up point. The guiding operations in **Toya Bungkah** charge from $100 per person (minimum numbers of two or four people apply). **Perama** also organize the climb (Rp750,000 per person, minimum two people); contact any of their offices.

Candi Dasa and Amuk Bay

CANDI DASA is a relaxed resort at the eastern end of **Amuk Bay**. There's a wide choice of accommodation and restaurants, and it's a good centre for snorkelling and diving as well as a convenient base from which to explore the east of Bali.

Originally centred on the lagoon, tourist developments now spread west around the bay, through the villages of **Senkidu**, **Mendira**, **Buitan** and

Manggis. Further west, just around the headland, the tiny cove of **Padang Bai** is popular as a laid-back tourist resort and is the access port for Lombok.

Following the destruction of the offshore reef in the 1980s (to produce lime for cement to fuel the tourist building boom), the beach in the centre of Candi Dasa washed away. Large jetties now protrude into the sea with pockets of white sand nestling behind, while the beaches to the west and east of the centre are a respectable size. There are reportedly plans to import sand from elsewhere in Bali to rehabilitate the beach even further. The vast majority of the resort offers excellent views of a clutch of tiny offshore islands with Nusa Lembongan and Nusa Penida rising mistily in the distance.

Arrival and information

Hotel development in the Candi Dasa area extends for about 8km along the main Denpasar–Amlapura road with much of the accommodation located on small lanes leading down to the sea. The entire coastal area is served by **public transport**, both buses and minibuses from Denpasar (Batubulan terminal) to Amlapura, and local bemos on shorter runs. **Shuttle buses** from the main tourist destinations serve Candi Dasa, and Perama has an office with daily arrivals from destinations on Bali and Lombok. Sample prices are Rp40,000 between Candi Dasa and Ubud, Kuta or Sanur and Rp100,000 to Lovina; see "Travel details" on p.271 for more. Fixed-price taxis serve Candi Dasa from Ngurah Rai Airport (Rp300,000; 2hr). The **tourist office**, in the main street close to the lagoon, seems to have somewhat erratic opening hours and staffing.

Accommodation

There's plenty of **accommodation** to suit every taste and pocket with many extremely attractive as well as functional places to stay. Most of the ones listed below do not have street addresses but all are keyed on the map.

Candi Dasa

Accommodation is spread about 1km along the main road running just behind the beach in central **Candi Dasa**. Beware of places that are close to the road and therefore noisy.

Agung Bungalows ☎&ℱ0363/41535. This is a decent budget choice as the bungalows have good-sized verandahs, fans, hot and cold water, and are located in a lush garden on the coast. ❷

Ashram Gandhi Canti Dasa ☎0363/41108, ⓦwww.ashramgandhi.com. This Gandhian ashram rents out bungalows between the lagoon and the ocean. Guests take as much or as little part in the daily round of puja, yoga, meditation and lectures as they wish, but may not smoke, drink or sunbathe nude; only married couples may share rooms. Charges include three vegetarian meals a day. Booking is essential. Volunteer placements are also possible. ❺

Dewa Bharata ☎0363/41090, ℱ41091. Good-value bungalows, all with hot water, plus a pretty pool and seafront restaurant in well-maintained gardens. Top-end rooms have a/c and sea views. ❹–❺

Dewi Bungalows ☎0363/41166, ℱ41177. Clean, tiled bungalows in a spacious garden close to the lagoon and the sea. All rooms have hot water; one has a/c. ❹

Geringsing ☎0363/41084. Four good-quality bungalows all with a/c and hot water in a family compound on the coast, some with sea views. ❹

Kelapa Mas ☎0363/41369, ⓦwww.kelapamas.com. Justifiably popular and centrally located, offering a range of clean bungalows set in a lovely garden on the seafront. Hot water and a/c are available. ❷–❹

Kubu Bali ☎0363/41532, ⓦwww.kububali.com. Excellent, well-furnished bungalows with deep verandahs. All have fan, a/c and hot water, and are widely spaced in a glorious garden ranging up the hillside to the lovely swimming pool at the top. Service is friendly yet efficient. ❻

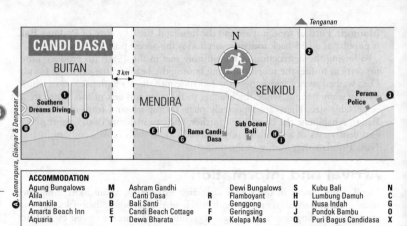

ACCOMMODATION

Agung Bungalows	M	Ashram Gandhi		Dewi Bungalows	S	Kubu Bali	N
Alila	D	Canti Dasa	R	Flamboyant	H	Lumbung Damuh	C
Amankila	B	Bali Santi	I	Genggong	U	Nusa Indah	G
Amarta Beach Inn	E	Candi Beach Cottage	F	Geringsing	J	Pondok Bambu	O
Aquaria	T	Dewa Bharata	P	Kelapa Mas	Q	Puri Bagus Candidasa	X

Pondok Bambu ☎0363/41534, ⓦwww
.pondokbambu.com. Comfortable bungalows all
with a/c and hot water in an attractive garden with
a small pool close to the beach. ⑤

Seaside Cottages ☎0363/41629, ⓦwww
.bali-seafront-bungalows.com. Small place offering
several standards of decent accommodation in a
pretty garden, from basic budget bungalows with
attached *mandi* to ones on the seafront with a/c
and hot water. ①–④

The Watergarden/Hotel Taman Air
☎0363/41540, ⓦwww.watergardenhotel
.com. Superb, characterful, excellently furnished
bungalows with deep verandahs, each
overlooking a lotus pond, set in an atmospheric,
lush garden. All have a/c and hot water. There's a
pretty, secluded swimming pool. Service is
excellent. ⑦–⑧

Forest Road

As the centre of Candi Dasa suffers more from road noise, the quiet of **Forest Road** is increasingly appealing and even *Puri Bagus* at the far end is only about ten minutes' walk from the centre.

Aquaria ☎0363/41127, ⓦwww.aquariabali.com.
Delightful rooms with a definite "wow" factor built
around a great pool on the coast. Fan or a/c are
available, all have hot water and lovely verandahs.
There's an attached spa. ⑤–⑥

Genggong ☎0363/41105. Bungalows plus rooms
in a two-storey block with big balconies and
verandahs. There's a choice of fan or a/c. Rooms
do vary so ask to see several. The big plus, though,
is the large garden and picturesque stretch of
white-sand beach just over the wall. ①–③

Puri Bagus Candidasa ☎0363/41131,
ⓦwww.puribagus.net. Well-furnished accommodation with a glorious pool, flourishing garden and
lovely spa. The ten deluxe rooms with sea views
are the ones to go for – well worth the additional

cost. For a more rural location, consider the sister
operation, *Puri Bagus Manggis* (see below). ⑦–⑧

Puri Oka Beach Bungalows ☎0363/41092,
ⓔpuri_oka@hotmail.com. Something of a work in
progress, this long-established place is undergoing
renovations. The basic bottom-end rooms may
lurch upmarket but currently offer amazing value
for a place with a pool and the top-end apartments
are absolutely stunning. ②–⑤

Sekar Anggrek ☎0363/41086, ⓦwww
.sekar-orchid.com. Smart little place with seven
clean, good-quality bungalows, all with fan, hot
water, and mosquito screens at the windows, in a
quiet seafront garden. The website is in German
but the photographs are helpful. ④

Senkidu and Mendira

The village of **Senkidu** is about 1km to the west of Candi Dasa, slightly detached and quiet, but still convenient for the centre. The adjacent village of

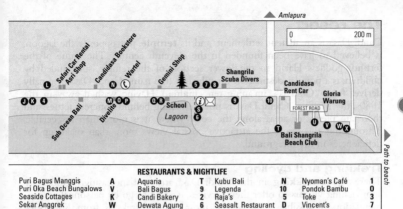

		RESTAURANTS & NIGHTLIFE					
Puri Bagus Manggis	**A**	Aquaria	**T**	Kubu Bali	**N**	Nyoman's Café	**1**
Puri Oka Beach Bungalows	**V**	Bali Bagus	**9**	Legenda	**10**	Pondok Bambu	**0**
Seaside Cottages	**K**	Candi Bakery	**2**	Raja's	**5**	Toke	**3**
Sekar Anggrek	**W**	Dewata Agung	**6**	Seasalt Restaurant	**D**	Vincent's	**7**
The Watergarden	**L**	Iguana Café	**4**	Mr Grumpy's	**8**	Watergarden Kafé	**L**

Mendira is further away and you'll need transport to get to Candi Dasa comfortably.

Amarta Beach Inn ☎0363/41230. Large, tiled bungalows, all with fans, set in a pretty garden facing the ocean at Mendira. The more expensive rooms have hot water. There's a beachside restaurant and plenty of space for sunbathing. ②–③

Bali Santi ☎0363/41611. Ⓦwww .balisanti.com. Good-value, clean, well-maintained budget accommodation in a lovely garden in Senkidu with fine coastal views. *Flamboyant* (☎0363/41886) is next door if they are full. ①–②

Candi Beach Cottage ☎0363/41234, Ⓦwww .candibeachbali.com. Top-price accommodation in Mendira in comfortable rooms or bungalows with all the facilities in attractive grounds with two beachside pools and a tennis court. Plenty of activities are on offer, including trekking and snorkelling. ⑦–⑧

Nusa Indah ☎0363/41062, Ⓦwww.nusaindah .de. Attractive rooms in a good garden setting just behind the beach at Mendira. There's a lovely pool. More expensive rooms are larger, and all have hot water. ⑤–⑥

Buitan and Manggis

If you stay further west at **Buitan** you'll need transport to reach central Candi Dasa; some hotels provide free shuttles. Further west again, most of **Manggis** village is spread inland, but it does offer two luxury hotels.

Alila Buitan ☎0363/41011, Ⓦwww .alilahotels.com. Impressive hotel situated in a picturesque, beachside coconut grove with rooms ranged around a gorgeous pool. The decor is stylish and minimalist chic, service is excellent and there's a spa. The hotel has an international reputation for its cooking school and plenty of activities are on offer with regular tai chi and yoga, and free shuttles. ⑧–⑨

Amankila Manggis ☎0363/41333, Ⓦwww .amanresorts.com. Jetset hideaway (rumour has it that Mick Jagger and Jerry Hall honeymooned here) featuring fabulous hillside villas with gorgeous coastal views. For Rp400,000 a day, at the manager's discretion, nonresidents can use the Beach Club facilities (which include a 45m pool), although you won't be allowed in the much-photographed three-tiered main pool up above. Prices from US$750. ⑨

Lumbung Damuh ☎0363/41553, Ⓦwww .damuhbali.com. Four wooden *lumbung*-style cottages in a lush garden on Buitan's coast. Bedrooms, with small fridges, are upstairs and bathrooms with hot water plus the sitting areas are down. The sign to Royal Bali Beach Club identifies the turning from the main road. There is home-cooked bread for breakfast and free use of boogie boards and canoes. ④–⑤

Puri Bagus Manggis ☎0363/41304, Ⓦwww .puribagus.net. Part of the small *Puri Bagus* stable, with just six attractive rooms in a rural setting in Manggis – the only accommodation in the village itself. There's a small swimming pool in the paddy-fields just across the road. Cooking, cycling and trekking can be arranged, and there's free transport to its beachside, sister hotel in Candi Dasa. ⑧

The resort

Candi Dasa is an ancient settlement, and its **temple**, just opposite the lagoon, is believed to have been founded in the eleventh century. The statue of the fertility goddess Hariti in the lower section of the temple, surrounded by children, is a popular destination for pilgrims (the name Candi Dasa originally derives from "Cilidasa", meaning ten children). Having washed away in the 1980s, the beach at Candi Dasa is now returning behind concrete jetties, and there are plenty of areas along the coast where it is more than respectable. Throughout the resort the attractive coastal views more than make up for deficiencies in the foreground.

Trekking and cycling

There's good **trekking** in the Candi Dasa area and increasingly guides are approaching visitors to offer their services, it's best to go by personnal recommendation if possible. One of the most popular treks is from Kastala to Tenganan which offers about three hours of easy walking with excellent rice-terrace views and with the chance to learn about the making of local palm wine by visiting a local household involved in production. M&G Trekking (T0363/41464 or 0813/315 3991, Emgtrekking@hotmail.com) is an established local firm with an office in Buitan and rates are Rp250,000 per person for the trip with a minimum of two people. Paleng's (T0817/471 9487, Wwww.eastbalionline.com) charges Rp300,000 for one person and Rp400,000 for two; all transport is included. Perama in Candi Dasa also offers trekking from Rp125,000 (T0363/41114, Wwww.peramatour.com).

M&G also arrange **cycling** tours starting at Besakih and taking in a largely downhill (55km) route to the coast at Amed for snorkelling before heading home (Rp700,000 per person, min 2 people). See "Listings" for information on **bicycle rental**.

Diving and snorkelling

Just off the coast, the tiny islands of **Gili Tepekong** (also known as Gili Kambing or Goat Island), **Gili Biaha** (also known as Gili Likman) and **Gili Mimpang** offer excellent **diving**, although it's not suitable for beginners as the water can be cold and the currents strong. There are several walls, a pinnacle just off Mimpang and the dramatic scenery of Tepekong Canyon, lined with massive boulders. The current is too strong for the growth of big coral, but the fish include barracuda, tuna, white-tipped reef shark, *mola mola* and manta ray.

The reef is gradually rejuvenating and there is now snorkelling just offshore, stretching for about a kilometre westwards from just in front of *Puri Bagus Candidasa*. Don't venture too far out and stay aware of your position at all times – the currents can be hazardous. The best places are off Gili Mimpang and Blue Lagoon on the western side of Amuk Bay, closer to Padang Bai (see p.254). Arrange snorkelling trips with local boat-owners; with negotiation the price is Rp200–250,000 for two hours for up to three people and including equipment to the islands off Candi Dasa or Pasir Putih (see p.249) or Rp250–300,000 to Blue Lagoon. Many dive shops take snorkellers along on dive trips; prices vary from $15 to $30 so shop around; always be clear whether or not equipment is included in the price.

As well as the local sites, Candi Dasa is conveniently located for diving trips to Padang Bai, Nusa Penida, Nusa Lembongan, Amed, Tulamben and Gili Selang ($60–80 depending on the distance). Candi Dasa is also a good place to take a course, as hotel swimming pools are available for initial tuition; PADI Open Water ($360–400), Advanced Open Water ($250–300) and Divemaster (contact them directly for prices) courses can all be arranged. Many places in Candi Dasa charge additional equipment rental ($5–15 per set per day) so check at the time of booking. Below are details of some dive companies in the area – all offer trips for experienced divers and some courses. See p.51 for general advice on choosing a dive operator.

Candi Dasa dive operators

Divelite ☎0363/41660, ⓦwww.divelite.com. Offering tuition in Japanese, Indonesian and English.

Pineapple Divers At *Candi Beach Cottage* ☎0363/41760, ⓦwww.bali-pineapple-divers .com. Also arranges two- and three-day package tours of dive sites around the island, including accommodation.

Shangrila Scuba Divers ☎0813/3733 5081, ⓦwww.divingatbalishangrila.com. At the *Bali Shangrila Beach Club* on the Forest Road and with a counter in town.

Southern Dreams Diving ☎0363/41506, ⓔsouthern@idola.net.id. On the road down to Buitan Beach offering mostly trips for experienced divers.

Sub Ocean Bali ☎0363/41411, ⓦwww .suboceanbali.com. In Senkidu, offering courses up to Divemaster plus Nitrox.

Eating, drinking and nightlife

Candi Dasa offers a great variety of **places to eat**, with plenty of good–quality food. Restaurants along the main road are noisy because of the traffic; some manage to mask the noise but the quietest places are on the coast. Quite a few places offer free transport, useful if you are staying away from the centre.

Aquaria ☎0363/41127, ⓦwww .aquariabali.com. Tiny restaurant overlooking the pool serves inventive, delicious food that is well above the norm. The fixed-price menu (Rp65,000 for three courses) changes daily but makes full use of local produce and offers vegetarian options. Also worth a visit for the lunchtime and daily snack menu.

Bali Bagus ☎0363/41363. Excellent value in attractive surroundings with set three-course meals from Rp39,950. Free transport in the Candi area.

Candi Bakery About 300m along the road to Tenganan. Serves the best iced coffee in Candi Dasa, as well as an appetizing selection of bread and cakes. Lunch and dinner is offered, with some German dishes such as *bratwurst, sauerkraut* and *bratkartoffel* (main courses Rp18–25,000).

Dewata Agung ☎0363/41204. Overlooking the lagoon, the extensive menu features the usual suspects but the food is well cooked and they offer a range of Balinese specialities. The set menus aren't the cheapest in town (Rp49,000) but they're worth it. Free transport in Candi Dasa.

Kubu Bali The vast menu covers seafood, Western, Chinese and Indonesian food (main courses Rp25,000 upwards) in attractive, relaxed surround-ings. Better tables are at the back near the fish ponds. There's a big list of drinks, too.

Nyoman's Café One of a trio of cheap and cheerful places on the road to Buitan beach, with a selection of Indonesian and Western favourites including local seafood (mains about Rp15,000).

Pondok Bambu This is an excellent spot for a sunset drink (cocktails Rp40–50,000, imported wine around Rp200,000 per bottle) and the food is good too although it's standard dishes with main courses Rp25,000 upwards.

Seasalt Restaurant at the *Alila* hotel ☎0363/41011, ⓦwww.alilahotels.com. The premier dining experience in eastern Bali, in an open-sided *bale* built with natural materials. The huge menu features Asian and international dishes but the East Balinese specialities are a major part – best sampled through the Balinese *Megibung* (a feast of eight dishes) for Rp180,000. Much of the produce is grown in the hotel's organic garden, and main courses are Rp60,000 upwards. The hotel's cooking school is justifiably renowned.

Vincent's ☎0363/41368, ⓦwww .vincentsbali.com. Lazy jazz on the music system and original artwork on the walls create an inviting atmosphere, although it isn't always easy to get a table. The Balinese, Indonesian and inter-national menu is enormous (starters Rp18–39,000, main courses Rp30–55,000) and extremely well presented and cooked. The salads are worth a special mention – fresh and scrumptious. Their offshoot, *Toke* (☎0363/41991, ⓦwww.tokebali .com), replicates many of the positives, with varia-tions, at the other end of town. Free transport in the Candi Dasa area.

Watergarden Kafé Offering a vast drinks list (cocktails about Rp45,000) and an eclectic assortment of well-cooked, well-presented Indonesian, international and seafood dishes including good steaks, with daily specials adding to the choice (mains Rp28–55,000). There are vegetarian options and nut-free and wheat-free dishes are available.

Nightlife

Nightlife is low-key in Candi Dasa: apart from a few late-opening restaurants, things are pretty quiet by 10pm. There's no club scene, and live music alternates between *Legenda* and *Iguana Café*. *Raja's* shows nightly videos and there are music videos, sports and films at *Mr Grumpy's*. It's not unknown for those in search of late-night entertainment to head for Padang Bai.

Massage and spas

Beach **massages** are available throughout the resort (Rp50,000/hour). There are also some fabulous spas. Pricer spas ($35–55 per hour) with a vast choice of massages and treatments are the *Alila* spa (T0363/41011) with beachside *bale* and indoor rooms, Ambiente Spa at the *Rama Candi Dasa* (T0363/41974) with fabulous treatment rooms, and Jaya Spa at the *Puri Bagus Candidasa* (T0361/41131) set amidst pools and fountains. The more affordable *Aquaria* (T0363/41127) offers massage, scrubs, hot stone treatments and crystal massages and facials in the oceanfront spa from Rp150,000.

Shopping

While nobody would describe Candi Dasa as a Mecca for **shopping**, there's a reasonable selection of crafts and textiles on sale. Asri Shop and Gemini Shop (daily 8am–10pm) are central **supermarkets**, selling everyday goods as well as souvenirs and the fixed prices serve as a good guide for your bargaining elsewhere. Heading eastwards on a retail trail from the Perama office, Gogos does a good range of **silver** items while the Geringsing Shop, near the hotel of the same name, is a treasure-trove of the old and not-so-old, including an extensive selection of **textiles** and **wooden carvings** from across Indonesia. Then check out the tiny shop at *The Watergarden* for some delightful items, especially jewellery, although it isn't cheap and, across the road, the shop attached to *Seaside Cottages* has a huge range of well-priced items as does Nadis 2 next to the Candidasa Bookstore. The shop in the warung telkom next to *Kubu Bali* boasts a selection of small pottery, wooden and bone items plus **jewellery** and some textiles including a few rolls of cloth sold by the metre. Kabeh Art and Edy Kites, together just west of *Raja's* are both worth a browse and while the **kites** are attractive and good-value at Rp90,000 for the largest size, they are not suited to long-distance transportation. Nusantara Archipelago, just east of *Vincent's*, has a small but excellent selection of **paper**, **wood** and **metal** items, all well crafted and tasteful and, slightly further east again, across the road this time, Maya sells a huge range of textiles including silk **batik** at the top of the price range (from Rp300–600,000) but with plenty of cheaper items as well.

If you're looking to splash out, the shop at the *Alila* hotel in Buitan, Alila Living (8am–8pm), has a fabulous selection including the natural toiletries that they use in the hotel, great clothes and books and some of the loveliest gift items you'll find in east Bali.

There's also a great choice of textiles and other crafts in the nearby village of **Tenganan** (see p.250), but if you can't get there the Ata Shop is about 200m along the Tenganan turning from the main road; they have a selection of baskets and textiles.

Listings

Bike rental Sub Ocean Bali in central Candi Dasa and Gloria Warung on Forest Road. Rp25,000 a day. Beware the busy traffic on the main road.

Books Several bookstores sell new and second-hand books; the Candidasa Bookstore has the largest selection.

Car and motorbike rental You'll be offered 'transport' every few yards along the main road, or else inquire at your accommodation. There are also well-established rental companies. Safari (℡0363/41707) in the centre of town; and Candidasa Rent Car (℡0363/41225) at the start of Forest Rd. The insurance included varies considerably. Prices are Rp90,000–100,000 per day for a Suzuki Jimney, Rp150,000 for a Kijang and Rp50,000–60,000 for a motorbike.

Charter transport To put together your own day-trip, you'll be looking at Rp350,000–400,000 per day for vehicle, driver and petrol, depending on your itinerary. Negotiate with the touts along the main street, ask at your accommodation or approach the car rental companies. One-way drops to destinations throughout Bali are a convenient and, if you're in a group, a reasonable way of moving on: Rp50,000 to Padang Bai, Rp200,000 to Amed, Rp250,000 to Ubud, Rp300,000 to the airport/Kuta area, Rp400–450,000 to Lovina. If you want to charter transport, Ketut Lagun (℡0812/362 2076) is a recommended driver.

Doctor Dr Nisa (℡0811/380645) is a highly regarded, English-speaking local doctor who will visit sick tourists on a private basis. Can also be contacted at Water Worx Dive Centre in Padang Bai. The nearest hospitals are at Amlapura, Semarapura or Denpasar (see p.95).

Exchange Moneychangers on the main street. Currently there's no international ATM but one may be installed soon in the petrol station just west of Candi Dasa. The next closest ones are Amlapura, Padang Bai (if it is working) and Semarapura.

Internet access On the main street (Rp400/min), although the dial-up connection is slow.

Phones There's a warung telkom (daily 7am–10.45pm) next to the *Kubu Bali* restaurant.

Police The police post is just west of Perama.

Post office Near the lagoon (Mon–Fri 8.30am–noon).

Tourist shuttle buses Plenty of places offer shuttle buses from Candi Dasa to destinations throughout Bali and Lombok. Perama (℡0363/41114, ℗www.peramatour.com; 8am–9pm) is the most established operator. See "Travel details", p.271, for a full list of destinations.

Tours Available at Perama, the tourist booths on the main road, or through hotels and car rental companies. The standard tours are: Amlapura (the palace, Tirtagangga and Tenganan), Besakih (Putung, Muncan, Besakih, Klungkung), Kintamani (Bangli, Kintamani, Penelokan, Tampaksiring, Gunung Kawi), Kuta (Kuta, Nusa Dua, Sanur, Uluwatu, sometimes including the sunset), Sangeh (Sangeh, Mengwi, Bedugul and Danau Bratan, Tanah Lot), Singaraja (Tirtagangga, Tulamben, Air Sanih, Lovina, Singaraja) and Ubud (Goa Gajah, Monkey Forest, Mas, Celuk, Ubud). It depends on the tour but prices range up to Rp600,000 for the ten-hour Lovina trip. Shop around and be clear whether prices quoted are per person or per vehicle. Alternatively, charter transport and put your own trip together (see above).

Around Candi Dasa

Take a trip to **Pura Gomang** for great views of the area. Catch an Amlapura-bound bemo for 3km, up the hill to the pass marked by a small shrine on the road. Concrete steps followed by a steep path head seawards to the temple at the top of the hill. Alternatively, Paleng's (℡0817/471 9487, ℗www.eastbalionline.com) organizes treks for Rp150,000 per person. Every two years, around October, four of the local villages – Bugbug, Bebandem, Jasi and Ngis – participate in a ritual battle near the top of Gomang Hill to settle an ancient dispute.

Some 6km northeast of Candi, **Pasir Putih** is a lovely but shadeless pure-white beach sheltered by rocky headlands. Take a bemo as far as Perasi, from where Jalan Pasir Putih (there's a tiny sign that's easy to miss) leads 3km to the coast via a ticket office (Rp2000 per person plus Rp1000 per vehicle). There are a few small warung renting out sun-loungers (Rp20,000) and snorkelling gear (Rp20–30,000) in addition to selling inexpensive food and drink. The beach is rumoured to be earmarked for a big resort development.

From Manggis, 6km west of Candi, a great road with fabulous views of the area – check the condition before setting off in a vehicle – heads up into the hills (see p.261).

Tenganan

The village of **TENGANAN** (admission by donation) is one of the Bali Aga communities of the island and adheres to traditional ways. Rejecting the Javani-zation of their land, the caste system and the religious reforms that followed the Majapahit conquest of the island in 1343, the **Bali Aga** or Bali Mula, meaning "original Balinese", withdrew to their village enclaves to live a life based around ritual and ceremony. Today, Tenganan is a wealthy village and the only place in Indonesia that produces the celebrated **gringsing** cloth.

Laid out on either side of broad cobbled avenues that run north–south, Tenganan rises in a series of terraces. All the house compounds have rooms and small *bale* around courtyards behind high walls. Despite the emphasis on tradition, however, you'll still see noisy motorbikes scurrying around the village and television aerials and satellite dishes crowding the skyline.

For a more in-depth visit to the village, JED, Village Ecotourism Network (℡0361/735320, ⓦwww.jed.or.id), arrange guided visits which include detailed insights into Tenganan and its people and customs.

The road up to Tenganan is a pleasant **walk** from the centre of Candi Dasa but **ojek** (Rp5000) wait at the bottom to transport you the 3km up to the village.

Rituals, ceremonies and festivals

Tenganan's inhabitants pursue a complex round of **rituals and ceremonies**, which are laid down in ancient texts and believed to prevent the wrath of the gods destroying the village. Most of the daily rituals are not open to the public, but there are many **festival** days where visitors are welcome (see sources of

▲ Pasir Putih Beach

The founding of Tenganan

A famous legend details the **founding of Tenganan**. In the days before the Majapahit invasion of Bali, **King Bedaulu** ruled the island. One day his favourite horse went missing, and the king offered a large reward for its return. The horse was eventually discovered dead near Tenganan and the king decided that he would give the local people the area within which the stench of the rotting animal could be smelled. One of the king's ministers was sent to adjudicate, and he and the village headman set out to decide the boundaries. The smell of the horse could be detected over a huge area. The lines were duly drawn and the minister departed. At this point, the devious village headman took out from under his clothes the piece of rotting horse meat with which he had fooled the minister. The limits of the village lands are still the ones set at that time, and cover more than ten square kilometres.

information on p.74). During the month-long Usaba Sambah festival, generally in May and June, a massive wooden swing, like a giant Ferris wheel, is set up by the young men of the village for the young girls to swing on. You may also see the *perang padan* or *mekare-kare*, a fight between combatants armed with shields of woven bamboo and weapons made of the thorny pandanus leaves.

Tenganan crafts

The most famous product of Tenganan is **gringsing** or double *ikat* (see p.458), a highly valued, brown, deep-red, blue-black and tan cloth, which Bhatara Indra, the god of creation, supposedly taught the women of Tenganan to weave. It can take many years to make one piece, and it is prized throughout Bali, as protection against evil. Many religious ceremonies require the use of the cloth, including tooth-filing (see p.463) and cremation.

In recent years, **basketwork** from *ata* grass has become another distinctive product of the village. This is an ancient skill, but since the 1980s it has become more commercial produced for export and sale throughout Bali. It can take a month to produce a basket: the grass is split and woven, boiled to tighten the weave, dried for up to a week and then smoked for three days over an open fire, turning every three hours, to give it its glossy, golden finish. You can see all the stages at I Nyoman Uking's Ata Shop (☏0363/41121) in the right-hand section of the village, the *banjar pande*. There's a small sign outside and Nyoman speaks English.

Traditional calligraphy is another attractive product of the village. Calendars and pictorial representations of traditional stories are incised on narrow lengths of *lontar* palm, which are then strung together to create a small hanging. Compare several, and it soon becomes easy to spot the most skilful work.

If you don't want to explore the workshops in the village, there is a good selection of **stalls** in the car park just outside the village gate selling well-made crafts.

Padang Bai

Deriving from two languages – *padang* is Balinese for grass and *bai* is Dutch for bay – **PADANG BAI**, the port for Lombok, nestles in a white sand cove crowded with fishing boats. It has developed into a small, laid-back resort. Ferries and tourist boats run regularly to **Lombok**; the jetty, Perama office, ferry office and car park are all at the western end of the bay, from where everything is within easy walking distance.

Arrival and transport

Bemos and **minibuses** arrive at and depart from the port entrance. Bemos serve Amlapura (via Candi Dasa) and Semarapura (also known as Klungkung) and minibuses serve Amlapura and Batubulan. Plenty of counters along the seafront offer tourist information, but these are commercial set ups; the nearest government tourist office is in Candi Dasa (see p.243). The ticket office for **Nusa Penida** is a little way east of the port; from 7am onwards, boats leave from the beach, when they're full, for Buyuk Harbour (Rp17,000) and there is a regular 1.30pm ferry from the ferry terminal, where the tickets are sold.

Perama **tourist shuttle buses** operate from their office (daily 7am–7pm; ⊕0363/41419) near the jetty (see "Travel details", p.271). Sample prices are Rp40,000 between Padang Bai and Ubud, Kuta or Sanur and Rp100,000 between Padang Bai and Lovina. There are plenty of other shuttle services advertised throughout the resort. Fixed-price taxis serve Padang Bai from Ngurah Rai Airport (Rp280,000; 2hr). There's a **post office** near the port entrance and **warung telkom** on the seafront (daily 7am–10pm). **Internet** services are widely available (Rp300 per min) but connection can be slow. Many seafront restaurants **change money**, and there's a BRI bank with an ATM. **Car rental** (Rp150,000 per day for a Suzuki Jimney, Rp200,000 for a Kijang) and **motorbike rental** (Rp50,000 daily) are easy to arrange; ask at your accommodation or any of the seafront tourist counters. The **police** post is by the port entrance.

Accommodation

A wide choice of **accommodation** is available in the village and along the road behind the beach. Watch out for renovations and new places as things move upmarket. Being near the beach has obvious attractions but upstairs rooms in the village accommodation, especially up on the hill, catch the breeze and have fine views. Downstairs rooms are cheaper but darker.

Bagus Inn ☎0363/41398. A good budget choice offering small rooms with attached bathroom in a friendly family compound. Plusher rooms are being added. **❶**

Darma ☎0363/41394. A clean family set-up in the village; a/c and hot water are available. **❶–❸**

🏃 **Kembar Inn** ☎0363/41364. Spotless tiled place in the village with plenty of sitting areas and a buffet breakfast. There's a/c and hot water in the more expensive rooms. **❶–❹**

Kerti Beach Inn ☎0363/41391, ✉kertibeachinn @yahoo.co.in. Near the beach; accommodation is in bungalows and two-storey *lumbung*-style bamboo-and-thatch barns. **❶**

Made Homestay ☎0363/41441, ✉mades_padangbai@hotmail.com. Clean, tiled rooms with fan and attached cold-water bathrooms in a two-storey block in a small compound, convenient for both the beach and the village. **❶**

Marco Inn ☎0813/3785 4486. Eight simple rooms set around a pretty little garden plus a kitchen and DVD/video room for the use of guests. **❶**

Padang Bai Billabong ☎0363/41399. Cheap-as-chips budget place without much style, but rooms are located in a wild garden near the beach. **❶**

Parta ☎0363/41475. Pleasant, clean village place offering some hot water and a/c, with a great communal sitting area on the top floor. **❶–❹**

Puri Rai ☎0363/41385, ⊛www.puriraihotel.com. Most upmarket place in town with large, tiled rooms with hot water and fan or a/c. Best rooms overlook the pool. **❹–❺**

🏃 **Serangan Inn II** ☎0363/41425. Spotless place built at the top of the village with good views. Catches the breeze, and there's a/c and hot water in the pricier rooms. **❶–❹**

The beaches

If you find the main beach too busy, head for the smaller, quieter bay of **Bias Tugal** (also known as Pantai Kecil), to the west. It has just a few tiny *warung*, although things may well change here as a five-star hotel has been planned. Follow the road past the post office and, just as it begins to climb, take the roadway to the left.

Alternatively, head east over the headland and take the left fork a couple of hundred yards beyond *Topi Inn* to the small, white cove of **Blue Lagoon**. *Warung Blue Lagoon* and *Shanthi Warung* provide shade and refreshment, rent out sun loungers and snorkelling gear and have showers. New construction is also underway over this side, but it's smaller scale.

It's possible to arrange **fishing** trips from Padang Bai; you'll be approached on the beach about this, or ask at your guesthouse. Beach **massages** are widely available (Rp30–40,000 per hour).

Temples

To the east of Padang Bai, the paved road around the bay climbs up to the headland, topped with three temples: **Pura Silayukti**, **Pura Telagamas** and

---

Moving on to Lombok

The following operate from Padang Bai. See p.356 for other routes to Lombok.

Ferry Every 90min; takes 4hr–4hr 30min. Rp24,000 with an extra charge for bicycles (Rp35,000), motorbikes (Rp5000) and cars (from Rp498,000). See p.39 for information on taking rental vehicles between the islands.

Tourist boat Perama operate a daily boat (with two days maintenance each month so check the schedule) at 1.30pm direct to the Gili Islands (4hr; Rp200,000) and on to Senggigi (5hr; Rp215,000).

Speed boat *Gili Cat* (Rp660,000; 2hr 30min) ☎0361/271680, ⊛www.gilicat.com or book at *Made Restaurant* at the front of *Made Homestay*.

Tourist buses Perama and other operators advertise throughout the resort and use the public ferry to Lembar, then tourist bus.

Pura Tanjunsari. They have links with the eleventh-century priests Empu Kuturan and his brother, Empu Bharadah, who was involved with the early history of Besakih (see p.237) and the defeat of the evil witch, Rangda (see box, p.226).

Eating and drinking

Seafood is the speciality in Padang Bai **restaurants**, with mahi mahi, barracuda, snapper and prawns on offer, depending on the catch, alongside the usual traveller's fare. Places tend to stop serving early, especially outside the busy months so it's best to start eating by about nine. *Padang Bai Café*, on the seafront, more than lives up to its promise of "The best seafood in town" and with main meals at Rp25–30,000, it's a catch. The shady café at *Topi Inn* has a menu several centimetres thick and great bread, cakes, coffee and a ton of imaginative vegetarian dishes supplement the more usual Western and Indonesian meals (mains Rp23–38,000 and baguettes from Rp18,000). Fill up water bottles here for Rp1000. The classiest dining experience in Padang Bai is at *Omang Omang*, which has a small menu of extremely well-cooked Western, Indonesian and Balinese food including splendid ice cream and desserts (mains mostly Rp28–59,000). For a more unusual, but tasty, concept *Ali in Bali* is an Arabic lounge-bar with just two items on the menu: a Dutch breakfast (Rp25,000) and Shoearma Doner Kebab (Rp29,000), spicy meat in tasty bread with sauces on the side. The bonus here is excellent views across to the beach. The long-standing *Ozone* in the village serves up philosophical sayings on the menu and walls alongside the usual fare; main courses are about Rp28,000, and you can also refill water bottles here.

Courses and workshops

If the appeal of sea, sun and sand falters, *Topi Inn* (⊤0363/41424, ⓦwww.topiinn.com) organize an enormous range of cultural and artistic workshops

---

Snorkelling and diving at Padang Bai

Several places in Padang Bai rent **snorkelling** equipment (Rp20,000 per day); the water in the bay is surprisingly clear, although the best snorkelling is at Blue Lagoon where you can snorkel off the beach, or you can charter a boat from Padang Bai to take you around the headland.

There are several **dive operations** in Padang Bai. The most experienced are Geko Dive (⊤0363/41516, ⓦwww.gekodive.com) and Water Worx (⊤0363/41220, ⓦwww.waterworxbali.com), both on the seafront. They offer the full range of PADI courses (in several languages), dives for experienced divers, both locally and further afield, and the Discover Scuba introductory day. Prices range from $40–50 for two dives in the Padang Bai area up to $80–90 for dives at the most distant locations such as Gili Selang or Nusa Penida and with prices in between for Candi Dasa, Amed and Tulamben. The PADI Open Water course is $300–320, the PADI Advanced Open Water course $225–250 and instruction up to Divemaster level is available. Both welcome approaches by email and can arrange airport transfers and offer advice on accommodation; combined diving/accommodation packages are also available. See p.51 for general advice on selecting a dive operator.

There are several dive sites at **Blue Lagoon**, around and beyond the headland to the east of the bay and plenty of hard and soft coral, including elephant and table corals – which attract eels, wrasses, turtles, flatheads and lion fish – plus there's a good chance of spotting sharks. There are plenty of species you won't see elsewhere in Bali; Spanish Dancers are frequently spotted on night dives. The operators in Padang Bai are also adept at finding *mola mola*.

(€8–€10 per person, minimum two people) including batik, *ikat*, basket weaving, Balinese dance, sculpture, cooking, *wayang kulit* and, if it all gets a bit much, coconut-tree climbing, among many others.

Nightlife

Padang Bai is a laid-back place and the **nightlife** is equally relaxed. *Babylon Reggae Bar* is a perennial favourite and *Zen Bar* offers friendly staff, a huge screen and an almost unbelievably eclectic range of music videos in attractive surroundings. *Omang Omang* also has regular live music and is hugely popular.

Goa Lawah and Kusamba

Near the coast 7km west of Padang Bai, **Goa Lawah** (Bat Cave; daily 8am–6pm; Rp10,000 including sarong rental; parking Rp1000) is a major tourist draw. The **temple**, probably founded by Empu Kuturan in 1007, is small but much revered by the Balinese, being one of the island's nine directional temples (see p.431); this one is dedicated to the southeast. The highlight is the **cave** at the base of the cliff, which heaves with fruit bats. The cave is supposedly the start of a tunnel that stretches 30km inland to Pura Goa in Besakih and is said to contain the cosmic *naga* Basuki. If you engage a local guide to show you round, establish the fee beforehand; Rp20,000 is reasonable.

Some 3km further west, the farming, fishing and salt-producing village of **KUSAMBA** spreads about 2km along the beach (see box, p.404, for more on salt production in Bali). From Kusamba, it's 17km east to Candi Dasa.

East of Candi Dasa

The area **east of Candi Dasa** offers lush rice terraces just a few kilometres from parched landscapes. The central volcanic mass of the island, most apparent in the awesome bulk of Gunung Agung, extends down to the gentler slopes of Gunung Lempuyang and Seraya at the far eastern end of the island, with settlements and roads clinging to the coast or the valleys.

The main road beyond Candi Dasa cuts inland, passing close to sleepy **Amlapura**, before climbing to **Tirtagangga**, crossing the hills to the north coast and continuing on the long coastal strip to Singaraja, via Tulamben, the main diving Mecca on Bali. You can follow this route by public transport, but to explore the countryside around **Iseh** and **Sidemen**, you'll need your own transport. The accommodation along the lengthy stretch of coast known as **Amed** is accessible on public transport, although with your own transport you'll have more opportunity to explore this burgeoning area more fully.

Amlapura

Formerly known as Karangasem, **AMLAPURA**, 40km east of Klungkung, was renamed after the 1963 eruption of Gunung Agung, when the outskirts of the town were flattened by the lava flow. (Balinese people sometimes change their names after serious illness in the belief that it will bring about a change of fortune.) A remote district capital, its relaxed atmosphere makes it a pleasant place for a day-trip but a visit to all the sights, **Puri Agung Karangasem**, **Puri Gede** and **Taman Sukasada** doesn't take long.

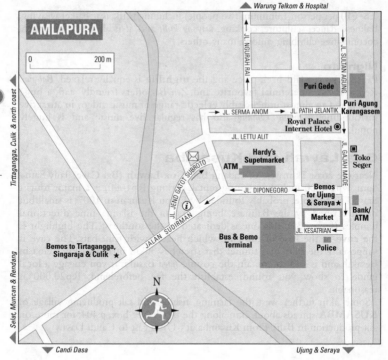

Some history

For much of its history, the far eastern **regency of Karangasem** was involved
with Lombok, only 35km across the Lombok Strait. Initially under the
authority of the *dewa agung* of Klungkung, Karangasem gradually developed its
independence and, during the late seventeenth century, wrested control of
Lombok from Muslim Sulawesi. Four Hindu rajas were installed to rule over
the Sasak population, but ended up fighting among themselves. In 1849, the raja
of Lombok, seeking to even old scores, provided four thousand troops to help
the Dutch in their attack against Karangasem (see p.419). The Lombok troops
ambushed and killed **Jelantik**, the hero of the Buleleng military, and the raja of
Karangasem and his family committed *puputan*. The raja of Lombok was
rewarded with the Karangasem regency, which he ruled from 1849 to 1893.
Following a series of adventures in Bali and Lombok, the colourful **Gusti Gede
Jelantik** was appointed as Dutch regent in 1894 and ruled until 1902,
succeeded by his son, Anak Agung Gede Jelantik. His descendants still occupy
palaces in Amlapura.

Puri Agung Karangasem and Puri Gede

Built at the end of the nineteenth century by the king of Karangasem, Anak
Agung Gede Jelantik, **Puri Agung Karangasem** (8am–5pm; admission by
donation, minimum Rp5000) has been undergoing renovation. Areas open to the
public at the time of writing include the **Maskerdam building**, a corruption of
the name "Amsterdam", as a tribute to the Dutch and the place where important
guests were received and now decorated with old photographs and paintings; the
Bale Kambang, formerly used for meetings, dancing and dining, which rises

from the middle of a pond and the **Bale Pewedaan**, scene of royal ceremonies including tooth filing. **Puri Gede** just across the road is also open to the public on a more informal basis; the caretaker will show you around. The palaces are a way to while away an hour or so in Amlapura but not worth a special journey.

Taman Sukasada

Situated at **Ujung**, 5km south of Amlapura, **Taman Sukasada** (7am–6pm; Rp10,000) is the largest, if not the most picturesque, of the three water palaces built by the last raja of Karangasem, Anak Agung Anglurah. It was built in 1921. Bemos run from Amlapura (see map). Recent renovations have re-created lakes, pavilions and statues in attractive gardens – there's a small *warung* inside. From Ujung the main road heads to Seraya and on to Amed (see p.262).

Practicalities

Public transport heading for Amlapura terminal completes a circle around the top of town, passing the **warung telkom** (7am–10pm) and **hospital** on the way up Jalan Ngurah Rai and Puri Agung Karangasem and Puri Gede on the way down. The **post office** is at Jalan Jend Gatot Subroto 25. **Exchange** facilities are at BRI on Jalan Gajah Made and there are international **ATMs** here and at the Hardy's shopping centre.

In the afternoon, Amlapura dies quickly so it's best to travel early as transport becomes very infrequent the later you leave. **Bemos** from the terminal serve Candi Dasa and Padang Bai (orange) and Selat, Muncan and Rendang (green). Bemos for Ujung and, occasionally, Seraya (blue) leave from the southern end of Jalan Gajah Made not far from the terminal. There are also **buses** and **minibuses** north to Singaraja, with some on to Gilimanuk. Bemos to Culik and Tianyar via Tirtagangga leave from the turn-off on the outskirts of town, as do dark red minibuses to Singaraja. This turning is marked by a huge black-and-white pinnacle, a monument to the fight for independence, which is adorned with a Garuda.

The **tourist office** is at Jalan Diponegoro 46 (Mon–Thurs 7am–3pm, Fri 7am–noon; ☎0363/21196), but they get very few callers. The **police** post is in the market on Jalan Kesatrian.

Most people stop off in Amlapura for a couple of hours on their way elsewhere. However, there is **accommodation** on Jalan Gajah Made at *The Royal Palace Internet Hotel* (☎0363/23246, ✉theroyalpalaceinternethotel@yahoo.com; ❸) which has cold-water fan rooms, in a small compound just south of Puri Gede. For **food**, *Toko Seger* further south on Jalan Gajah Made serves a small selection of inexpensive Indonesian dishes (from Rp10,000) and there are also *warung* near the market. Hardy's **shopping** centre is on Jalan Diponegoro.

Tirtagangga and around

Some 6km northwest of Amlapura, **TIRTAGANGGA**'s draws are its gorgeous Water Palace, its cool climate, and the surrounding ricefields and mountains. Treks to suit all levels of fitness and enthusiasm are easy to arrange and there is plenty of accommodation. Tirtagangga is served by **minibuses** and **buses** plying between Amlapura and Singaraja, and by Perama charters from Candi Dasa (Rp75,000 per person for a minimum of two people). See "Travel details", p.271, for more.

There are **moneychangers** in the village but rates are better in Candi Dasa and the nearest international **ATM** is in Amlapura (see above). There's a **warung telkom** (6am–9pm) next to the parking area and a **postal agent** on the track to the Water Palace from the main road.

TIRTAGANGGA

N

0 — 200 m

RESTAURANTS	
Good Karma	1
Puri Sawah	C
Tirta Ayu	D

ACCOMMODATION	
Cabé Bali	G
Dhangin Taman Inn	E
Kusumajaya Inn	B
Puri Prima	A
Puri Sawah	C
Rijasa	F
Tirta Ayu	D

Water Palace

Genta Bali Warung

▼ Temega, Amlapura & Ⓖ

Accommodation

All the **accommodation** listed is keyed on the map but it's also worth considering staying in the village of **Ababi** (see below). It's around 2km from Tirtagangga by road, but there are footpaths down to Tirtagangga in twenty minutes or less.

Cabé Bali ☎0363/22045, ⓦwww
.cabebali.com. Fabulous, characterful
accommodation offering tasteful bungalows, all
with hot water, in lovely gardens surrounded by
fields. There's a relaxed atmosphere, excellent,
friendly service and a swimming pool. Accessed
from Temega – about 1.5km south of Tirtagangga.
Look out for the sign opposite the market; it's
500m along a rough road into the paddy-fields. Ⓖ

Dhangin Taman Inn ☎0363/22059. Close to the
Water Palace with a good sitting area overlooking
the pools, this place has some decent rooms in a
cosy compound. ❶–❷

Good Karma ☎0363/22445. Clean, tiled rooms
set in a small garden in the paddy-fields. Enquire
at the restaurant of the same name close to the
main parking area. ❸

Kusumajaya Inn ☎0363/21250, ⓔjaya.ttrg
@yahoo.co.id. About 300m north of the centre of
Tirtagangga, on a hill; it's a climb of 98 steps to
reach the clean, tiled, cold-water bungalows from
the road. All have verandahs that make the most of
the splendid ricefield views. ❶–❷

Puri Prima ☎0363/21316. About 500m north of
the *Kusumajaya Inn*, most rooms have cold water
(one has hot) but all offer great views of Gunung
Lempuyang from the verandahs. Road noise can be
a bit intrusive as trucks labour up the road below.
❶–❹

Puri Sawah ☎0363/21847. Just 100m beyond
the Water Palace, on a track heading left from a
sharp turn in the main road. There are four rooms
with verandahs in a small, peaceful garden in a
lovely location among the fields. One room has hot
water. ❸–❹

Rijasa ☎0363/21873. Across the main road from
the track leading to the Water Palace, this is a
good-value, centrally located place with a neat row
of straightforward bungalows in an attractive
garden. ❶–❷

Tirta Ayu ☎0363/22503, ⓦwww
.hoteltirtagangga.com. Overlooking the Water
Palace, there are four large, luxurious bungalows
all with hot water, television, room safe and
attractive furnishings. ❽–❾

Ababi

North of Tirtagangga, the small, cool village of **ABABI** has plenty of **accommodation**, which is reached along a left-hand turn signed from the main road just over 1km from Tirtagangga. About 600m along this side road, another left onto a track leads 200m to the hidden *Geria Semalung* (☎0363/22116, ⓦwww
.geriasemalung.com; ❹), with four clean, tiled bungalows with hot water in a

great garden with stunning views. There's a small restaurant, **guides** are available for local treks (Rp25,000 per person per hour) and for Gunung Agung climbs ($120 for one or two people including transport). From here, it's about twenty minutes along footpaths to Tirtagangga.

Another 200m further along the road, another track to the left leads to two more places. Taking the left fork when the track divides brings you to ✷ *Pondok Batur Indah* (☎0363/22342; ❷), with four large, clean, tiled rooms with hot water in a small family compound with fine views to Gunung Lempuyang and Seraya. It's about fifteen minutes' walk down to Tirtagangga. Gede Wangsa is the trekking guide here and he offers short (2hr) and long (4hr) local treks for Rp50,000 and Rp70,000 per person. Telephone to arrange a pick-up in Tirtagangga. The right fork in the track brings you to *Pondok Lembah Dukuh* (☎0813/3829 5142, ❶–❹) with good-value rooms on the hill and in the ricefields below. Hot water is available. There are equally lovely views here, a short walk from Tirtagangga. Local trekking is available (Rp17,000 per person per hour) and Gunung Agung climbs can be arranged (Rp700,000 for two people including transport).

The Water Palace

Tirtagangga's **Water Palace** (daily 7am–7pm; Rp5000; ⓦ www.tirtagangga .com) was built in 1946 by Anak Agung Anglurah, the last raja of Karangasem, and is the finest manifestation of his obsession with pools, moats and fountains. It is an impressive terraced garden featuring glorious pools, water channels and fountains. Check the website for historic photographs and information, plus details of the restoration. You can swim in the upper, deeper pool (Rp6000) or a lower, shallower pool (Rp4000).

Trekking and recovering

It seems that every person in Tirtagangga is now a **trekking** guide. Go by personal recommendation or ask at your accommodation. One well-established guide is Komang Gede Sutama (contact him through *Good Karma* restaurant ☎0363/22445; see "Eating"), who offers two-hour as well as four- to five-hour walks (Rp25,000 per person per hour) as well as treks from Tirtagangga to Tenganan, to Amed via Pura Lempuyang and Gunung Seraya, and up Gunung Agung. Nyoman Budiarsa's shop at *Genta Bali Warung* (☎0363/22436) on the main road sells a **map** of local walks (Rp3000) and can arrange **guides** for local walking trips (Rp20,000 per person per hour) plus climbs up Gunung Agung.

It's all very well hauling your body up hill and down dale for several hours but if you are unused to exercise and suffer from some aches and pains the next day consider a **massage**; Tungtang from Ababi is highly recommended (☎0812/392 6321) at Rp70,000 per hour.

Eating

The **restaurants** below offer good-value food in pleasant surroundings. The *Rice Terrace Coffee Shop* attached to *Puri Sawah* is one of the quietest spots in the village and has excellent baguettes, salads, stuffed baked potatoes and all the usual Indonesian favouites with plenty of vegetarian choices (around Rp28,000 for a main course). And they also serve the best apple crumble in eastern Bali. Above the car park, the *Good Karma* restaurant has a relaxed atmosphere and a big tourist menu (mains Rp18–25,000). The location of the restaurant at *Tirta Ayu*, within the Water Palace grounds and looking down across the gardens and pools, is excellent as is the food from the vast menu including pizza (Rp30–55,000), sandwiches (Rp45,000) and salads

(Rp40,000). They are the only place serving wine in Tirtagangga (Rp50,000 per glass).

Pura Lempuyang Luhur

One of the *kayangan jagat* or directional temples of Bali (see p.431), giving protection from the east, **Pura Lempuyang Luhur** gleams white on the slopes of Gunung Lempuyang. It is among the most sacred temples on the island and offers some of the best views in Bali. Access is from Abang, north of Tirtagangga and the car park is 8km off the main road. Festival days are the best time to visit (see "Basics", p.74, for sources of information on festival dates) when the 1700 steps up to the temple swarm with worshippers, and extra public **bemos** run almost all the way to the temple. On other days, bemos only run from Abang to **NGIS TISTA**, about 2km off the main road.

It's a two-hour climb up the staircase to the temple, which is believed to be the dwelling place of the god Genijaya (Victorious Fire) but the view of Gunung Agung, perfectly framed in the *candi bentar*, makes it all worthwhile. The **courtyard** contains a stand of bamboo, and on festival days the priest makes a cut in the bamboo to release holy water. From the temple, a ninety-minute climb up another staircase brings you to the **summit** of Gunung Lempuyang, where there's another temple and even more spectacular views. The day after Galungan (see p.47) is the most popular time for local people to make a pilgrimage here.

The Amlapura–Rendang road

From Amlapura, a **picturesque road** heads about 32km west through Sibetan and Muncan, joining the main Semarapura–Penelokan road 14km north of Semarapura at Rendang. Public **bemos** ply the Amlapura–Rendang route, but without **private transport** the highlights of this area – Pura Pasar Agung above Selat and the rice terrace views around Iseh and Sidemen – are inaccesible.

Bebandem and westwards

Heading west from Amlapura, the city soon gives way to fields and, on clear days, the towering bulk of Gunung Agung appears startlingly close. About 9km west of Amlapura, the village of **BEBANDEM** holds a large cattle market every three days. Two kilometres west of Bebandem there's a sign off the main road to Desa Jungutan; an excursion along here brings you to **Tirta Telaga Tista** at **JUNGUTAN**, one of the water palaces built by the last raja of Karangasem. It's an artificial lake fed by a freshwater spring and was never as grand as Tirtagangga or Ujung. It hasn't been renovated but it's a quiet spot surrounded by ricefields.

Continuing west with excellent views of Gunung Agung along the way, the main road heads through **SIBETAN**, the *salak* centre of Bali. *Salak*, or snakeskin fruit, has a brown scaly skin hiding a crisp flesh with a fragrant apple flavour. There are supposedly fourteen different varieties of the fruit – all of which are identical to the untutored eye. It grows on an aggressively prickly palm about 3m high, usually planted among coconuts for shade; the main season is January to February. There are no tourist facilities here but visits can be arranged through JED, Village Ecotourism Network (☏0361/735320, ⓦwww.jed.or.id).

The small village of **PESANGKAN**, 9km west of Sibetan, bursts into activity every three days (even more so during the *salak* season) with its local market from 6–10am. A side road heads 1500m south to *Pondok Bukit Putung*, also known as *Hilltop*, which seems to lose all signs pointing out the route, but has brilliant views down to the coast from its **restaurant** terrace, where reasonably priced food (main courses Rp15–25,000) and drinks are available. Continuing past the restaurant a narrow road with glorious views winds 7km down through the villages of Bakung and Manggis to the main Candi Dasa–Semarapura road with gorgeous views of the entire area. Check the condition of the road locally before setting off, as it's sometimes impassable. There are no bemos, but ojek (Rp15–20,000) wait at the junction of this road with the main Candi Dasa road. For an excellent day-trip from Candi Dasa either get public transport around to Pesangkan via Amlapura and then walk down to the main Candi Dasa road or get an ojek up to *Pondok Bukit Putung* and walk back down.

Selat and around

A further kilometre west from Pesangkan, *Warung Makan Wayan* (10am–10pm) is an unmissable **refreshment** stop; Wayan is a larger than life character who serves Indonesian food (main courses Rp15–20,000) that is renowned among local people and visitors. The tables at the back have lovely rice terrace views.

Between one and two kilometres west the small village of **SELAT** marks the turn-off to **Pura Pasar Agung**, one of the nine directional temples of Bali. The temple was destroyed by the 1963 eruption of Gunung Agung and has been rebuilt. The road to the temple is an ear-poppingly steep climb ten kilometres through bamboo stands and acacia forests, in countryside scored by deep lava-carved gorges. From the car park, more than 330 concrete steps lead up to the temple. Rising in three terraces to the inner courtyard, it's impressive and dramatic, perched at 1200m on the slopes of Gunung Agung, and it is the starting-point for one of the routes up the mountain (see p.241). Officially only worshippers may enter the temple but on a quiet day, if you bring a sarong and sash you may be permitted to enter. Even if you're not going in or climbing Agung, hike to the entrance, it's an atmospheric spot with fabulous views.

There is basic **accommodation** at *Pondok Wisata Puri Agung* (T& F0366/23037; ❷–❸), on the east side of Selat just after the post office. This is the closest accommodation to Pura Pasar Agung if you are intending to climb Gunung Agung although the climb is easy to arrange from further away (see p.242). They offer ricefield **trekking** (Rp50,000–75,000 per person for two to three hours) and **climbs** up Gunung Agung (Rp350,000 for two people, Rp450,000 for three to four not including transport to Pura Pasar Agung, which is currently Rp125,000 for the return trip to the temple).

Iseh and Sidemen

From **DUDA**, just east of Selat, a beautiful road heads south through Iseh and Sidemen to Semarapura with ricefield views that are among the loveliest in Bali.

Artists Walter Spies (see p.192) and Theo Meier both lived in **ISEH** for some time, and Anna Mathews wrote her evocative *Night of Purnama* about her life in the village before and during the 1963 eruption of Gunung Agung.

Three kilometres south, **SIDEMEN** is a beautiful base to experience rural Bali, with extensive footpaths through the surrounding countryside. You can watch **endek-weaving** on foot looms at the *Pelangi* workshop (8am–5pm) in the centre of the village while the tiny shop opposite produces traditional **lontar-palm** paintings. If you want **to stay** in the area, a signed turning close to *Pelangi* leads to accommodation out in the ricefields. The road forks after 500m; 100m along the right-hand turn is *Pondok Wisata Lihat Sawah* (T0366/24183, Elihatsawah@yahoo.co.id; ❹–❺), an excellent place to stay with clean, tiled bungalows with great ricefield views – hot water is available. They arrange trekking guides for Rp35,000 per hour, give all guests a local map so they can head off independently, have Internet access (Rp12,000 per hour) and rent out motorcycles (Rp60,000 per day). The same owner has several houses along the other fork in the road offering accommodation: *Kubu Tani*, *Pondok Soria Moria* and *Abian Ayu* (③–④). All are well-built, clean and comfortable, have hot-water bathrooms, and take full advantage of the rice terrace views. Some have kitchen facilities.

Also along the left fork in the road from Sidemen, after 700m there's *Tanto Villa* (☎0812/395 0271, ⓦwww.tanto_villa.com; ④–⑤). The four rooms in the house are big, bright and well furnished, and boast private balconies. The attached *Kafé Ketut* offers a small Indo-Chinese and Western menu with mains Rp25–32,000. Another 600m along the road brings you to the *Nirarta Centre for Living Awareness* (☎0366/24122, ⓦwww.awareness-bali.com; ④–⑥), set up by psychologist Peter Wrycza. The accommodation is used by groups for courses but individual retreats are also available. Visit the website to read about the philosophical and spiritual base of the centre. The attached **restaurant** is semi-vegetarian (serving chicken and fish) and guests may join in the twice-daily Awareness Meditation sessions if they wish. Just opposite, the new *Uma Agung* (☎0363/41672, ⓦwww.umagung.com; ④) is another excellent choice. Bungalows are well-furnished and have hot water and lovely views. There's a small attached restaurant, and a spa is planned.

From Sidemen the road drops down another ten kilometres to Paksabali on the main Semarapura–Kusamba road.

Muncan and Rendang

About 4km west of Selat along the Amlapura–Rendang road, **MUNCAN** is a quiet little village and another possible base for climbing Gunung Agung (see p.241). West of Muncan, the valleys become narrower and deeper; the River Telaga Waja is used by Sobek rafting company (see ⓦwww.99bali.com /adventure/sobek). A further 4km west at the attractive village of **RENDANG**, the route joins the main Klungkung–Penelokan road, and there are bemos to Menanga for Besakih (see p.237). The new *Mahagiri* (☎0812/381 4775, ⒺMahagiri@yahoo.com; ⑤) has extremely attractive bungalows with hot-water bathrooms in a location to die for, looking straight across a stunning valley filled with rice terraces to Gunung Agung. Follow the signs from Menanga or from Rendang turn north alongside the football field. If you haven't time to stay, a lunch or drink stop is highly recommended.

Amed

The stretch of coast in the **far east of Bali** from Culik to Aas is known throughout Bali as **Amed** although this is the name of just one village in an area of peaceful bays, clear waters and stunning coastal views. Accommodation is spread along an eleven-kilometre stretch from Amed to Aas and, although it's developing fast, it's an ideal area for a peaceful few days of sunbathing, snorkelling and diving. Accommodation is mushrooming quickly as word spreads about the glorious coastline, peace and quiet and underwater attractions, and there's a great selection of excellent-value places to stay from classy hotels to budget backpacker bungalows. Lipah and Bunutan are the most developed areas, though even these remain quiet and low-key. The **beaches** are largely stoney and you'll share them with plenty of local boats (*jukung*) but it is the coral reefs and offshore wrecks that make this a great centre for divers and snorkellers.

Arrival and transport

Access to Amed is from **CULIK**, just over 9km northeast of Tirtagangga. All public transport between Amlapura and Singaraja passes through Culik.

Transport along the Amed coast, though, is slim. From Culik, **bemos** run via Amed to Aas in the morning; hard bargaining should get a fare of around Rp25,000 to Lipah Beach or use an ojek (Rp30,000 to Lipah Beach). Later in the day you'll need to use an ojek or charter a bemo (aim for about Rp25,000 per person for the charter). You can also use a Perama charter service from Candi Dasa (Rp75,000 per person, minimum two people). Staff at your accommodation can help arrange transport for your return or book Perama by ringing Candi Dasa or using the shuttle bus from *Amed Café* (✆0363/23473) near Jemeluk (three daily departures with destinations including Padang Bai €5, Ubud €10, the southern resorts plus the airport €10–15 and Lovina €12).

For the section from Aas south to Seraya you'll need your own vehicle. There are no **ATMs** (the closest is in Amlapura), but there are a few **money-changers** (Lipah, Bunutan and Jemeluk) offering poor rates – bring plenty of cash as very few hotels accept credit cards. There's no **post office**. There are a few **warung telkom** with **Internet** access (a warung telkom in Lipah, *Apa Kabar* in Bunutan and *Amed Café* near Jemeluk) but connection times are slow. Ask at your accommodation if you want to rent a **motorcycle** or *Amed Café* has them for Rp50,000 a day; they also have **bicycles** for Rp35,000 a day, but the gradients over some of the headlands are a bit extreme.

The coast

The first village after leaving Culik is **Amed**, 3km away, where life centres on fishing and salt production, which you can see at close quarters. A kilometre east is the hamlet of **Congkang** where salt has given way to fishing, and then **Jemeluk**, 6km from Culik, the diving focus of the area, with as much traffic during the day as you'll find anywhere along the coast as divers and snorkellers flock to the reef just offshore. From here it's over headland after headland to the villages of **Bunutan** and **Lipah Beach** both with plenty of accommodation and on to **Lean Beach**, **Selang**, **Ibus**, **Banyuning** and eventually **Aas** almost 15km from Culik.

Continuing around the coast from Aas, the country east and south of the mountains is too dry to grow rice and the only crops are peanuts, soya beans and corn, grown in the wet season. The scenery is dramatic, with hills sweeping up for hundreds of metres from the coast. The road turns inland at **Kusambi** about 4km from Aas and marked by a massive beacon. This is the most easterly point of Bali – on clear days Lombok is visible, 35km across the strait. Another 14km further on, the small market-town of **Seraya** features a grand temple dominated by the looming Gunung Seraya. From here the road heads down to the coast, where colourful boats line the beach. There is accommodation 4km southwest of Seraya from where it's just over a kilometre on to **Ujung**, 5km south of Amlapura (see p.257).

The entire **coastal route** from Culik around to Amlapura is about 45km. It's a lovely trip, winding in and out of the hills, but isn't something to try at night; motorcyclists should beware of some of the drops beside the road. Check the condition of the road before setting off from either direction.

Accommodation and eating

There is excellent **accommodation** around the coast to suit every budget and taste. Most have their own **restaurants** but there are plenty of dining options here, and the quality of food is high. All are keyed on the map.

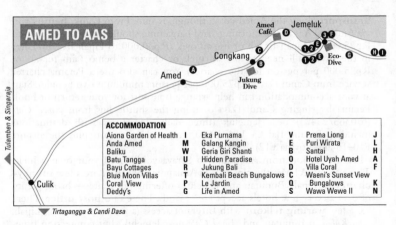

AMED TO AAS

Amed Café, Jemeluk, Congkang, Amed, Jungkung Dive, Eco-Dive

Tulamben & Singaraja

ACCOMMODATION

Aiona Garden of Health	I	Eka Purnama	V	Prema Liong	J
Anda Amed	M	Galang Kangin	E	Puri Wirata	L
Baliku	W	Geria Giri Shanti	B	Santai	H
Batu Tangga	U	Hidden Paradise	O	Hotel Uyah Amed	A
Bayu Cottages	R	Jukung Bali	D	Villa Coral	F
Blue Moon Villas	T	Kembali Beach Bungalows	C	Waeni's Sunset View	
Coral View	P	Le Jardin	Q	Bungalows	K
Deddy's	G	Life in Amed	S	Wawa Wewe II	N

Culik

▼ Tirtagangga & Candi Dasa

Amed, Congkang and Jemeluk

The villages of **AMED**, **CONGKANG** and **JEMELUK** all offer plenty of great accommodation in a prime location just behind the beach, but there are some excellent-value places across the road, just a couple of minutes' walk from the water.

This is a decent area for tourist facilities; there are several moneychangers in Jemeluk although rates are poor, the *Amed Café* (☎0363/23473, ⓦwww .amedcafe.com) has Internet access (7am–9pm; Rp500 per minute) and a supermarket, and operates shuttle buses.

At the far eastern end of the bay the neighbouring beachside restaurants *Villa Coral* and *Blue Star Café* are quiet, shady spots to hang out – both with the usual menus. The speciality, *ikan pepes bakar*, is recommended at the *Divers Café*. Nearby, *Sama-Sama* is also relaxed and friendly and right by the beach. *Café Garam*, attached to *Hotel Uyah Amed*, hosts Balinese dance/music every Wednesday and Saturday.

Eco-Dive ☎0363/23482, ⓦwww.ecodivebali.com. Basic bamboo-and-thatch rooms behind the dive shop. Hardened backpackers will relish the limited comfort, as well as the cheapest rooms in Amed. The dive shop is moving in 2009 so these rooms may not survive. ①

Galang Kangin ☎0363/23480. Extremely clean, good-value rooms in a two-storey block on the beach side of the road, all with lovely sea views, and cottages in a garden across the road. A/c and hot water are available. ④–⑤

Geria Giri Shanti ☎0819/1665 4874, ⓦwww.geriagirishanti.com. Four large, spotless bungalows above the road, all with fine verandahs, cold water and fans. Hot water is planned. Budget accommodation doesn't come much better than this. ②

Jukung Bali ☎0363/23470, ⓦwww.jukungbali .com A smashing little place with big bungalows with cold-water garden bathrooms, fans and deep

verandahs, just a few feet from the beach in a pretty garden. ④

Kembali Beach Bungalows ☎0817/476 8313, ⓦwww.kembalibeachbungalows.com. On the beach just oppposite Jukung Dive in Congkang, these great new bungalows are well-designed and set in a beachside garden with a lovely little pool. Superb value: most have a/c and hot water. There's good snorkelling off the beach. ④–⑤

Hotel Uyah Amed ☎0363/23462, ⓦwww.hoteluyah .com. The first place on the road from Culik, located in Amed behind the beach, which is crowded with salt-making paraphernalia. There are eight well-furnished bungalows with fan or a/c and solar-powered hot water, clustered around the small pool. ⑤

Villa Coral ☎0813/3852 0243, ⓦwww .balivillacoral.com. The best-quality accom-modation in Jemeluk with two beachfront villas and four rooms behind these, further from the beach. All have hot water and a/c. ④–⑥

3

EAST BALI | East of Candi Dasa

264

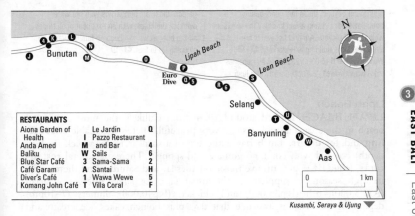

RESTAURANTS

Aiona Garden of Health	**I**	Le Jardin	**Q**
Anda Amed	**M**	Pazzo Restaurant and Bar	**4**
Baliku	**W**	Sails	**6**
Blue Star Café	**3**	Sama-Sama	**2**
Café Garam	**A**	Santai	**H**
Diver's Café	**1**	Wawa Wewe	**5**
Komang John Café	**T**	Villa Coral	**F**

Kusambi, Seraya & Ujung ▼

Bunutan

About 8km from Culik **BUNUTAN** has some of the loveliest accommodation in the area although places are quite spread out. Most people eat at or near to where they are staying. *Pazzo Restaurant and Bar* is the closest that Amed has to nightlife and is a busy bar featuring live music on Friday nights. The food is well cooked with Indonesian, Western and traveller's fare (mains Rp30–55,000), an extensive drinks list and there's a pool table too. Head to *Santai* if you feel like splashing out (mains Rp50–110,000) in an attractive setting but it's the coffees and desserts (Key Lime Pie and Chocolate Orgasm) that are worth shouting about. *Anda Amed's* restaurant has some creative and unusual choices, all of it tasty and well-executed (mains Rp30–70,000). *Aiona Garden of Health* hotel has a vegetarian restaurant open for lunch (noon–3pm) and dinner (5–7pm), reservations recommended, with the food supplemented by aloe vera and *kombucha* cocktails from plants grown in their garden; their wholegrain bread is also worth travelling for.

Aiona Garden of Health ☎0813/3816 1730, ⓦwww.aionabali.com. Three rustic bungalows in a lush garden by the beach, this place offers healing consultations and treatments in addition to massage, yoga and meditation. Potential guests should email before booking – minimum two-night stay. ❹

🏃 **Anda Amed** ☎0363/23498, ⓦwww .andaamedresort.com. The most well thought out and executed accommodation along the coast with lovely bungalows widely spaced on the hillside to give maximum privacy and make the most of the views. All have hot water and a/c. Probably the only hotel in Bali with pet ducks. Booking recommended. ❻–❼

Deddy's ☎0363/23510. Three good-value fan and cold-water bungalows set on the hillside. An additional three rooms across the road, near the beach, have a/c and hot water. ❸–❹

Prema Liong ☎0363/23486, ⓦwww.bali-amed .com. Four two-storey thatched cottages way up on the hillside with stunning views, fans, cold-water bathrooms and great lounging areas on deep verandahs. There's an eccentric bell system to call the staff up to collect refreshment orders. ❹

Puri Wirata ☎0363/23523, ⓦwww.diveamed .com. A large place with several standards of room and choice of fan or a/c. Cheaper rooms are closer to the road. The grounds stretch down to the coast and the views from the rooms vary enormously. Discounts for divers with the attached dive company. There's a great beach-front pool and spa. ❹–❻

Santai ☎0363/23487, ⓦwww.santaibali.com. Accommodation in Sulawesi-style wood, bamboo-and-thatch buildings with deep verandahs, the more expensive ones with ocean views. Rooms are in a two-storey building behind. All have a/c and hot water. There's a pretty pool. ❻–❼

Waeni's Sunset View Bungalows ☎0363/23515, ⓔmadesani@hotmail.com. Perched on a headland with views west to Gunung

Agung and beyond, these five good-quality bungalows have sitting areas to enjoy the views as well as DVD players. A/c and hot water are available. More building is underway. **④–⑤**
Wawa Wewe II ☎0363/23522, ⓦau.geocities.com/wawawewe1_2. Tucked away in a lush

garden, these a/c bungalows with hot water overlook the coast, with an excellent pool. Nearly all the bungalows can become family rooms sleeping up to four. **④–⑤**

Lipah Beach

LIPAH BEACH, located around 10km from Culik, is the most developed beach in the area, although it's still very peaceful. There's reasonable **snorkelling** and, for **divers**, Lipah Bay is the site of a small freighter wreck (6–12m depth) covered with coral, gorgonians and sponges. There are several **restaurants**; *Wawa Wewe* puts on live music on Tuesday and Saturday and there's cake in high season to supplement the usual fare; *Le Jardin* offers vegetarian (Rp25,000), fish (Rp35,000) and chicken (Rp40,000) dinners (7–10pm) depending on what is available that day; plus French cakes, ice cream and yoghurt to die for.

Bayu Cottages ☎0363/23495, ⓦwww.bayucottages.com. Popular, good-value rooms with fan and a/c, hot-water bathrooms and an attractive pool on the hillside at the far end of Lipah Beach. **④**
Coral View ☎0363/23493, ⓦwww.hiddenparadise-bali.com. Large, deep-verandahed bungalows in a lush garden with a lovely little pool. All have a/c and hot water and there are two-storey

family villas on the beachfront. *Hidden Paradise* (☎0363/23514) is nearby. Published prices are high but worth considering if you can negotiate a low-season discount. **⑥–⑦**
Le Jardin ☎0363/23507, ⓔlimamarie@yahoo.fr. Four good-value bungalows in a lovely garden with the beach a short walk away. The so-called cold water is usually warm from the tank. **④**

Lean, Selang, Banyuning and Aas

With **Lean** 11km from Culik, **Selang** almost 12km and **Banyuning** and **Aas** even further east, it's extremely quiet and while you'll mostly be staying put at night, there are a couple of restaurant options in Selang but no other tourist facilities. Snorkellers will enjoy the Japanese wreck just off the coast at Banyuning. *Sails* (☎0363/22006 or 0852/3710 2701) is a lovely **restaurant** up on the headland between Lean and Lipah with a bold minimalist design. Indonesian (Rp15–45,000) and Western (Rp45–70,000) food is described enthusiastically on the menu. There's free transport in the Amed area.

Baliku ☎0828/372 2601, ⓔbalidodo@yahoo.com. Across the road from the beach these villas are large and clean, all with a/c and hot water, and good views. There's an attractive swimming pool and a restaurant with Indonesian and Western food (mains Rp22–42,000). Also free transport to the restaurant in the Amed area and if you dine here there's free use of the showers and pool. **⑥**
Batu Tangga ☎0813/3858 9809, ⓦwww.batutangga.com. Huge, spotless rooms with a/c, hot water and deep verandahs in a fabulous cliffside location at the far end of Selang. There's a lovely pool set in a well-maintained garden. Restaurants are a short walk away. **⑥–⑦**
Blue Moon Villas ☎0812/362 2597, ⓦwww.bluemoonvilla.com. Accommodation in a lush garden on the headland beyond the beach at Selang. There are large, light rooms with a/c and

hot water, two great pools and some superb views. The attached *Komang John Café* is laid-back and recommended (mains Rp45–50,000, wine by the bottle). Trekking can be arranged here, and there is excellent snorkelling off the local beach, a short walk away. **⑥–⑦**
Eka Purnama ☎0813/3757 8060, ⓦwww.eka-purnama.com. On the hillside above the road, there are four bamboo bungalows with tiled roofs, large verandahs looking seawards, fan and cold-water bathroom. **④**
Life in Amed ☎0363/23152, ⓦwww.lifebali.com. On Lean Beach, this small place offers well-built, attractive cottages. All are attractively furnished, have a/c and hot water and are set in a small garden with a pool just behind the beach. Beachfront two-storey villas are available for larger groups and families. **⑥–⑧**

Seraya and Ujung

There are a couple of delightful places about 4km southwest of the village of **Seraya** and just over a kilometre from **Ujung**. There are ojek (Rp15,000 from Amlapura) and occasional bemos but you'll need transport to get anywhere; both places can arrange this.

Kebun Impian ☎0813/3872 1842, ⓦwww .holiday-rentals.co.uk/65990. The first place on the road from Ubung with three huge, clean, tiled fan rooms set in the garden or near the pool, which is just above the beach. Each has a fridge and DVD player. There is an attached restaurant. ❹–❺
Seraya Shores ☎0813/3841 6572, ⓔserayashores@hotmail.com. Seven large rooms all slightly different, all with fan, hot water, deep verandahs and attractive furnishings. There's a lovely garden with dramatic beach views and a pretty pool. Lunch is an additional Rp50,000 and dinner Rp100,000 – the only alternative is the restaurant nearby at *Kebun Impian*. ❼–❽

Diving at Amed

The main **diving area** is at Jemeluk: a massive sloping terrace of hard and soft coral, leads to a wall dropping to a depth of more than 40m. Gorgonians, fans, basket sponges and table coral are especially good, there's a high density of fish (including schools of red-tooth trigger fish and sergeant majors) with sharks, wrasses and parrotfish spotted in the outer parts, and the current is generally slow. Advanced divers can explore Gili Selang, the eastern tip of Bali, where a pristine reef, pelagics and exciting currents are the draw. Other dives in the area include the wreck at Lipah and a dramatic drift dive at Bunutan with the chance to see schools of barracuda and giant barrel sponges.

There are several **dive operators** around the coast. Although it is tempting to go with whoever is closest to your accommodation, see our general advice on p.51 on choosing an operator as all the established places will collect you from your accommodation. All operators offer trips for certified divers both local and further afield; $50–70 for two dives in Jemeluk/Lipah/Bunutan, $60–85 in Tulamben and $80 at Gili Selang. Introductory dives range from $50 to $90. Reviews for those who haven't dived for a while (around $75) and an introduction ($95) for those new to the sport are widely available as are the PADI Open Water course (around $375) and the Advanced Open Water course ($300). The Divemaster qualification is available at the most established shops.

Several of the places below offer packages/safaris which means completing a larger number of dives over four or five days in the Amed area. See the details on their websites. Among the most established operators in the area are:

Eco-Dive ☎0363/23482, ⓦwww.ecodivebali.com. With an office in Jemeluk, staff have tremendous local knowledge and offer dives for experienced divers and PADI courses up to Divemaster level. They offer English, French, Dutch, German and Indonesian. There is a move planned in 2009; the new office will be between *Amed Café* and *Bamboo Bali*.

Euro Dive ☎0363/23605, ⓦwww.eurodivebali.com. A smart office in Lipah, offering all PADI courses up to Divemaster, and English, French and Hungarian. Nitrox is available.

Jukung Dive ☎0363/23469, ⓦwww.jukungdivebali.com. With smart premises including a pool and small restaurant in Congkang offering all PADI courses up to Divemaster level. They have teaching manuals in Dutch, French, English and German. "Dive and Massage" packages are available.

Puri Wirata Dive School ☎/0363/23523, ⓦwww.diveamed.com. Attached to *Puri Wirata* in Bunutan and offering English, German, Indonesian and Dutch.

Shopping and other pastimes

Only the wildly optimistic would head to Amed for the **shopping** but with a pioneer spirit, and transport, there is a lot of excellent, good-value stuff available that is worth searching out. The gift shops at *Blue Moon Villas* and *Santai* have attractive textiles, baskets and jewellery while Trio Silver Workshop in Jemeluk and Krystal Mountain Jewellery in Lipah do what they say on the tin. *Hotel Uyah Amed* sells local salt in small quantities in pretty boxes and baskets and *Aiona Garden of Health* produces natural items including toiletries, mango jam and mango chutney.

If the beach gets too much, the **Shell Museum** at *Aiona Garden of Health* (2–4pm; Rp10,000 or Rp20,000 with guide) is the only one of its kind on the island and features shells from Bali, Sri Lanka and South Africa, including cowrie shells.

You'll be offered **massage** all along the coast (Rp60,000 per hour). However, if you fancy more pampering, the "a" Spa (☎0813/3823 8846, ✉aspatrad @yahoo.com; 10am–7pm), just opposite *Pazzo Bar* in Bunutan, gives treatments in a lovely garden *bale* including massages, scrubs, baths, manicures and pedicures. Prices are reasonable; the two-hour Traditional Lulur package costs $33. Some of the treatments are available in your hotel if you are staying at *Anda Amed*, *Blue Moon Villas*, *Life in Amed* or *Santai*.

Amed to Tulamben

Heading **north from Culik**, the parched countryside is cut with folds and channels, relics of the lava flow from the 1963 eruption of Gunuing Agung (see p.240), which rises dramatically inland. The coastline is attractive and two places are worth considering along here. At **Batu Belah**, 5km from Culik and signed from the main road, *Batu Belah Sekar Karang* (☎0817/975 5214, ⓦwww.eastbaliresort.com; ⓺) is a fabulous oasis with three good-value bungalows (all wheelchair friendly) with a/c, hot water, satellite TV and safety box. There's a restaurant and swimming pool and the Balinese/British owners provide fish and chips and meat pie and mashed potato alongside more usual Balinese fare (mains Rp25–50,000). The sea is crystal clear, snorkelling and fishing gear is for rent and boat trips can be arranged. The restaurant makes a great stop on any trip along the north coast – nonresidents can use the pool for Rp25,000 a day.

Two kilometres further west the diving specialists *Scuba Seraya Resort* (☎0813/3719 2820, ⓦwww.scubaseraya.com; ⓺–⓻) have beachside accommodation with a/c and hot water, a pool and a dive centre. One of Bali's best muck dives is just off the coast. From here it is 3km west to Tulamben.

Tulamben and around

The small village of **TULAMBEN**, about 10km northwest of Culik, has few attractions unless you're into **diving** or **snorkelling**. It's the site of the most popular dive in Bali, the **Liberty wreck**, attracting thousands of visitors every year. Built in 1915 in the US as a cargo steamship, the 120-metre-long *Liberty* was carrying a cargo of rubber and rail parts when she was torpedoed on January 11, 1942, 15km southwest of Lombok. Attempts to tow her to port at Singaraja failed and she filled up with water and was beached at Tulamben. In 1963, earth tremors accompanying the eruption of Gunung Agung shifted the hull off the beach into the water. Up to a hundred divers a day now visit the site, so it's worth avoiding the rush hours (11.30am–4pm). Night dives here are especially exciting.

Practicalities

Tulamben is easily **accessible** from either Singaraja or Amlapura by public minibus or bus. Perama in Candi Dasa serves Tulamben; see "Travel details", p.271, for information. Several **restaurants** offer the usual range of Indonesian and Western options, supplemented with a number of German specialities catering for the many German visitors to the area. The restaurants at *Tauch Terminal Resort* and *Matahari Resort* have pretty locations near the sea with *Tauch* winning for variety, presentation and the availability of *Häagen-Dazs* ice cream (mains Rp35–55,000).

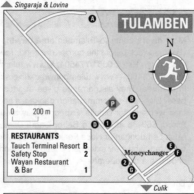

▲ Singaraja & Lovina

TULAMBEN

N

0   200 m

RESTAURANTS
Tauch Terminal Resort   B
Safety Stop   2
Wayan Restaurant
& Bar   1

Moneychanger

▼ Culik

ACCOMMODATION

Bali Coral Bungalows	C	
Matahari Tulamben Resort	F	
Paradise Palm Beach Bungalows	E	
Puri Aries	G	
Puri Madha	A	
Tauch Terminal Resort	B	
Tulamben Wreck Divers	D	

Safety Stop (with a pool table) and *Wayan Restaurant and Bar* on the main road both offer attractive surroundings and Indonesian and Western main courses in the Rp18–42,000 range. There's a **warung telkom** (8am–9pm) 250 metres east of the village and **Internet access** is available at a few spots including *Tulamben Wreck Divers* (2–9pm; Rp500 per min) and *Tauch Terminal Resort*, where Wi-Fi is also available. There's no post office – don't trust the post box on the main road. There's a **moneychanger** on the main road (9am–5pm) but it's better to bring enough cash with you; the closest **ATM** is in Amlapura.

Plenty of ladies on the beach offer **massages** (Rp60,000/hr). For more pampering the **spa** at *Tauch Terminal* is open to all (noon–7pm); it's relaxing and peaceful and a vast range of treatments is available in attractive rooms from 25 to 160 minutes (€10–49).

Most of the **accommodation** in Tulamben is between the sea and the Culik–Singaraja road, over a distance of less than 500m. Most rooms are functional and adequate as it is assumed that visitors will spend most of their time near or in the water.

Bali Coral Bungalows ☎&ℱ0363/22909. On the track leading to *Tauch Terminal Resort*. Set in a small area, rooms face seawards but only a few have sea views. Hot water and a/c are available. ③–④

Matahari Tulamben Resort ☎0363/ 22916, �🌐www.divetulamben.com. There are two standards of rooms: with fan and cold water or a/c and hot water. All lead off the track heading down to the sea. There's a small pool just behind the beachside restaurant. ②–④

Paradise Palm Beach Bungalows ☎0363/22910, �🌐www.paradise-tulamben.com. Long-established bungalows offering several standards of accommodation in the small garden compound, the most expensive having a/c and

hot water. There's a restaurant overlooking the sea. ①–④

Puri Aries ☎0363/23402. Eight basic bungalows set above the main road in a small compound. All have fan, cold-water bathrooms and verandahs, and are OK if you don't need to be next to the sea. ①

Puri Madha ☎0363/22921, ℱ23346. Very near the *Liberty* wreck. Older rooms are basic with fan and cold-water bathrooms while newer ones are attractive and offer a/c and hot water as well as ocean views. ①–④

🏃 **Tauch Terminal Resort** ☎0363/22911 or contact in southern Bali ☎0361/774504, �🌐www.tulamben.com. Large, attractive, lively establishment that fronts a long section of the coast. Features landscaped gardens, a pretty pool,

Diving at Tulamben

Most **divers** come to Tulamben on a day-trip but if you stay here you'll be able to dive the wreck before the hordes descend. *Tauch Terminal* (℡0363/22911, or contact in southern Bali ℡0361/774504, ⊕www.tulamben.com) and *Tulamben Wreck Divers* (℡0363/23400, ⊕www.tulambenwreckdivers.com) are among the most established in the area. They also arrange dives at sites throughout Bali using Tulamben as a base. Dive-and-accommodation packages and dive safaris are also available; check their websites for details. Expect to pay around $50 for two dives at Tulamben or Amed, $60–65 at Padang Bai or Candi Dasa, $75 at Pulau Menjangan and $85 at Nusa Lembongan or Nusa Penida, and $350 for a PADI Open Water course. Beware operators who offer extremely cheap dives and see p.51 for general guidelines about choosing a dive operator.

Dive sites

The **Liberty wreck** lies almost parallel to the beach, on a sandy slope about 30m offshore, and is encrusted with soft coral, gorgonians and hydrozoans plus a few hard corals, providing a wonderful habitat for around three hundred species of reef fish that live on the wreck and over a hundred species that visit from deeper water. The wreck is now pretty broken up and there are plenty of entrances letting you explore inside. Parts of the wreck are in shallow water, making this a good snorkelling site, too.

Although most divers come to Tulamben for the wreck, there are plenty of other excellent sites in the area – enough to dive for a week or more. The **Tulamben Drop-off**, sometimes called "The Wall", off the eastern end of the beach, comprises several underwater fingers of volcanic rock, which drop to 60m and are home to an enormous variety of fish, including unusual species such as comets, though it's also a good place for black coral bushes. Many divers rate this area at least as highly as the wreck itself – if not higher – although there can be more of a current to contend with. **Batu Kelebit** lies further east again and consists of two huge boulders with underwater coral-covered ridges nurturing a somewhat different but equally rewarding sealife; it's possibly the best local site for the bigger creatures such as shark, barracuda, jack, manta, *mola* and tuna. There are several other sites accessible from Tulamben; **Palung Palung** is about five minutes by boat and is suitable for beginners and experienced divers alike as it offers hard and soft coral and an excellent variety of small and large creatures from 3m to 40m depths. Batu Niti is slightly further with untouched hard and soft corals and an excellent range of coral fish. The site known as **Secret Seraya**, to the east, is a muck dive, on a sand and stone seabed and depends on having a good guide as it is otherwise easy to miss the extremely rare species here such as boxer crab, harlequin shrimp, ghost pipe fish and tiger shrimp. **Tulamben Coral Garden** and **Shark Point** are pretty self-descriptive with black-tip reef sharks the draw at the latter. All operators have their own favourite sites along the coast – check out their websites.

spa and busy dive centre. All rooms, the best in the area, have a/c and hot water, with good furnishings and balconies. ❻–❼

Tulamben Wreck Divers ℡0363/23400, ⊕www.tulambenwreckdivers.com. Just above the main road, these tiled and spacious a/c rooms

have hot water and are close to the attractive pool. There are also two spacious villas on the coast about 500m west of Tulamben, each with its own pool; one contains three rooms, which are rented out separately, and the other villa sleeps up to six. ❹–❻

North of Tulamben

From Tulamben it's a long haul along the parched north coast to Singaraja but there are excellent views of the mountains which appear much closer and more dramatic than when seen from the south. Cashew orchards are the most apparent vegetation. Heading on from Tulamben, the villages of **Tembok**, **Sembirenteng** and **Bondalem** offer accommodation (see p.299). From Bondalem, a pretty – although steep – back road leads to Kintamani (see p.285).

Travel details

Bemos and public buses

It's almost impossible to give the frequency with which bemos and public buses run: see Basics, p.36, for details. Journey times given are the minimum you can expect. Only the direct bemo and bus routes are listed.

Amlapura to: Air Sanih (2hr); Candi Dasa (20min); Culik (45min); Denpasar (Batubulan terminal; 2hr); Gianyar (1hr 20min); Gilimanuk (4–5hr); Lovina (3hr 30min); Padang Bai (45min); Semarapura (1hr); Seraya (40min); Singaraja (Penarukan terminal; 3hr); Tirtagangga (20min); Tulamben (1hr); Ujung (20min).

Bangli to: Denpasar (Batubulan terminal; 1hr 30min); Gianyar (20min); Singaraja (Penarukan terminal; 2hr 15min).

Candi Dasa to: Amlapura (20min); Denpasar (Batubulan terminal; 2hr); Gianyar (1hr); Padang Bai (20min); Semarapura (40min).

Culik to: Aas (1hr 30min); Air Sanih (1hr 30min); Amed (20min); Amlapura (45min); Bunutan (45min); Jemeluk (30min); Lipah Beach (1hr); Lovina (2hr 30min); Selang (1hr 15min); Singaraja (Penarukan terminal; 2hr 30min); Tirtagangga (30min); Tulamben (1hr).

Gianyar to: Amlapura (1hr 20min); Bangli (20min); Batur (40min); Blahbatuh (30min); Candi Dasa (1hr); Denpasar (Batubulan terminal; 1hr); Semarapura (20min); Ubud (20min).

Padang Bai to: Amlapura (45min); Candi Dasa (20min); Gilimanuk (3–4hr); Semarapura (30min).

Semarapura to: Amlapura (1hr); Besakih (45min); Candi Dasa (40min); Denpasar (Batubulan terminal; 1hr 20min); Gianyar (20min); Padang Bai (30min); Rendang (30min).

Tirtagangga to: Air Sanih (2hr); Amlapura (20min); Culik (30min); Lovina (3hr); Singaraja (2hr 30min); Tulamben (1hr).

Tulamben to: Air Sanih (1hr); Amlapura (1hr); Culik (30min); Lovina (2hr 30min); Singaraja (2hr); Tirtagangga (1hr).

Perama shuttle buses

The Direct Boat relates to the Perama boat direct from Padang Bai to the Gili Islands and Senggigi – other destinations are served by connecting bus.

Amed to: Candi Dasa (daily, min 2 people; 1hr–1hr 30min);

Candi Dasa to: Amed (daily, min 2 people; 1hr–1hr 30min); Bedugul (daily; 2hr–2hr 30min); Gili Islands Direct Boat (daily; 5hr) Ferry (daily; 6–7hr); Kuta/Ngurah Rai Airport (3 daily; 3hr); Lovina (daily; 3hr–3hr 30min); Mataram Direct Boat (daily; 6hr) Ferry (daily; 7–8hr); Padang Bai (3 daily; 30min); Sanur (3 daily; 2hr–2hr 30min); Senggigi Direct Boat (daily; 6hr) Ferry (daily; 7–8hr); Tirtagangga (daily; min 2 people; 1hr); Tulamben (daily, min 2 people; 2hr); Ubud (3 daily; 1hr 30min–2hr).

Padang Bai to: Candi Dasa (3 daily; 30min); Gili Islands Direct Boat (daily; 4hr) Ferry (daily; 5–6hr); Kuta/Ngurah Rai Airport (3 daily; 2hr 30min); Lovina (daily; 2hr 30min–3hr); Mataram Direct Boat (daily; 5hr) Ferry (daily; 6–7hr); Sanur (3 daily; 1hr 30min–2hr); Senggigi Direct Boat (daily; 4hr) Ferry (daily; 5–6hr); Ubud (daily 2hr–2hr 30min).

Tirtagangga to: Candi Dasa (daily, min 2 people; 45min).

Tulamben to: Candi Dasa (daily, min 2 people; 2hr).

Boats

Padang Bai to: Buyuk Harbour (Nusa Penida; 2 daily; 1hr); Gili Islands Perama Direct Boat (daily; 4hr); Lembar, Lombok (every 1hr 30min; 4–5hr); Senggigi Perama Direct Boat (daily; 5hr).

North Bali and the central volcanoes

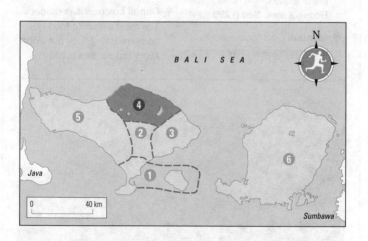

CHAPTER 4 # Highlights

* **Gunung Batur** Volcano set amidst dramatic scenery: a wonderful panorama from Penelokan or from the summit at sunrise. See p.277

* **Bali Botanical Gardens** Gorgeous highland area with hundreds of plant species – and an adventure park for the brave. See p.288

* **Danau Tamblingan** The quietest, smallest and most picturesque of the lakes in the Bedugul area. See p.290

* **Munduk** Cool temperatures, fine scenery and easy access make this an ideal base for exploration. See p.291

* **Singaraja** Bali's second city offers wide boulevards, a stimulating ethnic mix and bustling street-life. See p.293

* **Pura Meduwe Karang** The best example of the exuberant carving typical of northern temples. See p.297

* **Lovina** Laid-back beach resort offering something for everyone. See p.300

* **Damai Lovina Villas dinner** The most exquisite food in northern Bali, pricey but worth every rupiah. See p.308

▲ Canoe on Danau Batur

4

North Bali and the central volcanoes

eading into **north Bali** from the crowded southern plains, you soon enter a peaceful, cool and mountainous landscape. The centre of the island is occupied by the volcanic masses of the **Batur** and **Bedugul** areas, where dramatic mountains shelter crater lakes, and tiny villages line their shores. The **mountains** don't rival Gunung Agung in stature, but their accessibility and beauty are unbeatable. Most people come to the Batur area for the panorama from the crater rim or to trek up **Gunung Batur**, the most climbed peak in Bali, which still sends up occasional puffs of smoke. The Bedugul area offers more lakes, mountains and forests, but on a smaller scale. Several important, and stunning, temples are located on the shores of the **central lakes** and they are destinations for Balinese pilgrims and foreign day-trippers, especially **Pura Ulun Danu Bratan** on the shores of Danau Bratan. (The third of Bali's central mountain areas, Batukaru, is described on p.326, as access is via routes covered in Chapter 5.)

Beyond the mountains, the northern **coast** is arid and rugged as the mountains drop steeply to the coast with villages and roads squeezed between shore and mountain, although there are some areas of gentler hillsides and glorious rice terraces. Many visitors head straight for the resort of **Lovina**, which is the largest outside the Kuta–Legian–Seminyak conurbation but still retains a laid-back air.

For hundreds and possibly thousands of years, the north of Bali was the part of the island most open to foreign influence, as Indian, Chinese and Arab traders plied their wares through the north coast, most recently the port of **Singaraja**. This persisted into the early twentieth century with the start of the KPM steamship service from Java in 1924. However, the completion of Ngurah Rai Airport in 1969 shifted the tourist emphasis firmly to the south. Today, Singaraja, a bustling, modern city, is a major transport hub and is impossible to avoid. The **Gedong Kirtya** is the only *lontar* manuscript library in the world and warrants a quick stop in the city along with a visit to the restored Royal Palace of **Puri Agung Singaraja** next door.

The exuberant **temple carvings** of the north depict bicycle-riding, car-driving Dutch invaders and Balinese folk alongside religious figures. The best-known temples of the area – **Kubutambahan**, **Jagaraga** and **Sangsit** – are accessible and worth seeking out.

NORTH BALI & THE CENTRAL VOLCANOES

10 km

0

▲ Tulamben

Kubu

Gunung Agung (3142m) ▲

Besakih ✦

S. Yehunda

Blandingan

Pura Ulun Danu Batur

Tembok

Trunyan

Pura Jati

Songan

Gunung Abang (2153m) ▲

Abang

Sembirenteng

Les

Pacung

Pura Puncak Penulisan

Gunung Penulisan (1745m)

Penginyahan

Gunung Batur (1717m) ▲

Toya Bungkah

Buahan

Suter

Bangli ►

Sekardadi

Palikithing

Bondalem

Sembiran

Dausa

Danau Batur

Kedisan

S. Petanu

Ponjok Batu

Alassari

Tejakula

Kintamani

Pura Ulun Danu Batur

Penelokan

Bukti

Bulian

Catur

Bayunggede

S. Wos

Seribatu

Air Sanih

Pura Meduwe Karang ✦

Kubu-tambahan

Tamblang

Sawan

Bebitin

Lampu

Gunung Catur (2096m) ▲

S. Daya

S. Yeh Ayung

Punggang

Ubud ►

Catur

Jagaraga

Pura Dalem ✦

Pura Dalem Jagaraga ✦

Sukasada

Gitgit

Asah Gobleg

Danau Buyan

Pancasari

Pelaga

Pura Ulun Danu Bratan

Taman Rekreasi Bedugul

Baturiti

Pacung

Senganan

Pura Beji ✦

Sangsit

Singaraja

Lovina

Munduk

Danau Tamblingan

Candikuning

Gunung Pohen (2063m) ▲

Gunung Batukaru (2276m) ▲

Pura Luhur Batukaru ✦

Wongayagede

Buddhist Monastery

Gobleg

Gunung Sari

Dencarik

Bestala

Banyuatis

S. Saba

Pupuan

S. Yehbatan

Hot Springs

Munduk

Bestala

Rangdu

Mayong

Serrit

N

Gilimanuk ▼

The Singaraja–Gilimanuk road threads along the north coast, taking in Lovina, and public transport plies the three main southbound roads through the mountains to Denpasar – from Seririt via Pupuan, Singaraja via Bedugul, and Kubutambahan via Kintamani. With good **bus** links from Java, Denpasar and Amlapura and **bemo** connections within the area, most of the sights in the north are easy to get to on public transport, although your own vehicle opens up less accessible areas such as Danau Tamblingan and the back roads nearby. A good range of **accommodation** throughout the region makes this an ideal touring area.

Batur and Bedugul

The lakes within the volcanic craters of the **Batur** and **Bedugul** areas are the source of water for a vast area of agricultural land. They are also home to Ida Batara Dewi Ulun Danu, the goddess of the lake, and are pivotal to religious belief on the island. The cool mountain air, trekking opportunities and good transport links have long made this region a favourite with local and foreign visitors.

Gunung Batur and Danau Batur

The **Batur** area was formed thirty thousand years ago by the eruption of a gigantic volcano. The result is a spectacular area filled with volcanic peaks, craters and dramatic views. The view from the rim is what draws most visitors to the area. **Gunung Batur** (Mount Batur) rises 1717m from the floor of the crater with Danau Batur (Lake Batur) nestled beside it. There are many villages around the crater rim and lake, and sometimes the area is referred to as **Kintamani**, although this is the name of just one village. The highest points on the rim are **Gunung Abang** (2153m) on the eastern side, the third highest mountain in Bali, and **Gunung Penulisan** (1745m) on the northwest corner, with Pura Puncak Penulisan on its summit. Gunung Batur is an active volcano and every night, trekkers set off to climb the peak for the sunrise.

Toya Bungkah is the main accommodation centre and start of one route up the mountain. **Kedisan** also offers hotels, and is the starting point for boat trips across the lake to the Bali Aga village of **Trunyan**. South of Kedisan, **Buahan** is the quietest spot of all, and **Songan**, at the northern end of the lake, is the start of walks up to the crater rim.

Sadly, the Batur area has developed a reputation for hassles. However, the dramatic landscape makes it worth taking a deep breath, keeping a hold on your patience and heading upwards for at least a glimpse of its remarkable scenery.

The crater rim

Spread out along the crater-rim's road for 11km, the villages of **Penelokan**, **Batur** and **Kintamani** virtually merge. The road is one of the main routes

Eruptions at Gunung Batur

Gunung Batur has **erupted** more than twenty times since 1800. In 1917, a major eruption killed over a thousand people, but the lava stopped just outside the temple of Batur village, which was then situated in the crater beside the lake. Considering this a good omen, the population stayed put until August 3, 1926, when another eruption engulfed the village and the people were evacuated up onto the crater rim. The longest-lasting eruption took place in September 1963, a few months after the massive explosion of Gunung Agung (see p.240), and continued until May 1964. At Yehmampeh, on the road around the base of the mountain, you'll see lava flows from an eruption in March 1974. The newest crater, Batur IV, was formed during the eruption that started on August 7, 1994, and continues periodically. It's startling to see the volcano still smoking, but local belief is that it's better if Batur lets off a little steam regularly rather than saving it up for a major blow.

between the north and south coasts and public transport is frequent. If you're staying up here, the nights are chilly; at the very least, you'll need a sweater.

There's an **admission charge** to the crater area (Rp4000; Rp2000 per car or motorbike). The ticket offices are just south of Penelokan on the road from Bangli and at the junction of the road from Ubud and the rim road.

Practicalities

The crater rim is included in many **day-trips** from the major resorts. However, getting here independently is straightforward, with **buses** running between Singaraja (Penarukan) and Denpasar (Batubulan), via Bangli. The route from Ubud is served by brown (Kintamani) **bemos**. Kintamani is not on Perama's **tourist shuttle-bus** regular schedule but, with a minimum of two people, charters are available from Ubud (Rp75,000), Kuta (Rp100,000) and Sanur (Rp100,000); check their website (ⓦ www.peramatour.com) or enquire at any of their offices. Once in the area, there are plenty of bemos zipping along the rim. For something different, Sobek (ⓦ www.balisobek.com; $68) offers downhill **cycling** trips in the Gunung Batur area, and prices include transport to/from the southern resorts or Ubud.

The **post office** and **phone office** are close together just off the main road 2km north of Penelokan. It is difficult to **change money** although there is an international **ATM** in the car park of the *Lakeview* hotel. It is advisable to bring plenty of cash.

Penelokan

Literally meaning "Place to Look", the views from **PENELOKAN** (1450m) are majestic across a stark volcanic landscape: Danau Batur lies far below, with Gunung Batur and Gunung Abang towering on either side. Hundreds of tourists pass through Penelokan every day, attracting persistent **hawkers** selling everything imaginable.

If you tire of the view, or want to escape the sellers, the **Museum Gunungapi Batur** (Batur Volcano Museum; Mon–Fri 7am–noon; Rp5000) presents exhibits and photographs of the formation and history of the area.

Yayasan Bintang Danu, a local organization, runs the **tourist office** (ⓣ 0366/51730; daily 10am–3pm), almost opposite the turning down to Danau Batur.

Most people who **stay** overnight base themselves at the lake but, if your budget will run to it, go for the ⚞ *Lakeview Hotel* (ⓣ 0366/51394, ⓦ www.indo .com/hotels/lakeview; ❹–❺), right on the edge of the crater rim. There are no frills but it has stunning views, hot water and thick quilts, and the hotel can arrange sunrise treks up Gunung Batur. A couple of hundred feet below, on the road down to Kedisan, *Windu Sara* (℡0366/52467, ℻52468; ❹) has just four rooms but equally fine views and similar facilities.

The crater rim is packed with **restaurants** offering expensive buffet lunches to day-trippers. For something cheaper but still with great views, try *Warung Kopi* (mains Rp15–25,000), on the crater rim about 300m towards Kintamani from Penelokan tucked behind the expensive *Ramana*. Closer to Penelokan, on the opposite side of the road, *Wibisana* is also good value (main courses about Rp11,000).

Pura Ulun Danu Batur

About 4km north of Penelokan, **Pura Ulun Danu Batur** (admission by donation; sarong rental available) is the second most important temple on the island after Besakih and one of the highly venerated *kayangan jagat* (directional temples): this one protects Bali from the north. The eleven-day *odalan* festival (see p.434) is particularly spectacular.

The original temple was located down in the crater until the 1926 eruption of Gunung Batur, when the village and temple were rebuilt up here. The temple honours **Ida Batara Dewi Ulun Danu**, the goddess of the lake, who is said to control the water for the irrigation systems throughout the island and shares dominion of Bali with the god of Gunung Agung. A manuscript in the temple proclaims, "Because the goddess makes the waters flow, those who do not follow her laws may not possess her rice terraces." A virgin priestess selects 24 boys who serve the goddess as **priests** in the temple for life. The high priest, Jero Gde or Sanglingan, the earthly representative of the goddess of the lake, is

Climbing Gunung Abang

Thickly forested and lacking sweeping views on the way, climbing **Gunung Abang** (Red Mountain) is less popular than Batur. Allow three hours to get to the top from the start of the footpath and take enough food and water. A **guide** is recommended. Enquire at the trekking agencies in Toya Bungkah (see p.283; about \$55 per person), Yayasan Bintang Danu in Penelokan, Made Senter at *Miranda* losmen in Kintamani (Rp700,000 for up to four people) or the Association of Mount Batur Trekking Guides in Toya Bungkah (Rp350,000 per guide for a maximum of three people).

The route starts on the Suter road, which heads east around the rim from Penelokan, from just below the *Lakeview Hotel* (there are no public bemos along here). Approximately 4km from Penelokan, the road turns south away from the crater rim, but a rough track continues along the edge. Follow this track for 2km, passing **Pura Munggu** in the middle of the forest. The track eventually turns away from the crater rim; at this point, take the footpath straight in front of you that heads up the mountain. You'll pass the small forest temple, **Pura Manu Kaya**, about halfway, reaching **Pura Puncak Tuluk Biyu**, from where there are good views, at the summit.

A track continues down the other side of Gunung Abang to the far side of the crater above Songan. However, this path is long and little used; you definitely need a guide to attempt it.

selected by the virgin priestess. His days are spent making offerings to her on behalf of visiting pilgrims. Farmers or *subak* with plans for, or conflicts about, irrigation systems come to confer with the Jero Gde, whose word is accepted as final. The number of shrines is overwhelming for many visitors, but the most significant is the **eleven-roofed meru** in the inner courtyard, dedicated to both the goddess of the lake and the god of Gunung Agung. The drum in the *kulkul* tower in the outer courtyard is beaten 45 times each morning to honour the 45 deities worshipped in the temple.

Kintamani

Two kilometres north of Pura Ulun Danu Batur, **KINTAMANI** isn't particularly attractive and is too far north along the rim of the crater for the best views. It's famous for its breed of furry dogs and the huge market held every three days. Most people stay at the lakeside, where there is more accommodation, or in Penelokan, where the views are better. However, *Miranda* (☎0366/52022; ①) is the only budget accommodation on the rim. It's 100m north of the market; all public transport along the rim passes the door. The rooms are basic but clean and have attached *mandi* and squat toilet. The lounge cheers up when there are a few people staying and the open fire is lit. The owner, Made Senter, also works as a **trekking guide** for climbs up Gunung Batur (Rp400,000 for up to four people) and Gunung Abang (Rp700,000 for up to four people) and less strenuous trekking on the crater rim from (1–4 hours, Rp150,000 upwards depending on duration); prices include transport.

Pura Puncak Penulisan

About 5km north of Kintamani in the village of Sukawana, **Pura Puncak Penulisan**, also known as Pura Tegeh Koripan (admission by donation), built on the summit of Gunung Penulisan, is the highest temple on Bali and one of the most ancient, being referred to in ninth-century inscriptions. There are 333 steps to the top temple, **Pura Panarajon**, dedicated to Sanghyang Grinatha, a manifestation of Siwa and god of the mountains where *bale* shelter ancient lingga and statues from the eleventh to thirteenth centuries. These include a wedding portrait believed to portray the marriage of King Udayana and Queen Mahendratta, the source of the Rangda myth (see box, p.226).

Danau Batur

Home to **Ida Batara Dewi Ulun Danu** (or Dewi Danu for short), the goddess of the lake, **Danau Batur** is especially sacred to the Balinese. The waters from the lake, generated by eleven springs, are believed to percolate through the earth and reappear as springs in other parts of the island. Situated 500m below the crater rim, this is the largest lake in Bali, 8km long and 3km wide, and one of the most glorious: the villages dotted around its shores are referred to as *bintang danu* (stars of the lake). The shores are lined with the vegetable fields that provide the livelihood for these communities of market gardeners and fishermen.

The road to the lakeside, served by **public bemos**, leaves the crater rim at Penelokan. Bemos go as far as Songan on the western side of the lake and Abang on the eastern side; the tourist fare from Penelokan to any of the lakeside accommodation is about Rp5000 with bargaining. If you charter, you'll be looking at Rp20,000 per person. Be aware that the peace by the lake can be shattered by trucks ferrying stone from the quarry on the western side of Gunung Batur, although most of them use an alternative road that avoids the tourist developments.

For the safety of your vehicle, if travelling **by car or motorbike**, it's best to leave them in the care of your hotel or restaurant or take a driver to stay with it while you trek.

Kedisan

At the bottom of the steep descent, 3km from Penelokan, the road splits in the lakeside village of **KEDISAN**: the right fork leads to the jetty for boats to Trunyan and continues on to the villages of Buahan and Abang; the left fork goes to Toya Bungkah and Songan.

A few hundred metres from the junction, towards Toya Bungkah, *Hotel Segara* (T0366/51136, Ehotelsegara@plasa.com; ❷–❹) has good-quality **accommodation**, with hot water available. The hotel can arrange pick-ups from Penelokan (Rp15,000 per person), Kuta (Rp350,000 per car), Lovina (Rp300,000 per car) or Ubud (Rp200,000 per car). Confirm the cost when you phone to arrange it. Next door, *Hotel Surya* (T0366/51139; ❶–❷) also has decent rooms, some with hot water and lovely views. They also do pick-ups; free from local areas and from Ubud, Bangli, Besakih, Gianyar and Semarapura, Rp250,000 per car from Kuta and Rp200,000 per car from Candi Dasa and Lovina. Again confirm the cost when you phone ahead. A couple of hundred metres further on, the delightful 𝕵 *Hotel Astra Dana* (T0366/52091; ❶) has a dozen rooms by the lakeside; the most expensive have hot water and fabulous lake views. They offer free pick-ups from Penelokan. All of these places arrange Mount Batur climbs (Rp350–400,000 for two people).

Turning right at the bottom of the road from Penelokan brings you to the quietest part of the lake and the jetty for boats to Trunyan. See p.284 for accommodation further round this side of the lake.

Toya Bungkah and around

TOYA BUNGKAH, 8km from Penelokan, is the accommodation centre of the lakeside area and one starting-point for climbs up Gunung Batur. Its **hot**

Climbing Gunung Batur

Bear in mind that Batur remains **active** so only trek when it is safe. Check ⓦwww
.vsi.esdm.go.id for the current situation – it's mostly in Indonesian but it is clear if a
mountain is on alert.

There's a choice of **routes up Gunung Batur**. If you have your own wheels, the
easiest route is to drive to **Serongga**, off the Yehmampeh road, west of Songan.
From the car park, it's thirty minutes to an hour to the highest peak and largest crater,
Batur I. Steam holes just below the crater rim confirm that this volcano is far from
extinct, although the crater itself is grassed over.

The most common walking **routes** up to Batur I are from Toya Bungkah and Pura
Jati. The path from Pura Jati is shadeless and largely across old lava fields, while about
half of the ascent from Toya Bungkah is in forest. From Toya Bungkah, numerous paths
head up through the forest (one starts just south of *Arlina's*); after about an hour you'll
come out onto the bare slope of the mountain, from where you can follow the paths
that head up to the tiny warung perched on the crater rim way up on the skyline. This
is the steep bit, slippery with black volcanic sand. Allow two to three hours to get to
the top from either start and about half that time to get back down.

A **medium-length trek** involves climbing to Batur I, walking around the rim and
then descending by another route. The **long-trek** option, sometimes called the
Exploration (about 8hr in total) involves climbing up to Batur I, walking around the
rim to the western side, descending to Batur II, then to Batur III and down to Toya
Bungkah or Yehmampeh.

Practicalities

Climbing Batur is best in the **dry season** (April–Oct). The path becomes unpleasant
in the wet and the views clouded over. However, the wet season isn't unrelenting, and
you might be lucky and hit a few dry days.

In **daylight**, you don't need a guide if you're just climbing to Batur I from Toya
Bungkah or Pura Jati and you've a reasonable sense of direction. However, it's
unwise to climb alone and you should let somebody responsible know where you are

---

springs, **Toya Devasa**, (daily 8am–7pm; $6 including lunch), are clean and
attractive, with a cold-water swimming pool and smaller hot-water pools. About
4km before Toya Bungkah, **Pura Jati**, dedicated to the god Wisnu, has some
fine carvings, and it's near here that Magening, one of the eleven springs within
the lake, rises. Every five years, the festival of Bakti Pekelem involves the
sacrifice of animals to Dewi Danu through ritual drowning in the lake.
Changing money can be difficult, so bring cash. There's a **warung telkom**
(8am–11pm) but at the time of writing no **Internet** access.

Accommodation, eating and drinking

There is plenty of **accommodation** in Toya Bungkah. Several losmen have
inexpensive **restaurants** serving a good range of Western and Indo-Chinese
options, and lake fish (Rp15–28,000 for mains). *Arlina's* is a long-standing
favourite with well-cooked food, and *Volcano Breeze* is on a quiet track down
to the lake.

Arlina's ☎0366/51165. Friendly and popular, at
the southern end of town, with clean rooms (some
with hot water) and small verandahs. ❸
Lakeside Cottages ☎0366/51249, ⓦwww
.lakesidebali.com. Aptly named with large cottages
boasting lake views, hot water and TV, while

cheaper, cold-water rooms are further from the
lake. There's a swimming pool. ❷–❺
Nyoman Mawar *(Under the Volcano)*
☎0366/51166. In the village, with clean,
good-value rooms. Cold-water bathrooms
only. ❶

going. For the longer treks or the less well trodden paths, you do need a guide: routes are trickier and it's important to stay away from the most active parts of the volcano. However, most people climb **in the dark** to reach the top for the sunrise views over the lake to Gunung Abang and Gunung Rinjani on Lombok. You'll need to leave around 4–5am and a guide is vital, as it's easy to get lost in the dark.

Anyone who climbs Batur is under intense pressure to engage a local guide. These are organized into the **Association of Mount Batur Trekking Guides** (☏0366/52362), with offices in Toya Bungkah and at Pura Jati. However, it can be confusing dealing with them in spite of "fixed" prices supposedly displayed in the offices (from Rp200,000 per group of four people). If you do use them the best advice is to be absolutely sure what is included (for example, is breakfast extra), which trek you are doing and whether the price you have agreed is per person or for the group. Many people find it is more straightforward to deal with their hotel or with the trekking agencies.

Trekking agencies

Aside from the Association of Mount Batur Trekking Guides, you can get **information** about Gunung Batur from staff at your hotel and from **trekking agencies** in Toya Bungkah: Jero Wijaya at *Lakeside Cottages* (☏0366/51249, ⓦwww.lakesidebali.com) and *Arlina's* (☏0366/51165). It is $20–25 per person for the short trek, or $35–38 for the long one. Bali Sunrise 2001 (☏0818/552669, ⓦwww.balisunrise2001.com) arranges treks including pick-ups throughout Bali including Nusa Dua and Lovina ($45–80 per person depending on pick-up point, the trek and whether overnight accommodation in Toya Bungkah is included). There are minimum numbers required – usually two people.

In addition, all can arrange **other treks** in the area including Gunung Abang (see above); *Arlina's* offer Toya Bungkah to Besakih ($65) or to the sea ($90), *Lakeside* arrange trekking on the **crater rim** ($30–40 from the Toya Bungkah area, $55–65 from elsewhere in Bali) and Bali Sunrise 2001 offers Bedugul trekking (see p.287).

🏃 **Nyoman Mawar III** *(also known as Under the Volcano III)* ☏0366/3860 0081. Bungalows close to the lake with fabulous views; all are simple and clean, with cold water only. ❶

Pualam ☏0813/3813 2606. Quiet losmen, close to the hot springs, with simple rooms in a pleasant garden. ❶

Songan

At the northern end of the lake, 4km beyond Toya Bungkah, the village of **SONGAN** is the location of **Pura Ulun Danu Batur**, believed to be one of the oldest temples in Bali and not to be confused with the bigger, more important temple of the same name up on the crater rim. A ceremony is held here every ten years to honour the goddess of the lake, involving the ritual drowning of buffaloes, pigs, goats, chickens and geese, all adorned with gold ornaments. Not many bemos serve Songan and you may end up walking to or from Toya Bungkah; either follow the road or take the lakeside track.

Directly behind the temple in Songan, a **footpath** winds up onto the rim of the outer crater and you can follow tracks to explore the tiny villages of traditional bamboo huts whose inhabitants farm the steep, dry hillsides. There are some fine views down to the north coast, and back to Abang, Agung, and even – on a clear day – Rinjani on Lombok. With a good supply of food and water (it gets hotter the further down you go), the adventurous should be able to locate the paths down to the **north coast** where you can pick up public transport west to Air Sanih or east to Tulamben.

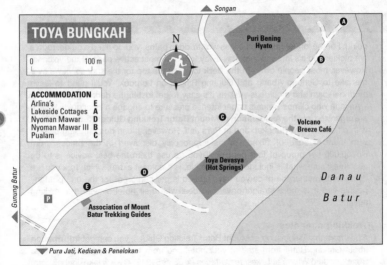

From the junction in the middle of Songan, a **road** circles the base of Gunung Batur, passing through **Yehmampeh** on its way round to Penelokan, a trip of about 26km. If you have your own transport, it's worth exploring for different but no less dramatic views of Gunung Batur. To the northwest of the volcano, **Pura Bukit Mentik** is known as Lucky Temple because lava from the 1974 eruption surrounded it but caused no damage. The lava fields from that eruption now supply the grey-black building stone *paras* and sand that is ferried continuously from the area.

Buahan and Abang

The most attractive section of road in the crater follows the eastern shore of Danau Batur beyond Kedisan, offering great views across the lake to Gunung Batur. A couple of hundred metres beyond the village of **BUAHAN**, 2km from the junction with the Penelokan road at Kedisan, *Hotel Baruna* (●–●) has clean, tiled rooms with stunning views across the lake. There may not be a sign, so look out for a small *bale* in a garden beyond the village.

From here the road edges between the lake and the cliffs, which rise up into the mass of Gunung Abang, and finally ends at the tiny village of **ABANG**, where a couple of shops sell soft drinks. From Abang, there's a lakeside footpath to Trunyan (4km).

Trunyan

Inhabited by Bali Aga people who rejected the changes brought about by the Majapahit invasion in 1343 (see p.415), **TRUNYAN** and its nearby cemetery at Kuban are well-established tourist attractions. Situated beside Danau Batur with Gunung Abang behind, there are two routes to the village: by boat from Kedisan or by a four-kilometre footpath from Abang village. The **boat trip** is beautiful but chilly and takes less than an hour. Tourists must charter boats from the pier at Kedisan. Prices (advertised as including a guide and all donations) are Rp261,000 for a boat for one, Rp131,750 per person for two people, Rp88,700 per person for three people – and so on, up to a maximum of seven people, at Rp39,500 per person. They head from the pier to Trunyan village, on to the cemetery, then Toya Bungkah and back to Kedisan.

The origin of the name "Trunyan" is disputed. Some say it derives from *taru*, meaning wood, and *munyan*, meaning perfume, referring to the banyan tree in the cemetery; others claim it derives from *turun hyang*, meaning descendants from heaven. There's no doubt that Trunyan was inhabited in ancient times: ninth-century copper inscriptions refer to a statue of a god named Bhatara Da Tonta that must be bathed, painted and decorated with jewellery. This possibly refers to a four-metre-high **statue** in the village temple, called Da Tonta by the people of Trunyan.

The village keeps many of the ancient **Bali Aga customs**, most notoriously disposing of dead bodies in pits covered only by a cloth and a rough bamboo roof and left to decompose in the air. The banyan tree in Trunyan's tiny **cemetery** at Kabuan, just north of the village and accessible only by boat, supposedly prevents the corpses from smelling. For many tourists, this is the reason for their visit, as grim as it may seem. All you're likely to see are a few artfully arranged bones, the towering banyan tree and the covered graves.

Apart from market gardening, the village's main source of income is from tourists, and although the boat fee is supposed to include donations some people have been asked for more. Trunyan can feel rather isolated and forbidding; it's advisable to take some small notes to give away.

Routes to the north coast

It's 40km from Kintamani down through the foothills to the **north coast** at Kubutambahan, one of the main north–south routes across the island. There's some pretty scenery, with mountains to the west and verdant valleys and forested ridges descending to the coast. The vegetation changes, too, as the hardier, high-altitude vegetables and crops give way to tropical growth.

The village of **PENGINYAHAN**, 19km from Kintamani, makes a good stopping place. The roadside *Restoran Coffeebreak*, owned by a Balinese–Dutch family, Ketut Widiada and his wife Paula, serves inexpensive Indonesian **food** and drinks. You can get directions here or hire a guide to three local **waterfalls**. Another forty minutes or so brings you to the north coast at Kubutambahan, from where Singaraja is 11km west and Air Sanih is 6km east.

The back road to Bondalem

If you have your own transport and want to avoid the busy main road, you can follow an attractive **back road** to the north coast that delivers you to

Cloves

It was the search for **cloves**, among other spices, that first drove Europeans to explore the Indonesian archipelago, and for hundreds of years they were one of the region's most lucrative exports. Native to certain islands of the Moluccas (the original "Spice Islands") clove production is now centred in Maluku, Sumatra, Sulawesi and Bali. You'll spot the tall trees in the hills around Bedugul, Tamblingan and Munduk and if you're there during harvest time, from August to October, you'll see death-defying pickers on rickety ladders and huge piles of drying cloves beside the road – buds that must be picked before the petals open, after which the amount of clove oil declines sharply.

Bali's cloves end up in Java for the manufacture of Indonesia's pungent **kretek cigarettes**. These consist of up to fifty percent cloves mixed with tobacco, and demand is so great that the former clove capital of the world now imports them from Madagascar and Zanzibar to supplement local production.

4

NORTH BALI AND THE CENTRAL VOLCANOES | Gunung Batur and Danau Batur

285

Bondalem, east of Air Sanih. It's a narrow, twisting and very steep 16km with some lovely views. It leaves the main road at the village of Lateng, 13km from the market at Kintamani, and 500m after the end of the village of Dausa; there's a sign pointing to Bondalem. The main road swings left on a sharp bend and there's a row of shops on the right at the start of this side road; it's worth checking if you've got the correct turning (which is known locally as the Tejakula road).

The road initially descends through vegetable gardens and stands of cloves, cocoa, coffee and avocado with great views of neighbouring ridges and westwards to the area around Gunung Batukaru. There are few villages; **Madenan** is a neat, cool settlement about 10km of the way down. After this, the temperature rises significantly, and coconut plantations stretch into the distance all the way to the north coast. The road reaches the main north-coast road at the village of **BONDALEM** (see p.299 for information on accommodation in the area). It's 15km west to Air Sanih, and 36km east to Tulamben via Sembirenteng and Tembok.

The Bedugul region

Neither as big nor as dramatic as the Batur region, the Danau Bratan area, often just called **Bedugul**, has impressive mountains, lakes and temples. The name refers to both the village and the surrounding area. It is a popular Indonesian destination; pilgrims make offerings at **Pura Ulun Danu Bratan** on the shores of **Danau Bratan**, while lowland dwellers come to the **Bali Botanical Gardens** in Candikuning for leisurely picnics or to swing through the trees at **Bali Treetop Adventure Park** and for watersports at the **Taman Rekreasi**

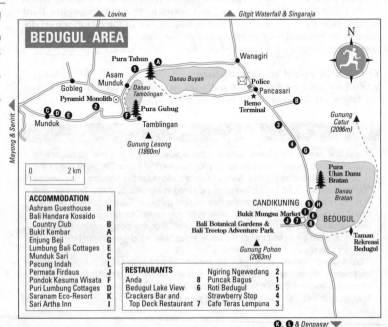

The Bedugul area offers plenty of opportunities for **trekking**; if you want a guide enquire at your accommodation, at the kiosk on the main road near the turning to the *Ashram Guesthouse* or at the Danau Buyan or Danau Tamblingan ticket offices where you'll find guides with printed price lists detailing an excellent range of treks. From Tamblingan there's a short two hours in the forest, returning by canoe on the lake (Rp280,000) up to eight hours strenuous trekking to Jatiluwih (Rp1million) although the most popular is probably the four-hour one-way trek over to Lake Buyan (Rp460,000). All prices are for one guide and up to four people and includes the loan of walking sticks. Transport isn't included; to tackle one of the longer treks charter a car and driver, drive to the start and get the driver to meet you at the finish.

Alternatively, agencies in Toya Bungkah (see p.283), *Puri Lumbung* and *Lumbung Bali Cottages* (see p.291) in Munduk and Sobek (@ www.balisobek.com; $55) run treks in the Bedugul area. Prices include transport.

Bedugul. The area attracts fewer foreign tourists and not many stay overnight although there's a reasonable range of **accommodation**.

Danau Bratan nestles in the lee of Gunung Catur, on the main Denpasar–Mengwi–Singaraja road 53km north of Denpasar and 30km south of Singaraja; no direct route links it to Batur. Approaching from the south, the road rises through a series of small villages. **Pacung** offers accommodation; just north of it, near the market in **Baturiti**, a road is signed to Senganan, which takes a picturesque route through Jatiluwih to the Batukaru region (see p.330). The main road completes another steep 8km north to the rim of an ancient volcanic crater at the market village of **Candikuning** then it descends through **Pancasari**, skirting the western shore of Danau Bratan. It climbs again to the pass out of the crater at **Wanagiri** (known locally as Puncak), where it begins the steep descent to the northern plains. The smaller, quieter **Danau Buyan** and **Danau Tamblingan** lie about 6km northwest of Danau Bratan.

All the lakes have superbly situated shoreside temples, and the area is dotted with attractive villages. There are **bus** services to and from Denpasar (Ubung; 1hr 30min) and Singaraja (Sukasada; 1hr 30min); however, having your own transport means that the lakes of Buyan and Tamblingan plus Munduk and Mayong on the way to the north coast, become easily accessible.

Candikuning and Danau Bratan

The small village of **CANDIKUNING**, situated above the southern shores of Danau Bratan, is home to one of the gems of central Bali, the **Bali Botanical Gardens**.

Candikuning's daily **market**, Bukit Mungsu, offers fruit, spices and plants alongside the usual tourist items. Have a look at the AdoptA Co-op shop in the corner, set up by five widows of the Bali Bomb; they sell a range of fun clothes including T-shirts. There's a **warung telkom** in the market and **moneychangers** in the market and in the car park at Pura Ulun Danu Bratan (rates are poor). For **tourist shuttle bus** tickets, the Perama office (☎ 0368/21011) is at the *Sari Artha* losmen, just below the market on the main road in Candikuning. Prices are Rp40,000 to Kuta, Ubud, Sanur or Lovina. It's also possible to arrange charter transport locally (at the *Ashram Guesthouse*, for example); it's around Rp350,000 per car to Lovina, Ubud, Kuta and other southern resorts.

Accommodation

Most accommodation in the area is in or near Candikuning village, although one of the best options is further afield.

Ashram Guesthouse ☏ 0368/21450. A large place on the lakeside with a range of options from basic rooms with shared cold-water bathrooms to comfortable bungalows with hot water, verandahs and good lake views. ❶–❸

Bali Handara Kosaido Country Club ☏ 0362/22646, ⓦ www.balihandarakosaido.com. The centrepiece is a 6434-yard par-72 golf course, which claims to be the only one in the world situated in the crater of a volcano. Rooms are heated and well furnished and have fabulous views over the course. Other facilities include tennis courts, a fitness centre and a spa. The view of Danau Buyan from the bar is glorious but, unless you have transport, it's a two-kilometre walk up the drive. It's $110 for a round of golf (guests half-price); equipment rental is extra. ❼–❾

Enjung Beji ☏ 0368/21490, ☏ 21022. Accommodation in well-furnished cottages set in an attractive garden on the lakeside, where there is also a restaurant; less expensive ones are on the road down to the compound. All have hot water. ❹–❻

Pacung Indah ☏ 0368/21020, ⓦ www.pacungbali.com. The nicest place to stay in the area is situated 9km south of Bedugul, just before the village of Pacung. The bungalows are comfortable and well furnished, with hot water and great views from the communal terrace. ❹–❻

Permata Firdaus ☏ 0368/21531. Just off the road to the Botanical Gardens, offering six good-value, simple rooms with hot water. ❶

Saranam Eco-Resort ☏ 0368/21038, ⓔ info_saranam@ehotelier.com. A large place across the road from *Pacung Indah*, rooms are comfortable with some good rice terrace views. Top-end bungalows are down in the ricefields; a cable car brings guests up to the main buildings, and there's a pretty little swimming pool. ❻–❼

Sari Artha Inn ☏ 0368/21011. Just north of the market, there's a choice of rooms with or without hot water, all with verandahs, set in a pretty garden but with no lake views. The Perama office is here. ❶–❷

Bali Botanical Gardens and Bali Treetop Adventure Park

A short walk along a side road from Candikuning, the **Bali Botanical Gardens** (Kebun Raya Eka Karya Bali; daily 8am–6pm; Rp3500; parking for cars Rp1500, for motorbikes Rp500; entry for cars Rp6000, motorbikes prohibited) cover more than 150 hectares on the slopes of Gunung Pohon (Tree Mountain) and include more than a thousand species of plants including **trees**, **bamboo** and **orchids**. This is also a rich area for **bird-watching** (see box, p.290). It gets busy at weekends and on holidays but during the week you'll see very few people. Visitors receive a leaflet/map but unless you've a particular interest, it's a great place just to wander.

One great reason to visit is the **Bali Treetop Adventure Park** (☏ 0361/852 0680, ⓦ www.balitreetop.com; $20, child $13) located inside the gardens, consisting of five circuits of ropeways, bridges, platforms and zip lines constructed up to 20m off the ground which the intrepid and not so intrepid (there's a circuit to suit every level of bravado) negotiate at their own pace. It's brilliant and suits families with small children as well as the adrenaline junkies. Booking is recommended, weekends and holidays are best avoided and packages are available from the southern resorts including transport, lunch and a visit to Pura Ulun Danu Bratan.

Danau Bratan

Situated at 1200m above sea level and thought to be 35m deep in places, **Danau Bratan** is surrounded by forested hills, with the bulk of Gunung Catur rising sheer behind. The lake becomes frenetic with watersports on holidays and at weekends – although the scenery more than compensates for the buzz of motorboats.

▲ Danau Batur

The lake (and its goddess) are worshipped in the temple of **Pura Ulun Danu Bratan** (daily 7am–5pm; Rp10,000, cars Rp5000), one of the most photographed and highly revered temples in Bali. Built in 1633 by the raja of Mengwi on a small promontory on the western shore of the lake, it's dedicated to Dewi Danu, source of water and hence fertility for the land and people of Bali. The temple consists of several shrines spread along the shore and perched on small islands, which appear to float on the surface of the lake, with the mountains rising behind. Closest to the bank, the eleven-roofed *meru* is dedicated to Wisnu and Dewi Danu, and the three-roofed *meru* just beyond it houses an ancient *lingam* to Siwa.

Taman Rekreasi Bedugul

The **Taman Rekreasi Bedugul** (daily 8am–5pm; Rp10,000, cars Rp5000, motorbikes Rp2000), on the southern shores of the lake, is signed "Bedugul" from the main road. This is a recreation park where you can indulge in water-skiing, parasailing and jet-skiing or rent a speedboat or rowing boat. Private boat operators also linger near the Taman Rekreasi and the *Ashram Guesthouse*; with a bit of bargaining you'll get a boat for about Rp150,000 per hour after 9am and Rp70–80,000 before this.

Eating and drinking

Most **restaurants** in the area cater for the **lunchtime** trade. The restaurant at the *Pacung Indah* hotel has the best views accompanying its buffet for Rp65,000 per person. For cheap food, a row of *kaki lima* (stalls) lines the road along the lakeside south of Pura Ulun Danu Bratan, and there are warung in the temple car park. *Crackers Bar and Top Deck Restaurant* is tucked away in Bukit Mungsu market, a quiet haven with a small menu of sandwiches, burgers, and fish and chips (Rp18–35,000) alongside a big choice of drinks. Near the market, *Roti Bedugul* has fabulous home-baked bread, sweet buns and cookies, while *Bedugul Lake View*, north of *Ashram Guesthouse*, provides a distant view of the lake and basic Indonesian food (mains around Rp18,500). *Strawberry Stop*, 2km towards Pancasari, dishes up strawberries with cream or ice cream, in milkshakes or in pancakes all from Rp8–10,000.

The birds of Bedugul

The Bali Botanical Gardens and the southern shores of Danau Bratan are home to an amazing variety of **birds**. The most common sightings are of the forest-dwelling **grey-cheeked green pigeon** and **blue-crowned barbet**, almost entirely green with a blue crown and yellow forehead. The barbet is found only on Java and Bali, and you'll hear its monotonous call from high in the forest canopy. You're also likely to see **flycatchers**, especially the snowy-browed flycatcher, which has a distinctive white line above the eye, a slate-blue back and orange breast. Flowering or fruiting trees attract a range of different birds: the gregarious **Philippine glossy starling**, with greenish-purple feathers, feeds in fruiting trees, while the tiny **yellow-throated hanging parrot**, green with a red rump, heads for buds and flowers. The **collared kingfisher** is also a regular, a noisy bird, giving a loud "chek chek" call. Iridescent blue-green in colour with white underparts and a white collar, it hunts for insects in open areas near water. Danau Tamblingan is particularly renowned for bird-watching, and you may spot babblers, woodpeckers, ground thrushes and malkohas if you take the path around the western edge of the lake.

Options in the **evenings** are fewer. In Candikuning, *Anda*, just across the road from the turning to the Botanical Gardens, is a good bet, offering inexpensive Indonesian and Chinese food, and in Pancasari the menu at *Cafe Teras Lempuna* has the usual fare plus lots of Japanese options (Rp30–40,000 for mains).

Danau Buyan

The best way to explore **Danau Buyan**, 6km northwest of Bedugul, is on foot, although you can drive 3km on the side road that heads west just to the north of the Pancasari bemo terminal to the ticket office (Rp3000, parking Rp2000). There are plenty of tracks in the area and there should be some local trekking guides at the ticket office offering fixed-price local treks. Don't wander too far off the beaten track on your own – it's easy to lose your sense of direction in the dense forest.

Danau Tamblingan and beyond

To reach **Danau Tamblingan**, take the road west from **Wanagiri**, 2km north of Pancasari, which runs along the ridge above the northern shore of Danau Buyan.

About 4km from Wanagiri, *Bukit Kembar* (☎0859/3610 0848, ✉princessdayu @yahoo.com; ➌) has six functional rooms with hot water; there's an attached restaurant. A kilometre further west, *Puncak Bagus* is a small restaurant with fine lake views from the sitting area across the road. The restaurant is located above the shoulder of land separating Danau Buyan and Danau Tamblingan.

Another two kilometres west the road divides at a monolithic, seemingly granite, **pyramid**, that now resembles an Inca ruin, which was built some years ago from recycled plastic. Take the left fork 3km down to the village of **TAMBLINGAN**, where the farmers grow vegetables, fish for carp and rear cattle on the *tunjung* (lotus) that grows on the lake. ⚡ *Pondok Kesuma Wisata* (☎0817/472 8826; ➍) has attractive, well-kept bungalows with hot water in a pretty garden. It's then a hundred metres to the car park and ticket office for **Danau Tamblingan** (Rp3000, parking Rp1000), from where it's ten minutes' walk down to the lakeside. On the shore, **Pura Gubug**, sporting eleven-, nine- and five-roofed *meru*, is dedicated to Dewi Danu. Pilgrims visit the three lakeside temples of Batur, Bratan and Tamblingan to worship the lake goddess and pray for good harvests. Footpaths lead around the shore; see p.287 for information on guided treks.

The scenic route to the north coast

Back at the pyramid above Tamblingan, the main road from Wanagiri turns away from the lakes as it continues west and descends through coffee fields and clove trees. It's just over a kilometre to the restaurant *Ngiring Ngewedang*, which has a glorious panorama. There's a small Indo-Chinese menu and sandwiches (Rp25–30,000). They roast and grind coffee and staff will explain the entire process. The road continues on down to Munduk (4km).

An **alternative scenic route**, even further off the beaten track, takes the road signed "Gobleg" from above Danau Tamblingan, 1.8km north of the pyramid. It descends slopes rich in banana, durian, papaya and jackfruit trees, to Gobleg, Asah Gobleg and then down through Selat before reaching the coast at **Anturan** towards the east of Lovina. Take a decent road-map to explore these byways.

Munduk

Three kilometres down from *Ngiring Ngewedang* there's a small sign for **Munduk waterfall** (Rp3000, parking Rp2000), only one of several waterfalls in the area – anyone staying at *Puri Lumbung Cottages* or *Lumbung Bali Cottages* (see box below) can arrange a trek to the others. The falls are far more impressive than those at the more famous Gitgit.

A kilometre north, the village of **MUNDUK** is an excellent base for exploring the area and arranging cultural classes (see box below). Munduk's most established **place to stay** is 乎 *Puri Lumbung Cottages* (☏0362/92810, ⓦ www .purilumbung.com; ❻–❼), which provides accommodation in replicas of the traditional *lumbung* (rice-storage barns) that stood on the site. They have hot water, fabulous views, are extremely well furnished and sit in lovely grounds. There's a **spa** and a moderately-priced restaurant attached. *Puri Lumbung Cottages* also administer several local **homestays** (❹–❺). A few hundred metres south, *Lumbung Bali Cottages* (☏0828/372 6458, ⓦ www.lumbung-bali.com; ❻) features comfortable, traditional bungalows in attractive gardens with an attached restaurant. The newest place, *Munduk Sari* (☏0828/372 2744, ⓦ www.munduksari.com; ❻–❽) is a few hundred metres north and has rooms, some with excellent views. There are several warung in the village as an alternative to **eating** at the hotels.

On to Mayong

Heading towards the north coast from Munduk you'll pass through the ridge villages of Gunung Sari and Banyuatis before reaching **MAYONG** (see p.312 for details of a detour inland from here through Bestala), where there's a

---

Munduk activities

A huge number of **activities** can be arranged at *Puri Lumbung Cottages* in Munduk, including trekking and sightseeing ($3–8.50 per hour for a guide for a group). The **treks** on offer take in waterfalls, springs, villages, coffee and clove plantations, rivers, *subak*, lakes and temples. An equally diverse variety of **sightseeing** trips are available. Activities and classes include massage ($8–17/hr), yoga (from $25/hr depending on the size of the group), cooking ($24 per person for an all-day class), Indonesian language, palm-leaf or bamboo weaving, fruit and flower arranging, woodcarving, painting, dancing and musical instrument classes ($10–20/hr depending on the size of the group) and spiritual discussions ($20/hr). Some of these activities are also available through *Lumbung Bali Cottages*.

roadside restaurant, 🎋 *Bali Panorama* (☎0813/3863 0449, ⊜mayong_bali @yahoo.com), serving mostly organic food (mains Rp21–37,500) from an enticing menu accompanied by lovely paddy-field views. It's generally open 9am to 6.30pm but will serve dinner on request. *Bali Panorama* also organize local treks of two or six hours (from Rp50,000 per hour depending on the group size) and three-hour cooking classes (Rp175,000 per person); contact them in advance for these activities. Jero Made Karsini Murjasa, the proprietor, is a keen conversationalist and always willing to offer advice on spiritual matters. From Mayong, the road continues to **Seririt** on the north coast.

The north coast

The **north coast** of Bali is a rugged and, in places, dramatic landscape, the northern flanks of the mountains dropping steeply towards sweeping black-sand beaches. The land is parched towards the east, where lava flows from the last eruption of Gunung Agung are still visible. To the west, more fertile soil and more rain results in some finely sculpted rice terraces.

The major settlement is **Singaraja**, once the busiest port on the island. Most tourists, however, come to the north for the beach resort of **Lovina**, west of Singaraja, a great place to relax or to use as a base for exploring the region. Increasing accommodation options to the east provide alternative, more isolated, bases.

Some history

While the north coast of Bali has been inhabited for centuries, with local villages mentioned in tenth-century inscriptions, the ascendancy of the area really began at the end of the sixteenth century, when **Ki Gusti Ngurah Panji Sakti** founded the northern kingdom of Buleleng. In 1604, he built a new palace called Singaraja and went on to gain control of Karangasem, Jembrana and parts of eastern Java, in addition to his own kingdom. These dominions expanded even further when, in 1711, the throne was taken by his son-in-law **Gusti Agung Sakti**, the raja of Mengwi, who established a joint Mengwi–Buleleng kingdom, which flourished for most of the eighteenth century.

In 1846, the invading **Dutch** directed their First Military Expedition against the north of the island defeating the Balinese in 1849 and taking over the administration of Buleleng. This encouraged European journalists, merchants and scholars to visit and settle in the area, while the south of the island was still battling against the Dutch. In attempting to make the colony profitable, the Dutch built roads, improved irrigation systems and encouraged coffee as a cash crop. However, it was not all plain sailing: in 1864, **Ida Made Rai** rebelled in Banjar, near Seririt, and it took the Dutch until 1868 to subdue him and his followers.

As the Dutch strengthened their hold, the administrative importance of the north grew. When they combined Bali and Lombok into one regency in 1882, Singaraja was established as the capital. During World War II, the invading **Japanese** also made their headquarters here, but when the Dutch subsequently returned to the island, they moved their capital to Denpasar due to its proximity to the new airport and the larger population.

Singaraja and around

The second largest Balinese city after Denpasar, **SINGARAJA** has an airy spaciousness of broad avenues, large monuments and colonial bungalows set in attractive gardens. With a population of over 100,000, it is home to Hindus, Muslims and Buddhists. Behind the old harbour you can still see the shophouses and narrow streets of the original trading area; Jalan Hasanuddin is known as Kampung Bugis and Jalan Imam Bonjol as Kampung Arab after the Muslim Bugis settlers from Sulawesi whose descendants still live in the area.

Accommodation isn't great in Singaraja and there are only a couple of sights, but you can spend a few interesting hours exploring here, best done as a day-trip from Lovina. All points eastwards are easily accessible, including the fabulous temples of **Pura Meduwe Karang** – best of the bunch – **Sangsit** and **Jagaraga**, and further along the north coast to the resorts of **Air Sanih** and **Tulamben**.

Arrival, orientation and information

Singaraja has three bus and bemo terminals: **Sukasada** (also called Sangket) to the south of the town, serving Gitgit, Bedugul and Denpasar (Ubung terminal); **Banyuasri** on the western edge serving Lovina, Seririt and Gilimanuk; and **Penarukan** in the east, for services along the coast via Tulamben to Amlapura, and inland along the road to Kintamani, Penelokan (for the Batur area) and on to Denpasar (Batubulan terminal) via Bangli. For information on travelling to and from **Ngurah Rai Airport**, see the box on p.100.

Small bemos (flat rate Rp5000) ply main routes around town linking two of the terminals – light brown between Banyuasri and Penarukan, dark red between Sukasada and Banyuasri, and blue between Sukasada and Penarukan. There are no metered taxis.

Spread out along the coast and stretching inland for several kilometres, the main thoroughfare of **Jalan Jen Achmad Yani/Jalan Dr Sutomo** is oriented east–west and will eventually take you out onto the road to Lovina, while **Jalan Gajah Made** is oriented north–south and heads, via Sukasada, inland to Bedugul. The major junction where these two main roads meet has the market, restaurants, banks, post office and night market all within walking distance: it feels as much like the town centre as anywhere.

The **tourist office** is south of the town centre at Jl Veteran 23 (Mon–Thurs 8am–3pm, Fri 8–11am; ℡0362/25141, ⓦwww.northbalitourism.com). Staff may be able to produce a brochure, map and calendar of events. Bemos heading to Sukasada terminal pass the eastern end of Jalan Veteran, 100m from the office.

Accommodation

The **hotels** in Singaraja cater for Indonesians. *Wijaya*, Jl Sudirman 74 (℡0362/21915, ℻25817; ❶–❹), has clean, tiled rooms and is conveniently close to Banyuasri terminal. A/c and hot water are available.

The City

Singaraja's best-known attraction is esoteric, but surprisingly interesting. A couple of kilometres south of the town centre the **Gedong Kirtya,**

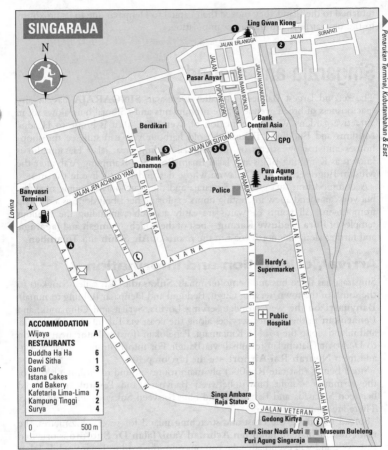

SINGARAJA

N

Ling Gwan Kiong

JALAN ERLANGGA

JALAN SURAPATI

Penarukan Terminal, Kubutambahan & East

JALAN DIPONEGORO

JALAN IMAM BONJOL

JALAN HASANUDIN

JL DURIAN

Pasar Anyar

Berdikari

JALAN DR SUTOMO

Bank
Central Asia

GPO

JALAN KARTINI

JALAN DEWI SARTIKA

Bank
Danamon

JALAN PRAMUKA

Pura Agung
Jagatnata

JALAN JEN ACHMAD YANI

Banyuasri
Terminal

Police

Lovina

JALAN UDAYANA

JALAN GAJAH MADE

JL KARTINI

JALAN NGURAH RAI

Hardy's
Supermarket

Public
Hospital

JALAN SUDIRMAN

Singa Ambara
Raja Statue

JALAN GAJAH MADE

JALAN VETERAN

Gedong Kirtya

Puri Sinar Nadi Putri   Museum Buleleng
Puri Agung Singaraja

Sukasada Terminal, Beratan & Bedugul ▼

ACCOMMODATION
Wijaya · · · · · · · · · · · · A
RESTAURANTS
Buddha Ha Ha · · · · · · 6
Dewi Sitha · · · · · · · · · 1
Gandi · · · · · · · · · · · · · 3
Istana Cakes
 and Bakery · · · · · · · 5
Kafetaria Lima-Lima · · 7
Kampung Tinggi · · · · · 2
Surya · · · · · · · · · · · · · 4

0 ———— 500 m

Jl Veteran 20 (Mon–Thurs 7.30am–3.30pm, Fri 7am–2.30pm; donation
expected), is the only library of **lontar manuscripts** in the world. These are
texts inscribed on leaves from the *lontar* palm (see box, p.295). It contains
over six thousand texts on religion, customs, philosophy, folklore, medicine,
astrology and black magic, written in Balinese, Old Javanese and Indonesian.
Established by L.J.J. Caron, the Dutch Resident of Bali, and opened in 1928,
this is a scholarly place, but visitors are welcome; a member of the library
staff will show you around. There are also manuscripts from India and Burma
as well as *prasasti*, inscribed bronze plates from the tenth century, which are
amongst the oldest written records on Bali.

Just around the corner the Royal Palace of **Puri Agung Singaraja**, also known
as Puri Gede Buleleng (Jl Mayor Metra 12 ☏0362/22974, ✉purisingaraja
@hotmail.com; daily 9am–5pm; entry by donation), is the restored palace of the
former royal family of Buleleng. Rebuilt at the beginning of the twentieth century,
there are excellent displays and photographs of previous rulers and their historical
context. The most interesting relate to Anak Agung Panji Tisna (1908–78), the **last
Raja of Buleleng**, novelist, founder of Lovina and converted Christian who

narrowly escaped execution by the occupying Japanese army during World War II. His descendants still live in the palace.

At the front of the palace the **Museum Buleleng** (as above) displays paintings, ancient artifacts found within Buleleng and assorted other bits and piecese: an antique car and an ancient typewriter to name just two. Some of the material is set in context but much of it remains quite enigmatic to the casual visitor. Also attached to the palace, **Puri Sinar Nadi Putri** (as above) is a small weaving workshop producing attractive, weft *ikat* cloth.

A larger **weaving workshop** is **Berdikari**, Jl Dewi Sartika 42 (daily 8am–5pm), which produces top-quality silk and cotton *ikat* – you can see photographs of all the recent Indonesian presidents wearing their cloth. Scarves (from Rp300,000) and sarongs (from Rp587,000 for cotton to a million rupiah for silk) are on sale. If you want to watch the weavers, come before 4pm.

Keep your eyes open as you amble around the city; **Singa Ambara Raja**, the winged lion symbol of Buleleng district, is a source of great pride to the citizens of Singaraja, and you'll notice its image everywhere.

Almost in the middle of town, on Jalan Pramuka, **Pura Agung Jagatnata** is grand and modern with every available surface covered in typically northern effusive decoration. The *candi bentar* rises dramatically for 15m, and the main shrine, the *padmasana* to the Supreme God, Sang Yang Widi, in the inner courtyard, is even higher. Take along a sarong and scarf just in case it's open, but very often it is closed.

North of Jalan Jen Achmad Yani, in the midst of a maze of alleys, the market, **Pasar Anyar**, is a treasure-trove selling pretty much everything available in the north of the island including food, clothes and household goods. Continue north to the **waterfront**, site of the ancient harbour of Buleleng. It's hard to imagine the days when this was the busiest port on Bali. A monument, **Yudha Mandala Tama**, shows an independence fighter and commemorates an incident in 1945 during the independence struggle when the Balinese resistance attempted to lower a Dutch flag that was flying on the coast. They succeeded but were spotted and fired on by a Dutch navy vessel offshore, killing one man. Just around the corner, the Chinese temple, **Ling Gwan Kiong** (admission by donation), is a colourful, atmospheric confection of shrines, statues, plaques and bridges.

Lontar manuscripts

Preparing the leaves of the **lontar palm** or *punyan ental* for inscription is a lengthy process. After removing the central rib, the leaves are soaked in water for three days to destroy the chlorophyll and brushed to remove dirt, before being boiled with traditional herbal ingredients to increase flexibility and strength. The leaves are slow-dried to prevent wrinkling, pressed for ten days, cut to the required size (35–40cm long and 3–4cm wide), and punched with three holes for threading. The palms are bound between thin wooden boards, pressed, and their edges coloured red with *kincu* to deter insects. Storing for about six months after binding produces the perfect texture.

The text is engraved using a sharpened iron tool and carbon black from a lamp is rubbed into the inscription to make it visible. Due to the humidity on Bali, the manuscripts only last between fifty and a hundred years, so decaying manuscripts are copied onto new palm leaves, ensuring the survival of this ancient art. It is also possible to watch *lontar* palms being inscribed in the village of Tenganan near Candi Dasa (see p.250).

Eating, drinking and nightlife

The largest concentration of **restaurants** is at Jl Jen Achmad Yani 25, a small square set back from the road; the Chinese restaurant *Gandi* is a good bet, as is *Surya*, at the entrance to the square, selling Padang food at Rp6–7,000 per plate. Further west along the same street *Kafetaria Lima-Lima* at no. 55A has cheap Indonesian food and drink (mains about Rp6000). Across the road, *Istana Cakes and Bakery* at no. 64 dishes up sweet buns and fluorescent coloured cakes. During the day *Buddha Ha Ha* on Jalan Gajah Made, just south of the main post office, features mostly vegetarian Indonesian dishes for Rp6–7000. On the waterfront there are several, very similar, restaurants built on stilts over the water – a great spot to catch the breeze with fine coastal views. *Dewi Sitha* offers Indonesian main courses at Rp15–22,000 and better-value set meals (Rp19–30,000). For really cheap eats, *Kampung Tinggi*, just east of the bridge on the main road east out of Singaraja, is lined with food stalls every afternoon (2–8pm), some of which have a basic written menu. At the western end of Singaraja, the restaurants that line Jalan Pemaron Pura Penimbangan are accessible from the city (see p.307 for details).

As darkness falls, the **night market** in the Jalan Durian area springs into life with fruit, vegetable and food stalls; this is the only local nightlife and a pleasant way to spend the evening.

Listings

Banks and exchange Bank Central Asia on Jl Dr Sutomo (exchange counter Mon–Fri 10am–2pm) is most convenient for exchange and there's also an international ATM. Several other ATMs, including Bank Danamon on Jl Jen Achmad Yani and at Hardy's.

Bus tickets (long-distance) Menggala, Jl Jen Achmad Yani 76 (☎0362/24374), operates daily night buses to Surabaya (Rp110,000; 8hr), leaving at 7pm, arriving at Probolinggo and Pasuruan in East Java, access points for the Bromo region, in the middle of the night. Safari Dharma Raya, Jl Jen Achmad Yani 84 (☎0362/23460), leaves every afternoon at 3pm for the 24-hour trip to Jakarta (Rp250,000). Puspa Rama, Jl Jen Achmad Yani 90 (☎0362/22696), operates daily buses to Surabaya (7.30pm; 8hr; Rp110,000) and Malang (7.30pm; 9–10hr; Rp120,000). They also sell tickets for the daily bus that leaves Gilimanuk at 5pm for Yogyakarta (12hrs; Rp160,000).

Doctors & hospital Rumah Sakit Umum (the public hospital), Jl Ngurah Rai ☎0362/41046. Many of Singaraja's medical facilities, including doctors and pharmacies, are concentrated nearby.

Internet access Warnet, Jl Dewi Sartika 32A (6am–12midnight; Rp4000/hr).

Phones The main phone office is at the southern end of Jalan Kartini (see map).

Post office The main post office is at Jl Gajah Made 156 (Mon–Thurs 8am–3pm, Fri 8am–1pm, Sat 8am–noon). Poste restante service is to the above address, Singaraja 81113, Bali. Also a Western Union agent. A smaller post office is south of *Wijaya* hotel at Jl Sudirman 68A, a short walk from Banyuasri terminal.

Supermarket Hardy's (6am–10.30pm), the closest that Singaraja boasts to a mall, is three floors of local shopping including a supermarket.

South of Singaraja

Just to the **south** of the city, the village of **BERATAN**, 2km beyond Jalan Veteran towards the Sukasada terminal (bemos to Sukasada pass the door) is known for its silverwork. There are a few shops on the main road but if you are seriously interested, Celuk (see p.172) is a better bet.

Further south, 10km along the road to Bedugul and spread over a three-kilometre stretch are three well-signposted waterfalls at **Gitgit** (daily 8am–5.30pm; Rp3000, parking Rp2000 at each). All buses between Singaraja (Sukasada terminal) and Denpasar via Bedugul pass here. The most southerly falls are the Twin Falls, while the Multi-tiered Fall is fairly unimpressive. The main fall is a forty-metre single drop. Local belief suggests that couples coming to Gitgit will eventually separate – but it doesn't seem to deter hordes of visitors.

East of Singaraja

Many of the villages and the wealth of carved temples to the **east of Singaraja** can be visited on a day-trip from Lovina: all lie on bemo or bus routes.

Sangsit

Some 8km east of Singaraja, a side road north leads 200m to the pink-sandstone **Pura Beji** (admission by donation, sarong rental included) of **SANGSIT**. Dedicated to Dewi Sri, the rice goddess, it's justly famous for the exuberance of its carvings and every surface drips with animals, plants, masks, humans and monsters both old and new.

About 400m to the northeast across the fields from Pura Beji, you'll spot the red roofs of **Pura Dalem Sangsit**. The front wall of the temple vibrantly depicts the rewards that await the godly in heaven and, more luridly, the punishments awaiting the evil in hell: stone blocks on the head, women giving birth to strange creatures, and sharp penises descending through the tops of skulls. The village of Sangsit straggles 500m north from here to a black-sand beach.

Jagaraga

Back on the main road, 500m east of the Sangsit turning, the road to **JAGARAGA** heads 4km inland to the village. Bemos serve the village from Singaraja (Penarukan terminal).

Jagaraga was the site of two immense battles between the Balinese and the Dutch. In 1848, the Balinese, led by Jelantik, won with huge loss of life, their 16,000 troops fighting with lances and kris against 3000 well-armed Dutch. The two forces met here again in 1849, when the Dutch finally took control of Buleleng (see p.419). The temple **Pura Dalem Jagaraga**, about 1km north of the village, is dedicated to Siwa the destroyer and his wife Durga and renowned for the pictorial carvings on its front walls. Those on the left show village life before the Dutch invasion – kite-flying, fishing, climbing coconut trees. Next to these are the Dutch arriving in cars, boats, planes and on bicycles, destroying the community. On the right-hand side is a much-photographed carving of two Dutch men driving a Model T Ford, being held up by bandits. Nearby are statues of uniformed Dutch officers and the legendary Pan Brayut (see box, p.194). On the inside wall the crocodile eating the man is taken to represent the Dutch conquering Bali.

Pura Meduwe Karang

The most spectacular temple in the area is **Pura Meduwe Karang** (admission by donation, sarong rental included) at **KUBUTAMBAHAN**, 11km east of Singaraja and 300m east of the junction with the Kintamani road. If you only visit one temple in the north, this is the one to go for. Dedicated to Batara Meduwe Karang, the temple ensures divine protection for crops grown on dry land, such as coconuts, maize and groundnuts. It's built on a grand scale: the terraces at the front support 34 figures from the *Ramayana* (see p.444) including the giant Kumbakarna battling with hordes of monkeys from Sugriwa's army.

Inside, the walls are decorated with **carvings** of Balinese folk, including elderly people and mothers with babies. In the inner courtyard, and typical of northern temples, a large rectangular base links the three central shrines, called the *bebaturan*. It is here you'll find one of the most famous carvings on Bali: a cyclist (possibly the Dutch artist W.O.J. Nieuwenkamp, who first visited Bali in 1904 and explored the island on a bicycle) wearing floral shorts, with a rat about to go under the back wheel, apparently being chased by a dog.

Air Sanih and around

Further east, 6km from Kubutambahan, the tiny beach resort of **AIR SANIH**, also known as Yeh Sanih, is the location of cold **springs** (daily 7am–7pm; Rp3000), which are believed to originate in Danau Bratan. They are surrounded by gardens and there are changing rooms. All public transport between Singaraja and Amlapura passes through.

Accommodation

With two notable exceptions much of the **accommodation** in the area is purely functional. If you just need a bed, *Puri Rahayu* (☎0362/26565; ❶–❷) is just over 200m east of the springs with bungalows in a small compound and a restaurant attached. All have cold water and a/c is available. *Hotel Tara* (☎0362/26575; ❶–❷) is on the coast 600m east of the springs, with a row of basic tiled bungalows with a choice of fan or a/c, all facing seawards.

There's accommodation worth travelling for at ⚲ *Cilik's Beach Garden* (☎0362/26561, ⓦwww.ciliksbeachgarden.com; ❼–❽) 200m east of the springs, and the real gem in the area, with two bungalows, one villa and one *lumbung*-style cottage. All have hot water and are set in fabulous gardens overlooking the coast – a truly magical hideaway.

It is also worth the effort needed to reach *Mimpi Bungalows* (☎0813/3857 9595, ⓦwww.mimpibali.com; ❹), 700m inland along a well-marked turning just to the east of the springs. Bungalows are comfortable, have fan and hot water and are set around a lovely pool. The rooftop restaurant has a great panorama over the area and there is a spa offering treatments at around Rp80,000.

East from Air Sanih

About 12km east of Air Sanih, the road climbs over a headland at **PONJOK BATU** with great views along the coast. The **temple** here was founded by the sixteenth-century Javanese priest Nirartha (see pp. 320 & 416). It is said that while sitting on a rock Nirartha saw a wrecked ship below. All the crew were dead on the beach but, using his spiritual powers, he brought them back to life. Following this miracle, the local people noticed that the rock where Nirartha had been sitting shone with a magical light and a temple was founded here. Now, all Balinese drivers stop to pray and receive a blessing.

About 300m west of the temple, *Puri Bagus Ponjok Batu* is a small **restaurant** perched above the road with good views and a breeze. There's a small menu of Indonesian food including grilled fish and chicken (mains Rp22–30,000).

Just 1.5 km west of the temple it's impossible to miss the exuberant decoration on the outside of the **Art Zoo**, the northern gallery of the American-born artist **Symon** (ⓦwww.symonbali.com), displaying his characteristically dramatic and sensual pictures of naked young men and women. He also has a gallery in Ubud (see p.195).

Less than 1km east of the temple, in the village of **ALASSARI**, *Pondok Sembiran Bungalows* (☎0362/24437, ⓕ21108; ❹), signed towards the coast from the main road, is an attractive setup in a quiet location. All accommodation has a/c and hot water, some is by the beach and some about 300m inland where there's a pretty pool. Nearby, accessed via the same side road, *Villa Boreh* (☎0812/385 8813, ⓦwww.bali-villa.org; room ❺, villa ❼–❾) is a magical spot just along the coast.

At the time of writing there are six gorgeous villas, each slightly different, set well apart in a luscious garden just behind the beach and with two great swimming pools. Rooms in a large house are also available. There's an offshore reef for snorkelling and an attached spa using Villa Boreh products. Prices are reasonable (two-hour Balinese massage Rp180,000) and spa clients do not have to be staying at the hotel although advanced booking is necessary.

Continuing east, the land becomes increasingly dry and barren, and views of the outer rim of the Batur crater dominate the inland skyline. From Pacung, 2km east of Ponjok Batu, it is 3km inland to **SEMBIRAN**, an ancient Bali Aga village, along with Trunyan (see p.284) and Tenganan (see p.250), but today little distinguishes it from any other village in Bali.

A hundred metres beyond the Sembiran turning in **PACUNG**, the *Surya Indigo Handweaving Centre* (Ⓦwww.surya-indigo.com; Mon–Sat 10am–4pm) is well worth a stop. Producing striped *bebali* cloth in cotton and silk using all local materials and natural dyes (many of the plants are in the garden) and woven on traditional *cagcag* (backstrap) looms, it is possible to see every stage in the process and learn about the co-operative. Cloth is produced for export but some may be for sale – a cotton *bebali* (180cm by 60cm) retails at about Rp200,000 and silk at Rp300,000.

Bondalem and around

Another kilometre east brings you to **BONDALEM**. On the west side of the village *Bali Mandala Resort* (Ⓣ0362/28508, Ⓦwww.balimandala.com; ⑥) is in a great coastal location with a small swimming pool. All bungalows have hot water, and there's a two-storey restaurant, with fine views, serving Balinese and international food. There are often groups here attending meditation and yoga courses but individuals seeking peace and quiet are also welcome – reservations required. An on-site **Wellness Spa** offers Balinese healing, meditation, yoga and counselling. *Bali Mandala* is signposted from the main road, but it's 800m through a maze of lanes so you'll probably need to ask for directions. On the eastern side of Bondalem village a sign indicates a quiet **back road** that leads 26km up to Kintamani (see p.285).

The small village of **TEJAKULA**, 3km east of Bondalem, is worth a stop for the building that has become known as its **horse bath**, an elaborate white-stone confection that is a cross between a public bathing area and a temple – you'll need a sarong and sash to enter. It is 100m south of the road, marked by a large pink statue in the centre of the village. In reality the only horses who ever bathed here belonged to the kings of Buleleng and the site was a sacred temple long before that. The village is a sleepy backwater these days but local historians claim that the area had trading links with distant lands as far back as the first century AD, when it far outstripped the later trading ports of Padang Bai and Benoa in fame and influence; numerous local finds of foreign relics support their case. There's excellent accommodation here at *Bali Beach Villas* (Ⓣ0362/26561, Ⓦwww.cbg-tejakula.com; ⑥), an outpost of *Cilik's Beach Garden* in Air Sanih. There are two comfortable, beautifully furnished bungalows next to the beach. Look out for the "*CBG Beach Resort*" sign pointing seawards at the western end of the village.

A kilometre east of the village, a discreet sign points to *Gaia-Oasis* (Ⓣ0812/385 3350, Ⓦwww.gaia-oasis.com; ⑥), a haven of tranquillity offering spiritual and physical healing in a brilliant location with comfortable accommodation. There is no vehicle access and the final 500m is completed on foot. There are regular yoga and meditation sessions and a range of therapies is available. *Gaia* also operate a small property in the hills nearby – see website for details.

About two kilometres beyond here at **LES**, a sign points inland to **Yeh Mempeh** or Waterfall, questionably dubbed the highest waterfall in Bali. It's 1.5km through the village to a parking area. Pay a donation at the warung on the corner and follow the concreted path to the side for about twenty minutes through the forest. Follow the water channel until, about fifteen minutes in, you'll realize the concrete path is below and to the right. Join it again and you'll soon reach the falls. Even in the dry season it is picturesque as the water bounces down the rock face into an icy pool at the bottom.

Sembirenteng and Tembok

About 7km beyond Tejakula, just east of **SEMBIRENTENG**, *Alam Anda Dive and Spa Resort* (☎0812/465 6485, @www.alamanda.de; ⑥–⑨) is a vibrant, place, largely but not solely, used by divers. There are two reefs just offshore and day-trips to other dive sites. Plenty of other activities are also available including tours and cookery sessions and there's a spa and a pool right beside the beach. Accommodation is as plush or basic as you require with a/c and hot water available. One apartment is wheelchair friendly. The **restaurant** is attractive and cool-serving Western and Indonesian food supplemented by some German favourites – as well as Häagen-Dazs ice cream (main courses Rp26–60,000). It's a good place to stop on a drive along the north coast.

Just over a kilometre further east at **TEMBOK** the *Poinciana Resort* (☎0812/385 9951, @www.poinciana-resort.com; ⑤–⑦) is completely secluded on the coast with a/c and hot-water accommodation, set in a pretty garden around a pool. The attached restaurant serves Indonesian and Western fare (main courses Rp25–40,000). It's a great spot and be prepared for complete relaxation.

Another 3km further east, the super-luxurious *Spa Village Tembok* (☎0362/32033, @www.spavillage.com; ⑨) features fabulously designed accommodation in Bali-modern style. The pool is glorious, landscaping is superb and there are a vast number of treatments available from Bali and Malaysia (the home of the *Spa Village* concept). This is one of the most gorgeous hotels in the east and north of Bali and prices start at $400, all inclusive including a daily spa treatment. However, it is pretty isolated – 22km east to Tulamben.

Lovina and around

Stretching along 8km of black-sand beach, **LOVINA** is the largest resort in Bali outside the Kuta–Legian–Seminyak conurbation. Beginning 6km west of Singaraja, the resort encompasses six villages: from east to west, **Pemaron**, **Tukad Mungga**, **Anturan**, **Kalibukbuk**, **Kaliasem** and **Temukus**. Kalibukbuk is the centre of Lovina and is bursting with accommodation and restaurants, located on several side-roads leading down to the coast, including one about 1.5km east known as **Banyualit**. While the peak season (June–Aug & Dec) is busy, Lovina remains far less frantic than the southern resorts, although there's some nightlife available.

The potential of the area was spotted by the last raja of Buleleng, Anak Agung Panji Tisna, who built the *Tasik Madu Hotel* at Kaliasem in the 1960s and devised the name Lovina. Today, activity centres on the beach, with **snorkelling**, **diving** and **dolphin-watching** as diversions. Lovina is an ideal base for exploring the whole of the north coast as well as the volcanic areas inland.

▲ Fishermen at Lovina

On Independence Day (Aug 17) you can witness local **buffalo races** (*sapi gerumbungan*), the only place on Bali where the colourful tradition can be seen, apart from at Negara. Keep an eye open in case the races staged at other times for tourists are reinstated.

Lovina is one stop on the annual **Sail Indonesia** (ⓦ www.sailindonesia.net) three-month sailing rally through Indonesia from July to September. It's an amazing hoopla when the hundreds of yachts hit town with loads of special events and activities (check website for dates).

Arrival, information and transport

Getting to Lovina is easy: inter-island **buses** from Java to Singaraja pass through, as do Gilimanuk–Singaraja and Amlapura–Gilimanuk services and all local buses and **bemos** from the west of the island. From Denpasar, you can come on Denpasar (Ubung)–Singaraja services via Pupuan or on minibuses to Seririt and then swap onto local bemos. From the east of Bali, you'll come via Singaraja, from whose Banyuasri terminal it's a short bemo ride (Rp5000). As the resort is so spread out, it's well worth pinning down where you want to stay initially. Perama **tourist shuttle buses** serve the resort. See "Travel details", see p.312 for a full list of destinations. Sample prices are Rp70,000 to the southern resorts and Ubud and Rp100,000 to Candi Dasa or Padang Bai. Perama's office is in Anturan (a short walk from the Anturan accommodation) – it's an additional Rp5000 to be dropped off elsewhere. Check with other shuttle-bus operators whether they drop off more centrally. Fixed-price taxis are available direct from **Ngurah Rai Airport** for Rp450,000. For more information on travelling to and from the airport, see the box on p.100.

Lovina's **tourist office** (ⓣ 0362/41910 mornings only; Mon–Sat 8am–8pm) is on the main road at Kalibukbuk. The monthly **tourist paper** *Lovina Pages* is worth picking up around the resort. During daylight hours there are frequent **bemos** between Singaraja and Seririt, but after dark you'll need to negotiate with the transport touts, unless your hotel or restaurant offers transport. A huge number of places offer **vehicles for rent** or charter (see "Listings") and there are **bicycles** for rent, but the Singaraja–Seririt road is very busy.

Accommodation

Lovina has **accommodation** options for every budget and taste but it's spread over a wide area and it's best to avoid the noisy main road. There are restaurants throughout the resort but if you want any semblance of nightlife then you'll want to be within reach of Kalibukbuk.

Pemaron and Tukad Mungga

Putri Sari, on the main road, marks the eastern end of Lovina. The accommodation in **Pemaron** and **Tukad Mungga** (where the beach is known as Pantai Happy) ranges from budget cheapies to top-class choices. It's an extremely quiet area. The turning for Pantai Happy is opposite a split gateway and sign for Tukad Mungga. The beach is scruffy but it's a pleasant 15–20-minute walk along to Anturan, not least to admire the beachside villas that now occupy the seafront.

Happy Beach Inn ☎0362/41017. Four functional, cheap rooms with attached cold-water bathrooms close to the beach in a small but pleasant garden. ❶

Kubu Lalang ☎0362/42207, ⓦkubu .balihotelguide.com. Traditional bungalows, all with fan but with the option of hot water, in a pretty garden just behind the beach midway between Pantai Happy and Anturan (5–10min walk in each direction). There's also access from the main road. ❷–❹

Puri Bagus Lovina ☎0362/21430, ⓦwww .puribagus.com. The most luxurious hotel on the Lovina coast offers large, airy villas in extensive grounds towards the far eastern end of the resort. There's a good pool, a library and a gorgeous spa surrounded by pools and fountains. ❽–❾

Puri Bedahulu ☎0362/41731. Next to the beach at Pantai Happy with a pretty garden. Comfortable bungalows have elegant Balinese carvings, and hot water and a/c is available. ❶–❷

Anturan

The small fishing village of **Anturan** remains much quieter than Kalibukbuk and the villagers are well used to tourists wandering around. There are plenty of hawkers but it's all relaxed and amiable. To get there, take the turning almost opposite the petrol station and the Anturan health centre (*Puskesmas*). All the listed accommodation is within ten minutes' walk of the Perama office, just west of the turning.

Bali Taman Resort and Spa ☎0362/41126, ⓦwww.balitamanlovina.com. A big operation with good-quality accommodation and lots of facilities including a spa. The top-end bungalows with sea views are excellent. There's free transport in the Lovina area. ❻–❼

Bayu Mantra ☎0362/41930, ⓦwww.balitour .jimdo.com. Clean, tiled, fan-cooled bungalows in a large, quiet garden a short walk from the beach. Hot water is available. ❶

🏃 **Gede Homestay** ☎0362/41526. Good-quality accommodation in two rows of well-kept bungalows in an excellent location just behind the beach. There's a small restaurant and sunbathing area. A/c and hot water are available. ❶–❸

Mandhara Chico ☎0362/41271. Close to the beach, the best rooms are the two beachfront

bungalows with verandahs facing seawards. Hot water and a/c are available. ❶–❷

Puspa Rama ☎0362/42070, Ⓔagungdayu @yahoo.com. A small row of clean rooms, one with a/c and some with hot water, set in a large garden a short walk from the beach. ❶–❷

Sri Homestay ☎0813/3757 0692. All the bungalows face the ocean and some have hot water. Access is via a track from the main road or via the beach. ❷–❸

Villa Agung Beach Inn ☎0362/41527, ⓦwww .agungvilla.com. Rooms, all with hot water, are set back from the sea behind the small swimming pool. The real draw is the upstairs lounge offering great ocean views. A/c is available. ❸–❹

Banyualit

The **Banyualit** side-road, Jalan Laviana, is 1.5km east of Kalibukbuk and is quiet. The beach here is pretty with plenty of local fishing boats. There are enough restaurants to eat at a different place every night for a week and the *Volcano Club*, Lovina's main nightlife, is also easily accessible.

Aneka Lovina ☎0362/41121, ⓦwww .anekahotels.com. West of the Banyualit turning, 15min walk from Kalibukbuk. Pleasant, comfortable mid-range accommodation in a two-storey building or thatched bungalows, set in attractive gardens with a beachside pool and spa. ⑤–⑥

Juni Arta ☎0362/41885. Rather tucked away, access is via a path from the beach end of Jalan Laviana, these are good-quality, good-value bungalows in a peaceful spot. All rooms have cold water, and there's a choice of fan or a/c. ①–②

Lupa-Lupa Lovina Cottages ☎0362/41698, ⓔjade@s7.dion.ne.jp. A tiny beachside place with its own track from the Singaraja–Seririt road. There are two simple but good-quality rooms with fan and hot water and a two-storey villa with a/c and hot water. All have sea views. ③–⑤

Mas Bungalows ☎0362/41773, ⓦwww .masbungalows.com. All rooms have hot water and are decorated with local textiles. A/c is available and there's a large pool. ②–③

Ray ☎0362/41088. Tiled rooms in a two-storey building with balcony or verandah looking out onto a decent garden. All have fan and hot water is available. There's a small spa. ②–③

Sartaya ☎0362/42240, ⓔkembarsartaya @hotmail.com. Two rows of good-quality, good-value, clean, tiled bungalows, some with hot water and a choice of fan or a/c, facing each other across a small garden. ①–②

Suma ☎0362/41566, ⓦwww.sumahotel .com. Offers a range of clean, well-maintained rooms, from fan and cold-water options up to lovely a/c and hot-water ones. The pool is excellent, the gardens pretty and there's Internet access for guests (Rp200 per minute). Booking recommended. ③–⑤

Kalibukbuk

Centered around two side-roads, Jalan Bina Ria and a parallel road a few hundred metres to the east Jalan Mawar, also known as Jalan Ketapang or Jalan Rambutan, **Kalibukbuk** is the centre of Lovina and chock-full of accommodation, restaurants and tourist facilities. The entrance to Jalan Mawar is at the crossroads marked by traffic lights (the only ones in Lovina) virtually opposite *Khi Khi Restaurant* on the main road. A beachfront walkway links the ocean ends of Jalan Mawar and Jalan Bina Ria.

Astina ☎0362/41187, ⓔselisakadek@hotmail .com. Decent bungalows in a large garden near the beach at the end of Jalan Mawar. A/c and hot water are options and there's an attractive pool with a restaurant nearby. ②–④

Damai Lovina Villas ☎0362/41008, ⓦwww.damai.com. Four kilometres inland in a beautiful hillside location. Accommodation, service and ambience are all elegantly luxurious and the best in Lovina. The eight superbly appointed, characterful bungalows, furnished with antiques, are widely spaced in glorious gardens. There's a spa and lovely pool and the restaurant is one of the delights of northern Bali. Villas with butler service are available across the valley. ⑥

Harris Homestay ☎0362/41152. A popular budget gem tucked away off Jalan Bina Ria. Just five good-value, good-quality rooms, all with fan and attached cold-water bathrooms. ①

Padang Lovina ☎0362/41302, ⓔpadanglovina @yahoo.com. Central but quiet accommodation in a two-storey block just off Jalan Bina Ria. The downstairs rooms have hot water and a/c and upstairs fan and cold water. Guests can use the pool at *Pulestis*. ②–④

Pulestis ☎0362/41035. With a grand entrance on Jalan Bina Ria, this guesthouse offers comfortable rooms with a choice of hot or cold water, fan or a/c, and the pool has a fun waterfall feature. Excellent value. ①–④

Puri Bali ☎0362/41485, ⓦwww.puribalilovina .com. A variety of rooms, in an attractive, quiet garden on Jalan Mawar with an excellent pool; more expensive ones, closer to the pool, have a/c and hot water. ②–④

Puri Manik Sari ☎/ⓕ0362/41089. Mostly fan-cooled bungalows with hot water in a pretty garden set far enough back from the road to avoid the noise. There's one with a/c. ①–②

Rambutan ☎0362/41388, ⓦwww.rambutan .org. Halfway down Jalan Mawar, this long-standing Lovina favourite offers well-furnished,

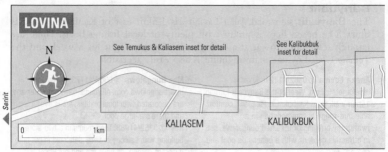

LOVINA

N

0 _____ 1km

See Temukus & Kaliasem inset for detail

See Kalibukbuk inset for detail

KALIASEM   KALIBUKBUK

KALIBUKBUK

Patung Lumba
Lumba

N

JALAN BINA RIA

Spice Dive

Angsoka

JALAN MAWAR

@ 777
Internet

Biyu
Gallery

Nirwana
Gallery

Kristop
Shop

Benny
Tantra

Rahayu
Pharmacy

Khi Khi
Restaurant

0 _____ 100 m

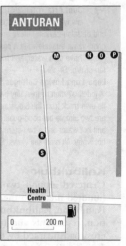

ANTURAN

N

Health
Centre

0 _____ 200 m

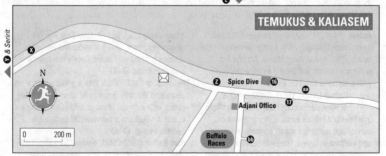

TEMUKUS & KALIASEM

N

0 _____ 200 m

Spice Dive

Adjani Office

Buffalo
Races

ACCOMMODATION

Aditya Beach Resort	Z	Bayu Mantra	R	Lupa-Lupa Lovina		Puri Bali	E	Rini	D
Agus Homestay	X	Damai Lovina Villas	L	Cottages	cc	Puri Bedahulu	V	Rumah Cantik	bb
Aneka Lovina	ee	Gede Homestay	M	Mandhara Chico	N	Puri Manggala	aa	Sartaya	gg
Astina	C	Happy Beach Inn	U	Mas Bungalows	ii	Puri Manik Sari	K	Suma	dd
Bagus Homestay	Y	Harris Homestay	I	Padang Lovina	J	Puspa Rama	S	Sea Breeze	B
Bali Taman Resort		Juni Arta	ff	Pulestis	T	Rambutan	G	Cottages	
and Spa	Q	Kubu Lalang		Puri Bagus Lovina	W	Ray	hh	Sri Homestay	P

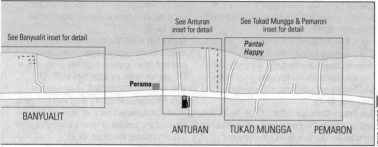

See Banyualit inset for detail

See Anturan inset for detail

See Tukad Mungga & Pemaron inset for detail

Pantai Happy

Perama

BANYUALIT

ANTURAN

TUKAD MUNGGA

PEMARON

TUKAD MUNGGA & PEMARON

Pantai Happy

Putri Sari

0   200 m

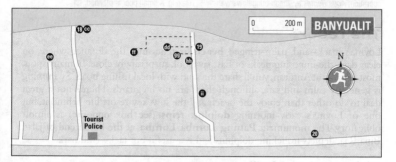

0   200 m

BANYUALIT

Tourist Police

		RESTAURANTS & BARS					
Taman Lily's	F	Barakuda	6	Kopi Bali	5	Santhi Bar	2
Villa Agung		Bu Warung	11	Kubu Lalang	T	Sea Breeze	3
Beach Inn	O	Café Spice	16	Kwizien	17	Spunky's Bar & Restaurant	18
Villa Jaya	A	Damai Lovina Villas	L	Le Madre	8	Volcano Club	20
		Jasmine Kitchen	7	Lovina Bakery,		Warung Bambu Pemaron	15
		Jax Bar and Grill	14	Bistro & Deli	12	Warung Bintang Bali	1
		Kakatua	4	Poco Bar Evolution	10	Warung Indra	19
		Kantin Bar & Restaurant	13	Rambutan	G	Zigiz	9

spotless bungalows from budget to luxury in a beautiful garden with two pools and an attractive restaurant. ③–⑦

🏃 **Rini** ☎0362/41386, Ⓦrinihotel .homepage.dk. Several standards of extremely clean accommodation in a pretty garden on Jalan Mawar. A/c and hot water are available, and there's a salt-water pool with a poolside restaurant. ②–④

Sea Breeze Cottages ☎0362/41138. Beside *Sea Breeze* restaurant in a great beachside position, the attractive wooden bungalows behind the pretty

pool (nonresidents Rp20,000) have a/c and hot water. The more basic rooms are tucked further away. ③–⑤

Taman Lily's ☎0362/41307, Ⓦwww .balilovinahotel-tamanlilys.com. A row of six excellent-value, spotless bungalows, with fans or a/c, and hot water, on Jalan Mawar. ②–③

Villa Jaya ☎0362/700 1238, Ⓦwww.villajaya .com. Attractive, quiet place a short walk from Jalan Mawar. Six rooms in a block, all clean and tiled with hot water and a choice of fan or a/c. There's a dinky pool and attached restaurant. ②–④

Kaliasem and Temukus

Heading west from Kalibukbuk the main road through the villages of **Kaliasem** and **Temukus** runs close to the coast, which is lined with hotels and guesthouses. However, only consider places that are set far enough back to avoid road noise. The western end of Lovina is marked by *Agus Homestay* on the coast although there is one place, *Bagus Homestay*, 1km or so further west, somewhat adrift from the main resort.

Aditya Beach Resort ☎0362/41059, Ⓦwww .adityalovina.com. Large mid-range place with an attractive pool. The most expensive, and best, rooms are close to the sea. ⑤–⑥

Agus Homestay ☎ & Ⓕ0362/41202. A small, clean place at the far western end of the main Lovina development. The best rooms have verandahs that face the ocean. All have a/c and hot water. ③

🏃 **Bagus Homestay** ☎0362/93407, Ⓕ93406. Situated 1.5km west of its sister operation, *Agus Homestay*. Clean bungalows with

a/c and hot water in a lovely garden with a good beachside pool. ②–④

Puri Manggala ☎0362/41371, ⒺPurimanggala @hotmail.com. Neat, simple rooms in a small, friendly family compound. Hot water and a/c are available. ①–③

Rumah Cantik ☎0362/42159, Ⓦwww .lovinacantik.com. Four large, comfortable, well-furnished rooms, all with balcony or verandah, in Kaliasem village although only a short walk from the sea, surrounded by an attractive garden for relaxing. A small pool is planned. ⑥

The resort

Lovina's black-sand, palm-fringed **beach** stretches into the distance where, on clear days, the imposing peaks of East Java look surprisingly close. In many spots, most notably at Anturan, you'll share the sand with local fishing boats. Swimming is generally calm and safe, although there are no lifeguards. There's not a great deal to do other than enjoy the beach and the low-key resort life behind it, but one of Lovina's early-morning **dolphin trips** (see box opposite) is almost obligatory. The monument **Patung Lumba Lumba**, at the beach end of Jalan Bina Ria, depicts frolicking dolphins and is a useful but tacky landmark.

Diving and snorkelling

Situated between Pemuteran and Pulau Menjangan to the west and Tulamben and Amed to the east, Lovina is an ideal base for **diving**. The local reef, perhaps unfairly, has a reputation as being uninteresting for experienced divers, though there's an excellent range of fish, and tyres, an old car and a small boat have been placed on the reef and are encouraging coral growth. Note that the Lovina reef is too far from the shore to swim to; you'll need a boat.

There are plenty of **operators**, all arranging trips for qualified divers, introductory dives and courses. See p.51 for general information about choosing dive companies. However, Spice Dive (☎0362/41509, Ⓦwww.balispicedive.com) in

Dolphin trips

Lovina is famous (or infamous) for dawn trips to see the **dolphins** that frolic off the coast: opinions are evenly split between those who think it's grossly overrated and those who consider it one of the best things on Bali.

A flotilla of simple *prahu* hewn from a single tree-trunk with a bamboo stabilizer on each side head out to sea at dawn, providing lovely views of the coast and the central mountains. The ensuing scenario is comical, as one skipper spots a dolphin and chases after it, to be followed by the rest of the fleet, by which time, of course, the dolphin is often long gone. It's pretty much the luck of the draw, some days there is little to see while on others the dolphins cavort around and under the boats in a grand display. If you can see the funny side, it's a good trip, and very, very occasionally **whales** have been spotted.

Prices are fixed and you'll currently **pay** Rp50,000 per person for the two-hour trip; book directly with the skippers on the beach or through your accommodation. There's a maximum of four passengers per boat. If you arrange snorkelling at the same time, you'll come back to land for breakfast and then head out again afterwards.

Kaliasem and on Jalan Bina Ria is the longest-established operator and the resort's only PADI five-star dive centre. They offer courses from the PADI Open Water (€250) up to Divemaster and Assistant Instructor level. Local hotel pools are available for early training. Fun dives in the Lovina area, Pulau Menjangan, Tulamben and Amed are all available (€35–€65) as dive packages, introductory dives, refresher sessions and courses for children from the age of eight years with a specially trained instructor and special gear.

Your losmen can also arrange **snorkelling trips**, or you can approach the boat skippers on the beach; expect to pay Rp50,000 for one and a half to two hours to the local reef. Most of the dive shops take snorkellers along on dive trips further afield if they have space; this is more expensive but offers greater variety. Shop around and see where the operators are heading the next day.

Eating, drinking and nightlife

There's a high turnover of **restaurants** in Lovina – the favourite today may well be extinct tomorrow – and a healthy level of competition ensures plenty of good "Happy Hour" deals, especially around Jalan Bina Ria. The quality and variety of food is excellent with something for every taste and pocket. As an alternative to tourist places try the Singaraja night market (see p.296) or, a couple of kilometres towards Singaraja, Jalan Pemaron Pura Penimbangan, where there is a host of local restaurants specializing in seafood and Indonesian food. *Cosy Resto*, *Ranggun Sunset* and *Casablangka* are all worth a try. Head towards the sea at the first set of traffic lights after leaving Banyuasri terminal heading towards Lovina.

Kalibukbuk

Barakuda On Jalan Mawar, specializing in well-cooked, good-value seafood including fish (Rp17,500), squid (Rp21,500), crab (Rp25,000), prawns (Rp25,500) and lobster (Rp155,000), served with one of eleven Balinese or Chinese sauces. The set meals are excellent value, from Rp85,000 for two. There are plenty of vegetarian, pork and chicken options as well.

Bu Warung Probably the best-value food in Kalibukbuk, this tiny place on the main road has a small menu of around a dozen well-cooked mains (Rp10,000–12,500). There are also sandwiches, pancakes, and fried bananas and pineapple.

Jasmine Kitchen Outstanding restaurant serving fabulous Thai food (mains up to Rp39,000) in relaxed surroundings just off Jalan Bina Ria. Everything is delectable but desserts (Rp18,000) and coffee are exceptional and staff are lovely.

Kakatua Imposing place in a huge *bale* surrounded by water features on Jalan Bina Ria with an equally huge menu spanning the globe and taking in Asian, European and Mexican dishes. Mains are Rp20–50,000 and while the expertise is inevitably spread thin, the food is pleasant and there's a lively atmosphere.

Kopi Bali Popular, cheap and cheerful place with well-cooked food towards the ocean end of Jalan Bina Ria. Featuring a big menu of the usual fare and, with nasi goreng at Rp12,900, this is an excellent place for big appetites with small budgets.

Kwizien ⓦwww.balikwizien.com. This relative newcomer to top-end dining in Lovina is a bit of a hotchpotch; stylish touches beside the kitsch, some things well-done, others less so. The menu emphasises meat with some fish options (mains Rp40–125,000) and although there aren't many desserts, they are delicious.

🏃 **Le Madre** Little spot on Jalan Mawar serving excellent Italian food (the cook used to work at *La Lucciola* restaurant in Seminyak) but with Indonesian and Balinese fare as well. Service is friendly, and focaccia is baked daily. Mains are Rp25–35,000 and pizzas Rp28–40,000.

Lovina Bakery, Bistro and Deli Attached to the deli serving those tasty morsels from home that you can't live without plus excellent homebaked bread, salads, sandwiches, pizzas and a small menu of Western dishes including fish, steaks and goulash (mains (Rp48–85,000). There are plenty of drinks; a bottle of Veuve Clicquot goes for Rp1 million, but there are lots of cheaper tipple both alcoholic and non.

Rambutan The restaurant of this hotel is tucked away near the pool but it's worth searching out for relaxed surroundings, mellow music, and an extensive drinks list. The menu features Balinese and Indonesian favourites plus some good Western choices including English sausages in the mixed grill, steaks and pork chops. Most mains are Rp35–45,000.

Santhi Bar Shady chill-out spot at the beach end of Jalan Bina Ria. Drinks (alcoholic and non) are cheap and there's a good-value menu of Indonesian and Western food with mains up to Rp25,000.

Sea Breeze On the beach and great for sunset drinks, with an excellent menu of Western, Indonesian and seafood dishes including soups, salads and sandwiches (mains Rp25–55,000). Cakes and desserts are great – crumble, brownies, lemon meringue pie, lemon cheesecake and chocolate mousse – although they're not all available every day. Quality acoustic music regularly accompanies the setting sun.

Warung Bintang Bali At the end of Jalan Mawar close to the beach, a relaxed and popular place with friendly staff and a big good-value menu of the usual travellers' fare with mains Rp18–24,000.

Further afield

Café Spice Beside the beach at Spice Dive in Kaliasem, divers and non-divers enjoy this shady spot. The menu includes seafood, Western and Indo-Chinese meals (mains Rp23–39,000) plus plenty of snacks, soups, shakes and juices, with some unusual choices including Norwegian fish soup and spinach terrine, and there's excellent home-made bread.

🏃 **Damai** ☎0362/41008. The restaurant attached to the luxury *Damai Lovina Villas* offers the most exquisite dining in northern Bali, if not the entire island. The menu is imaginative, innovative, well cooked, and fabulously presented. Meals are meticulously prepared and service is friendly yet discreet. The $39 five-course dinner is a feast beyond words – and it changes daily. The drinks list is extensive and equally imaginative. Opt to dine beside the pool if the weather is fine.

Kubu Lalang ☎0362/42207. On the coast at the eastern end of Lovina, with a free boat transfer for lunch or dinner for a minimum of four people from elsewhere in the resort (two hours' notice required and it depends on the tide). The imaginative menu is huge with all meals described in appetizing detail, including plenty of vegetarian choices. Mains from Rp28–40,000 and set meals are available.

Spunky's Bar and Restaurant In an unbeatable beachfront location in Banyualit, next to *Lupa-Lupa Lovina Cottages*, the menu is the usual travellers' dishes.

Warung Bambu Pemaron ☎0362/27080 or 31455. On the road down to *Puri Bagus Lovina* at the eastern end of Lovina, serving an excellent range of Balinese and Indonesian food with mains Rp24–35,000. A *rijsttafel* (Rp90,000 per person) and "Romantic Buffet" (Rp105,000 per person) are available for a minimum of two diners but should be ordered in advance. Balinese dancing accompanies dinner twice a week (Wed & Sun). There is original art for sale and cooking classes are available (see below). Free transport in the Lovina area.

Warung Indra Neat, friendly little place with just four tables on Jalan Laviana in Banyualit featuring a vast menu of Western and Indonesian standards; nothing is more than Rp20,000 and there are plenty of vegetarian choices.

Nightlife

Anybody coming to Lovina for energetic **nightlife** is in for a disappointment; after a day on the beach, most people eat a leisurely dinner and head off to bed.

The only established nightspot is the *Volcano Club* on the main road near Banyualit; opening varies with the season – look out for local adverts. There's regular **live music** in the *Poco Bar Evolution* and *Zigiz* bars on Jalan Bina Ria, and around the corner *Jax Bar and Grill* and *Kantin Bar and Restaurant*.

Shopping

There are plenty of **shops** along Jalan Bina Ria, Jalan Mawar and the main road in Kalibukbuk. Secondhand **bookshops** abound and the *Jakarta Post* **newspaper** arrives in the afternoon at Kristop Shop on the main road.

There is a vast array of **textiles**, **paper** and **wood** items – a fair representation of most of the crafts of Bali – all labelled with fixed prices at Nirwana Gallery on the main road slightly east of the junction with Jalan Bina Ria. Nearby, Biyu Gallery, on the main road to the west of the junction of Jalan Bina Ria, sells a selection of stuff from across Indonesia; textiles and statues predominate but it's a treasure-trove and prices range from Rp40,000 to several millions. Take a look at Durian, next to *Rambutan* on Jalan Mawar, packed full of textiles, carvings and **jewellery**; several other little shops along here are also worth a browse including Suga Gallery for art. Jalan Bina Ria has a clutch of fashionable little places; Bambooh specializes in sparkly things (belts, bags, jewellery, purses), Touch of Bali has well-designed **bags** and, across the road, Mimpi's jewellery is pretty. One unusual shop is Benny Tantra on the main road, with hand-painted and cartoon **T-shirts** (Rp70–90,000 for printed ones, Rp250,000 for hand-painted ones) and great cartoon postcards (Rp2500). Across the road from here Warung Seni stocks original art. At the luxury end, *Damai Lovina Villas* retail their own beautiful **toiletries** – prices are on a par with those in the West.

Massage and treatments

As well as beach massages, there are many places offering a range of **massages and treatments**. Bali Samadhi Spa (☎0813/3855 8260, ⊛www.balisamadhi .com) is off Jalan Mawar, Agung's (☎0362/42018, ⊛www.lovina-spa.com) on the road to *Damai Lovina Villas* and Araminth Spa (☎0362/41901, ⊛www .arunaspa.com) all have extensive spa menus and prices from Rp60,000 for a massage. The Jaya Spa at *Puri Bagus Lovina* is a step up in terms of luxury, with prices to match (from Rp175,000).

Regular **yoga** sessions (Mon–Thurs 8am; ☎0819/1562 5525, ⊜akarbali @peacemail.com; Rp50,000) operate at the Banana Plantation in Kaliasem; enquire at the Akar Shop in Jalan Bina Ria.

Cookery courses

Taking a **cookery class** for a couple of hours is a popular activity here. Most include a trip to the market and you get to eat your efforts. Classes can be tailored for you; for example, all have a vegetarian option. The price depends partly on the menu you choose to cook and there's usually a minimum number of two participants required. Adjani (☎0812/385 6802, ⊜ad-janibali@telkom .net) is well-established and has an office in Kaliasem. Prices vary from Rp150,000 to Rp175,000 per person. *Barakuda* restaurant (☎0362/41405, ⊜restaurant_barakuda@hotmail.com) on Jalan Mawar offers classes in Balinese cooking and Balinese seafood consisting of four main courses (Rp75–85,000 per person) or seven main courses (Rp135–175,000) and all classes include black rice pudding. *Warung Bambu Pemaron* (☎0362/27080 & 31455, ⊜warungbambu @gmx.net) run a selection of classes including one that only prepares sweets (Rp300,000 per person). In Banyualit, Penny's Cooking Classes can be booked at *Suma's* (Rp150,000 for four dishes). Putu's Cooking (☎0813/3856 3705) is advertised throughout the resort (Rp150,000 per person).

Listings

Bicycle rental On Jalan Mawar next to Suga Gallery, Rp20,000 per day.

Car and motorbike rental and charter transport Available throughout the resort from established firms and from people who'll approach you on the street. Costs are Rp90–100,000/day for a Suzuki Jimney and Rp150-200,000 for a Kijang. Insurance deals vary and are only available with established companies. Motorbikes are also widely available (Rp30,000–40,000 per day). Established companies include Yuli Transport (☎0362/41184) on Jalan Mawar, and Dupa, on the main road (☎0362/41397), where Made Wijana (☎0813/3856 3027) is a safe, reliable and recommended driver. If you want to charter a vehicle plus driver, you'll be looking at Rp300–350,000 per day including petrol. It's also possible to arrange one-way drops to destinations throughout Bali (Rp225,000 to Pemuteran, Rp250,000 to Tulamben, Amed, Batur, Bedugul or Gilimanuk, Rp275,000 to Ubud, Rp300,000 to the south Bali resorts or airport and Rp350,000 to Candi Dasa, Padang Bai or Tirtagangga). If there are several of you, this can be good value.

Exchange and banks Moneychangers throughout the resort. There's an international BCA ATM on the main road in Kalibukbuk.

Internet and phone access Offered by many places (8am–10pm; Rp400/min). 777 Internet on Jalan Mawar and Spice Dive on Jalan Bina Ria, both burn CDs and DVDs (for digital photographs), print text and photographs, and work with USB devices such as memory sticks. They also offer telephone services.

Long-distance buses See p.296 for operators from Singaraja or Perama who book buses to other parts of Indonesia, including Jakarta (Rp285,000), Surabaya (Rp120,000) and Yogyakarta (Rp200,000).

Pharmacy Rayahu Pharmacy (9am–9pm) on the main road, and there is a doctor attached.

Police ☎0362/41010. On the main road to the east of Kalibukbuk; see map, p.304.

Post office The post office (Mon–Thurs 8am–3pm, Fri 8am–1pm, Sat 8am–12noon) is about 1km west of Kalibukbuk. For poste restante, have mail addressed to you at the Post Office, Jalan Raya Singaraja, Lovina, Singaraja 81152, Bali. Several places in Kalibukbuk sell stamps.

Tours Available throughout the resort, at Rp250,000–500,000 per car. The main ones on offer include Singaraja (Pura Beji, Jagaraga, Sawan, Kubutambahan, Ponjok Batu and Hot Springs), Kintamani (Pura Beji, Kubutambahan, Penulisan, Penelokan and Toyah Bungkah), Eastern Bali (Pura Beji, Kubutambahan, Penulisan, Besakih, Tenganan, Candi Dasa and Tirtagangga) and Sunset (Gitgit, Danau Bratan, Taman Ayu and Tanah Lot). Consider chartering a vehicle and driver and putting together your own itinerary.

Travel agents/shuttle buses The Perama office is at Anturan (daily 8am–10pm; ☎0362/41161). There are shuttle buses to destinations on Bali and Lombok and charters (minimum two people) available to Tulamben (Rp100,000), Amed (Rp125,000), Pemuteran (Rp100,000), Penelokan (Rp125,000) and Candi Dasa/Padang Bai (Rp135,000). There are plenty of other companies advertising shuttle services.

Around Lovina

There are plenty of attractions around Lovina; several are accessible on public transport – such as the **Buddhist monastery** and **hot springs** at Banjar – while the area inland from Seririt is better explored with your own transport. A kilometre beyond the western limits of Lovina, Jalan Singsing leads 1km south to the **Singsing (Daybreak) waterfalls**, only really worth a look in the rainy season and not nearly as dramatic as other falls in the region.

Buddhist monastery and hot springs

Bali's largest **Buddhist monastery** lies 10km southwest of Lovina and can be combined with a visit to the hot springs at Banjar, which are on a parallel road slightly further west. Catch any westbound bemo to **Dencarik**, where ojek wait to take you the last, steep 5km. This is the main grape-growing region in Bali and you'll see the cultivated vines in the fields beside the road.

▲ Golden Buddha at Brahmavihara Arama

The **Brahmavihara Arama** (rarely closed; donation includes sarong rental), built in 1970, is a colourful confection in a wonderful hillside setting. A glorious gold Buddha is the centrepiece of the main temple flanked by carved stone plaques showing scenes from Buddha's life. There's a pictorial Buddhist grotto showing him meditating, an attractive Buddhist stupa and a hilltop replica of the temples in Borobodur in East Java.

Just a few hundred metres back down the hill from here, *Banjar Hills Retreat* (☎0815/5808 3880, ⓦwww.banjarhillsbali.com; ❸) is a great place to stay with comfortable bungalows in a hillside location and there's a pretty swimming pool and attached restaurant.

From the temple you can walk to the **hot springs** (daily 8am–6pm; Rp3000, parking Rp2000). Head back downhill and take the first road to the left. After a few hundred metres – with fine views of the mountains of East Java in the distance – you'll reach a major crossroads and the market of **BANJAR TEGA**. Turn left and a highly decorated *kulkul* tower will now be on your right. After about 200m you'll see a sign for the "Air Panas Holy Hot Spring" pointing you to a left turn. From here it's a pleasant one-kilometre walk to the springs where the water has a slight sulphur smell and a silky softness. There are lockers, showers, changing rooms and *Restoran Komala Tirta* has a small Indo–Chinese menu (mains Rp17–25,000) overlooking the pools. Weekends and holidays can get a bit busy. From the springs it's a 3km walk back to the main road or take an ojek from the market.

Inland from Seririt

With your own transport, you can take an interesting **inland drive** through the countryside south of **Seririt**, 12km west of Lovina, initially along the Denpasar road. The road climbs through paddy-fields and fields of grapes, splitting after 7km at **Rangdu**. The right-hand fork heads across the mountains via Pupuan to the south coast, while the left fork goes through **Mayong**, Banyuatis and Gunungsari to Munduk and on up to Danau Tamblingan and Danau Buyan.

Taking this left fork for just under 3km, you'll reach a small left turn signed "Desa Bestala" which leads to the village of **Bestala**, where you should turn left by the statue of the independence fighter. The road then winds down into the valley, across the river and up the other side to the hamlet of **Munduk Bestala**, famous for its durians (Jan and Feb are the main season). Turn right at the T-junction in the village and if you've a decent map it is possible to navigate to **Pedawa** and **Sidetapa**, two Bali Aga villages, which still retain their narrow lanes, high-walled compounds and gates. For guided walks around Mayong, see *Bali Panorama* restaurant in Mayong (see p.292). For guided walks in the Sidetapa area, contact Adjani in Lovina (see p.309); it is Rp200,000 per person (minimum of two people required) and involves two to three hours trekking plus visits to the Buddhist temple and hot springs at Banjar.

Travel details

Bemos and public buses

It's almost impossible to give the frequency with which bemos and public buses run: see Basics, p.36, for details. Journey times given are the minimum you can expect. Only the direct bemo and bus routes are listed; for longer journeys, you'll have to go via either Singaraja or Denpasar.

Air Sanih to: Amlapura (2hr); Culik (1hr 30min); Gilimanuk (3hr); Singaraja (Penarukan terminal; 30min); Tirtagangga (2hr); Tulamben (1hr).
Bedugul to: Denpasar (Ubung terminal; 1hr 30min); Singaraja (Sukasada terminal; 1hr 30min).
Kintamani to: Bangli (1hr); Denpasar (Batubulan terminal; 2hr); Singaraja (Penarukan terminal; 1hr 30min); Ubud (40min).
Lovina to: Amlapura (3hr 30min); Gilimanuk (2hr 30min); Jakarta (Java; 24hr); Malang (Java; 9–10hr); Probolinggo (for Bromo; 6–7hr); Seririt (20min); Singaraja (Banyuasri terminal; 20min); Surabaya (Java; 8hr); Yogyakarta (Java; 12hr).
Penelokan to: Bangli (45min); Buahan (30min); Denpasar (Batubulan terminal; 1hr 30min); Gianyar (50min); Singaraja (Penarukan terminal; 1hr 30min); Songan (45min); Toya Bungkah (30min).

Singaraja (Banyuasri terminal) to: Gilimanuk (2hr 30min); Lovina (20min); Seririt (40min); Surabaya (8hr); Yogyakarta (Java; 12hr).
Singaraja (Penarukan terminal) to: Amlapura (3hr); Culik (2hr 30min); Denpasar (Batubulan terminal; 3hr); Gianyar (2hr 20min); Penelokan (1hr 30min); Kubutambahan (20min); Sawan (30min); Tirtagangga (2hr 30min); Tulamben (1hr).
Singaraja (Sukasada terminal) to: Bedugul (1hr 30min); Denpasar (Ubung terminal; 3hr); Gitgit (30min).

Perama shuttle buses

Bedugul to: Kuta (daily; 2hr 30min–3hr); Lovina (daily; 1hr 30min); Sanur (daily; 2hr–2hr 30min); Ubud (daily; 1hr 30min).
Kintamani to: Kuta, Ubud, Sanur (charter; 1–2hr; min 2 people).
Lovina to: Bedugul (daily; 1hr 30min); Candi Dasa (daily; 3hr–3hr 30min); Gili Islands, Lombok (daily; 8hr); Kuta/Ngurah Rai Airport (daily; 3hr); Mataram, Lombok (daily; 9hr); Padang Bai (daily; 2hr 45min); Sanur (daily; 2hr 30min–3hr); Ubud (daily; 3hr 30min–4hr).

West Bali

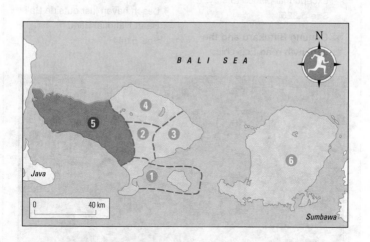

BALI SEA

N

Java

0   40 km

Sumbawa

CHAPTER 5   Highlights

✳ **Tanah Lot** Perched like a sea bird on a wave-lashed rock, this is Bali's most visited temple. See p.320

✳ **Subak Museum, Tabanan** Fascinating insight into Bali's rice-farming culture. See p.323

✳ **Yeh Gangga** A dramatic stretch of remote black-sand beach with just a couple of exceptional places to stay. See p.325

✳ **Gunung Batukaru and the Jatiluwih road** Eco-chic accommodation on the slopes of Bali's second highest mountain, an atmospheric garden temple, and luscious rice terraces. See p.326

✳ **Snorkelling off Pulau Menjangan** National-park island with crystal waters and spectacular, abundant, shallow reefs. See p.341

✳ **Pemuteran** Small, relaxed beach haven just outside Bali Barat National Park. See p.344

▲ Jatiluwih ricefields

5

West Bali

S parsely populated, mountainous, and in places extremely rugged, **west Bali** stretches from the northwestern outskirts of Denpasar across 128km to Gilimanuk at the island's westernmost tip and encompasses the districts of Tabanan, Jembrana and western Buleleng. Once connected to East Java by a tract of land (now submerged beneath the Bali Strait), the region has always had a distinct Javanese character. When East Java's Hindu Majapahit elite fled to Bali in the sixteenth century, the Javanese priest Nirartha started his influential preaching tour of Bali from the west – leaving the region with a stunning trinity of clifftop temples at **Tanah Lot**, **Rambut Siwi** and **Pulaki**. More recently, west Bali's Muslim population has increased so much that in Jembrana, and especially the region to the west of Negara, mosques now seem to outnumber temples and a good percentage of the male population leaves the house wearing a small black *peci*.

Apart from making the obligatory visits to the big attractions just west of Denpasar – **Pura Tanah Lot**, Mengwi's **Pura Taman Ayun** and **Sangeh Monkey Forest** being the main draws – few tourists linger long in west Bali, choosing instead to rush through on their way to or from Java, via the ferry service at Gilimanuk. Yet the southwest coast holds some fine black-sand beaches, and some good surf at **Lalang Linggah** and **Medewi**, while the cream of Bali's coral reefs lie off the northwest coast around **Pulau Menjangan** (Deer Island), near the little beach haven of **Pemuteran**. Bali's only national park, **Bali Barat National Park**, is also here, home to the endangered Bali starling and many other bird species. The island's second highest peak, the sacred **Gunung Batukaru**, dominates many west Bali vistas and its southern slopes nourish the most fertile paddies in Bali, not least in the area around **Jatiluwih**, focus of a famously scenic drive. Bali's rice-growing culture is celebrated in a museum in nearby **Tabanan**. For areas that lie in Batukaru's rain shadow however, the picture is quite different, with both the extreme west and some stretches of the northwest suffering from arid and infertile land.

Despite the lack of tourist centres in the west, there are several exceptional **hotels** both on the coast and in inland villages, most of them quiet and well off the usual tourist route. The southwest coast is served by **bemos** from Denpasar's Ubung bemo terminal, and the northwest coast by bemos from Singaraja: both services terminate at **Gilimanuk**, from where car ferries shuttle across the Bali Strait to Java.

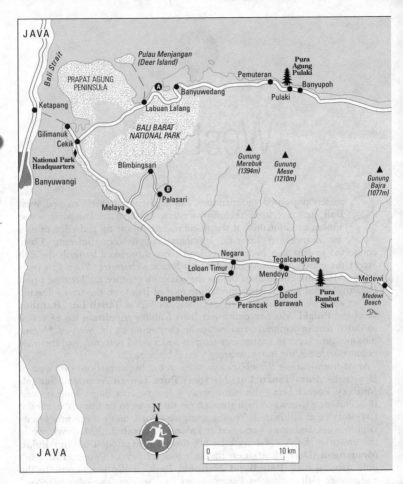

The southwest

From the **Ubung** bemo terminal in Denpasar's northwestern suburbs, all westbound bemos follow the busy main road through an almost continuous urban sprawl of nondescript little towns. After 15km, the conurbation becomes more distinctive as it shapes into **Kapal**, which, as you can't fail to notice, is one of the shrine-making centres of Bali: the sidewalks here are lined with every conceivable permutation in stone, concrete and wood, some roofed with wiry black *ijuk* thatch made from sugar-palm fibres. The road branches just west of Kapal, the northbound fork being a major artery for Bedugul and Singaraja via the seventeenth-century temple complex at **Mengwi**, with a side road to the **Sangeh Monkey Forest**. Continuing west towards Gilimanuk, the road reaches a crossroads at Kediri, access point for the coastal temple of **Pura Tanah Lot**. Kediri lies on the outskirts of **Tabanan**, the district capital, from where you can get transport to **Yeh Gangga beach** and the royal palace at **Krambitan**.

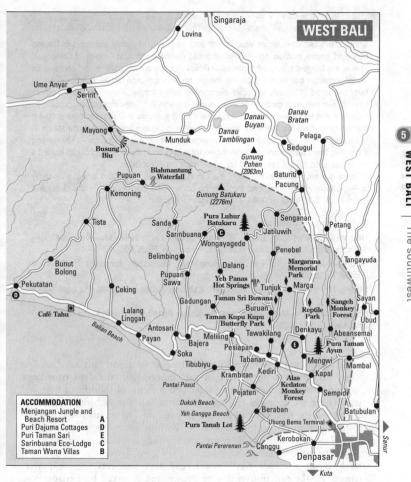

ACCOMMODATION

Sangeh Monkey Forest

Monkeys have a special status in Hindu religion, and a number of Balinese
temples boast a resident monkey population, respected by devotees and duly
fed and photographed by tourists. The **Monkey Forest** (Bukit Sari) in the
village of **SANGEH**, 21km north of Denpasar, is the most atmospheric of
these, its unruly inhabitants the self-appointed guardians of the slightly eerie
Pura Bukit Sari (daylight hours; donation). According to local legend, the
forest was created when Rama's general, the monkey king Hanuman,
attempted to kill Rama's enemy Rawana by squashing him between two
halves of the sacred Mount Meru. In the process, part of the mountain fell to
earth at Sangeh, with hordes of Hanuman's simian retainers still clinging to
the trees, creating Bukit Sari and its monkey dynasty. The temple was built
some time during the seventeenth century, among sacred nutmeg trees that
tower forty metres high. It is best appreciated in late afternoon, after the tour
buses have left, when both forest and temple take on a ghostly aspect, missing

from the island's other monkey forests. Whatever time you visit, take heed of the signs warning you to beware of the unnervingly confident **monkeys**: keep cameras and jewellery out of sight and remove all food from bags and pockets. There are no paths through the forest, but a track almost circles its perimeter and the temple compound is easy to find. The weathered and moss-encrusted grey-stone temple is out of bounds to everyone except the monkeys, but beyond the walls you can see a huge *garuda* statue, stonecarved reliefs and tiered, thatched *meru*.

Sangeh is on a minor northbound road that connects Denpasar with Kintamani via the junction village of Petang, and is served by **bemos** from the small Wangaya terminal in central Denpasar (see p.83). With your own transport, Sangeh is an easy drive from Mengwi, 15km southwest, or a pleasant forty-minute ride from Ubud. Sangeh also features on every **tour** operator's programme, often combined with Mengwi and Tanah Lot, and sometimes Bedugul.

Mengwi and around

The town of **MENGWI**, some 18km northwest of Denpasar, has a glittering history as the capital of a once powerful kingdom and is the site of an important temple, **Pura Taman Ayun**. From the early seventeenth century until the late nineteenth, the wily, battle-strong rajas of Mengwi held sway over an extensive area, comprising parts of present-day Badung, Tabanan and Gianyar districts. Their fortunes eventually waned however and in 1885 the kingdom of Mengwi was divided between Badung and Tabanan. Descendants of the royal family still live in the Mengwi area, and one of their palaces, **Puri Taman Sari** in nearby

Umabian, now operates as a high-class homestay. Also near Mengwi is the important **Margarana memorial**, erected in honour of Bali's anti-Dutch freedom fighters.

Pura Taman Ayun

The state temple of the former kingdom of Mengwi, **Pura Taman Ayun** (daily during daylight hours; Rp3000, kids Rp1500) is thought to have been built by Raja I Gusti Agung Anom in 1634. Designed as a series of terraced courtyards, the complex is surrounded by a moat – now picturesquely enhanced by weeds and lilies – to symbolize the mythological home of the gods, Mount Meru, floating in the cosmic ocean. The **inner courtyard** is encircled by its own little moat and is inaccessible to the public except at festival time, although the surrounding wall is low enough to give a reasonable view of the two-dozen multi-tiered **meru** within. The most important are the three that honour Bali's holiest mountains; their positions within the courtyard correspond to their location on Bali in relation to Mengwi. Thus, the eleven-roofed structure in the far northwest corner represents Gunung Batukaru; the nine-roofed *meru* halfway down the east side symbolizes Gunung Batur; and Batur's eleven-roofed neighbour honours Gunung Agung. The Batur *meru* has only nine tiers because the mountain is significantly lower than the other two.

Pura Taman Ayun is just east off the main Mengwi–Singaraja road and easily reached by **bemo** from Denpasar's Ubung terminal (30min). Coming from Gilimanuk or other points on the west coast, you'll need to change bemos at Tabanan's Pesiapan terminal.

Puri Taman Sari

One very good reason to visit this area is to stay at the *puri* (palace) of a branch of the Mengwi royal family. Located in the tiny village of **UMABIAN**, about 5km northwest of Pura Taman Ayun, ⚜ *Puri Taman Sari* (℡0361/261240, Ⓦwww.balitamansari.com; ❺–❻) has a traditional design but plenty of modern comforts. The compound features pavilions for sleeping, cooking and ceremonial activities, plus half a dozen delightful a/c guest rooms, and overlooks a classic rice-terrace panorama. The *puri* ethos is that guests should get involved in the normal daily life of this typical high-caste household, where activities include making offerings, watching dance rehearsals, attending late-night village gamelan practice and helping to cook. The rural environs are a pleasure to explore on foot or by bicycle and Alas Kedaton Monkey Forest is also nearby. Access to *Puri Taman Sari* is via Denkayu on the Mengwi–Bedugul–Singaraja road, but phone for directions.

Reptile and Crocodile Park

Unless you have a real passion for crocodiles, there's little point making the trek to the overpriced and poorly designed **Taman Buaya dan Reptil**, known as the **Reptile and Crocodile Park** (daily 9am–6pm; $10), which is home to four kinds of croc and eight species of lizard but is far inferior to the Reptile Park in Batubulan, described on p.170. This park is 8km north of Mengwi on the Bedugul road and served by all Ubung–Singaraja and Ubung–Seririt bemos.

Margarana Memorial Park

When Indonesia began fighting the Dutch for independence immediately after World War II, resistance in Bali was spearheaded by the young army officer **Gusti Ngurah Rai**, whose plan was to gather forces from all over the island on the slopes of Gunung Agung (see "History", on p.423, for more detail). The most famous battle of this campaign, the Margarana *puputan* (fight to the death), took place in Marga, about 6km north of Mengwi, on November 20, 1946, and ended with the death of Ngurah Rai and all 96 of his men. The battlefield has now been turned into the **Margarana Memorial Park**, or Taman Pujaan Bangsa Margarana (daily 8am–4pm; donation), dedicated to Ngurah Rai and the other 1371 independence fighters who died between 1945 and 1950, the vast majority of them from the Tabanan area. Just inside the entrance to its pleasantly landscaped grounds, four statues brandish traditional weapons while a fifth unfurls the flag of independence. At the heart of the park stands a red-brick shrine displaying a small photograph of Ngurah Rai (now a national hero, and the man after whom the airport is named) and inscribed with the words of his letter of no surrender, which ends with the cry "Freedom or death!". Beyond the shrine stretches row upon row of neat gravestones.

Nearly every schoolchild on the island has visited the memorial but few tourists make the effort. Access by public transport involves taking any Denpasar (Ubung)–Bedugul–Singaraja **bemo** as close as you can to Marga, then walking the 2km west of the main road to the monument.

Pura Tanah Lot and around

Dramatically marooned on a craggy wave-lashed rock sitting just off the southwest coast, **Pura Tanah Lot** really does deserve its reputation as one of Bali's top sights. Fringed by frothing white surf and glistening black sand, its elegant multi-tiered shrines have become the unofficial symbol of Bali, appearing on a vast range of tourist souvenirs, while its links with several other coastal temples afford it an especially holy status. It's a huge tourist trap of course, particularly at sunset, and a busy tourist village encircles the temple approach, but get there early morning and it's still a striking sight.

Access is fairly easy by public bemo and there are several places to stay around the temple, but most visitors come on organized day-trips from the resorts in the south.

The temple

Pura Tanah Lot (daily during daylight hours; Rp10,000, plus Rp5000/2000 per car/motorbike) is said to have been founded by the wandering Hindu priest **Nirartha**, who sailed to Bali from Java during the sixteenth century. Legends describe how he was drawn to the site by a light beaming from a holy spring, but his arrival was not welcomed by the local priest, who demanded that the rival holy man leave. In response, Nirartha meditated so hard that he pushed the rock he was sitting on out into the sea. This became the Tanah Lot "island". He dedicated his new retreat to the god of the sea and transformed his scarf into poisonous snakes to protect the place. Ever since, Pura Tanah Lot has been one of the holiest places on Bali, closely associated with several other important temples along this coast, including Pura Rambut Siwi and Pura Luhur Uluwatu.

Because of its sacred status, only bona fide devotees are allowed to climb the temple stairway carved out of the once-crumbling but now artificially enhanced rock face and enter the compounds; everyone else is confined to the patch of grey sand around the base of the rock, which gets submerged at high tide. When the waters are low enough, you can take a sip of **holy water** (*air suci*) from the spring that rises beneath the temple rock (donation requested) or view the holy coral **snakes** that frequent nooks in the cliff face. Otherwise, your best option is to climb up to the mainland **clifftop** for the best viewing angle. Most people loiter at the cliffside restaurants immediately to the south of the temple rock, but if you follow the clifftop path northwest instead, you'll be rewarded with a panoramic view of the Bukit plateau on Bali's southernmost tip. The coast path continues north past small weather-beaten shrines that watch over the wild grey sands below and eventually reaches Yeh Gangga, about two hours' walk away (see p.325).

Practicalities

Though there are occasional bright-blue **bemos** from Denpasar's Ubung terminal direct to Tanah Lot, you'll probably end up having to go via **KEDIRI**, 12km northeast of the temple complex on the main Denpasar–Tabanan road. All Ubung (Denpasar)–Gilimanuk bemos pass through Kediri (about Rp3000; 30min), whose bemo station is at the crossroads where the road branches left for Tanah Lot, right for central Tabanan and straight on for Gilimanuk via the bypass. Bright blue Kediri–Tanah Lot bemos (about Rp5000; 25min) run fairly regularly in daylight hours, more frequently in the morning.

If travelling independently from Kuta, the prettiest **route to Tanah Lot** is via Kerobokan and Beraban, passing through classic rice terraces and traditional villages. Alternatively, come via the *subak* rice museum in nearby Tabanan (see p.323), or make a slight detour to the ceramic-producing village of Pejaten (see p.322).

There's an **ATM**, several **exchange** booths and a wartel in Tanah Lot's tourist village, in front of *Dewi Sinta Cottages* hotel. The **Kecak dance** is performed in the temple complex every Saturday night at sunset (Rp50,000).

5

WEST BALI | The southwest

The sacred and the profane

The construction in the mid-1990s of the *Nirwana Golf and Spa Resort* within 500m of Pura Tanah Lot marked a new low in the relationship between **property developers** and Balinese villagers. In Bali, there are long-standing religious laws about how close to a temple one can build, and the relative scale and status of the secular building must also be appropriate. When it became obvious that the *Nirwana* team had circumvented these rules, huge protests erupted in the press and on the streets.

This was the first time there had been such strong and widespread **opposition to tourist development** on Bali. Protestors argued that by building a tourist resort here, one of the island's most important temples was being treated as nothing more than an ornament for the pleasure of foreign eyes – a serious case of disrespect. In addition, it was reported that farmers who refused to sell their ancestral land to make way for the project were forced out by underhand means (including blocking irrigation channels to make the land infertile) and that several small temples were destroyed. Nonetheless, commercial interests prevailed and the *Le Meridien Nirwana* is now one of Bali's most successful luxury hotels.

With hundreds of jobs at stake and a desperate desire for the tourist dollar, the *Nirwana* controversy is typical of the tensions that have dogged Bali ever since the first tourists arrived in the 1930s. As land gets more expensive, it is left to outside **investors** with little regard for Bali's religious heritage to bankroll new projects and impose their own conditions. On the other hand, cash injections like this are good for the Balinese economy and it's unclear whether local investors would be any more ethical. For a more complete view of the effect of tourist development in Bali, see p.466.

Accommodation and eating

Tanah Lot all but dies after the last tour bus pulls away at about 7.30pm, so there's little incentive to stay here overnight, though there are a few **hotels** to choose from. The most convenient is the welcoming *Dewi Sinta Cottages*, located in the tourist village beside the temple approach (℡0361/812933; Fan ❸ A/c ❺). Its fan and a/c bungalows are set in a soothing tropical garden with swimming pool; the fan rooms have the best views, overlooking the pool and the ricefields. Set well away from the commercial clutter, about 700m back along the access road from the temple car park, *Pondok Wisata Astiti Graha* (℡0361/812955; ❶) is surrounded by ricefields and offers clean if rudimentary en-suite rooms. On an entirely different scale, the super-swanky five-star *Le Meridien Nirwana Golf and Spa Resort* (℡0361/815900, ⓦwww.bali.lemeridien.com; ❼–❾) occupies extensive grounds with views of Pura Tanah Lot, and has three swimming pools (strong currents make swimming in the sea dangerous here) and a highly-praised Greg Norman–designed 18-hole golf course (℡0361/815960, ⓦwww.nirwanabaligolf .com; $130).

The coastal path alongside the temple complex is packed with **restaurants** affording prime views and predictably inflated prices, but a better option is the *Dewi Sinta Restaurant* in the tourist village. A much cheaper option is *Depot Dini* next to *Pondok Wisata Astiti Graha*, about 650m before the Tanah Lot car park, where nasi goreng costs just Rp12,000.

Pejaten

About 6km northeast of Tanah Lot and signposted west off the Kediri–Tanah Lot road, the ceramic-producing village of **PEJATEN** is famous as the place where most Balinese roof tiles and roof-crown ornaments (*ketu*) are made. Of more interest to tourists is the distinctive Pejaten **ceramic ware**, particularly the bowls, plates and little pots designed with distinctive frog, gecko and monkey embellishments and glazed in pastel greens, blues and beiges. Although Pejaten ceramics are sold in the big resorts, you should get better prices and a bigger choice in the village itself, particularly at Tanteri's Ceramic shop in Banjar Simpangan in the centre of the village (ⓦwww .tanteri-ceramic.com). There are kilns dotted all over the village, each of them fuelled by coconut husks, which lie in piles along the roadside – about as industrial as rural Bali gets. To have a look inside one of the workshops, follow the signs for CV Keramic.

Tabanan and around

Despite being the former capital of the ancient kingdom of Tabanan and the administrative centre of Bali's most fertile district, **TABANAN** is a medium-sized town with little to encourage a protracted stop. Its one outstanding feature is the **Subak Museum**, an ethnographic exhibition about rice farming in Bali. Otherwise, Tabanan's main claim to fame is that it was once home to the outstanding dancer I Ketut Marya, known as **Mario**, remembered for his astonishing performances of the Kebyar, which he reinvented and popularized in the 1920s (see p.445); he is commemorated at the Gedong Marya theatre in the town centre.

Historically, the kingdom of Tabanan was always one of the more stable power centres, holding out against the Dutch until the last possible moment when, in 1906, the colonialists launched their offensive on southern Bali and then – irked by the refusal of the Tabanan royal house to outlaw *suttee* (self-immolation of bereaved wives) – marched on Tabanan. The raja of Tabanan and his crown prince decided to negotiate rather than commit *puputan*, but the

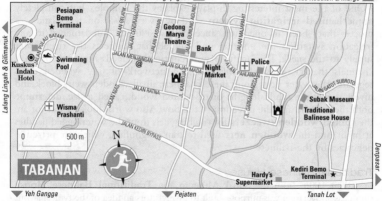

Dutch refused to make a deal and, rather than face exile to Lombok or Madura, the regents committed suicide inside Denpasar prison. Little now remains of the former kingdom, as the Dutch sacked Tabanan's main *puri*, leaving only the subsidiary palace at Krambitan, 8km away.

Practicalities

All Ubung (Denpasar)–Gilimanuk **bemos** bypass Tabanan town centre, dropping passengers at the **Pesiapan terminal**, a major transport hub on the northwest edge of town. Bright-yellow city bemos shuttle from Pesiapan into the town centre (Rp3000), 1.5km east, where you'll find most of the banks, ATMs and currency exchanges, plus Internet access and the post office, on Jalan Gajah Mada and its continuation, Jalan Pahlawan. Several regional bemo services run out of Pesiapan, including to Krambitan, Kediri (for Tanah Lot; Rp3000) and Taman Ayun (Mengwi), plus occasional services to Yeh Gangga. For **accommodation**, you could do worse than the *Kuskus Indah Hotel* (℡0361/815373; ❶–❷), whose clean fan and a/c rooms are located just a few metres west of the Pesiapan bemo station at Jalan Pulau Batam 32. But for an extended stay in the area, Yeh Gangga beach, 8km southwest (see p.325), and Lalang Linggah (Balian beach; see p.331), further west again, are much more enticing options.

Subak Museum and Traditional Balinese House

Tabanan's two most interesting, though under-visited, sights are both located on the eastern edge of town, within 100m of each other. The Subak Museum is signposted off the main Tabanan road in **BANJAR SENGGULAN**, 1.5km east of Tabanan town centre and about the same distance west of the Kediri T-junction; the **Traditional Balinese House** is signed from the Subak Museum itself. Coming from Ubung, either alight at the Kediri junction and walk the 1.5km, or switch to a town-centre bemo at the Pesiapan terminal.

Subak Museum

Tabanan district has long been a major rice producer, and the **Subak Museum** or **Mandala Mathika Subak** (Mon–Thurs & Sat 8am–4.30pm, Fri 8am–1pm; donation requested) celebrates the role of the rice-farmers' collectives (the *subak*) by describing traditional farming practices and exhibiting typical agricultural implements.

One of the most interesting displays explains the complex but completely unmechanized **irrigation system** used by every *subak* on the island – a process that's been in operation since at least 600 AD. Fundamental to any irrigation system is the underground tunnel that connects the river water supply to the *subak*. This artificial watercourse then feeds hundreds of small channels that crisscross the *subak* area. A network of tiny wooden dams regulates the water flow along these channels: small wooden weirs block and divert the water, while lengths of castellated wood, called *tektek*, determine both the volume and the direction of the flow. Also worth looking out for are the **spiked wooden tweezers** for catching eels from the waterlogged paddies at night, and the **wooden nets** used to trap dragonflies, which are prized as delicacies by the Balinese.

Traditional Balinese House

Less than 100m from the Subak Museum, the **Traditional Balinese House** (hours as above; free) was purpose-built to give visitors an idea of the typical layout of a village home, comprising a series of thatched *bale* (pavilions) in a walled compound. Each *bale* has a specific function and its location is determined by the sacred Balinese direction *kaja* (towards the sacred Gunung Agung mountain) and its counterpoint *kelod* (away from the mountain, or towards the sea). There are no labels or guides here, but for more information on sacred Balinese architecture and an annotated plan of a traditional house compound, see p.461.

True to form, the **family temple** occupies the *kaja* corner, to the far left of the entrance gate. To the right of the temple, the open-sided *bale dangin* is reserved for ceremonial functions such as marriage and funeral rites. The enclosed, windowless pavilion along the left-hand (north) wall of the compound is the *bale daja* for sleeping, and next to that, immediately to the left of the entrance gate, stands the open-sided multifunctional pavilion, which can be adapted for sleeping. Straight ahead of the entrance gate in the middle of the compound, the only two-storey *bale* has an enclosed rice-storage barn upstairs and a breezy social space or guestroom below. The kitchen pavilion or *paon* stands to the right of the entrance in the *kelod* corner, diagonally opposite the temple, and contains a few traditional cooking implements made from bamboo and coconut wood; the nearby *bale* along the right-hand (south) wall is for rice milling. There's no bathroom, as villagers traditionally do their ablutions outdoors.

Taman Kupu Kupu Butterfly Park

About 5km north of Tabanan, in the village of **WANASARI** on the road to Gunung Batukaru, **Taman Kupu Kupu Butterfly Park** (daily 8am–5pm, last entry 4pm; $6, kids $3) houses an impressive variety of butterfly species from all over Indonesia in its small but prettily landscaped garden. The best time to visit is in the morning when the butterflies flit around most energetically. All Tabanan–Penebel **bemos** go past Taman Kupu Kupu, departing from the Tawakilang terminal, which is 2km north of Tabanan town centre on the Penebel road and accessed by a town-centre bemo from central Tabanan or Pesiapan terminal.

Tunjuk

The tiny, very traditional village of **Tunjuk**, about 7km northeast from Tabanan's Tawakilang bemo terminal and junction (or 3km west of the Margarana Memorial), hosts an interesting and pretty authentic "village life" programme organized through **Taman Sri Buwana** (reserve ahead on

⊤0361/742 5929, ⊛www.balivillagelife.com; $49 including transfers). It features visits to the local elementary school and a typical house compound that is home to fifteen different families (all related) each with their own kitchen, *lumbung*, general *bale* and sleeping pavilion; there's also a rice-farming demonstration, a walk through the ricefields, and lunch.

Alas Kedaton Monkey Forest

Less interesting than Sangeh Monkey Forest, **Alas Kedaton** (daily 8am–6pm; Rp10,000, kids Rp5000), 3km north of the Kediri junction, is only worth a visit to get close to its resident monkeys, who are not as aggressive as many of their cousins elsewhere in Bali. The temple here is a *pura dalem*, or temple of the dead, out of bounds to tourists, and the monkeys only congregate in the patch of forest along its perimeters. Beware of getting landed with a guide, whose main concern will be steering you to the souvenir stalls on the edge of the temple car park. Access to Alas Kedaton is via Kediri: either take a bemo from Denpasar's Ubung terminal to Kediri, then charter another one for the final 3km, or drive to Kediri, then follow signs for Marga.

Yeh Gangga beach

Heading west out of Tabanan, nearly every minor road that branches off south leads to the coast, a barely developed stretch of black sand notable for its strong currents and weird offshore rock formations. One of the most appealing sections is at **YEH GANGGA**, 10km southwest of Tabanan, whose two exceptionally attractive places to stay make this a good base from which to explore the area if you have your own transport. The currents here make the sea too dangerous for swimming, but it's a dramatic scene, punctuated by huge eroded rocks, and the beach stretches for miles in both directions. You can walk along the coast to Tanah Lot in under two hours, and the Pejaten ceramics village (see p.322) is within easy cycling distance.

The access road to Yeh Gangga is signposted off the main road about 4km west of the Kediri junction, or reach it via back roads from Tanah Lot. Occasional Yeh Gangga **bemos** depart Tabanan's Pesiapan terminal (45min) but you may have to charter one (about Rp20,000).

At the end of the road you'll come to relaxed, unpretentious ⚜ *Bali Wisata Bungalows* (⊤0361/7443561, ⊛www.baliwisatabungalows.com; ❸–❹), whose half a dozen large, spacious, fan- and a/c **bungalows** are set in a wild shorefront garden of cacti and windblown shrubs, with nothing but the sea and the rice-paddies in sight. Many of the bungalows have separate living areas and some have kitchen facilities; all have great views. There's a large salt-water swimming pool and massage service, plus plenty of info on local activities, motorbike rental, daily transport into Tabanan, and a good restaurant.

About 1km northwest along the coast, beyond the rock with a hole, is *Waka Gangga* (⊤0361/416256, ⊛www.wakaexperience.com; ❸), the nicest of the idiosyncratic *Waka* group of small luxury hotels. Its ten exquisite, circular bungalows are scattered across terraced rice-paddies and beautifully constructed from dark woods, rough-cut stone and natural fabrics; each has a garden bathroom and huge glass windows affording panoramic 270-degree views of the ocean and ricefields. There's a swimming pool, restaurant and spa as well.

Krambitan and around

Midway between the main road and the coast, the village of **KRAMBITAN**, 8km southwest of Tabanan, lacks obvious attractions, but makes a pleasant base as it's a typically Balinese environment that rarely sees foreign overnight visitors. Pretty villages, fine rice-paddy landscapes and empty beaches are all within cycling distance, and you also get the chance to sleep in a royal palace. Turquoise **bemos** connect Krambitan with Tabanan's Pesiapan terminal, taking about thirty minutes. If driving from Kuta or Denpasar, take the back road via Kerobokan, Beraban and Pejaten for the most scenic route.

In the late seventeenth century, Krambitan became the home of a branch of the **royal family** of Tabanan, and some of their descendants still live here. Deprived of a political role, some of the rajas' offspring have turned to tourism, transforming a section of one of their palaces into compact but elegant guest **accommodation**. The palace compound of *Puri Anyar Kerambitan* (T0361/812668, Egiriputri@serunibali.com; 4) is an impressively grand composition of elaborate carvings and tropical garden courtyards, within which are several *bale* for paying guests, each one furnished with a huge four-poster bed and garden bathroom; rooms must be reserved in advance as this is still very much a family home. On request, *Puri Anyar* can also host one-day cultural programmes that incorporate demonstrations in dance, traditional games, kite design, and making offerings.

Another descendant of the Tabanan royal family lives just around the corner at **Puri Agung Wisata**, which you can visit for a small donation. Though Puri Agung (literally "big" or "main" palace) is the most important of the Tabanan palaces, it's less stylish than *Puri Anyar*, but worth a look for the special tooth-filing pavilion and family temple compound. It's a popular venue for tourists' wedding parties.

Both Krambitan and the neighbouring village of **PANARUKAN** have a reputation for their outstanding dancers, who sometimes give **dance performances** at *Puri Anyar* (call for details). They are particularly renowned for their Calonarang, a ritual cleansing Barong and Rangda dance in which almost half the village participates and for their *tektekan* bamboo percussion orchestra.

North to Gunung Batukaru

Much of inland southwest Bali lies in the shadow of massive **Gunung Batukaru** (sometimes spelled Batukau; 2276m), the second highest mountain on the island after Gunung Agung and one of the holiest. All west-Bali temples have a shrine dedicated to the spirit of Gunung Batukaru, and on the lower slopes of the holy mountain itself stands the beautiful **Pura Luhur Batukaru**, Bali's directional temple (*kayangan jagat*) for the west and the focus of many pilgrimages.

Gunung Batukaru and its hinterland is the **wettest** region of Bali, and the dense tropical rainforest that clothes the uppermost slopes has been designated a nature reserve, a particularly rewarding area for **bird-watching**. Lower down, on the gentler slopes that effectively stretch all the way to Tabanan, 21km southeast of Pura Luhur, the superior soil provides some of the most productive agricultural land on the island: the rice terraces around **Jatiluwih** are particularly scenic. Because of Batukaru's cool, damp microclimate, it's worth bringing warm clothes and rain gear up here, even if you're only making a brief visit to Pura Luhur Batukaru (817m above sea level) or are planning to stay in comfort either in the nearby village of **Wongayagede** or in eco-chic style in **Sarinbuana**.

Transport practicalities

From Tabanan, with your own transport, you have a choice of two main **routes to Pura Luhur Batukaru**. The following account describes a circular tour to the temple and back, going up via Penatahan and Wongayagede and returning via Jatiluwih, Senganan and Penebel. Sarinbuana is accessed by a different road described on p.330.

There are no public **bemos** to Pura Luhur Batukaru, though there is a service that goes as far as Jatiluwih, via Penebel, and you may be able to charter the same bemo on to Pura Luhur. The Tabanan–Penebel–Jatiluwih bemos leave from the bemo terminal at Tawakilang, 2km north of Tabanan's town centre – approximately hourly in the mornings, less frequently after noon.

Most **tour** operators offer trips to Pura Luhur Batukaru, usually taking in the Jatiluwih rice terraces and either Pura Taman Ayun at Mengwi or Bedugul's Pura Ulun Danu; all prices include transfers from the main southern resorts. Sobek (℡0361/844 6194, @www.99bali.com/adventure/sobek) run guided **mountain-bike** trips down the side of Gunung Batukaru for US$53; SeeBali Adventures do bicycle and **quad-bike** tours through the cacao plantations and ricefields (see below for details); and Big Tree Farms hosts six-course **firefly suppers** at its organic farm near Jatiluwih (℡0361/461978, @www.bigtreebali .com; May–Sept only; Rp500,000).

Tabanan to Wongayagede (via Yeh Panas)

Beyond Tabanan the main route **to Wongayagede** and Pura Luhur Batukaru passes the butterfly park in Wanasari (see p.324) and continues via archetypal Balinese scenes of shrub-lined villages and rice terraces before reaching a junction at **BURUAN**. The right-hand fork will take you up to Gunung Batukaru via Penebel, Senganan and Jatiluwih, and is described in reverse on p.330.

A short distance along the left-hand fork and you reach the village of **PENATAHAN**, site of the sulphurous **Yeh Panas Hot Springs** and the *Yeh Panas Natural Hot Spring and Spa Hotel* (℡0361/262356, @info@archipelhomes .com; ❺) whose comfortable a/c bungalows are built high on the hillside for optimum rice-terrace views. Day-guests can use the hotel springs for Rp100,000, but for a free soak in a more natural hot spring, continue past the hotel for a few hundred metres, along the road to Pura Luhur, and follow the tiny sign that points you 100m west down a track to a traditional pool.

There's a chance to engage more energetically with the landscape in the village of **TENGKUDAK**, a few kilometres north of Yeh Panas, where the profession-ally run SeeBali Adventures (℡0361/794 9693, @www.seebaliadventures.com; $69 including transfers) leads **quad-bike** and bicycle excursions ("the more mud the better") through cacao plantations and ricefields. At the northern edge of the village, about 500m before the road enters Wongayagede, the Catholic church (*gereja*) of St Martinus de Pons now draws its congregation from just five local Christian families, and is likely to be locked, but the facade is an interesting example of Balinese Christian architecture. Several Christian motifs have been carved on to an otherwise typical red-brick facade and the whole structure is crowned with a four-tiered Hindu-style *meru* tower.

Wongayagede

A night or two in **WONGAYAGEDE**, the village nearest to Pura Luhur Batukaru, is a rewarding experience. Remote and extremely scenic, it offers ample opportunity to explore the tranquil countryside and make the challenging trek up Gunung Batukaru.

Climbing Gunung Batukaru

Because of the sacred status of Gunung Batukaru, most local villagers make the long trek up to the **summit** temple of this holy mountain once a year on the occasion of their own village temple ceremony. A few tourists also **climb** to the top, but it's quite an undertaking: a guide is essential and the best month is July, with the November–March rainy season being out of the question because of dangerously slippery trails, not to mention the high leech population. Gunung Batukaru is a long-extinct volcano and the dense **rainforest** that covers the slopes offers few clearings from which to admire the view, but a knowledgeable guide will point out some of the countless, interesting plants, birds and butterflies, and perhaps even one of the resident rhesus monkeys. Constant shade and low-lying cloud make the atmosphere damp and the trails potentially hazardous whatever the season, so bring warm clothes, rainwear, and decent shoes.

Of the several **routes** up Gunung Batukaru, the most accessible start from hotels in Sarinbuana (see p.330), Wongayagede (see below) and Sanda (see p.349). The Sarinbuana route is the easiest (about 4hr to the top, though it has been done in two and a half) and Sanda the most taxing (about 6hr), though all three routes converge at a point known as Munduk Ngandang for the final tough two-and-a-half-hour slog to the summit. For an easier hike, consider simply doing the route to Munduk Ngandang and back. The descent from the summit usually takes three to five hours; some people take it more gently and camp near the top.

Guides for Batukaru treks can be arranged through the above-mentioned hotels, or with the guys who hang around Pura Luhur Batukaru in Wongayagede. They all offer short hikes partway up the slopes to various of the mountain's shrines as well as return day-hikes to the summit; arrangements for overnight summit treks should be discussed direct. The **temple guides** charge per guide and do not supply water or food (note that beef is not permitted on the mountain): Rp100,000 per guide per hour for 1–3hr or Rp900,000 for the day-return to the summit. **Hotels** tend to charge per participant and provide food and water and may also supply more than one guide per group: about Rp250,000 per person for a four-hour hike including lunch or Rp500,000 per person to the summit and back, inclusive.

The village is 2km south of the temple car park and the only **place to stay** here is the exceptionally tranquil ⚐ *Prana Dewi* (☎0813/3866 0154, ⓦwww .balipranaresort.com; ⑥), signposted west off the main road through the village (north of the side road to Jatiluwih). Occupying an idyllic, inspirational spot within the ricefields and enjoying views of majestic Gunung Batukaru, *Prana Dewi*'s thirteen stylish bungalows are thoughtfully designed with traditional features, picture windows, verandahs and four-poster beds, and widely spaced amidst the garden's streams and ponds; there are no fans or a/c as it's cool up here at 636m. The **restaurant** is worth visiting in its own right: it shares the same views and serves home-grown red rice, organic vegetables, salads and brown bread as well as curries (Rp35,000–50,000) and pasta. You can arrange **guides** for the Gunung Batukaru trek here (see box above), as well as for less taxing local walks. *Prana Dewi* also holds regular **yoga retreats** ($180 for three days full-board).

Pura Luhur Batukaru

Usually silent except for its resident orchestra of cicadas and frogs, **Pura Luhur Batukaru** (donation requested) is one of Bali's nine directional temples, the guardian of the west, and does full justice to its epithet the "Garden Temple". The grassy courtyards are planted with flowering hibiscus, Javanese ixora and cempaka shrubs, and the montane forest that carpets the slopes of Gunung Batukaru encroaches on the compound's perimeters to the north, east and west. The monuments are encrusted with moss, and a web of paths fans out to solitary shrines set further into the forest. Batukaru's **bird** population finds plenty to feed on here, so you're likely to see bright green woodpecker-like barbets, scarlet minivets, olive-green grey-headed flycatchers, and possibly even scarlet-headed flowerpeckers in the temple treetops.

Pura Luhur Batukaru is thought to have become a holy site in the eleventh century and was later consecrated by the rajas of the kingdom of Tabanan who made it into their state temple and dedicated shrines here to their ancestral gods. In 1604, the rival rajas of Bululeng razed the shrines and, although devotees continued to worship at the ruins, the temple was not fully renovated until 1959. Many of the thatched *meru* now standing inside the **inner sanctuary** still represent a particular branch or ancestor of the Tabanan royal family. The most important shrine though is the unusual seven-tiered pagoda, which is dedicated to Mahadewa, the god of Gunung Batukaru. To the east of the main temple compound, a large square **pond** has been dug to represent and honour the gods of nearby Danau Tamblingan, which lies immediately to the north of Gunung Batukaru. Only Batukaru's priests are allowed access to the tiny island shrine in the middle of the pond, which they reach by means of a makeshift raft on a pulley. Pura Luhur continues to play a very important role in the lives of Balinese Hindus. Members of local *subak* groups come here to draw holy water from the pond for use in agricultural ceremonies, and at the annual Galungan festivities truckloads of devotees travel long distances to pay their respects and lay their offerings.

In deference to Pura Luhur's extremely sacred status, visitors are requested to obey the strict **rules of admission** posted at the entrance. Aside from the usual prohibitions, such as menstruating women and those who have been recently bereaved, Batukaru also bars pregnant women and new mothers (who are considered ritually impure for 42 days after the birth), as well as "mad ladies/gentleman".

▲ Temple sculptures at Pura Luhur Batukaru

Wongayagede to Tabanan (via Jatiluwih)

The road to Jatiluwih branches east from Wongayagede about 2.5km south of Pura Luhur, and then winds through some of the most famous rice-paddy vistas on Bali, offering expansive panoramas over the broad and gently sloping terraces and, afternoon cloud cover permitting, background shots of Gunung Batukaru as well. This whole area is known as **JATILUWIH**, after the hamlet of the same name, and has been designated a tourist site which means every visitor has to pay a Rp10,000 toll to drive through it. The road twists through ever more lush landscapes, dense with banana trees, *kopi bali* coffee plantations, fields of chilli peppers and tomato plants, ferns and *dadap* trees, plus the occasional chicken farm. Several **restaurants** make the most of the glorious vistas, the best positioned and best value of which is *Café Jatiluwih*, 7.5km from the Wongayagede junction.

About 11km from Wongayagede, the road arrives at the **SENGANAN** road junction. The quickest route to the north or south coasts is the northeast (left) fork, a good, fast 7.5-kilometre road that feeds into the main Denpasar–Bedugul–Singaraja artery at Pacung, 6km south of Bedugul and 25km north of Mengwi. For the slower, more scenic route to Buruan and Tabanan, take the southbound (right) fork that runs via the sizeable market town of **PENEBEL**.

Sarinbuana Eco-Lodge

Secreted away in an even more remote spot on the southwestern slopes of Gunung Batukaru, 22km northwest of Tabanan, is the delightful ☀ *Sarinbuana Eco-Lodge* (☎0361/743 5198, ⓦwww.baliecolodge.com; ❺–❻ Family house for four ❼), an exceptional **place to stay** that's run by committed expat environmentalists. There's contemporary jungle-chic accommodation in five bungalows dotted around a garden clearing in the rainforest, with rooms designed to make the most of the jungle surround-sound (including dozens of different birds) and views across unadulterated forest. The *Lodge* is a genuinely, award-winning, **environmentally conscious** project; it grows its own organic fruit and veg, runs an interesting programme of village-based cultural workshops, and organizes guided walks including up to the summit of Gunung Batukaru (see p.328). They can also arrange orang-utan trekking holidays on Sumatra. There are natural swimming pools in the grounds, and a waterfall, and *Lodge* staff can also fix up cheaper **homestay accommodation** in the village (❷).

Sarinbuana Eco-Lodge is located at 750m above sea level, on the edge of the *banjar* of **BIAHAN** in Sarinbuana village. Coming from south Bali or Ubud, access is via a road that begins 7km west of Tabanan, at kilometre-stone 30, and runs 15km north via the villages of Gadungan and Dalang; you can also get there via **BAJERA** further west, but phone or email for directions. Sarinbuana village itself is a couple of kilometres beyond the *Lodge* and holds great spiritual significance to the Balinese people who go there to collect holy water.

The coast road to Negara

Few tourists venture further west than Tanah Lot, but the stretch of coast beyond Tabanan holds some nice surprises at the black-sand beaches of **Balian** and **Medewi**. The spectacular cliff-side temple of **Pura Rambut Siwi** is almost as stunningly located as Tanah Lot but far less crowded with visitors, while **Negara**'s hinterland is of interest for its traditional fishing boats, Bugis architecture and Sunday-morning bull-racing.

The main road divides 16km west of Tabanan at the village of **ANTOSARI**, splitting the thundering westbound Gilimanuk and Java traffic from the vehicles heading to Seririt and the north coast. The northbound road, served by Ubung (Denpasar)–Seririt buses and bemos, climbs through some impressive mountain scenery and is described on p.348.

To Lalang Linggah and Balian beach

Heading west through Antosari and along the base of the mountain ridge, the road to Gilimanuk drops right down to the coast, affording fine sea views with shadows of southeast Java on the horizon, along with tantalizing inland panoramas of paddy-fields. You can make more of these views by stopping off at *Soka Indah* (T0361/7463106; ➋), located in **Soka** where the road hits the coast (kilometre-stone 45). The uninviting, tour-group-oriented restaurant here is better than it looks and, if you follow the path from the car park down to the sea (Rp2000 for non-guests), you'll find a couple of large, surprisingly secluded, comfortable bungalows with fine sea views.

About 10km west of Antosari, the Gilimanuk road zips through **LALANG LINGGAH**, the village closest to **Balian beach**, a spiritually charged spot at the mouth of the Balian River. Its caves and headlands are frequented by priests and shamen while the three surf breaks attract committed waveriders. The area is a pleasantly low-key, uncommercialized place to hang out, with some appealing accommodation, though take local advice on the vicious current, which makes nearly all of this beach too dangerous for casual swimmers. Fields of rice run down to the grey-sand beach, spiked by occasional cashew trees and stands of clove, cinnamon and cocoa bushes. There are a few tracks to explore here and inland, up the course of the river, or just head west along the thirty-kilometre-long beach.

All Ubung (Denpasar)–Gilimanuk **bemos** and buses pass through Lalang Linggah; they take about an hour and a quarter from Ubung or about half an hour from Medewi. Coming from the north coast you can take any Seririt–Ubung bemo as far as Antosari and then change onto the Ubung–Gilimanuk service.

Accommodation

Lalang Linggah has a growing amount and range of **accommodation** which caters mainly to surfers. None of it is more than five minutes' walk from the sea, with some set along the village road that runs down to the coast and others along the narrow shorefront road itself. Aside from those places listed here, there are also a number of expat villas with rooms available for rent. All the following are accessed via the narrow village road that runs south off the main Gilimanuk road, signed to *Gajah Mina*.

Balian Breezes Village road T0817/344 520, W www.balianbreezes.com. Villa accommodation comprising two good-quality, self-contained a/c rooms (one upstairs, one down), a kitchenette and a small pool. ➎

Balian Segara Shorefront road T0859/3536 8404. Four simple, concrete, surfers' bungalows, with bathrooms, just above the surf. ➋

Balian Surfer Homestay Village road T0361/747 4633, W www.baliansurfer.com. A genuine

homestay in a modern village house, offering just a handful of rooms with and without private bathrooms. ➋–➌

Gajah Mina West off the village road T0812/381 1630, W www.gajahminaresort.com. A chic and rather romantic walled hideaway of seven artfully designed bungalows and a couple of family suites, each with French windows leading to a private garden terrace, with easy access down to the beach and the river. There's a luxurious pool here, and a restaurant serving French-influenced cuisine. ❼–❽

Pondok Pisces Shorefront road and riverside ☎ 0813/3879 7722, ⓦ www .pondokpiscesbali.com. Run by an Australian–Indonesian couple, this welcoming little place offers a range of comfortably designed accommodation (all of it fan-cooled) in two different locations. Three bungalows overlook the surf break (one is a very spacious private house, one a two-storey bungalow and the other a charming, authentic, hand-carved wooden house shipped over from Timor), while another couple of two-storey bungalows enjoy a tranquil garden location down beside the Balian River. Swimming in the river is safe and a pool is also planned. *Pondok Pisces* also runs a charity foundation to help educate local kids: for details see Basics, p.61. ❹–❻

Medewi beach

As it skirts the coastline, the 25km stretch of road between Lalang Linggah and Medewi beach crosses more than a dozen rivers, each one streaming down from the Batukaru mountain range, watering kilometre after kilometre of stunningly lush land en route. Rice-paddies dominate the landscape, some even dropping to the shoreline, but this area is also a major coconut-growing region as well as a big producer of vanilla pods, cloves, cocoa beans and coffee. If you like tofu, a pleasant and very popular place for a **meal** with sea breezes is *Café Tahu* at kilometre-stone 60, where you can choose from twenty different Indonesian soups, stir-fries, curry and salad dishes all based around *tahu*, most of which cost under Rp10,000.

MEDEWI village sits on the main Tabanan–Gilimanuk road at kilometre-stone 72, served by frequent bemos (about 2hr from Ubung), and is famous for its surf. The black-sand shore is primarily a fishing beach, but is fronted by a small enclave of sea-view bungalows catering mainly to **surfers**: the light current and fairly benign waves makes this a popular spot for novices. You can also rent boats here, for snorkelling or fishing.

Accommodation

CSB Beach Inn About 600m east of central Medewi, via beach or road ☎ 0813/3866 7288. A quiet, well-kept losmen with ten large, clean, en-suite fan and a/c rooms offering views over the shorefront ricefields and the 300m track through them that leads down to the beach. Rooms with fan ❸ With a/c ❹

Homestay G'de Medewi beachfront ☎ 0812/397 6668. Friendly, super-cheap accommodation in eight primitive but perfectly acceptable en-suite rooms in a rickety two-storey block right on the shore. ❶

Hotel Pantai Medewi, aka **Medewi Beach Cottages** Medewi beachfront ☎ 0365/40029. The cheapest fan rooms here are twice as pricey as *G'de*'s and half as nice, though their more expensive a/c cottages occupy seafront positions and are set in pleasant gardens with a swimming pool. Rooms with fan ❷ With a/c ❺–❻

Puri Dajuma Cottages In Pekutatan, 5.5km east of central Medewi by road, or 20min walk along the shore ☎ 0365/43955, ⓦ www.dajuma.com. Attractive, rather luxurious seafront hotel whose 18 a/c bungalows are surrounded by a tropical garden, with pool, spa and *hammam*, and are pleasingly furnished with four-poster beds and garden bathrooms. Also runs a programme of cultural workshops and interesting trips around this untouristed region. ❽

Pura Rambut Siwi

When the sixteenth-century Hindu priest Nirartha sailed across from Java, he paused at this spot 16km west of modern-day Medewi and claimed it as holy. On leaving, he donated a lock of his hair to the villagers, who duly erected a temple and named it **Pura Rambut Siwi**, "the temple for worshipping the hair". This temple is now the most important in Jembrana district and is easily reached by the Denpasar–Gilimanuk **bemo**, which drops you at the head of the

750-metre access road to the temple. You'll be asked by the Brahman temple caretakers to wear a sash and give a donation, and in return they will offer to guide you around.

Nirartha's hair is enshrined, along with some of his clothing, in a sandalwood box buried deep inside the central three-tiered *meru*. This shrine is the focus of the inner courtyard, which is inaccessible to casual visitors but can be admired from alongside its south-facing **kori agung**. Built in tiers of solid red brick and ornamented with fierce stonecarvings of open-mouthed Bhoma, the gateway gives direct access to the cliff face and frames a stunning view of the Bali Strait. The figure that stands in the middle of the stairway, staring out to sea with his right arm raised, is said to be looking sorrowfully at Java (you can see Mount Bromo quite distinctly from here), bemoaning the ascendance of Islam over the Hindu kingdom of Majapahit. Gently stepped garden terraces of frangipani and stubby palm trees connect the outer *candi bentar* with the **shrine to Dewi Sri**, goddess of rice and of water and hence of prosperity, that balances on the cliff edge. Descending the rock-cut steps to the charcoal-black-sand beach, you'll find a string of tiny cave temples tucked into the cliff face to the left of the stairway.

Negara and around

Formerly the home of the Jembrana royal family and still the administrative capital of Jembrana district, **NEGARA** is graced with wide boulevards, a large number of mosques and a noticeably Islamic feel – though not a plethora of must-see sights. Historically, this was the main port of entry for the Javanese and the islanders of Madura, off northeast Java, who would sail through the Bali Strait to the estuary at Perancak and then head up the Ijo Gading River into the town. Negara's Muslims, already well established here by the nineteenth century, came mostly from southern Sulawesi; many were of **Bugis** origin, descendants of a seafaring race with a reputation as fearsome pirates. Traditional Bugis-style housing – raised, elongated wooden structures with distinctive carved panels and window frames – still features in the area, notably in the **Loloan Timur** neighbourhood, signed just south of Negara town centre.

Flamboyantly decorated **Madurese-style fishing boats** are still used in Negara's ports and are worth a look. Although now owned by wealthy Balinese or Javanese living in the area, the boats retain the traditional features, their masts festooned with tassels, fairy lights, portraits of heroes, windchimes and pennant flags. More importantly, these wide-bottomed hardwood workhorses are phenomenal load carriers and, working in twos, can haul in a lucrative fifty tonnes of fish per pair each night – quite a catch when sold on for around Rp7000/kg. During the day, most of these boats anchor close to the fish factory at **PANGAMBENGAN**, which is 7km southwest of central Negara and signed both from the main Gilimanuk road and from Loloan Timur. Other Madurese-style boats shelter further east, in the **PERANCAK** estuary, beside Pura Perancak, about 20km southeast of central Negara or 9km west of Delod Berawah (for access to which, see below). Pura Perancak commemorates the landing of the influential Javanese Hindu priest Nirartha here in the sixteenth century.

Negara's only other significant attraction is its traditional **bull races** or *mekepung*, which were probably also introduced from Madura, where similar races are still held. Decked out in strings of bells and decorative harness, the bull pairs are hitched to carts and thrashed along a four-kilometre dirt track, encouraged by whip-happy jockeys. Local races are staged in **DELOD BERAWAH**

every second and fourth Sunday morning (7am–noon), with alternate Sundays being practice days; there are also occasional big competitions. To reach Delod Berewa, drive 7km east along the highway from Negara town centre to Tegal-cangkring, then follow the signs south for 2.5km. Both *Puri Dajuma Cottages* and *Hotel Pantai Medewi* in Medewi organize trips to the races.

Practicalities

All Denpasar–Gilimanuk **bemos** pass through Negara town centre, arriving at the bemo terminal north of the market on Jalan Pahlawan. Hardly any tourists **stay** here, but those that do usually choose the *Wira Pada Hotel* (℡0365/41161; ❶–❷), which is centrally located at Jalan Ngurah Rai 107 and has decent enough fan and a/c rooms set around a yard. It also runs a reasonably priced streetside Sino-Indonesian **restaurant**. There are several ATMs and a money changer nearby. The dozens of cute-looking, discreetly shrub-shrouded little *penginapan* **bungalows** that line the Delod Berawah–Perancak road are designed for local couples needing a few hours on their own, but an overnight stay is possible (❷).

The far west

Beyond Negara, the landscape of the **far west** changes dramatically, becoming noticeably drier and more rugged. The thickly forested, cloud-capped mountain slopes shelter very few villages and much of the land is protected by Bali's Forestry Department, with the most important habitats conserved as **Bali Barat National Park**. Few tourists explore the park – the only one on the island – but it can be rewarding for bird-watchers and also harbours some of Bali's best coral reefs, around **Pulau Menjangan (Deer Island)**.

If you're arriving overland from Java, the port town of **Gilimanuk** will be your first introduction to Bali. Other than Bali's most famous chilli-chicken restaurant there's little to detain you in the town itself, but the Menjangan reefs and Pemuteran beach are just a few kilometres away, and good transport connections enable you to head either straight to Lovina and the north coast or to Denpasar and the south.

Palasari and Blimbingsari

While Muslims have long been accepted into western Balinese society, **Christians** have historically had a frostier reception. Under the Dutch colonialists' "cultural preservation" policy, all Christian missionaries were barred from practising on the island, but by 1932 the American Christian and Missionary Alliance (CMA) had nonetheless made several hundred converts, mostly within the Chinese community but also among those of "pure Balinese" ethnicity. The CMA's approach was fundamentalist, encouraging converts to destroy Hindu temples and question the iniquities of the caste system, to which Hindu leaders responded by forbidding Hindus from having any contact with Balinese Christians. Tensions escalated and by 1939 the Dutch had banned the CMA altogether and exiled the Christian community to a remote, inhospitable area of uninhabited jungle high up in the mountains of west Bali, some 30km northwest of Negara.

Against massive odds and with an amazing pioneering spirit, the Protestants hacked the cross-shaped village of **BLIMBINGSARI** out of this patch of jungle and built a huge modern church at its core, still the mother church for Bali's entire Christian community. Some 5km southeast, the Catholics did the same at **PALASARI**. Both missions were founded on the principle of contextualization, so many elements of Balinese Christian practice have distinctly Balinese-Hindu roots, including church architecture, dress, and thanksgiving offerings, an interesting achievement given that Balinese culture has long been held as inextricable from Balinese religion. Balinese music and dance, for example, are taught in Blimbingsari and Palasari, but the characters and stories are taken from the Bible rather than from the *Ramayana* and *Mahabharata*, and the churches up here blend Balinese and Western European architecture to dramatic effect. Both modern-day settlements are, however, in decline, with populations of no more than two thousand apiece dependent on local cacao and coconut plantations, and a younger generation forced to seek employment elsewhere.

The two communities are accessible, and signposted, via a road that runs inland from near Melaya on the main Tabanan–Gilimanuk road. There's no regular bemo service to either place, though gangs of **ojek** usually hang around the main road turn-offs. Several families in Blimbingsari offer informal homestay accommodation to visiting Christians, but the only **hotel** is the ultra-luxurious *Taman Wana Villas* (☎0365/40970, ⓦwww.bali-tamanwana-villas .com; ⑨), just beyond Palasari, and clearly signed all the way from the main Gilimanuk road 8km away. Its circular villas occupy a breathtaking spot overlooking the Palasari reservoir, surrounded by ricefields and palm groves, with the distant peaks of Gunung Klatakan and Gunung Bakingan and the waters of the Bali Strait all visible from the restaurant.

Gilimanuk

Situated on the westernmost tip of Bali, less than 3km from East Java, the small, ribbon-like town of **GILIMANUK** is used by visitors mainly as a transit point for journeys to and from Java. A 24-hour ferry service crosses the Bali Strait so few travellers bother to linger, and there's nothing much to see here except the silhouettes of Java's great volcanoes across the water. The **Bali Strait** is a notoriously difficult stretch of water to negotiate: although Bali and East Java are so close, the water is just 60m deep, and the current treacherous. (Despite this, it is occasionally swum; as of May 2006, the world record is 29 minutes and 30 seconds). During the Ice Ages, it's likely that a land bridge connected the two islands, which both rest on the continental plate known as the Sunda shelf, enabling humans and other animals to walk back and forth between the two – something which may become a reality once more, if the controversial plans to construct a modern-day Bali–Java bridge ever come to fruition.

Skeletons and pottery shards found around Gilimanuk show that this area was inhabited at least as far back as 3000 BC and some of the Neolithic remains are on show at one of the archeological sites near the bay, **Museum Situs Purbakala Gilimanuk** (Mon–Fri 7am–5pm; donation). The display is rather desultory however, and there's no English-language information.

The one significant attraction round here is the chance to "**muck dive**" the cold, shallow, silty waters of Gilimanuk's **Secret Bay**, just east of the port, where juvenile fish and rare marine species are prolific and especially rewarding for macro-photographers. Any dive operator in Pemuteran (see p.346) or the south (see p.146) can organize a trip.

The other big draw for locals is Gilimanuk's reputation for producing the finest **ayam betutu** (steamed chilli-chicken) on Bali. And the most famous purveyor of them all is *Asli Warung Men Tempeh* (10am–4pm), whose simple warung at the back of the old bemo station is always crowded with fans, some of whom travel miles for the pleasure. The late Men Tempeh's fiery recipe, now reproduced by her husband, entails slathering the chicken in an exhilaratingly mouth-blasting mix of garlic, galangal, turmeric, ginger, chilli and shrimp paste and serving it with extra *sambal* (Rp45,000). There are several copycat outlets in the old bemo terminal, but the original is at the back.

Practicalities

Gilimanuk's **bus and bemo terminal** is across from the ferry terminal and operates frequent services to and from Denpasar's **Ubung** terminal, 128km away (dark green; buses Rp17,000, bemos Rp25,500), via **Negara** (Rp5000/7000) and the southwest coast; **Singaraja,** 88km away (dark red; Rp11,500/17,500), via **Lovina**; **Padang Bai** (bus Rp24,500); and **Amlapura** (bus Rp23,500).

Accommodation in Gilimanuk is not tourist-oriented, as it's intended mainly for minimal overnight stops (which includes the brothel trade) or for long-stay contract workers. If you have to spend the night, try the friendly *Nusantara Gilimanuk Guest House* (☎0365/61405; Fan ❸ A/c ❹), which has seven adequate rooms running off a corridor (no external windows) and a misleadingly striking minimalist grey-stone entrance. Alternatively, there's the 18-room *Pondok Wisata Lestari* losmen and restaurant (☎0365/61504; Fan ❶ A/c ❹), about 2km southeast of the port along the road to Cekik, or 1.5km north of the Bali Barat National Park headquarters.

There's only one **ATM** in Gilimanuk that takes foreign cards and it's in the ferry terminal compound.

Map of Gilimanuk showing: Ferry Terminal for Boats to Java, Ketapang, Bali Strait, ATM, Bus & Bemo Terminal, Gilimanuk Bay, Split Gate, Police, Jalan Muhara, Asli Warung Men Tempeh, Jalan Raya Gilimanuk, Bank, Museum Situs Purbakala Gilimanuk, Market, Bemo Stop, Nusantara Gilimanuk Guest House, 0 approx. 200 m

Bali Barat National Park

Parts of westernmost Bali are protected as **Bali Barat National Park (Taman Nasional Bali Barat)**, whose 19,000 hectares of savannah, rainforest, monsoon forest, mangrove swamp and coral

Pondok Wisata Lestari, ▼ *Cekik, Pemuteran & Denpasar*

Crossing to Java

Crossing the Bali Strait between Bali and Java is easy: there are no formalities, and onward transport facilities from both ports are frequent and efficient. If you're travelling quite a way into Java, to Probolinggo (for Mount Bromo), for example, or to Surabaya, Yogyakarta or Jakarta, the easiest option is to get an all-inclusive ticket from your starting point in Bali. The cheapest **long-distance buses** run out of Denpasar's Ubung station (see p.318), with pick-up points in Tabanan, Negara and sometimes Gilimanuk, but there are also more expensive **tourist shuttle buses** and **bus-and-train** combinations operating from tourist centres.

Ferries shuttle between Gilimanuk and Ketapang (East Java) and back again 24 hours a day (every 20min; 45min including loading and docking). **Tickets** are issued as you board: for foot passengers they cost Rp6000 (Rp4200 for kids), for motorbikes Rp15,000–33,600 (including rider), and cars Rp96,000 (including driver and passengers). Note that most car-rental agencies on Bali prohibit tourists from taking their vehicles to other islands (see p.39 for more).

Arriving in **Ketapang**, the Banyuwangi Baru train station is about 100m north of the ferry terminal and runs services to Surabaya Kota, Probolinggo and Yogyakarta. The central bus stations for cross-Java travel are in the much larger nearby town of **Banyuwangi**, 8km south of Ketapang and served by frequent bemos from the ferry terminal.

reef are home to a range of small animals, prolific marine life and approximately 160 species of bird – including the elusive and endangered **Bali starling**, Bali's one true endemic creature. This was also once the province of the Bali tiger, but the last one was shot here in the 1930s. Some published maps show the national park as extending a great deal further, but in reality the park is encircled by forest that comes under the jurisdiction of the provincial forestry department.

Just a fraction of the national park is open to the public and its biggest attraction by far is **Pulau Menjangan** (**Deer Island**), whose spectacular **coral reefs** draw snorkellers and divers from all over Bali. On dry land, encroachment and illegal tree-felling has degraded some of the forest and the handful of rarely-trekked **trails** are only worth it for the reasonably rewarding bird-watching, though you can also take a boat trip through the shoreline mangroves. Grey macaques live in the roadside forests and can often be seen waiting for titbits from passing drivers.

Practicalities

All dark-green Ubung (Denpasar)–Gilimanuk **bemos** pass the national park headquarters at Cekik, 3km south of Gilimanuk, as do all dark-red Singaraja–Gilimanuk bemos; both routes are also useful for access to trailheads.

Anyone who enters Bali Barat National Park must be accompanied by a park guide and have a permit. Both can be arranged through either the national park headquarters or the branch office at the Labuan Lalang jetty. The **national park headquarters** (daily 8am–5pm) is conveniently located at **CEKIK**, beside the Denpasar–Gilimanuk–Singaraja T-junction, 3km south of Gilimanuk; for details of the branch office at the Labuan Lalang jetty, see p.341.

Most of the **guides** are English-speaking and knowledgeable about the flora and fauna of Bali Barat; they don't necessarily need to be booked in advance. The basic fee is Rp190,000 for a two-hour hike for up to two people (Rp350,000 for three to five people), or Rp440,000/660,000 for a seven-hour hike. Specialist bird-watching excursions are also available (2–4hr;

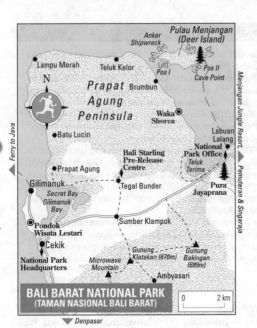

Rp390,000/550,000). If you don't have your own transport you'll also be expected to pay for any necessary bemo or boat charters. Having arranged a guide, the fee for most treks should include the Rp20,000 national park **permit**.

All the hotels in Pemuteran, 28km northeast of Cekik, organize **day-trips** to the park.

Accommodation and eating

Rangers generally don't allow visitors to **camp** in the park, but you can ask for permission to pitch your tent at Labuan Lalang's beach or, if student and other groups aren't in residence, at the Cekik national park headquarters, though there are few facilities at either spot and you'll have to pay extra for a shower. Otherwise, the closest decent **guesthouse** is *Pondok Wisata Lestari*, about 1.5km north of the park headquarters on the road into Gilimanuk; see p.336 for details. Alternatively, make for the appealing accommodation at Pemuteran (see p.344), 28km along the road towards Singaraja.

There are also a few upmarket **resorts** on the fringes of the park, closer to Labuan Lalang than Cekik, all of which offer guided walks and diving and snorkelling excursions. The fourteen elegantly simple wilderness bungalows at *Waka Shorea* (☎0362/94666, ⚑www.wakaexperience.com; ⑧) are just across the water from Pulau Menjangan on the shore of the Prapat Agung Peninsula, only accessible by hotel shuttle-boat from the Labuan Lalang jetty area. A couple of kilometres east of Labuan Lalang, at kilometre-marker 17, the *Menjangan Jungle and Beach Resort* (☎0362/94700, ⚑www.menjangan.net; ⑨) was reportedly built under such strictly enforced restrictions that many of its buildings incorporated existing trees rather than having them cut down. It's a top-end resort, constructed entirely from Kalimantan timber, with spectacularly indulgent rooms in luxury sea-view villas (from $484) and some disappointingly ordinary, terraced "monsoon forest" rooms set around a swimming pool near the resort's riding stables.

Other than at the resorts, there are no warung or **food** hawkers inside the national park, but a *bakso* and noodle cart sets up outside the Cekik park headquarters every day. The nearest restaurant is at *Pondok Wisata Lestari*, 1.5km north up the road to Gilimanuk, or there are several warung at the Labuan Lalang jetty, 13km east of Cekik.

The Prapat Agung trail

If your main interest is bird-spotting, opt for a trek on the **Prapat Agung Peninsula** (1–2hr; best in the early morning), whose monsoon forest harbours a large **bird population**, including flocks of the common yellow-vented bulbul, and the loud-chirping black-naped oriole. Other possible sightings include parakeets and fantails; the green jungle fowl; the pinky-brown spotted dove, which has a distinctive call; the black drongo, completely black save for its red eyes; and the tiny, bright-yellow-breasted olive-backed sunbird. This peninsula is also home to the last few Bali starlings that remain in the wild and to the Bali Starling Pre-Release Centre, a captive breeding project that can sometimes be visited with prior permission.

Gilimanuk Bay boat trip

The Tegal Bunder trail combines nicely with a boat trip round mangrove-lined **Gilimanuk Bay**. Tiny *jukung* for two people cost Rp200,000 for two hours and should be arranged through the national park guides; you have to pay the standard permit fee on top. Note that the current off this shore is dangerously strong so it's not advisable to swim here, and sunbathing isn't that tempting either, as the beaches seem to end up with all the plastic bottles and other debris washed in across the Bali Strait.

Mangroves are best seen at low tide, when their exposed aerial roots form knotted archways above the muddy banks. Not only are these roots essential

The Bali starling

With its silky, snow-white feathers, blue eye patches, black wing and tail tips and delicate soft crest, the **Bali starling** or Rothschild's Myna (*leucopsar Rothschildi*) is a strikingly beautiful bird and the provincial symbol of Bali. It's Bali's only remaining endemic creature and survives in the dry monsoon forests and savannah grasslands that characterize the Prapat Agung Peninsula of Bali Barat National Park. Sadly however, its looks have been its downfall, for Bali starlings make docile and very pretty pets, fetching up to US$4000 when sold, and have now been hunted almost to extinction. With just 54 wild birds estimated to be left living wild in Bali Barat as of 2007, the Bali starling (*jalak putih Bali* in Bahasa Indonesia) is now officially classified as **critically endangered**.

Another crucial factor is **habitat**. The Bali starling is exceptionally sensitive to changes in its surroundings and requires a very stable habitat to survive. During the breeding season, Bali Barat's entire population is found in a small, extremely arid area of less than three square kilometres around Brumbun on the Prapat Agung Peninsula. But human activity, both legal and illegal, in this area of the national park seems to have had a bad effect on the birds' nerves.

To try and reverse the population decline, a **captive breeding programme** was established at the Bali Starling Pre-Release Centre on the Prapat Agung Peninsula. Though it has successfully released some birds into the existing habitat area around Brumbun, the project has been beset by problems, including being robbed of nearly all its birds by an armed gang in 2000. (As a result, tourists now need to apply for a special permit to see the birds at the Centre.) Now a rival (and therefore controversial) breeding programme has been established by the Friends of the National Parks Foundation (🌐 www.fnpf.org) and the Begawan Giri Foundation, miles away from the increasingly degraded forests of Bali Barat, on the relatively remote south-Bali island of **Nusa Penida**. The founders seemed to have made at least one important break-through there by persuading leaders of all 35 villages on the island to make it an offence against *awig-awig* traditional law to poach or kill the Bali starlings; by May 2007, 49 birds had been released on Nusa Penida.

The only other places you can see Bali starlings in Bali are in **aviaries** at the Bali Bird Park in Batubulan (see p.171) and at the Museum Blanco in Ubud (see p.196), both of which run small captive breeding programmes.

parts of the trees' breathing apparatus, but they also reclaim land for future mangroves by trapping debris into which the metre-long mangrove seedlings can fall. In this way, mangrove swamps also stabilize shifting mud and protect coastlines from erosion and the impact of tropical storms.

Boatmen should be able to get you close enough to the mangroves to spot resident **fiddler crabs**, named after the male's massive reddish claw that it uses to threaten and to communicate, and is said to be so strong it can open a can of beans. You might see **mudskippers** as well, specially adapted fish who can absorb atmospheric oxygen when out of the water, as long as they keep their outsides damp – which is why they spend a lot of time slithering through the mangrove mud. **Crab-eating or long-tailed macaques** hang out along the shore, too, filling their outsized cheek pouches with fruit, mussels, small mammals and crabs (they're very good swimmers and divers).

On the exposed reef you'll see **sea cucumbers**, **sea horses**, and various species of **crab**, as well as heaps of seashells. You might also spot some elegant dark-grey **Pacific reef egrets**.

Teluk Terima

The two-hour walk around **Teluk Terima**, the bay west of the Labuan Lalang jetty and park office, passes through monsoon forest and coastal flats fairly similar to those at Tegal Bunder. It's a fruitful area for early-morning sightings of sea eagles, dollar birds and even the rufous-backed kingfisher, plus monkeys, deer and metre-long iguanas.

The Gunung Klatakan trail

The **Gunung Klatakan**–Gunung Bakingan trail (7hr) is the most popular and strenuous of the Bali Barat hikes. It starts at the Sumber Klampok ranger post and ascends the slopes of Gunung Klatakan and Gunung Bakingan, before returning to the main road a few kilometres east of Sumber Klampok. En route you pass through an area known as Watu Lesung, where grinding stones, possibly dating back to prehistoric times and now considered to be holy, were found. For the most part, the trail follows a steep incline through **tropical rainforest** that leaves few clearings through which to view the surrounding peaks. The forest is thick with ferns, vines, spiky-stemmed rattan and viciously serrated pandanus palms, plus various epiphytic orchids, including the elegantly long-stemmed, white-sepalled madavellia orchid. You're unlikely to spot much **wildlife** on this trail, but you'll probably hear the black monkeys swinging through the uppermost canopy, and you may stumble across a fearsome-looking wild boar – short-sighted and a bit stupid, boars tend to charge in a straight line until they hit an obstacle, regardless of where their prey happens to be, so just run away in zigzags if you encounter one. The most dramatic of the **birds** up here are the southern pied hornbill – with a black head, white breast and tail feathers, and a pronounced casque on its yellow beak – and the wreathed hornbill, which has a much smaller casque on its beak and no white breast. Other commonly sighted birds include the multicoloured banded pitta, the bluey-grey dollarbird with its distinctive red beak, the talking mynah, and the red-and-green jungle fowl.

Pulau Menjangan (Deer Island)

By far the most popular part of Bali Barat National Park is **Pulau Menjangan (Deer Island)**, a tiny uninhabited island 8km off the north coast, whose shoreline is encircled by some of the most spectacular **coral reefs** in Bali. Most visitors rate this as the best snorkelling spot on Bali, and divers place it high on their list too. Many divers and snorkellers come on organized **tours** from the south, at least a three-hour drive away (US$100 for two dives, $50 for snorkellers), but it's cheaper and less tiring to base yourself at the nearby north-coast resorts of Pemuteran or Lovina, where prices average $80 for two dives or $40 for snorkellers. For snorkellers it can work out even cheaper to head to Labuan Lalang, the access port for Menjangan, and club together with other tourists to hire a boat. As the island comes under the jurisdiction of the national park, hiring a guide is essential, but both the guide and boat transport can be arranged at the jetty in Labuan Lalang without first checking in at the Cekik headquarters.

All snorkelling boats anchor off Menjangan's southeastern corner. If you take lunch, you can picnic on the beach there; there's no food or water on **the island**, nor any shade. Nor is there anything much to see, save for a small shrine and a freshwater spring. Brahmans from the mainland make pilgrimages here in search of medicinal herbs and a path encircles the flat, sandy-soiled island, which can be covered in about an hour.

Menjangan practicalities

The departure point for Pulau Menjangan is **LABUAN LALANG**, just east of Teluk Terima, 13km from Cekik and 15km west of Pemuteran. To get there, take any Singaraja-bound **bemo** or **bus** from Gilimanuk (30min) or Cekik (20min), or any Gilimanuk-bound bemo or bus from Lovina (2hr) or Pemuteran (30min). If you're coming from the southwest coast, take any Ubung (Denpasar)–Gilimanuk bus or bemo to Cekik, then change onto the Singaraja-bound service. There's a small **national park office** at Labuan Lalang (daily 8am–3pm), as well as several **warung** where you can have a meal and buy food and water to take with you.

The **hiring of boats** to Pulau Menjangan is well organized and should be arranged through the national park office in the Labuan Lalang car park. Boats can be hired at any time of day up to about 3pm (underwater visibility is best in the morning); they hold up to ten people and prices are fixed at Rp310,000 for a round trip of up to four hours, which includes thirty minutes journey-time each way. In addition to boat rental, you must pay Rp60,000 for a national park guide, who usually snorkels with you, plus Rp20,000 per person for the national-park entry fee. The boat can be hired for as many extra hours as you like for Rp40,000 per hour (plus extra for the guide), and you can rent mask, fins and snorkel from the office for Rp50,000 a set. There are occasional reports of **thefts** from the boats while snorkellers are underwater, so leave valuables in the car or the hotel and bring minimal money out with you, or keep it in a waterproof neck-pouch.

The Menjangan reefs

The clear, shallow water between Labuan Lalang and Pulau Menjangan is protected from excessive winds and strong currents by the Prapat Agung Peninsula, and its **reefs** are mostly in good health, not least because patrols by national park officials and local dive operators has helped put a stop to the highly destructive practice of dynamite fishing. The reefs form a band 100m to 150m around the coastline, offering seven different **dive** sites, with drop-offs of 40m to 60m, first-class wall dives, and superb visibility ranging from 15m to 50m. Two of these sites, off the southeastern corner of the island, offer outstanding **snorkelling**: at Pos II, the extensive reef wall drops down around 50m but tops out very near the surface and is a phenomenally rich trove of sea fans and soft and hard corals visited by masses of reef fish, parrot

Life on the reef

Coral reefs are living organisms composed of a huge variety of marine life forms, but the foundation of every reef is its ostensibly inanimate **stony coral** – hard constructions such as boulder, cabbage patch, mushroom, bushy staghorn and brain coral. Stony coral is composed of colonies of polyps – minuscule invertebrates that feed on plankton, generally depend on algae and direct sunlight for photosynthesis, and extract calcium carbonate (limestone) from sea water to reproduce. The polyps use this calcium carbonate to build new skeletons outside their bodies – an asexual reproductive process known as budding – and this is how a reef is formed. It's an extraordinarily slow process, with colony growth averaging somewhere between 0.5cm and 2.8cm a year.

Fleshy, plant-like **soft coral**, such as dead man's fingers and elephant's ear, is also composed of polyps, but with flaccid internal skeletons built from protein rather than calcium. The lack of an external casing means the polyps' vivid colours are much more visible, and as they do not depend on direct sunlight they flourish at greater depths, using tentacles to trap microorganisms. **Horny coral**, or gorgonians, like sea whips and sea fans, are a cross between stony and soft coral, while **sea anemones** have the most obvious, and poisonous, tentacles of any member of the coral family, using them to trap fish and other large prey.

The algae and plankton that accumulate around coral colonies attract a catalogue of **reef fish**. Most are small, with exotically patterned skins for camouflage against the coral, and flattened bodies, broad tails and specially adapted fins for easy manoeuvring around the tiniest crannies. **Butterfly fish** are typically well designed: named for the fluttering movements of their thin, flat, yellow, white and black bodies, they can swim backwards and some also have elongated snouts for nosing into crevices. **Moorish idols** are easily recognized by the long pennant fin that trails from the dorsal fin, their pronounced snout, and dramatic black, yellow and white bands of colour. There are around one hundred species of **surgeonfish**, each with its own distinctive markings, but they all have a sharp blade on either side of the tail-base, which becomes erect when antagonized and can inflict serious damage. The slender, pipe-like **trumpetfish** grows up to 75cm long, has elongated jaws and is a skilful and frequently spotted daytime predator. With the help of a bird-like beak, which is in fact

fish, clams, nudibranchs and all manner of other reef dwellers. At nearby Cave Point, the reef features lots of nooks and crannies, some of which are accessible to snorkellers. Elsewhere, in among the expansive sea fans, enormous barrel sponges and black tree corals so distinctive of this area, the reefs teem with yellowback fusiliers, puffer fish, barracuda and silvery jacks. There's also an old **shipwreck** lying 45m deep off the western tip of the island, frequented by sharks and rays as well as by Moorish idols, sweetlips and snappers. It's a small *prahu*, known as the "Anker", but is rarely visited because it's too deep for normal PADI divers. The wreck's anchor is only about 6m deep, and features on some dive excursions, but is some way from the ship itself.

Pura Jayaprana

For the best aerial view of Pulau Menjangan, stop off at **Pura Jayaprana** (donation), 12km east of Cekik and 1km west of Labuan Lalang. The temple itself is unimpressive, but its location at the top of a long flight of steps is superb, with panoramas that take in the island, its translucent waters, and the shadows of the coral reefs beneath. Pura Jayaprana enshrines the grave of the eponymous local seventeenth-century folk hero who was murdered because several teeth fused together, the ubiquitous **parrot fish** scrapes away at the coral, leaving characteristic white scars, and then grinds the fragments down with another set of back teeth – which is considerably damaging to a reef.

Larger, less frequent visitors to Bali's and Lombok's reefs include the **moray eel**, whose elongated jaws of viciously pointed teeth make it a deadly predator; it hunts mainly at night and often holes up in coral caves during the day. The similarly be-fanged **barracuda** can grow to two metres. **Sharks** are more common, and it's also sometimes possible to swim with a **manta ray**, whose extraordinary flatness, strange wing-like fins, and massive size – up to 6m across and weighing some 1600kg – make it an astonishing presence. Weighing up to twice as much as rays, **mola mola** (also known as **oceanic sunfish**) are phenomenal sights, measuring some 3m top to bottom and about 2.5m end to end. They are extremely rare, but are occasionally spotted off Nusa Lembongan; they're very short-sighted so can often be inspected at close quarters. **Turtles** occasionally paddle around reef waters, too, but are fast becoming endangered in Bali (see p.134).

The reefs of Bali and Lombok also support countless species of **invertebrates**, including multi-celled, multi-hued **sponges**, both encrusting and free-standing; and a thousand-plus species of hermaphroditic, shell-less mollusc known as **nudibranchs** or sea slugs, which come in an arresting array of patterns and shapes and live in shallow waters. The hideous slug-like **sea cucumber** lies half-buried on the sea bed where it constantly ingests and excretes so much sand and mud that the combined force of those sea cucumbers in a three-square-kilometre area can together redis-tribute one million kilogrammes of sea-bed material a year.

Of the reef's numerous spiny echinoderms, the commonest **sea urchins**, which also tend to live in shallow areas near shore, are those with evil-looking black spines up to 35cm in length, though some varieties are covered in short, blunt spines or even excruciatingly painful flower-like pincers. The magnificent **crown-of-thorns starfish** is also protected by highly venomous spines, which sheath the twenty or so "arms" that extend from its body and can measure up to 50cm in diameter. Disas-trously for many reefs, the crown-of-thorns starfish feeds on coral, destroying as much as fifty square centimetres of stony coral in a 24-hour period.

the king wanted to marry the young man's wife. The wife, Layonsari, remained faithful to the memory of her dead husband and chose suicide over marriage to the king. The young couple's grave is enclosed in a glass case in the shrine's inner courtyard, watched over by kitsch doll-like statues representing Jayaprana and Layonsari.

The northwest coast

East of Cekik, the main Gilimanuk–Singaraja road emerges from Bali Barat National Park at Teluk Terima and runs along the narrow strip of the **northwest coast** between the sea and the mountains, passing Labuan Lalang, access point for Pulau Menjangan (Deer Island; described above), and 8km further east, the uninspiring hot springs at **Banyuwedang**. The terrain gets more interesting beyond Banyuwedang, with dramatic mountain slopes dominating inland views as far as **Pemuteran**, a peaceful beach haven offering plenty of opportunities for snorkelling and diving. Continue east and you'll soon reach an even smaller hideaway at **Ume Anyar**, before the road divides: head east for Lovina and Singaraja (covered in Chapter 4) or south for the cool, refreshing hills around **Sanda** and **Belimbing**.

Pemuteran and around

East of Banyuwedang, the great craggy folds of Bali Barat's north-facing ridges rise almost perpendicular from the roadside, and in the foreground of this amazing setting sits the little fishing village of **PEMUTERAN**, 28km east of Cekik. It's a pleasantly low-key area to stay and a good place to base yourself for diving and snorkelling (both nearby and at Pulau Menjangan), plus the small cluster of lovely, if mostly rather pricey, shoreside hotels here make a conscious effort not to upset the village ambience. You can swim and snorkel in the safe, calm waters off the tree-shaded black-sand beach and make trips to the national park.

Practicalities

All dark-red Gilimanuk–Singaraja **bemos** pass through Pemuteran and will drop you in front of your chosen hotel; they take about thirty minutes from Labuan Lalang (or 1hr 20min from Lovina). If coming from Ubud or the south-coast resorts, your fastest option is to take a **tourist shuttle bus** to Lovina and then hop on to a bemo. Some tiny private charter planes use the Let. Kol. Wisnu airstrip in Pegamatan, 4km west of Pemuteran.

There's a well-provisioned local store on the main road between Reef Seen and *Sari Amertha Villa* and broadband **Internet** access at most of the top hotels, most cheaply for non-guests at *Sari Amertha* and *Taman Sari*. The nearest banks and ATM are in Gilimanuk, but you can **change money** and traveller's cheques at *Rare Angon* homestay. The **Pemuteran Clinic** next to *Sari Amertha* is open 24 hours, but for any major ailments you'll have to go to one of the hospitals in Singaraja or Denpasar.

Accommodation

Nearly all Pemuteran **accommodation** occupies beachfront land, with access via the Gilimanuk–Singaraja road. *Taman Sari*, *Pondok Sari* and *Taman Selini* are all at the western end of Pemuteran, within a minute's walk of each other along the shore, a bit further by road; *Rare Angon* is across the road from *Taman Sari* and *Sari Amertha Villa* a little way further east, on the sea. About 1km further east again along the road, you reach *Jubawa Homestay* and *Matahari Beach*; *Segara Bukit* is out on its own in Banyupoh, another 4km further east.

In high season, much of the **accommodation** gets booked up by diving tours, so it's best to reserve as far ahead as possible. Divers and snorkellers at Reef Seen Aquatics dive school can stay at their five terraced shorefront a/c bungalows (⑤) and if they're not busy, non-divers can stay there for a bit extra.

Jubawa Homestay 800m east of *Sari Amertha* and 200m west of *Matahari Beach* ☎ 0362/94745. One of Pemuteran's cheapest options, with eight unexpectedly attractive fan and a/c bungalows set back from the road behind the restaurant, in a neat little garden beneath the mountains, about 400m from the beach. The interiors are smartly furnished in dark wood and have decent bathrooms. ④

Matahari Beach Resort and Spa 1km east of *Sari Amertha* ☎ 0362/92312, ⓦ www .matahari-beach-resort.com. Accommodation in this luxury beachfront complex comprises 32 very classy private villa compounds furnished with four-poster beds and pretty garden bathrooms. But the real attraction is the exceptionally elegant spa complex, reminiscent of a Roman bathhouse, with its own lotus-pond tea pavilion, as well as private massage rooms and a gym. The hotel also has a swimming pool and a beachfront bar. ⑨

Pondok Sari Between *Taman Sari* and *Taman Selini* ☎ 0362/94738, ⓦ www.pondoksari.com. A lovely collection of 30 large, stylishly designed, semi-detached a/c cottages all with attractive open-roofed garden bathrooms spaced around a beautiful mature tropical garden that runs down to the beach. Also has five deluxe options plus a pool and a spa. ⑥–⑦

Rare Angon Western end of Pemuteran, across the road from *Taman Sari* ☎0362/94747, ✉rareangon @yahoo.co.id. The best located of Pemuteran's cheaper options, across the road and just 200m from the main beach area, this tiny homestay currently has just three bungalows (though four more are planned). The a/c bungalows are especially attractive, furnished with a four-poster bed, local textiles and garden bathroom. It's set back from the road, behind the Greek-accented restaurant. Rooms with fan ③ With a/c ④

Sari Amertha Villa Eastern end of central Pemuteran ☎0813/3758 2258, ⓦwww .balitamansari.com. Set up by *Taman Sari* as a timeshare outfit whose villas are available to all, this place is a good spot for families. Its fourteen 2-, 3- and 4-bedroom a/c villas all have private pools and are set around a very spacious seafront garden that also has its own large pool and restaurant. Some villas have kitchen facilities. Two-bed villas can also be rented out by the room. Per room ⑥–⑦ 2-bedroom villas ⑨

Segara Bukit Seaside Cottages 5km east of *Sari Amertha* in Banyupoh ☎0362/94749. One of the cheapest places to stay in the area – and by far the cheapest shoreside option – with sixteen perfectly pleasant fan and a/c rooms ranged around a small garden fronting a sandy beach, not far from a fish farm. Also has a pretty seafront pool, a restaurant, and car and motorbike rental. Rooms with fan ② With a/c ④

Taman Sari ☎0362/93264, ⓦwww.balitamansari .com. Another lovely place to stay, with attractive terraced bungalows, spacious, detached a/c bungalows with shady verandahs and garden bathrooms, plus several deluxe suites. Has a pool and a good Thai restaurant. ⑤–⑧

Taman Selini Immediately east along the shore from *Pondok Sari* ☎0362/94746, ⓦwww .tamanselini.com. Tiny, elegant outfit with eleven rather chic bungalows, all furnished with four-poster beds, large garden bathrooms, and day beds on the spacious verandahs. Mango trees grow in the beachfront garden, and there's an inviting sea-view pool and a Greek restaurant. ⑦

▲ Pemuteran beach

All the hotels have **restaurants** serving freshly caught seafood, as well as the usual range of tourist and Indonesian standards. *Taman Selini's* menu of Greek dishes includes recommended mezze sets for Rp45,000 (the Greek owner also runs the *Pantarei* restaurant in Legian); *Rare Angon's* Balinese owner also spent a dozen years in Greece and serves cheaper Greek classics (mezzes from Rp8000, sate and tuna kebabs Rp12,000–20,000); and *Taman Sari* restaurant specializes in Thai food. For cheap and cheerful Balinese standards, there are several small warung alongside the main road, including *Badini*, across the road from *Taman Selini*, which is locally famous for its fresh fish and great *ayam kecap* (chicken marinated in soy sauce).

The *Matahari Beach* stages frequent classical Balinese **dance** performances for diners at its very expensive restaurant, or you can watch a similar performance by local village girls at *Pondok Sari* restaurant on most Saturday evenings at 7pm (they also rehearse at Reef Seen, Sat 3–5pm & Sun 9am–noon).

Snorkelling and diving

The chief activities in Pemuteran – apart from lying on the black-sand beach – are **snorkelling and diving**. Although there are some impressive reefs within easy reach of Pemuteran's shore, most divers and snorkellers agree that they are outclassed by those at nearby **Pulau Menjangan**.

Pemuteran reefs

Some of the **Pemuteran reefs** have suffered considerable damage over the last decade, ascribed to a combination of bad practices by local fishermen and unavoidable environmental factors. In an attempt to try and do something about this, hotels and dive operators have established a very successful **coral-growing experiment**, the award-winning Karang Lestari Pemuteran project (ⓦwww.globalcoral.org), just off the Pemuteran shore. Using the pioneering "Biorock" process of electrical mineral accretion, this involves encouraging new growth by continuously passing a low electrical current through the stony coral, causing minerals to build up at about four times the normal speed. Any snorkeller can observe the experiment – the largest of its kind in the world – in the reefs in front of *Pondok Sari* and *Taman Sari*, where more than forty large, differently configured, cage-like steel structures lie on the sea bed, bound with wires; here, in amongst the groves of deathly grey coral, you can see the abundant new growth, which is much more colourful. To help support the project, you can buy a donor's Biorock tag from any of the dive shops for Rp30,000. See p.381 for more on the Biorock process.

There are a number of healthier, more interesting **reefs** within fifteen minutes' boat ride of the Pemuteran shore, where divers and snorkellers can expect to encounter a huge variety of reef fish, including bright blue dancers, black-and-white-striped damsel fish, and shoals of silver fusilier, as well as snappers and the occasional white manta ray or shark. Reef Seen Aquatics dive centre has mapped out the most rewarding areas, with Napoleon (5m) and Tunkad (3m) best for snorkellers but also good for deep dives.

Dive centres

Pemuteran's **dive centres** all run diving and snorkelling trips to local reefs as well as to Pulau Menjangan; some also go to Gilimanuk's Secret Bay, to Puri Jati near Seririt, and to Tulamben on Bali's east coast. Several do night dives, nitrox diving, and macro-photography trips. On the beach in front of the hotels, between *Sari Amertha* and *Taman Selini,* you'll find Reef Seen

Aquatics (℡0362/93001, ⓦwww.reefseen.com); Werner Lau at both *Pondok Sari* and *Matahari Beach Resort* (℡0812/385 9161, ⓦwww.wernerlau.com); and Bali Diving Academy Pemuteran at *Taman Sari* (℡0812/387 5121, ⓦwww.scubali.com).

A single boat **dive** on the Pemuteran reefs averages US$40 including all equipment; two dives around Pulau Menjangan or in Secret Bay cost about $80 inclusive. Dive courses average $390 for the four-day PADI Open Water. **Snorkelling** trips cost Rp110,000 per person to the Pemuteran reefs (2hr), or about Rp400,000 per person to Menjangan (6hr), though small groups of snorkellers will probably find it cheaper if less convenient to arrange boats from Labuan Lalang (see p.341). All snorkelling equipment is rented through the village association booth on the beach between *Pondok Sari* and *Taman Sari* (Rp50,000 for three hours).

Other activities

All the Pemuteran hotels organize **day-trips** to local sights as well as **hikes** through Bali Barat National Park (from Rp250,000 per person). Reef Seen Aquatics dive centre runs sunrise cruises for **dolphin-watching** (Rp110,000 per person for 2hr) but, although the early-morning skies are worth the dawn start, dolphin sightings are far from guaranteed.

Reef Seen also runs a **turtle-hatching** project at its dive centre (Rp25,000 donation, plus Rp75,000 to release a turtle). Green, Olive Ridley and hawksbill turtles all have nesting sites in the Pemuteran area, but all three species are fast becoming endangered (see box, p.134), and their eggs are particularly prized. To combat this, Reef Seen purchases eggs from fishermen for a little above market price and the turtles are hatched and reared before being released off the Pemuteran coast.

To Seririt and the road south

Seven kilometres east of Pemuteran, the stark charcoal-grey stone of **Pura Agung Pulaki** peers down from the top of a weatherworn cliff face, making for a good viewpoint. The temple's history dates back to the days of the sixteenth-century Javanese priest Nirartha, but the buildings are modern and overrun by a band of grey macaques. Most bemo drivers stop here on their first trip of the day to make an offering at the temple's roadside shrine and get sprinkled with holy water dished out by the attendant priest.

With its cool sea breezes, relatively temperate climate and moderately fertile soil, the stretch of the northwest coast between Pulaki and Seririt, 30km to the east, is ideal for **vines** and Bali's main wine-producer, Hatten Wines, has a big vineyard in this area, where grapes are harvested year-round. The other significant industry around here is **pearl farming**. Should you be in the market for a $15,000 string of cultured south-sea pearls, or simply a $65 misshapen teardrop, you might want to visit the Atlas North Bali Pearl visitor centre and gallery, 12km east of Pemuteran in the village of Penyabangan. Tours are offered daily (from 9.30am–3.30pm; 1hr; Rp65,000, kids Rp40,000; ⓦwww .atlassouthseapearl.com.au) and feature an introduction to the four-year growing process and advice on how to distinguish real from fake pearls and freshwater from seawater ones.

Seririt

The town of **SERIRIT** is chiefly of interest to travellers as a junction and for its banks and ATMs (which are all at the east end of town, next to the post office and clinic). The main north-coast road slices through the town centre, travelled by frequent dark-red Gilimanuk–Lovina–Singaraja bemos (Lovina is 13km to the east); this is also the departure point for the scenic back-road to Munduk, Danau Bratan and Bedugul (see p.291). Most importantly though, Seririt stands at the head of the most westerly route between the north and south coasts, described below, and served by frequent Seririt–Ubung (Denpasar) bemos.

Ume Anyar and Puri Jati

About 1.5km west of Seririt, 33km east of Pemuteran, in the village of **UME ANYAR**, a couple of signs point you north off the main road to two quite different places to stay, *Zen Resort Bali* and *Ratu Ayu Villas*. The local beach, sometimes known as **PURI JATI**, or PJ, is scruffy though fine for swimming but is most famous as a **muck-diving** destination (the practice of diving in sandy-bottomed bays in search of the elusive marine life that hides there). It's rich in juvenile fish and rare species and particularly good for macro-photography, so several dive operators around Bali run trips here.

Zen Resort Bali (☎0362/93578, ⓦwww.zenresortbali.com; ❸), 600m from the road and about the same distance from the beach, commands fine views over surrounding vineyards and to the sea beyond and makes a tranquil **place to stay**, not least because of the extensive programme of 28 different Ayurvedic therapies offered here. Its thirteen a/c rooms are stylishly contemporary (the "sunset"-view ones are best and enjoy huge terraces and sunken patio baths) and there's also a beautiful infinity pool, daily yoga sessions plus dolphin-watching and mountain tours. Some 700m further down a rough track, the rather remote *Ratu Ayu Villas* (☎0812/383 6891, ⓔlumbung@dps .centrin.net.id; ❺) are secluded in a hollow, five minutes' walk from the sea, on a site imbued with great spiritual history and power. The five bungalows are simply but artistically designed, with balconies offering inspiring views of the ricefields, the sea and the distant mountains. Established by one of the owners of *Puri Lumbung* in Munduk (see p.291), *Ratu Ayu* also emphasizes cultural, spiritual and educational tourism and arranges workshops with local musicians.

To the south coast

The road from Seririt to the south coast commands some breathtakingly lovely views as it crosses through the mountains, rice-growing valleys and small hilltop villages of Bali's central spine. Seven kilometres south of Seririt the road branches southeast for Mayong and Danau Tamblingan, an area that's described on p.291. On the southbound road, the first great viewpoint comes 12km south of Seririt, after **BUSUNG BIU**, where you can stop in a lay-by to admire the vista of rice terraces tumbling down into the valley, framed by the peaks of Gunung Batukaru to the southeast.

The road divides at the village of **PUPUAN**, 22km south of Seririt, the site of a hundred-metre-high waterfall called **Blahmantung**. Despite the height, the falls are less than spectacular, only really worth visiting in February or March when water levels are high from several months of rain. The 1.7-kilometre-long access road is steep and rutted, signed just beyond the southernmost limit of Pupuan; you can walk it in about half an hour.

Pupuan to Pekutatan (via Tista)

From Pupuan, the more westerly route takes you on a slow, twisting course west via the ridgetop settlements of **KEMONING** (where you can veer off south, via Ceking and Bangal, down a road that ends just west of Balian beach;

see p.331) and **Tegalasaih**, and then south through clove plantations to **TISTA**. Beyond Tista, the road parallels the Pulukan River and soon passes right through the middle of an enormous fig tree at **Bunut Bolong** (a famous local sight but not worth a special trip). About 10km south of the tree, the road comes to a T-junction at **PEKUTATAN** on the main Tabanan–Gilimanuk road, 2km east of Medewi beach (see p.332).

Pupuan to Antosari (via Sanda and Belimbing)

The easterly branch of the road from Pupuan drops down through similarly eye-pleasing mountainscapes, affording especially impressive views of Gunung Batukaru to the east. On the way, you'll pass dozens of **coffee plantations** (the *robusta* variety, known and drunk locally as *kopi bali*), many of them protected by liberal plantings of spindly-looking dadap ("coral") trees. The almost-circular leaves of the fast-growing *dadap* are commonly used in offerings, but those that are allowed to fall provide vital fertilizer for the coffee plants, while the roots simultaneously anchor the soil and prevent erosion. **Cacao** is also a big crop round here, and **cloves** too, which you often see drying on mats beside the road.

In the village of **SANDA**, about 30km from Seririt, one former coffee plantation has been turned into a small, charmingly colonial-style **hotel** and **restaurant**, *Sanda Butik Villas* (℗0828/372 0055, ⓦwww.sandavillas.com; ❼), whose eight stylish rooms are tastefully decorated with Balinese accents; have enormous enclosed verandahs that overlook the neighbouring plantations. A small patch of the original coffee plantation has also been incorporated into the hotel garden and there's a saltwater pool here, too, though the 761m elevation on the slopes of Gunung Batukaru means the temperature in Sanda is always refreshingly cool. In the early mornings you get grand views of Batukaru, and it's possible to hire a guide here for the strenuous trek from the village to the summit and back (see p.328 for more on climbing Gunung Batukaru), as well as for other local trips.

Some 10km further south, overlooking a pretty valley in the village of **BELIMBING**, sits the *Cempaka Belimbing* **hotel** (℗0361/7451178, ⓦwww.cempakabelimbing.com; ❼), whose best a/c valley-view villas enjoy a fine panorama of palm groves, paddy-fields and the peaks of Gunung Batukaru; furnishings in all rooms are a little faded however, and the cheaper rooms are fan only, though they all have use of the swimming pool. Even if you don't stay you can soak up the glorious views from a seat in the *Warung Sari Wisata* **café**, 50m north across the road from *Cempaka Belimbing*.

About 10km south of Belimbing, the road meets the Denpasar–Gilimanuk highway at **Antosari** (see p.331), 16km west of Tabanan.

Travel details

Bemos and public buses

It's almost impossible to give the frequency with which bemos and public buses run: see Basics, p.36, for details. Journey times given are the minimum you can expect. Only direct bemo and bus routes are listed; for longer journeys, you'll have to go via either Denpasar's Ubung terminal (see p.318), Gilimanuk (see p.335), or Singaraja's Banyuasri terminal (see p.293). The nearest shuttle bus service runs out of Lovina on the north coast (see p.310).

Gilimanuk to: Amlapura (4hr); Antosari (2hr 15min); Cekik (10min); Denpasar (Ubung terminal; 3hr 15min); Kediri (for Tanah Lot; 2hr 45min); Labuan Lalang (for Pulau Menjangan;

25min); Lalang Linggah (for Balian beach; 2hr 15min); Pemuteran (1hr); Lovina (2hr 15min); Medewi (1hr 45min); Negara (1hr); Padang Bai (5hr); Seririt (1hr 30min); Singaraja (Banyuasri terminal; 2hr 30min); Tabanan (2hr 30min).
Pemuteran to: Cekik (50min); Gilimanuk (1hr); Labuan Lalang (for Pulau Menjangan; 30min); Lovina (1hr 15min); Seririt (45min); Singaraja (Banyuasri terminal; 1hr 30min).
Ubung (Denpasar) to: Antosari (1hr); Bedugul (1hr 30min); Cekik (3hr); Gilimanuk (3hr 15min);

Jakarta, Java (24hr); Kediri (for Tanah Lot; 30min); Lalang Linggah (for Balian beach; 1hr 15min); Medewi (1hr 30min); Mengwi (30min); Negara (2hr 15min); Singaraja (Sukasada terminal; 3hr); Solo (Java; 15hr); Surabaya (Java; 10hr); Tabanan (35min); Yogyakarta (Java; 15hr).

Boats

Gilimanuk to: Ketapang (East Java; every 20min; 45min).

6

Lombok and the Gili Islands

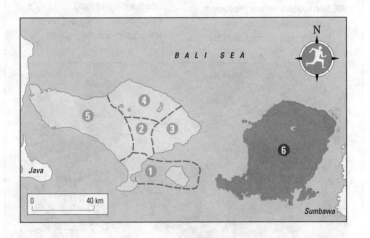

CHAPTER 6

Highlights

* **Crafts** Pottery, textiles, woodcarving and basketware are on sale in craft villages scattered across Lombok. See p.363

* **Senggigi** Lombok's relaxed main resort, with some of the island's best hotels and restaurants. See p.368

* **Gili Islands** Three perfect islands off the northwest coast, each very individual in character. See p.376

* **Sembalun valley** Picturesque upland valley far off the tourist trail, surrounded by impressive mountain peaks. See p.393

* **Gunung Rinjani** Highest mountain on the island, offering adventurous and rewarding trekking. See p.394

* **Sapit** Pretty village on the southern slopes of Rinjani, ideal for chilling out for a while. See p.400

* **South-coast beaches** Hidden coves nestle between rocky headlands all along Lombok's south coast, while big swells attract surfers. See p.408

▲ Lombok woodcarving

Lombok and the Gili Islands

ocated 35km due east of Bali, **Lombok** is inevitably compared with its more famous neighbour, although it differs in almost every way – physically, culturally, linguistically and historically. Lombok also offers a very different experience for the visitor with lots of wide-open spaces, plenty of unspoilt beaches and less traffic and pollution. Things are changing fast, but Lombok's essential character remains intact and accessible to visitors rather than buried beneath a veneer of tourist development.

The majority of Lombok's 2.4 million inhabitants are the indigenous Muslim **Sasak** people. About ten percent of the population are Balinese, mostly settled in the west of the island where their distinctive temples and household architecture are apparent. The two cultures appear to coexist relatively amicably, but it doesn't take long to discern less amiable emotions below the surface – perhaps not surprising given historical events and the fact that many of the economic advantages of increased tourism have eluded the native Sasak.

From the seventeenth century onwards, Lombok came increasingly under **Balinese influence**, after the Balinese had helped the Sasak aristocracy defeat invaders from Sumbawa. Infighting among the rajas of the four Lombok principalities – Pagasangan, Pagutan, Mataram and Cakranegara – further weakened the hold of the Sasak rulers. In 1830, **Ratu Agung** acceded to the throne of Mataram, and over the next thirteen years brought the whole of Lombok under his rule. In 1849, he also gained control of Karangasem in East Bali in return for supplying troops to the Dutch. He was succeeded by his brother, Ratu Agung Ngurah, in 1872. However, Ratu Agung Ngurah had bold military ambitions in Bali. He pushed his demand for soldiers from the local populace too far and the residents of Praya **rebelled** in 1891. This unrest spread quickly and the Dutch intervened, eventually invading Lombok in 1894 and bringing the entire island under colonial rule until Indonesian independence.

Measuring 80km by 70km, Lombok is slightly smaller than Bali and divides into three geographical regions. The mountainous **north** is dominated by the bulk of **Gunung Rinjani**, at 3726m one of the highest peaks in Indonesia; trekking here is easily organized and highly satisfying. The **central plains**, about 25km wide, contain most of the population and the most productive agricultural land as well as the major road on the island, linking the west and east coasts. The only city on Lombok, a conurbation of the four towns of

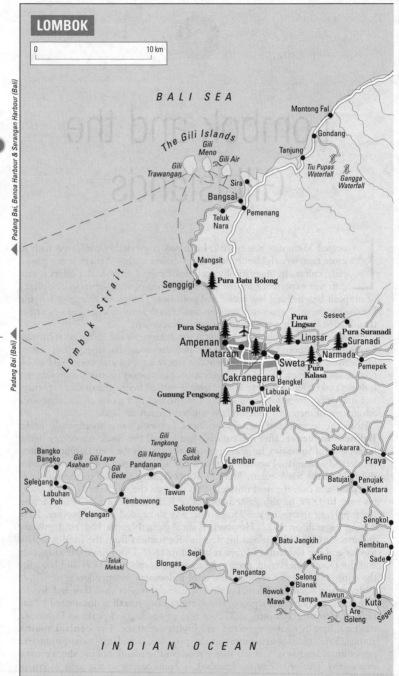

LOMBOK

0   10 km

BALI SEA

Montong Fal

Gondang

The Gili Islands

Gili
Meno
Gili Air

Gili
Trawangan

Tanjung

Tiu Pupas
Waterfall

Gangga
Waterfall

Sira

Bangsal

Pemenang

Teluk
Nara

Mangsit

Senggigi

Pura Batu Bolong

Pura Segara

Pura
Lingsar

Seseot

Ampenan

Pura Suranadi
Suranadi

Mataram

Lingsar

Sweta

Narmada

Cakranegara

Pura
Kalasa

Pemepek

Bengkel

Gunung Pengsong

Labuapi

Banyumulek

Gili
Tangkong
Gili Nanggu

Gili
Sudak

Bangko
Bangko

Gili Gili Layar
Asahan

Gili
Gede

Pandanan

Lembar

Sukarara

Praya

Selegang

Batujai

Penujak
Ketara

Labuhan
Poh

Tembowong

Tawun

Pelangan

Sekotong

Sengkol

Batu Jangkih

Rembitan

Keling

Sade

Teluk
Mekaki

Sepi

Blongas

Pengantap

Selong
Blanak

Rowok
Mawi

Mawun

Kuta

Tampa

Are
Goleng

Seger

INDIAN OCEAN

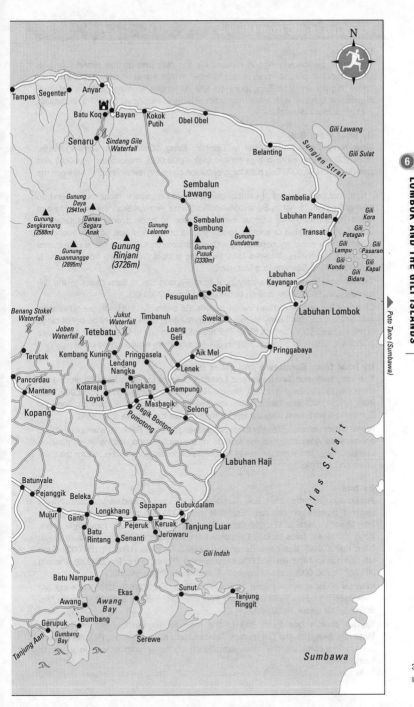

N

Tampes

Segenter

Anyar

Batu Koq

Bayan

Kokok Putih

Obel Obel

Senaru

Sindang Gile Waterfall

Belanting

Gili Lawang

Gili Sulat

Sungian Strait

Sembalun Lawang

Sambelia

Gunung Daya (2941m)

Gunung Sengkareang (2588m)

Danau Segara Anak

Gunung Lelonten

Sembalun Bumbung

Labuhan Pandan

Transat

Gili Kora

Gili Petagan

Gunung Buanmangge (2895m)

Gunung Rinjani (3726m)

Gunung Pusuk (2330m)

Gunung Dundatrum

Gili Lampu

Gili Kondo

Gili Pasaran

Gili Kapal

Gili Bidara

Labuhan Kayangan

Pesugulan

Sapit

Labuhan Lombok

Benang Stokel Waterfall

Jukut Waterfall

Timbanuh

Swela

Pringgabaya

Joben Waterfall

Tetebatu

Loang Geli

Terutak

Kembang Kuning

Pringgasela

Aik Mel

Pancordau

Lendang Nangka

Lenek

Mantang

Kotaraja

Rungkang

Rempung

Kopang

Loyok

Masbagik

Bagik Bontong

Pomotong

Selong

Alas Strait

Labuhan Haji

Batunyale

Pejanggik

Beleka

Mujur

Ganti

Longkhang

Sepapan

Gubukdalam

Pejeruk

Keruak

Tanjung Luar

Batu Rintang

Senanti

Jerowaru

Gili Indah

Batu Nampur

Ekas

Sunut

Awang

Awang Bay

Tanjung Ringgit

Gerupuk

Bumbang

Tanjung Aan

Gumbang Bay

Serewe

Sumbawa

By plane

Mataram's Selaparang Airport is currently the only one on the island (Lombok International Airport at Praya is due to open in 2010) and its only direct **international flights** are from Singapore on Silk Air (thrice weekly). Regular **internal flights** link Lombok with other international hubs in Indonesia (see "Travel details" p.412, for more details).

By boat from Bali

Slow ferry From Padang Bai to Lembar. Every 90min; takes 4hr–4hr 30min. Rp24,000 with an extra charge for bicycles (Rp35,000), motorbikes (Rp5000) and cars (from Rp498,000). See p.39 for information on taking rental vehicles between the islands.

Note that bemo drivers at Lembar port are hard bargainers: most tourists end up paying far more to get to Bertais/Mandalika/Sweta terminal than the correct fare of about Rp15,000. These hassles are one reason to book directly to Mataram or Senggigi with Perama or another tourist-shuttle company; if you haven't booked in advance, you could try negotiating with the driver/conductor on the shuttle buses that meet the ferries. Metered taxis serve the port; a typical fare from Lembar is Rp50–60,000 to Cakranegara/Mataram.

Tourist boat Perama run a daily boat from Padang Bai at 9am direct to the Gili Islands (5hr; Rp200,000) and on to Senggigi (7hr; Rp200,000).

Charters Between Amed and the Gili Islands. Be aware that the boats are often small with one engine, don't carry radios, and that mobile phones may well be out of range in the middle of the Lombok Strait. For the return trip talk to Dean on Gili Meno (see p.385) and Ozzy Shop (see p.386) on Gili Air, who have twin-engined boats.

By boat from Sumbawa and other islands

The ferry between Sumbawa and Lombok Departs Labuhan Lombok around the clock (every 40mins; Rp12,500, bicycle Rp19,500, motorbike from Rp32,000, cars from Rp251,500) and takes ninety minutes to two hours to reach Poto Tano on Sumbawa's northwest coast, a few kilometres from the island's main road.

From other islands The Indonesian passenger line, Pelni (Ⓦwww.pelni.co.id), operates services between the islands of the archipelago, calling at Lembar on Lombok. See "Travel details" p.411 for details of destinations and p.363 for the Pelni office on Lombok.

By bus

Public bus Sumatra, Java, Bali, Sumbawa and Flores to Bertais/Mandalika/Sweta terminal. Several services daily. Expect to pay Rp375,000 for a/c and reclining seats from Jakarta (Java) to Lombok (2days/2nights), Rp285,000 from Yogyakarta (Java; 22hr). Other a/c fares include Denpasar (Bali; 6–8hr; Rp150,000); Surabaya (Java; 20hr; Rp200,000); Sumbawa Besar (6hr; Rp90,000); Bima (12hr; Rp150,000); Sape (all Sumbawa; 14hr; Rp190,000); Labuhanbajo (Flores; 24hr; Rp250,000); Padang (4D/3N; Rp750,000) and Medan (both Sumatra; 4D/4N; Rp950,000).

Minibus Pancasari, Jl Panca Usaha, BlockA 8 (Ⓣ0370/665 0555) operate a/c minibuses (11 seats) three times daily from their office at the back of Mataram Mall to Sumbawa Besar. Rp90,000.

Tourist shuttle bus From Bali to the main tourist destinations on Lombok: Mataram, Senggigi, the Gili Islands, Tetebatu and Kuta, Lombok. Perama (Ⓦwww.peramatour.com) are the most established company with offices in all major tourist areas.

Ampenan, Mataram, Cakranegara and Sweta, a pleasant, user-friendly place, is at the western end of this main road. Attractive villages in the southern foothills of Rinjani, such as Tetebatu and Sapit, and many of the craft villages including Sukara for textiles and Penujak and Penakak for pottery, are easily accessible from this cross-island corridor. Further south again there is a range of hills, around 500m high, behind the sweeping bays and pure white sands of the southern beaches, all of which can be explored from Kuta, the accommodation centre of the south and surfing centre of the island.

The mainland resort of Senggigi, located on a rugged stretch of the west coast, is easily accessible from Bali by sea or air. Several groups of islands lie off the Lombok coast. The trio of Gili Islands – Trawangan, Meno and Air – off the northwest coast, are the most popular for visitors in search of sea, sun and sand. Those off the southwest peninsula and the northeast coast are also becoming more accessible.

Lombok's economy is largely agricultural, producing rice, cassava, cotton, tobacco (a major export), soya beans and chilli peppers. Historically the island has found it impossible to support its burgeoning population, and thousands have died in famines, reportedly 50,000 in one as recently as 1966. Consequently, many people have moved to other Indonesian islands as part of the government's transmigrasi scheme (see p.424). The government is also encouraging diversification: pumice, cultivated pearls, seaweed and sea cucumber are growing in economic importance, and income from the pottery industry and tourism is rising annually.

The tourist presence on Lombok is nowhere near as pervasive as in Bali and it is easy to find remote villages, unspoilt coastline and people still living traditional lives. However, accommodation is variable; five-star luxury is confined to Senggigi, Gili Trawangan, the *Oberoi* on the northwest coast and *Novotel Lombok* in the south. Elsewhere choices are fewer and simpler, although in many cases no less appealing.

For regular information, the monthly *Lombok Times* (Ⓦwww.lomboktimes .com) is widely available in tourist areas and online. For reliable Gili island information on Bali visit Island Promotions, Shop 12, Poppies Lane 1, Kuta (Ⓣ0361/753241, Ⓦwww.gili-paradise.com; 9am–10pm). They can also book transport and accommodation and have a hotel booking site Ⓦwww.gili-hotels .com.

West Lombok

West Lombok – stretching from the remote southwest peninsula, through the port of Lembar, to the city of Ampenan–Mataram–Cakranegara–Sweta, then north to the established resort of Senggigi and the small village of Bangsal (access port for the Gili Islands) – offers plenty of facilities for tourists. With Lombok's only airport and its major port and bus station in this area, most visitors pass through at some point and a high proportion come to Lombok purely for Senggigi or the Gili Islands.

Lombok tours

If time is limited, you may want to join a **tour**. The biggest range is available in Senggigi, but it's also easy to devise your own itinerary and charter a vehicle and driver (see p.375) or a boat to the Gili Islands (see p.375).

Typically, the tours take a **full day** (8–10hr). Prices vary enormously. Check whether prices quoted are per person or for the vehicle, whether lunch is included, the size of the group and whether you'll be travelling by bus, minibus or car. Popular itineraries include:

Southern tour Narmada, Sukarara, Penujak, Rembitan or Sade, Kuta and Tanjung Aan.

Northern tour Senaru via Pusuk, Segenter and Sindang Gile waterfall.

Central/Eastern tour Sembalun valley, Puncak Pass, Sapit and Masbagik.

Gili Islands Snorkelling around the islands.

Gili Nanggu By boat from Senggigi or road to Tawun, and then boat to the island for snorkelling.

Four-cities tour Half-day (4hrs). Nusa Tenggara Provincial Museum, Mayura Water Palace, Pura Meru, Narmada, Lingsar and a shopping centre or market.

Tour operators
Bidy Tour ☎0370/632127, ✉bidytour@indo.net.id. Senggigi office.
Coconut Cottages ☎0370/635365, ⓦwww.coconuts-giliair.com
Indonesia Holidays Travel Service ☎0370/665 5710
Lomata Tours and Travel ☎0370/646494
Perama Senggigi ☎0370/693007, ⓦwww.peramatour.com

Ampenan-Mataram-Cakranegara-Sweta and around

The four towns of **AMPENAN, MATARAM, CAKRANEGARA and SWETA**, with a population of around 250,000, form one large city area that stretches over 8km from west to east. It's pretty big but broad streets and low-rise buildings give it a spacious air while straightforward local transport makes it easy to get around.

Laid out around three parallel roads, which stretch from **Ampenan** on the coast through **Mataram** and **Cakranegara** to **Sweta** on the eastern edge, the roads change their names several times along their length. The most northerly is Jalan Langko–Jalan Pejanggik–Jalan Selaparang, which allows travel only in a west–east direction for an extensive stretch. Running parallel to the south, Jalan Tumpang Sari–Jalan Panca Usaha–Jalan Pancawarga–Jalan Pendidikan, allows only east–west travel for a part of its length. The third, Jalan Brawijaya–Jalan Sriwijaya–Jalan Majapahit, two-way for most of the way, skirts to the south of these and is the location of the central post office and tourist office.

Arrival and information

Selaparang Airport (☎0370/622987) is on Jalan Adi Sucipto at Rembiga, a couple of kilometres north of Mataram. There's an exchange counter, open for all international arrivals, and post office (Mon–Thurs 11am–3pm, Fri

AMPENAN-MATARAM-CAKRANEGARA

▲ *Lingsar* ▲ *Bertais/Mandalika/Sweta Terminal*

RESTAURANTS

Aroma	5
Dirgahayu	6
Dua Em	1
Kristal	3
Mataram Mall	4
Murah Meriah	8
Pizza Hut	2
Seafood Ikan Baru 99	7

ACCOMMODATION

Crocodile River Cottages	A
Grand Legi Mataram	F
Lombok Raya	C
Puri Indah	E
Red Pepper Inn	B
Hotel Viktor	D

▲ *Pusuk, Gunung Sari & Bangsal*

▲ *Senggigi & A*

Chinese Cemetery
Pura Segara
Bemos to Senggigi

Kebon Roek Bemo Terminal & Market

Selaparang Airport
International Terminal
Domestic Terminal

Sayang Sayang Art Market

Lombok Handicraft Centre

RUNGKANG JANGKOK

CAKRANEGARA

Slamet Riady
Puri Mayura
Pura Meru
Cakranegara Market

Lombok Pottery Centre

MATARAM

KAMASAN

AMPENAN

Perama

Immigration Office

West Nusa Tenggara Provincial Museum

Police

Pelni

JALAN JEND SUDIRMAN
JALAN DR. SUTOMO
JALAN ADI SUCIPTO
JALAN UDAYANA
JALAN HOS COKROAMINOTO
JALAN A. RAHMAN HAKIM
JALAN PANCAWARGA
JALAN PEJANGGIK
JALAN LANGKO
JALAN PENDIDIKAN
JALAN SUPRAPTO
JALAN MAJAPAHIT
JALAN PANJI TILAR NEGARA
JALAN AIRLANGGA
JALAN SRIWIJAYA
JALAN BUNG KARNO
JALAN TRANS MIGRASI
JALAN KEBUDAYAAN
JALAN PEJANGGIK
JALAN PANCA USAHA
JALAN HASANUDIN
JALAN GEDE NGURAH
JALAN SELAPARANG
JALAN TUMPANG SARI
JALAN BRAWIJAYA
JALAN PABEAN
JALAN KOPERASI
JALAN SONOKLING
JALAN ADI SUDARSO
JALAN INDUSTRI

Kali Jangkok
Kali Ancar
Kali Ancar

▲ *Lembar & 8*

▼ *Sekarbela*

N

RESTAURANTS / ACCOMMODATION

A
B
C
D
E
F

1
2
3
4
5
6
7
8

0   1 km

8–11.30am, Sat 8–11am). Luxury hotels and travel agents have **accommodation** booking counters just outside the arrivals hall; shop around for the best rate. There's a **taxi** counter with fixed-price fares (Mataram Rp27–40,000; central Senggigi Rp50,000; north Senggigi Rp70–90,000; Bangsal Rp95,000; Sekotong Rp190,000–225,000; Tetebatu Rp180,000; Labuhan Lombok Rp210,000; Senaru Rp300,000; Sembalun Rp350,000; maximum four people). For lower prices walk out of the airport gates (about 200m) and hail a metered taxi on the road. A few black **bemos** serving Kebon Roek bus terminal in Ampenan (heading to the right) pass along the road in front of the airport. See p.376 for public transport details from the airport to Bangsal (for the Gili Islands).

If you're arriving by bus or bemo from anywhere except Senggigi, you'll come into the island's main **bus terminal** on the eastern edge of the city area, known variously as **Bertais**, **Mandalika** or **Sweta**, where bemos, local buses and long-distance inter-island services to Sumbawa, Flores, Bali, Java and Sumatra all jostle for space. Arriving **from Senggigi**, you'll come into the **Kebon Roek terminal** in Ampenan. These two bus terminals are linked by the frequent yellow bemos that zip around the city.

The most helpful **tourist office** is the Provincial Tourist Service for West Nusa Tenggara, which is tucked off Jalan Majapahit in the south of the city, at Jl Singosari 2 (Mon–Thurs 7am–2pm, Fri 7–11am, Sat 7am–2pm; From 8am during Ramadan; ☎0370/634800). They may be able to rustle up some leaflets, maps and advice about travel in Lombok and Sumbawa. Yellow bemos heading via "Kekalik" pass the end of Jalan Singosari as they run along Jalan Majapahit.

City transport

Bright yellow **bemos** (Rp3000) ply numerous routes between Kebon Roek terminal in Ampenan and Bertais/Mandalika/Sweta terminal from early morning until late evening. Most follow the Jalan Langko–Jalan Pejanggik–Jalan Selaparang route heading west to east, and Jalan Tumpang Sari–Jalan Panca Usaha–Jalan Pancawarga–Jalan Pendidikan heading east to west, although there are plenty of variations.

The horse-drawn carts here, unlike the ones on Bali, have small pneumatic tyres and are called **cidomo**; they cover the back routes and aren't allowed on the main streets. Negotiate the fare beforehand.

There are plenty of easily identifiable official metered **taxis**. Flagfall is Rp3850 and a trip across the city is unlikely to be more than Rp20,000.

Accommodation

There's a good range of **accommodation**, although with one exception none is oriented solely towards foreign visitors. Few tourists stay here since Senggigi is only a few kilometres up the road but a night or two here provides an excellent introduction to Indonesian city life. **Cakranegara** is the commercial heart of the city but the two options in the west are worth considering. Avoid the bottom-end places that dot the city area – they are "short time" places and don't welcome tourists.

Crocodile River Cottages ☎0370/664 6440, ⓦ www.lombok-cottages.com. Five gorgeous Javenese teak bungalows set on the river bank in the village of Jati Sela just north of Ampenan. All are fan cooled with hot-water bathrooms,

beautifully decorated and have plenty of lounging areas. Although signed from Meninting, it can be tricky to find. ⑥

Grand Legi Mataram Jl Sriwijaya 81 ☎0370/636282, ⓦ www.grandlegihotels.co.id.

Elegant hotel with attractive gardens, good rooms with a/c, hot water and satellite TV, and an excellent pool. Free airport transfers. ⑤–⑥

Lombok Raya Jl Panca Usaha 11 ⓣ0370/632305, ⓔlombokraya_htl@telkom.net. Convenient for Mataram Mall, this busy upmarket place has tiled rooms overlooking an attractive pool and garden, all with a/c and hot water. ⑥–⑦

Puri Indah Jl Sriwijaya 132 ⓣ0370/637633, ⓕ637669. A bit out of the way, but reasonable value with the added bonus of a small pool. There's a choice of fan or a/c rooms but no hot water. ①–②

Red Pepper Inn (Losmen Tjabe Merah) Gang Sawah, Jl Saleh Sungkar ⓣ0370/636150, ⓕ637635. Turn east 200m north of the traffic lights in Ampenan at the junction of the Senggigi road with the market/airport turning. Two rows of clean fan rooms with attached cold-water bathroom set in a neat garden. The Dutch-speaking manager welcomes foreign visitors. ①

Hotel Viktor Jl Abimanyu 1 ⓣ0370/633830. Decent a/c rooms on both sides of the road in Cakra, some with hot water. Free tea and coffee at all times. ①–②

The City

In the far west of the Ampenan-Mataram-Cakranegera-Sweta city area, the old port town of **AMPENAN** flourishes around the mouth of the Kali Jangkok. It's the liveliest part of the city, with narrow streets, a **market** and a bustling atmosphere. Early Chinese and Arab traders settled here in a maze of shop-houses, although international trading has long since ceased and Ampenan is now home to a fishing community. It's also the jumping-off point to Senggigi a few kilometres up the coast. Kebon Roek market and the narrow lanes behind the main crossroads easily provide a few hours, gentle exploration.

The **West Nusa Tenggara Provincial Museum**, Jl Panji Tilar Negara 6 (Tues–Sun 8am–2pm; Rp1000), is worth a brief visit. The exhibits, with only a few labelled in English, range from displays about the geological formation of Indonesia and the various cultural groups of Nusa Tenggara to household, craft and religious items.

It's a pleasant walk out to the **coast** at the end of Jalan Pabean despite the nearby industrial area. A few hundred metres north on the main road, the extensive **Chinese cemetery** is a reminder of the people who died in the purges in 1965 (see p.423) and an indication of the affluence of many of the Chinese community today.

Mataram and Cakranegara

Merging into Ampenan to the east, **MATARAM** is the capital of West Nusa Tenggara province as well as the district of Lombok Barat (West Lombok). It's full of imposing government buildings on broad, tree-lined avenues, but there's little of tourist interest.

East again, **CAKRANEGARA**, usually known as Cakra (pronounced *chakra*), was the capital of Lombok in the eighteenth century during the height of the Balinese ascendancy on the island, and was the site of savage fighting during 1894 that culminated in Dutch victory. Today, it's the commercial capital of Lombok, with shops, markets, hotels and the frantic **Mataram Mall** – a great place to mingle with local families and youngsters at leisure. The **market** is probably the friendliest in the area.

Built in 1744 during the rule of the Balinese in West Lombok, the **Puri Mayura** (Mayura Water Palace), on Jalan Selaparang (daily 8am–6pm; Rp5000), is pleasant if you're looking for a bit of peace. The centrepiece of the palace was the bale kambang (floating pavilion), the meeting hall and court of justice, set in the middle of a large artificial lake, which has now been replaced by a modern version. Pura Jagatnatha within the grounds houses some exuberant carvings and is especially popular with worshippers during a full moon. It is important to fix a price with local guides here before you use their services.

Across the main road, **Pura Meru** (donation; sarong and scarf available) also known as Pura Mayura, is the largest Balinese temple on the island, built in 1720 by Prince Anak Agung Made Karang in an attempt to unite the various Hindu factions on Lombok. The *candi bentar* displaying scenes from the *Ramayana* is the highlight of the temple although the towering *meru* are also attractive. It teems with activity during ceremonies but is otherwise deserted.

Eating and drinking

There are great-value **places to eat** throughout the cities area. Although Lombok is predominantly Muslim, if you visit **during Ramadan** many of the places below remain open during the day with a curtain at the window discreetly shielding diners. **Street food** offers the liveliest eating experience; after dark Jalan Pejanggik, just east of Mataram Mall, comes to life with stalls and the north end of Jalan Udayana in Rembiga is the area for sate stalls. The adventurous might want to head to Bengkel, south of the city, where stalls line the road in the late afternoon/evening. You'll see plenty of cars and lorries drawn up alongside. The speciality is *sop kuda*, horse soup, known for its aphrodisiac properties – well, those *cidomo* horses don't live forever.

Aroma Jl Palapa I 2, Cakranegara. A long-standing favourite with residents and visitors alike, serving excellent Chinese food, with seafood a speciality. Main courses Rp30–65,000.

Dirgahayu Jl Cilinaya 10. Local restaurant in the road alongside Mataram Mall with a big Indonesian menu (take the dictionary). Excellent for cheap eats; nasi campur is Rp6000.

Dua Em Jl Transmigrasi 99. Traditional Sasak food. This one is for the adventurous; the food is beyond hot and all body parts are dished up. *Otak* is brains; *paru* is liver; *jeroan* is entrails and *sate sum-sum* is bone-marrow sate (main courses Rp20–25,000).

Kristal Jl Pejanggik 22a, Cakranegara. There's a big Chinese, Indonesian and seafood menu, including lots of vegetarian dishes. Main meals Rp12–25,000.

Mataram Mall Jl Pejanggik, Cakranegara. *McDonald's*, *KFC*, *Swensen's* ice-cream stall and *Delicio Bakery and Cafe* are ground-floor stalwarts, but explore the upper floors for other bakeries and stalls. *Pizza Hut* is just across Jalan Pejanggik.

Murah Meriah Out of the city at Bengkel (taxi drivers will know it), a big selection of well-cooked, appetizing local food is laid out Padang style and diners choose their dishes. Fish, chicken, seafood, beef, tofu, tempe and lots of vegetables are all served with a delicious *sambal*. About Rp25,000 per person.

Seafood Ikan Baru 99 Jl Subak III 10. Signed off Jalan Panca Usaha about 300m east of *Lombok Raya* hotel. Grilled fish (*ikan bakar*) is the speciality. It's clean, lively and prices are excellent. Fish is sold by weight; an *ons* is 200g and a 1kg fish is plenty for two people,

Shopping

Shopping can be fun throughout the city area whether you prefer local markets, malls or small shops and this area, alongside Senggigi, is where you'll find the biggest array of things to buy. Remember you have to get your purchases home. Tourist shops throughout Lombok can arrange packing and shipping, but it is expensive (see Basics, p.58).

Markets

There are several **markets** in the city area; surrounding the Bertais/Mandalika/Sweta bus terminal, Kebon Roek in Ampenan, and in Cakranegara (probably the friendliest). All are great for a view of everyday life and a sample of pretty much everything that Lombok has to offer, from foodstuffs and household goods to clothes and textiles. The market in Gunung Sari (see p.364) is easily accessible from the cities.

Crafts and textiles

The best one-stop craft centre is the **Sayang Sayang Art Market** (daily 9am–6pm), on Jalan Jend Sudirman, with stalls selling a big variety of handicrafts ranged around a car park. It's a livelier offshoot of the Lombok Handicraft Centre also known as Sayang Sayang, which is around the corner, on Jalan Hasanudin at Rungkang Jangkok (see map, p.359).

The local workshop Slamet Riady (℡0370/631196; Sun–Fri 8am–6pm, Sat 8am–2pm, but the weavers don't work on Sunday) produces **ikat** cloth at Jl Tanun 10, just off Jalan Hasanudin in Cakranegara. The process is the same as that used in Bali (see p.458), and the *ikat* is very similar.

Pottery

Lombok **pottery** has an international reputation for style and beauty, and the **Lombok Pottery Centre**, Jl Sriwijaya 111a (℡0370/640351, ⓦwww.lombokpottery.com; Mon–Fri 9am–4pm), is the showroom of the Lombok Craft Project, which was established in 1988 and has fuelled the renaissance of pottery on the island. The showroom stocks a small range of top-quality products (Rp25–75,000) although sadly, some of the loveliest are prototypes and not for sale.

Pearls and jewellery

An increasingly popular purchase is the **pearls** cultivated in the farms dotted along the Lombok coastline. They're sold by weight and come in a variety of sizes, shapes and colours. The place to start is Sekarbela, a couple of kilometres south of Mataram with shops lining the main road west from the junction of Jalan Gajah Made and Jalan S. Kaharudin. The other area to look is along Jalan Lingkar Selatan at Karang Genteng, a few kilometres south. It is best to shop Monday to Saturday, as many shops shut on Sundays.

For **gold** and **silver jewellery**, head for Kamasan (see map, p.359), north of Mataram, where pretty much every family works in the business. Workshops and small shops around Jalan H.O.S. Cokroaminoto are responsible for quite a lot of the jewellery on sale in Bali and Lombok. Look out for Miza Silver at Jalan H.O.S. Cokroaminota 61; the turning into the village is opposite.

Listings

Airlines Airlines serving Lombok have ticket counters at the airport and/or offices in the city area. Batavia, Jl Pejanggik 88 ℡0370/648998; Citilink Garuda International, Jl Pejanggik 42–44, ℡0370/638259; Indonesia Air Transport, Selaparang Airport ℡0370/639589; Lion Air/Wings Air, Selaparang Airport ℡0370/662 7444, 24hr reservation 0804-1-778899, ⓦwww.lionair.co.id; Merpati, Jl Pejanggik 69 ℡0370/621111, Selaparang Airport ℡0370/633637, ⓦwww.merpati.co.id; Silk Air ⓦwww.silkair.com, *Hotel Lombok Raya*, Jl Panca Usaha 11 ℡0370/628254, Selaparang Airport ℡0370/63624; Trigana Air, Selaparang Airport ℡0370/616428. For international airline offices in Bali, see p.101.

Banks and exchange All the large Mataram and Cakra banks change money and traveller's cheques. The most convenient are BCA,

Jl Pejanggik 67 ℡622587; BNI, Jl Langko 64 ℡0370/622788; Bank Danamon, Jl Pejanggik ℡0370/622408. All have international ATMs. The main post office is a Western Union agent.

Boats Pelni, Jl Industri 1, Ampenan ℡0370/637212, ⓦwww.pelni.co.id (Mon–Fri 8am–3pm, Sat 8am–1pm).

Buses Buy tickets for inter-island departures at the Bertais/Mandalika/Sweta terminal. Perama can advise on fares and timings and can book tickets for you.

Car rental The best choice and prices are in Senggigi (see p.375).

Consulates The closest consulates are all on Bali (see p.66).

Dentist Dr Darmono, Jl Kebudayan 108, Mataram (℡081/836 7749), speaks good English. Call him directly to make an appointment. If you can't get through on his mobile, contact him from 8am–4pm on ☎0370/636852 and from 4–9pm on ☎0370/643483. Clinic opening times are 8am–noon & 5–9pm.

Departure tax Leaving Lombok by air: Rp30,000 (domestic), Rp100,000 (international).

Hospital The public hospital, Rumah Sakit Umum, Jl Pejanggik 6, Mataram ☎0370/623498, has a daily (9–11am) tourist clinic.

Immigration office Kantor Imigrasi, Jl Udayana 2, Mataram ☎0370/632520.

Internet access Deddy's Internet (9am–9pm; Rp6000/hr), walk through the cassette shop at the front of Mataram Mall.

Phones The main phone office is at Jl Langko 23, Ampenan (daily 24hr).

Photographic services For transferring images to CD/DVD, top-quality printing and photographic supplies, Diamond Digital, Cakra Plaza Blok C1, Jl Pejanggik, Cakranegara.

Police Senggigi Tourist Police ☎0370/632733.

Post office Lombok's main office is at Jl Sriwijaya 21, Mataram (Mon–Sat 8am–7pm, Sun 8am–noon). Another at Jl Langko 21, Ampenan (Mon–Sat 8am–7pm). For poste restante, the Senggigi post office is more used to dealing with tourists.

Recompression chamber Jl Adi Sucipto 13B (24hr hotline ☎0370/660 0333).

Supermarket Hero in the Mataram Mall (daily 10am–9pm).

Taxi Lombok Taxis ☎0370/627000.

Travel companies See box, p.358, for the standard Lombok tours. Perama, Jl Pejanggik 66, Mataram ☎0370/635928, ⓦwww .peramatour.com.

Out of the city

There are several enjoyable **excursions** from the city area; to the north, the road to Pemenang via Pusuk and, to the south, places that lie on or near the road to Lembar. All are accessible by bus or bemo from the Bertais/Mandalika/Sweta bus terminal.

Other feasible day-trips inland, to Narmada and Lingsar, are covered in the Central Lombok section (see p.396).

To the north

Heading north out of Mataram on the Pemenang road, it's a couple of kilometres to **GUNUNG SARI**, the location of a vibrant, daily morning market selling every variety of produce and goods Lombok offers. From here the road climbs up through the forest to the **Pusuk Pass**, and hordes of aggressive monkeys. Then it's 10km down to the plains and the village of **Pemenang**. Roadside stalls sell *tuak manis*, a local drink made from palm sap, and from February to April the durian sold here are regarded as especially sweet.

To the south

The *pura* on the summit of **Gunung Pengsong** (admission by donation, sarong and scarf required), 6km south of Mataram, is one of the prettiest Balinese temples in Lombok. It's a twenty-minute climb to the tiny temple at the top of the hill. A local guide will accompany you and expect a tip. The Balinese community on Lombok believe that the earliest Balinese settlers on the island landed in this area and the temple hosts regular ceremonies.

Labuapi and Banyumulek

About 7km south of Mataram, on the main road that leads to Lembar and nearby side roads, the small village of **LABUAPI** is lined with woodcarving workshops and showrooms specializing in masks. **BANYUMULEK**, 2km south of Labuapi, is one of the three main **pottery** centres on the island. Stretching west from the main road to Lembar, it's an easy one-kilometre walk from the junction at Rumak, marked by traffic lights and the enormous mosque, Masjid Jami' Asasuttaqwa, to the pottery workshops and showrooms; cidomo serve the route. Showrooms are open daily 8am–5pm and you can

Bali and Lombok are separated by the 35-kilometre-wide Lombok Strait, which is over 1300m deep in places. An imaginary boundary, the **Wallace Line**, runs through it, marking a division between the distribution of Asian and Australasian wildlife.

Between 1854 and 1862, the British naturalist **Sir Alfred Russell Wallace** travelled throughout the Indonesian archipelago. Encountering differences between the wildlife on Bali and that on Lombok, he suggested that during the Ice Ages, when the levels of the world's oceans dropped, animals ranged overland from mainland Asia down through Sumatra and Java to Bali. However, reaching the waters of the Lombok Strait, they could go no further. Similarly, animals from the land masses to the south roamed as far as Lombok on the other side of the strait.

Some evidence supports this idea. Bali and the islands to the west have creatures mostly common to mainland Asia (rabbits, monkeys, tigers), while the wildlife on Lombok and the islands to the east is more characteristic of Australia and New Guinea (parrots, marsupials, platypus and lizards). For example, the **yellow-crested cockatoo**, a native of Australia, and the **rainbow lorikeet** and **red-cheeked parrot** are found no further west than Lombok.

However, later research showed that many animal species are common to both Bali and Lombok; you're likely to see crab-eating macaques and silvered leaf monkeys both in Bali Barat National Park and on the slopes of Gunung Rinjani. Opinion has now shifted away from Wallace's theory and today naturalists refer not to Wallace's Line but to a zone of transition from the Asian type of animal life to the Australasian; in honour of Sir Alfred, this is known as "Wallacea".

usually see the potters in action. Fashions change fast; currently designs incorporating sections of engraving, aluminium decoration, eggshells and rattan are popular.

Lembar and the southwest peninsula

The main west-coast port on Lombok is the huge natural harbour of **Lembar**, 22km south of Mataram. It's industrial, swarming with traffic and there is no reason to linger. With enticing offshore islands and a glorious coastline, the **southwest peninsula** is easily accessible from Lembar but in beauty and atmosphere feels a million miles away. **Bangko Bangko** at the tip of the peninsula is legendary among surfers as the location of the Desert Point break, regarded as the best in the world by some. Even if you follow only part of the road out here, you'll get a feel for this arid land with its sparse population. The road is suitable for cycling as traffic is light and there are places to get food and water; however, it is shadeless in parts. See p.373 for organized cycling trips.

Lembar

LEMBAR, the port for Bali (see p.356 for ferry details), has nothing to detain travellers. The best **accommodation** if you get stranded is the bungalows at *Tidar* (℡0370/681444; ❶–❷), who are well-used to travellers arriving at all hours. They have eight functional rooms and a restaurant with a small Indonesian menu (mains Rp5–15,000). It's a bold orange and black so easily spotted on the side road from the port to the main road. There's a small **tourist office** (7am–5pm) tucked away behind the warung that line the car park in the port.

Bemos run between the Bertais/Mandalika/Sweta terminal and the port at Lembar (Rp15,000 if you bargain hard) and also from the main road outside the port. Metered **taxis** wait on the road outside the port; you'll be looking at Rp50–60,000 to Mataram/Cakranegara.

The southwest peninsula

It's only around 23km from Lembar to Bangko Bangko, at the tip of the peninsula. However, the road meanders around the picturesque northern coast for 50km or more. It's in good condition until 2km past *Hotel Bola Bola Paradis* but then deteriorates fast, eventually turning into sandy tracks as you approach Bangko Bangko, although improvements are promised. The scenery is great: many of the **beaches** are glorious and clusters of paradise **islands** are visible offshore.

Public **bemos** to the southwest peninsula leave from the large Terminal Segenter 500m north of the port at Lembar, at the junction of the main road and the turning to Bangko Bangko via Sekotong (this turn is marked with hotel signs for *Hotel Bola Bola Paradis* and *Sundancer*). Bemos operate from here to Labuhan Poh at least hourly until sunset (Rp20,000) but be aware that some terminate at Sekotong. **Chartered bemos** charge Rp300–400,000 for

▲ Nirvana Roemah Air restaurant, Sekotong

Bangko Bangko. The cost of a metered **taxi** from Lembar to Tawun is Rp50–60,000.

Heading towards Sekotong, you've a choice of two roads. The sea-level, longer route (*Bawah* on the road signs) traces the outline of the massive harbour, much of which is black sand lined with mangroves, while the shorter, busier one (*Atas* on the road signs) winds inland through rolling hills – all distances below assume you take this road. The large village of **SEKOTONG**, 11km from Lembar, marks the junction of the Bangko Bangko road with a tiny road that heads 11km south to Sepi on the south coast (see p.409). If you have your own transport, enquire locally about road conditions before setting off along here. Sekotong is also the location of one of the more unusual accommodation options in Lombok: *Nirvana Roemah Air* (℡0370/660 8060; ℗www .floatingvilla.com; ❼) has two bungalows, one attached to the land and the other floating in the sea. They have cold-water bathrooms, fans and electricity – plus a telephone with which to communicate with the mainland; room service is an option. They certainly score on novelty value, but in February and March large waves make some guests rather queasy. The attached restaurant (8am–10pm), on stilts over the water, makes a good refreshment-stop with Indonesian food from Rp18,000 and Western from Rp27,000. The set menus are good value (from Rp54,000). The same menu is available at the Gili Sudak offshoot (℡0828/364 9621); you can either get a boat from *Nirvana* or combine it with a snorkelling trip from Tawun.

Tawun and around

Past Sekotong, the views of the offshore islands become more enticing as you reach the village of **TAWUN**, 19km from Lembar. This is a sweeping white-sand bay, from where you can look across to Gili Sudak, Gili Tangkong and Gili Nanggu. There are only charter boats to **Gili Nanggu** (20min; Rp100,000 per boat one way; max 6 people). The boat captains rent out **snorkelling** gear (Rp50,000 per set), and all-day snorkelling trips to Gili Nanggu (Rp187,500 per boat) or to several of the islands (Rp210,000) are the reason most people come to the area. There's a Rp5000 entrance fee to the island, collected on the beach; Rp10,000 buys access to fresh-water showers. The only accommodation is at *Gili Nanggu Cottages and Bungalows* (℡0370/623783, ℗www .gilinanggu.com; ❹–❺) with a choice of fan or a/c, and a moderately priced **restaurant** attached. It's ideal for total relaxation or trips to nearby islands: Gili Tangkong to the east and Gili Poh, the miniscule desert-island lookalike, to the west. Slightly further east, **Gili Sudak** is also worth a visit for great coral and a multitude of fish.

Just 2km around the coast from Tawun, in the village of **Labu**, *Hotel Sekotong Indah* (℡0370/660 1921; ❷) has functional fan and cold-water bungalows just across the road from the beach.

Another 2km west you'll be unable to miss the gigantic, blue-roofed *Sundancer* (℗www.sundancerresort.com) development, which will eventually include residential villas, holiday homes and a hotel, ranging up the hillside at **Pandanan**, 23km from Lembar. Dive Zone (℡0370/660 3205, ℗www .divezone-lombok.com) operate from the jetty here, the only operator in these waters, which offers sites for all levels of experience. Dive/accommodation packages are available.

Tembowong to Bangko Bangko and Pandana

Moving west again, **TEMBOWONG**, 12km from Tawun, provides access to **Gili Gede**, the largest offshore island visible from here. Local boats charge

Rp5–10,000 per person each way (free transport if you are staying). You can stay at *Secret Island Resort* (☎0818/0376 2001, ⓦwww.secretislandresort.com; ❹–❺), which has simple fan rooms as well as a larger villa. There's snorkelling off the beach or trips to other sites can be arranged. Kayaking is available and there's a pool table.

A further 2km west, **PELANGAN** is the largest village in this part of the peninsula. An enticing track, suitable only for motorcycles, heads south for 5km to the bay of Teluk Mekaki on the south coast. Improvments to make it passable by cars were promised for 2008; check locally before trying it. A couple of kilometres beyond Pelangan, *Palm Beach Gardens* (☎0370/668 3350, ⓔaniehof @web.de; ❶) is a magical spot, with gorgeous coastal views, snorkelling just off the beach and three spotless bungalows. Booking is vital from June to September and December to January. Almost next door *Hotel Bola Bola Paradis* (☎0817/578 7355, ⓦwww.bolabolaparadis.com; ❹–❺) has three standards of room, all with fan and some with hot water. The attached restaurant serves well-prepared and -presented Indonesian and Western food (mains Rp35–70,000). **Boat** trips are available (from Rp300,000 per boat for 3hr).

From here, the condition of the road declines markedly. Five kilometres from Bola Bola, *Desert Point Lodges* (☎0818/0379 0044, ⓦwww.desertpointlodges .com; ❸) features wood, thatch and bamboo *lumbung* set in a small garden across the road from the beach at **Batu Putih**, 7km from Pelangan. The road follows the shore for another 3km to **LABUHAN POH**, where the glorious bay appears almost circular, enclosed by hills, headlands and islands, all fringed with white sand. *Aman Gati Hotel* (☎361/480777 or 0817/572 0699; ❹) is close to the beach with eye-boggling views east and west and to Gili Asahan just offshore. The bungalows have a/c and DVD/TV if all that sun and scenery get too much.

From here it is about six kilometres to the white-sand bay of **BANGKO BANGKO** lined with fishermen's huts via the hamlet of **Selegang**. From mid-May to September, and again in December, hundreds of **surfers** converge here from across the globe in search of the elusive, ultimate wave, **Desert Point**, just offshore. Alternatively, access is on a liveaboard boat charter from Bali.

This is a harsh landscape supporting only a tiny population: the place buzzes during surf season but it's otherwise as remote and isolated a spot as you'll find in Lombok with fine views across to Nusa Penida and a wonderful sense of being at the end of the earth. From here, you've no alternative but to turn around and head back the way you've come.

Senggigi and the northwest coast

Covering a lengthy stretch of coastline, **SENGGIGI**, with sweeping bays separated by towering headlands, is an attractive and laid-back beach resort, awash with good-quality accommodation and restaurants, and low-key nightlife. Although proximity to the airport at Mataram makes it a convenient first- or last-night destination, the excellent Lombok roads also make it an ideal base to explore the rest of the island. It's a relaxed resort, although there are plenty of hawkers in the central areas (see box, p.372).

The inaugural **Lombok International Triathlon** (ⓦwww.lomboktriathlon .com) took place in and around Senggigi in October 2007 and attracted an international field. It is scheduled to take place annually in late October. It's a highlight of the Senggigi year and not to be missed if you are in the area as participant (it is described as "the toughest triathlon in Asia") or observer.

Arrival and orientation

Senggigi is served by **bemos** from Ampenan throughout the day (every 15–20min); pick them up on Jalan Saleh Sungkar just north of the turn-off to Kebon Roek terminal in Ampenan. Metered taxis zip between the city and the resort. From the **airport**, fixed-price taxis charge Rp50–90,000 to Senggigi, depending on destination. Perama **tourist shuttle buses** and the **Perama boat** operate to Senggigi from the main Bali and Lombok tourist destinations; see "Travel details", p.411, for more. Using the Perama boat you'll pay Rp200,000 from Padang Bai or Rp240,000 from Ubud, if using public ferry and tourist shuttle bus it is Rp60,000 and Rp100,000 respectively.

The southern end of Senggigi is five kilometres north of Ampenan, and a few hotels are spread out along the next four kilometres until the main concentration of hotels, which stretches for about a kilometre from the *Graha Senggigi* to the *Sheraton Senggigi Beach Resort*. Low-density development continues for another 7km to the most northerly development, *Bulan Baru* at Lendang Luar. **Bemos** (Rp5000) ply the coastal road as far as here during the day, and metered blue **taxis** operate throughout the area from early morning to late at night; a ride from central Senggigi to Lendang Luar costs about Rp16,000 and to Mangsit Rp10–12,000

The nearest government **tourist office** is in Mataram (see p.360). The resort is lined with "tourist information" places, which are commercial companies offering tours and vehicle rental.

Accommodation

There's plenty of **accommodation** in Senggigi from budget to five-star luxury. Bemos operate throughout the resort in daylight hours but if you stay outside the central area, you'll depend on taxis or restaurant transport to move around in the evenings. The most attractive area is **north Senggigi**, where the hotels are more spread out. In **central Senggigi**, there's plenty happening, with bars and restaurants on your doorstep. **South Senggigi** has the advantage of being closer to the city area and airport.

South Senggigi

Batu Bolong Cottages ☏0370/693198, ⓔbbcresort_lombok@yahoo.com. Just north of Pura Batu Bolong on both sides of the road in attractive gardens, there is good-quality furnishing and hot water. A/c is available and some rooms have fine coastal views. ❷–❹

Batu Layar Bungalow ☏0370/692235. Clean, tiled bungalows with fans and most with hot water in an attractive garden set back from the road. It's a short walk to the beach, and there's free evening transport to central Senggigi. ❶–❷

The Beach Club ☏0370/693637, ⓔthebeachclublombok@hotmail.com. This

---

Trips to Sumbawa, Komodo and Flores

Travel agencies on Lombok and the Gili Islands advertise boat trips via **Sumbawa** and **Komodo** to **Flores**, including **snorkelling**, **trekking**, sightseeing, and a visit to the Komodo dragons. Diving can be arranged on some trips. Conditions on board can be pretty basic and comforts few. Prices vary, starting at Rp1,000,000 per person for a three-to-five-day trip. If possible, go by personal recommendation, and be clear where the trip ends and how you'll move on (air transport out of Labuanbajo on Flores can be difficult to arrange). The following sell trips: Perama (ⓦwww.peramatour.com; contact any office); Suarmanik Kencana (☏0376/21738) and agents in the Gili Islands and Senggigi; Lomata Tours and Travel (☏0370/646494) and agents in the Gili islands and Senggigi.

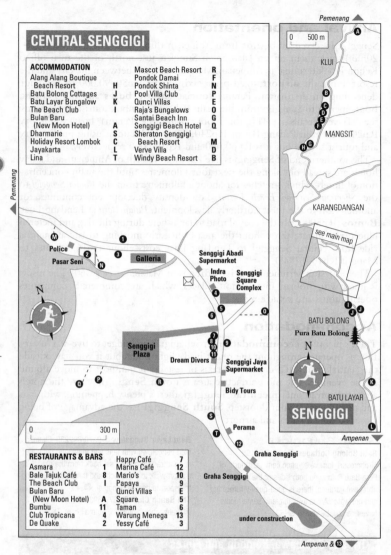

CENTRAL SENGGIGI

ACCOMMODATION

Alang Alang Boutique Beach Resort	H	Mascot Beach Resort	R
Batu Bolong Cottages	J	Pondok Damai	F
Batu Layar Bungalow	K	Pondok Shinta	N
The Beach Club	I	Pool Villa Club	P
Bulan Baru (New Moon Hotel)	A	Qunci Villas	E
Dharmarie	C	Raja's Bungalows	O
Holiday Resort Lombok	L	Santai Beach Inn	G
Jayakarta		Senggigi Beach Hotel	Q
Lina	T	Sheraton Senggigi Beach Resort	M
		Verve Villa	D
		Windy Beach Resort	B

RESTAURANTS & BARS

Asmara	1	Happy Café	7
Bale Tajuk Café	8	Marina Café	12
The Beach Club	I	Mario's	10
Bulan Baru (New Moon Hotel)	A	Papaya	9
		Qunci Villas	E
Bumbu	11	Square	5
Club Tropicana	4	Taman	6
De Quake	2	Warung Menega	13
		Yessy Café	3

popular bar south of the centre also has attractive thatch-and-bamboo bungalows with a/c and hot water. There's a pretty swimming pool as well. ❹

Jayakarta ℡0370/693045, ⓦjayakartahotelsresorts .com. Enormous, busy hotel at the southern end of Senggigi with five standards of top-end rooms and fantastic swimming pools. ❺–❽

Central Senggigi

Dharmarie ℡0370/693050, ℗693099. Attractive bungalows in large, centrally located

beachfront grounds. All have a/c and hot water. More expensive bungalows boast sea views. ❹

Lina ℡0370/693237. Long-standing favourite in a tiny seafront compound in central Senggigi, just opposite the Perama office. All rooms have a/c, but only the more expensive have sea views and hot water. ❷–❸

Mascot Beach Resort ℡0370/693365, ⓔmascot@telkom.net. Central but quiet place in huge grounds fronting the beach. All the bungalows have a/c, hot water and huge verandahs. ⑤–⑦

Pondok Shinta ℡0370/693563. Central, budget place tucked away in a small garden offering clean, fan rooms with good verandahs. Great value. ❶

Raja's Bungalows ℡0812/373 4171, ℮Rajas22 @yahoo.com. Off the road to the mosque, four clean, tiled budget bungalows with fan and attached cold-water bathrooms set in a lush garden. ❷

Senggigi Beach Hotel and Pool Villa Club ℡0370/693210, ⓦwww.senggigibeach .aerowisata.com. Occupying an entire promontory in central Senggigi, the rooms are excellent, and there's an attractive pool plus several bars and restaurants, tennis courts and a Mandara spa. The super-plush *Pool Villa Club* (℡0370/693210, ⓦwww.poolvillaclub.aerowisata.com) is attached but set in its own grounds. It has sixteen fabulously appointed two-storey villas with direct access to the elegant pool. Published prices in the *Pool Villa Club* start at $380. Hotel ⑦–⑧ Club ⑨

Sheraton Senggigi Beach Resort ℡0370/693333, ⓦwww.sheraton.com/senggigi. The best luxury hotel in town is a peaceful enclave in central Senggigi with a great swimming pool and lush grounds. All rooms have verandahs or balconies facing seawards. There's a spa, several bars and restaurants, health club and children's playground. Villas with their own pools are available. ⑧–⑨

North Senggigi

Alang Alang Boutique Resort ℡0370/693518, ⓦwww.alang-alang-villas.com. Atmospheric place 4km north of central Senggigi. All accommodation has a/c and hot water but the more expensive bungalows are far better value than the rooms. The gardens are glorious, with a pretty pool. ⑦–⑧

🏃 **Bulan Baru (New Moon Hotel)** ℡0370/693785, ℮bulanbaru@hotmail .com. At Lendang Luar, 7km north of central Senggigi. Spotless bungalows with a/c and hot water situated in a pretty garden with a pool. It's fabulously peaceful, and Setangi beach, with decent snorkelling, is nearby. There's an excellent restaurant and service is friendly and efficient. ❸

Holiday Resort Lombok ℡0370/693444, ⓦwww.holidayresort-lombok.com. In extensive, attractive grounds, this upmarket place 5km north of central Senggigi has several standards of rooms, all with the comfort and facilities to be expected at this end of the market. Two-bedroom self-catering villas are across the road from the main hotel. There's a giant swimming pool (Rp100,000 for nonresidents), kiddy club, beachside spa, dive shop, and several bars and restaurants. ⑥–⑦

Pondok Damai ℡ & ⓕ0370/693019. On the coast 4km north of central Senggigi, in a quiet spot with good-value, fan-cooled bamboo-and-thatch bungalows built on a tile base in a lovely garden. Hot water in the more expensive rooms. ❸

Qunci Villas ℡0370/693800, ⓦwww.quncivillas .com. Designer accommodation, all with a/c and hot water, decorated with original art. Welcoming gay as well as mixed-sex couples in a cosy beachside garden 4km north of central Senggigi, with an excellent pool and beachside restaurant. Private villas also available for rent. ❼

Santai Beach Inn ℡0370/693038, ⓦwww .santaibeachinn.com. Popular thatched fan and cold-water bungalows plus a couple of large family rooms with hot water set in an atmospheric garden on the coast at Mangsit. Meals (booking needed) are eaten communally; the menu caters for fish-eating vegetarians but they can also cater for vegans – meat-eating guests are welcome to dine elsewhere. Bookings are only accepted for the large rooms, but phone ahead, as they do get full. ❷–❹

Verve Villa ℡0370/693500, ⓦwww.vervevilla .com. Designer chic hits Lombok with these wow-factor rooms in a villa set beachside, just behind a great little pool at Mangsit, 4km north of the centre. High ceilings, open-plan bathrooms and eye-catching decoration and art all add to the allure. ⑧

🏃 **Windy Beach Resort** ℡0370/693191, ⓦwww.windybeach.com. Several standards of well-furnished, traditional bungalows in a great garden with a stunning beachside pool (Rp20,000 for nonresidents), 5km north of central Senggigi. All rooms have hot water and a/c is available. You can rent snorkelling equipment – there are a couple of good spots nearby. ❹–❺

The resort and around

Life in Senggigi centres on the **beach** or swimming pool during the day and the restaurants and bars in the evening. The only local sight is **Pura Batu Bolong**, a kilometre south of the centre of Senggigi ranged around a rocky promontory with fabulous views along the coast. The main part of the temple is built over an archway in the rock, the hole through which virgins

They don't mean to spoil your holiday

Walk along the street or beach or eat at a beachside or streetside restaurant in central Senggigi and you'll be approached by one or more of the local **hawkers** selling T-shirts, sarongs, watches, jewellery, paintings, bookmarks, tours, transport and pretty much anything else you can imagine. It can be irritating, but it's worth bearing a few things in mind. Despite the tourist gloss, many people in Lombok are poor and the employment opportunities are few. Jobs in hotels and restaurants are like gold dust, government jobs depend on having connections, and there's not enough work in the commercial sector to meet demand. Farming is tough and family land is often insufficient to support all the people dependent on it. Youngsters come to Senggigi in the hope of scraping a living and getting a toe-hold in the tourist industry – and perhaps meeting a future spouse from overseas.

Suggestions for coping:

• Acknowledge people and remain polite and calm. A simple "No, thank you" is usually enough.

• If you say you'll look at things tomorrow or later, then you should do so.

• If you start bargaining and the seller agrees your price, you are then obliged to buy.

• Talk to the sellers; you'll get a fascinating insight into Lombok life.

were once supposedly sacrificed to appease the gods. Nowadays, it's a peaceful spot, a favourite with local fishermen.

Diving and snorkelling

There are many operators in the resort, several also have offices in the Gili Islands (see p.380, 385 & 386). Senggigi is a good diving base if you want the comforts of a resort and don't mind the additional cost and travel time to **dive** around the islands. Most companies keep their boats at Teluk Nara, about 20km (30mins by road) north of Senggigi. Companies vary greatly in what they charge; this makes it especially important to heed the general guidelines (see p.51) on choosing an operator and not simply opting for the cheapest. It is also worth checking the trip times involved – some companies head straight out to the dive sites from Teluk Nara, others spend considerable time collecting other clients from the Gili Islands before the diving starts.

The dive sites closer to Senggigi (Nipah Slope, Malimbu Cave and Alang-Alang Wall) are not visited as much as sites further afield.

Qualified divers will **pay** $35 for the first dive and $30 for subsequent dives. A PADI Open Water course is about $350, a PADI Advanced Open Water course $275. Check whether equipment rental is included in the price.

Most operators run **snorkelling** trips to the Gili Islands; you go along with the divers and have to be fairly self-reliant in the water. Expect to pay up to $15, including equipment and lunch. Blue Marlin is the exception; they have guided snorkelling tours ($20 for one, $30 for two), a big advantage for the less confident.

In case of accidents there is a **recompression chamber** in Mataram, Jl Adi Sucipto 13B (24hr hotline ☏0370/660 0333).

Dive operators

See p.380, p.385 and p.386 for Gili island operators.

Blue Marlin ☏0370/692003, ⊛www.diveindo .com. At *Senggigi Beach Hotel* (☏0370/693210),

Alang-Alang (☏0370/693911) and *Holiday Resort Lombok* (☏0370/693719).

Dive Indonesia ☏0370/693367, ⊛www .diveindonesiaonline.com. Office in the Galleria in Senggigi; see map, p.370.

Dive Zone ℡0370/660 3205, ⓦwww
.divezone-lombok.com. There's a booking counter
in Bidy Tours next to Senggigi Jaya Supermarket.
Diving in the Sekotong (see p.367), Kuta
(see p.405) and Blongas (see p.409) areas.

Dream Divers ℡0370/693738, ⓦwww
.dreamdivers.com. Also at the *Sheraton Senggigi
Beach Resort* and *The Santosa*. As well as the
usual trips and courses they arrange liveaboards
on the 24-metre *Moana* to Komodo and West
Papua/the Moluccas (see website for details).

Adventure activities

Use the high-speed boat between Bali and the Gili Islands (see p.377) for an
exciting introduction to the island. Once you are there, the **Rinjani trek** is the
biggest Lombok adventure. See p.394 for details and note that it is easy to
arrange the trek from Senggigi with transport to and from the resort included.
Closer to home, Lombok Biking Tour (℡0370/692164), with an office next to
Bumbu restaurant, offer a range of guided **cycle tours** in West Lombok from
$18–32 per person (minimum 2 people) including guide, equipment and
transport to the start. Senggigi Surf (℡0819/1703 2384) in central Senggigi
arrange **surfing** lessons (Rp250,000 per day all inclusive) and rent out
(Rp100,000 per day) and repair boards. For **watersports**, *Sunset House Homestay*
(℡0370/692020, ⓦwww.sunsethouse-lombok.com) south of Senggigi next to
the *Beach Club*, has jet skis from Rp200,000 for 15 minutes and just along the
coast, the other side of the *Beach Club*, Flicker Air and Water Sport (℡0828/370
4440) offers banana-boat rides, jet skis and parasailing.

Spas and treatments

There are plenty of **massages** and **spa treatments** available from beach
massages (Rp60,000 per hour) to pampering of undiluted luxury. At the top
end the Mandara Spa at the *Senggigi Beach Hotel* (℡0370/693210 ext 8122) has
an international reputation, great treatment rooms and a private pool, but with
a Balinese massage at $36 for 50min, prices match the ambience. The beachfront
spas at *Sheraton Senggigi Beach Resort* (℡0370/693333 ext 2120) and *Holiday
Resort Lombok* (℡0370/693444) have extensive spa menus, from $25 per hour
for massage. Rumah Bunga Spa (℡0370/665 3531) in the Senggigi Plaza
complex is quiet and pretty with a range of good-value treatments (massages
from Rp75,000 per hour) and have several packages on offer.

The road north

With your own transport, the spectacular **coastal road north** from Senggigi
to Pemenang (24km) makes a great day out, passing through small villages
behind sweeping bays amidst stands of coconut palm. Travelling through the
bays of Karangdangan, Mangsit, Malimbu, Teluk Kodek, Nippah and Teluk Nara,
there are fine views of the Gili Islands – tiny white specks atop a turquoise sea
– and across to Gunung Agung on Bali in clear weather. However, the road is
steep, with bad bends and sheer drops, and is especially hazardous at night.

Pemenang marks the turn-off to Bangsal, from where boats depart to the Gili
Islands. Only a couple of kilometres beyond Pemenang lies the stunning beach
at Sira.

Eating, drinking and nightlife

A wide range of **restaurants** in Senggigi offer high-quality international cuisine
at decent prices. For budget eating, the beach at the end of the road to *Senggigi
Beach Hotel* comes alive in the afternoons with **sate sellers** and makeshift shelters.
It's very popular with local people; ten sate sticks and a parcel of rice costs
Rp15,000. During Ramadan all tourist places remain open.

Asmara ☎ 0370/693619. This long-standing Senggigi favourite is a tasteful, relaxed place serving excellent Western (Rp28–125,000) and Indonesian (Rp28–50,000) dishes. There's good home-made bread for breakfast, and also baby and children's meals. The set-lunch menu is a great deal (Rp35,000). Free pick-up throughout Senggigi.

Bale Tajuk Café Cheap and cheerful place opposite *Papaya*. No mains are over Rp40,000 and there's a big menu of Indonesian, Western and Sasak food. The "King of Rinjani" (Rp125,000) is a Sasak meal for two.

The Beach Club A great beachside chill-out bar south of the centre with a pool table and satellite TV, plus a small menu of well-cooked food (Indonesian mains Rp25–28,000, burgers Rp40,000, sandwiches Rp25–30,000) and a huge drinks list. Come for a snack and stay all day.

Bulan Baru (New Moon Hotel) At Lendang Luar, 7km north of central Senggigi. The menu describes Indonesian, Thai and Western dishes (including bangers and mash for homesick travellers) in mouth-watering detail (mains Rp28–48,000) and served by welcoming staff. This is a good spot for lunch, with soups, salads, sandwiches and rolls (Rp12–16,000), and Setangi beach is nearby.

Bumbu Small, popular place in central Senggigi. Thai food is excellent, but tell the waiters if you can't cope with industrial quantities of chilli. There are plenty of other options, including steaks and sandwiches, mains Rp20–40,000.

De Quake Stylish, beachside bar/restaurant in the Pasar Seni serving Pan Asian cuisine with lots of seafood (mains Rp35–42,000, salads Rp24–29,000, soups Rp21–27,000) from a menu that is refreshingly different from most of the others in Senggigi. Desserts to die for (Rp20,000).

Happy Café Excellent live music in a friendly atmosphere, with a large bar, a vast drinks menu and an extensive menu of well-priced Indonesian, Chinese and Western food (mains Rp15–75,000). Popular with foreign tourists and Indonesians alike.

Mario's High-ceilinged, dark wood bar serving plenty of drinks and with a hefty menu of

Indonesian and Western food with a German slant including five varieties of sausages, (mains Rp30–60,000). There are draft beers and excellent teas and coffees.

Papaya Quality live music plus an Indonesian, Western and Chinese menu – the Chinese dishes come in small, medium or large servings (Rp24–111,000). There's plenty of seafood, peaking with the "King of Seafood" for two for Rp244,500. Thin and crispy pizzas are a speciality (Rp39,000).

Qunci Villas ☎ 0370/693800, ⓦ www.quncivillas .com. Dine beachside or in the small restaurant near the pool. There's a small menu with minimal description but the food is excellent, covering Asian and international options (mains Rp45–55,000) supplemented by a huge drinks list including cocktails and wine. Lunch has a Mexican slant alongside salads, soups and sandwiches (Rp44,000 upwards).

Square ☎ 0370/664 4888, ⓦ www.squarelombok .com. Top-end two-storey bar and restaurant on the main drag. There's a huge menu; starters such as beef carpaccio wade in at Rp40,000 and Chinese, Indonesian and Western main courses, including imported lamb and steak mean that you can, but needn't break the bank (Rp30–135,000). Desserts are equally intricate; Grand Marnier crème brûlée at Rp40,000 for example, and the drinks list matches the food in size and range.

Taman ☎ 0370/693842. Imposing two-storey place on the main road in central Senggigi with a huge, appealing global menu (mains Rp20–95,000) and a gigantic, wide-ranging wine list covering the Old World, New World and Indonesia. There's an attached deli/bakery.

Warung Menega A simple place on the coast 3km south of Senggigi with delectable seafood sold by weight or in good-value set meals (Rp70–140,000 including drinks); lobster, prawn, crab, squid, clams, snapper, tuna, barracuda are all on offer.

Yessy Café ☎ 0370/693148. Cheap drinks (Aussie wine Rp28,000 per glass, large Bintang Rp16,000) and a big menu of good-value food (mains Rp27–34,000) make this small place a popular, lively spot.

Nightlife

The **nightlife** in Senggigi, the only on mainland Lombok, is extremely sedate in keeping with the sensibilities of the local Muslim population and the tourist profile here. *Marina Café* features live music, sometimes featuring big bands from Jakarta and attracts a mix of local people, expats and tourists. *Club Tropicana* is also open nightly, but Friday and Saturday are busiest. It's popular with visitors from other parts of Indonesia who spend the weekend in Senggigi, boosting Saturday-night numbers.

Shopping

Senggigi boasts plenty of shops selling **crafts** including textiles, jewellery, basketware and items from across the archipelago, as well as Western clothes and bags aimed at the tourist market, although there isn't the quality or variety that you'll find in Bali – more than one Lombok visitor has flown to Bali on a day-trip for retail therapy. Don't forget there are also shops and markets in nearby Ampenan-Mataram-Cakranegara-Sweta (see p.362). If you are in the market for furniture, try the shops along the road from Senggigi to Ampenan. All the shops can arrange shipping, but see p.58.

Asmara Collection Attached to *Asmara* restaurant, selling a range of good-quality Indonesian items big and small, new and old including furniture, handicrafts and textiles.

Bayan Lombok Just north of *Taman* restaurant, they have one of the best selections of crafts in Senggigi including wooden lacquered masks, boxes and trays, all at great prices.

Lex Bookshop Secondhand bookshop opposite *Asmara* restaurant. Excellent selection of books in all European languages.

Mandara Spa Even if you can't afford the treatments, the spa products are gorgeous and well-packaged, and with prices starting at Rp18,000, they won't break the bank.

Pamour Large place with good-quality stuff that is worth an extended rummage around over all its three floors. The furniture is downstairs but they also stock loads of other small items that are much more transportable.

Pasar Seni The tiny stalls and shops that make up the art market sell a selection of pretty much everything that is available in Lombok. Excellent for browsing.

Senggigi Surf Near Senggigi Abadi supermarket. They sell a good selection of surf clothes plus secondhand boards (from Rp750,000) and accessories.

Sudirman Almost opposite *Happy Café*. Long established in Senggigi, selling antiques from across Indonesia. Staff know what they are selling, and what it is worth.

Listings

Airlines See p.363 for details of airlines serving Lombok. Information on international airline offices in Bali is on p.101.

Boats Perama (☎0370/693007, ⊛www.peramatour.com, 6am–10pm) operate a daily boat to Gili Trawangan at 9am (1hr 30min; Rp70,000). If you're interested in arranging a boat to the Gili Islands for fishing or snorkelling, negotiate with the captains on the beach. Rp350,000 for two islands, Rp400,000 for all three.

Buses Perama (☎0370/693007, ⊛www.peramatour.com; 6am–10pm) are the longest-standing of the companies offering tourist shuttles to Bali and Lombok destinations. See "Travel details" on p.411. Other companies advertise along the main street. Perama can advise on inter-island bus journeys and book tickets. See p.356 for inter-island buses from the Bertais/Mandalika/Sweta terminal.

Car and bike rental Plenty of places rent vehicles with and without drivers. Kotasi is the local transport co-operative. Check the insurance at the time of renting. It's worth shopping around, but general prices are: Suzuki Jimneys (Rp150,000/day), Kijangs (Rp250,000), motorbikes (Rp35,000–75,000 without insurance) and bicycles (Rp25,000–30,000).

Chartering a vehicle including driver costs Rp250,000–300,000 per day with the customer paying for the fuel. It's best to go by personal recommendation. Highly recommended local drivers include Hasan Nur (☎081/854 8227, ⊜hsn_y @yahoo.com), Made (☎0370/667 9679 or 0812/372 5415) and Mudzakir (☎0370/640170 or 0813/3977 5211).

Dentist You'll need to go to Ampenan-Mataram-Cakranegara-Sweta (see "Listings", p.363).

Doctor *Senggigi Beach Hotel* ☎0370/693210 (24hr). See p.364 for hospitals in Ampenan-Mataram-Cakranegara-Sweta.

Exchange International ATM near Senggigi Abadi supermarket. Moneychangers (daily 10am–10pm) on the main street.

Internet and phone access Several Internet cafés along the main street (daily 8am–10pm; Rp300/min), also offering telephone services. Planet Senggigi, north of *Taman* restaurant, is reliable and can work with USB devices like digital cameras.

Left luggage Perama (Rp10,000/item/week), or most accommodation will store stuff if you're coming back to them.

Police Tourist Police ℡0370/632733, on the main road.

Post office In the centre of Senggigi (Mon–Thurs 7.30am–5pm, Fri & Sat 7.30am–4pm). Poste restante is available at the Post Office, Senggigi, Lombok 83355, West Nusa Tenggara.

Supermarkets In the centre, Senggigi Abadi and Senggigi Jaya (daily 8.30am–9.30pm), which sell necessities, postcards and souvenirs. The English-language *Jakarta Post* arrives in the afternoon.

Tour companies See p.358 for information on Lombok tours and operators.

The Gili Islands

Strikingly beautiful, with white-sand beaches lapped by brilliant blue waters and circled by coral reefs hosting myriad species of fish, each of the **Gili Islands** has its own character.

Of the three, **Gili Trawangan** best fits the image of a "party island". With a vast array of accommodation, restaurants and nightlife, it attracts the liveliest visitors although outside the June to September and December high seasons it is perfectly possible to have a quiet stay. If you want to get away from it all, head for the smallest and quietest of the islands, **Gili Meno**, which has no nightlife and much less accommodation – but still some excellent places to stay. Closest to the mainland, **Gili Air** fits somewhere between the two in atmosphere, with weekly parties in high season, plenty of facilities in the south, and more peace and quiet the further round the coast you go.

Accommodation prices vary dramatically depending on the season and are more fluid than anywhere else on Bali or Lombok. A bungalow costing Rp150,000 in February or October will cost Rp400,000 or even more from June to September and in December. It is essential to make reservations in the high season or face a long, possibly fruitless, search for a bed. It is advisable to reserve the most popular places at any time.

For reliable **Gili island information** on Bali visit Island Promotions, Shop 12, Poppies Lane 1, Kuta (℡0361/753241, ⓦwww.gili-paradise.com; 9am–10pm). They can also book transport and accommodation and have a hotel booking site, ⓦwww.gili-hotels.com.

All the island beaches are public. The local people are Muslim and public nudity is **offensive**. Although they are more used to seeing scantily clad Western women (and men) on the Gili Islands than in any other part of Lombok, you should cover up when you move away from the beach.

Pemenang and Bangsal

The access port for the Gili Islands is **BANGSAL**, 25km north of Senggigi, a 1.5-kilometre cidomo ride or a shadeless walk from **PEMENANG**, 26km beyond the Ampenan-Mataram-Cakranegara-Sweta area. Pemenang is served by **bemos** and **buses**: all transport between Ampenan-Mataram-Cakranegara-Sweta and points around the north coast passes through. **From the airport**, turn left on the main road outside the airport, head straight across the roundabout and, 500m further on, at the traffic lights, turn left and catch any bus heading north, which will drop you at Pemenang. **From Senggigi**, there's no public bemo service along the coastal road north to Pemenang. A gate at Bangsal stops all vehicles 500m from the harbour itself, so prepare to **walk** the final bit or bargain with the cidomo drivers (Rp5000 per cidomo is fair).

Volcanoes and ricefields

Situated in one of the most seismically active areas on the planet, Bali and Lombok's mountains, crater lakes and soaring rice terraces have been created over millennia by volcanic eruptions large and small, and have now become iconic images of both islands. These mountains and lakes, clustered in the north of the island, are highly revered by the Balinese, who have built temples to honour their gods and goddesses. Pilgrims and foreign visitors mingle in these dramatic interior landscapes, which are an invigorating contrast to the beaches and coastal plains.

Gunung Agung

The highest mountain on Bali, **Gunung Agung** (3142m), is the spiritual centre of the island. Many Balinese Hindus prefer to sleep with their heads towards the mountain and it is always the corner of a ricefield closest to the mountain that is the first to be planted. The classically conical mountain is impossible to miss from anywhere in eastern Bali. Most visitors enjoy its dramatic profile from afar, as a stunning backdrop to lowland rice terraces. For a closer look, the temples of **Besakih** and **Pura Pasar Agung**, high on the flanks of the mountain, make the stark grandeur of the peak even more apparent. The fit and adventurous can engage a guide for the hard overnight slog to the summit for sunrise and views that take in much of the island. Agung is worthy of respect; it last erupted in 1963 (see p.240) with deadly and long lasting results, and solidified lava flows are still visible today.

Besakih Temple with Gunung Agung ▲

Segara Anak lake on Gunung Rinjani ▼

Gunung Rinjani

Rising to 3726m, **Gunung Rinjani** on Lombok is one of the highest peaks in Indonesia and is the most challenging and rewarding trek on either island. It takes three tough days to reach the summit and get back. However, there are plenty of shorter – but equally rewarding – treks. Hike to the rim of Gunung Rinjani's crater, which contains the lake of **Segara Anak** and the peak of **Gunung Baru**, which rises dramatically from the waters. This route only requires an overnight trek, albeit with a 2000m ascent. Considered sacred by both Hindus and Wetu Telu Muslims, the lake is the focus of pilgrims from both religions.

Gunung Batur

The almost lunar landscape around **Gunung Batur** (1717m) in north Bali draws hundreds of tourists every day. The views are stunning. Batur's dramatic, and still active, volcanic cone rises beside the vast lake of **Danau Batur**, all set inside an outer crater. Treks to the top for sunrise take a bit of puff but most people can do it in only two or three hours and hikers are rewarded by fabulous views of the peaks of Abang, Agung and Rinjani. After the descent, the hot springs beside the lake are ideal for easing tired muscles. The temple of **Pura Ulun Danu Batur** is also a must-see. In 1926, following a major eruption of Batur, the temple was relocated from the lakeside to the crater rim. Its new location is no less dramatic as it's frequently shrouded in mist.

Lakes and temples

Pura Ulun Danu Bratan is the most photographed temple on Bali and with good reason. It is built on a series of islands and the shrines appear to float on the surface of the lake, while forested mountains rise behind. It's a gorgeous spot but certainly not peaceful as scores of pilgrims and busloads of tourists add to the traffic on the nearby main road – in addition to the motorboats on the lake.

The nearby lakes of **Buyan** and **Tamblingan** are less accessible and less frequented but equally beautiful. They boast small but pretty lakeside temples and the peaceful setting adds to their allure. Buyan and Tamblingan are ideal for lakeside strolls or more adventurous forays into the surrounding forest with local guides (see p.287). Bird spotting is particularly rewarding here.

▲ Looking across Danau Batur to Gunung Batur

▼ Pura Ulun Danu Bratan

The furthest west of Bali's volcanic peaks, the slopes and summit of **Gunung Batukaru** are jungle-covered and lack the dramatic views that reward other mountain hikes. **Pura Luhur Batukaru** is the temple on its forested slopes. What Gunung Batukaru lacks in drama it more than makes up for by its mysterious atmosphere amidst the foliage and the trees.

Ricefields

The quintessentially Indonesian landscape of verdant ricefields is common throughout the islands, but in places the sheer loveliness of the scenery is breathtaking. In plenty of areas it is possible to gaze in awe from a car window, a restaurant or a hotel verandah. However, nothing beats getting out there and walking through the beauty. Less vertiginous and demanding than scaling volcanoes, are the **ricefield treks** ranging from a few hours to all-day excursions. Our favourite areas include Jatiluwih (see p.330), Sidemen (see p.261), Tirtagangga (see p.257).

Rooms with a view

You don't need to stir an inch to enjoy the mountain views from these hotels.

Lakeview, Penelokan. Startling views of Danau Batur and the four craters of the mountain (see p.278).

Mahagiri, Rendang. Stunning views of Agung (see p.262).

Rinjani Mountain Garden, Bayan, Lombok. Camp in the garden here and in the morning get startling mountain views (see p.393).

Prana Dewi, Wongayagede. A classic vista of ricefields and forest, framed by Gunung Batukaru (see p.328).

Alam Jiwa, Nyuhkuning, Ubud. Enjoy dramatic long-range views of Gunung Agung from the bathtub and the balcony (see p.184).

Whichever boat you use to get to the Gili Islands, the chances are you'll get your feet wet; the boats anchor in the shallows and passengers wade to and fro.

Bangsal

Public boats operate between Bangsal and the islands throughout the day, leaving when full (7.30am–4.30pm; journey time 20–45min). **Shuttle boats** depart at 8.15am from Gili Trawangan and Gili Air and 4.30pm from Bangsal. You can also charter a boat, for a maximum of ten people, for single or return, or trips to more than one island. Prices are fixed and displayed in the ticket offices at Bangsal and on the islands.

	To Gili Air	To Gili Meno	To Gili Trawangan
Public boat	Rp7000	Rp7500	Rp8000
Shuttle boat	Rp21,000	Rp22,000	Rp23,0000
Charter (one way)	Rp135,000	Rp145,000	Rp155,000

Note that prices after dark escalate; they are displayed in some places but not others. It's Rp40,000 between Bangsal and Gili Trawangan and Rp25-30,000 between the islands. Most people end up chartering after dark.

Senggigi and elsewhere on Lombok/Bali

From Senggigi Daily Perama boat at 9am (Rp70,000; 2hr). Charters are available from Senggigi (see p.375), approach the boat captains on the beach. It's a great trip but the boats are small and it gets rough on the return trip in the afternoon. Sometimes weather conditions make the trip impossible.

Tourist shuttle bus/public ferry combination Tickets between the Gili Islands and all main tourist destinations on Bali and Lombok are widely advertised. Perama customers can use the Perama boat between Padang Bai and Senggigi/Gili Islands or public ferries and buses. Other companies use public ferries.

Whichever operator you use, there is no direct public or tourist shuttle boat from the islands to Senggigi – you go to Bangsal and proceed overland. You'll walk from the port at Bangsal to the gate on the main road, where you'll be collected by the shuttle bus operator.

From Serangan Harbour to Gili Trawangan: Daily *Mahi Mahi* boat (Rp550,000; 2hr 30min); book through Island Promotions (℡0818/0530 5632).

From Benoa to Gili Trawangan, Gili Meno, Gili Air. Daily *Blue Water Express* boat runs June to October (Rp690,000, 2hrs; ℡0813/3841 8988, ⊛www.bwsbali.com). Low-season discounts apply.

From Padang Bai to Gili Trawangan: Daily *Gili Cat* (Rp660,000; 2hr 30min; ℡0361/271680, ⊛www.gilicat.com).

From Amed on Bali Increasing numbers of skippers arrange charters to the islands. Be aware that the boats are often small with single engines, don't carry radios, and mobile phones may well be out of range in the middle of the Lombok Strait. For the return trip talk to Dean on Gili Meno (see p.385) and Ozzy Shop (see p.386) on Gili Air, who have twin-engined boats.

Sadly, Bangsal has developed a reputation as a place full of **hassle** for tourists; there have even been punch-ups. Keep your cool: the Gilis are worth it. The **ticket office** (8am–4.30pm) for all boats to the islands is right on the seafront; it's organized, and there's a printed price-list covering public boats, shuttles and charters. Buy your ticket only from there; ignore anybody who tries to persuade you otherwise. It's also useful to know that everything on sale in Bangsal is also on sale on the Gili Islands, including water, mosquito coils and return boat tickets. Ideally, get your own bag onto and off the boats; if you cannot manage this, you should negotiate with the porters before you let them touch the bags – and be clear whether you're talking about rupiah, dollars, for one bag or for the whole lot.

Bangsal has a few **restaurants**, a moneychanger and one **place to stay**, the *Taman Sari* (☎0370/646934; ❶), just by the gate with functional rooms opening onto a small garden.

Island transport and practicalities

None of the islands has a particular **crime** problem, although some years ago there were attacks on women during and after the parties on Gili Trawangan. Do take reasonable precautions (see p.64). Many of the bungalows feature locking drawers or safe deposit boxes for your valuables. There are no **police** on the islands, although Satgas (beach security) on Gili Trawangan have a role in tourist security: it's the role of the *kepala desa*, the headman who looks after Gili Air and Gili Meno, and the *kepala kampung* on Gili Trawangan, to deal with any problems. If you need to make a police report (for example, for insurance), go to the police on the mainland (at Tanjung or Ampenan).

Snorkelling and diving

The **snorkelling** and **diving** around the Gili Islands is some of the best and most accessible in Lombok. The islands are fringed by **coral reefs** and visibility is generally around 15m. The **fish** life is the main attraction and, with more than 3500 species estimated to live in the Indonesian waters, there's certainly plenty of variety; species include white- and black-tip reef shark, cuttlefish, moray eel, lobster, manta ray, Napoleon wrasse and bumphead parrotfish. **Turtles** have become increasingly common and it's a rare dive that spots none. There are more than a dozen **sites** around the islands, with exotic names such as Shark Point, Deep Turbo, Turtle Heaven, Deep Halik and Manta Point. Talk to the dive guides to find out the best site depending on local conditions and your experience and interests. There are good snorkelling spots just off the beaches of all the islands.

There are **dive operations** on all the islands, and many of their **instructors** are from overseas, offering tuition and dive-guiding in all European languages. Most operators have PADI materials in several languages.

There's a price agreement, with all the operators on all the islands charging identical rates; however, they vary in approach and atmosphere and you should

---

"Hopping island" boat service

The **"hopping island"** boat service between all three Gili Islands does one circuit, Air–Meno–Trawangan–Meno–Air, in the morning, and another in the afternoon. It's fast and conveniently timetabled, and so makes a day-trip to another island straightforward. The fare for any one leg of the route is Rp18,000; for a two-leg journey (Air–Trawangan), it's Rp21,000.

Gili Air to Gili Meno Departs 8.30am & 3pm.
Gili Meno to Gili Trawangan Departs 9.50am & 4.20pm.
Gili Trawangan to Gili Meno Departs 9.30am & 4pm.
Gili Meno to Gili Air Departs 9.50am & 4.20pm.
If you wish to **charter** a boat on the islands, prices are displayed at the ticket offices.

choose carefully (see p.51 for general advice). Check at the time of booking whether the price includes equipment rental. If you're a qualified diver, expect to pay $35 per dive ($30 for second dives and discounts for five or more), $60 for Discover Scuba and a PADI Open Water course is $350; PADI Advanced Open Water course $275, Divemaster $650.

The **liveaboard** *Moana* is operated by Dream Divers to Komodo and West Papua/the Moluccas; the *Ikan Biru* is owned by Blue Marlin and operates to Komodo and the Java Sea. Prices are competitive; enquiries and reservations should be made as far in advance as possible.

Dive companies take **snorkellers** on trips for about $10. Snorkel gear is widely available for Rp25,000 per day; check it carefully before you take it. You can buy good-quality gear on the islands in the dive shops.

All divers off the Gili Islands pay a one-off **reef tax** of Rp30,000 to the Gili Eco Trust, which works to protect the reefs around the islands.

Take **safety precautions** seriously as the nearest hospital is in Mataram. In case of accidents there is a **recompression chamber** in Mataram at Jl Adi Sucipto 13B (24hr hotline ☎0370/660 0333).

Note, too, that **offshore currents** are hazardous. Dive operators are alert to this but if you're snorkelling or swimming off the beach you're at risk: it's easy to get carried out further than you intend and then be unable to get back. Never imagine that you can swim between the islands; there have been drownings.

Gili Trawangan

GILI TRAWANGAN, the largest of the islands and the furthest from the mainland, attracts the greatest number of visitors and is very developed. The southeast of the island is wall-to-wall bungalows, restaurants and dive shops, although it is still low-key and relaxing away from high season. For quieter surroundings, head further north.

Island **transport** is by cidomo; fix a price beforehand. There are **bicycles** for rent (Rp10–25,000 per hour) but quality varies. Only a tiny section of road in the southeast corner is paved, so be prepared for sandy cycling – the wider your tyres the better and a basket can be handy to save you wearing a day-pack.

A **walk** around the island, less than 3km long by 2km at the widest part, takes four hours or less. There's not much to see on the west side other than the occasional monitor lizard and giant cacti, ixorea, eucalyptus and palms. Take some water; there's a stretch of the west coast where there's nowhere to get a drink. Inland, the 100m **hill** is the compulsory expedition at sunset – follow the tracks from the southern end of the island for views of Gunung Agung, Gunung Abang and Gunung Batur on Bali, with the sky blazing behind.

Diving, snorkelling, watersports and horse-riding

The northern end of the east coast is the most popular for **snorkelling**: most people hang out here during the day, and there are plenty of restaurants nearby. Local boat captains offer **glass-bottomed boat** and snorkelling trips to sites around all three islands (10.30am–3pm; Rp60,000 per person including mask and snorkel; minimum seven people).

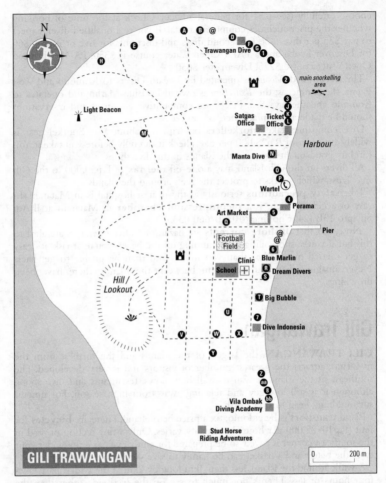

ACCOMMODATION

Alam Gili	C	Flush	F	Ozzy Homestay	D
The Beach House	aa	Gili Villas	Q	Pesona	S
Beach Wind	K	Good Heart	B	Pondok Lita	U
Big Bubble	T	Karma Kayak	E	Pondok Sederhana	V
Blue Beach Cottage	I	Kelapa Kecil	G	Sagita	J
Desa Dunia Beda	H	Kelapa Luxury		Sama-Sama	O
Dream Divers	R	Villas	M	Sirwa	L
Edy Homestay	Y	Manta Dive	N	Tir Na Nóg	Z
Emalia	P	Marta's	X	Vila Ombak	bb
		Maulana	W	Villa Almarik	A

RESTAURANTS & BARS

The Beach House	aa	Pesona	S
Blue Marlin Café	6	Recchi Living	
Coco	4	Room	3
Café Wayan		Rudy's	7
and Bakery	1	Tir Na Nóg	Z
Dream Divers	R	Warung Bu'de	8
Horizontal Lounge	2		
Karma Kayak	E		
Kikinovi	5		

Dive operators

All the operators offer **dives** for qualified divers and courses, and have their own pools for the early stages of training. They're all on the east coast so go along and have a chat to see where you feel most at home; see p.379 for information on pricing. They all offer Dive-and-Stay packages combining diving with accommodation.

Big Bubble ⊤ 0370/625020, ⓦ www
.bigbubblediving.com. Friendly place owned by
two British women. Groups are kept small so it's
easier to individualize dives to suit guests or take
advantage of quiet sites. Join them for volleyball at
the end of every afternoon on the court in front of
the dive shop.

Blue Marlin ⊤ 0370/632424, ⓦ www.diveindo
.com. British owned, offering courses up to PADI
IDC (Instructor Development Courses) and IANTD
(International Association of Nitrox and Technical
Divers) Instructor Training Course level. They have
expertise in technical diving.

Dive Indonesia ⊤ 0370/644174, ⓦ www
.diveindonesiaonline.com. Courses up to PADI
IDC; all divers are loaned dive computers to use.

Dream Divers ⊤ 0370/603 4496, ⓦ www
.dreamdivers.com. Courses up to PADI IDC. Dive
instruction offered in German and English.

Manta Dive ⊤ 0370/643649, ⓦ www.manta-dive
.com. British-owned company with highly
respected local dive-guides. Courses up to PADI
Divemaster level are on offer, and there's always
lots of Divemaster trainees around who give the
place a good buzz. They offer day-trips to the more
distant Tunang Wall with some excellent coral –
suitable for all levels of experience.

Trawangan Dive ⊤ 0370/649220, ⓦ www
.trawangandive.com. Located at the quieter north
of the island, they pride themselves on taking good
care of divers (fruit, water and towels on boats).
They cater well for all levels of experience as well
as offer technical diving and underwater photography in addition to all the usual dives and courses.

Vila Ombak Diving Academy ⊤ 0370/638531,
ⓦ www.hotelombak.com. Don't be deterred by its
location in a smart hotel – prices are the same as
elsewhere. All divers are provided with a computer
attached to their regulator.

Watersports and horse-riding

The Gili waters are just crying out for **watersports** although there isn't much
on offer. Karma Enquire at Manta Dive about windsurfing and sailing. Karma
Kayak offer guided **kayaking** trips ($20 per half-day) which are tailored to
individual levels of experience.

There's also **horse-riding** from Stud Horse Riding Adventures
(⊤ 0370/639248) who offer lessons (30min; Rp150,000) or guided riding
around the island (Rp250,000 per hour).

Accommodation

There's a great choice of attractive **accommodation**, from quality budget
places, to bungalows with hot water and air conditioning if you want a bit
more comfort, right up to top-end places such as *Vila Ombak* and *Desa Dunia
Beda*, the only hotel options. Bear in mind that we have indicated **high-
season** prices, many of which are crazy. Outside of the main rush from July
to September, prices are more than reasonable and many are slashed in half, if
not more.

More so than anywhere else on Lombok, **villas** are an increasing option. *The
Beach House* (⊤ 0370/642352; ⓦ www.beachhousegilit.com), *Gili Villas*

Biorock

The waters off the Gili Islands and Pemuteran in northern Bali (see p.346) are the
location of some Biorock installations aimed at stimulating **coral growth** in the area
and rejuvenation of the reef, following previous damage and bleaching. The
equipment consists of steel bars, plus copper wiring that is attached to electrodes.
A small current is transmitted through the wiring, crystallizing the minerals in the
seawater into limestone, the building block of reefs, on the bars. This becomes a
perfect breeding-ground for coral, which can also be stimulated by the introduction
of live coral fragments. Measurements have shown that coral growth occurs three
to five times faster than when nature is left to her own devices. For more information
on Biorock, check out the Global Coral Reef Alliance (ⓦ www.globalcoral.org).

(☎0812/376 4780 ⊛www.gilivillasindonesia.com) and *Kelapa Luxury Villas* (☎0812/375 6003, ⊛www.kelapavillas.com) are well established.

The southeast corner, known as **central**, is closest to the restaurants and parties, though many lack views and sea breezes. A lot of excellent budget places are in the village behind the main drag. Further north, beyond the boat landing area, the beach is the most attractive on the island and is the main hang-out spot during the day.

Given the local climate, gleaming new bungalows quickly fade unless they're maintained. For that reason, keep an eye out for **new places**, whether or not they're listed here: they're likely to be a good, clean bet.

The east coast

The Beach House ☎0370/642352, ⊛www .beachhousegilit.com. This restaurant in the southeast also has a huge variety of attractive rooms. Some accommodation is disabled-friendly with ramps, bars, etc. ④–⑥

Beach Wind ☎0812/376 4347, ⓔcae_ beachwind@hotmail.com. Well-priced bungalows with a hot-water option. Prices include breakfast, which, party-goers may appreciate, is available until noon. ④–⑤

Big Bubble ☎0370/625020, ⊛www .bigbubblediving.com. Well-decorated and maintained, good-value bungalows in two price-brackets in the garden behind the dive shop. All are cold-water, and a/c is an option. ③–⑤

Blue Beach Cottage ☎0819/1675 8116. Wood-and-thatch bunaglows just across the track from a lovely section of beach. The best and priciest are at the front; a/c and hot water are available. ④–⑥

Dream Divers ☎0370/603 4496, ⊛www .dreamdivers.com. Bungalows and rooms above and behind the dive shop in central, so in the heart of the action. ③–④

Flush (no phone). Two budget rooms with good verandahs in a two-storey wood-and-thatch building in a great location just behind the main snorkelling beach of the island. ③

Kelapa Kecil ☎0812/375 6003, ⊛www .kelapavillas.com. Three, tiny but well-planned rooms with all facilities and mod-cons just behind a small plunge pool in a great location behind the beach. The only rooms on the island where you can lie in bed and look out to sea. ⑥

Manta Dive ☎0370/643649, ⊛www.manta-dive .com. Behind the dive shop. Stylish wooden bungalows, with all mod-cons including hot water and a/c based loosely on a traditional Lombok rice-barn design. ④–⑥

Ozzy Homestay ☎0812/371 8039. Good-quality rooms with verandahs set in a quiet garden close to the main snorkelling area. All have cold water but there is a choice of fan or a/c. ③–⑤

Pesona ☎0370/660 7233, ⊛www.pesonaresort .com. Attractive, thoughtfully designed bungalows in a pretty garden behind the restaurant. All have TV/DVD player, a/c plus fan, hot water and verandahs with hammocks. There's a lovely pool. ⑥

Sama-Sama ☎0812/376 3650, ⊛www .thesamasama.com. Two bungalows and two larger *lumbung*-style places, all with a/c and hot water in a garden setting not far from the boat landing area. ④–⑥

Sirwa ☎0819/1724 6125. A row of small, basic bungalows, some with a/c, across the track from the main sunbathing beach – a good budget option. If they are full, consider *Sagita* (☎0812/373 1832) to the north or *Emalia* (☎0819/1713 4470) to the south. ②–③

Tir Na Nóg ☎0370/639463, ⊛www.tirnanogbar .com. Rooms in two-storey buildings behind the restaurant; all have hot water and a/c. Right in the middle of the action. ④–⑤

Vila Ombak ☎0370/642336, ⊛www .hotelombak.com. The best hotel on the island is a central, stylish place with accommodation in two-storey *lumbung* (with excellent verandahs and sitting areas) or less characterful bungalows, all with a/c and hot water. The garden is extensive and there's a good pool (Rp75,000 for nonresidents). ⑧

The village

Edy Homestay ☎0812/373 4469. Good budget choice with neat, clean rooms in a friendly compound in the village. A/c and hot water are available. Breakfast is served at any time, which should suit party-goers. Look at *Maulana* across the road if they are full. ④–⑤

🏃 **Marta's** ☎0812/372 2777, ⓔmartas_trawangan@yahoo.com.

Great-quality two-storey accommodation in the village, all with a/c and hot water, and lovely verandahs with day-beds looking onto a pretty garden with a pool. ❺
Pondok Lita ☎0370/648607. An excellent, clean budget choice in the village. Rooms, set around a

small garden, have fan and cold-water bathrooms. There's one with a/c. ❷–❹
Pondok Sederhana ☎0813/3953 6047. Excellent village choice with a row of neat, fan, cold-water bungalows in a pretty, fenced garden. ❹

The north coast

Alam Gili ☎0370/630466, ⓦwww.alamgili.com. Delightful bamboo, wood-and-thatch bunaglows in a quiet garden in the north with a tiny swimming pool. All have fan and hot water. An offshoot of the *Alam Indah* hotel in Ubud. ❻
Desa Dunia Beda ☎0370/641575, ⓦwww .desaduniabeda.com. Six gorgeous fan-cooled wooden bungalows with traditional furniture in a large garden with a stylish pool. This is the furthest-flung accommodation on the island and the only TV is in the family villa. It'll cost Rp30,000 or so for a cidomo from central. ❼
Good Heart ☎0812/376 3491, ⒺEgoodheart-trawangan@hotmail.com. Stylish wood-and-palm bungalows with a/c,

satellite TV and hot water with excellent *bale* across the track for relaxation. ❼
Karma Kayak ☎0818/0364 0538, ⓦwww .karmakayak.com. Excellent bungalows with a/c in the far north which are well-built, thoughtfully designed and in a fabulous location. A cidomo from central costs Rp15–20,000 and staff can contact drivers when necessary. ❺
Villa Almarik ☎0370/638520, ⓦwww .almarik-lombok.com. Hotel with 20 a/c and hot-water rooms in the northeast. There's a small garden and a sunbathing area across the track near the beach. The swimming pool is pretty (nonresidents can use it if they eat meals at the restaurant). ❼–❽

Eating, drinking and nightlife

The east coast is lined with **restaurants** and **bars** with the greatest concentration south of the jetty where there is a continuous line just above the beach. The quality and variety of food is excellent and prices are reasonable, with **seafood BBQs** widely available. Select your dinner from the fish that is laid out on ice; price depends on weight.

The Beach House Stylish two-storey beachside place with a large, eclectic menu of tasty sandwiches (Rp25–35,000), salads (Rp25–35,000), pasta (Rp25–30,000), Indonesian (Rp25–40,000) and Western dishes such as fish and chips (Rp40,000) and pork chop with apple sauce (Rp45,000). The drinks menu is equally vast with an enormous selection of imported booze. Their bottle shop has an excellent selection.
Blue Marlin Café At the dive shop with tables near the pool or the beach. The menu is large and food well cooked (mains around Rp45,000, baguettes or salads are Rp30-35,000). Their barbecued seafood has a lot of fans.
Café Wayan and Bakery Great for bread, croissants, cinnamon rolls and other highly calorific baked goods. There are also excellent salads Rp10–31,000, pizzas Rp29–37,000, pasta Rp29–37,000 and other European mains, up to Rp52,000. Located near the main chill-out beach, so it is excellent for daytime snacks.
🕴 **Coco** Illy coffee (Rp15–18,000), cakes including mango cheeecake, and brownies

(Rp6–15,000), salads (Rp28–30,000), baguettes (Rp25–38,000). There's even a loyalty card for addicts.
Dream Divers Attached to the dive shop, there's a wide selection of fish on display for the barbecue with side-dishes from the buffet of rice, potatoes, vegetables and salad. The rest of the huge menu is eclectic, covering Europe and Asia, all at decent prices. Mains are Rp22–45,000. There's also an Indonesian rice table (Rp80,000) for two) on offer.
Horizontal Lounge They get full marks for style as this modern bright, white place looks very different from everywhere else. The menu covers Middle Eastern, Thai, Chinese, Italian, Indian and Western options (mains Rp45–70,000). It's matched by an equally large drinks list, with lots of imported wines.
Karma Kayak A delightful spot in the far north of the island; schedule a stop here on any circumnavigation of Trawangan with excellent and imaginative tapas (Rp11–26,000). From May to mid-September, this is the prime sunset-viewing spot – come for a drink and stay for dinner.

Kikinovi A sparkly, grey-haired lady cooks up ten pots or so of mostly local food every lunchtime and sells it in the art market. You point to what you want, and pay afterwards. At time of writing that was Rp10–15,000 depending on her mood.

Pesona Excellent, surprisingly authentic Indian food with *rogan josh, dopiaza, kofta, masala, biryani* and *dosas* (Rp39–55,000). Seating by the beach or in the restaurant – *sheeshas* are available Rp90–125,000 for after dinner.

Recchi Living Room The surroundings are simple but the food is excellent and great value (mains Rp25–50,000) and covers Western (pizza, pasta, moussaka, steaks) and local options – the

chef worked in five–star hotels before seeking out the quiet island life. All is carefully and intricately prepared and presented, and the service is lovely.

Tír Na Nóg Popular Irish bar with beer, darts, movies and sport plus an ambitious menu which is great for comfort food such as Irish fry breakfast (Rp38,000), Irish casserole (Rp37,0000), bangers and mash (Rp35,000), and steak and Guinness pie (Rp40,000). The drinks list includes bottled Guinness and Irish whiskey. Outdoor *bale* all have individual TV screens and guests select their own DVDs from a vast choice.

Warung Bu'de A favourite among expat divers on the island – good, cheap eats at Rp5000 per plate in a tiny place just north of *Vila Ombak*.

Nightlife

Gili Trawangan is renowned for its high-season **parties**, and full-moon parties in the low season, which get going at about 11pm. Venues are advertised on flyers around the island: at time of writing Monday is *Blue Marlin Café*, Wednesday *Tír Na Nóg* and Friday is *Rudy's*. *Tír Na Nóg* and *Rudy's* don't close until late anyway, if they close at all, and, apart from the parties, are the late-night venues of choice. You'll be offered any and all **drugs** on the island – see p.64

Please note that, for reasons of **personal safety**, women should not leave late-night venues or parties alone.

Listings

Bus tickets Perama (daily 7am–10pm) is near the jetty and many other companies advertise shuttle tickets.

Exchange There are no ATMs. Moneychangers line the main strip but rates are better on the mainland. Dive companies offer advances on Visa and MasterCard – useful in an emergency but you will pay ten percent for this.

Internet Several places offer access (Rp400/min; minimum 5min) but connection can be slow and unreliable – it's worse in cloudy weather.

Medical The *Pak Mantra* (nurse) at the clinic is experienced with first aid and traveller's ailments

– it's best to enquire through your accommodation first as the nurse is occasionally off the island. There's also Clinic Vila Ombak, just south of the hotel of the same name (daily 8am–5pm).

Phones The wartel is open 7am–midnight.

Post There's a postal agent in the *Pasar Seni*.

Shopping Several shops sell and exchange secondhand books in European languages and there's a small art market (*Pasar Seni*) for clothes and crafts. Plenty of small shops sell everyday necessities. Beach hawkers offer pearl jewellery.

Gili Meno

GILI MENO, two kilometres long and just over a kilometre wide, is the most tranquil of the islands, with a local population of just 350 and no nightlife. It takes a couple of hours to stroll around the island, and walking and the sea are the only pastimes.

Boats arrive at the section of beach designated as the **harbour** on the east coast – you'll know you are there when you see the red handpainted sign nailed to a tree – and the boat ticket office is under the same tree. You can **change money** at two kiosks, one south of *Mallia's Child* and one further north. There's a **wartel** (daily 8am–10pm) with **Internet** access (see map), but phone lines aren't reliable and connection is slow. The Perama agent is the *Kontiki* hotel and other **shuttle–bus** tickets are widely advertised.

The **snorkelling** is good along the east coast; go in at *Royal Reef Resort* and drift down to *Kontiki* in the south. Take care as there may be boat traffic in the harbour. The other option is to start snorkelling at the yellow light beacon in the north of the island, swim left and let the current take you round to the west coast over the Meno Wall and down to the disused Bounty jetty. See p.379 for a warning about **offshore currents**. Chartering a boat allows you to venture further afield; ask on the beach (about Rp200,000 per person for a minimum of two people off Gili Meno, Rp350,000 for all three islands). Equipment is available on the island but a lot has seen (far) better days (Rp20,000 per day).

For **diving**, consult Blue Marlin Dive (☎0370/639980, ⓦwww.diveindo .com); they offer courses up to Divemaster. For **boat trips**, search out Dean (☎0813/3950 9859), one of the boat captains; he's often in front of the Blue Marlin dive shop. He'll take you out on fishing trips, to see dolphins (best in March–Aug & Nov; from Rp200,000 to Rp400,000 per person). You can charter him to Senggigi (Rp400,000 per boat, maximum four people) and to Amed in Bali (Rp550,000 per person), but see the warning on p.356.

Accommodation

Budget through to luxury **accommodation** is available, mostly spread along the east coast.

Amber House ☎0813/3757 9728, ⓔamber_house02pm@hotmail.com. Thatch-and-bamboo bungalows in a shady garden, set slightly back from the beach towards the north of the island. A quiet choice, cheaper with salt-water showers and more expensive with fresh-water showers. ❶–❸

Biru Meno ☎0813/3975 8968. At the southern end of the island just behind the beach, 10min walk from the harbour. These good-quality bungalows have great verandahs, fans and attached cold-water bathrooms. ❹–❺

Gazebo ☎ &ⓕ0370/635795. Ten bungalows with lots of dark wood and plenty of furniture set in a shady grove, with fan or a/c but no hot water. There's a pretty pool near the beach. ❺–❼

Good Heart ☎0813/3955 6976. Well-built, well-furnished *lumbung*-style accommodation with good verandahs but you'll need to climb ladders to get down to the bathroom. They are in an isolated location in the north of the island and face the garden rather than the sea. ❸

Kontiki ☎0370/632824. Close to a good beach, bungalows are tiled, with fans and attached cold-water bathrooms. There's one with a/c. ❹–❺

Mallia's Child ☎0370/622007, ⓦwww .gilimeno-mallias.com. Traditional beachside

bungalows with fine sea views from the verandahs, which are also close to the harbour. All with fan and cold water. ❸–❹

Royal Reef Resort ☎&ⓕ0370/642340. Close to the harbour, these good-quality, well-furnished bungalows, set in a large garden, have fans and good verandahs. ❹

Sunset Gecko ☎0813/5356 6774, ⓦwww. thesunsetgecko.com. Well-built, attractive wood-and-thatch accommodation in the quiet north just behind the beach and with some great views. ❶–❺

Tao' Kombo' ☎0812/372 2174, ⓔtao_kombo @yahoo.com. Set in a garden 200m behind the beach, with a large bar and communal area. Four bungalows have fans and fresh-water showers. There are also two *brugak* (open-sided sleeping platforms) with mattress, screen, mosquito net and shared bathrooms. *Brugak* ❶ Bungalows ❸

🏃 **Villa Nautilus** ☎0370/642143, ⓦwww .villanautilus.com. The most modern and stylish, light and airy rooms on any of the three islands. Five villas with front walls made of glass doors that open onto the deck and an abundance of natural materials. All have a/c and hot water. ❼

Eating and drinking

There are plenty of **places to eat** and all of the places below have fine views of the beach, of neighbouring islands and, from the east coast, across to the Lombok mainland. *Balenta* at the top of the island specializes in Sasak food

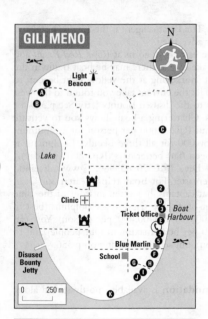

GILI MENO

Light Beacon

Lake

Clinic

Ticket Office

Boat Harbour

Blue Marlin

School

Disused Bounty Jetty

0   250 m

(Rp11–20,000), *Ya Ya* on the way north has Indonesian and Western options' while *Family* and *Jali Café* are both good choices offering the usual travellers' fare near the harbour. *Bibi's Café* attached to *Villa Nautilus* serves the best pizzas on the island (Rp35–45,000) and *Mallia's Child*, next door, is always reliable (mains Rp15–25,000). In the **evening**, *Rust Bar and Restaurant* and *Jungle Bar* at *Tao' Kombo'* is the place to hang out, with cool music and plenty of drinks.

Gili Air

Closest to the mainland, **GILI AIR** stretches about 1.5km in each direction. Atmospherically, it sits between lively Gili Trawangan and peaceful Gili Meno. It takes a couple of hours to complete a circuit on foot, and there are great views across to Sira beach on the mainland. Although accommodation is spread around most of the coast, it's concentrated in the southeast corner where the **beach** is most popular, with excellent **snorkelling**. Snorkelling gear is widely available for rent: try Ozzy Shop (Rp25,000 per day). For snorkelling further afield, **boat trips** (Rp70–75,000 per person including equipment; 9.30am–2.30pm), which take in sites off all three islands, are advertised pretty much everywhere, or ask at Ozzy Shop, or Bhalgiaz (☎0813/5357 7103) at *Gita Gili* who charges Rp350,000 per boat, or on the beach.

For **diving**, operators include Dream Divers (☎0370/634547, ⓦwww.dreamdivers.com), Manta Dive (☎0813/5305 0462, ⓦwww.manta-dive.com) and Blue Marlin (☎0370/634387, ⓦwww.diveindo.com) who have a great pool. Prices are the same as those on the other islands and all courses up to Divemaster are available on the island. They take snorkellers along on suitable dive trips (Rp25,000) but the priority is the diving so you need to be able to look after yourself.

Ozzy Shop rents **bicycles** (Rp25,000 per day) and they also sell a great little island map (Rp3000) – it's surprisingly easy to lose your bearings if you wander inland.

There's no **ATM** on the island but a few **moneychangers** near the harbour and up the east coast – rates are poor. There's a **wartel** (daily 8am–10pm) behind *Villa Karang Hotel* and another at Ozzy Shop, where there is also **Internet access** (Rp400 per min, minimum Rp4000) but connection is unreliable and often slow – it's known to be worse in cloudy weather for some unfathomable reason.

There is a **clinic** (see map) with a nurse in attendance most days (7–9am & 5–7pm) who is fine for first aid and has a limited supply of medicines. Otherwise the closest hospital is in Mataram. The **Perama office** (7am–1pm & 2–6pm; ☎0370/637816 or 0818/0527 2735) is next to *Villa Karang Hotel*. The **ticket office** for public boats is at the land end of the jetty in the harbour (see p.377 for prices). Charters from Gili Air to Senggigi are Rp400,000 one way for one to three people; enquire at your accommodation or the boat captains on the beach. There's no **post office**; take mail back to the mainland.

Accommodation

There's plenty of good-value **accommodation**. Use a cidomo to reach the more far-flung spots when you arrive with your bags; it's Rp15,000 from the harbour to *Coconut Cottages*, Rp20,000 to *Hotel Gili Air*.

▲ View from the Gili Islands towards the mainland

Abdi Fantastik ⓉⒹ0370/636421. In a fine location on the east coast; the wood-and-thatch bungalows are basic but have fans and mosquito nets, and there are sitting areas overlooking the water. ❸

🏃 **Coconut Cottages** Ⓣ0370/635365, Ⓦwww.coconuts-giliair.com. Attractive, clean and well-maintained bungalows in a huge garden haven set back from the coast. All have hot water and a/c is available. Staff are lovely, there's a great restaurant (see below) and this is the place for total relaxation. ❹–❺

Gili Air Santay Ⓣ0818/0375 8695, Ⓦwww .giliair-santay.com. Popular, good-quality traditional cottages set 100m back from the coast in a shady garden. *Brugak* (open platforms) on the beach for relaxing. ❷–❹

Gita Gili Ⓣ0813/3955 3395. Convenient for the harbour, with thatch, wood and bamboo bungalows facing the sea. All have attached cold-water bathroom and fans. ❸

Gusung Indah Ⓣ0812/378 9054. Close to the coast, with two standards of bungalows facing seawards, some with squat toilets. There are good *brugak* and an excellent bar. *Sandy*, nearby, is similar although they also have two rather fine new A-frame places at the front. ❹

Hotel Gili Air Ⓣ0370/634435, Ⓦwww.hotelgiliair .com. The most upmarket option on the island with four standards of bungalow, all with hot water and with a/c in the more expensive. The swimming pool is lovely (Rp50,000 for nonresidents or spend Rp50,000 on lunch) and the location peaceful. Look at several rooms, as the priciest aren't the nicest. Negotiate big discounts when it's quiet. ❺–❼

Lombok Indah Basic budget place with bamboo, wood-and-thatch bungalows on the northeast coast, just behind the beach, convenient for the weekly parties at nearby *Legend*. ❷

Matahari Good choice if you want total isolation on the far northwest coast. The older bungalows are showing their age but the new A-frame ones, still with fan and cold water, are clean and have great verandahs. ❸–❹

Mawar Ⓣ0813/6225 3995. Excellent budget choice with four clean bungalows a short walk from the harbour. All have fan and cold water, deep verandahs with hammocks and decent furnishings. ❷–❸

Nina Ⓣ0819/1612 6343. Bamboo, thatch and wood cottages in a neat garden just on the edge of the southeast corner. All have fan and cold water and decent verandahs. There's an excellent two-storey *lumbung* with a great balcony and sitting area downstairs. *Corner Cottages* offer similar cottages nearby. Access is through *Corner Cottages*. Cottages ❶ *Lumbung* ❺

Resota Ⓣ0859/3618 5928, Ⓔmarini_resota @yahoo.co.uk. Traditionally built bungalows with deep verandahs for relaxing. A decent budget choice, close to the harbour. ❷

Sejuk Cottages Ⓣ0370/636461, Ⓔsejukcottages @hotmail.com. Great-value, clean, thoughtfully designed and well-maintained cottages (all have cold water, the most expensive have a/c) in a shady garden behind the coast. ❹–❺

Sunrise Ⓣ & Ⓕ0370/642370. On the southeast corner. Accommodation is in two-storey *lumbung* barns with sitting areas upstairs and down. The ones at the front have good sea-views. All have cold-water attached bathrooms and fans. There are some bigger family rooms. ❸–❹

Villa Karang Hotel Ⓣ0370/637328, Ⓔvillakarang @indo.net.id. In a big compound near the harbour with several standards of accommodation; a/c and hot water are available. The ones at the front have good sea-views. ❹–❺

Eating, drinking and nightlife

There's a fine range of **restaurants**, offering good-value Indonesian, Asian and Western food. The most popular places during the day are the **bars** and **restaurants** that line the east coast; all have stunning views across to Gunung Rinjani on the mainland. Towards the south *Zipp's* and the *Chill Out Bar* just outside Dream Divers have enthusiastic regulars – and these are the spots for late-night drinking also. Moving north, the Thai food (Rp20–30,000) is highly recommended at *Gili Air Santay* although it's only one section of a vast global menu. If you are on an expedition around the island, aim for *Mirage Coffee Bar and Bakery*, a laid-back oasis in the far north with tasty home-made bread, sandwiches (Rp20–35,000), mezze including hummus (Rp45,000), brie on toast (Rp15,000) and full English breakfast (Rp35,000). This is an ideal sunset spot from June to August.

The most imaginative dining is at the *Frangipani Garden Restaurant* at *Coconut Cottages*, with seating in the main restaurant or in *brugak* in the garden. It has appetizing and well-presented Western and local cuisine as well

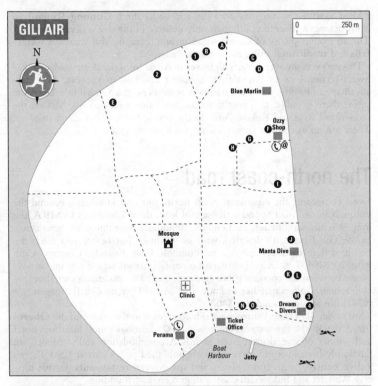

GILI AIR

N

0   250 m

Blue Marlin

Ozzy Shop

Mosque

Manta Dive

Clinic

Dream Divers

Ticket Office

Perama

Boat Harbour   Jetty

ACCOMMODATION						RESTAURANTS & BARS	
Abdi Fantastik	**F**	Hotel Gili Air	**A**	Sandy	**C**	Chill Out Bar	**4**
Coconut Cottages	**H**	Lombok Indah	**B**	Sejuk Cottages	**G**	Frangipani Garden Restaurant	**H**
Corner Cottages	**L**	Matahari	**E**	Sunrise	**M**	Gili Air Santay	**I**
Gili Air Santay	**I**	Mawar	**O**	Villa Karang		Legend	**1**
Gita Gili	**J**	Nina	**K**	Hotel	**P**	Mirage Coffee Bar and Bakery	**2**
Gusung Indah	**D**	Resota	**N**			Zipp's	**3**

as seafood. A set menu (Rp100,000 for two) needs to be ordered the day before and is a feast of **Sasak food**. Sasak buffets for ten or more people are also available.

Gili Air has weekly **parties** at *Legend* on Wednesdays during the high season. At the time of writing there were also **dark-moon parties** in February and August; enquire at your guesthouse about the current situation.

North Lombok

Dominated by the volcanic mass of Gunung Rinjani and its neighbours, the villages in **north Lombok** nestle in the foothills of the mountains or perch along the black-sand coastline.

Most tourists visit the area on a day-trip or to climb **Gunung Rinjani**, an easily arranged adventure, although only possible in the dry season (May–Oct). The area offers plenty of accommodation, and there are also attractive **water-falls** and **traditional villages** for the less energetic.

This area is easily accessible, with **buses** to Anyar from the Bertais/Mandalika/Sweta terminal or to Bayan from Labuhan Lombok in the east. The main advantage of having your own transport is to access the Sembalun valley more easily; there is public transport from the Sembalun valley to Aik Mel on the cross-island road and Kokok Putih in the north, but services aren't frequent. There are no **exchange** facilities after you leave Bangsal.

The north-coast road

From Pemenang, the coast road heads north. Just two kilometres beyond the village, a signed road opposite the school leads three kilometres to **SIRA**, the longest white-sand **beach** on Lombok. Blindingly beautiful, with views across to the Gili Islands, it's deserted, with no facilities. Just before you reach the beach, a left turn brings you to Lombok Golf Kosaido Country Club (℡0370/640137, @siregolf@mataram.wasantara.net.id), where verdant fairways gleam between the coconut palms (green fees are $80, excluding cart, shoe and club rental). Golfers may like to know that Manta Dive on Gili Trawangan (see p.381) can arrange rounds for $40.

Just under 4km from Pemenang, a side road leads to the coast and the **Oberoi** (℡0370/638444, @www.oberoihotels.com; ⑨), Lombok's most luxurious hotel and winner of several prestigious awards. Accommodation and ambience are fabulously luxurious and service superb; published prices start at $290. There's a **dive centre**, tennis court, library and **spa**. Several **restaurants** provide top-class Western and Indonesian cuisine in gorgeous surroundings.

If you can't afford this but appreciate comfort, *Medana Resort* (℡0370/628000, @http://medanaresort.com; ⑦) is about 500m before the *Oberoi*. There are six luxurious a/c bungalows with deep verandahs in a lush garden, plus a large pool. There's Internet access plus TV and DVD players, snorkelling gear, mountain bikes, a sailboat and glass-bottomed boat for rent. The beach is a few minutes' walk away.

Tanjung and around

Back on the main road, four kilometres further east, **TANJUNG** is the largest settlement around the north coast. It's an attractive town with a daily morning market of stalls overflowing with local produce.

About 4km beyond, in the small village of **GONDANG**, a sign to **Tiu Pupas waterfall** points inland, although it's further than the 4km claimed. The track is rough in a maze of confusing lanes, but the falls are glorious, tumbling 40m down a semicircular, sheer rock-face into a deep pool. However, in the dry season (May–Nov) the water reduces to a trickle and the pool becomes a muddy puddle. **Gangga waterfall**, also known as **Selelos**, is a trek for the adventurous, about an hour's walk beyond Tiu Pupas. Two kilometres east of Gondang a sign points seawards to *Pondok Pantai* (℡0812/375 2632, @www.pondok-pantai.com; ❶–❷), a delightful coastal spot almost a kilometre from the main road in a pretty garden. Accommodation is in wood, thatch and bamboo bungalows and moderately priced meals are available. It doesn't get much more peaceful than this.

About five kilometres beyond Gondang in a hamlet called **Montong Fal**, just as the road turns inland, *Pondok Nusa Tiga* (☎0819/3317 1386; ❶) comprises simple rooms with good views, and the owners provide directions for local walks taking in waterfalls, coffee and cocoa plantations and traditional villages.

The village of **TAMPES**, ten kilometres beyond Montong Fal, bursts into activity every Wednesday morning for a traditional market. It's a twisty 27km from here to Anyar.

Segenter, Anyar and around

Almost at the northern tip of the island, 4km west of Anyar, the welcoming traditional, fenced village of **SEGENTER** is 2km inland. Park just outside the gate and a guide will meet you. You'll be taken inside one of the houses to see the eating platform, stone hearth and the *inan bale*, a small house-within-a-house where newlyweds spend their first night, but which is otherwise used to store rice. At the end of the visit you'll be expected to make a **donation** to the village and sign the visitors' book.

The road from Segenter to **ANYAR** touches the coast here and there at pretty beaches lined with *jukung*, but much of it passes inland through cashew orchards with great views across the lower slopes of Gunung Rinjani.

The small village of **BAYAN**, four kilometres south of Anyar, is the site of Masjid Kuno Bayan Beleq, the **oldest mosque** on Lombok, said to be pre-1700, a kilometre east of the junction with the road to Batu Koq. You can't go in, but even from outside it's striking: a traditional bamboo-and-thatch building atop a circular stone-and-concrete citadel. Many of Lombok's more orthodox Muslims are uncomfortable that this ancient symbol of their religion is located in an area dominated by the Wetu Telu religion (see p.437). Buses from Mandalika/Bertais/Sweta and Labuhan Lombok terminate in Bayan.

East of Bayan, the road winds eight kilometres through the foothills of Gunung Rinjani, offering fine views of the volcano and soon giving way to the arid terrain of the east of Lombok. From **KOKOK PUTIH**, also known as Kalih Putih, a small junction with a few shops, buses run to the Sembalun valley, an alternative access-point for treks up Rinjani. The main road around the north coast continues for another 10km to Obel Obel and on to the east coast (see p.402).

Gunung Rinjani and around

Despite deforestation across much of Lombok, an extensive area of forest remains on the slopes of **GUNUNG RINJANI** (3726m), and stretches over 65km across the north of the island. The **climb** up Rinjani, taking in **Danau Segara Anak**, the magnificent crater-lake, measuring 8km by 6km, is the most energetic and rewarding trek on either Bali or Lombok. Climbs start from either **Senaru** or **Sembalun Lawang** depending on the itinerary – and there are plenty to choose from. If you want to reach the summit, Sembalun Lawang is the best base. If you just want to see Danau Segara Anak from the crater rim, the easiest access is from Senaru.

Batu Koq and Senaru

The small villages of **BATU KOQ** and **SENARU**, south of Bayan (about 86km from Mataram), offer cool temperatures in refreshing contrast to the

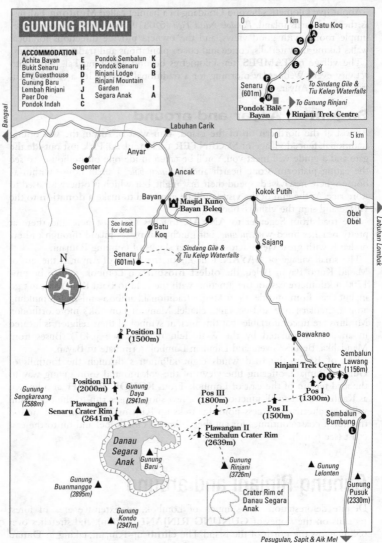

GUNUNG RINJANI

ACCOMMODATION

Achita Bayan	**E**	Pondok Sembalun	**K**
Bukit Senaru	**H**	Pondok Senaru	**G**
Emy Guesthouse	**D**	Rinjani Lodge	**B**
Gunung Baru	**F**	Rinjani Mountain	
Lembah Rinjani	**J**	Garden	
Paer Doe	**L**	Segara Anak	**I**
Pondok Indah	**C**		

Batu Koq

Senaru (601m)

To Sindang Gile & Tiu Kelep Waterfalls

To Gunung Rinjani

Pondok Bale Bayan

Rinjani Trek Centre

Bangsal

Labuhan Lombok

Labuhan Carik

Anyar

Segenter

Ancak

Bayan

Masjid Kuno Bayan Beleq

Kokok Putih

Obel Obel

See inset for detail

Batu Koq

Senaru (601m)

Sindang Gile & Tiu Kelep Waterfalls

Sajang

N

Bawaknao

Position II (1500m)

Gunung Sengkareang (2588m)

Position III (2000m)

Gunung Daya (2941m)

Plawangan I Senaru Crater Rim (2641m)

Sembalun Lawang (1156m)

Rinjani Trek Centre

Pos III (1800m)

Pos I (1300m)

Pos II (1500m)

Sembalun Bumbung

Danau Segara Anak

Gunung Baru

Plawangan II Sembalun Crater Rim (2639m)

Gunung Buanmangge (2895m)

Gunung Rinjani (3726m)

Gunung Lelonten

Gunung Pusuk (2330m)

Gunung Kondo (2947m)

Crater Rim of Danau Segara Anak

Pesugulan, Sapit & Aik Mel

north-coast heat. Both are reached by bemo (Rp10,000) or ojek (Rp15–20,000) from Bayan, a few kilometres to the north.

Just south of *Pondok Senaru*, a small path heads east to the river and **Sindang Gile waterfall** (Rp2000). It's a lovely spot and the main fall is about 25m high. **Tiu Kelep** is another waterfall a further hour beyond the first, where the water pours down in a double horseshoe shape. You should probably take a dip here; local belief is that you become a year younger every time you swim behind the falls.

It's worth visiting the **traditional village** in Senaru, a fenced compound with houses of bamboo and thatch at the end of the tarmacked road. The villagers still live a very simple life. A villager will show you around, and you'll be expected to make a donation and sign the visitors' book. For gentle exercise through the immediate area, the **Senaru Panorama Walk** (3hr) or **Rice Terraces and Waterfalls Walk** (1.5hr) are guided by local women. Ask at the Rinjani Trek Centre. Prices depend on the group size, for example, one person alone on the Senaru Panorama Walk costs Rp170,000 but Rp43,000 as one of a group of eight or more.

Accommodation

The **accommodation**, with one notable exception, is spread for several kilometres along the road through Batu Koq and Senaru. Most are basic concrete and tile with attached cold-water bathrooms often with squat toilets; breakfast may or may not be included in the price. Places on the east of the road generally have the best views towards the mountain. All will store your stuff while you climb and have small **restaurants** attached, serving simple Indonesian, Sasak and travellers' fare.

Achita Bayan Concrete-floored bungalows with mountain and garden views. Some squat and some Western toilets. ❶–❷

Bukit Senaru Well-spaced bungalows in a pleasant garden. They're bigger than many in the area, and have Western toilets. ❷

Emy Guesthouse ☏0817/575 0585. Four simple rooms within a large house. All are adequate if not plush. ❶

Gunung Baru ☏0817/572 4863. Small setup not far from the start of the trail with a few simple, tiled bungalows. ❶

Pondok Indah ☏0817/578 8018, ⊛www .lombok-rinjanitrek.com. Decent bungalows, all with deep verandahs set in a pleasant garden. The more expensive rooms are better quality and have Western toilets. ❷–❸

Pondok Senaru ☏0818/0362 4129. The biggest setup in the area, offering decent accommodation,

all set in a pretty garden, with a huge restaurant. Hot water is available. ❸–❹

Rinjani Mountain Garden ☏0818/569 730, ⓔrinjanigarden@hotmail.de. The best place to stay in the area but less accessible than the other accommodation; head past the old mosque in Bayan and at the sharp left turn in the road go straight on along a small motorable road for 4km to the village of Teres Genit. Luxury camping (all equipment provided) in a fabulous garden with great views, spotless showers (solar-heated warm water) and a swimming pool. ❸

Segara Anak ☏0817/575 4551, ⊛rinjanitrekking .com. The first place on the road from Bayan. There are fine panoramas from the verandahs of the more expensive bungalows. The same company owns *Rinjani Lodge* 50metres further up the hill with equally fine views. ❶

Sembalun Lawang and Sembalun Bumbung

Set in countryside that is unique in Lombok, **SEMBALUN LAWANG** is accessed via a steep 16km road from Kokok Putih or an equally steep, 16km road north from Sapit on the other side of the mountains. The Sembalun area is a high, flat-bottomed mountain valley surrounded by hills. The people of this area are said to be directly descended from the Majapahit dynasty of Java. There are buses between Sembalun Lawang and Aik Mel (Rp40,00) and minibuses and ojek (Rp20,000) from Kokok Putih to Sembalun Lawang.

The area is known for **handweaving** and it's possible to visit local weavers – ask in your accommodation. It's also possible to arrange the leisurely Sembalun Village Walk (4hr) and for **gentle trekking**, the Sembalun Wildflowers Walk involves one night camping and is best from May to October. Enquire at the Rinjani Trek Centre or with local trek organizers for current prices.

There are a few **places to stay** in the area. Just 200m along the path to Rinjani, *Lembah Rinjani* (☏0818/0365 2511; ❸) has clean rooms with verandahs facing Rinjani and they can provide hot water in a bucket for bathing. There's an attached restaurant. Next door, *Pondok Sembalun*

Trekking on Rinjani is not for the frail or unfit and shouldn't be attempted without adequate food and water. A guide is essential (see below) and you must **register** at the Rinjani Trek Centres at Senaru or Sembalun Lawang and pay the national park admission fee (ⓦ www.rinjaninationalpark.com; Rp50,000) when you set off.

Climbing Rinjani is something to think about before you leave home as basic **equipment** is needed; it is highly advisable to bring your own **walking boots** (Rinjani is not for those wearing trainers), a head torch that leaves your hands free and take loads of snacks and sweets even if food is provided. If you haven't got a seriously warm, windproof jacket with you, make sure you rent one. The Rinjani Trek Centres rent out radios but, increasingly, mobile telephones are being relied on as **emergency backup**; make sure one or the other are available in your party.

Routes

The shortest trek is **from Senaru** to the **crater rim**. This starts at the top of the village at 601m up through the forest via rest stops with small *bale*; **Pos II** is at 1500m and **Pos III** at 2000m; then you'll leave the forest for the steep slog up to the rim at 2641m. Most people take six to seven hours (or more to get to the rim from Senaru). If you sleep up here, there is a sheltered camp area about 30 minutes below the rim itself, allowing you to easily reach the rim the next morning for sunrise. From the rim there are classic views across Segara Anak to Gunung Baru. You can return to Senaru from here.

For a longer trek, a path (2hr) descends into the crater to **the lake**, at 2050m. It is steep and scary at the top with some metal handrails and some ropes instead of handrails, but it gets better further down. You can bathe in the lakeside hot springs.

From the lake, you can return the same way to Senaru or there's a different path (3hr; pretty steep but not as bad as previous descent) to the rim on the Sembalun side at 2639m and a site called **Plawangan II** where everyone aiming for the summit overnights. From there it's an extraordinarily steep haul up to the **summit of Rinjani** (another 3–4hr plus and 3hr back down). Try to reach the summit for sunrise; it clouds over soon after.

The shorter route to Plawangan II and then to the summit is to climb **from Sembalun Lawang** on the northeast side of the mountain, starting on the track next to the Rinjani Trek Centre. It takes seven to eight hours to Plawangan II and you attack the summit the next morning.

The most complete exploration of the mountain involves a **round trip**; the **recommended route** is to ascend from Sembalun Lawang, taking in the summit, then the lake and descending to Senaru – this has the advantage of getting the most exhausting ascent over while you are fresh and enabling you to soak tired muscles in the hot springs at the lakeside afterwards. This takes four days and three nights.

Even more extensive trips, up to six days and five nights in length, taking in the summit and exploring the caves around the lake are available from some operators.

(ⓣ 0852/3956 1340; ❶) has four simple, thatched rooms but no Rinjani views and a telephone mast in front.

South of the village is a patchwork of fields and vegetable gardens before the valley closes in, the mountain walls rising steeply on all sides. Some 4km south of Sembalun Lawang is **SEMBALUN BUMBUNG**, an attractive village with houses clustered around the mosque in the shadows of the surrounding mountains. At the far southern end of the village, *Paer Doe* (ⓣ 0852/3977 8818; ❶) is a tiny **homestay** with four basic rooms in a pretty garden just opposite the football field. There are great views of the local mountains from the garden.

Rinjani trips

If you want to put your trek together **independently**, it is perfectly possible to arrange a guide (Rp100,000 per day) and porters (Rp60,000) at the Rinjani Trek Centres (guides and porters should all be licensed). You can also rent equipment at the trek centres and you'll need to buy your own food and food for the porter and guide.

There are a multitude of **trek organizers** in Senggigi, Senaru and Sembalun Lawang. They all offer a similar selection of all-inclusive climbs: to the crater rim from Senaru (two days, one night), to the rim and then down to the lake from Senaru (two nights/three days), the shortest route to the summit and then the lake to and from Sembalun Lawang (three days, two nights) and the longer version (four days, three nights) heading up from Sembalun and then back down via the lake and crater rim to Senaru.

The number of **organizers/agencies** offering all-inclusive treks is utterly bewildering as is the range of prices quoted, which at the end of the day depend on your bargaining ability. Be warned that everyone you speak to will flourish a piece of paper stating "Published prices" under your nose – you should still bargain. Prices depend on the trek and the size of the group but should include guide, porters, equipment (including sleeping bags and tents) and meals. Transport should be included in treks arranged in Senggigi, as should return transport if you are doing a round trip.

Questions to ask

- What exactly is and is not included in the price?
- How many porters and guides are included (you don't want to have to carry your stuff out of guilt about the size of the load the poor old porter is weighed down with)?
- What are they planning on feeding you?
- Will the person you are talking to (and presumably like and trust) be going with you?
- Will your group be part of a larger group or going independently?

If time is limited you'll arrange the trek in Senggigi or even on the Internet before you arrive on the island but it is inevitably cheaper in Senaru or Sembalun Lawang. Typically **published prices** in Senaru or Sembalun for one person on the four day/three night summit and lake trek are Rp2,300,000 down to Rp1,500,000 for the two day/one night crater-rim trip, while in a party of two the prices are Rp1,400,000 down to Rp900,000 per person and in a party of three or more Rp1,175,00 per person down to Rp823,000.

Trekking organizers

In **Senggigi** check out John's Adventures (ⓦwww.lombok-rinjanitrek.com in Bidy Tours Office), Rinjani Trekking Club (ⓣ0370/693202, ⓦwww.info2lombok.com) and Planet Senggigi Internet (ⓣ0370/693921), all on the main street, also driver Made (ⓣ0370/667 9679 or 0812/372 5415), who is also a registered trekking guide.

In **Senaru** check out the Rinani Trek Centre and other local organizers; in **Sembalun,** the Rinjani Trek Centre and *Lembah Rinjani* (ⓣ0818/0365 2511).

From Sembalun Bumbung, the mountain road winds for 15km across Gunung Pusuk to Pesugulan, the turn-off for Sapit, Swela and on to Pringgabaya or Aik Mel on the cross-island road. This road is prone to closure due to landslides; check on its status before heading out. There's **public transport** on this route and also via Kokok Putih from Bayan and from Labuhan Lombok to the valley.

It is possible to arrange one-way **charters** from the valley (Rp150,000 to Labuhan Lombok and Rp300–350,000 to most other Lombok destinations) at *Lembah Rinjani* (see above).

Climbing Gunung Rinjani

The **summit of Gunung Rinjani** is reached by relatively few trekkers; the majority are satisfied with a shorter, less arduous trip to the **crater rim**. From here there are fabulous views of the turquoise crater-lake, **Danau Segara Anak** (Child of the Sea), and the perfect cone of **Gunung Baru** (New Mountain) rising from it. It is also possible to descend to the lakeside and ease aching muscles in scalding **hot springs**. The lake is considered to be the abode of the gods, and Wetu Telu pilgrims come on nights of the full moon while Balinese Hindus make offerings to the lake during the Pekelem festival (during the full moon of the fifth Balinese month).

Having lain dormant since 1906, Gunung Baru **erupted** in August 1994, closing the mountain for several weeks. Gunung Rinjani itself has been inactive since 1901, apart from a few periodic puffs of smoke. However, the mountain should be treated with respect, and its weather is notoriously unpredictable.

Central Lombok

The broad corridor of **central Lombok** occupies the middle of the island from the west to east coast between Gunung Rinjani to the north and a range of lower hills to the south. This is the densely populated agricultural heartland of the island.

Stretching for 74km from Ampenan–Mataram–Cakranegara–Sweta to Labuhan Lombok, the main highway on the island passes close to many of the most attractive destinations such as the pretty villages of **Tetebatu** and **Sapit** in the foothills, **Lendang Nangka** on the plains where travellers can experience a real homestay, and the cultural and religious sights at **Narmada**, **Pura Lingsar** and **Suranadi**. The craft villages dotted throughout the area offer the chance to see potters and weavers at work.

Well served by **bemos and buses**, much of the centre is accessible without your own transport. Note that there are very few exchange facilities east of Sweta.

Narmada and around

The small market town of **NARMADA** is 7km east of Sweta and served by frequent bemos from the Bertais/Mandalika/Sweta terminal. The attraction here is the gardens of **Taman Narmada** (daily 7.30am–5.30pm; Rp5000, swimming Rp3300), very popular with local families, especially at weekends. Built in 1805 by the raja of Mataram, Anak Gede Karangasem, it includes a replica of Gunung Rinjani and its crater lake, made for the raja when he became too old to climb the real volcano to make his offering to the gods. More cynical commentators claim that he built the lake to lure local women to bathe while he watched from his pavilion. The grounds are extensive, and there's a swimming pool. The Balinese temple here, **Pura Kalasa**, is the focus of the celebration of Pujawali (usually in Nov or Dec), when offerings of ducks are made to the lake.

The aqueduct at the side of the lake is one of the few remnants of Dutch occupation on the island. If you use a local guide to show you round, Rp20,000 is a reasonable fee – agree it beforehand.

The gardens lie on the south side of the main road opposite the bemo terminal and daily market.

Pura Lingsar

A few kilometres northwest of Narmada and easily reached by bemo, **Pura Lingsar** (daily 7am–6pm; admission by donation) was built around 1714 and rebuilt in 1874. Local guides will approach you; Rp15,000–20,000 is a fair price. The temple is used by Hindus as well as the Muslim Wetu Telu (see p.437). The furthest north, and highest, courtyard is the Hindu one guarded by fierce monsters at the *candi bentar*, while the Wetu Telu area has a pond overlooked by a vivid statue of Wisnu, home to well-fed eels, which emerge for hard-boiled eggs brought by devotees. The Pujawali festival is also celebrated here (Nov or Dec), and is followed by a mock battle between Hindus and Muslims throwing *ketupat* (rice wrapped in leaves) at each other.

Few tourists stay, but there is **accommodation**. About 1.5km west of the turning to the temple on the back road from Narmada to Cakranegara *Puri Lingsar Bungalows* (℡0370/671652; ❶) has basic bungalows offering fan, attached bathroom and deep verandahs in an attractive garden – the best ones are furthest from the road. Some 500m beyond the turning to the temple, *Losmen Ida* (℡0817/570 3220; ❶) has tiled rooms with fan and attached *mandi* and squat toilet.

Suranadi

Situated about 300m above sea level, **SURANADI** is seven kilometres north of Narmada at the site of a freshwater spring. The temple, **Pura Suranadi**, is a pilgrimage site for Hindus as the saint Nirartha is believed to have located the springs while in a trance. Almost next to the temple is a small forest area, **Hutan Wisata Suranadi**, which is a reasonable picnic spot.

Suranadi Hotel (℡0370/636411; ❸–❹) has **accommodation** overlooking the swimming pool (nonresidents Rp8000). The more expensive bungalows, with hot water, are the best value. The **restaurant** near the pool offers a small Indo-Chinese menu (mains Rp15–30,000).

Seseot and around

With your own transport, the attractive village of **SESEOT** is accessible from Suranadi. Head up the road past the Hutan Wisata Suranadi, turn right at the T-junction and continue uphill. After about 5km you'll reach Seseot, whose location next to the river is the main attraction. There are plenty of places for a quiet picnic beside the river – either follow the path beside the mosque down to the river or cross the road bridge at the top of the village to the other side. Bemos also run to Seseot from Narmada. A kilometre further on, the forest at **AIK NYET** is another attractive destination.

For an altogether different atmosphere, the *GEC Rinjani Country Club* (℡0370/633488, ⓦwww.lombokgolf.com; ❻–❼), also known as *Padang Golf*, sits about a kilometre from the main cross-island road at **Golong** (there's a sign at Sedau, 5km east of Narmada). There's accommodation with hot water and a/c and there are tennis courts, a spa and a large swimming pool (Rp10,000 for nonresidents). This is one of two 18-hole **golf courses** on the island. Green fees are $40 during the week, $70 at weekends excluding caddy fees and equipment rental.

Benang Stokel

If you fancy a little light trekking, head to the waterfalls at **BENANG STOKEL**, north of the main cross-island road at Pancordau. It's three kilometres to the village of Terutak where you'll register and pay admission (Rp2000) and negotiate a guide (Rp40,000) who will lead you through the local rice terraces with fine views of Rinjani, for about half an hour. It's a quiet spot that gets few visitors. You can stand under the wide and impressive falls and head another 500 metres to the Benang Kelambu falls, which are even bigger and more dramatic.

Tetebatu and around

TETEBATU is situated on the southern slopes of Gunung Rinjani, 50km from Sweta (11km north of the main cross-island road), with stunning views of the volcano across terraced fields lush with rice in the rainy season and tobacco in the dry; the area is dotted with the tall drying towers for the tobacco. At an altitude of 400m, the area is cool but not cold and it's excellent for a few days' relaxation or as a base from which to explore the centre of the island.

On public transport, get off the **bemo** or **bus** at Pomotong on the main road and either take a bemo (Rp10,000) or an ojek (Rp15,000) to Tetebatu. Alternatively, you can reach Tetebatu by **Perama charter** from Mataram (ⓦwww .peramatour.com; Rp90,000 per person, minimum two people).

From Tetebatu, you can explore nearby waterfalls and craft villages: the *Green Orry* and *Pondok Tetebatu* (see below) rent motorcycles (Rp50,000 per day self-drive or Rp80,000 with driver) or vehicle charters (Rp300,000–350,000 per day including driver and petrol). Guides for local treks can be arranged at all the accommodation – the most usual trek is through the local monkey forest to Jukut Waterfall (Rp75,000–100,000 per person for 4–6hr) or there are shorter two-hour treks closer to home (Rp50,000 per person). **Charter transport** to other Lombok destinations is widely available (Rp300–400,000 depending on distance).

It isn't easy to change money locally and at the time of writing there was no public **telephone** or **Internet** access.

Accommodation and eating

Accommodation is on the main road to *Wisma Soedjono* from Kotaraja and the road to the east, Waterfall Street. It's all basic (all have cold-water bathrooms unless stated) and functional but adequate. Most have **restaurants** attached and

there are a couple of other eating options; *Bale Bale Cafe* and *Salabuse* are on the main road. The menus feature Indo-Chinese and travellers' fare, plus some Sasak options (main courses Rp12–30,000). The best views are from the restaurants at *Cendrawasih* and *Hakiki*.

Cendrawasih ☎0828/364 6158. Attractive *lumbung*-style barns in a lush garden on Waterfall Street. ❷

Green Orry ☎0376/632233, ℱ632255. More than 20 tiled, clean bungalows in a cosy compound on Waterfall Street. ❸

Hakiki ☎0818/0373 7407. In the middle of paddy-fields at the eastern end of Waterfall Street, two-storey traditional *lumbung* with excellent verandahs. Some squat toilets and some Western toilets. ❶–❷

Pondok Bulan ☎0376/632581. Tiny place on Waterfall Street with three basic tiled bungalows. ❶

Pondok Tetebatu ☎0819/1771 6445. Small but clean, tiled rooms in two rows facing across a small garden with welcoming staff. ❶

Wisma Soedjono ☎0828/370 1750, ℮neni-benny @yahoo.co.id. The home of Dr Soedjono, the first doctor in eastern Lombok, occupies extensive grounds at the top of the village. There's a range of accommodation and this is the most upmarket option in the area, and the only place with hot water. There's also a swimming pool. ❶–❸

Jukut and Joben waterfalls

With your own transport you can follow the road east from Tetebatu to **Kembang Kuning**, from where it's six kilometres to **Jukut waterfall** (Rp20,000, parking Rp1000). To reach it, you need to walk the last couple of kilometres along a steep path with little shade. The water falls 20m into a circular pool surrounded by towering walls covered in undergrowth. It's cool and shady nearby. Enquire locally about the advisability of going alone, as robberies have been reported here. If you want to get here via footpaths from Tetebatu, you'll need a guide. From Kembang Kunung, a seven-kilometre back road leads to Lendang Nangka.

Northwest of Tetebatu, **Joben waterfall**, also known as Otak Kokok Gading, is much less dramatic. The water falls only a short distance and is fed into an open-air shower block. It's believed locally, however, that this is a sacred place and that the water will turn cloudy if you're ill.

Kotaraja, Loyok and Rungkang

The bustling village of **KOTARAJA** lies 5km south of Tetebatu. The name means "City of Kings", referring to ancient times when the kingdom of Langko fell to Balinese invaders and the royal family fled here. The area is known for its blacksmiths, but you'll have to ask for directions and come early to see them at work.

A centre for bamboo basketware, **LOYOK** is just a few kilometres south of Kotaraja. Several workshops sell an excellent range of local goods including bags, lamps and boxes, and even the children plait basketware as they walk along the road.

Pottery is produced at **RUNGKANG**, just east of Loyok. Arrive early in the workshops to see the pots being moulded over stones and beaten into shape with a flat stick. Made from the local grey clay, the pots turn an attractive mottled orange-black colour when fired, and are surprisingly light.

Lendang Nangka and beyond

Developed as a tourist destination by retired teacher Haji Radiah, **LENDANG NANGKA** is a farming community four kilometres north of the main cross-island road, and served by cidomo and ojek (Rp5000) from Bagik Bontong. Although the scenery is not as picturesque as Tetebatu, the village is welcoming and this is a great place to experience village life and to practise your Indonesian or Sasak. There's a wealth of walks through the ricefields around the village, and visitors get a map with suggestions for local excursions.

Established in 1983, *H.Radiah's* (T0819/1577 0442; ❷ full board) is a **homestay** in the middle of the village, tucked away behind the school, so ask for directions. You can stay in rooms in the original family compound or in larger, newer rooms in a house nearby with other family members. It's great to be part of a household and have the rare opportunity of meeting Sasak women in their home environment. Many visitors enjoy an afternoon walk with owner Radiah. Sannah, Radiah's wife, cooks traditional Sasak food and she's used to visitors in the kitchen.

Penakak and around

Further east, the hamlet of **PENAKAK** lies just off the main road, 1.5km east of the domes, spires and minarets of the mosque, Masjid Al-Jami Al-Akbar, on the main cross-island road in the centre of **Masbagik**. The turning is signed from the west. Penakak is one of the three main pottery villages on Lombok, and the road through the village is lined with potteries. The range of goods produced is enormous; the potteries will ship goods overseas.

Pringgasela and Timbanuh

Some 5km north of **Rempung** on the cross-island road is the local weaving centre of **PRINGGASELA**. Local women make both *songket* and *ikat* cloth on simple backstrap looms (see p.458 for more), and there are plenty of workshops in the village. Access to Pringgasela is from Rempung by ojek or cidomo. For an excursion well off the beaten track, if you have your own transport, the road up to **Timbanuh**, 8km north of Pringgasela via Pengadangan, ascends to the foothills of Rinjani through coffee, banana and rambutan plantations. It's a picturesque trip to the road-end on a ridge with spellbinding views across to Sumbawa.

Sapit

Situated at 1400m on the southern slopes of Gunung Pusuk, the small village of **SAPIT** is a quiet retreat with wonderful views down to the east coast. It's 16km from Sembalun Lawang (2–3hr by daily bus; Rp10,000) but public transport depends on road conditions; it is prone to landslides and blocking. It's the same distance from the cross-island road, either via Aik Mel or Pringgabaya (Rp10,000 from either on bemo but they are more frequent from Aik Mel). There's **accommodation** at ⚘ *Hati Suci* (T0370/636545, Wwww.hatisuci.tk; ❷) and nearby *Balelangga* (same contact; ❶–❷) which are both run by the same family; they have simple bungalows in lovely gardens with great views to the coast and Sumbawa. Each has a small **restaurant** offering a basic menu (mains Rp17–20,000), and staff will direct you for walks to waterfalls and the monkey forest and, for the hardy, the 15km trek across to the Sembalun valley (see p.393).

From Sapit the **mountain road** climbs 11.5km up along a forested ridge to the pass, surrounded by towering peaks and with great views back towards Sapit and ahead down to Sembalun Bumbung in the valley below (see p.394). There are ojek from Sapit to the Sembalun valley (Rp20–25,000).

East Lombok

With an arid climate, sparse population and few facilities, not many visitors linger in **east Lombok** although if you're heading to or from Sumbawa you'll pass through the small port of **Labuhan Lombok**. While there's little to detain you for long, the accommodation near **Labuhan Pandan** offers total relaxation and the opportunity for trips to the uninhabited islands off the coast.

Labuhan Lombok and around

LABUHAN LOMBOK, 75km east of Mataram, is possibly the least interesting town in Lombok, although its near-circular bay is attractive. Boats to Sumbawa depart from the **ferry terminal**, Labuhan Kayangan, a long 3.5 kilometres around the south side of the bay; take a local bemo (Rp3000) or ojek (Rp5000). **Kayangan Hill**, on the south side of the bay, has good views inland and across to Sumbawa.

Buses run along the cross-island road between Bertais/Mandalika/Sweta terminal and Labuhan Lombok with some continuing on to the ferry terminal (Rp25,000). Travelling between Labuhan Lombok and Kuta involves changing first at Kopang, on the main road, and then again at Praya.

A decent **place to stay** is *Hotel Melati Lima Tiga*, Jl Kayangan 14 (☎0376/23316; ❶), about 150m from the town centre on the road to the ferry terminal. The rooms are a bit box-like and lack fans but are adequate, although bathrooms, with *mandi* and squat toilet, are shared. There are **warung** nearby. There's a **wartel** at *Hotel Melati Lima Tiga* and, if you head to the main road and turn left, the **post office** is 100m along on the right. There's a local **Perama office** on the coast side of the road to the harbour (☎0376/292 4534 and 0813/3991 1345).

North of Labuhan Lombok

Travelling north from Labuhan Lombok, the scenery quickly becomes parched and villages are few and far between. The best time to see the area round to Obel Obel is at the end of the rainy season in April/May when it greens up a bit. The towering mahogany trees 5km from Labuhan Lombok are welcome shade and are widely believed to be the largest such specimens in Lombok.

Labuhan Pandan and the islands

In the area of **LABUHAN PANDAN**, 13km north of Labuhan Lombok, look out for **Pantai Pulo Lampu** beach at Transat – popular at weekends but

---

Moving on to Sumbawa

The **ferry to Sumbawa** departs Labuhan Lombok around the clock (every 40mins; Rp12,500, bicycle Rp19,500, motorbike from Rp32,000, cars from Rp251,500) and takes ninety minutes to two hours to reach Poto Tano on Sumbawa's northwest coast, a few kilometres from the main road across the island. Alternatively, you can book **long-distance bus** tickets from Bertais/Mandalika/Sweta terminal through to destinations on Sumbawa (see p.356).

6

LOMBOK AND THE GILI ISLANDS | East Lombok • Labuhan Lombok and around

401

otherwise peaceful. Bemos (Rp5000; charter Rp30,000 per vehicle) and ojek (Rp15–20,000) run here from Labuhan Lombok and the port. The only **accommodation** is at *Pondok Gili Lampu* (☎0818/0363 7405; ●), which has basic wood-and-thatch bunaglows in a garden behind the beach. It is possible to organize boat trips here to the islands for snorkelling (bring your own gear), fishing or sightseeing (from Rp300,000 per boat for a maximum of 6 people) or camping (from Rp300,000 for two people for one night all inclusive).

There are two groups of **islands** off the northeast Lombok coast. The most southerly are **Gili Petangan** and its satellites, Gili Lampu, Gili Kondo and Gili Bidara, which have beaches as well as coral walls and attract many varieties of fish; further north are the larger islands **Gili Sulat** and **Gili Lawang**, surrounded by coastal mangrove, without any beaches but with a large array of offshore coral. All are uninhabited and preserved from buildings by a government ban, although some boat trips from Lombok east to Sumbawa and Flores use them for camping.

Sambelia and around

Just north of Labuhan Pandan, the village of **SAMBELIA** is a traditional settlement of Bugis people who originate from Sumbawa, with some wooden houses built on stilts – although they're gradually being replaced by concrete and brick dwellings. The views of Gili Sulat and Gili Lawang from here around to **BELANTING** are enticing across the Sungian Strait.

Moving north around the coast the road twists and turns through the hills for 33km from Sambelia to Kokok Putih via **OBEL OBEL**, a tiny oasis among the folds of the barren hills. From Kokok Putih a road branches south to Sembalun Lawang (see p.393) and the coast road continues west to Bayan (see p.391).

South Lombok

The largely undeveloped **south coast** of Lombok is extraordinarily beautiful, with mile upon mile of picturesque bays of pure white sand separated by rocky headlands. Known to surfers for several years, **Kuta** is a low-key development and from here you can explore the fabulous coastline west and east. **The far east of the southeast peninsula** is well off the beaten track, and realistically only accessible with private transport. If you're restricted to public transport, you can still reach the inland villages specializing in pottery, weaving and carving, such as **Sukarara**, **Penujak** and **Senanti**, and the traditional villages of **Sade** and **Rembitan**.

The new **Lombok International Airport** near Praya, due to be opened in 2010, is linked with resort development in the south and it looks likely that the whole region will change out of all recognition in the near future.

The issue of **safety for tourists** in the south of Lombok periodically gains a high profile. The overwhelming majority of people have a great trip with no problems and increased security on the beaches has helped. Ask in Kuta about the current situation. It is always worth taking a local person with you as a driver or passenger – they know the area well.

Celebrated on Lombok and the more distant islands of Sumba and Savu, this annual festival centres around the seaworm, *eunice viridis*, known locally as *nale* or **nyale**. The worms live attached to rocks in the ocean, but at roughly the same time every year, on the 19th day of the tenth Sasak month (February to March), they begin their sexual cycle and release brightly coloured male and female sexual parts, which rise to the surface ready for fertilization, turning the ocean into a seething mass of fluorescent spaghetti. The number of worms is believed to indicate the success of the next rice harvest, and it is estimated that around 100,000 people travel to the south coast of Lombok at this time to gather the worms (they are believed to be aphrodisiacs either grilled or raw) and to enjoy traditional singing, dancing, poetry and a re-enactment of the *Putri Nyale* or *Mandalika* legend. This tells how a beautiful princess, distraught because of the number of suitors who were fighting over her hand in marriage and loath to upset any by refusing them and risk plunging her country into war, flung herself into the sea where her hair was changed into *nyale* seaworms.

Nyale is celebrated in Kuta and some of the villages on the southeast peninsula and the shores of Awang Bay.

Praya and the craft villages

The pleasant market town and transport hub of **PRAYA**, 22km southeast of Sweta, is accessible by **bus** from Bertais/Mandalika/Sweta terminal. With the bus terminal three kilometres northwest of the centre, most visitors bypass the town completely and there's little reason to linger. However, there are international **ATMs** in the town centre. If you need a **place to eat**, *Ria*, opposite the banks on Jalan Jend Sudirman, on the west corner of a shopping centre, is inexpensive and famed in southern Lombok for goat sate, which appears on the menu as *nasi gudeg* – you'll get a plate of rice, sate and sauce, and a bowl of mutton soup (about Rp20,000 for a meal including soft drink). However, there are also plenty of vegetarian options.

South and west of Praya

On the road to Selong Blanak, **PENUJAK**, 6km southwest of Praya, is one of the three major pottery villages on Lombok. There are plenty of workshops on and behind the main road and there's a sign for the Lombok Crafts Project just south of the large bridge across the river. Ceramics in a variety of designs and patterns are available, in all shapes and sizes, up to 1m tall, and you can watch the potters at work if you come early in the day.

Directly west of Praya the village of **SUKARARA** produces the widest range of textiles on Lombok including highly coloured *songket* cloth using backstrap looms and *ikat* cloth using foot looms (see p.458). The subtle *ikat* shades are produced by vegetable dyes from indigo, spinach, betel nut, pineapple, tamarind, saffron, jasmine root and bay leaves. Children begin learning from the age of seven to master the huge number of designs, which they weave from memory. Local girls must be skilled weavers in order to be considered marriageable; men only weave using foot looms. A sarong and scarf set can take up to five months to weave. Patuh Art Shop (Ⓦ www.lombokexotic.com/patuh_artshop.htm) sells an enormous range of textiles from the local co-operative. Bargaining is vital but *songket* tablecloths (you'll start bargaining at Rp350,000), *ikat* bedspreads

(Rp850,000) and the most intricate of *songket* sarong and scarf sets (Rp4.5million) are all available. You can get dressed up in local costume for a souvenir photograph and you can ask for someone (ask for Billy) to take you on a walk through the village to see the earlier stages of the process and explain some of the motifs in the weaving (Rp15–20,000 tip is appreciated).

East of Praya

East of Praya, the main road across the south of the island heads to Gubukdalam, and most of the **villages** of interest are near it. With bemos plying the route, access to most is straightforward.

Turning south at **Ganti**, 16km east of Praya the road heads to the coastal village of **BATU NAMPAR** on Awang Bay where people make their living from fishing and seaweed cultivation; see p.162 for an alternative route to the bay. It's a rough road and tourists are a rarity but the views of the bay are excellent: you can see across to Ekas on the southeast peninsula. Local brides and grooms sail around the rock called **Linus**, just off the shore, as part of the wedding ceremony.

East of Ganti

Back on the main road, 6km east of Ganti at Longkhang, a signed turning leads for several kilometres to the village of **Senanti** where woodcarving is the speciality and workshops create a large variety of carvings big and small. One common one shows three figures climbing on top of each other. Legend tells how three brothers were hunting in the forest. One of them, Doyan Medaran, was waiting for his brothers beside a deer that he had killed when a giant appeared. Doyan Medaran was so frightened that he climbed up a massive tree to hide from the giant who, after devouring the deer, disappeared into the forest. Doyan Medaran remained stuck in the tree until his brothers came along and rescued him by climbing on to each others' shoulders.

Known for its canoe-making, the village of **KERUAK**, another 4km east, has workshops east of the village in the hamlet of Batu Rimpang, south of the road to Tanjung Luar. Hand tools are used to create dugout canoes from vast tree trunks.

The right turn to **TANJUNG LUAR** is just under 6km east of Keruak, from where it's a couple of kilometres to this attractive fishing village with

Making salt

On parts of the Lombok coast and on Bali, at Kusamba and Amed, you'll see the salt beds and piles of salt that are evidence of one of the most backbreaking occupations on the islands – **salt-making**. Vast quantities of salt water are hauled from the sea in buckets and poured into specially dug ponds, close to the shore. When the water has evaporated, the salty, sandy residue is placed in hollowed-out palm-tree trunks and mixed with more seawater. The water becomes saturated with salt and the thick brine is poured off and evaporated to form salt crystals. You may see large bamboo baskets suspended from frames at salt-making sites: the liquid from the wet salt crystals, which contains soluble impurities, drips down a string hanging from the baskets, leaving pure salt crystals behind.

The rainy season halts salt production and high tides can flood the salt pools. A typical family can make around 25kg of salt a day, but salt is cheap to buy and many former salt-producing areas are now turning to seaweed farming as a more lucrative way of earning a living.

Bugis houses built on stilts and a harbour packed full of boats. You can watch cormorants diving for fish and admire the great views around the wide sweep of the coastline.

Kuta and around

The only tourist development on the south coast is **KUTA**, 54km from Mataram and 32km from Praya, a tiny fishing village situated behind a sweeping, white-sand beach. It's ideal for a few quiet days by the sea and especially suitable if you like wild coastal scenery and turbulent surf. The beach is framed by rocky headlands, and **Seger** and **Tanjung Aan** beaches are within walking or cycling distance. Apart from the Sunday and Wednesday **markets**, the area is extremely quiet.

Kuta has local **surf** breaks but is also an excellent base to explore the rest of the south coast. Most of the bays west of Kuta, from Mawun to Blongas, are glorious for sightseeing although the surf can be erratic. East of Kuta there are breaks off the coast of the southeast peninsula near **Serewe**, inside the southern headlands of the stunningly lovely **Awang Bay**, also known as Ekas Bay, and **Gumbang Bay**, also called Grupuk Bay, a short drive from Kuta. You can charter boats from Gerupuk and Awang or base yourself at Ekas.

Coming from the west, **buses** run to Praya from the Bertais/Mandalika/ Sweta terminal. From Praya, bemos run either to Sengkol, where you can change, or right through to Kuta. From the east of Lombok, bemos run to Praya via Kopang on the main cross-island road. Perama offer **tourist charters** to Kuta from Lembar or Mataram (Rp90,000 per person, minimum two people).

Kuta days revolve around the beach or pool. The small row of **shops** on the road behind the beach sell crafts and clothing; *Prabu Bagus* in the village is also good for crafts. You can hire **surf boards** at *Mimpi Manis* and Kimen Surf in the village (Rp20,000 per day) and arrange **fishing** trips from *Mimpi Manis* (Rp250,000 for 3 hrs, Rp600,000 all day) – they'll grill your catch for dinner. For something totally different **horse-riding** is available (℡0819/3316 2226, ⓦwww.horseridingkuta.canalblog.com; Rp300,000 per hour).

The only **diving** operator in the area, Dive Zone (℡0370/660 3205, ⓦwww .divezone-lombok.com) at *Novotel Lombok*, know of sites for all levels of experience. Dive/accommodation packages are available.

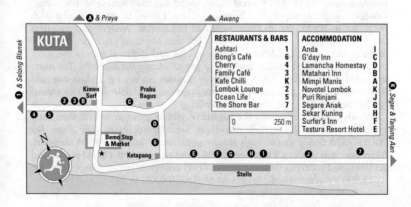

KUTA

▲ Ⓐ & Praya   ▲ Awang

Ⓐ & Selong Blanak

Kimen Surf   Prabu Bagus

Bemo Stop & Market

Ketapang

Stalls

RESTAURANTS & BARS	
Ashtari	1
Bong's Café	6
Cherry	4
Family Café	3
Kafe Chilli	K
Lombok Lounge	2
Ocean Life	5
The Shore Bar	7

ACCOMMODATION	
Anda	I
G'day Inn	C
Lamancha Homestay	D
Matahari Inn	B
Mimpi Manis	A
Novotel Lombok	K
Puri Rinjani	J
Segare Anak	G
Sekar Kuning	H
Surfer's Inn	F
Tastura Resort Hotel	E

0   250 m

Ⓦ Seger & Tanjung Aan

Accommodation

Kuta's **accommodation** covers all price ranges. The main road runs just inland from the beach and accommodation is spread for about 500m on the far side of the road, so don't expect cottages on the beach. There are also places in the village.

Anda ⊕0370/654836. Clean, tiled budget rooms set in a shady garden. A/c is available. ❷

G'day Inn ⊕0370/655342. Five well-kept rooms with attached cold-water bathrooms in a friendly family compound in the village. ❶

Lamancha Homestay ⊕ & ⊕0370/655186. Family place in the village, a short walk from the beach, comprising three rooms with attached *mandi* and squat toilet. ❶

Matahari Inn ⊕0370/655000, ⊜mas_ully @yahoo.com. A big selection of rooms in a lush garden; hot water and a/c is available and top-end villas are huge. Considerable effort has been made with decor and decoration. ❸–❺

Mimpi Manis ⊕081/836 9950, ⊛www .mimpimanis.com. Just over 1.5km north of the beach on the way to Sade, this spotless place is run by a Balinese–English family. Choose between a/c or fan rooms or a two-storey house. There are DVD players, an extensive selection of films and safety boxes. ❶–❷

Novotel Lombok ⊕0370/653333, ⊛www .novotel-lombok.com. Stunningly located 3km east of Kuta on Seger beach, accommodation is in low-rise buildings or bungalows in lovely grounds with four pools. All rooms have garden rather than ocean views and you'll pay more for an outside verandah. The top-end villas are glorious. It's a fairly isolated spot, but there are several bars and restaurants, a business centre, dive centre, plenty of organized activities and a spa. ❼–❾

Puri Rinjani ⊕0370/654849, ⊕654852. Clean rooms in a big garden; hot water and a/c are available. ❷–❹

Segare Anak ⊕0370/654846, ⊛www .kutalombok.com. This long-standing favourite has a big choice of rooms, some with a/c but all with cold water, set in a lovely garden with a dinky pool. Safe deposit boxes are available. ❶–❸

Sekar Kuning ⊕0370/654856. Clean, cold-water, fan rooms in a small garden. ❶

Surfer's Inn ⊕0370/655582, ⊛www .lombok-surfersinn.com. A big choice of good-quality rooms ranged around a pretty pool; hot water and a/c are available and all have verandahs. Appealing for surfers and landlubbers alike. ❷–❺

Tastura Resort Hotel ⊕0370/655540, ⊜tastura@mataram.wasantara.net.id. Bungalows in a huge garden with a pool. All rooms have a/c, hot water and deep verandahs. You can negotiate big discounts when it is quiet. ❺–❼

Eating, drinking and entertainment

All Kuta's losmen have **restaurants** but there are plenty of other eating options. The most brilliant place to eat is *Ashtari* (8.30am–6pm), at the top of the hill on the road west from Kuta – the views are spectacular, the food is excellent and the small vegetarian menu of sandwiches, salads and Indonesian dishes (mains around Rp18,000) is great value. Along the road west from the village, *Lombok Lounge*, *Family Café*, *Cherry* and *Ocean Life* are all pretty similar with mains up to Rp35,000 on their menus of Indonesian, Western and traveller's fare featuring plenty of seafood. *Bong's Café* is in the same price range but the menu is vast, taking in Mexican, German, Thai and Italian alongside the more usual choices; the food is fine and you've got to admire the ambition. For more upmarket dining, *Kafe Chilli* at *Novotel Lombok* serves up Indonesian and Western dishes with pizza and pasta featuring strongly (Rp50–70,000 for mains) just behind the beach in elegant surroundings.

Nobody comes to Kuta for the **nightlife**, which is just as well, as there isn't any, although you'll find live music on Saturday nights in *The Shore Bar* (⊕0817/575 5653) in the high season until about 2am; free local transport. Alternatively, if you've a TV in your hotel room you can rent a DVD player (and get unlimited access to their exhaustive DVD collection) from *Mimpi Manis* for Rp25,000 a night (refundable deposit of Rp250,000).

▲ The south coast near Kuta

Listings

Books Big secondhand book selection at *Mimpi Manis*.

Changing money *Anda* and *Surfer's Inn* change money.

Charter transport Ask at your accommodation. Costs depend on your itinerary and most people use charters for one-way drops; Rp200,000 to Mataram/the airport, Rp250,000 to Senggigi, Rp300,000 to Bangsal. Motorcycles are available at *Mimpi Manis* at Rp35–50,000 per day, but there's no insurance in Kuta. Decent bicycles cost Rp25,000 per day from *Mimpi Manis*.

Internet access Available in *Ketapang*, *Anda* and *Segare Anak* (Rp4–500/min).

Phones No public phone access.

Post *Segare Anak* is a postal agent and you can use them for poste restante; get mail addressed to you at Segare Anak, Kuta Beach, Lombok Tengah, Nusa Tenggara Barat 83573. The nearest post office is in Sengkol.

Shuttle bus tickets *Segare Anak* (☎0370/654846) are Perama agents.

Inland from Kuta

The traditional village of **SADE**, 6km north of Kuta on the Sengkol road, sees hordes of visitors (admission by donation). Guides (tip expected, Rp10–15,000) explain all the delights, such as the buffalo-dung foundations of the houses. The *lumbung* barns and traditional houses are picturesque and faithfully preserved, but it feels a bit like a theme park and you'll be asked to buy things or to take photographs of people – all at a price.

Just up the road, 1km to the north, **REMBITAN** also welcomes visitors but seems less artificial. Rembitan is regarded by some as having the oldest mosque on the island (although Bayan in the north is more widely accepted to have that honour; see p.391). Some years ago, there was a big fire near the mosque. It did not burn, however, and children later reported having seen figures clad in white surrounding and protecting the building. The belief in the mystical properties of the mosque grew, and when the roof was repaired many local people took part of the old one as protection for their homes. One of the Nine Walis believed to have brought Islam to Indonesia is supposedly buried close to Rembitan at **MAKAM NYATO**, and on Wednesdays pilgrims visit the grave, shaded by frangipani and banyan trees.

There are a couple of **batik workshops** on the road between Sade and Rembitan. At Rembitan Sasak Art Gallery (☎0817/579 5883; 8am–6pm), you can see the process and courses are also available. The variety of images includes characters from the *Ramayana*, primitive motifs, traditional scenes and modern designs. Prices range from Rp150,000 for the small pieces up to Rp750,000 for the biggest – you need to bargain.

West of Kuta

The coast **west of Kuta** has some of the loveliest beaches on the island. You'll need your own transport and be prepared for a leisurely trip and some wrong turnings. The road deteriorates further west; check the state it's in before setting off.

The road west out of Kuta climbs for a couple of kilometres. The views from the *Ashtari* restaurant at the top of the hill back across the entire Kuta area is one of the most dramatic in southern Lombok.

Some 6km out of Kuta you'll pass the "MTR 64" road marker (indicating 64km to Mataram). Just under 1km west of this, look out for a dirt track heading off to the coast. After 2km, it reaches the coastal village of **ARE GOLENG**. The beach here is about 400m long, and a tiny island, **Gili Nungsa**, sits out in the bay.

The next beach west is **Mawun** (cars Rp4000, motorbikes Rp2000), 9km from Kuta and reached by a two-hundred-metre-long sealed road a couple of hundred metres beyond the "MTR 66" marker. The bay is enclosed by rocky headlands, with the water fading from turquoise to a vibrant blue. There are usually a few hawkers plying their wares.

A kilometre further west, the main road reaches the gently curving **Tampa** beach backed by flat scrub, and there isn't much shade – but it's pretty deserted.

Access to the beach at **Mawi**, about 3km west of Tampa, takes persistence. Take the next sealed road branching off seaward (if you reach the "MTR 75" marker, you've gone too far). It's more than three kilometres on a rapidly deteriorating track to the white-sand beach (cars Rp2000), a favourite with surfers, and separated from nearby **Rowok** by a rocky outcrop. From here there are great views plus the impressive sight of Gili Lawang offshore – three pinnacles rising sheer out of the ocean.

Selong Blanak and around

Back on the road, after three kilometres you reach the beach at **SELONG BLANAK**, 15km from Kuta, also accessible via Penujak from Praya (24km). It is a fabulous curving beach a couple of kilometres long with superb views west along the coast, and it's popular with local people. For a more peaceful location, the two beaches visible to the west are **Tomangomang**, nearest to Selong Blanak, and **Serangan**, both accessible by tracks.

From Selong Blanak, the road west to Pengantap curves 18km inland and is an adventure. It climbs up steeply into the coastal hills through mahogany and teak stands with fine views of the surrounding countryside. After about three kilometres it splits at the tiny village of **Keling**. The right fork leads north to Penujak while the left fork continues on westwards through tiny hamlets of bamboo-and-thatch houses, reaching the village of **Montong Sapah** after another 6km. The road deteriorates further west but there are some fabulous panoramas. Another 9km brings you to the village of **PENGANGTAP**, a row of thatched houses just behind the beach. The turquoise shallows are filled with the frames for seaweed farming and the harvest dries on the beach. From Pengangtap, the road again curves away from the coast, arriving at **SEPI** after 5km, another tiny coastal hamlet, which is served by bemos from Lembar via Sekotong, and by trucks east to Keling. From Sepi, you can continue 1km west to **BLONGAS BAY**, where there's isolated accommodation only accessible by boat, at *The Lodge @ Belongas Bay* (☎0370/645974, ⓦwww .thelodge-lombok.com; ❻) located just behind the beach, with fans and hot water, but booking is most efficient through Dive Zone. Dive Zone (☎0370/660 3205, ⓦwww.divezone-lombokcom) offer diving in this area although the most famous sites, the Cathedral and the Magnet, require significant levels of competence as conditions can be difficult. Dive/accommodation packages are available.

The "road" marked on several maps west to Teluk Mekaki was, in early 2008, no more than a rough, impassable track but government plans to improve roads in the area may change the situation. Inquire locally.

Alternatively, follow the steep road that climbs northwards from Sepi through the coastal hills. The road gradually improves, the density of population increases and, after 11km, you reach Sekotong where you can turn west to Bangko Bangko or north to Lembar.

East of Kuta

Easily accessible from Kuta and, at a push, walkable if you have no transport (bicycles are a good idea) the white-sand beaches of **Seger** and **Tanjung Aan** are picture-postcard perfect. Seger is closest to Kuta (1km) and the location of *Novotel Lombok*. Tanjung Aan, 5km from Kuta, comprises two smaller beaches, **Aan** to the west and **Pedau** to the east, separated by a rocky outcrop, Batu Kotak. As their popularity has grown, the beaches now host hawkers and public toilets but few other facilities.

Past Tanjung Aan, the small fishing village of **GERUPUK**, just under 8km from Kuta, perches on the western shores of Gumbang Bay. **Lobster** and seaweed (see p.162 for information on seaweed farming) are the main sources of income. *Gerupuk Surf Bungalows, Lakuen* (☎0817/470 4161, ⓦwww .lakuen.net; ❻) are behind the beach at the end of the road in from Kuta and good-quality bungalows are ranged around a pretty pool; there's a surf school and spa. Next door, the *Surfer's Café* is on the edge of the beach and catches a great breeze.

From Gerupuk, you can look across the huge bay to **BUMBANG** on the eastern shore, and you can rent a boat for sightseeing in the bay (Rp100,000 per boat for two hours) and snorkelling gear is also available to rent. The more adventurous can charter a boat around to Ekas from here (Rp500,000 for a day-trip), which takes at least ninety minutes each way. Inquire on the beach.

The thriving fishing village of **AWANG**, 16km east of Kuta, is well worth the trip to see **Awang Bay**, a massive inlet, also known as Ekas Bay, 10km long and 8km wide in parts. As the road descends into the village, you'll spot the island of Linus, just off Batu Nampar at the northern end of the bay,

Ekas across on the southeast peninsula, and see all the way south to the open sea. You can charter boats from Awang to Ekas, an easier option than tackling the rough roads (Rp250,000 return). An international harbour is under construction so the **beach** is hardly pristine, but the views are great. Contact local captain Alex Taurus (℡0819/740 4115), for snorkelling trips in the bay (Rp350,000 per day for two people) but you must bring your own equipment. Alternative access to Awang is via a better-quality road from Mujur east of Praya.

⑥ The southeast peninsula

Lombok's isolated **southeast peninsula** is as far off the beaten track as it is possible to get on Lombok. Travel isn't easy but the coastal views, especially the startling scenery of Awang Bay, make it worthwhile if you have your own transport – it isn't feasible on public transport. The road to the peninsula leaves the southern main road at **SEPAPAN**, about 500m west of Keruak, and is signposted to "Jerowaru, Tanjung Ringgit, Kaliantan and *Heaven on the Planet*". Fill up with fuel at the nearby petrol station and bear in mind that travel is slow, as the road surface deteriorates the further south you go.

The first village is **JEROWARU**, where the road splits – turn right at the southern end of the village, 4km from the main road. The landscape is arid, with glimpses of the east coast as the road completes a dogleg around it. To continue south, turn left after another 1.5km at the Masjid Al-Muntaha mosque in the village of Tutuk. Carry on south to the village of Pemongkang and head on through it. South of the village, 5km from the turn by the mosque, there's a major junction. The sign points straight on to Kaliantan, Tanjung Ringgit and Pantai Cemara and right to Ekas and Pantai Surga.

Following the Ekas road, after another 7.5km, *Heaven on the Planet* (℡0812/370 5393, ⓦwww.heavenontheplanet.co.nz; ⑨ all inclusive including some activities), the only accommodation on the peninsula, is signed off the main road – it is just over two kilometres along a steep, rutted and rocky track to the clifftop with footpaths to two local beaches. There's a wide range of choices, from small bungalows with outside bathroom through larger, better equipped ones with remarkable views up to *Reef Palace*, the most luxurious place with views that must be seen to be believed. *Ocean Heaven* is nearby on the coast with bungalows just behind the beach in a coconut grove. Booking is essential, transport is included from elsewhere on Lombok and there's a minimum two-night stay. Access is only by boat from Awang in the rainy season and more comfortable by that route at any time. Snorkelling equipment is provided and diving is available. The local dive-site is Walls of Heaven, an underwater cliff dropping sheer to 50m. Motorbikes are available for rent and tours are available. Nearby, at the tiny village of **EKAS**, just behind the shoreline, people make their living from fishing and seaweed farming. Irregular **bemos** link Ekas and the main road at Sepapan.

It's another six kilometres down to the southern tip of the peninsula at **SEREWE**, a tiny fishing and seaweed-farming village. The scenery doesn't compare with the grand panorama you get from *Heaven on the Planet*.

Taking the other fork back at Pemongang, the road to **TANJUNG RINGGIT**, the southeastern tip of Lombok, is long and rough, and you'll need to check en route to be sure of finding the right turning – consider renting a boat from Tanjung Luar on the east coast rather than driving. Tanjung Ringgit is reputed to be a magical place, with large caves believed to be the home of a demon. There is some startling coastal scenery and a few World War II canons dotted around, but the long trek back the way you've come is the only option at the end of the day.

Travel details

Buses and bemos

It's impossible to give the frequency with which bemos and public buses run: see Basics, p.36, for details. Journey times given are the minimum you can expect. Only direct bemo and bus routes are listed.

Ampenan to: Senggigi (20min).
Bayan to: Bertais/Mandalika/Sweta terminal (2hr 30min); Pemenang (2hr); Senaru (20min).
Bertais/Mandalika/Sweta terminal to: Bayan (for Gunung Rinjani; 2hr 30min); Bima (Sumbawa; 12hr); Denpasar (Bali; 6–8hr); Dompu (Sumbawa; 10hr); Jakarta (Java; 2D/2N); Labuanbajo (Flores; 24hr); Labuhan Lombok (2hr); Lembar (30min); Medan (4D/4N); Padang (Sumatra; 4D/3N); Pemenang (for the Gili Islands; 1hr); Pomotong (for Tetebatu; 1hr 15min); Praya (for Kuta; 30min); Ruteng (Flores; 36hr); Sape (Sumbawa; 14hr); Sumbawa Besar (Sumbawa; 6hr); Surabaya (Java; 20hr); Yogyakarta (Java; 22hr).
Kuta to: Praya (1hr); Sengkol (30min).
Labuhan Lombok to: Bayan (2hr); Bertais/Mandalika/Sweta terminal (2hr); Kopang (for Praya; 1hr); Sembalun Lawang (2hr 30min).
Lembar to: Bertais/Mandalika/Sweta terminal (30min); Sekotong (1hr); Selegang (3hr); Tawun (2hr); Tembowong (2hr 30min).
Pemenang to: Bayan (2hr); Bertais/Mandalika/Sweta terminal (1hr 30min).
Praya to: Bertais/Mandalika/Sweta terminal (30min); Gubukdalam (1hr 30min); Kuta (1hr).
Sapit to: Aik Mel (1hr); Pringgabaya (1hr); Sembalun Lawang (2hr).
Sembalun Lawang to: Kokok Putih (1hr); Aik Mel (2hr).
Senggigi to: Ampenan (20min).

Perama shuttle buses – using the public ferry

Gili Islands to: Candi Dasa (Bali; daily; 7hr 30min–8hr); Kuta, Bali/Ngurah Rai Airport (Bali; daily; 10hr); Lovina (Bali; daily; 12hr; min 2 people);

Padang Bai (Bali; daily; 6hr 30min–7hr); Sanur (Bali; daily; 10hr); Senggigi (daily; 3hr); Ubud (Bali; daily; 8hr).
Mataram to: Bangsal (daily; 2hr; min 2 people); Candi Dasa (Bali; daily; 5hr 30min–6hr); Kuta, Bali/Ngurah Rai Airport (Bali; daily; 8hr 30min); Kuta, Lombok (2 daily; 2hr; min 2 people); Lovina (Bali; daily; 10hr; min 2 people); Padang Bai (Bali; daily; 4hr 30min–5hr); Sanur (Bali; daily; 8hr); Senggigi (daily; 30min; min 2 people); Tetebatu (2 daily; 2hr; min 2 people); Ubud (Bali; daily; 8hr).
Senggigi to: Bangsal (daily; 2hr; min 2 people); Candi Dasa (Bali; daily; 5hr 30min–6hr); Kuta, Bali/Ngurah Rai Airport (Bali; daily; 8hr 30min); Kuta, Lombok (2 daily; 2hr; min 2 people); Padang Bai (Bali; daily; 4hr 30min–5hr); Sanur (Bali; daily; 8hr); Senggigi (daily; 30min; min 2 people); Tetebatu (2 daily; 2hr; min 2 people); Ubud (Bali; daily; 8hr).

Perama shuttle boat

Senggigi to: Padang Bai (Bali; daily; 5–6hr); Gili Islands (daily; 2hr).

Pelni ferries

Lembar Fortnightly services to: KM *Awu*: Ende (Flores; 32hr); Kalabahi (Alor; 57hr); Kupang (Timor; 44hr); Lewoleba (Lembata; 64hr); Makassar (Sulawesi; 95hr); Maumere (Flores; 72hr); Nunukan (Kalimantan; 6D+20hr); Parepare (Sulawesi; 4D+18hr); Tarakan (Kalimantan; 6D+12hr); Waingapu (Sumba; 24hr).
KM *Tilongkabila*: Baubau (Sulawesi; 61hr); Benoa (Bali; 4hr); Bima (Flores; 15hr); Bitung (Sulawesi; 4D+20hr); Kendari (Sulawesi; 3D+1hr); Kolonedale (Sulawesi; 3D+20hr); Labuanbajo (Flores; 24hr); Luwuk (Sulawesi; 4D+1hr); Makassar (Sulawesi; 37hr); Raha (Sulawesi; 66hr).

Other ferries

Bangsal to: Gili Islands (several times daily; 20–45min).
Gili Air to: Bangsal (daily; 20min); Gili Meno (daily; 20min); Gili Trawangan (daily; 40min).

Gili Meno to: Bangsal (daily; 30min); Gili Air (daily; 20min); Gili Trawangan (daily; 20min).

Gili Trawangan to: Bangsal (daily; 45min); Gili Air (daily; 40min); Gili Meno (daily; 20min).

Labuhan Lombok to: Poto Tano (Sumbawa; every 40min; 1hr 30min).

Lembar to: Padang Bai (Bali; every 90min; 4hr–4hr 30min).

Planes

Selaparang Airport (Mataram) to: Denpasar (Bali; 12 daily; 30min); Jakarta (Java; daily; 3hr); Singapore (6 weekly; 2hr 30min); Surabaya (Java; 4 daily; 50min); Yogyakarta (Java; daily; 1hr 15min).

Contexts

Contexts

History

T wo tiny islands, Bali and Lombok have been buffeted by powerful empires throughout history, and their fortunes have often been tied to those of their larger neighbours, Java and Sumbawa. More recently the islands have been subsumed in the fate of the vast Indonesian archipelago. Relations between Bali and Lombok have often been turbulent, and the origins of their present cultural, religious and economic differences are firmly rooted in past events.

Beginnings

Homo erectus, a distant ancestor of modern man, arrived in Indonesia around half a million years ago during the **Ice Ages**. At this time glaciers advanced from the polar regions and the levels of the oceans fell exposing **land bridges** between the islands and the land masses of Southeast Asia and Australia. Homo erectus moved across these land bridges into and through Indonesia. The fossilized bones of "Java Man" from this period were found in Central Java and stone axes and adzes have been discovered on Bali.

Homo sapiens appeared around 40,000 years ago and were cave-dwelling hunter-gatherers whose rock paintings have been found in the far east of the archipelago. The **Neolithic** era, around 3000 BC, is marked by the appearance of more sophisticated stone tools, agricultural techniques and basic pottery. Remains from this period have been found at Cekik, in the far west of Bali.

From the seventh or eighth centuries BC, the **Bronze Age** spread south from southern China. Famed for bronze casting, decorated drums have been found throughout the Indonesian archipelago. The most famous example in Bali, and the largest drum found anywhere in Southeast Asia, is the **Moon of Pejeng**. It is nearly 2m wide and housed in a temple just east of Ubud. **Stone sarcophagi** from this period are on display in the Bali Museum in Denpasar and the Museum Arkeologi in Pejeng.

Early traders and empires

From at least 200 BC, **trade** was a feature of life across the archipelago. The earliest written records in Bali, metal inscriptions or *prasasti* dating from the ninth century AD, reveal significant Buddhist and Hindu influence from the Indian subcontinent, shown also by the statues, bronzes and rock-cut caves at Gunung Kawi and Goa Gajah.

The most famous event in early Balinese history occurred towards the end of the tenth century when a princess of East Java, Princess **Mahendratta**, married the Balinese king **Udayana**. Their marriage portrait is believed to be depicted in a stone in the Pura Tegeh Koripan near Kintamani. Their son, **Erlangga**, born around 991 AD, later brought the two realms together until his death in 1049.

In the following centuries, control of Bali was won by the Javanese and then wrested back by Balinese rulers. By 1300 Bali was being ruled domestically, by **King Bedaulu**, based in the Pejeng district, east of Ubud.

Little is known of the ancient history of **Lombok**, although it is known that the kingdom of Selaparang controlled an area in the east of the island for a period.

The Majapahit

One of the most significant dates in Balinese history is 1343 AD, when the island was colonized by **Gajah Mada**, the prime minister of the powerful Hindu **Majapahit** kingdom of East Java. Establishing a court at Samprangan in eastern Bali, the first Majapahit ruler of Bali was **Sri Dalem Kapakisan**. They introduced a caste system to the island and Balinese who did not accept this established their own villages. Their descendants, known as the **Bali Aga** or *Bali Mula*, the "original Balinese", still live in separate villages, such as Tenganan near Candi Dasa and Trunyan on the shores of Danau Batur, and adhere to ancient traditions.

Kapakisan was succeeded by his son, **Dewa Ketut Ngulesir**, who set up his court in **Gelgel**, in east Bali. Throughout the fifteenth century, Islam gained influence on Java and when the Majapahit fell in 1515, many of its Hindu followers – priests, craftsmen, soldiers, nobles and artists – fled east to Bali, flooding the island with **Javanese cultural ideas** and reaffirming Hindu practices.

Given the huge influence of **Islam** at this time, it is unclear why the faith did not spread to Bali, especially as it moved further east to Lombok, Sulawesi and Maluku. It could be that Islam spread along trade routes: with poor harbours and few resources, Bali was largely bypassed and the tide of Islam swept east, although there are small Muslim communities on the island.

An ancient text detailing the history of the Majapahit dynasty lists **Lombok** as part of its empire, and the villages in the Sembalun valley on the eastern flanks of Gunung Rinjani consider themselves directly descended from the Majapahit dynasty, claiming that the brother of a Majapahit raja is buried in the valley.

Bali's Golden Age

Dewa Ketut Ngulesir was succeeded by his eldest son, **Batu Renggong**, who became king, or **dewa agung** (literally meaning "great god"), in 1550 and the title of *dewa agung* continued through succeeding generations until the twentieth century. During Batu Renggong's reign the Gelgel kingdom ruled an empire from Blambangan in Java in the west to Sumbawa in the east. This period coincided with a cultural renaissance in Bali and, as a result, is often referred to as the **Golden Age**. The Javanese Hindu priest **Nirartha** achieved a great following on Bali at this time.

Eventually, the glory faded and other kingdoms within Bali rose to prominence, most notably **Gianyar** under Dewa Manggis Kuning in the seventeenth century.

Foreigners and trade

Lacking the spices of the eastern isles, Bali appears not to have been in the mainstream of the archipelago's early trading history. The **Chinese** visited Bali, which they knew as Paoli or Rice Island, in the seventh century, but by this time trade had been established on nearby islands for a thousand years. Bali became known to **Europeans** at the end of the fifteenth century when Portuguese, Spanish and English explorers came in search of the lucrative Spice Islands. They marked Bali on their maps as Balle, Ilha Bale or Java Minor, but rarely stopped, although Sir Francis Drake is reported to have visited in 1580.

The first documented contact between Europeans and the Balinese occurred in the sixteenth century. The **Portuguese**, having won the race for the Spice Islands, turned their eyes towards Bali, and in 1588 dispatched a ship from

Malacca, aiming to construct a fort and trading post on the island. The ship hit a reef just off Bali and sank with huge loss of life. The survivors were treated kindly by the *dewa agung* but not permitted to leave the island. Portuguese attempts at establishing contact were not repeated.

On February 9, 1597, four **Dutch** ships under the command of Commodore Cornelius Houtman anchored off Bali and three sailors landed at Kuta including Aernoudt Lintgens, whose report of his experiences is the first account by a Westerner of the island. The other two crew members were so entranced that they did not return to the ship.

The Dutch came again in 1601, when Cornelis Heemskerk arrived with a letter from the prince of Holland requesting **formal trade relations**, which the *dewa agung* accepted. The VOC, or **Dutch East India Company**, was formed in 1602, and its headquarters founded in Batavia (modern-day Jakarta) in 1619, from where the Dutch trading empire expanded as far as Sumatra, Borneo, Makassar and the Moluccas.

From then until the beginning of the nineteenth century, European eyes were on the far larger islands of the archipelago and Bali was largely ignored, as it produced little of interest to them. The exception was **slaves**, who were sold through Kuta to Dutch merchants from Batavia and French merchants from Mauritius.

The situation in Lombok

During the seventeenth century, the west of Lombok was invaded by the **Balinese** from Karangasem in the far east of Bali, and the **Makassarese** of Sulawesi, who had conquered Sumbawa in 1618 and invaded the east of the island. The first major conflicts between the two invaders occurred in 1677 when the Balinese, assisted by the indigenous **Sasak** aristocracy, defeated the Makassarese.

From the end of the seventeenth to the mid-nineteenth century, the Balinese struggled to secure control over Lombok. In 1775, **Gusti Wayan Tegah**, who had been placed on the throne by the raja of Karangasem, died, and disagreements over the succession resulted in four rival principalities in the west vying for control: Pagasangan, Pagutan, Mataram and Cakranegara. Meanwhile the Sasak aristocracy in the east of the island faced little interference in their affairs.

Eventually, in 1838, the raja of Mataram, **Ratu Agung K'tut**, triumphed over the other principalities and also brought the east of Lombok under his control. He also further expanded his kingdom by providing four thousand troops to support the Dutch in their fight against Karangasem in eastern Bali. This ensured the defeat of the ruling dynasty in Karangasem and, in payment for his help, the Dutch gave him the right to put his own nominee on the throne.

European turmoil and Dutch interest

Conflicts in Europe at the turn of the nineteenth century had massive repercussions in Bali. In 1795, **French** troops under Napoleon conquered the Netherlands, thus acquiring **Dutch** possessions overseas. The Dutch colonies in Southeast Asia were placed under the control of a governor-general appointed by Napoleon. This governor was subsequently defeated by the **British**, who had their own interests in the area, and the British Lieutenant-Governor of Java, **Sir Thomas Stamford Raffles**, administered the region. However, British rule was short-lived. Napoleon was defeated at Waterloo in 1815 and, as part of the peace settlement, the Indies were returned to the Dutch.

Dutch incursions

By the mid-1830s, the Dutch interest in Bali had intensified. The Danish trader **Mads Lange** had set up a trading post in Kuta supplying rice, which both Bali and Lombok produced to excess, to British-held Singapore. The Dutch evolved a plan to start trading with Bali, with the aim of gaining political control before the British. In 1839 they established an agent in Kuta with the agreement of the raja of Badung. In 1840, the Dutch envoy, **Huskus Koopman**, began a series of visits with the aim of eventually gaining Dutch sovereignty over the island.

The Dutch also wanted to abolish Balinese *tawan karang* or reef rights, which had been a long-term grievance. The Balinese had always asserted their right to goods salvaged from shipping wrecked on the island's reefs, much of which was

▲ 19th-century photo of the prince of Buleleng, with his daughter

Dutch. The plundering of the Dutch vessel *Overijssel*, wrecked on the Kuta reef on July 19, 1841, particularly outraged the Dutch.

By 1843, Koopman, a skilled operator, had made **treaties** with the kingdoms of Badung, Klungkung, Buleleng, Karangasem and Tabanan, agreeing to a Dutch trade monopoly. The rajas failed to realize that they had also given the Dutch sovereignty over their lands and surrendered reef rights. Following Koopman's retirement, a new commissioner arrived in 1844 to finalize the treaties, but it soon became apparent that there were huge differences in Dutch and Balinese understandings. Most kingdoms did ratify the treaties, but **Buleleng** and **Karangasem** stood firm. A further Dutch mission came the following year, including a military officer whose brief was to assess the Buleleng defences. At a meeting in Singaraja in May 1845, Gusti Ketut Jelantik, brother of the rajas of Buleleng and Karangasem, stated, "Not by a mere scrap of paper shall any man become the master of another's lands. Rather let the kris decide."

Dutch military victory

On June 26, 1846, the **First Dutch Military Expedition** arrived off the Buleleng coast with 3500 men and issued an ultimatum to the raja of Buleleng to comply with all the Dutch demands. On June 28, the military force landed and marched into Singaraja. The rajas of Buleleng and Karangasem came to Singaraja to negotiate and eventually signed a surrender, agreeing to Dutch sovereignty and to paying costs for the victor's military expedition.

The Dutch departed, believing they had achieved their objectives, and left behind a small garrison until the compensation was paid. However, this fitted in with Jelantik's plan, and he continued to prepare for future battle. Meanwhile, nothing was paid to the Dutch, and ships that foundered continued to be plundered by the Balinese. On March 7, 1848, the governor-general of the Dutch East Indies sent ultimatums to Buleleng, Karangasem and Klungkung demanding compensation, payment of war debts, the destruction of defence works and, in the case of Buleleng, the delivery of Jelantik to them. The ultimatums were ignored, and the **Second Dutch Military Expedition** arrived off the northern coast at Sangsit on June 8, 1848, with almost three thousand troops. Having quickly overcome the defences on the coast, the well-armed force marched towards **Jagaraga** where Jelantik had organized his army of around 16,000, armed largely with kris and lances. The Dutch were eventually put to flight, at a cost of around two hundred dead and wounded. The Balinese suffered over two thousand casualties but on June 10, 1848, the Dutch sailed back to Batavia.

The following year, in the **Third Dutch Military Expedition**, the Dutch used almost their entire military force in the Indies to overcome the Balinese. Around seven thousand troops landed in Buleleng on April 4, 1849. Negotiations failed and on April 15, the Dutch attacked the fortress at Jagaraga and defeated the Balinese with the loss of only about thirty men to the Balinese thousands. Jelantik and the rajas of Buleleng and Karangasem fled east. With four thousand additional troops from Lombok, the Dutch attacked Karangasem first. On their arrival at the palace on May 20, the raja of Karangasem, Gusti Gde Ngurah Karangasem, his family, and followers, all committed **puputan** (ritual suicide). The raja of Buleleng, accompanied by Jelantik, fled to the mountains of Seraya, where they were killed in further fighting.

Dutch troops then headed west towards Semarapura where the *dewa agung* signed an **agreement** on July 13, 1849. The Balinese recognized Dutch sovereignty and accepted that *tawan karang* was prohibited, and in return the Dutch agreed to leave the rajas to administer their kingdoms and not to base garrisons on the island. A feast on July 15 sealed the agreement.

The strengthening of the Dutch position

Initially, the Dutch left matters pretty much alone. They regarded themselves as having sovereignty over the whole island but largely left the kingdoms of the south and the east alone, basing themselves in the north. During the 1850s they strengthened their hold and placed Dutch controllers over the rajas of Buleleng and Jembrana.

From their administrative capital in **Singaraja**, the Dutch made some improvements to irrigation, planted coffee as a cash crop and outlawed slavery and the tradition of *suttee*, whereby widows would throw themselves on the funeral pyres of their dead husbands. They also quelled **local rebellions**, such as the 1864 uprising in the village of Banjar, close to modern-day Lovina.

Meanwhile, with the Dutch concentrated in the north, the kingdoms of Klungkung, Badung, Gianyar, Mengwi, Bangli and Tabanan in the south were weakened by internal conflicts and fighting with each other. They increasingly turned to the Dutch for protection from their neighbours.

Rebellion and the Dutch in Lombok

In Lombok, meanwhile, Ratu Agung K'tut continued to rule. The **west** of the island was relatively harmonious, but in the **east** the frustrated Sasak aristocracy deeply resented their Balinese masters and there were failed rebellions in 1855 and 1871. In 1872, Ratu Agung K'tut was succeeded by his younger brother, **Ratu Agung Ngurah**.

The **rebellion of 1891** was more successful. For many years, Ratu Agung Ngurah had vied with the *dewa agung* of the Balinese kingdom of Klungkung over claims to the title of Supreme Ruler of Bali. In 1891, he decided to take action, but his demand for several thousand Sasak troops was met with resistance in **Praya**, and a local Sasak aristocrat was executed. On August 7, 1891, several thousand Sasaks surrounded and burned the palace of the Balinese district chief and rebellion spread quickly. By September 22, 1891, Balinese rule had been overthrown throughout East Lombok.

Hostilities between the Balinese and the Sasak aristocracy dragged on for years, gains being made and then lost, until mid-1894, when the Dutch army landed in West Lombok.

On the night of August 25, 1894, Balinese forces attacked the Dutch camp in the **Mayura Palace** at Cakranegara, where around nine hundred soldiers were camped. The Dutch escaped with heavy casualties, but they soon received reinforcements and, aided by the Sasaks from the east, proved too strong for the raja. Mataram was razed to the ground. Some members of the royal family surrendered while others committed *puputan*. The Dutch took control of the entire island, including the district of Karangasem on Bali, which had been under the raja's control.

Further confrontation in south Bali

The Dutch had wanted to emphasize their control of the **south of Bali** for many years, but it wasn't until the turn of the twentieth century that they made their move. On May 27, 1904, a schooner, the *Sri Kumala*, under Dutch protection, hit the reef just off Sanur. The owner complained to the Dutch Resident in Singaraja that copper and silver coins had been stolen from the ship. The

Resident decreed a **blockade** of Badung and ordered that the raja of Badung, Gusti Gde Ngurah, should pay compensation.

The raja of Tabanan defused the blockade by allowing goods to be imported through ports further north, and the situation dragged on until July 1906, when the Dutch delivered ultimatums threatening military action. Dutch forces landed at Sanur, and by September 20, 1906, had advanced to **Badung** (modern-day Denpasar). Gusti Gde Ngurah realized defence was useless and arranged the traditional **puputan**. An eyewitness account from a Dutch observer, Dr van Weede, in his book *Indies Travel Memories*, describes the event:

The ruler and the princes with their followers, dressed in their glittering attire, with their krises girded on, of which the golden hilts were in the form of Buddha statues and studded with precious stones; all of them were dressed in red or black and their hair was carefully combed, moistened with fragrant oils. The women were wearing the best clothes and accessories that they had; most of them wore their hair loose and all had white cloaks. The prince had his palace burned down and had everything that was breakable destroyed.

When at nine o'clock it was reported to him that the enemy had penetrated Denpasar from the North, the tragic procession of 250 people started to move; each man and woman carried a kris or long lance, also the children who had the strength to do it, while the babies were carried in their arms. Thus they walked to the north along the wide road bordered by tall trees, meeting their destruction.

The prince walked in front, carried on the shoulders by his followers according to custom, and silently ... until all of a sudden, at a turning in the road, the dark line of our infantry was visible before them. Immediately a halt was commanded and Captain Schutstal ordered the interpreters to summon the arriving party to a halt with gestures and with words. However these summons were in vain, and in spite of the repeated warnings the Balinese went over to a trot.

Incessantly the Captain and the interpreters made signs, but it was in vain. Soon they had to realize that they had to do with people who wanted to die. They let them approach to a hundred paces, eighty, seventy paces, but now they went over to a double quick step with couched lances and raised krises, the prince always in front.

A longer delay would have been irresponsible in view of the safety of our men, and the first salvo was given; several killed men remained at the place. One of the first to fall was the ruler; and now one of the most horrible scenes one could imagine took place.

While those who were saved continued the attack, and the shooting on our part for self-defence remained necessary, one saw lightly wounded give the death-blow to the heavily wounded. Women held out their breasts to be killed or received the death blow between their shoulders, and those who did this were mowed down by our rifle fire, other men and women got up to continue the bloody work. Also suicides took place there on a big scale, and all seemed to yearn for their death: some women threw as a reward for the violent death which they desired from them gold coins to the soldiers, and stood straight up in front of them, pointing at their heart, as if they wanted to be hit there; if no shot was fired they killed themselves. Especially an old man was busily stepping over the corpses, and used his kris left and right until he was shot down. An old woman took his task and underwent the same fate, however, nothing helped. Always others got up to continue the work of destruction.

This scene was repeated later the same day at the palace of the prince of **Pemecutan**. Estimates of the number of people killed that day vary between four hundred and two thousand. Having defeated Badung, on September 27, the Dutch marched on to **Tabanan**, where the raja and crown prince surrendered and were imprisoned, where they both committed suicide rather than face exile.

The completion of Dutch control

On April 28, 1908, Dutch troops in **Semarapura** witnessed a scene similar to the Badung *puputan* two years earlier. Reports tell how the *dewa agung* stabbed his royal kris into the ground expecting its power to rent the ground asunder or bring torrential rain to destroy the enemy. Nothing happened and around two hundred members of the royal household committed suicide that day; the remainder were exiled.

At this point the raja of **Bangli** realized a pretext would soon be found to attack him and, in October 1908, requested that his kingdom should have the same status as Gianyar and Karangasem and become a Dutch Protectorate. When this was approved in January 1909, the whole of the island of Bali came under **Dutch control**.

Colonial rule

The *puputans* of 1906 and 1908 caused a stir in Europe and the United States and pressure was put on the Dutch to moderate their policies. They ruled with a philosophy they called the **Ethical Policy**, which they claimed upheld Balinese values. Traditional rulers remained as regents under the authority of the Dutch administration, although not all of the old royal families were amenable to this; in Buleleng, it was not until several generations after the Dutch conquest that an obliging member of the royal family could be found.

Under the Dutch, engineers, doctors and teachers were introduced to the colony. In addition, Bali was spared the less enlightened **agricultural policies** that had turned large parts of Java into plantations. Big businesses were discouraged from Bali, although the steamship line KPM began encouraging **tourism** on the island from 1924 onwards.

Lombok under the Dutch

The situation on **Lombok** deteriorated markedly following the Dutch victory in 1894, and brought the population to the point of starvation more than once. The Dutch were determined to rule profitably: they taxed the population harshly and introduced **compulsory labour** for projects such as road-building. In addition to land tax, there were **taxes** on income and on the slaughter of animals. These were initially payable in local currency, but eventually they were demanded in Netherlands Indies currency (NIC). The Chinese rice-exporters were one of the few groups on the island who traded in NIC, and increasing amounts of rice needed to be sold to raise money for taxes. Consequently, a high proportion of food grown on the island was exported, and local rice consumption dropped by a quarter. By 1934, it was estimated that a third of the population were **landless and destitute**.

World War II and independence

Following the bombing of the American Fleet in Pearl Harbour on December 7, 1941, Japan entered **World War II** and moved quickly through Asia. The **Japanese** fleet arrived off Sanur on February 18, 1942, were unopposed on their march to Denpasar and took control of Bali without a fight. Java and Sumatra had fallen by March 9.

The Japanese **occupation** was hard but relatively short-lived as the Dutch were expelled from the country. It also showed the occupied islanders that the Dutch colonialists could be defeated.

Throughout the war years, the idea of liberation grew and, on August 17, 1945, three days after the Japanese surrender, Indonesia made its **Declaration of Independence** in an announcement by President **Sukarno**. Some Balinese were strong supporters of independence but many were uncertain about joining a republic dominated by Muslim Java.

The fight for independence

Returning to their colony in March 1946 the **Dutch** faced ferocious fighting on Java. On Bali guerrilla forces, the most famous of which was led by **Gusti Ngurah Rai**, harried the Dutch relentlessly, despite suffering massive losses in a famous battle near Marga in Tabanan. Ngurah Rai is remembered as a hero: Bali's airport is named after him and the Marga battlefield, where he died, is now a memorial park.

However, the Dutch were also under a different sort of attack. The US questioned the Dutch expenditure of Marshall Plan aid (money allocated to European countries for reconstruction after the war) on fighting to keep the Indies. Finally, in January 1949, the UN Security Council ordered the Dutch to withdraw their troops and negotiate. In December 1949, the United States of Indonesia was legally recognized, dissolving the following year to form the **Republic of Indonesia**, with Sukarno as president.

The Sukarno years

The early years of independence were not kind to Indonesia. The economic situation was disastrous as inflation, corruption and mismanagement ran riot. Martial rule was instituted, and parliament was abolished in 1959 with the introduction of what Sukarno labeled as **guided democracy**. 1963 saw a catastrophic war against Malaya to try to prevent the creation of the Federation of Malaysia.

Although Sukarno's mother was Balinese, the Balinese felt neglected by the government in Jakarta, which, in turn, was suspicious of Balinese Hinduism. Sukarno visited his palace at Tampaksiring regularly, with a massive entourage that demanded to be fed, entertained and then sent away with gifts. During the 1960s, a groundswell of resentment against the government grew in Bali. The Balinese began to believe that a state of spiritual disharmony had been reached, and a huge purification ceremony, **Eka Dasa Rudra**, was held in 1963 against the backdrop of a rumbling Gunung Agung, which eventually erupted and laid waste to much of the east of the island.

Later events in Jakarta piled disaster upon disaster in Bali. In 1965 **Major-General Suharto** seized power after a mysterious attempted coup that was blamed on the communist party (PKI). It unleashed a bloodbath in the country with actual or suspected members of the PKI and their sympathizers the main targets, along with the Chinese population. At least half a million people were killed across Indonesia: an estimated 100,000 on Bali and 50,000 on Lombok. Around 200,000 were imprisoned, mostly without trial, more than half of them for ten years or more while their families were stigmatized well into the 1990s. Suharto officially became the second president of Indonesia in March 1968, a position he held for over thirty years.

Indonesia under Suharto

Suharto's **New Order** policy of attracting foreign investment, curbing inflation and re-entering the global economy was largely successful. It was helped enormously by Indonesia's massive **natural resources** of copper, tin, timber and oil, and foreign investment established manufacturing industries. The **economic situation** of the country improved and the material prosperity of the average Indonesian rose.

However, the economic benefits came with a massive price as alongside this the government acquired almost complete control. **Political opposition** in the form of student or Islamic activists was crushed and the **media** silenced. The fearful memory of the events of 1965 lingered for decades. In every election from 1971 to 1997 the government party, Sekretariat Bersama Golongan Karya, known as **Golkar**, won the majority of seats in the House of Representatives (*Dewan Perwakilan Rakyat*) and then re-elected Suharto as president.

Initially introduced as a policy during Dutch colonial times, the Indonesian government continued the practice of transmigration, or **transmigrasi** – the relief of population pressure in some parts of the archipelago, most often Java, by settling other, less-populated islands. The issue is still being debated as human rights' groups and environmentalists claim that land has been taken from indigenous peoples and massive deforestation occurred; they also say that it is an attempt to "Javanize" the ethnically diverse Indonesians. Ethnic tensions in settled areas continue.

The **economic crisis** of the late 1990s that decimated the economies of Southeast Asia savaged Indonesia as well. Prices of imports (including food) rose sharply, and a series of riots in early 1998, centred on Java, targeted Chinese businesses – long the scapegoats of Indonesian unrest. Gradually, Indonesian anger turned against President Suharto and his family, who were seen to have been the biggest winners in the Indonesian economic success story.

Student rioting in May 1998 led to more widespread unrest and, eventually, to **Suharto's resignation** on May 21. He spent the ten years until his death on January 27, 2008, dodging corruption charges – in 2000 he was judged as unfit to stand trial. Transparency International, an international anti-corruption organization, estimates that he stole US\$15–\$35billion, possibly topping the worldwide list of corrupt politicians.

After Suharto

Following Suharto proved a tough job. The next two presidents, **B.J. Habibie** and **Abdurrahman Wahid**, known as **Gus Dur**, lasted only short periods of time and on July 23, 2001, **Megawati Sukarnoputri** became president. Megawati – darling of the Balinese, to whom she is known simply as Mega – was regarded in Bali with something approaching fanaticism, based on the fact that her maternal grandmother (Sukarno's mother) was Balinese. Starting her presidency on a wave of optimism, she proved to be ineffectual and far less charismatic in leadership than she had been in opposition.

However, Indonesia hit the world headlines on **12 October, 2002**, for far more tragic reasons than its political situation, when bombs planted in the heart of tourist Bali, at the *Sari Club* and *Paddy's Irish Bar* in Kuta, exploded, killing more than two hundred people, the majority of them tourists but with dozens of Indonesian victims also. A third bomb exploded outside the US consulate in Denpasar but caused little damage and no injuries. The attacks were carried out by members of the Islamic militants organization Jemaah

Islamiah. The perpetrators included Amrozi bin Nurhasyim, who gained global notoriety when he punched the air after being sentenced to death; he was one of three who received the death penalty. At the time of writing the three had exhausted all their appeals but the sentences had not been carried out. Dozens of others received prison sentences. The bombing of the *Marriot Hotel* in Jakarta in May 2003, the Australian Embassy in Jakarta in 2004 and Jimbaran and Kuta in 2005 emphasized to Indonesians and the wider world that fundamentalist forces are at large in the largest Muslim nation in the world.

Whatever Megawati's failings, she did lay the foundations for Indonesia's **first-ever direct presidential election** in 2004, in which 114 million voters across 14,000 islands voted her out of the job in favour of **Susilo Bambang Yudhoyono**, commonly known as **SBY**.

With 61 percent of the vote he was a popular winner and early signs were positive although later on the gloss wore off. He received international approval for his peace deal with the Aceh separatists. However, the separatist struggle in West Papua is unresolved and inflation, corruption, terrorism and nepotism are the concerns of every Indonesian – of whom more than sixteen percent live below the poverty line. With elections due again in 2009, only time will tell whether this president has more longevity than his last three predecessors. His chances hinge on whether the electorate consider he has kept to his 2004 pledge to fight corruption and create jobs.

Religion

Some 92 percent of Balinese are Hindus. In contrast, Lombok is only three percent Hindu and the vast majority of its inhabitants are Muslim.

Religious activity permeates almost every aspect of **Balinese** life. Every morning, tiny palm-leaf offerings are laid down for the gods and spirits who need 24-hour propitiation; in the afternoons, processions of men and women parade the streets en route to temple celebrations, towers of offertory fruit and rice cakes balanced on their heads. Temple compounds dominate the horizons of every village, and the desire to entice and entertain the deities inspires daily performances of dance and gamelan music.

While Islam is as pervasive on **Lombok** as Hinduism is on Bali, it has a much more austere presence. You'll hear the call to prayer five times a day, and streets are often deserted on Fridays around noon, when a large proportion of the population go to the mosque. Marriage and circumcision are celebrated, but the exuberant and frequent festivals of Balinese Hinduism have no Muslim equivalents.

Balinese Hinduism

Though it's not a proselytizing faith, **Balinese Hinduism** is a demanding one, which requires participation from every citizen. Despite certain obvious similarities, Balinese Hinduism differs dramatically from Indian and Nepalese Hinduism. Bali's is a blend of theories and practices borrowed from Hinduism and Buddhism, grafted onto the far stronger indigenous vision of a world that is overrun by good and bad spirits. The Balinese have practised ancestor worship and followed animist cults ever since the Stone Age and consequently only the most complementary aspects of the newer Asian theologies have been adopted.

Early influences

The **animism** of the Stone- and Bronze-Age Balinese probably differed very little from the beliefs of their twenty-first-century descendants, who worship sacred mountains and rivers and conduct elaborate rituals to ensure that the souls of their dead ancestors are kept sweet. In among these animist practices are elements borrowed from the **Mahayana Buddhism** that dominated much of Southeast Asia in the eighth century – certain Buddhist saints, for example, some of which are still visible at Goa Gajah, and a penchant for highly ornate imagery. The strongest influences arrived with the droves of **East Javanese Hindu priests** who fled Muslim invaders en masse in the early sixteenth century. High-caste, educated pillars of the Majapahit kingdom, these strict followers of the Hindu faith settled all over Bali and quickly set about formalizing the island's embryonic Hindu practices. Balinese Hinduism, or **agama Hindu** as it's usually termed, became the official religion, and the Majapahit priests have, ever since, been worshipped as the true Balinese ancestors.

As Bali's Hinduism gained strength, so its neighbouring islands turned towards Islam, and Bali is now a tiny Hindu enclave in an archipelago that contains the biggest Islamic population in the world. Hindu Bali's role within the predominantly Muslim Indonesian state has always been problematic. As part of its code of national law (*pancasila*), the Jakarta administration requires that all Indonesian faiths be monotheistic and embrace just one God – a proviso that doesn't sit easily with either Hindu or animist tenets. After concerted theological and political wranglings, however, Bali's Hindu Council came up with an acceptable compromise. By emphasizing the role of their supreme deity, **Sanghyang Widi Wasa** (who manifests himself as the Hindu Trinity of Brahma, Siwa and Wisnu), the Council convinced the Ministry of Religion that Bali was essentially

▲ Temple offerings

monotheistic, and in 1962 Balinese Hinduism was formally recognized by Jakarta. As a result, many new Balinese temples were dedicated to a unifying force – Jagatnata or "Lord of the World"; two typical examples of *pura Jagatnata* can be seen in Denpasar and Singaraja.

The beliefs

At the root of *agama Hindu* lies the fundamental understanding that the world – both natural and supernatural – is composed of opposing forces. These can be defined as good and evil, positive and negative, pure and impure, order and disorder, gods and demons, or as a mixture of all these things, but the crucial fact is that the forces need to be balanced. The desire to achieve **equilibrium** and harmony in all things dictates every spiritual activity. **Positive forces**, or *dharma*, are represented by the gods (*dewa* and *bhatara*), and need to be cultivated, entertained and honoured with offerings, dances, beautiful paintings and sculptures, fine earthly abodes (temples) and ministrations from ceremonially clad devotees. The **malevolent forces**, *adharma*, which manifest themselves as earth demons (*bhuta*, *kala* and *leyak*) and cause sickness, death and volcanic eruptions, need to be neutralized with elaborate rituals and special offerings.

To ensure that malevolent forces never take the upper hand, elaborate purification rituals are undertaken for the exorcism of spirits. Crucial to this is the notion of **ritual uncleanliness** (*sebel*), a state which can affect an individual (during a woman's period, for example, or after a serious illness), a family (after the death of a close relative, or if twins are born), or even a whole community (a plague of rats in the village ricefields, or a fire in village buildings). The whole island can even become *sebel*, and **island-wide exorcisms** are held every new year (*Nyepi*) to restore the spiritual health of Bali and all its people. The 2002 Kuta bombing caused the whole island to become ritually unclean, and as well as a huge purification ceremony at Ground Zero a month after the attack, exorcism rites were also performed simultaneously across the island. Other regular, very elaborate island-cleansing rituals are performed every five, ten and twenty-five years, climaxing with the centennial *Eka Dasa Rudra* rite, which is held at the mother temple, Besakih. In addition, there are all sorts of **purification rituals** (*yadnya*) that Balinese must go through at various significant stages in their lives (see p.462).

The focus of every purification ritual is the ministering of **holy water** (*agama Hindu* is sometimes known as *agama tirta*, the religion of holy water). Ordinary well or tap water can be transformed into holy water by a *pedanda* (high priest), but water from certain sources is considered to be particularly sacred – the springs at Tirta Empul in Tampaksiring and on Gunung Agung, for example, and the water taken from the lakeside Pura Danu Batur.

As the main sources of these life-giving waters, Bali's three great **mountains** are also worshipped: the highest, and the holiest, of the three is Gunung Agung, associated with the sun god Surya, and site of Bali's most sacred mother temple, Besakih; Gunung Batur and Gunung Batukaru also hold great spiritual power. Ever since the Stone Age, the Balinese have regarded their mountains as being the realm of the deities, the sea as the abode of demons and giants, and the valleys in between as the natural province of the human world. From this concept comes the Balinese sense of direction and **spatial orientation**, whereby all things, such as temples, houses and villages, are aligned in relation to the mountains and the sea: **kaja** is the direction towards the mountains, upstream, and is the holiest direction; **kelod** is the downstream direction, the part that is closest to the sea and therefore impure.

An important practical tenet of *agama Hindu* is **Tri Hita Karana**, the need to constantly work towards harmony between the three dimensions of daily life – spiritual, social and environmental – fostering a three-way balance between humans and God, humans and humans, and humans and the environment (both cultural and physical). This philosophy is even applied within the tourist industry, which runs a Tri Hita Karana award system for hotels that achieve this balance in design and operation.

Finally, there are the notions of karma, reincarnation, and the attaining of enlightenment. The aim of every Hindu is to attain **enlightenment** (*moksa*), which unites the individual and the divine, and brings liberation from the endless cycle of death and rebirth; it is only attainable by pure souls, and can take hundreds of lifetimes to attain. Hindus believe that everybody is **reincarnated** according to their **karma**, karma being a kind of account book that registers all the good and bad deeds performed in the past lives of a soul. Karma is closely bound up with caste and the notion that an individual should accept rather than challenge their destiny.

The gods

All Balinese **gods** are manifestations of the supreme being, **Sanghyang Widi Wasa**, a deity who is often only alluded to in abstract form by an empty throne-shrine, the *padmasana*, that stands in the holiest corner of every temple. Sanghyang Widi Wasa's three main aspects manifest themselves as the Hindu trinity: Brahma, Wisnu and Siwa.

Brahma is the Creator, represented by the colour red and often depicted riding on a bull. His consort is the goddess of learning, **Saraswati**, who rides a white goose. As the Preserver, **Wisnu** is associated with life-giving waters; he rides the *garuda* (half-man, half-bird) and is honoured by the colour black. Wisnu also has several avatars, including **Buddha** – a neat way of incorporating Buddhist elements into the Hindu faith.

Siwa, the Destroyer, or more accurately, the Dissolver, is associated with death and rebirth, with the temples of the dead and with the colour white. He is sometimes represented as a phallic pillar or lingam, and sometimes in the manifestation of **Surya**, the sun god. Siwa's consort is the terrifying goddess **Durga**, whose Balinese personality is the gruesome widow-witch **Rangda**, queen of the demons. The son of Siwa and Durga is the elephant-headed deity **Ganesh**, generally worshipped as the remover of obstacles.

Brahma, Wisnu and Siwa all have associated lesser deities or *dewi* (*dewa* if male), many of them gods of the elements and of the physical world. **Dewi Sri** is the goddess of rice, worshipped at tiny shrines in the paddy-fields and honoured at significant stages throughout the agricultural year. **Dewi Danu** (more formally known as Ida Batara Dewi Ulun Danu) is the goddess of the crater lake – honoured with temples on the shores of the three volcanic lakes Bratan, Batur and Tamblingan, and so important to rice-growers as a source of vital irrigation that annual pilgrimages are made to all three temples. **Dewa Baruna** is the unpredictable god of the sea, and **Dewi Melanting** the goddess of commerce and prosperity.

The demons

Demons also come in a variety of manifestations. The forces of evil are personified by a cast of **bhuta** and **kala**, invisible goblins and ghosts who inhabit eerie, desolate places like the temples of the dead, cemeteries, moonless sea-shores and dark forests. Their purpose is to wreak havoc in the human world, causing horrible lingering illnesses and ruinous agricultural and economic disasters, preying on the most vulnerable babies, and entering villagers' minds and turning them insane. But they are not invincible and can be appeased with **offerings** just as the gods can – the difference being that the offerings for these demons consist mainly of dirty, unpleasant, unattractive and mouldy things, which are thrown on the ground, not placed respectfully on ledges and altars. Demons are notoriously greedy too and so the Balinese will often waste a dash of *arak* (rice liquor) on the ground before drinking, or drop a few grains of rice to the floor when eating.

Various other strategies are used to repel, confuse and banish the *bhuta* and *kala*. Most entrance gates to temples and households are guarded by fierce-looking statues and ugly demonic images designed to frighten off even the boldest demon. Many gateways are also blocked by a low brick wall, an **aling-aling**, as demons can only walk in straight lines, and so won't be able to zigzag around it. *Bhuta* and *kala* get particular pleasure from entering a person's body via their various orifices, so certain temples (especially in the north) have covered their walls in pornographic carvings, the theory being that the demons will have so much fun penetrating the carved simulation orifices on the outside walls that they won't bother to try their luck further inside the temple compound.

In addition to the unseen *bhuta* and *kala*, there are the **leyak**, or witches, who take highly visible and creepy forms, morphing into headless chickens, bald-headed giants, monkeys with rows of shiny gold teeth, fireballs and riderless motorbikes. *Leyak* can transform themselves effortlessly, and most assume the human form during the daytime, leading outwardly normal lives. Only at night do they release their dark spirits to wreak havoc on unsuspecting islanders, while their human shell remains innocently asleep in bed. Even in their human form, *leyak* cannot be killed with knives or poisons, but they can be controlled by harnessing the white magic practised by shamanic *balian* and priests.

The temples

The focus of every community's spiritual activity is the **temple**, or *pura*, a temporary abode for the gods that's open and unroofed to invite easy access between heaven and earth. Major religious ceremonies take place inside the *pura*, and members of the community spend a great deal of their time and income beautifying the sanctuary with carvings, and consecrating offerings at its altars.

To outsiders, Balinese temples can seem confusing, even unimpressive: open-roofed compounds scattered with shrines and altars, built mainly of limestone and red brick, and with no paintings or treasures to focus on. But there are at least 20,000 temples on the island and many do reward closer examination. Every structure within a temple complex is charged with great symbolic significance, often with entertaining legends attached, and many of the walls and gateways are carved with an ebullience of mythical figures, demonic spirits and even secular scenes. (Note that when **visiting a temple**, you must be appropriately dressed, even if there's no one else in the vicinity; see p.55 for details.)

The reason there are so many temples in Bali is that every *banjar* is obliged to build at least three. At the top of the village – the *kaja*, or holiest end – stands the **pura puseh**, the temple of origin, which is dedicated to the founders of the community. For everyday spiritual activities, villagers worship at the **pura desa**, the village temple, which always stands at the heart of the village, and is often also used for community events. (In some communities, the *pura puseh* and the *pura desa* are combined within a single compound.) The trio is completed by the **pura dalem**, or temple of the dead, at the *kelod* (unclean) end of the village, which is usually dedicated either to Siwa, or to the widow-witch Rangda. Larger villages will often have other temples as well, perhaps including a **pura melanting** for the gods of wealth and commerce, and a small agricultural temple or shrine, a **pura subak**, dedicated to the rice goddess, Dewi Sri.

Bali also has nine directional temples, or **kayangan jagat**, which protect the entire island and all its people. They're located at strategic points across Bali, especially on high mountain slopes, rugged cliff-faces and lakeside shores: Pura Ulun Danu Batur is on the shores of Danau Batur (north); Pura Pasar Agung on Gunung Agung (northeast); Pura Lempuyang Luhur on Gunung Lempuyang (east); Goa Lawah near Candi Dasa (southeast); Pura Masceti near Lebih (south); Pura Luhur Uluwatu on the Bukit (southwest); Pura Luhur Batukaru on Gunung Batukaru (west); Pura Ulun Danu Bratan on the shores of Danau Bratan (northwest); and Besakih on Gunung Agung (centre). The most important of these is **Besakih** – the mother temple – as it occupies the crucial position on Bali's holiest, and highest mountain, Gunung Agung; the others are all of equal status, and islanders are expected to attend the anniversary celebrations (*odalan*) of the one situated closest to their home.

Temple layout

Whatever the size, status or particular function of a temple, it will nearly always follow a prescribed layout (see temple plan overleaf), adhering to the precepts of **religious architecture** minutely described in the ancient *lontar* texts. All Balinese temples are oriented *kaja–kelod*, and are designed around two or three courtyards, each section divided from the next by a low wall punctuated by a huge, and usually ornate, gateway.

In many temples, particularly in north Bali, the **outer courtyard** (*jaba*) and **middle courtyard** (*jaba tengah*) are merged into one. These courtyards represent the transition zone between the human and the divine worlds, containing special pavilions for the preparation of offerings and the storing of temple paraphernalia, as well as for cockfights and the less sacred dance performances (such as those for tourists). The extremely sacred **inner courtyard**, *jeroan*, houses all the shrines, and is the focus of all temple rituals. All offerings are brought here, prayers are held in front of the shrines, and the most sacred dances are performed within its confines. The *jeroan* is quite often out of bounds to the lay community and opened only during festivals.

Every *pura* contains several ritual structures. **Bale** (pronounced "ba-leh") are raised, open-sided pavilions, usually built of wood and thatched with black sugar-palm fibre. These are practical buildings for seating devotees or gamelan players, and for storing things. **Gedong** is the generic term for the squat, often cube-shaped shrines that are generally made of brick, with thatched roofs. Each *gedong* is dedicated to a particular deity or ancestor, and sometimes contains a symbolic image. The elegant pagoda-style shrines that tower over every temple wall are known as **meru**, after the sacred Hindu peak Mount Meru, home of the gods. Each *meru* has a small wood or brick base beneath a multi-tiered roof thatched with thick black sugar-palm fibre. There's always an odd number of roofs (three, five, seven, nine or eleven), the number indicating the status of the god to whom the *meru* is dedicated.

Priests

The only people who are conversant with all the rituals of *agama Hindu* are the **high priests**, or *pedanda*, men and a few women of the Brahman caste who

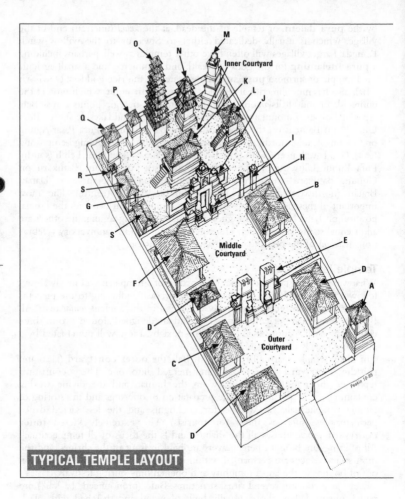

Inner Courtyard

Middle
Courtyard

Outer
Courtyard

Peakin 10-95

TYPICAL TEMPLE LAYOUT

spend years studying the complex theology. This knowledge sets them apart from others and so the *pedanda* and family usually live in a special compound (*griya*) that stands slightly separate from the rest of the community.

Only the most important ceremonies are presided over by a *pedanda*. Wreathed in clouds of incense and dressed all in white, save for bejewelled mitres on their heads and multiple strings of beads around their necks, the *pedanda*'s role is to invoke the spirit of the supreme deity with a complicated ritual performance of chanting, hand gestures and the periodic ringing of a small handbell. With legs folded into a half-lotus and eyes closed, the *pedanda* can spend hours chanting the appropriate mantras in an ancient tongue – either the old Javanese language, Kawi, or the similarly esoteric Sanskrit – which mean nothing to the lay people who generally just pause for a brief prayer before moving on.

The scholarly *pedanda* are also traditionally the only people to understand the complexities of the Balinese calendar system (for more on which, see p.48) and so they are consulted over the timing for major events – such as the most

A: Kulkul Drum tower. Tall roofed tower that contains the wooden bell or "drum" (*kulkul*) used to summon members of the *banjar* to festivals, meetings and, in the past, into battle. The drum is made from a hollowed-out log slit down the middle.

B: Wantilan Performance pavilion for cockfights and dances.

C: Bale gong Gamelan pavilion where musicians play during temple events, and store their instruments.

D: Bale All-purpose pavilion, used for meetings and for resting.

E: Candi bentar The split temple gate. Designed to represent a tower that has literally been split down the middle, with various symbolic meanings: the material world has been split so that the human body can enter the spiritual realm; the left side represents femaleness, the right, maleness; if an evil spirit tries to pass through, the two halves will come together to crush it.

F: Paon Kitchen. Open-sided pavilion where festival offerings are prepared.

G: Kori agung (or **paduraksa**) Central covered gateway to the inner courtyard, usually approached by a flight of steps and topped with a sculpted tower. The central wooden door is officially only for the use of the deities and their representatives so is kept locked except at festival times. Its archway is crowned with the grotesque fanged head of **Bhoma**, child of the earth or son of the forest, whose role is to ward off demons.

H: Raksasa Metre-high demon statues. Usually paired on either side of gateways, *raksasa* wield clubs and act as a deterrent to malevolent spirits.

I : Side gate For access to the inner courtyard.

J: Aling-aling Low, freestanding wall. Located directly in front of the *kori agung*'s central doorway, this is the last line of defence against unwanted demons: evil spirits can only walk in straight lines, so the *aling-aling* will block their path.

K: Gedong paruman or **pepelik** Empty pavilion reserved for the gods to watch temple festivities.

L: Gedong pesimpangan The principal shrine honouring the village founder or important local deity.

M: Padmasana Lotus throne. An empty stone throne built into the summit of a tall, sculpted tower, which is reserved for the supreme deity **Sanghyang Widi Wasa** whenever he descends to earth. Always located in the corner that's closest to the holiest mountain, Gunung Agung (usually the northeast corner). The tower is supported by the cosmic turtle, Bedawang, and two *naga*, or mythological sea serpents, which are central to the Balinese creation myth. **Bedawang** carries the world on his back (when he gets restless, he shakes the earth's foundations, so causing earthquakes), while **Naga Basukih** and **Naga Anantaboga** act as his steadying agents and represent human needs, namely food, shelter, clothing and security.

N: Meru Gunung Agung Three-roofed (occasionally eleven-roofed) shrine, dedicated to Bali's holiest mountain.

O: Meru Sanghyang Widi Wasa Eleven-roofed shrine dedicated to the supreme deity.

P: Meru Gunung Batur One-roofed (occasionally nine-roofed) shrine dedicated to the sacred Batur mountain.

Q: Gedong Maospahit Shrine honouring the Javanese Majapahit (or Maospahit) people, who are considered the spiritual ancestors of the Balinese and are usually represented by a sculpture of a deer's head or a carved or real pair of antlers.

R: Taksu Stone pillar. The seat for the *taksu* (life force or spirit) which occasionally descends to inhabit the bodies of certain worshippers, sending them into a trance so that they can convey messages between the gods and the humans.

S: Bale piasan Pavilions where offerings are laid.

auspicious day for laying the foundation stone of a house or office, for example, or for holding a cremation ceremony.

It is the job of the **village priest**, the *pemangku*, to attend to the more mundane spiritual activities of the community. *Pemangku* are nearly always male, though their wives also help. Easily recognized by his white apparel and formal white *udeng* headdress, the *pemangku* spends a great deal of time at the temple, sweeping the grounds, repairing the buildings and, in the run-up to the *odalan* and other local celebrations, preparing the *pura* for the reception of offerings and necessary rituals. At the time of the *odalan*, it is the *pemangku* who invites the gods to partake of the offerings, and he and his wife then dispense holy water to the worshippers. Their other main duty is to advise the community on appropriate offerings and rituals for every occasion: if a household is struck down by sickness, for example, or if a family suddenly has some good fortune, they will ask the *pemangku* to help them express their sorrow or thanks. It is the *pemangku* who appears at the beginning of every dance performance (even the

Traditional dress

It is customary for Balinese men and women to wear **traditional dress** whenever they attend temple festivals, cremations, weddings, birth rites and other important rituals; men also wear temple dress if playing in a gamelan orchestra and occasionally for *banjar* meetings too.

The traditional outfit for **women** is a lacy, close-fitting, long-sleeved blouse (*kebaya*) and a tightly wound sarong (*kain kamben*), set off by the all-important sash (*selempot*) around the waist, which symbolically contains the body and its physical appetites. It's currently fashionable to wear a vividly coloured bustier under the **kebaya**, and some women don flamboyant hair-pieces as well. For some big festivals, women from the same community will all wear the same-coloured *kebaya* to give their group a recognizable identity.

Men also wear a type of sarong (*kamben sarung*) plus a formal, collared shirt (generally white but sometimes batik) or a starched jacket-like shirt. The man's sash (*selempot*) is often hidden under the shirt, but the more important item for him is the hip-cloth (*saput*), which is often yellow and usually knee-length and is worn over the sarong. Men also wear a headcloth (**udeng**), which they tie in whatever way they like, but generally leaving a triangular crest on top (shops sell ready-tied *udeng*). As with the sash, the *udeng* symbolically concentrates the mental energies and directs the thoughts heavenwards, via the perky cockscomb at the front.

---

tourist ones) to bless the performers with sprinklings of holy water, and it is his job too to awaken the dancers out of their trances.

Temple festivals

Aside from the daily propitiation of the household spirits, *agama Hindu* requires no regular act of collective worship, no daily mass or weekly service, and so, for much of the year, Bali's 20,000 temples remain deserted, visited only by the village *pemangku* and perhaps the occasional curious tourist. But this all changes on the occasion of the temple's anniversary celebrations, or **odalan**, a three-day devotional extravaganza held at every temple either once every 210 days (every Balinese calendar year; see p.48 for an explanation of this) or once every 354–356 days (the *saka* year). With at least three temples in every community, any visitor who spends more than a week on the island will be certain to see some kind of festival. Most temples welcome tourists to the celebrations, provided they dress respectably (see p.55) and wear the temple sash, and that they don't walk in front of praying devotees.

As well as the temple anniversary celebrations, there are numerous island-wide religious festivals, the most important of which are *Nyepi* and *Galungan-Kuningan*, described on p.47. Although the majority of the other rituals – birth celebrations, tooth filing, marriage and death – that punctuate every Balinese Hindu's life also have strong religious ramifications, most of these are conducted inside the family compound, and are described on pp.462–464.

The larger, wealthier and more important the temple, the more dramatic the *odalan* celebrations. Whatever the size, the purpose is always to invite the gods down to earth so that they can be entertained and pampered by as many displays of devotion and gratitude as the community can afford. In the days before the *odalan*, the *pemangku* dresses the temple statues in **holy cloths**, either the spiritually charged black-and-white *kain poleng*, or a length of plain cloth in the colour symbolic of that temple's deity. Meanwhile, the women of the community begin to construct their offering towers, or *banten*, and to cook ceremonial food.

Odalan are so important that everyone makes a huge effort to return to their home village for their own temple festival, even if they live and work far away; most employers will automatically give their Balinese staff time off to attend. **Celebrations** start in the afternoon, with a procession of ceremonially clad women carrying their offerings to the temple. Sometimes the gods will temporarily inhabit the body of one of the worshippers, sending him or her into a trance and conveying its message through gestures or words. Elsewhere in the temple compound, there might be a cockfight and some gamelan music, and sacred dances are often performed as well. After dark, a shadow play, *wayang kulit*, is often staged.

Offerings

The simplest **offerings** are the ones laid out every day by the women of each house, and placed at the household shrine, at the entrance gate, and in any crannies thought to be of interest to *bhuta* and *kala*. These offerings, called **canang**, are tiny banana-leaf trays, pinned together with bamboo splinters and filled with a symbolic assortment of rice, fruit, flowers and incense. The flowers are always red or pink, to represent the Hindu god Brahma, and white for Siwa, with the green of the banana leaf symbolizing Wisnu. Though it's still common for women to make their own *canang*, an increasing number buy theirs at the market. Offerings for the gods are always placed in elevated positions, either on specially constructed altars or on functional shelves, but those meant for the demons are scattered on the ground. When the devotee places the gods' offering, she sprinkles holy water over it and wafts the incense smoke heavenwards. This sends the essence of the *canang* up to the appropriate god and ensures that he comes down immediately to enjoy it. Once the essence has been extracted, the *canang* loses its holiness and is left to rot.

In the run-up to festivals and celebrations, the women of each *banjar* band together to create great towers of fruit and rice cakes, tiny rice-dough figurines, and banners woven from palm fronds. The most dramatic of these are the magnificent **banten**, built up around the trunk of a young banana tree, up to

---

Cockfights

Because certain Hindu rituals require the shedding of fresh sacrificial blood to placate evil spirits, every temple's purification ceremony is prefaced by a **cockfight**, which attracts massive crowds and even larger bets. Providing you wear suitable temple dress and can stand the gore, tourists are quite welcome to attend.

Prize cocks can earn both their owners and the temple tidy sums of money – and plunge losing gamblers into debilitating debt – and you'll see men of all ages and incomes preening their birds in public. When not being pampered, the birds are kept in bell-shaped bamboo baskets, often in quite noisy public places such as by the roadside, so that they won't be scared or distracted when in the ring.

Fights generally take place in the temple's special cockfighting pavilion or *wantilan*. Complicated **rules** written on ancient manuscripts specify the days on which fights may take place, and describe the detailed classification system under which the birds are categorized. Before the fight, a lethal 11- to 15cm-long blade, or *taji*, is attached to the left ankle of each bird. This is considered a sacred weapon and cockfights are meant to be won and lost by skilful use of the *taji*, not just by brutish pecking. Fights last for a maximum of five rounds, and the winning bird is the cock who remains standing the longest – even if he drops dead soon after. The owner of the winning cock gets the body of the losing bird plus his opponent's share of the central fund.

three metres high. *Banten* cannot be reused, but once they've done service at the temple they can be dismantled and eaten by the families who donated them.

On the occasion of major island-wide festivals, such as *Galungan-Kuningan*, or at the Balinese New Year, *Nyepi*, Bali's villages get decked out with special banners and ornamental poles, designed to attract the attention of the deities living on Gunung Agung and invite them onto the local streets. The banners, known as **lamak**, are amazing ornamental mats, often up to three metres long and woven in bold symbolic patterns from fresh green banana leaves. The most common design centres round the **cili** motif, a stylized female figure thought to represent the rice goddess Dewi Sri, with a body formed of simple geometric shapes and wearing a spiky headdress. Seven days before the great *Galungan* festival begins, special bamboo poles, or **penyor**, are erected along the streets of every village, each one bowed down with intricately woven garlands of dried flowers and palm leaves, which arch gracefully over the roadway. Attached to the *penyor* are symbolic leafy tassels, and offerings of dried paddy sheaves and coconut shells.

Bali's other faiths

Islam is Bali's second religion, practised by around six percent of the population. The island has around two thousand mosques, the majority of which are in the west and north, in the communities of people who have moved across the Bali Strait from Java.

Bali's tiny **Christian** population makes up less than one percent of the population and is centred on two communities on a remote mountainside in west Bali (see p.334). There are nine **Buddhist** temples, the most famous of which is the Thai-style Theravada Buddhist sanctuary in the northern village of Banjar (see p.311). Although the 2005 census shows that only half a percent of the population is Buddhist, mainstream Balinese Hinduism incorporates a number of Buddhist teachings and practices. Because **Confucianism** is not monotheistic, it's not officially recognized by the Indonesian government and so is effectively illegal. Most Chinese temples on Bali are therefore Theravada Buddhist, but suffused with enough Confucian elements to retain a distinctly Chinese character. The major Chinese temples are located near the coast and in the biggest commercial centres – close to the homes of the original Chinese traders and settlers; the most notable are in Kuta, Tanjung Benoa and Singaraja.

Lombok and Islam

Indonesia is the largest **Muslim** nation in the world, and almost ninety percent (around 182 million) of its population follow the faith. On Lombok, 85 percent of the islanders are Muslim, most of the remainder are Balinese Hindus. A tiny minority of Lombok's Muslims adhere to Wetu Telu (see below) but as it is not officially recognized, numbers of followers are unknown.

On Lombok, you'll see that women dress modestly, but are not strictly veiled; the centre and east of the island are the most devout, but even here you'll see some women without head-coverings and relatively few with their entire body covered. The **mosque** is the centre of the Muslim faith, and prayers on Friday at noon pretty much empties the villages (see p.55 for etiquette required when visiting a mosque). Many new, extremely grand mosques are under construction throughout the island. Thousands of islanders every year manage to afford the millions of rupiah needed for a pilgrimage to Mecca.

It is still unclear exactly how Islam came to Indonesia, but it seems likely that it spread along trade routes, probably via traders from Gujarat in India who had converted to Islam in the mid-thirteenth century, and by the sixteenth century it had arrived in Lombok. Traditionally, the arrival of Islam in Java is thought to have more exotic roots, brought by nine Islamic saints or *wali sangga*, one of whom is believed to be buried near Rembitan in the south of Lombok.

Wetu Telu

Followers of **Wetu Telu** – the title translates as "three times", possibly referring to the number of daily prayer-times – adhere to the central tenets of Islam, such as belief in Allah as the one God and Muhammad as his prophet, but diverge significantly from the practices of orthodox Muslims, who, because they pray five times a day, are known as "Wetu Lima".

For the Wetu Telu, the older traditions of **ancestor worship** and **animism** persist and there are many similarities with Balinese Hindu beliefs and practices; both worship at Pura Lingsar, and Wetu Telu believe that **Gunung Rinjani** is the dwelling place of the ancestors and the Supreme God and make pilgrimages to the mountain. Many Wetu Telu observe a three-day fast rather than the full month of **Ramadan**. The most important Wetu Telu rituals are **life-cycle ceremonies** associated with birth, death, marriage and circumcision, as well as rituals connected with agriculture and house-building. Their most important annual festival is **Maulid**, Muhammad's birthday.

Throughout their history, the Wetu Telu have been subjected to varying degrees of pressure to conform to mainstream Islamic ideas. During the civil unrest in 1965 anyone less than scrupulously orthodox was in danger of being regarded as communist and there were attacks against the Wetu Telu. These days many Wetu Telu profess to follow orthodox Islam while also carrying out their Wetu Telu observances under the label of *adat*, customary practices.

Traditional music and dance

C

M
usic and dance play an essential part in daily Balinese life, and as a visitor you can't fail to experience them, either at a special tourist show, in rehearsal or at a temple festival. Ubud and its neighbouring villages have long had a reputation for their superb dance troupes and gamelan orchestras, and villagers now supplement their incomes by doing regular **shows** in the traditional settings of temple courtyards and village compounds. None is exactly authentic, as most comprise a medley of highlights from the more dramatic temple dances, but the quality is generally high and spectators are given English-language synopses. Ubud is also the place to take introductory lessons in the performing arts. To see wholly authentic performances you'll need to find out about imminent temple festivals or attend rehearsals, most of which take place in the local *banjar* after sundown; you'll probably be welcome to watch. There's a vibrant tradition of music and dance on Lombok, too, rarely witnessed by casual visitors to the island, since it's associated almost exclusively with religious practices.

Balinese performing arts

Traditionally, **Balinese** dancers and musicians have always learnt their craft from the experts in their village and by imitating other performers. Since the 1960s, however, arts students have also had the option of attending a government-run high school and college dedicated to the performing arts. The month-long Bali Arts Festival (⊛ www.baliartsfestival.com; see p.93), held every summer in Denpasar, showcases the best in the performing arts, staging both new and traditional works performed by professional arts graduates as well as village groups.

Balinese gamelan music

The national music of Bali is **gamelan**, a jangly clashing of syncopated sounds once described by the writer Miguel Covarrubias as being like "an Oriental ultra-modern Bach fugue, an astounding combination of bells, machinery and thunder". The highly structured compositions are produced by a group of 25 or more musicians seated cross-legged on the ground at a variety of bronze percussion instruments – gongs, metallophones and cymbals – with a couple of optional wind and stringed instruments. All gamelan music is written for instruments tuned either to a five- or (less commonly) a seven-tone scale, and most is performed at an incredible speed: one study of a gamelan performance found that each instrumentalist played an average of seven notes per second.

"Gamelan" is the Javanese word for the bronze instruments, and the music probably came over from Java around the fourteenth century; the Balinese duly adapted it to suit their own personality, and now the sounds of the Javanese and Balinese gamelan are distinctive even to the untrained ear. Where Javanese gamelan music is restrained and rather courtly, Balinese is loud and flashy, boisterous and speedy, full of dramatic stops and starts. This modern Balinese style, known as **gong kebyar** (*gong* means orchestra, *kebyar* translates, aptly, as lightning flashes), has been around since the early 1900s, emerging at a time of great political upheaval on the island, when the status of Bali's royal houses was irreparably dented by Dutch colonial aggression. Until then, Bali's music had been as palace-oriented as Javanese gamelan, but in 1915 village musicians from north Bali gave a public performance in the new *kebyar* style, and the trend spread like wildfire across the island, with whole orchestras turning their instruments in to be melted down and recast in the new, more exuberant, timbres.

Gamelan orchestras are an essential part of village life. Every *banjar* that can afford to buy a set of instruments has its own *seka* or **music club**, and there are said to be 1500 active *gong kebyar* on the island. In most communities, the *seka* is open only to men (the all-female gamelan of Peliatan is a rare exception), but welcomes players of any standard between the ages of about eight and eighty. **Rehearsals** generally happen after nightfall, either in the *bale banjar* or in the temple's *bale gong* pavilion. There's special *gong* music for every occasion – for sacred and secular dances, cremations, *odalan* festivities and *wayang kulit* shows – but players never learn from scores (in fact, few *gong* compositions are ever notated), preferring instead to have it drummed into them by repetitive practice. Whatever the occasion, *gong* players always dress up in the ceremonial uniform of their music club, and make appropriate blessings and ritual offerings to the deities. Like dancers, musicians are acutely conscious of their role as entertainers of the gods.

Gamelan instruments

The type of music that a *seka* plays depends on the make-up of its particular gamelan orchestra, and every *gong* on the island sounds slightly different. Tuned-in Balinese can supposedly find their way around the island in the dark by recognizing the distinctive tones of the various local gamelan.

Although the *gong kebyar* is by far the most popular style of music in Bali – and therefore the most common type of orchestra – there are over twenty other different ensemble variations. The smallest is the four-piece **gender wayang**, which traditionally accompanies the *wayang kulit* shadow-play performances; the largest is the old-fashioned classical Javanese-style orchestra comprising fifty instruments, known as the **gamelan gong**. Most gamelan instruments are huge and far too heavy to be easily transported, so many *banjar* also possess a portable orchestra known as a **gamelan angklung**, designed around a set of miniature four-keyed metallophones, for playing in processions and at cremations or seashore ceremonies. There are also a few "bamboo orchestras", particularly in western Bali, where they're known as **gamelan joged bumbung** and **gamelan jegog**, composed entirely of bamboo instruments such as split bamboo tubes, marimbas and flutes.

The *gong kebyar* is made up of at least 25 instruments, and always features half-a-dozen tuned gongs, several sets of metallophones, two drums, a few sets of cymbals and one or more flutes. The leader of the orchestra is always one of the two **kendang** players (a double-ended cylindrical drum), whose job it is to link the different elements of the orchestra, and to take leads from the dancers. Cast in bronze and set in beautifully carved jackfruit-wood frames, often painted red and decorated with gold leaf, metal xylophones or **metallophones** create the distinctive clanging and shimmering gamelan sound. They come in a variety of forms, but are all designed around a series of bronze bars or keys (the smallest has four, the biggest fourteen) that are strung loosely together and suspended over bamboo resonators. Players strike each key with a small wood- or metal-tipped mallet held in the right hand, while simultaneously dampening the last key with the finger and thumb of the left hand. Since the *kebyar* is often played incredibly fast, metallophone players need phenomenal coordination to move up and down the "keyboard", striking and dampening two different keys at the same time.

Centre-stage is nearly always dominated by the row of ten or more linked bronze kettle-gongs (flattened bells with knobs on the top): the **trompong**. The large bronze **gong**, suspended from a frame at the back of the orchestra, marks off the beginning and end of each melody. Other minor and occasional instruments include different-sized cymbals (**cengceng**), bamboo flutes (**suling**), and the classical two-stringed violin, the **rebab**. Some orchestras feature guest spots from the **genggong**, a simple palm-wood jew's-harp, whose haunting vibrations sound a bit like the didgeridoo and ismost popularly used for the frog dance.

Discography of traditional music

Most tourist CD shops on Bali sell some traditional music; otherwise try Ganesha Books in Ubud (@www.ganeshabooksbali.com), which also offers international shipping.

Angklung Sidan (Bali Stereo). Ceremonial classics played by a small, light, processional gamelan orchestra.

Bali: Gamelan and Kecak (Nonesuch). A fine cross-section, including *gong kebyar*, *gender wayang*, *kecak* and *genggong*.

The Best of Gamelan Bali Parts 1 and 2 (Rick's/Maharani). Including music for the Jauk demon dance, and the rarely heard wooden xylophone, the *gambang*.

Degung Instrumental: Sabilu-lungan (SP Records). Not strictly Balinese, but played in every tourist restaurant and shop, this is typical Sundanese (west Javan) *degung*

featuring the softer gamelan and a prominent bamboo flute.

Gamelan Gong Kebyar of "Eka Cita" Abian Kapas Kaja (King World Music Library). A terrific example of the Balinese *kebyar* style.

Gamelan Semar Pegulingan: The Heavenly Orchestra of Bali (CMP). Sonorous recording of the gentle, older gamelan from Kamasan.

Jegog of Negara (King World Music Library). A bamboo ensemble from west Bali.

Music for the Gods (Rykodisc). Fascinating music from the 1940s, recorded by anthropologists Bruce and Sheridan Fahnestock.

Traditional dance-dramas of Bali

Most Balinese **dance–dramas** have evolved from **sacred rituals**, and are still performed at religious events, with full attention given to the offertory and devotional aspects. Before the show begins, a *pemangku* (village priest) sprinkles the players and the performance area with holy water, and many performances open with a Pendet, or welcome dance, intended for the gods. The exorcist Barong–Rangda dramas continue to play a vital function in the **spiritual practices** of every village, and the Baris dance re-enacts the traditional offering up of weapons by village warriors to the gods to invest them with supernatural power. Some of the more secular dance-dramas tell ancient and **legendary stories**, many of them adapted from the epic Hindu morality tales, the *Ramayana* and the *Mahabharata*, that came from India more than a thousand years ago.

Others are based on **historical events**, embellishing the romances and battles of the royal courts of Java and Bali between the tenth and the fourteenth centuries.

There are few professional **dancers** in Bali; most performers don costumes and make-up only at festival times or for the regular tourist shows. Dancers learn by imitation and repetition, the instructor often holding the pupil against his or her body and manipulating limbs until the exact angles and tensions are reproduced to perfection. Personal expression has no place in the Balinese theatre, but the skilful execution of traditional moves is much admired, and trained dancers enjoy high status within the community.

▲ Dance performance at Ubud Palace

Female dancers keep their feet firmly planted on the ground, their legs and hips encased in restrictive sarongs that give them a distinctive forward-angled posture. They express themselves through a vocabulary of controlled **angular movements** of the arms, wrists, fingers, neck and, most beguilingly, the eyes. Each pose and gesture derives from a movement observed in the natural rather than the human world. Thus, a certain type of flutter of the hand may be a bird in flight, a vigorous rotation of the forearms the shaking of water from an animal's coat. Dressed in pantaloons or hitched-up sarongs,

The Mahabharata

Like its companion piece the *Ramayana*, the **Mahabharata** is an epic moral narrative of Hindu ethics that came to Indonesia from India in the eleventh century. Written during the fourth century AD by the Indian poet Vyasa, the original poem is phenomenally long, at over 100,000 verses. The **Balinese version** is translated into the ancient poetic language of Kawi and written on sacred *lontar* books kept in the Gedong Kirtya library at Singaraja. Its most famous episodes are known to every Balinese and reiterated in paintings, sculpted reliefs, *wayang kulit* dramas and dances.

At the heart of the story is the conflict between two rival branches of the same family, the Pandawas and the Korawas, all of them descendants of various unions between the deities and the mortals. The five **Pandawa brothers** represent the side of virtue, morality and noble purpose, though they each have their own foibles. The eldest is **Yudhisthira**, a calm and thoughtful leader with a passion for justice, whose one vice – an insatiable love of gambling – nonetheless manages to land the brothers in trouble. Then comes **Bhima**, a strong, courageous and hot-headed fighter, whose fiery temper and earthy manner make him especially appealing to the Balinese. The third brother, **Arjuna**, is the real hero; not only is he a brave warrior and an expert archer, but he's also handsome, high-minded, and a great lover. Arjuna's two younger brothers, the expert horseman **Nakula** and the learned **Sahadeva**, are twins. Their rivals are their cousins the **Korawas**, who number a hundred in all, and are led by the eldest male **Durodhana**, a symbol of jealousy, deviousness and ignoble behaviour.

An early episode in the *Mahabharata* tells how the Pandawa boys are forced by the usurping Korawas to give up their rightful claim to the throne. Banished to the mountains for a minimum of thirteen years, the Pandawas grow up determined to regain what is theirs. Meanwhile, both families engage in countless adventures, confrontations with gods and demons, long journeys, seductions and practical jokes. A particular favourite is the exploit known as **Bhima Swarga**, in which Bhima is dispatched to Hell to rescue the souls of his dead father and stepmother. While there, he witnesses all sorts of horrible tortures and punishments, many of which are graphically depicted on the ceilings of Semarapura's Kerta Gosa. When Bhima returns to earth with the souls of his relatives, he's immediately sent off to Heaven in search of the holy water needed to smooth his dead parents' passage there. This episode is known as **Bhima Suci** and features the nine directional gods, as well as a dramatic battle between Bhima and his own godly (as opposed to earthly) father, Bayu.

Finally, a full-scale battle is declared between the two sets of cousins. On the eve of the battle, Arjuna suddenly becomes doubtful about the morality of fighting his own family, and confides as much to his friend and charioteer Krishna. Krishna, who is actually an avatar of the Hindu god Wisnu, then launches into a long theological lecture, in which he explains to Arjuna that the action is the all-important factor, not the result, and that because Arjuna is of the warrior caste, his duty is to fight, to act in a manner that's appropriate to his destiny. This episode of the *Mahabharata* is known as the **Bhagavad Gita**, and encapsulates the core Hindu philosophy of caste, and the notions of karma and destiny. Duly persuaded, Arjuna joins his brothers in battle, and at the end of eighteen bloody days the Pandawa brothers are victorious.

the **male dancers** are much more energetic, and whirl about a lot, emphasizing their manliness by opening shoulders and limbs outwards, keeping their knees bent and their heads high.

Most dramas are performed either within a temple compound, or in the outer courtyard of a noble family's palace. The **costumes and masks** give immediate clues to the identity of each character – and to the action that is to follow. Some dramas are performed in a combination of contemporary Bahasa Indonesia and the ancient literary Kawi language, while others stick to modern speech – perhaps with a few humorous English phrases thrown in for the tourists.

In the last sixty years, the Balinese dance repertoire has expanded quite considerably, not least because of the efforts of one of the island's most famous performers, the late I Ketut Marya. Better known as **Mario**, he was also a highly imaginative choreographer, adapting old forms to suit the modern mood, and most famously to fit the modern *kebyar* gamelan style in the 1920s.

Baris

The **Baris** or **Warrior Dance** can be performed either as a solo or in a group of five or more, by a young woman, or more commonly a young man. Strutting on stage with knees and feet turned out, his centre of gravity kept low, the Baris cuts an impressive figure in a gilded brocade cloak of ribboned pennants, which fly out dramatically at every turn. In his performance, he enacts a young warrior's preparation for battle, goading himself into courageous mood, trying out his martial skills, showing pride at his calling and then expressing a whole series of emotions – ferocity, passion, tenderness, rage – much of it through his eyes.

Traditionally, the solo Baris has always improvised a lot, leading the gamelan rather than following it. In its original sacred form, known as the Baris Gede, this was a devotional dance in which soldiers dedicated themselves and their weapons to the gods.

Barong–Rangda dramas

Featuring the most spectacular costumes of all the Balinese dances, the **Barong–Rangda dramas** are also among the most sacred and important. Essentially a dramatization of the eternal conflict between the forces of good and evil, the dramas take various forms but nearly always serve as ritualized exorcisms.

The mythical widow-witch character of **Rangda** represents the forces of evil, and her costume and mask present a frightening spectacle (see p.226 for Rangda's story). The **Barong** cuts a much more lovable figure, a shaggy-haired creature with a bug-eyed expression and a mischievous grin on his masked face, something like a cross between a pantomime horse and a Chinese dragon. The Barong Ket (lion) is his most common persona, but you might also see Barong Macan (tiger), Barong Bangkal (wild boar) and Barong Celeng (pig). All Rangda and Barong **masks** are invested with great sacred power and treated with extreme respect; when not in use, they're wrapped in sacred cloth and stored in the temple.

Barong–Rangda dramas can be self-contained, as in the Calonarang (see below), or they can be just one symbolic episode in the middle of a well-known story like the *Mahabharata*. Whatever the context, the format tends to be similar. Rangda is always called upon by a character who wants to cause harm to a person, family or village (unrequited love is a common cause). She generally sends a minion to wage the first battles, and is then forced to appear herself when the opposition calls in the Barong, the defender of the good. In this final

Written in Sanskrit around the fourth century BC, the 24,000 verses that comprise the **Ramayana** have since fired the imaginations of writers, artists, dramatists and theologians right across Southeast Asia. Like the other great Hindu epic, the *Mahabharata*, the *Ramayana* has been translated into the classical Javanese Kawi language and transcribed on to sacred *lontar* texts.

It's essentially a morality tale, a dramatization of the eternal conflict between the forces of good (*dharma*) and the forces of evil (*adharma*). The forces of good are represented by Rama and his friends. **Rama**, the hero, is a refined and dutiful young man, handsome, strong and courageous, who also happens to be an avatar of the god Wisnu. Rama's wife, **Sita**, epitomizes the Hindu ideals of womanhood – virtue, fidelity and love – while Rama's brother, **Laksmana**, is a symbol of fraternal loyalty and youthful courage. The other important member of the Rama camp is **Hanuman**, the general of the monkey army, a wily and athletic ape who is unfailingly loyal to his allies. On the opposing side, the forces of evil are mainly represented by the demon king **Rawana**, a lustful and devious leader whose retainers are giants and devils.

The story begins with Rama, the eldest son of the king, being banished to the forests for thirteen years, having been cheated out of his rightful claim to the throne by a scheming stepmother. Sita and Laksmana accompany him, and together the trio have various encounters with sages, giants and seductresses.

The most crucial event in the epic is the **abduction of Sita** by Rawana, a crime that inspires the rather unwarlike Rama to wage battle against his enemy. A favourite subject for dances and carvings, the episode starts with Sita catching sight of a beautiful golden deer and imploring her husband Rama to catch it for her. The golden deer turns out to be a decoy planted by Rawana, and the demon king duly swoops down to abduct Sita as soon as Rama and Laksmana go off to chase the animal. The distraught Rama determines to get Sita back and, together with Laksmana, he sets off for Rawana's kingdom. En route he meets Hanuman, the monkey general, who agrees to sneak him into Sita's room at Rawana's palace and **give her Rama's ring** (another popular theme of pictures and dramas). Eventually, Rama, Laksmana, Hanuman and his monkey army all arrive at Rawana's palace and, following a big battle, Sita is rescued and Rawana done away with.

confrontation, the Barong enters first, occasionally joined by a monkey who teases him and plays tricks. Suddenly, Rangda appears, fingernails first, from behind the central gateway. Flashing her magic white cloth, she harasses the Barong, stalking him at every turn. When the Barong looks to be on his last legs, a group of village men rush in to his rescue, but are entranced by Rangda's magic and stab themselves instead of her. A priest quickly enters before any real injury is inflicted. The series of confrontations continues, and the drama ends in stalemate: the forces of good and evil remain as strong and vital as ever, ready to clash again in the next bout.

The **Calonarang** is an embellished version of the Barong–Rangda conflict, grafted on to an ancient legend about the daughter of a witch queen whom no one will marry because they're scared of her mother. The witch queen Calonarang is a manifestation of Rangda who, furious at the lack of suitors for her daughter, demands that her followers wreak destruction in all the villages. This drama is acted out on a regular basis, whenever there are considered to be evil forces and impurities affecting the community, and sometimes the whole neighbourhood takes part, the men parading with hand-held *kulkul* drums and the women filing in to make offerings at the temple shrines.

There's also an unusual human version of the Barong, called **Barong Landung** ("Tall Barong"). These are huge puppets, one male and one female, each one operated by a single performer. The male puppet looks forbidding, his masked face is black, and he has a fanged, grimacing mouth. As a representation of the legendary Jero Gede, a giant from Nusa Penida who brought disease and misfortune to Bali, this enormous figure is also meant to scare away any similar giants. Jero Gede is always accompanied by a far sweeter-looking female puppet, known as Jero Luh, who wears a white mask with a smiling face and faintly Chinese eyes. Together they act out a bawdy comic opera, which has exorcist purposes as well.

Kebyar

A great wave of artistic experimentation hit Bali in the 1920s, particularly in north Bali, where a group of young musicians came up with a vibrant and much brasher type of gamelan music, the **kebyar**, whose energetic rhythms inspired the talented young dancer Mario to choreograph a new piece. He performed this dance while seated on the ground and so called it **Kebyar Duduk** (Seated Kebyar). It's a stunningly camp piece of theatre, starring just one man, who alternately flirts with the gamelan, plays the kettle-gongs (*trompong*) that are placed in front of him, and flutters his fan in beguiling self-dramatization. Some years later, a slightly different version of this dance was invented, the **Kebyar Trompong**, in which the dancer sits and plays the *trompong* for only part of the performance, in between mincing coquettishly about the stage and making eyes at the audience.

Kecak

Sometimes called the **Monkey Dance** after the animals represented by the chorus, the **Kecak** gets its Balinese name from the hypnotic chattering sounds made by the a cappella choir. Chanting nothing more than "cak cak cak cak", the chorus of fifty or more men uses seven different rhythms to create the astonishing music that accompanies the drama. Bare-chested, and wearing lengths of black-and-white-check *kain poleng* cloth around their waists and a single red hibiscus behind the ear, the men sit cross-legged in five or six tight concentric circles, occasionally swaying or waving arms and clapping hands in unison. The **narrative** itself is taken from a core episode of the *Ramayana*, centring around the kidnap of Sita by the demon king Rawana, and is acted out in the middle of the chorus circle, with one or two narrators speaking for all the characters.

Although frequently attributed to the German artist and musician Walter Spies, the main creative force behind the Kecak was the famous Baris dancer **I Wayan Limbak**, who lived in Bedulu in Gianyar. In 1931, he developed the chants from the Sanghyang trance dances, in which the chorus chants the "cak cak cak" syncopation as part of the trance-inducing ritual, and created accompanying choreography to flesh out the episode from the *Ramayana*.

Legong

Undoubtedly the most refined of all the temple dances, the **Legong** is rather an acquired taste, characterized by the restrained, intricate weavings of arms, fingers, torsos and heads. It's always performed by three prepubescent girls who are bound tightly in sarongs and chest cloths of opulent green or pink, with gilded crowns filled with frangipani blossoms on their heads. The Legong is considered the acme of Balinese femininity and Legong dancers have always enjoyed a special status in their village, a reputation that endures long after they retire at the onset of menstruation. In the past, many a Legong dancer has ended up as a raja's wife or, latterly, as an expatriate artist's muse.

The dance evolved from a highly sacred Sanghyang trance dance and takes several different forms. By far the most common is the **Legong Keraton** (Dance of the Court), based on a classical twelfth-century tale from Java. It tells the story of King Laksem, who is holding a princess, Rangkesari, captive against her will. Rescue is on the way in the form of Prince Daha, who plans to wage battle against King Laksem. The princess tries to dissuade the king from going to war, but he sets off anyway. As he leaves, he is attacked by a raven, an extremely bad omen, after which he duly loses the battle and is killed.

The **performance** begins with a solo dance by a court lady, known as the *condong* (dressed in pink and gold). She picks up two fans from the ground in anticipation of the arrival of the two *legong* (literally "dancer"). Dressed identically in bright green and gold, the two Legong enact the story, adopting and swapping characters with no obvious distinction. The *condong* always returns as the raven, with pink wings attached to her costume. The final fatal battle is never shown on stage.

Oleg Tambulilingan

Translated as the **Bumblebee Dance**, the Oleg Tambulilingan is one of the most vivacious, humorous and engaging dances of the Balinese repertoire but unfortunately doesn't get performed that often. It's a flirtation dance, performed by a man and woman who act as courting bumblebees sipping honey in a flower garden, the man sexually obsessed with the female, desire burning in his eyes, the female coquettish and eventually compliant.

The Oleg Tambulilingan was invented in 1952 by the late, great dancer Mario. The female role is complicated, needing a highly skilled performer, and so is often taken by a former Legong dancer.

Sanghyang: trance dances

The state of **trance** lies at the heart of traditional Balinese dance. In order to maintain the health of the village, the gods are periodically invited down into the temple to help in the exorcism of evil and sickness-inducing spirits. The deities reveal themselves by possessing certain individuals, sometimes communicating through them with words, which may have to be interpreted by a priest, and sometimes taking over the whole physical being so that the medium is moved to dance or to perform astonishing physical feats. The chosen medium is put into a trance state through a combination of priestly chants and protective mantras, intoned exhortations by the a cappella choir, and great clouds of incense wafted heavenwards to attract the gods' attention. Trance dances are traditionally only performed when the village is suffering from a particularly serious bout of sickness or ill fortune – the versions that are reproduced at tourist shows have none of the spiritual dynamism of the real thing, though it is said that performers do sometimes slip into trance even then.

One of the most common trance dances is the **Sanghyang Dedari** (Angel Deity), which probably inspired the popular courtly dance, the Legong. In the Sanghyang Dedari, two young girls become possessed and perform a complicated duet with their eyes closed; though they have never learnt the steps, the girls usually perform in sync, sometimes for up to four hours. In the Sanghyang Dedari performed at tourist shows, however, the girls have almost certainly rehearsed the dance beforehand and probably do not enter a trance state at all. They wear the same tightly bound green and gold sarongs as the Legong dancers, and dance to the haunting backing vocals of an a cappella chorus of men and women.

In the **Sanghyang Jaran** (Horse Deity), one or more men are put into a trance state while the temple floor is littered with burning coconut husks. As they enter the trance, the men grab hold of wooden hobbyhorse sticks and then gallop frantically back and forth across the red-hot embers as if they were on real horses. The all-male Kecak chorus fuels the drama with excited a cappella crescendos until, finally, the exhausted hobbyhorse riders are awoken by the priest.

Topeng: mask dances

In the **Topeng** or **Mask Dance**, the performer is possessed by the spirit of the mask (for more on which, see p.457). Before every entrance, the Topeng actor sprinkles holy water on his mask and recites a mantra. Women never participate in Topeng: female roles are played by men, and most actors play several characters in each drama.

Topeng **storylines** usually centre around popular folk tales or well-known episodes from history, and the characters are immediately recognizable. Refined and **noble characters** always wear full masks, usually painted white with almond-shaped eyes, and heavy eyebrows for the men. They communicate with elegant gestures of the hands, arms and head, and move with rather grand, often swaggering bravado. A royal servant always acts as a narrator figure, speaking on behalf of the voiceless nobles, and he, like the coarser **clowns** and **servants**, wears a half-mask and baggy shapeless clothing in which to roll about the floor and engage in comic antics.

One of the most popular mask dances is the **Topeng Tua**, a touching solo in which an elderly retired first-minister recalls his time in the king's service. His mask is fringed with straggly white hair and beard, and his gait is frail and wavering. Another favourite tourist Topeng is the **Frog Dance** – performed to the evocative music of the Balinese jew's-harp or *genggong* – which tells how a frog turns into a prince. In the **Jauk**, the soloist portrays a terrifying demon-king who leaps mischievously about the stage as if darting from behind trees and pouncing on unsuspecting villagers. His red or white mask has bulging eyes and a creepy smile and he flashes his foot-long fingernails menacingly throughout.

Wayang kulit: shadow puppet shows

Wayang kulit or **shadow puppet shows** are typically staged as entertainment following large ceremonial events such as weddings, cremations or temple *odalan*. The stories are often taken from the *Mahabharata*, but improvisation and topical jokes keep the art alive and a skilled and witty *dalang* (puppeteer), nearly always a man, can attract huge crowds and keep them entertained into the early hours. The performance takes place behind a white cloth screen illuminated by flaming torches and may star as many as sixty different **wayang** (puppets), which are always made from buffalo hide and mounted on a stick. (You can see the workshops of some well-known *dalang* in Sukawati, described on p.172.) As in many other Balinese dramas, *wayang* characters are either refined and noble (royals, holy men and women, heroes and heroines) or coarse and vulgar (clowns and servants). The refined characters speak in the ancient courtly language of Kawi, while the coarse characters use Balinese.

Amazingly, the **dalang** not only manipulates each of his many *wayang* himself, but speaks for each one of them as well, displaying an impressive memory for lines and an extraordinary range of different voices. At the same time he also conducts the special four-piece orchestra that accompanies his performances, the *gender wayang*. Not surprisingly, *dalang* are greatly revered and considered to have great spiritual power.

The torch-lit **screen** represents the world in microcosm: the puppets are the humans that inhabit it, the torch represents the sun, and the *dalang* acts as god. Puppets who represent good characters always appear to the right of the *dalang*, and those who are evil appear on his left. A leaf-shaped fan-like puppet, symbolizing the tree of life, marks centre stage and is used to indicate the end of a scene as well as to represent clouds, spirits and magical forces.

Lombok music and dance

Lombok has a rich heritage of music and dance. The indigenous Sasak traditions have been subject to many influences, both Hindu and Islamic, direct from Bali and Java, and through Buginese and Makassarese traders. The resulting melange of puppetry, poetry, song and dance is varied, but largely inaccessible to tourists. There are **no cultural shows** like those on Bali, but you may stumble across a wedding or other celebration on your travels.

Lombok's gamelan music

Lombok's traditional **gamelan** music is similar to Bali's, though some of the orchestras are different. The **gamelan gong Sasak** resembles the *gamelan gong*, but may be combined with the unusual **gamelan grantang**, consisting of bamboo xylophones. The **gamelan oncer** is also widely used, and accompanies the Gendang Beleq dance, in which instrumentalists carry and play large drums and dance a dramatic and confrontational duet.

Gamelan tawa-tawa and **barong tengkok** are used in processions during life-cycle celebrations such as weddings or circumcision and other festivities such as national holidays. The usual gongs and drums are accompanied by eight sets of cymbals attached to decorated lances for marching with. The gamelan *barong tengkok* from central Lombok actually has gongs suspended within a Barong figure, and traditionally plays at wedding ceremonies, while the bride and groom are paraded on wooden horses. **Gamelan rebana** consists of up to twenty different drums, which mimic the traditional sound of gamelan music, but without the use of bronze instruments. More unusual is the **gamelan klentang**, made up entirely of iron instruments. Other musical ensembles that are seen on the island include **kecimol** and **cilokaq**, consisting of an oboe (*preret*), flutes, lutes, violins and drums, and are often played to accompany Sasak poetry.

Lombok's performance arts

In contrast to the huge academic interest in Balinese performance art, Lombok dance has been studied far less although the **dances** generally cover the same range of themes as those on the neighbouring island. The **Gandrung**, for instance, is a demonstration of **love**. It is performed mainly in central Lombok by a solo female dancer who selects a man to join her in the performance.

Lombok also has examples of **trance dances**. The **Suling Dewa**, accompanied by flutes and song, is found in the north of the island, and used to induce spirits to enter the local shaman and bless the village. The **Pepakon**, from east

Lombok, causes the sick to become possessed so that their illness can be removed from them.

Processional dances also occur. The **Batek Baris** is performed in Lingsar, among other places, the dancers wearing costumes mimicking Dutch army uniforms and carrying wooden rifles while they lead a procession to the sacred springs. The **Tandang Mendet** takes place rarely, and only in the mountain village of Sembalun Bumbung, and heads a procession to the grave of a Majapahit ancestor buried in the valley.

Other dances take place traditionally at certain times of year; for example, the **Tandak Geroq**, in east Lombok usually occurs after the hard work of the harvest.

As in Bali, some dances in Lombok are based on **legends**. The **Telek** is based very broadly on the tale of a princess who falls in love with a humble man; the **Kemidi Rudat** on the *Thousand and One Nights* stories, complete with colourful characters and clowns; and the **Kayak Sando** (with masks) on the Panji stories from Java in which a prince undertakes numerous adventures in search of his lost bride.

More a **martial art** than a performing art, but still a massive spectator draw, **peresean fighting** involves two men attacking each other with long rattan canes with only buffalo-skin shields to defend themselves – this is for real as the injuries show.

Modern Balinese music

The past decade has seen an explosion in the popularity of modern Balinese music – on Bali itself, throughout Indonesia, and even abroad. There are two main genres: Balinesia, in which the Balinese artists **sing in Indonesian**, and Balibali, in which they **sing in Balinese**. Albums by musicians from both genres far outsell their Western competition in Bali now, and concerts are often as well attended as those of the major national (mainly Javanese) bands.

The cultural impact of this boom has been significant. Instead of feeling marginalized and crowded out by Java, Balinese youth now have a channel through which they can express themselves; they can at last voice their disappointment with the political elite and epidemic corruption.

There is also a new pride in the Balinese language, whose "cool" status has been given a boost by artists singing in Balinese. The growing indie scene has opened up people's eyes to the possibility of doing something different from the Balinese norm and this is reflected in the trend for all things rockabilly and punk, from new independent clothing shops (*distro*) selling original fashion and music paraphernalia, to chopper-style motorbikes and lowrider pushbikes.

Balinesia

Balinesia emerged in the mid-80s with rock bands who favoured covers and drew large crowds. To be an AC/DC wannabe, to cover Gary Moore's songs, to shred guitar as fast as Rainbow's Ritchie Blackmore was considered ultracool.

But the Balinesia breakthrough came in 2003 when punk-rock band **Superman Is Dead (SID)** released their debut album *Kuta Rock City* with a major label, Sony Music Indonesia (now Sony BMG Indonesia) – an enormous deal for Bali. They were the first Balinese band to make it big outside Bali and the first to record mostly in English. They toured Australia in 2007 and continue to be huge in Bali.

Grunge band **Navicula** followed SID onto a major label with their album *Alkemis*, in Indonesian and English. Their live performance is like experiencing a wall of sound and with their focus on social and environmental issues they are the new hippies of the island, commanding great respect, especially from the young.

Virtuoso guitarist **Balawan** plays jazz with an ethnic touch and has performed frequently overseas, from Europe to Japan. His side band, Balawan & Batuan Ethnic Fusion, mixes jazz and Balinese music, using traditional gamelan instruments, *kendang* (drums) and bamboo flutes alongside guitars, drums and keyboards. Balawan is a master of finger-tapping and the only guitarist in Indonesia who plays double-neck guitar with two independent hands (eight-finger touch style). His major label debut is aptly titled *Magic Fingers*.

Rockabillies **The Hydrant** are an exciting band to see live and have a significant fanbase outside Bali in major Indonesian cities such as Jakarta, Surabaya and Yogyakarta. Their major label debut, *Rockabilly Live*, is in Indonesian and English.

Mixing punk and rockabilly, "psychobilly" band **Suicidal Sinatra** are massive in Bali and have enjoyed a similarly positive reception nationwide – the current craze for psychobilly began in Bali before hitting the rest of Indonesia. They have reached an international audience via the compilation album *Tropicalize 2*, which features their song "White Shoes" alongside tracks by big international names like Jack Johnson and Michael Franti & Spearhead.

Saharadja is the most famous world-music act from Bali. They are often invited to collaborate with other Indonesian bands and to participate in music festivals around the country.

Balibali

The **Balibali** phenomenon is unique in Indonesia and the music tends to be edgy and controversial. Although Balibali artists only sing in Balinese, their popularity is not as limited as you might expect because of the tightknit Balinese communities on Lombok, Kalimantan, Sumatra and Sulawesi.

Balibali began with the folk-style bands of the 1960s and came of age in the mid-80s when several artists released pop-rock style albums in Balinese and began writing more risqué lyrics, perhaps due to Western influences. But the big shake-up came in 2003 when Lolot 'N Band released *Gumine Mangkin*. **Lolot**, the singer, was a complete original with his punk-rock attitude and confrontational Balinese lyrics totally unlike the plaintive style common to the genre. He invented so-called alternative rock in Bali and pushed the boundaries with songs such as "Bangsat" ("Bastard"), a social protest anthem against the grasping Indonesian authorities whose refrain says: "Fuck, stop fighting/Look at the price of food commodities that are rising/Fuck, stop fighting/Look at the marginalized people, they are the victims".

CONTEXTS | Modern Balinese music

Discography

Modern Balinese music is hard to find outside Indonesia, but within Bali the best sources are major **record-store** chains such as Disc Tarra, local records shops and *distro*.

Punk rock/Alternative rock
Superman Is Dead *Black Market Love* (Balinesia; some lyrics in English)
Suicidal Sinatra *Boogie Woogie Psychobilly* (Balinesia; a few lyrics in English)
The Hydrant *Rockabilly Live* (Balinesia; a few lyrics in English)
Lolot 'N Band *Meong Garong* (Balibali)
Bintang *Playboy Funky* (Balibali)
Nanoe Biroe *Suba Kadung Matulis* (Balibali)

Grunge/Metal
Navicula *Beautiful Rebel* (Balinesia; a few lyrics in English)
Parau *Surga Bencana* (Balinesia; a few lyrics in English)

Jazz/World music
Balawan *Magic Fingers* (Balinesia; a few lyrics in English)
Sahardja *One World* (Balinesia; lyrics mainly in English)

Reggae
Joni Agung & Double T *Melalung* (Balibali)

Hip-hop
[XXX] *Jingkrak Jingkrak* (Balibali)

Pop
Dek Ulik *Rindu Ngantosang Janji* (Balibali)
Widi Widiana *Kilang Kileng* (Balibali)

Lolot remains one of Bali's rock giants but these days it's **Nanoe Biroe** who's the biggest Balibali rock star, commanding a legion of fanatical fans known as "Beduda" who see him as a hero, a prophet even. All over Bali, you'll come across countless young men wearing "President of Beduda" T-shirts, bearing a Nanoe version of the famous Che Guevara silhouette. "Beduda" is Balinese for dung beetle and so Nanoe has cleverly positioned himself as the leader of marginalized people.

Among other styles within the Balibali genre, **[XXX]** is Bali's only hip-hop band, a long-time popular act with very decent record sales. The island's top reggae artists are **Joni Agung & Double T**; their records also sell well and they are constantly on tour around Bali. Dreadlocked Joni is quite a local celebrity. Diva **Dek Ulik** is also popular locally, especially among women. Her debut album of 2005, *Rindu Ngantosang Janji*, sold over 50,000 copies, a first for a Balinese female soloist.

Venues, further info and music festivals

The main live-music **venues** for Balinese bands are in Kuta and Denpasar, and are detailed in the relevant accounts. For gig **listings** check the fortnightly English-language magazine *the beat* (@www.beatmag.com), available for free throughout south Bali, and the online music directory *Musikator* (@www.musikator.com). For news, **info** and gossip about the music scene in Indonesia, see @www.arocksociety.com, @www.deathrockstar.info, @www.suicideglam.net and @www.lagubali.com. You can also watch Balinese bands on **Bali Music Channel**, a local version of MTV, and hear them on the many dedicated local music radio stations.

Modern music **festivals** in Indonesia depend solely on corporate sponsorship and occur quite frequently though not at fixed times of the year. Those worth keeping an eye out for include Bali Jamfest, a huge two-day event featuring every major Balinese artist, and Soundrenaline, a touring Indonesian version of Australia's "Big Day Out" which invites a lot of local bands to join in. The annual Kuta Karnival, usually held in September (see p.100) also features several stages and a stimulating mix of Bali and national band line-ups.

Rudolf Dethu and Sarah Forbes

Arts and crafts

T he desire to make things look good – and to make beautiful things – is so ingrained in the Balinese way of life that there is no separate Balinese word for "art" or "artist". Villagers have traditionally considered it their unquestioned duty to honour both their gods and their rajas with attractive objects and buildings. Although highly skilled, the **carvers**, **sculptors**, **weavers** and **painters** who decorated Bali's temples and palaces were never paid for their work, and would earn their living as farmers or traders, just like everybody else. By the 1930s, however, the rajas had lost a great deal of their power and foreign tourists were gradually taking their place as **patrons of the arts** – and paying for the work. Over time, artists began to carve and paint secular subjects, to experiment with new materials, to express themselves as individuals and to sign their own work. Making paintings and carvings became a full-time, and relatively lucrative, job, and the arts and crafts industry is now one of the most profitable on Bali.

Lombok lacks the dynamic artistic heritage of Bali, and as a predominantly Islamic island that forbids the depiction of the human form, has virtually no indigenous fine art. However, there is a thriving crafts tradition.

For general information on **where to buy** arts and crafts in Bali and Lombok, see p.58; for an introduction to the crafts and their producers see the colour insert "The Crafts of Bali and Lombok".

Balinese painting

Art historians group traditional **Balinese painting** into five broad **schools**: *wayang* (also known as classical or Kamasan), Ubud, Batuan, Young Artists, and Modern or Academic.

Wayang or Kamasan style

The earliest Balinese painters drew their inspiration from the *wayang kulit* shadow plays, re-creating puppet-like figures on their canvases and depicting episodes from the same religious and historical epics that were played out on the stage. Variously known as the **wayang style**, the **classical style** or the **Kamasan style** (after the village most noted for its *wayang*-style art), this is the most traditional genre of Balinese art, and the one that's been the least influenced by Western techniques and subjects. The oldest-known examples are temple scrolls, curtains and astrological charts from the mid-seventeenth century, though these survive only through descriptions in contemporary literature. The finest and most famous *wayang*-style pictures are those that adorn the ceilings of the **Kerta Gosa** (Law Courts) and the Bale Kambung (Floating Pavilion) in the old palace of Semarapura (see p.232), which were probably painted in the early nineteenth century and have been retouched several times.

All *wayang*-style pictures are packed full of people painted in **three-quarter profile**, with caricature-like features and angular, puppet-like poses. There is no perspective, and stylized symbols indicate the location; in lengthy narratives, the pictures are divided into scenes by borders composed of rows of mountains, flames or walls. Traditional *wayang* artists limit their palette to red, blue, yellow, black and white, creating the hallmark muted effect. Because of all the stages involved in a *wayang*-style picture, most modern paintings are produced by a team, with the senior artist drawing the outlines in black while assistants fill in the colours.

As with the *wayang* puppets, the **characters** in the paintings are instantly recognizable by their facial features and hairstyles and by their clothes, stance and size. Convention requires, for example, that "refined" characters (heroes, heroines and other people of noble birth) look slightly supercilious whatever the occasion – in love, in battle, in anger or in joy – and that their bodies be svelte and elegant. "Coarse" characters, on the other hand, like clowns, servants and demonic creatures, have bulbous eyes, prominent teeth and chunky bodies.

The *wayang* style is still popular with modern artists: some stick faithfully to classical themes, while others experiment more freely. The traditional school is centred on the village of **Kamasan** near Semarapura, the home of the original Kerta Gosa artists and subsequent generations of restorers, as well as the most famous living artist of the Kamasan school, **I Nyoman Mandra**. Commercially minded Kamasan artists now apply their talents to more portable artefacts, such as small cloth pictures and reproductions of traditional calendars.

Ubud style

Although *wayang*-style pictures were occasionally peppered with incidents taken from everyday life, few artists took much interest in secular subjects until the early decades of the twentieth century. In the 1930s, however, Balinese painters started to experiment with more **naturalistic techniques**, including perspective and the use of light and shadow, and to reproduce in acrylics the events witnessed at the market, the temple, the village and the ricefields. As tourists and expatriate artists began taking a commercial interest in the works, painters made their pictures a more portable size and framed them as well. As the hub of this experimentation was Ubud, the style has been dubbed **Ubud style**.

Despite its innovations, the Ubud style retains many typical *wayang* features, particularly the overwhelming sense of **activity** that characterizes the canvases (a concept described in Balinese as *rame*), with every character engaged in some transaction or chore or conversation, and any intervening space taken up with detailed miniature reproductions of offerings or scavenging dogs. Every palm leaf and blade of grass is painstakingly delineated, every sarong pattern described, but people are rarely given much individuality, their faces usually set in a rather stylized expression.

The two expatriate artists most commonly associated with the emergence of the Ubud style are the German **Walter Spies** and the Dutchman **Rudolph**

Art galleries

Ubud is the centre for all things arty and not only houses the majority of Bali's best art museums but is also home to dozens of artists' studios, both local and expat. The best collection of Balinese painting on the island is housed in the **Neka Art Museum** in Ubud (see p.192), where you'll get an excellent introduction to all the major styles, and see some of the finest Balinese pictures in existence. Other worthwhile Ubud art museums include the **Seniwati Gallery of Art by Women** (see p.189), which is dedicated to paintings by women living in Bali; the Agung Rai Museum of Art, **ARMA** (see p.199), whose collection covers choice works from the past three hundred years; the **Museum Puri Lukisan** (see p.187), which features select paintings and woodcarvings from the 1930s on; and **Museum Rudana** (see p.174), which is good for contemporary art. Outside Ubud, head for the **Gunarsa Museum of Classical and Modern Art** near Semarapura (see p.234). For unrivalled examples of classical Balinese art, visit the old **Taman Gili** palace in Semarapura (see p.232).

Bonnet. Both men lived in the Ubud area in the 1930s and were involved in setting up the arts group Pita Maha, which was instrumental in encouraging innovation and individual expression. Most of the best-known Ubud-style artists are represented in the major Ubud art museums, among them the highly rated **Anak Agung Gede Sobrat**.

Pengosekan style

During the 1960s, a group of young painters working in the Ubud style and living in the village of Pengosekan on the outskirts of Ubud came up with a new approach, subsequently known as the **Pengosekan style**. From the Ubud-style pictures, the Pengosekan school isolated just a few components, specifically the **birds**, **butterflies**, **insects** and **flowering plants**, and magnified them to fill a whole canvas. The best Pengosekan paintings look delicate and lifelike, generally depicted in soothing pastels, and reminiscent of classical Japanese flower and bird pictures. To see some of the finer pictures, you can either go to the showroom run by the descendants of the original Pengosekan artists, in their village, to the Seniwati Gallery in Ubud or the commercial Agung Rai Gallery in Peliatan.

Batuan style

In contrast to the slightly romanticized visions of village events being painted by the Ubud-style artists in the 1930s, a group of painters in nearby Batuan were taking a more quizzical approach. Like the *wayang* artists, **Batuan-style** painters filled their works with scores of people, but on a much more frantic and wide-ranging scale. A single Batuan-style picture might contain a dozen apparently unrelated scenes – a temple dance, a rice harvest, a fishing expedition, an exorcism, and a couple of tourists taking snapshots – all depicted in fine detail that strikes a balance between the naturalistic and the stylized. By clever juxtaposition, the best Batuan artists, such as the Neka Art Museum exhibitors **I Wayan Bendi**, **I Made Budi** and **Ni Wayan Warti**, can turn their pictures into amusing and astute comments on Balinese society. Works by their precursors, the original Batuan artists, **Ida Bagus Made Togog** and **Ida Bagus Made Wija**, focused more on the darker side of village life, on the supernatural beings that hung around the temples and forests, and on the overwhelming sense of men and women as tiny elements in a forceful natural world.

Young Artists style

A second flush of artistic innovation hit the Ubud area in the 1960s, when a group of teenage boys from **Penestanan** started producing unusually expressionist works, painting everyday scenes in vibrant, non-realistic colours. They soon became known as the **Young Artists**, a tag now used to describe work by anyone in that same style. The boys were encouraged by Dutch artist **Arie Smit**, who settled in Penestanan in the 1960s, gave them materials and helped organize exhibitions. The style is indisputably childlike, even naive: the detailed, mosaic-like compositions of scenes from daily life are crudely drawn with minimal attention to perspective, outlined in black like a child's colouring book, and often washed over in weird shades of pink, purple and blue.

All the major museums have works by some of the original Young Artists from the 1960s, the most famous of whom include **I Ketut Tagen**, **I Wayan Pugur**, **I Nyoman Londo**, **I Nyoman Mundik** and **I Nyoman Mujung**. The Neka Art Museum in Ubud devotes a whole gallery to Arie Smit's own work.

Academic and Bali modernism

Bali's modern artists, both indigenous and expatriate, are sometimes labelled as **Academic**, meaning that they've studied and been influenced by Western modernism but have settled in Bali and paint Balinese subjects. Many of the best-known are graduates from the Yogyakarta Academy of Fine Arts in Java, and some are or have been part of the **Sanggar Dewata Indonesia** art movement, whose style – loosely defined as Balinese Hindu abstract expressionism – has been the dominant form of modern Balinese painting since the 1970s. Although the style has been somewhat devalued by the countless poor-quality abstracts sold in souvenir shops across Bali, works by the most famous Academics – including **Affandi**, **Anton H** and **Abdul Aziz**, all from Java, the Sumatran-born **Rusli**, and from Bali, **Made Wianta**, **Nyoman Gunarsa**, **Nyoman Erawan** and **Made Budiana** – are on show at the Ubud museums and the Gunarsa Museum near Semarapura. Of these important modern artists, Made Wianta is probably the best-known internationally; famous for his multimedia pieces and performance art, he represented Indonesia in the Venice 2003 Biennale, with a video installation on the Kuta bombings.

Woodcarving

The idea that woodcarvings could be purely ornamental or expressive didn't gather credence until the early years of the twentieth century, when Balinese carvers began both to take a greater interest in **secular subjects** and to court the burgeoning tourist market with carvings of nudes, lifelike animals and witty portraits. The most popular styles were quickly copied, and a whole new artistic genre evolved in just a few years.

By the mid-1930s however commercialization had set in and standards were slipping, so a group of influential artists and collectors established the **Pita Maha** foundation to encourage Bali's best carvers to be more experimental. One of these carvers was **Ida Bagus Nyana**, from the village of Mas, who, from the 1930s to the 1960s, produced works in a range of innovative styles, including abstract elongated human figures, erotic compositions of entwined limbs, and smooth, rounded portraits of voluptuously fat men and women. His son, **Ida Bagus Tilem**, continued to experiment and was particularly famous for his highly expressive pieces fashioned from contorted roots and twisted branches. Works by both artists are on show at the outstanding Nyana Tilem Gallery in Mas (see p.173). The Jati artist **I Nyoman Cokot** developed a "free-form" style that made turned monstrous branches into weird, otherworldly creatures, while his son, **Ketut Nongos**, lets his supernatural beings emerge from the contours of weatherworn logs and gnarled trunks.

The legacy of these innovative artists can be seen in almost every souvenir shop in Bali, many of which sell goods that suffer from the exact same lowering of artistic standards that hit Bali in the 1930s. Few **contemporary woodcarvers** have attained the same status as the stars of the Pita Maha and are now more often grouped by village rather than by individual reputation. The village of Mas, for example, is renowned for its high-quality unvarnished figurines, as well as for traditional *topeng* and *wayang wong* masks (see p.173).

Masks

Carved wooden **masks** play a hugely significant role in traditional Balinese dance-dramas. Many of them are treated as sacred objects, wrapped in holy cloth and stored in a high place within the temple compound when not being used, and given offerings before every public appearance. There's even an annual festival day for all masks and puppets, called Tumpek Wayang, at which actors and mask-makers honour their masks with special chants and offerings. Such is the power generated by certain masks, that some mask-makers enter a trance while working.

The main centres of mask-making on Bali are **Mas** and **Singapadu**. The best **material** is the pale wood of the *pule* (milkwood) tree and the mask-maker usually cuts the timber himself, but only after he's made special prayers of apology and thanks to the tree. The carving of any mask usually takes about two weeks. Old-school mask-makers still make their own paints from natural substances, but most now rely on commercial pigments; hair is either goat's hide or horsehair, and tusks are carved from the bones of wild boars or from water-buffalo horns.

Traditional masks fall into three categories: human, animal and supernatural. Most **human** masks are made for performances of the *Topeng*, literally "Masked Drama" (see p.447), and have a sacred, a symbolic and a narrative role. **Animal** masks feature a lot in the *Wayang Wong* dance-dramas, which take most of their stories and characters from the Hindu epic the *Ramayana*. Most sacred of all are the fantastical Barong and Rangda masks, worn by the **mythical creatures** who represent the forces of good and evil and who appear in almost every drama to do battle with each other.

Stonecarving

The prime function of **stonecarvings** has traditionally been to entice and entertain the gods and to ward off undesirable spirits and evil forces. The **temples** in the south are generally quite restrained in their use of carved ornamentation, being built mainly from red brick with just a few sections of carved volcanic tuff or *paras* (though Batubulan's Pura Puseh is a remarkable exception), but the northern temples, which are often built entirely from the easy-to-carve *paras*, flounder beneath a riot of reliefs and curlicues. Many of the classic northern temples are just a short bemo ride from Singaraja, and include the Pura Dalem in Jagaraga, Pura Beji and the Pura Dalem in Sangsit and, most famously, Pura Meduwe Karang at Kubutambahan.

Rajas and high-ranking nobles also commissioned fantastic carvings to embellish their **palaces** (*puri*). Few outlasted the early twentieth-century battles with the Dutch, but one notable survivor is the Puri Saren Agung (Ubud Palace). This was once the home of the culturally refined Sukawati family, and they employed Bali's most skilful stonecarver, **I Gusti Nyoman Lempad** (see p.189), to decorate the walls, gateways and shrines in the *puri* compound. These days, **hotels** are the modern *puri*, and many of the older, grander ones were built in the Bali-baroque *puri-pura* style, with plenty of exuberant stone-carved embellishments.

Gateways normally feature the most elaborate carvings, as these have a symbolic as well as a practical function, dividing the outer from the inner world, whether they're leading to the inner temple courtyard, or giving access to palace compounds or hotels. The Hindu trinity (Brahma, Wisnu and Siwa) are rarely depicted in stone, but a number of their spiritual relatives and manifestations crop up regularly. Lively scenes of secular life are also common. **Sculptures** of *raksasa* giants often guard temple gates but most other freestanding stonecarvings are destined for local gardens or tourists' homes; the vast majority are made in the workshops of Batubulan.

Traditional textiles

Traditional **fabrics** are still fashionable for clothes and furnishings in Indonesia and continue to be hand-woven in some areas of Bali and Lombok.

Textiles also have **ritual and traditional** uses here. On Lombok, the *kain usap*, a square cotton cloth either covered in geometric motifs or with alternating wide bands of floral patterns and narrow bands of geometric ones, is used to cover the face of the dead, while the striped, rectangular *lempot* stole is used to carry small children. Coarsely woven cotton striped *kombang* is particularly sacred; it's made with a continuous warp, which is cut through in the course of religious ceremonies such as the naming of a child or hair-cutting, and the fringes are tied with old Chinese coins for good fortune.

Ikat

Easily recognized by the fuzzy-edged motifs it produces, **ikat** weaving is common throughout Indonesia, woven either on backstrap, foot-pedal or, increasingly, on semiautomatic looms, from either silk, cotton or rayon. The word *ikat* derives from the Indonesian verb "to tie", and the technique is essentially a sophisticated tie-dye process. Bali is quite unusual in favouring **weft-ikat**, or **endek**, in which the weft yarn (the threads running across the fabric) is tie-dyed into the finished design before the warp begins. This produces a blurred edge to the predominantly geometric and abstract designs, and the fabric is popular for cushion covers and bedspreads, as well as for sarongs and other clothes. On Lombok, footlooms are used in the workshops of **Cakranegara**, while backstrap looms predominate in the villages of **Sukarara** and **Pringgasela**.

Warp-ikat (in which the threads that run lengthwise are tie-dyed) is more common elsewhere in Indonesia, including on Sumba and Flores, whose distinctive textiles are widely sold in south-Bali resorts, mostly as hangings, runners or bedspreads. The warp-*ikat*s of **east Sumba** are woven with bold humanoid motifs and images of real and mythological creatures and are usually dyed in combinations of indigo and deep red. **Flores** designs are typically geometric and non-figurative, in browns, ochres and dark reds, while those from Timor are usually indigo and white or deep red and white, and often feature crocodiles, fish and stylized human forms. A good way to display lengths of cloth at home is on the special carved **wooden hangers** sold in some *ikat* and souvenir shops; most are made in Lombok and Kalimantan.

Warp- and weft-*ikat* are complicated enough, but **double-ikat**, or **gringsing**, involves dyeing both the warp and the weft threads into their final designs before they're woven together; a double-*ikat* sarong can take five years to complete. There are just three areas in the world where this method is practised – India, Japan, and **Tenganan** in eastern Bali. Not surprisingly, *gringsing* is exceedingly expensive to purchase, and has acquired an important ritual significance. At first glance, *gringsing* can look similar to the warp-*ikat* of Flores, because both use the same dye combinations, but the Tenganan motifs have a highly charged spiritual meaning, and their geometric and floral designs are instantly recognizable to the people of Bali.

The art of embroidered *ikat*, or supplementary weft weaving, is known as **songket** and uses gold and silver metallic yarn to add tapestry-like motifs of birds, butterflies and flowers onto very fine silk (or, increasingly, rayon or artificial silk). *Songket* sarongs are worn on ceremonial occasions, and the brocaded sashes worn by performers of traditional Balinese dance are always made from *songket*. **Sukarara** in Lombok is the best place to see *songket* being woven.

Batik

Despite being more fashionable than *ikat* for everyday wear, nearly all **batik** fabric is imported from Java, as there's very little traditional batik produced in Bali or Lombok.

The batik **technique** involves drawing patterns in dye-resistant wax on to lengths of fabric, dyeing the fabric, then stripping off the wax to expose the undyed areas. Wax is then often reapplied in different places, and the fabric dyed with a different colour, repeating the process until the finished design is achieved. The royal Javanese cities of **Yogyakarta** and **Solo** have long been centres of high-quality batik. Coloured mainly with rust brown and indigo dyes against a cream or white background, the patterns adorning Yogyakarta/Solo batik tend to be either abstract, or compositions of graceful birds and flowers. Birds and flowers also appear a lot in the batiks from **Pekalongan**, on Java's north coast, but these artists use more colours, particularly blues, pinks and greens, and the designs show Chinese and Arabic influences. Some batik is now screen-printed rather than waxed, and the results are generally less good, especially as the dyes on screen-printed fabrics don't penetrate to the reverse side.

While batik is perfectly acceptable attire for most formal occasions; a special version called **perada** is used for ceremonial outfits and ornaments. This is the gold-painted cloth that you'll see fashioned into temple umbrellas, adorning some sacred statues, and worn by Legong dancers and other performers of religious dances. The background colour of *perada* fabric is nearly always bright green or yellow, sometimes purple, and on to this is painted or stamped a symbolic design (usually stylized birds or flowers) in either gold-leaf paint or, more commonly today, a bronze- or gold-coloured pigment imported from Europe.

Village life and traditions

The majority of people on Bali and Lombok live in villages. People employed in the cities or tourist resorts may well commute and even those whose villages are far away still identify with them and return for particular festivals each year.

Balinese village layout

Orientation in Bali does not correspond to the compass points of north, south, east and west. The main directions are **kaja** (towards Gunung Agung, dwelling place of the gods) and **kelod** (away from the mountain). The other directions are *kangin* (from where the sun rises), and its opposite, *kauh* (where the sun sets).

All Balinese villages are oriented *kaja–kelod* and the locations of the three village temples, *pura dalem*, *pura puseh* and *pura desa* (see p.430), are determined on this axis.

House compounds

Each Balinese house compound is built within a confining wall. When a son of the family marries, his wife usually moves into his compound, so there are frequently several generations living together, each with their own sleeping quarters, but otherwise sharing the facilities. Most domestic activities take place outside or in the partial shelter of **bale**, raised platforms with a roof. The different structures of the compound are believed to reflect the human body: the family shrine (*Sanggah Kemulan*) is the head, the *bale* are the arms, the courtyard is the navel, the kitchen and rice barn are the legs and feet, and the garbage tip, located along with the pig pens outside the *kelod* wall, is the anus. The Traditional Balinese House museum in Tabanan (see p.324) is a good example of a typical compound.

Initially all prospective house-builders consult an expert in the Balinese calendar to choose auspicious days for buying land and beginning construction. The architect or master builder (*undagi*) follows rules laid down in ancient texts, taking a series of **measurements** from the body of the **head of the household** and using these to calculate the exact dimensions of the compound. Before building starts, offerings are placed in the foundations so that work will proceed smoothly. When the building work is finished, further ceremonies must take place before the compound can be occupied. The final ceremony is the **melaspas**, an inauguration ritual that "brings the building to life".

Sasak villages

Balinese people living on Lombok retain their traditional house compounds as do the Bugis people, who have settled along Lombok's eastern and southern coasts and live in wooden houses constructed on tall piles. The indigenous **Sasak** people of Lombok also have their own architectural style.

Traditional Sasak villages are walled enclosures, with a gateway that is closed at night. **Houses**, made of bamboo with a thatch roof that slopes down

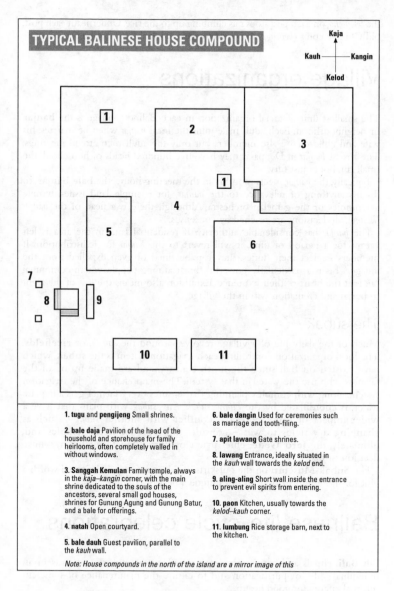

TYPICAL BALINESE HOUSE COMPOUND

Kaja

Kauh ⟶ ⟵ Kangin

Kelod

1   2   3

1

4

5   6

7

8   9

10   11

1. tugu and **pengijeng** Small shrines.

2. bale daja Pavilion of the head of the household and storehouse for family heirlooms, often completely walled in without windows.

3. Sanggah Kemulan Family temple, always in the *kaja–kangin* corner, with the main shrine dedicated to the souls of the ancestors, several small god houses, shrines for Gunung Agung and Gunung Batur, and a bale for offerings.

4. natah Open courtyard.

5. bale dauh Guest pavilion, parallel to the *kauh* wall.

6. bale dangin Used for ceremonies such as marriage and tooth-filing.

7. apit lawang Gate shrines.

8. lawang Entrance, ideally situated in the *kauh* wall towards the *kelod* end.

9. aling-aling Short wall inside the entrance to prevent evil spirits from entering.

10. paon Kitchen, usually towards the *kelod–kauh* corner.

11. lumbung Rice storage barn, next to the kitchen.

Note: House compounds in the north of the island are a mirror image of this

almost to the ground, are built on a base of mud and dung, and may have none or only a few windows, with a verandah on at least one side. Traditionally, the cooking hearth and eating area are inside the house, along with a walled-off room, the *inan bale*, generally used for storage, although this is also the place where newlyweds spend their first night.

The symbol of Lombok, the **lumbung rice barn**, with its bonnet-shaped roof, is a feature of only the south of the island. They are built in rows, on four piles, with a thatch roof and only one small opening high up. A circular wooden disc, the *jelepreng*, on each post stops rats climbing up to the rice. Underneath each post, old Chinese coins (*kepeng*) are buried for good luck and protection.

Village organizations

The smallest unit of social organization in each Balinese village is the **banjar** or neighbourhood. Each adult male joins the local *banjar* when he marries; his wife and children are also members but only the adult men attend meetings. The largest *banjar* in Denpasar may have five hundred heads of household, the small rural ones just fifty.

Typically, the *banjar* meets monthly in the meeting house, the **bale banjar**, to discuss anything of relevance to the *banjar*, for example land issues, temple ceremonies or the gamelan orchestra. Although there is a head of the *banjar* (*kliang*), all decisions are reached by consensus.

The *banjar* has considerable authority. If residential land in the area is left vacant for a period of time, it will revert to the *banjar* for redistribution. If members neglect their duties, they can be fined or even expelled from the village. This is a particularly powerful threat among people where communal life is at the heart of their existence. Expulsion also means the loss of the right to burial and cremation within the village.

The subak

Much of the daily life of a village revolves around the *sawah*, or **ricefields**. The local organization controlling each irrigation system is the **subak**, which have existed on Bali since the ninth century, and are made up of all the farmers who use the water in that system. The maintenance of the irrigation system, along with complex planning that ensures every farmer gets adequate water, is coordinated by the *kliang subak*. Any *subak* with plans that have a wider impact or cause potential conflict with another *subak* – such as changing dry fields to wet – consults the regional water temples and, ultimately, the **Jero Gede**, chief priest of Pura Ulun Danu Batur, whose decision is final.

The **Subak Museum** on the outskirts of Tabanan (see p.323) is well worth a visit for more information on this unique aspect of Balinese life.

Balinese life-cycle celebrations

On **Bali**, rituals and ceremonies are carried out at important points in an individual's life for purification and to ensure the maintenance of sufficient spiritual energy for good health.

The first life-cycle ritual, **pegedong-gedongan**, takes place about six months after conception, when the fetus has a human form, and emphasizes the hope for a long, healthy life. Subsequent **birth rituals** focus on the placenta, which is buried inside a coconut wrapped in sacred white cloth near the gateway of the parents' household. A rock is placed over the spot to protect it, and regular offerings are made there.

Following the birth, the parents and child are regarded as unclean (*sebel*), and cannot participate in religious practices. For the mother and baby, this lasts 42 days; for the father, it lasts until the baby's umbilical cord drops off, when the **kepus pungsed** ritual is carried out. The cord is wrapped in cloth, placed in an offering shaped like a dove and suspended over the baby's bed, along with a small shrine dedicated to Sanghyang Panca Kumara, son of Siwa, who is invoked as the child's protector. There are further ceremonies at twelve and 42 days and then, after 105 days, it's **telubulan**, a large, elaborate ceremony at which the child is named, and may be given an amulet to guard against evil spirits.

The child's **first birthday**, *oton*, occurs after 210 days (a Balinese year in the *wuku* calendar; see p.48), and is the first occasion that the child is allowed contact with the ground, and may be accompanied by a ritual hair-cutting ceremony. The next ceremony, **maketus**, takes place when the child's milk teeth fall out. Sanghyang Panca Kumara, who has been protecting the child since birth, is relieved of his duties, and the child is now guarded by the family ancestors.

Tooth filing

The **tooth-filing ritual**, *mapandes*, which preferably takes place before marriage, is a huge celebration with guests, music and lavish offerings. It is considered vital, and the elderly, and even the dead, have been known to have their teeth filed if they have never had it done. The aim is to remove coarse behaviour from the person and rid them of lust, greed, anger, drunkenness, confusion and jealousy, in order that they will lead a better life and be assured a more favourable reincarnation. The upper canine teeth or fangs and the four teeth in between are filed down.

Marriage

There are two **marriage** options. The most correct is *mamadik*, when the marriage is agreed between the two sets of parents and a huge financial outlay for lavish ceremonies is involved. Much more common is *ngerorod* or *malaib* – elopement. The man and woman run off and spend the night together, not so secretly that nobody knows, but with sufficient subterfuge that the girl's parents can pretend outrage. The following morning the couple are married in a private ceremony. More elaborate rituals and a reception may be hosted later the same day by the boy's parents. The girl's parents will not be invited as there is supposed to be bad feeling between the two sides. However, three days later the two sets of parents meet at the *ketipat bantal* ceremony, and are reconciled.

Traditional healers

Known as *balian* in Bali and *dukun* in Lombok, **traditional healers** are a vital adjunct to Western medicine on the islands. Illness is believed to stem from a lack of balance between the patient and the spirit world; for example, a patient may have paid insufficient respect to a god. There are many different kinds of *balian*, ranging from the most practical *balian tulang* (bonesetters), *balian manak* (midwives) and *balian apun* (masseurs), to the more spiritual, including *balian taksu*, mediums who enter a trance to communicate with the spirit world and *balian kebal*, who work with charms and spells, making love potions and magical amulets to protect the wearer against spiritual attack. *Balian* are also consulted to find out which ancestral souls have been reincarnated in the bodies of newborn babies, and which days are auspicious for certain events.

Cremation

The ceremony that visitors to Bali are most likely to witness is **cremation** (*pengabenan* or *palebonan*). The Balinese believe that the soul inhabits a temporary receptacle, the body, during life on earth. After death, the body must be returned to the five elements of solid, liquid, energy, radiance and ether to ready the soul for reincarnation.

Following death, the body is usually buried, sometimes for years, while the **preparations** for the cremation are made. Poorer families often share in the cremation ceremonies of wealthier families as costs are crippling. The entire extended family and *banjar* is involved in preparations. Animals are slaughtered, holy water acquired and gamelan, dancers and puppet shows organized. An animal-shaped, highly decorated sarcophagus is built to hold the body. The cremation tower, representing the Balinese universe, supported by the turtle, Bedawang, and the two *naga*, Basuki and Anantaboga, is also built, with tiers similar to the roofs on the *meru* in temples. A *bale* at the base of the tiers houses an effigy of the dead person.

Accompanied by the bamboo **gamelan angklung**, the sarcophagus and cremation tower are carried to the cemetery and twirled around many times en route to ensure that the soul is confused and cannot return home to cause mischief for the family. At the cremation ground the sarcophagus and tower are burned and the ashes carried to the sea or to a stream that will carry them to the ocean. Further ceremonies are needed after three days and twelve days, finishing with the ritual of *nyagara-gunung*, when the family take offerings to important sea and mountain temples.

▲ Funeral pyre at a royal cremation, Ubud

Sasak life-cycle ceremonies

Some of the ceremonies performed in Sasak communities on **Lombok** are associated with the more orthodox adherents to Islam, while others are associated only with Wetu Telu followers. The Wetu Telu **birth ceremony** of *adi kaka* is similar to the Balinese one involving the placenta. A few days after birth, the **naming ceremony** of *buang au* or *malang mali* takes place. A ritual **hair-cutting ceremony**, *ngurisang*, is also obligatory for a young child, although the age it takes place is variable.

The most important ceremony for a Muslim boy is his **circumcision** (*nyunatang*), which often takes place in the Muslim month of the Prophet Muhammad's birthday, accompanied by much ceremony and feasting.

There are three **marriage** options in Sasak culture: a marriage arranged by the families, one between cousins, or an elopement. Whichever occurs, the man's family pays a price (in cows, money, rice, betel nut, coconut, a white sarong and old Chinese coins) for the bride, who moves to their house. During the wedding ceremony, the couple are often carried on a sedan chair, and accompanied by a gamelan orchestra.

Under the laws of Islam, the dead are **buried**, rather than cremated. According to Wetu Telu custom, the dead are ritually washed and wrapped in a white sarong, carried to the cemetery, and buried with the head towards Mecca. A death in the family sets in motion a whole cycle of rituals. The most important is **deena nitook**, seven days after the death, **nyatus** after a hundred days, and the final event, **nyiu**, a thousand days after death, when the grave is sprinkled with holy water, commemorative stones are placed on it and offerings such as toothbrushes and clothes are made to ensure the deceased is comfortable in heaven.

The impact of tourism

Debates about the **effects of tourism** on Bali and Lombok have been running for decades. Back in the 1920s and 1930s, soon after the first tourists arrived, some local commentators decried the tendency of visitors to take photographs of bare-breasted Balinese women and damage island roads with their motor cars. In fact **nostalgia** for a more peaceful Bali is even older than that; an ancient document describes a Javanese mystic who, visiting Bali in 1500, complained that it was no longer quiet enough to practice meditation.

The history of tourism

Tourism in Bali effectively started in 1924 when KPM, the Royal Packet Navigation Company, established weekly **steamship services** connecting Bali with Batavia (Jakarta), Singapore, Semarang, Surabaya and Makassar, with visitors to Bali using the government rest-houses dotted around the island. Bali received 213 visitors that year, and the numbers, with a few blips, have continued to rise until the all-time high of more than 2.5 million visitors in 2007. This number includes the hundreds of thousands of Indonesian tourists, who are as fond of Bali as people from outside the country.

In 1928, KPM opened the first **hotel** on the island, the *Bali Hotel* in Denpasar (now the *Inna Bali*), an air link to Surabaya was established in 1933, a daily ferry between Java and Gilimanuk was launched in 1934 and the airport at Tuban opened in 1938. By the 1930s several thousand tourists each year were visiting, some of whom settled on the island. Many were artists, such as Walter Spies and Miguel Covarrubias, and anthropologists, including Margaret Mead and Gregory Bateson. They focused on the artistic and religious aspects of Balinese life, encouraging the Balinese to produce works of art that would appeal to tourists and, through their writing, painting, photography and film-making, enhancing the worldwide image of Bali as a paradise.

The Japanese invasion during World War II, followed by the struggle for independence, halted the tourist influx, but under President Sukarno and later President Suharto and his New Order, the **promotion of tourism** became official government policy supported by bodies such as the World Bank and the International Monetary Fund. The inauguration of **Ngurah Rai Airport** on August 1, 1969, marked the beginning of mass tourism on the island; it is now the second-busiest airport in the country, after Jakarta.

In 1972, the government-owned **Bali Tourist Development Corporation (BTDC)** was formed and built the resort of **Nusa Dua**, aimed at closeting high-spending tourists away from local people. The market responded and the number of visitors climbed from 30,000 in 1969 to 700,000 in 1989.

However, the tourists didn't all stay hidden away. By the 1970s **Kuta** had become a surfer's Mecca and local people in the small fishing village turned their homes into small hotels. Not everyone was happy; noting their ragged clothes (or lack of them) the surfers were labelled as hippies, drug addicts and practitioners of free love and the negative impact of tourism on the island was contemplated fearfully.

There was also concern about the **over-commercialization** of arts and culture for tourist consumption. Dances, for example, were shortened and changed to suit tourist tastes; it was a rare visitor who could enjoy a five-hour performance or appreciate dancers coming out of their trance by eating live chickens. During this time the slogan, often repeated since, "Tourism for Bali, not Bali for tourism" was coined and in the 1970s the annual Bali Arts Festival was inaugurated to encourage the Balinese to appreciate their own culture.

However, the advance of tourism continued apace. In 1971 about 60 percent of the island's income was contributed by agriculture and around 33 percent by tourism. By 2000, agriculture contributed less than 20 percent and tourism over 62 percent. Bali is one of the wealthiest of Indonesia's provinces and average income on the island exceeds that on neighbouring Java.

Brand Bali

Bali has an extremely high **global profile**. It is regularly voted one of the top island destinations in the world and Balinese-style restaurants, interiors, gardens, spas, handicrafts, jewellery and villas are now on offer from Los Angeles to Lisbon. Inevitably other Indonesian destinations, in particular Lombok, are marketed as "the next Bali" or "beyond Bali".

The image of Bali as a peaceful **paradise** has been sorely tested in recent years, especially in 2002 and 2005 when the island was dragged into the apparent clash between radical Islam and the West. Without Bali's high profile and the global interest in the island, it is unlikely that the island would have held any interest for the bombers.

Following the Kuta bombing on October 12, 2002, the island emptied of tourists overnight. However, when it was discovered that the bombers were Muslims, the Hindu population of Bali, following the example set by political, religious and intellectual leaders, made no moves against Muslim communities or individuals on the island and in fact placed the blame elsewhere. Many Balinese interpreted the bombing as an indication that the gods were angry with Bali and on November 15, 2002, a huge purification ceremony was carried out to resolve the problem. The annual commemoration service has always been an inter-faith service.

With an estimated 80 percent of the population relying on tourism for their living in some way or another, the economy nose-dived. Workers in tourist businesses were laid off or put on part-time, even apparently unconnected businesses such as garages noticed the effects – with less money to spend car-owners couldn't afford services or oil changes. By June 2003, a World Bank report estimated that the average Balinese income had dropped by forty percent. The fate of Lombok, inextricably linked to that of its more famous neighbour, mirrored Bali exactly. However, within a year there were signs of recovery aided by messages to the world that Bali was safe, open for business and, in fact, needed tourists to return and support the island. The recovery was even more remarkable given the start of the war in Iraq, the SARS outbreak, the advent of bird flu in Asia and the introduction of visas on arrival for visitors to Indonesia after a twenty-year open-door policy.

When suicide bombers struck again on October 1, 2005, in Kuta and Jimbaran, tourist arrivals plummeted again. Still, once again, Bali recovered and, as noted above, arrivals in 2007 were the highest ever.

Economy versus culture

Whatever the **economic benefits** to the island, in studies by Universitas Udayana (the University of Bali), some Balinese people described tourism as a tempest battering their coasts. Particular concerns related to tourism damaging **religion**; they condemned the desecration of temples by tourists and the fact that Balinese involved in the industry neglected their religious duties. One commentator noted, "Tourism is the fire that cooks your breakfast and the fire that burns down your house."

Even when tourism is thriving, the financial advantages are not evenly spread and there remain significant pockets of poverty on the island. Similarly, profits from multinational hotel chains flood out of the island to Jakarta and abroad. Equally concerning to many Balinese, the island is now a magnet for migrants from across Indonesia. Some people describe Kuta beach as *universitas pantai*, the beach university. Although many of the traders, from all across Indonesia, have no formal education, they end up as skilled, multilingual communicators with sales skills second to none and proceed to take jobs from the Balinese. Like migrants everywhere, they have an impressive drive to succeed. A local phrase tells that, "... *the migrant sells beef balls to buy land, while the Balinese sells land to buy beef balls*." Some tourist businesses prefer to employ non-Balinese rather than cope with Balinese staff needing to take time off to attend religious ceremonies.

However, as families grow and land-holdings are divided among more family members, many people in Bali can no longer earn a living from agriculture; the tourist sector offers opportunities at all levels from chambermaids to managers and Bali is now an exporter of skilled staff for the hospitality industry. Commentators have noted that the increased wealth of the Balinese is very often spent in highly traditional ways – in particular, on elaborate religious ceremonies.

Environmental concerns

Tourism also generates major **environmental concerns**. It is estimated that a thousand hectares of agricultural land are lost to tourist development every year. The cultivation of rice is the basis of agriculture on Bali, **water** is a life-or-death issue. One five-star hotel room is estimated to consume 500 litres of

---

Responsible tourism organizations

Many organizations are working to raise awareness of the impact of tourism throughout the world, and encourage responsible travelling. They all have sections devoted to Bali or Lombok or deal with issues that are directly relevant to the islands.

Ethical Traveler ⓦ www.ethicaltraveler.com

Global Anti-Golf Movement ⓦ www.antigolf.org/english.html

Indonesian Ecotourism Network ⓦ www.indecon.or.id

Partners in Responsible Tourism ⓦ www.pirt.org

Tourism Concern ⓦ www.tourismconcern.org.uk

water each day. Recent fears relate to the Balinese water table being polluted by salt water due to overuse and uncontrolled development.

Particular concerns have arisen about the effects of tourist developments on the island's **coral reefs**, with efforts to reverse damage already underway in the waters off Pemuteran and the Gili Islands. Global awareness of the environmental problems of **golf courses** is growing.

More than eleven thousand new **vehicles** head out onto the Balinese roads each month, increasing noise and air pollution and decreasing the quality of life.

In general, Balinese objections to tourist developments have failed to halt plans. The development of *Le Meridien Nirwana* near Tanah Lot, the building of the Garuda Wisnu Kencana (GWK) statue near Jimbaran, and the land reclamation around **Pulau Serangan** (Turtle Island) all evoked loud objections but building went ahead regardless. As tourist numbers rise again and investors' confidence grows, only time will tell whether opposition voices to new proposals will have any more impact than in the past.

Social changes

Social change has inevitably followed the influx of tourism. Michel Picard, author of *Bali: Cultural Tourism and Touristic Culture*, suggests that Bali has now become a "**touristic culture**" whereby the Balinese have adopted the tourists' perceptions of themselves and their island as their own, and have "come to search for confirmation of their 'Balinese-ness' in the mirror held to them by the tourists".

There are also concerns about **HIV/AIDS** (more than 3000 cases are estimated on Bali, among the highest in Indonesia) and **drug addiction**. ECPAT (@www.ecpat.net), a global organization working to abolish the commercial sexual exploitation of children, has reported that Bali has a reputation as a **child sex tourism** destination and is also a major destination for trafficked girls and women.

However, many of the problems are those of any developing country and, while many articulate the negative side of tourism, many of the people in the villages are keen to develop tourist facilities that will bring visitors, and their money, to them. The Indonesian government agrees and Bali is hoping to attract 2.5 million foreign visitors in 2008 and each following year.

The situation in Lombok

A small trickle of tourists started arriving on **Lombok** in the 1980s and local people set up small losmen around Senggigi, the Gili Islands and, later, around Kuta. By 1989, there were over 120,000 visitors annually, and by the late 1990s there were double that figure – but still only a fifth of the number of visitors to Bali.

Outside of the Senggigi area, development on the island has been slow and not without its controversies. Many Sasak people consider the gap between Muslim morals and those of their Western visitors is unacceptably wide, while the tourist job market has been increasingly dominated by the better-qualified Balinese. Sasak people in particular – forced out of education due to poverty – have little chance of landing anything but the most menial work.

Plans to build a new **international airport** outside Praya were at one point shelved following huge local protest and the reoccupation of the land by its previous owners. However, it is now steaming ahead, due for opening in 2010, and likely to spark resort and road development. The airport developers have promised to build a mosque and plan to attract more Middle-Eastern tourists, but reservations have been expressed about the potential increase in visitors.

Concern has also been repeatedly expressed about the island's **overreliance** on tourism, but with few resources to draw upon, there's little else to rely on for income.

Books

While plenty has been written on the culture, temples, and arts and crafts of Bali, there has been little coverage of Lombok.

We have included publishers' details only for books that may be hard to find outside Indonesia. Ganesha (@www.ganeshabooksbali.com) in Ubud offers an online ordering service. Titles marked 🏃 are particularly recommended; "o/p" means out of print.

Travel

Vicki Baum *A Tale from Bali*. Occasionally moving, and always interesting, semi-factual historical novel based on the events leading up to the 1906 *puputan* in Denpasar.

Elizabeth Gilbert *Eat, Pray, Love*. This insightful, funny journey of self-discovery, now a bestseller, climaxes in Ubud with various life-changing encounters of the sensual and spiritual kind.

🏃 **William Ingram** *A Little Bit One o'Clock: Living with a Balinese Family* (Ersania Books, Ubud, Bali). Warm, funny, warts-and-all portrait of the author's life with an Ubud family in the 1990s. Both the author and his adoptive family still live in Ubud and are involved in the Threads of Life Textile Arts Center.

🏃 **Louise G. Koke** *Our Hotel in Bali* (Pepper, Singapore). The engaging true story of two young Americans who built the first hotel on Kuta beach, in 1936. Some of the book's black-and-white photos are now displayed in Ubud's Neka Art Museum.

🏃 **Anna Mathews** *Night of Purnama*. Moving description of village life in the early 1960s, focusing on events in Iseh and the surrounding villages from the first eruption of Gunung Agung until the Mathews left in 1963. Written with affection and a keen realization of the gap between West and East.

Hickman Powell *The Last Paradise*. An American traveller in the late 1920s interleaves lively accounts of Balinese customs and festivals with a few spicy anecdotes.

🏃 **K'tut Tantri** *Revolt in Paradise*. The extraordinary, if in places somewhat embellished, story of British-born artist and adventurer Muriel Pearson, who became an active member of the Indonesian independence movement between 1932 and 1947, for which she was imprisoned and tortured by the Japanese invaders.

Adrian Vickers (ed) *Travelling to Bali: Four Hundred Years of Journeys*. One-stop anthology that includes accounts by early Dutch, Thai and British adventurers, as well as excerpts from writings by the expat community in the 1930s, and the musings of late twentieth-century visitors.

Culture and society

🏃 **Susan–Jane Beers** *Jamu: The Ancient Indonesian Art of Herbal Healing*. Fascinating look at the role of herbal medicine (*jamu*) in Indonesia, with features on how and why *jamu* works plus interviews with those who make and use it.

Lawrence Blair (ed) *Bali: Paradise Rediscovered* (iBal, Bali). A refreshingly modern take on the coffee-table view of Bali: a team of photographers was let loose on Bali for ten days in 2003 and Bali's top essayists write about what they shot.

🏃 **Miguel Covarrubias** *Island of Bali*. An early classic (first published in 1937) in which the Mexican artist and amateur anthropologist explores everything from the daily routines of his adopted village household to the religious and philosophical significance of the island's arts, dramas and music.

🏃 **Dr A.A.M. Djelantik** *The Birthmark: Memoirs of a Balinese Prince* (Tuttle Publishing). Fascinating, lively autobiography of the son of the last raja of Karangasem, who was born in east Bali in 1919, became Bali's most influential doctor, and lived through Dutch rule, World War II, the eruption of Gunung Agung and the communist killings.

🏃 **Fred B. Eiseman Jr** *Bali: Sekala and Niskala Vols 1 and 2*. Seminal, essential, wide-ranging anthologies of cultural and anthropological essays by an American resident of Bali.

David J. Fox *Once a Century: Pura Besakih and the Eka Dasa Rudra Festival* (Penerbit Sinar Harapan, Citra, Indonesia). Fabulous colour pictures, and an erudite but readable text, make this an excellent introduction to Besakih both ancient and modern. Also includes accounts of the 1963 Eka Dasa Rudra festival and the eruption of Gunung Agung.

Michael Hitchcock and I Nyoman Darma Putra *Tourism, Development and Terrorism in Bali*. Scholarly but readable account of the emergence of Bali as a globally known brand in tourism and the impact of this on the island. The authors also look at the effects of the 2002 and 2005 bombs on tourism and Balinese perceptions of tourism.

A.J. Bernet Kempers *Monumental Bali: Introduction to Balinese Archaeology and Guide to the Monuments*. A fairly highbrow analysis of Bali's oldest temples and ruins.

Gregor Krause *Bali 1912* (January Books, New Zealand). Reprinted edition of the original black-and-white photographs that inspired the first generation of arty expats to visit Bali. The pictures were taken by a young German doctor and give unrivalled insight into Balinese life in the early twentieth century.

🏃 **Michel Picard** *Bali: Cultural Tourism and Touristic Culture*. Fascinating, readable but ultimately depressing analysis of the effects of tourism upon the people of Bali.

Adrian Vickers *Bali: A Paradise Created*. Detailed, intelligent and highly readable account of the outside world's perception of Bali, the development of tourism, and how events inside and outside the country have shaped the Balinese view of themselves as well as outsiders' view of them.

History

Alfons van der Kraan *Lombok: Conquest, Colonization and Underdevelopment 1870–1940*. A detailed investigation into Lombok's complex relationship with Bali, its neighbour and conqueror, and subsequently with its Dutch rulers. A scathing attack on colonialism

and its devastating effect on the local populace.

🏃 **Robert Pringle** *A Short History of Bali*. An incisive, history of Bali from the prehistorical era to the 2002 bomb, with focus on social, cultural and environmental developments.

Art, crafts and music

Philip Cornwel-Smith *Property of the Artist: Symon* (PT Sang Yang Seni, Ubud, Bali). Lively, innovatively designed monograph of the expat Ubud artist Symon.

Edward Frey *The Kris: Mystic Weapon of the Malay World.* Small but well-illustrated book outlining the history and making of the kris, along with some of the myths associated with this magical weapon.

John Gillow and Barry Dawson *Traditional Indonesian Textiles.* Beautifully photographed and accessible introduction to the *ikat* and batik fabrics of the archipelago; a handy guide if you're thinking of buying cloth in Bali or Lombok.

Brigitta Hauser-Schaüblin, Marie-Louise Nabholz-Kartaschoff and Urs Ramseyer *Balinese Textiles.* Thorough and gloriously photographed survey of Balinese textiles and their role within contemporary society.

Garret Kam *Perceptions of Paradise: Images of Bali in the Arts* (Yayasan Dharma Seni Neka Museum, Bali). Ostensibly a guide to Ubud's Neka Art Museum, this is actually one of the best introductions to Balinese art.

Jean McKinnon *Vessels of Life: Lombok Earthenware.* Exhaustive and fabulously photographed book about Sasak life, pottery techniques and the significance of the items they create in the lives of the women potters.

Idanna Pucci *Bhima Swarga: The Balinese Journey of the Soul.* Fabulously produced guide to the *Mahabharata* legends depicted on the ceiling of Semarapura's Kerta Gosa. Illustrated with large, glossy colour photographs and a panel-by-panel description of the stories, which makes the whole creation much easier to interpret.

Anne Richter *Arts and Crafts of Indonesia.* General guide to the fabrics, carvings, jewellery and other folk arts of the archipelago, with some background on the practices involved.

Michael Tenzer *Balinese Music.* Well-pitched introduction to the gamelan, covering theory, practice and history, as well as anecdotes from Balinese musicians.

Lifestyle

Gianni Francione and Luca Invernizzi Tettoni *Bali Modern: The Art of Tropical Living.* A celebration of modern Balinese architecture, from the tasteful to the ostentatious.

Rio Helmi and Barbara Walker *Bali Style.* Sumptuously photographed paean to all things Balinese, from bamboo furniture to elegant homes.

William Warren and Luca Invernizzi Tettoni *Balinese Gardens.* Gorgeously photographed homage to (mostly) modern gardens in the south of the island, with informed introductions to classical gardens, Balinese flora, offerings, and the role of the garden in Balinese culture.

Made Wijaya and Isabella Ginanneschi *At Home in Bali.* The beautiful homes of Bali's beautiful (mainly expatriate) people.

Food and cookery

Heinz von Holzen and Lother Arsana *The Food of Bali* (Tuttle Publishing). Sumptuously illustrated paperback on all aspects of Balinese cuisine, including the religious and cultural background. The bulk of the book comprises recipes for local specialities – everything from snail soup to unripe-jackfruit curry.

Janet de Neefe *Fragrant Rice*. The Australian co-founder of Ubud's *Casa Luna* restaurant paints an enticing picture of life with her Balinese husband and family, interweaving her cultural observations with recipes for local dishes, from gado-gado to smoked duck.

Jacqueline Piper *Fruits of South-East Asia: Fact and Folklore*. Although only 94 pages long, this is an exhaustive, well-illustrated book, introducing all the fruits of the region together with the influence they have had on arts and crafts, and the part they have played in religious and cultural practices.

Travellers' guides

Dr Nick Jones *The Rough Guide to Travel Health*. Pretty much everything you need to know, in a pocket-sized, pack-friendly format.

Jane Marsden (ed) *Shopsmart Bali and Lombok*. Exhaustive guide to the shops, markets, arts, crafts, fashions, furniture and everything else for the shopaholic on Bali and Lombok.

Natural history

John MacKinnon *Field Guide to the Birds of Borneo, Sumatra, Java and Bali*. The most comprehensive field guide of its kind.

Victor Mason *Bali Bird Walks* (o/p). Delightful, highly personal, offbeat guidebook to over a dozen walks in the Ubud area, with the focus on flora and fauna, particularly birds.

David Pickell and Wally Siagian *Diving Bali: The Underwater Jewel of Southeast Asia*. Beautifully photographed and detailed account of everything you'll ever need to know about diving in Bali including plenty of detailed maps.

Fiction

Vern Cook (ed) *Bali Behind the Seen: Recent Fiction from Bali*. Short stories by modern Balinese and Javanese writers, many of whom explore the ways in which Bali is changing.

Diana Darling *The Painted Alphabet*. Charming, sophisticated reworking of a traditional Balinese tale about young love, rivalry and the harnessing of supernatural power.

Garrett Kam *Midnight Shadows*. A teenage boy's life in 1960s Bali is turned upside down first by the devastating eruption of Gunung Agung and then by the vicious, divisive, anti-communist violence that swept the island.

Odyle Knight *Bali Moon: A Spiritual Odyssey*. Riveting tale of an Australian woman's deepening involvement with the Balinese spirit world as her romance with a young Balinese priest draws her onto disturbing ground. Apparently based on true events.

Christopher J. Koch *The Year of Living Dangerously*. Set in Jakarta in the last year of President Sukarno's rule and climaxing in the days leading up to the 1965 takeover by Suharto and the subsequent violence, this story compellingly details ethnic, political and religious tensions that are still apparent in Indonesia today.

Putu Oka Sukanta *The Sweat of Pearls: Short Stories about Women of Bali* (Darma Printing, NSW, Australia). Though all the stories were written by a man, the vignettes of village life are enlightening, and the author is a respected writer who spent many years in jail because of his political beliefs.

Language

Language

Language

On your travels through Bali and Lombok you'll hear a vibrant mix of languages; the national language of Indonesia, known locally as Bahasa Indonesia and in English as Indonesian, as well as the indigenous languages of Balinese and Sasak (on Lombok), which are just two of more than 700 native languages and dialects spoken throughout the Indonesian archipelago. In practical terms, Indonesian will help you to communicate effectively, and everyone on the islands is at least bilingual, but a few words of Balinese or Sasak used appropriately will get you an extra warm welcome.

Bahasa Indonesia

Until the 1920s, the lingua franca of government and commerce was Dutch, but the emerging independence movement adopted a form of Bahasa Malay as a unifying language and by the 1950s, this had crystallized into **Bahasa Indonesia**, which is taught in every school and understood throughout Bali and Lombok.

Bahasa Indonesia is written in Roman script, has no tones and uses a fairly straightforward grammar – all of which makes it relatively easy for the visitor to get to grips with. The *Berlitz Indonesian Phrasebook and Dictionary* is a pocket-sized **phrasebook** that includes a dictionary of useful words as well as information on pronunciation and grammar. Of the numerous **teach yourself** options, Sutanto Atmosumarto's *Colloquial Indonesian: The Complete Course for Beginners* (Routledge) includes a book plus CD, and *Learn Indonesian* euroTalkinteractive CD and DVD (ⓦ www.eurotalk.com) is a beginner's course that has a printable dictionary and allows learners to compare their voices with those of native speakers. Several dictionaries are available: outside Indonesia, the *English-Indonesian Dictionary* and *Indonesian-English Dictionary* by Echols and Shadily (Cornell University Press) are comprehensive; inside the country, you might want to get hold of the more portable, though not pocket-sized, **dictionary** *Kamus Lengkap Inggeris-Indonesia, Indonesia-Inggeris* (Hasta Penerbit).

Grammar and pronunciation

For **grammar**, Bahasa Indonesia uses the same subject-verb-object word order as in English. The easiest way to make a question is simply to add a question mark and use a rising intonation. **Nouns** have no gender and don't require an article. To make a noun **plural** you usually just say the noun twice, eg *anak* (child), *anak-anak* (children). **Adjectives** always follow the noun. **Verbs** have no tenses: to indicate the past, prefix the verb with *sudah* (already) or *belum* (not yet); for the future, prefix the verb with *akan* (will).

Vowels and diphthongs

a is a cross between f**a**ther and c**u**p

e as in **a**long; or as in p**a**y; or as in g**e**t; or sometimes omitted (selamat pronounced "slamat")

i as in bout**i**que; or as in p**i**t

o as in h**o**t; or as in c**o**ld

u as in b**oo**t

ai as in f**i**ne

au as in h**ow**

Consonants

Most are pronounced as in English, with the following exceptions:

c as in **ch**eap

g is always hard, as in **g**irl

k is hard, as in English, except at the end of the word, when you should stop just short of pronouncing it. In written form, this is often indicated by an apostrophe; for example, beso' for besok.

Useful words and phrases

Greetings and basic phrases

The all-purpose greeting is **Selamat** (derived from Arabic), which communicates general goodwill. If addressing a married woman, it's polite to use the respectful term **Ibu** or **Nyonya**; if addressing a married man use **Bapak**.

Selamat pagi	Good morning (5–11am)
Selamat siang	Good day (11am–3pm)
Selamat sore	Good afternoon 3–7pm)
Selamat malam	Good evening (after 7pm)
Selamat tidur	Good night
Selamat tinggal	Goodbye
Sampai jumpa lagi	See you later
Selamat jalan	Have a good trip
Selamat datang	Welcome
Selamat makan	Enjoy your meal
Selamat minum	Cheers (toast)
Apa kabar?	How are you?
Bagus/Kabar baik	I'm fine
tolong	please (requesting)
silakan	please (offering)
Terima kasih (banyak)	Thank you (very much)
Sama sama	You're welcome
Ma'af	Sorry/excuse me
Tidak apa apa	Never mind/no worries
Siapa nama anda?	What is your name?

Nama saya...	My name is...
Dari mana?	Where are you from?
Saya dari...	I come from...
Bisa bicara bahasa Inggris?	Do you speak English?
Saya tidak mengerti	I don't understand
Ada...?	Do you have...?
Saya mau...	I want/would like...
Tidak mau	I don't want it/No thanks
Apa ini/itu?	What is this/that?
satu lagi	another
cantik	beautiful
besar/kecil	big/small
pacar	boyfriend or girlfriend
bersih/kotor	clean/dirty
dingin	cold
mahal/murah	expensive/inexpensive
sepat/lambat	fast/slow
turis	foreigner
teman	friend
bagus/buruk	good/bad
panas	hot (water/weather)
pedas	hot (spicy)
berapa?	how?
lapar/haus	hungry/thirsty
sakit	ill/sick
kawin/bujang	married/single
laki-laki	men
perempuan or wanita	women
bukan	no (with noun)
tidak (or tak)	not (with verb)

buka/tutup	open/closed
lelah	tired
banyak	very much/a lot
apa?	what?
kapan?	when?
dimana?	where?
siapa?	who?
mengapa?	why?
ya	yes

Getting around

Dimana...?	Where is the...?
Saya mau pergi ke...	I'd like to go to the...
Berapa kilometre?	How far?
Berapa jam?	How long?
Berapa harga karcis ke...?	How much is the fare to...?
Kemana bemo pergi?	Where is this bemo going?
Bila bemo/bis berangkut?	When will the bemo/bus leave?
Dimana ini?	Where is this?
estop!	stop!
disini	here
kanan	right
kiri	left
terus	straight on
lapangan terbang	airport
bank	bank
pantai	beach
terminal	bemo/bus station
sepeda	bicycle
bis	bus
mobil	car
kota	city/downtown
datang/pergi	to come/go
mengendarai	to drive
masuk/keluar	entrance/exit
ferry	ferry
bensin	fuel (petrol)
dokar/cidomo	horse cart
rumah sakit	hospital
losmen	hotel
pasar	market
sepeda motor	motorbike
ojek	motorbike taxi

dekat/jauh	near/far
apotik	pharmacy
wartel/kantor telkom	phone office
kantor polisi	police station
kantor pos	post office
restoran/rumah makan/warung	restaurant
toko	shop
taksi	taxi
karcis	ticket
kantor turis	tourist office
desa	village
jalan kaki	to walk

Accommodation and shopping

Berapa harga...?	How much is...?
kamar untuk satu orang	a single room
kamar untuk dua orang	a double room
Ada kamar yang lebih murah?	Do you have a cheaper room?
Boleh saya lihat kamar?	Can I look at the room?
tidur	to sleep
membeli/menjual	to buy/sell
uang	money
apakah ada...?	is there...?
ac	air conditioning
kamar mandi	bathroom
makan pagi	breakfast
kipas	fan
air panas	hot water
kelambu nyamuk	mosquito net
kolam renang	swimming pool
kamar kecil/wc	(pronounced "waysay") toilet

Numbers

nol	0
satu	1
dua	2
tiga	3
empat	4
lima	5
enam	6
tujuh	7

delapan	8	jam tiga	3.00
sembilan	9	jam empat lewat	4.10
sepuluh	10	sepuluh	
sebelas	11	jam lima kurang	4.45
duabelas, tigabelas, empatbelas	12, 13, 14, etc	seperempat	
		jam setengah tujuh	("half to seven") 6.30
duapuluh	20		
duapuluh satu, duapuluh dua, duapuluh tiga	21, 22, 23, etc	... pagi	... in the morning
		... sore	... in the afternoon
		... malam	... in the evening
tigapuluh, empatpuluh, limapuluh	30, 40, 50, etc	menit/jam	minute/hour
		hari	day
seratus	100	minggu	week
duaratus, tigaratus, empatratus	200, 300, 400, etc	bulan	month
		tahun	year
seribu	1000	hari ini/besok	today/tomorrow
duaribu	2000, 3000, 4000, etc	kemarin	yesterday
sepuluhribu	10,000	sekarang	now
dua puluhribu, tiag puluhribu, empat puluhribu	20,000, 30,000, 40,000, etc	belum	not yet
		tidak pernah	never
		sudah	already
seratusribu	100,000	Hari Senin	Monday
dua ratusribu, tiga ratusribu, empat ratusribu	200,000, 300,000, 400,000, etc	Hari Selasa	Tuesday
		Hari Rabu	Wednesday
		Hari Kamis	Thursday
sejuta	1,000,000	Hari Jumaat	Friday
dua juta, tiga juta, empat juta	2,000,000, 3,000,000, 4,000,000, etc	Hari sabtu	Saturday
		Hari Minggu	Sunday

Time and days of the week

Jam berapa?	What time is it?
Kapan dia buka/ tutup?	When does it open/ close

Menu reader

General terms

makan	to eat	garpu	fork
makan pagi	breakfast	sendok	spoon
makan siang	lunch	piring	plate
makan malam	evening meal	gelas	glass
daftar makanan	menu	minum	drink
Saya seorang vegetaris	I am vegetarian	tolong tanpa es	without ice, please
		tolong tanpa gula	without sugar, please
Saya tidak makan daging	I don't eat meat	dingin	cold
		panas	hot (temperature)
pisau	knife	pedas	hot (spicy)

| asam manis | sweet-and-sour | enak | delicious |
| goreng | fried | Saya injin bayar | I want to pay |

Meat, fish and basic foods

ayam	chicken	kecap asam	sour soy sauce
babi	pork	kecap manis	sweet soy sauce
bakmi	noodles	kepiting	crab
buah	fruit	nasi	rice
es	ice	petis	fish paste
garam	salt	sambal	hot chilli sauce
gula	sugar	sapi	beef
ikan	fish	soto	soup
itik	duck	telur	egg
jaja	rice cakes	tenggiri	king mackerel
kambing	goat	udang	prawn
kare	curry	udang karang	lobster

Everyday dishes

ayam goreng	fried chicken		vegetable, meat, fish and sometimes egg
bakso	meat ball soup		
bakmi goreng	fried noodles with vegetables and meat	nasi goreng	fried rice
		nasi pecel	steamed green vegetables with spicy peanut sauce and rice
botok daging sapi	spicy minced beef with tofu, tempeh and coconut milk		
		nasi putih	plain boiled rice
cap cai	mixed fried vegetables	nasi sela	steamed rice and sweet potato
es campur	fruit salad and shredded ice		
		pisang goreng	fried bananas
gado-gado	steamed vegetable with a spicy peanut sauce	rijsttafel	Dutch/Indonesian spread of six to ten different meat, fish and vegetable dishes with rice
ikan bakar	grilled fish		
ikan goreng	fried fish		
ikan pepes	spiced fish steamed in banana leaf	rujak	hot, spiced fruit salad
		rujak petis	vegetable and fruit in spicy peanut and shrimp sauce
kangkung	water-spinach		
krupuk	rice or cassava crackers, usually flavoured with prawn		
		tahu goreng telur	tofu omelette
		saté	meat or fish kebabs served with a spicy peanut sauce
lalapan	raw vegetables and sambal		
lontong	steamed rice in a banana-leaf packet	sayur bening	soup with spinach and corn
lumpia	spring rolls	sayur lodeh	vegetable and coconut-milk soup
nasi campur	boiled rice served with small amounts of	urap-urap/urap timum	vegetables with coconut and chilli

Balinese specialities

ayam betutu	steamed chilli-chicken
babi guling	roasted suckling pig
betutu bebek	smoked duck
lawar	raw meat, blood and spices
megibung	Balinese rijsttafel
sate languan	ground fish, coconut, spices and sugar cooked on a bamboo stick

Sasak specialities

ayam taliwang	fried or grilled chicken served with a hot chilli sauce
beberuk	raw eggplant and chilli sauce
cerorot	rice flour, palm sugar and coconut milk sweet, wrapped into a cone shape
geroan ayam	chicken liver
gule lemak	beef curry
hati	liver
kelor	vegetable soup
lapis	rice flour, coconut milk and sugar dessert, wrapped in banana leaves
olah olah	mixed vegetables and coconut cream
otak	brains
pangan	coconut milk and sugar dessert
paru	lungs
pelecing	chilli sauce
satay pusut	minced beef and coconut sate
sayur nangka	young jackfruit curry
sum-sum	bone marrow
tumbek	rice flour, coconut milk and palm sugar dessert, wrapped in coconut leaves
usus	intestines
wajik	sticky rice and palm-sugar sweet

Fruit

apel	apple
buah anggur	grapes
jeruk manis	orange
jeruk nipis	lemon
kelapa	coconut
mangga	mango
manggis	mangosteen
nanas	pineapple
nangka	jackfruit
pisang	banana
semangkha air	watermelon

Drinks

air jeruk	orange juice
air jeruk nipis	lemon juice
air minum	drinking water
arak	palm or rice spirit
bir	beer
brem	local rice beer
kopi	coffee
kopi bal	black coffee
kopi susu	white coffee
susu	milk
teh	tea
tuak	rice or palm wine

Bahasa Bali

The Balinese language, **Bahasa Bali**, has three main forms: High (*Ida*), Middle or Polite (*Ipun*), and Low (*Ia*). The form the speaker uses depends on the caste of the person he or she is addressing and on the context. If speaking to family or friends, or to a low-caste (Sudra) Balinese, you use **Low Balinese**; if addressing a superior or a stranger, you use **Middle or Polite Balinese**; if talking to someone from a high caste (Brahman, Satriya or Wesya) or discussing religious affairs, you use **High Balinese**. If the caste is not immediately apparent, then the speaker traditionally opens the conversation with the euphemistic question "Where do you sit?", in order to elicit an indication of caste. However, in the last couple of decades there's been a move to popularize the use of Polite or Middle Balinese, and disregard the caste factor. For more on castes and how to recognize them, see p.56.

Despite its numerous forms, Bahasa Bali is essentially a **spoken language**, with few official rules of grammar and hardly any textbooks or dictionaries. However, there's the *Practical Balinese Phrasebook and Dictionary* by G. Spitzing (Tuttle), available internationally. All phrases and questions given below are shown in the Middle or Polite form, unless otherwise stated.

Useful words and phrases

Sira pesengan ragane?	What is your name?	becik	good
		jeroan	house
Lunga kija?	Where are you going?	rabi	husband
Kija busan?	Where have you been?	tan, nente	no
Kenken kebara?	How are you?	pantu, beras, ajengan	rice
Napa orti?	How are things?		
Becik	(I'm/everything's) fine	sirep sare	to sleep
Tiang gele	I am sick	alit	small
Napi punika?	What is that?	timpal, isteri	wife
corah	bad	inggih, patut	yes
ageng	big	siki, diri	1
putra, putri	child	kalih	2
rauh, dateng	to come	tiga	3
ngajeng, nunas	to eat	pat	4
jaen	delicious	lima	5
panyaman, pasa metonan	family	nem, enem	6
		pitu	7
ajeng-ajengan, tetedan	food	kutus	8
		sia	9
switra	friend	dasa	10
lunga	to go		

Sasak

The language of Lombok is **Sasak**, a purely oral language that varies quite a lot from one part of the island to another. However, even a few words of Sasak are likely to be greeted with delight. The following should get you started.

There's no Sasak equivalent to the Indonesian **greetings** Selamat pagi and the like. If you meet someone walking along the road, the enquiry "Where are you going?" serves this purpose even if the answer is blatantly obvious.

Useful words and phrases

Ojok um bay?	Where are you going?
Lampat-lampat	Just walking around
Rinjani wah mo ojok um bay	I'm going to Rinjani
Um bay tao...?	Where is...?
Berem bay khabar?	How are you?
Bagus/solah	I'm fine
Berem bay seeda?	And you?
Upa gowey de?	What are you doing?
Pira kanak de?	How many children do you have?
Yak la low	See you (I'm going)
Nday kambay kambay	No problem
Nyeri too!	Go away!
belek/kodek	big/small
semeton mama/ semeton nine	brother/sister
kanak/bai	child/grandchild
peteng/tenang	dark/light
kanak nine/ kanak mame	daughter/son
maik	delicious

betjat/adeng-adeng	fast/slow
kantje	friend
takoot	frightened
berat/ringan	heavy/light
beneng	hot
lapar	hungry
semame/senine	husband/wife
ndarak	nothing
goro	thirsty
telah	tired
djelo sine	today
djema	tomorrow
sirutsin	yesterday
ndarak	none
skek	1
dua	2
telu	3
empat	4
lima	5
enam	6
pitook	7
baluk	8
siwak	9
sepulu	10

Glossary

adat Traditional law and custom.

alang-alang Tall, tough, sharp-edged Imperata cylindrical grass widely used for thatching roofs.

aling-aling Low, freestanding wall built directly behind a gateway to deter evil spirits.

Arjuna The most famous of the five heroic Pandawa brothers, stars of the epic Hindu tale, the *Mahabharata*.

bale Open-sided pavilion found in temples, family compounds and on roadsides, usually used as a resting place or shelter.

bale banjar Village **bale** used for meetings.

balian (or **dukun**) Traditional faith healer, herbalist or witch doctor.

banjar Village association or council to which all married men in the neighbourhood are obliged to belong; membership averages 100 to 500.

Barong Ket Mythical lion-like creature who represents the forces of good.

Barong Landung Ten-metre-high humanoid puppets used in temple rituals and dances.

bemo Local minibus transport.

Bhoma (or **Boma**) The son of the earth and repeller of evil spirits.

bhuta (and **kala**) Invisible demons and goblins, the personification of the forces of evil.

brugak Open-sided pavilion in Lombok found in family compounds and on roadsides and used as a resting place or shelter.

Calonarang Exorcist dance-drama featuring the widow-witch Rangda.

candi Monument erected as a memorial to an important person, also sometimes a shrine.

candi bentar Split gateway within a temple compound.

cidomo Horse-drawn cart used as a taxi on Lombok.

dalang Puppet master of *wayang kulit* shadow plays.

danau Lake.

desa Village.

dewa/dewi God/goddess.

Dewi Pertiwi Earth goddess.

Dewi Sri Rice goddess.

dokar Horse-drawn cart used as a taxi in a few Balinese towns.

dukun See **balian**.

dulang Wooden stand/pedestal used for offerings.

endek *Ikat* cloth in which the weft threads are dyed to the final pattern before being woven.

Erlangga (sometimes **Airlangga**) Eleventh-century king from East Java, son of the mythical widow-witch Rangda.

Galungan The most important Bali-wide holiday, held for ten days every 210 days in celebration of the triumph of good over evil.

gamelan Orchestra or music of bronze metallophones.

Ganesh Hindu elephant-headed deity, remover of obstacles and god of knowledge.

gang Lane or alley.

Garuda Mythical Hindu creature, half-man and half-bird, and the favoured vehicle of the god Wisnu.

gedong Building.

genggong Crude bamboo wind instrument, played like a jew's-harp.

geringsing Weaving technique and cloth, also known as double *ikat* because both the warp and the weft threads are dyed to the final design before being woven.

gunung Mountain.

Hanuman Monkey-god and chief of the monkey army in the *Ramayana* story; an ally of Rama's.

Ida Batara Dewi Ulun Danu (also just **Dewi Danu**) The goddess of the lakes in the centre of the island.

ikat Cloth in which the warp or weft threads, or both warp and weft threads, are tie-dyed to the final pattern before being woven: see also **endek** and **geringsing**.

jalan (Jl) Road.

jukung Traditional wooden fishing boat with outriggers.

kain poleng Black-and-white checked cloth used for religious purposes, symbolizing the harmonious balancing of good and evil forces.

kaja Crucial Balinese direction (opposite of kelod), which determines house and temple orientation; towards the mountains, upstream.

kala same as bhuta.

kantor pos General post office.

kantor telkom Government telephone office.

Kawi Ancient courtly language of Java.

kayangan jagat Highly sacred directional temple.

Kebo Iwa Mythical giant credited with building some of Bali's oldest monuments.

Kecak Spectacular dance-drama often referred to as the Monkey Dance.

kelod Crucial Balinese direction (opposite of kaja), which determines house and temple orientation; towards the sea, downstream.

kepeng Old Chinese coins with holes bored through the middle.

ketu Terracotta crown-shaped roof ornament.

kori agung See paduraksa.

Kumakarma Brother of the demon king, Rawana, in the *Ramayana* story.

Kuningan The culmination day of the important ten-day Galungan festivities.

kris Traditional-style dagger, with scalloped blade edges, of great symbolic and spiritual significance.

kulkul Bell-like drum made from a large, hollow log slit down the middle and suspended high up in a purpose-built tower in temples and other public places.

Legong Classical Balinese dance performed by two or three pre-pubescent girls.

leyak Witches who often assume disguises.

lontar Palm-leaf manuscripts on which all ancient texts were inscribed.

losmen Homestay or guesthouse.

lumbung Barn used for storing rice, raised high on stilts above a platform, and with a distinctive bonnet-shaped roof.

Mahabharata Lengthy Hindu epic describing the battles between representatives of good and evil, and focusing on the exploits of the Pandawa brothers.

mandi Traditional scoop-and-slosh method of showering, often in open-roofed or "garden" bathrooms.

meru Multi-tiered Hindu shrine with an odd number of thatched roofs (from one to eleven), which symbolizes the cosmic Mount Meru.

moksa Spiritual liberation for Hindus.

naga Mythological underwater deity, a cross between a snake and a dragon.

nusa Island.

odalan Individual temple festival held to mark the anniversary of the founding of every temple on Bali.

ojek Motorcycle taxi.

padmasana The empty throne that tops the shrine-tower, found in every temple and dedicated to the supreme god Sanghyang Widi Wasa.

paduraksa (or kori agung) Temple gateway to the inner sanctuary, like the candi bentar, but joined together rather than split.

pancasila The five principles of the Indonesian constitution: belief in one supreme god; the unity of the Indonesian nation; guided democracy; social justice and humanitarianism; and a civilized and prosperous society. Symbolized by an eagle bearing a five-part crest.

paras Soft, grey volcanic tuff used for carving.

pasar Market.

pasar seni Literally art market, usually sells fabrics and non-foodstuffs, and sometimes artefacts and souvenirs.

pawukon See wuku.

peci Black felt or velvet hat worn by Muslim men.

pedanda High priest of the Brahman caste.

pemangku Village priest.

perada Traditional gold, screen-printed material used for ceremonial garb and temple umbrellas.

prahu Traditional wooden fishing boat.

prasasti Ancient bronze inscriptions.

pulau Island.

puputan Suicidal fight to the death.

pura Hindu temple.

pura dalem Temple of the dead.

pura desa Village temple.

pura puseh Temple of origin.

puri Raja's palace, or the home of a wealthy nobleman.

Raksasa Mythical Hindu demon-giant with long teeth and a large club, often used to guard temple entrances.

Rama Hero of the **Ramayana** and an avatar of the god **Wisnu**.

Ramayana Hugely influential Hindu epic, essentially a morality tale of the battles between good and evil.

Rangda Legendary widow-witch who personifies evil and is most commonly depicted with huge fangs, a massive lolling tongue and pendulous breasts.

Rawana The demon king who represents the forces of evil (**Rama**'s adversary in the **Ramayana**).

raya Main or principal ("Jalan Raya Ubud" is the main Ubud road).

saka Hindu calendar, which is divided into years made up of between 354 and 356 days; runs eighty years behind the Western Gregorian calendar.

Sanghyang Widi Wasa The supreme Hindu god; all other gods are a manifestation of him.

Saraswati Goddess of science, learning and literature.

sarong The anglicized generic term for any length of material wrapped around the lower body and worn by men and women.

sawah Ricefields.

sebel Ritually unclean.

shophouse Shuttered building with living space upstairs and shop space on ground floor.

Siwa (Shiva) Important Hindu deity; "The Destroyer" or, more accurately, "The Dissolver".

sok Square-lidded basket used for offerings or storage.

songket Silk brocades often woven with real gold or silver thread.

subak Irrigation committee or local farmers' council.

suttee Practice of widows choosing to burn themselves to death on their husbands' funeral pyres.

swastika Ancient Hindu and Buddhist symbol representing the wheel of the sun.

teluk Bay.

Topeng Masked dance-drama, performed with human masks.

tuak Rice or palm wine.

wantilan Large pavilion, usually used for cockfights and dance performances.

wartel Phone office.

warung Foodstall or tiny streetside restaurant.

wayang kulit Shadow-puppet play.

Wisnu (Vishnu) Important Hindu deity – "The Preserver". Usually shown with four arms, holding a disc, a conch, a lotus and a club, and often seated astride his vehicle, the **Garuda**.

wuku (or pawukon) Complex Balinese calendar system based on a 210-day lunar cycle.

Travel
store

ROUGH
GUIDES

Small print and Index

A Rough Guide to Rough Guides

Published in 1982, the first Rough Guide – to Greece – was a student scheme that became a publishing phenomenon. Mark Ellingham, a recent graduate in English from Bristol University, had been travelling in Greece the previous summer and couldn't find the right guidebook. With a small group of friends he wrote his own guide, combining a highly contemporary, journalistic style with a thoroughly practical approach to travellers' needs.

The immediate success of the book spawned a series that rapidly covered dozens of destinations. And, in addition to impecunious backpackers, Rough Guides soon acquired a much broader and older readership that relished the guides' wit and inquisitiveness as much as their enthusiastic, critical approach and value-for-money ethos.

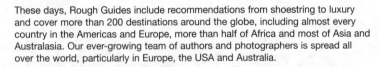

These days, Rough Guides include recommendations from shoestring to luxury and cover more than 200 destinations around the globe, including almost every country in the Americas and Europe, more than half of Africa and most of Asia and Australasia. Our ever-growing team of authors and photographers is spread all over the world, particularly in Europe, the USA and Australia.

In the early 1990s, Rough Guides branched out of travel, with the publication of Rough Guides to World Music, Classical Music and the Internet. All three have become benchmark titles in their fields, spearheading the publication of a wide range of books under the Rough Guide name.

Including the travel series, Rough Guides now number more than 350 titles, covering: phrasebooks, waterproof maps, music guides from Opera to Heavy Metal, reference works as diverse as Conspiracy Theories and Shakespeare, and popular culture books from iPods to Poker. Rough Guides also produce a series of more than 120 World Music CDs in partnership with World Music Network.

Visit www.roughguides.com to see our latest publications.

Rough Guide travel images are available for commercial licensing at www.roughguidespictures.com

Rough Guide credits

Text editor: Christina Valhouli
Layout: Sachin Tanwar
Cartography: Amod Singh
Picture editor: Harriet Mills
Production: Vicky Baldwin
Proofreader: Diane Margolis
Cover design: Chloë Roberts
Photographer: Martin Richardson
Editorial: London Ruth Blackmore, Alison
Murchie, Andy Turner, Keith Drew, Edward Aves,
Alice Park, Lucy White, Jo Kirby, James Smart,
Natasha Foges, Róisín Cameron, Emma Traynor,
Emma Gibbs, James Rice, Kathryn Lane, Monica
Woods, Mani Ramaswamy, Joe Staines, Peter
Buckley, Matthew Milton, Tracy Hopkins, Ruth
Tidbal; **New York** Andrew Rosenberg, Steven
Horak, AnneLise Sorensen, April Isaacs, Ella
Steim, Anna Owens, Sean Mahoney, Paula
Neudorf, Courtney Miller; **Delhi** Madhavi Singh,
Karen D'Souza
Design & Pictures: London Scott Stickland, Dan
May, Diana Jarvis, Nicole Newman, Mark Thomas,
Emily Taylor; **Delhi** Umesh Aggarwal, Ajay Verma,
Jessica Subramanian, Ankur Guha, Pradeep

Thapliyal, Anita Singh, Nikhil Agarwal
Production: Rebecca Short
Cartography: London Maxine Repath, Ed
Wright, Katie Lloyd-Jones; **Delhi** Jai Prakash
Mishra, Rajesh Chhibber, Ashutosh Bharti, Rajesh
Mishra, Animesh Pathak, Jasbir Sandhu, Karobi
Gogoi, Alakananda Bhattacharya, Swati Handoo
Online: Narender Kumar, Rakesh Kumar,
Amit Verma, Rahul Kumar, Ganesh Sharma,
Debojit Borah, Saurabh Sati, Ravi Yadav
Marketing & Publicity: London Liz Statham,
Niki Hanmer, Louise Maher, Jess Carter, Vanessa
Godden, Vivienne Watton, Anna Paynton, Rachel
Sprackett, Libby Jellie, Jayne McPherson, Holly
Dudley; **New York** Geoff Colquitt, Katy Ball; **Delhi**
Ragini Govind
Manager India: Punita Singh
Reference Director: Andrew Lockett
Operations Manager: Helen Phillips
PA to Publishing Director: Nicola Henderson
Publishing Director: Martin Dunford
Commercial Manager: Gino Magnotta
Managing Director: John Duhigg

Publishing information

This sixth edition published September 2008 by
Rough Guides Ltd,
80 Strand, London WC2R 0RL
345 Hudson St, 4th Floor,
New York, NY 10014, USA
14 Local Shopping Centre, Panchsheel Park,
New Delhi 110017, India
Distributed by the Penguin Group
Penguin Books Ltd,
80 Strand, London WC2R 0RL
Penguin Group (USA)
375 Hudson Street, NY 10014, USA
Penguin Group (Australia)
250 Camberwell Road, Camberwell,
Victoria 3124, Australia
Penguin Books Canada Ltd,
10 Alcorn Avenue, Toronto, Ontario,
Canada M4V 1E4
Penguin Group (NZ)
67 Apollo Drive, Mairangi Bay, Auckland 1310,
New Zealand
Cover concept by Peter Dyer.

Typeset in Bembo and Helvetica to an original
design by Henry Iles.

Printed and bound in China

© Lesley Reader and Lucy Ridout

No part of this book may be reproduced in any
form without permission from the publisher except
for the quotation of brief passages in reviews.

512pp includes index

A catalogue record for this book is available from
the British Library

ISBN: 978-1-85828-428-6

The publishers and authors have done their
best to ensure the accuracy and currency of
all the information in **The Rough Guide to
Bali & Lombok**, however, they can accept
no responsibility for any loss, injury, or
inconvenience sustained by any traveller as a
result of information or advice contained in the
guide.

1   3   5   7   9   8   6   4   2

Help us update

We've gone to a lot of effort to ensure that the
sixth edition of **The Rough Guide to Bali &
Lombok** is accurate and up to date. However,
things change – places get "discovered", opening
hours are notoriously fickle, restaurants and
rooms raise prices or lower standards. If you
feel we've got it wrong or left something out,
we'd like to know, and if you can remember the
address, the price, the hours, the phone number,
so much the better.

Please send your comments with the subject
line "**Rough Guide Bali & Lombok Update**"
to ⓔ mail@roughguides.com. We'll credit all
contributions and send a copy of the next edition
(or any other Rough Guide if you prefer) for the
very best emails.
Have your questions answered and tell others
about your trip at
ⓦ community.roughguides.com

SMALL PRINT

Acknowledgements

The authors would like to thank the following people:

From Lesley, many thanks to everyone who gave so generously of their time, knowledge and hospitality. Special thanks to Ketut Lagun, Made Wijana, Made, Mudzakir, Gemma and Made, Phil Smith and Nils Normann. And, as always, to Yau Sang Man.

From Lucy, special thanks to: Wayan Artana, Simon & Brigid Grigg; Rudolf Dethu and Sarah

Forbes; Meghan Pappenheim; Linda vant Hoff; and Ted and Lillen Kruuse-Jensen.

Thank you to those readers who took the time to write and email with their comments and suggestions. Many thanks also to the staff at Rough Guides.

Photo credits

All photos © Rough Guides except the following:

Front cover
Terraced ricefields © Hilarie Kavanagh/Getty

Back cover
Decorative umbrellas, temple festival, Mas
© James Green/Getty

Inside back cover
Pura Dalem Penataran Ped, Nusa Penida, Martin
Richardson © Rough Guides

Introduction
p.8 Swimming with Mola-Mola © Seapics.com

Things not to miss
01 Mount Rinjani © Romain Cintract/Hemis/
   Corbis
05 Gamelan orchestra © Adina Tovy/Robert
   Harding
07 South Lombok beaches, Tanjung Aan
   © Michael S. Yamashita/Corbis
08 Sunrise from Gunung Batur © Lesley Reader
10 Kerta Gosa paintings © Lesley Reader
11 Gili Islands © Sang Man
13 Kecak dance © Corbis
17 Nusa Lembongan © Carlotta/Alamy
19 Nusa Penida's south coast © Lesley Reader
20 Surfing, Kuta beach © Mark A Johnson/Flirt
   Collection/Photolibrary.com
21 Gunung Agung © Jim Holmes/Axiom
23 Fine Dining © Hu'u www.huubali.com

25 *Ritual Flirtation Dance* by Dewa Putu Bedil,
   courtesy of the Neka Art Museum
26 Barong-Rangda dance © Lesley Reader
27 Pemuteran © Seapics.com
31 Diving and snorkelling © Lesley Reader

Colour section: The crafts of Bali & Lombok
Potter at work, Lombok © Lesley Reader
Baskets woven from ata grass © Lesley Reader

Colour section: Volcanoes and ricefields
Besakih Temple © Lesley Reader
Hikers descend into the crater of Mount Rinjani
   © Erick Danzer/OnAsia
Pura Ulun Danu Temple, Lake Bratan © Karen
   Gentry/istockphoto.com

Black & white
p.137 Paragliding at Tanjung Benoa
   © Lucy Ridout
p.329 Pura Luhur Batukaru © Lesley Reader
p.352 Lombok woodcarving © Lesley Reader
p.366 Floating restaurant, Lombok southwest
   coast © Sang Man
p.386 Gili Islands boat and cloudy skies
   © Lesley Reader
p.407 Kuta Beach, Lombok © Lesley Reader
p.418 Gusti Ngura K'tut Djilantik, Prince
   of Buleleng, with his daughters c.1870
   © Koninklijk Instituut voor de Tropen,
   Tropenmuseum, Netherlands

SMALL PRINT

Selected images from our guidebooks are available for licensing from:

ROUGHGUIDESPICTURES.COM

Index

Map entries are in colour.

I

INDEX

503

INDEX

New Things to sell:

SOUTHBALL

pg98 <u>Bali Museum</u> - Denpasar (closed sunday)
Puppet Show in evening
pg93 Pasar Badung(?)
114 Kuta's Waterbom Park(?)
Seafood waring/ jimbaran
Legong Performance - at the Villas?
pg81 Jalang Monkey Forest

Things to return to:

~ Ubud

Map symbols

maps are listed in the full index using coloured text

– – – –	Chapter division boundary		🗐	Fuel station
═══	Main road		@	Internet access
═══	Minor road		ⓘ	Tourist information
◀═══	One-way street		☎	Telephone office
▬▬▬	Restricted access/ Pedestrianized street		✉	Post office
= = =	Unpaved road		⊞	Hospital/Clinic
- - - - -	Path		℗	Parking
▥▥▥	Steps		◉	Accommodation
────	River		▪	Restaurant/bar
– – –	Ferry route		⬤	Swimming
⊠—⊠	Gate		⌇	Surf break
) (	Bridge		⤛	Diving/snorkelling area
▲	Mountain peak		⊙	Statue
☼	Crater		♦	Shelter
ﻼﻼ	Reef		⛳	Golf course
☀	Waterfall		🌲	Temple
⋀⋀	Spring		🌲	Chinese Temple
◠	Cave		🕌	Mosque
⋇	Swamp		▮	Building
⋇	View point		▭	Market
☀	Lighthouse		▬	Hotel compound
✈	Airport		⊣⊢	Church
★	Bemo stop		▦	Park
♦	Point of interest		⸙	Mangrove swamp
			⸪	Beach